Broadcasting, Cable, the Internet, and Beyond

An Introduction to Modern Electronic Media

Seventh Edition

Joseph R. Dominick
University of Georgia, Athens (Retired)

Fritz Messere
State University of New York, Oswego

Barry L. Sherman

Mc Graw Hill

Connect
Learn
Succeed™

BROADCASTING, CABLE, THE INTERNET, AND BEYOND, SEVENTH EDITION

Published by McGraw-Hill, a business unit of The McGraw-Hill Companies, Inc., 1221 Avenue of the Americas, New York, NY 10020. Copyright © 2012 by The McGraw-Hill Companies, Inc. All rights reserved. Previous editions © 2008, 2004, and 2000. No part of this publication may be reproduced or distributed in any form or by any means, or stored in a database or retrieval system, without the prior written consent of The McGraw-Hill Companies, Inc., including, but not limited to, in any network or other electronic storage or transmission, or broadcast for distance learning.

Some ancillaries, including electronic and print components, may not be available to customers outside the United States.

This book is printed on acid-free paper.

1 2 3 4 5 6 7 8 9 0 DOW/DOW 1 0 9 8 7 6 5 4 3 2 1

ISBN 978-0-07-351203-7
MHID 0-07-351203-6

Vice President & Editor-in-Chief: *Michael Ryan*
Vice President, EDP: *Kimberly Meriwether David*
Editorial Director: *Beth Mejia*
Publisher: *David Patterson*
Sponsoring Editor: *Susan Gouijnstook*
Executive Marketing Manager: *Pamela S. Cooper*
Senior Project Manager: *Lisa A. Bruflodt*
Editorial Coordinator: *Nikki Weissman*
Design Coordinator: *Margarite Reynolds*
Cover designer: *Carole Lawson*
USE Cover Image Credit: *McGraw-Hill Companies, Inc./Jill Braaten, photographer; Imagestate Media (John Foxx); Lourens Smak/Alamy; OJO Images/Getty Images; Corbis/Punchstock; © Digital Vision/Getty Images (thumbnails, left to right); Radius Images/Alamy (background)*
Buyer: *Nicole Baumgartner*
Media Project Manager: *Sridevi Palani*
Compositor: *Aptara®, Inc.*
Typeface: *10/12 Palatino*
Printer: *R.R. Donnelley*

All credits appearing on page or at the end of the book are considered to be an extension of the copyright page.

Library of Congress Cataloging-in-Publication Data

Dominick, Joseph R.
    Broadcasting, the internet, and beyond: an introduction to modern electronic
media/Joseph R. Dominick, Fritz Messere, Barry L. Sherman. —7th ed.
        p. cm.
    Rev. ed. of: Broadcasting, cable, the Internet, and beyond. 6th ed. © 2008.
    ISBN-13: 978-0-07-351203-7
    ISBN-10: 0-07-351203-6
    1. Broadcasting—United States. 2. Internet—United States. 3. Telecommunication—United
States. I. Messere, Fritz. II. Sherman, Barry L. III. Dominick, Joseph R. Broadcasting, cable, the
Internet, and beyond. IV. Title.

HE8689.8.D66 2011
384.0973—dc22   2011000792

www.mhhe.com

Once again, to Candy, Eric, and Jessica, and to the memory of Barry L. Sherman

About the Authors

Joseph R. Dominick received his undergraduate degree from the University of Illinois and his PhD from Michigan State University in 1970. He taught for four years at Queens College, City University of New York, before going to the College of Journalism and Mass Communication at the University of Georgia, where from 1980 to 1985 he served as head of the Radio-TV-Film Sequence. Dr. Dominick is the author of three books in addition to *Broadcasting, Cable, the Internet, and Beyond* and has published more than 40 articles in scholarly journals. From 1976 to 1980, Dr. Dominick served as editor of the *Journal of Broadcasting*. He has received research grants from the National Association of Broadcasters and from the American Broadcasting Company, and has served as media consultant for such organizations as the Robert Wood Johnson Foundation and the American Chemical Society.

Fritz Messere received both undergraduate (1971) and graduate degrees (1976) from the State University of New York. He is the dean of the School of Communication, Media, and the Arts at Oswego State University and professor of broadcasting and telecommunications. In addition to *Broadcasting, Cable, the Internet, and Beyond*, Messere is the coauthor of four books about media, media production, and technology. He has broad experience in radio and television production and media management. Messere served as faculty fellow and senior fellow at the Annenberg Washington Program in Communications Policy and on the National Experts Panel on Telecommunications for the Rural Policy Research Institute. He also served as external assistant to FCC Commissioner Mimi Wayforth Dawson.

Barry L. Sherman (1952–2000) was a professor in the Grady College of Journalism and Mass Communication at the University of Georgia. From 1986 to 1991 he served as chair of the Department of Telecommunication. Dr. Sherman was named director of the George Foster Peabody Awards in 1991, a position he held until his death. In addition to *Broadcasting, Cable, the Internet, and Beyond*, Dr. Sherman was the author of *Telecommunications Management: The Broadcast and Cable Industries* and *The Television Standard*. His writings also appeared in a variety of scholarly and professional publications. Dr. Sherman was active in many professional organizations, including the Broadcast Education Association, the International Radio and Television Society, and the Museum of Broadcast Communications.

Preface

There's a scene in Lewis Carroll's *Alice's Adventures in Wonderland: Through the Looking Glass* that is relevant to today's electronic media. Alice and the Red Queen are running fast but are staying in the same spot. Alice is perplexed at their lack of progress, but as the Red Queen explains, "[I]t takes all the running you can do, to keep in the same place. If you want to get somewhere else, you must run at least twice as fast as that!"

Given the pace of change in today's media world, professionals, teachers, students, and textbook writers must feel a lot like Alice: They must run as fast as they can just to keep up with the changing media landscape. In that connection, the seventh edition of *Broadcasting, Cable, the Internet, and Beyond* is a sprint to bring the book up to speed with the electronic media's current situation. Consider that the bulk of the previous edition of this text was written in 2007, when

- Facebook had about 12 million members; it had more than 500 million in 2010.

- YouTube was barely more than a year old and was boasting that the site was getting 100 million views per day. In 2010 that number had increased to 2 billion.

- Hulu.com had yet to appear.

- Google was just a search engine. In 2010 it announced it was entering the TV business.

- The iPhone had just been announced, and the iPad hadn't been invented yet.

- Video clips were showing up on a relatively small number of Web sites. Now they are everywhere.

- The vast majority of people watched TV on a TV set. Only a few watched on their computers or iPods.

- Just slightly more than 10 percent of U.S. households had HDTV. In mid-2010 about 65 percent of households had high-definition sets.

- TV was still broadcasting analog signals.

- Revenue at local TV stations was more than 20 percent higher than in 2010. Network TV revenue was about 10 percent higher in 2007 than in 2010.

- The average gross domestic product (GDP), a key measure of the economy, had been 7 percent in 2006. In 2009 it was less than 1 percent.

- The unemployment rate was 4.6 percent. As of mid-2010, it was more than double that 2007 figure.

This list could be expanded, but the point is probably already clear: Things are changing so fast it is difficult to keep up. Hence the need for a new edition.

NEW AND IMPROVED

There are two major changes to the seventh edition. First, in response to reviewer and user feedback, Chapter 14, the chapter about international communication, has been eliminated. Users suggested that this material would be more appropriate for a more advanced course. We do not, however, totally ignore the international dimension. We have moved the information most relevant to an introductory text into other appropriate chapters. Second, Chapter 6, previously titled "The Internet and New Media Today," has been totally overhauled. Rather than trying to cover the structure, organization, content, economics, and social consequences of the Internet (topics that would require an entire book or two to address adequately), we have refocused the chapter so that it now looks at the basics of the Internet, the Internet's impact on traditional media, and the growth of social media and then discusses audio and video on the Web, a topic most of interest to the ever-changing electronic media.

In addition to these major changes, Chapter 1 ("History of Broadcast Media") has been updated to include the impact of the recession at decade's end, new technology, including HDTV and mobile TV, and the changing legal and regulatory environment ushered in by a new administration in Washington. Chapter 2 ("History of Cable, Home Video, and the Internet") now traces the development of the DVD and Blu-ray disk along with a discussion of the history of portable media. Chapter 3 ("Audio and Video Technology") has received a major makeover and now includes an extended discussion of digital audio and video production, transmission and storage techniques, and a description of wireless technology. This chapter attempts to convey the specialized information that is needed by today's student without becoming overly technical.

Chapter 4 ("Radio Today") examines the changing competitive environment of the modern radio station and includes an updated look at the industry's current economic situation as well as discussions of changes in radio programming, ownership, and organization. The chapter concludes with a section about the impact of mobile devices and the Internet on the traditional radio station. Chapter 5 ("Broadcast and Cable/Satellite TV Today") looks at the changes that have transformed contemporary broadcast and cable/satellite television, including digital transmission, mobile media, TV programs delivered via the Internet, and the struggle between broadcasters and cablecasters over retransmission fees. As mentioned earlier, Chapter 6 ("The Internet, Web Audio, and Web Video") now focuses on TV and radio carried via the Web.

Chapter 7 ("The Business of Broadcasting, Cable, and New Media") has been revised to reflect how the traditional broadcasting/cable business has been affected by changing economic conditions and emerging media. The chapter also contains a new section about Internet advertising challenges and opportunities. Chapter 8 ("Radio Programming") updates the current status of radio programming with a special emphasis on the impact of MP3 players, Internet radio stations, and social media. Chapter 9 ("TV Programming") examines the current state of television news and entertainment programming, including a new discussion of the effects of social media on news coverage and the latest trends in TV production.

Chapter 10 ("Rules and Regulations") discusses the debate over "network neutrality," the continuing issues regarding copyright and the Internet, and the back-and-forth between the FCC and the courts concerning broadcast indecency. Chapter 11 ("Self-Regulation and Ethics") looks at the ongoing debate over what is acceptable in broadcast television and the efforts of the industry to promote the V-chip. Chapter 12 ("Ratings and Audience Feedback") has been updated to reflect the expanded use of local market People Meters, C3 ratings, and the current methods of measuring the Internet and mobile TV audiences. Finally, Chapter 13 ("Effects") now contains the latest research concerning violent video games and the impact of the electronic media, particularly social media, on the political process.

BOXED INSERTS

The seventh edition continues the use of thematically organized boxed inserts to present expanded examples and discussions of topics mentioned in the text or interesting snapshots of industry leaders. Dozens of new boxes have been added. For example,

- Chapter 5 ("Broadcast and Cable/Satellite TV Today") includes a new box about the issue of diversity in TV station ownership.
- Chapter 6 ("The Internet, Web Audio, and Web Video") contains a new box about podcasting.
- A new box in Chapter 7 ("The Business of Broadcasting, Cable, and New Media") looks at the economics behind NBC's failed attempt with a prime-time version of the Jay Leno show.
- Chapter 10 ("Rules and Regulations") has a new Issues box that examines the continuing decline of libel cases filed against the electronic media.
- The pros and cons of the pressure group the Parents Television Council are discussed in a new box in Chapter 11 ("Self-Regulation and Ethics").

Web Support

As with the sixth edition, each chapter of the book is supported by an interactive Web site that students can use to supplement the material found in the text. The site has been updated and includes a study guide, practice tests, chapter summaries, key terms, and links to other relevant sites. For more information, see the McGraw-Hill Web site at www.mhhe.com/dominickbib7e.

Something Familiar

The seventh edition continues to use the same organizational structure that was introduced in the fifth edition.

- Part One ("Foundations") examines the history of the electronic media and introduces audio and video technology.

- Part Two ("How It Is") is an overview of the electronic media: radio, television, cable, and the Internet. Each of the three chapters in this section follows a common organization. Each surveys the structure of the media, looks at economic and social forces that influence their operation, examines current issues, and closes by outlining various career options.

- Part Three ("How It's Done") opens with a chapter that describes business aspects of each medium. Subsequent chapters concentrate on programming and how broadcasters and cablecasters select and schedule content that appeals to audiences that advertisers want to reach.

- Part Four ("How It's Controlled") looks at the regulatory process. The first chapter in this section discusses the rationale behind regulation, examines the FCC and other forces that shape electronic media regulation, and reviews the key federal and local laws that influence the day-to-day operations in the industry. The next chapter looks at self-regulation and examines how industry practices and ethics influence what the audience sees and hears.

- The final section, Part Five ("What It Does"), focuses on the audience. The first chapter in this section explains how ratings are determined, while the following chapter examines the social impact of the electronic media.

Moreover, every chapter has been updated and revised to reflect changes to this dynamic area. Charts and tables contain the most recent data available.

As was our goal in the previous editions, we continue our attempt to create a book that is concise but still contains sufficient depth of coverage. Again, as before, we have tried to maintain a conversational writing style that students will find interesting. Finally, we reiterate our hope that the seventh edition fulfills the goal we first set when the first edition appeared: to produce a textbook that is informative and that captures some of the excitement, exhilaration, and immediacy that characterize this industry.

Acknowledgments

Naturally, writing any book requires a gestation period in which the authors spend quite a bit of time doing research, fretting, writing, rewriting, and (sometimes) pacing. Family members are very supportive during the birth of any new edition, and we would be remiss if we did not thank those who put up with this behavior.

Many people helped by giving us up-to-date information about the industry and helping us understand the trends that are constantly moving the media in new directions. We are grateful to Rick Yacobush at Clear Channel Radio in Syracuse, Jack Myers for sharing some of his immense knowledge of the media business, Fred Vigeant of WRVO-FM, Tanya Dessereau at Veronis Suhler Stevenson, Andy Rainey of the Radio Advertising Bureau, Rick Greenhut at iBiquity Digital Corporation, Cliff Kobland for his insights about media, and Arielle Glott for her research help.

And, of course, thanks to all those who reviewed the previous edition for their helpful suggestions:

Robert Affe, Indiana University
Ann Catalano, Niagara County CC
Wyoming Rossett, Great Basin College
Christine Stover, Oakland University
Matthew Brent Goken, Illinois Central College
John Morris, University of Southern Indiana
Sharon A. Evans, Western Illinois University
Michael Morgan, University of Massachusetts
John Cooper, Eastern Michigan University
Anthony (AJ) Miceli, Gannon University
Siho Nam, University of North Florida
Bill Renkus, University of Florida

The crew members at McGraw-Hill are really wonderful. We would like to thank our development editors, Craig Leonard and Nikki Weissman, and our project manager, Lisa A. Bruflodt.

Finally, this is the third edition to be published after the untimely death of our friend and coauthor, Barry Sherman. Once again, we hope we have produced a book that Barry would be proud of.

Joseph R. Dominick
Fritz Messere

Brief Contents

Detailed Contents

**Part Two
How It Is**

4

Radio Today   85

5
Broadcast and Cable/Satellite TV Today   109

6
The Internet, Web Audio, and Web Video   136

Part Three
How It's Done

Part Four
How It's Controlled

10
Rules and Regulations   237

Part Five
What It Does

List of Boxes

Broadcasting, Cable, the Internet, and Beyond

Part One | Foundations

Introduction

Keeping up with the fast-changing world of electronic media continues to be a challenging task. In the few years since the last edition of *Broadcasting, Cable, the Internet, and Beyond,* the following are just some things that have occurred:

- The popularity of video-sharing sites on the Internet has skyrocketed. YouTube alone streams more than 5 billion video streams a month. More than 24 hours of video are uploaded every minute.

- Hulu.com, featuring clips of and full-length broadcast and cable programs, premiered and quickly became the second most popular online video site.

- Television broadcasting went all-digital.

- The satellite radio companies XM and Sirius merged.

- About 40 percent of U.S. households have acquired digital video recorders.

- Comcast announced plans to merge with NBC Universal.

- High-definition TV sets went down in price and up in popularity. As of 2010, more than half the households in the United States had sets that could receive high-definition signals.

- 3-D TV sets became available.

- The ratings of TV news programs continued to fall as more people turned to the Internet for news.

- Mobile video was becoming more popular thanks in part to Apple's development of the iPhone and the iPad.

- A U.S. court of appeals ruled that the FCC's indecency policy was unconstitutional.

- An economic recession caused advertising revenue to decline, and many broadcasters and cable organizations cut jobs.

This list could be extended, but by now the point is probably clear: All of the developments just mentioned suggest that the world of electronic media will continue to change and have a great effect on society. This, in turn, suggests that it is important for students to appreciate these changes and what they mean for the future.

Students will note that all the chapters in this book end with a section called "Suggestions for Further Reading." This introduction is different. We will end it with some suggestions for reading further—reasons why you should keep reading the rest of the book:

- Many of you will go into careers in the electronic media. This book presents a foundation of information for you to build on as you pursue your professional goals.

- For those of you who do not intend to become media professionals, knowledge of the electronic media will help you become intelligent consumers and informed critics of radio, TV, and online media. The electronic media are so pervasive in modern life that everyone should know how they are structured and what they do.

- Finally, all of you will spend the rest of your lives in the Information Age, in which the creation, distribution, and application of information will be the most important industry. The electronic media are at the core of the Information Age. Everybody benefits from the scholarly study of an industry that will be a crucial part of business, education, art, politics, and culture.

In sum, the authors hope that what you learn from this book will be liberating in the traditional sense of a liberal education: We hope that the knowledge that you acquire will free and empower you in this new era.

History of Broadcast Media   1

Quick Facts

First radio broadcast: Reginald Fessenden, Christmas Eve, 1906

First radio network company: NBC, 1926

First "Top 40" radio broadcasts: 1952

First public demonstration of TV: 1939 World's Fair

Cost of first TV commercial: $4 (1941)

Cost of commercial minute in 2010 Super Bowl: $5.2 million

"What hath God wrought?"

That was the message sent by wire from Washington, D.C., to Baltimore one spring day in 1844. Using a code made up of dots and dashes, Samuel Morse had demonstrated the potential of his new communication device—the telegraph. For the first time in history, it was possible to send a message across long distances almost instantaneously.

"Come here, Watson. I need you."

Thirty-four years after Morse's invention, Alexander Graham Bell uttered those words into a telephone, a device that could send the human voice through a wire, making it even easier to communicate at a distance. Both the telegraph and the telephone are radio's ancestors, and their evolution anticipated many factors that would shape radio. Specifically,

- Both the telegraph and the telephone businesses supported themselves through commercial means.
- Big corporations came to dominate both industries.
- Both the telephone and the telegraph were point-to-point communication media. They sent a message from one source to one receiver.

Radio started off as a point-to-point medium until people discovered the advantages of broadcasting—sending the same message to many people simultaneously. But we're getting ahead of the story.

THE INVENTORS

In the late 19th century, efforts were under way to liberate electronic communication from the wire. Physicists such as James Maxwell and Heinrich Hertz demonstrated the existence of electromagnetic radiation—energy waves that traveled through space. Other researchers investigated the nature of these mysterious waves. None of them, however, was able to perfect a system of wireless communication. The creation of such a system—radio—was due to the efforts of many inventors. There are three, however, whose contributions bear special mention: Marconi, Fessenden, and De Forest.

Marconi and Wireless

Guglielmo Marconi, who came from a wealthy and cultured Anglo-Italian family, had seen a demonstration of the mysterious radio waves while a college student. Enthralled with the new discovery, young Marconi started experimenting with radio transmitters and receivers. Eventually he was able to send a radio signal more than a mile.

Marconi was aware of the commercial possibilities of his experiments. He realized that the biggest potential use for his wireless communication system would be in situations where it was impossible to use traditional wire telegraphy: ship-to-ship and ship-to-shore communication. Accordingly, he traveled to Great Britain, the leading maritime country of the period, and applied for a patent. The British granted him a patent for his wireless telegraphy system in 1896, and Marconi formed his own company to manufacture and sell his new device.

As his company became successful, Marconi turned his efforts toward increasing the range of his signals. In December 1901 he successfully transmitted a wireless signal—three short beeps, the letter *S* in Morse code—across the Atlantic, a distance of more than 2,000 nautical miles. The age of radio was dawning.

Fessenden and the Continuous Wave

Keep in mind that Marconi was sending wireless telegraphy—dots and dashes. No one was yet able to send the human voice via radio waves. For this to occur, someone had to develop a new way of generating radio signals. Marconi used a technique that generated radio waves by making a spark jump across a gap between two electrodes. This was fine for Morse code, but the human voice was another matter. To transmit voice, or music or other sounds, what was needed was the generation of a continuous radio wave that could be transformed to carry speech.

Reginald Fessenden, a Canadian-born electrical engineer, came up with the solution. Working with the General Electric Company, he built a high-speed alternator, a piece of rotating machinery much like those used to generate alternating current for household use.

Fessenden tested his alternator on Christmas Eve 1906. Wireless operators on ships up and down the eastern coast of the United States were amazed when through their headphones they heard a human voice speaking to them. It was Fessenden explaining what was going on. After some violin music and readings from the Bible, the inventor wished his audience a merry Christmas and signed off.

Guglielmo Marconi was able to build a lucrative communications empire on his wireless invention. Here a successful Marconi listens to radio signals in the wireless room of his personal yacht, *Electra*.

This first "broadcast" caused a mild sensation and marked a major technological breakthrough. As dramatic as the change from typewriter to word processor, the shift from the spark gap to the continuous-wave transmitter ushered in a new age for radio. Radio waves could now carry more than just dots and dashes.

De Forest and the Invisible Empire

Around 1910, the most popular way of receiving radio signals was to use something called a **crystal set.** Scientists had discovered that some minerals, such as galena, possessed the ability to detect radio waves. Moving a tiny wire, called a cat's whisker, over a lump of galena allowed the listener to hear the faint sounds of wireless telephony, as radio broadcasts were called back then. Crystal sets were cheap and easy to assemble, but they had one big drawback: They couldn't amplify weak incoming signals.

If radio was to become a mass medium, something better was needed: a receiver that would boost the level of weak signals and make radio listening easier.

Lee De Forest found the answer during his experiments with something called a Fleming valve. This device looked like an ordinary lightbulb. It consisted of a plate and a thin wire and was used to detect radio waves. De Forest discovered that a small wire grid inserted between the plate and the wire acted as an amplifier that boosted weak radio signals until they were easily detected. Hooking together two or three such devices could amplify signals millions of times. De Forest, realizing the potential of his invention—which he named the **audion**—for radio, wrote in his diary that he had "discovered an Invisible Empire of the Air." De Forest's invention made galena obsolete. The audion moved radio into the electronic age.

The inventor tried to create a market for his audion by using publicity stunts such as broadcasting phonograph records from the Eiffel Tower in Paris and a performance from the New York Metropolitan Opera. These early demonstrations had few listeners, but they did show that broadcasting was possible. It would take a few more years, however, before that idea gained wide acceptance.

De Forest's invention also got him into legal trouble. The Marconi company sued him, claiming that his audion infringed on its patents to the Fleming valve. Another patent battle over the audion dragged on for more than 20 years before reaching the Supreme Court. De Forest eventually sold rights to the audion, for a modest $50,000, to AT&T, which wanted to use it to amplify the signal of long-distance phone calls, and he turned his attention to other areas.

The audion contributed to improvements in transmission as well as reception. It subsequently was refined into the vacuum tube and formed the basis for all radio transmission until the 1950s, when it was replaced by the transistor and solid-state electronics.

BOARDROOMS AND COURTROOMS

Now that radio had been successfully demonstrated, the next step was to refine it and make it commercially rewarding. Accordingly, the next phase of broadcasting's evolution was marked by the activities of corporations more than of individuals. It's a tangled story, complicated by legal feuds, conflicting claims, politics, and war. It's also an important phase: Decisions made during this period permanently shaped radio's future.

Legal Tangles

To begin, let's review the situation as of 1910. Radio was still thought of as a point-to-point communication device—much like the telegraph and the telephone. Despite De Forest's demonstrations, broadcasting, as we know it today, did not exist. Radio's main use was still ship-to-ship and ship-to-shore communication.

Although Marconi's company (British Marconi) and its American subsidiary (American Marconi) dominated the business, other companies were interested in radio: General Electric, AT&T, and Westinghouse. Each of these companies held patents on certain elements necessary to manufacture radio transmitters and receiving sets, but no one company had patents that covered the entire process.

Predictably, each company produced its own version of the inventions patented by the others so it could enter the business. The result was a long and costly legal battle over patent infringements. Had something drastic not happened, radio's evolution might have been severely hindered.

Radio Goes to War

Something drastic—World War I—was not long in coming. The military benefits of radio were apparent from the start of the conflict. The U.S. Navy had equipped all of its warships with radio and operated three dozen coastal radio stations. When the United States entered the war in 1917, the government, in the interests of national security, gave the navy complete control over all radio operations, including all commercial stations.

This move had two important consequences for radio. First, the navy assumed responsibility for patent infringement. This meant the various companies involved could pool their discoveries to improve radio communication. This is exactly what happened, and by the war's end in 1918, the technology was vastly improved. Second, during the war the navy had taken control of 45 coastal radio stations and eight high-power transmitters owned by American Marconi. When the war ended, the navy was reluctant to give them back because it was convinced that such an important function as international radio communication should not be controlled by a company (American Marconi) that was in turn controlled by a foreign power (Britain). In fact, bills were introduced in Congress to give the navy exclusive control over radio's future. Obviously some important decisions had to be made.

Birth of RCA

The first decision was what to do about the navy. Commercial interests in the United States were opposed to any governmental intrusion into the free enterprise system and did not want the navy controlling a potentially lucrative business. Consequently the bills giving the navy control over radio were never brought to a vote. Unlike some other countries, the United States chose not to put radio under direct governmental control.

The second problem was what to do about American Marconi and a possible British monopoly. To make matters worse, with the navy out of the picture, all the prewar patent problems immediately resurfaced. The ultimate solution to the problem was suggested by the navy: Buy out American Marconi and start a new company. Representatives from the U.S. government went to General Electric, the company with the most resources and financial clout, to handle the deal. After much tough negotiating, the management at Marconi agreed to the plan. Marconi would sell its American subsidiary to a new company—the Radio Corporation of America (RCA). Note that RCA would still be in the business of point-to-point communication and planned to make its money by sending wireless telegraphy and telephony to U.S. and international customers.

The next step was to solve the patents problem. Ultimately RCA entered into a cross licensing agreement with GE, AT&T, and Westinghouse that enabled each company to use the others' discoveries. The companies also agreed to divide the market: GE and Westinghouse would manufacture radio equipment, and RCA would sell it. AT&T would build the transmitters.

Ironically, just as these new agreements were falling into place, it became clear that the real future of radio would not be in point-to-point communication but in broadcasting—providing news and entertainment to the general public. Because of this, all the agreements that were negotiated among these companies would soon fall apart as radio headed in a new direction.

BROADCASTING'S BEGINNINGS

Radio burst on the scene in the 1920s and soon became a national craze. There were several cogent reasons for the incredible growth of this new medium:

1. An audience of enthusiastic hobbyists, thousands of them trained in radio communication during the war, was available and eager to start tinkering with their crystal sets.

2. Improvements during the war gave radio better reception and greater range.

3. Big business realized that broadcasting might make money.

Its beginnings were modest. In 1920 Frank Conrad, an engineer for Westinghouse, began experimental broadcasts from his Pittsburgh garage. Conrad's programs, consisting of phonograph recordings and readings from the newspaper, became popular with listeners who were picking up the broadcast on crystal sets. Westinghouse noticed the popularity of Conrad's program and began manufacturing radio sets that were sold by a local department store. As sales of radio sets increased, Westinghouse moved Conrad from his garage to a studio on the roof of the company's tallest building in Pittsburgh. This new station was licensed by the Department of Commerce and given the call letters of KDKA (it's still on the air today, making it the oldest operating station). Conrad had established that there was a market for radio broadcasting.

Westinghouse quickly started other stations in Chicago, Newark, and other cities. RCA, GE, and AT&T also started radio stations. As the year 1922 began, 28 were stations actively broadcasting; six months later there were 378; and by the end of the year, 570. Receiving sets were selling quickly; by the end of the decade almost half of the homes in America had a working radio.

The tremendous growth brought problems. For the listener, the biggest annoyance was interference. Only a few frequencies available gave good reception, and many stations were operating on them, which caused great difficulty for the listener as the competing signals interfered with one another.

At the corporate level, the problem was money. The cross-licensing agreement did not anticipate broadcasting. In 1923 RCA made $11 million from selling radio sets and only $3 million from its wireless telegraphy operation. AT&T, prohibited from manufacturing radio sets by the agreement, was obviously displeased. Friction soon developed between the members of the cross-licensing agreement over who had the right to do what. After a four-year imbroglio, the parties agreed to a plan that ultimately solved the problem. AT&T left the broadcasting business and sold its assets to the other companies involved in the agreement. In return, AT&T would be granted a monopoly over the wire interconnections that were used to link stations together into a network (see the "Radio Networks" section). RCA won the right to manufacture radio sets and acquired WEAF, the powerful New York City station formerly owned by AT&T.

RADIO'S FAST TIMES: THE 1920s

Things happened quickly for radio in the 1920s. In eight years, from 1920 to 1927, radio went from a fad to a major industry and a major social force. We

The control room and studio of KDKA, Pittsburgh, generally considered to be the oldest broadcasting station in the nation. Note that early broadcasters had to be careful about loose wires.

have already noted how big business got involved with early radio. The three other major developments of this period that helped to shape modern radio were the development of radio advertising, the beginning of radio networks, and the evolution of radio regulation.

Advertising

When broadcasting first started, nobody thought too much about how it was supposed to make money. Most of the early broadcasters were radio and electronics manufacturers. For these companies, radio was simply a device to help sell their products. Other businesses that owned large numbers of early radio stations were newspaper publishers and department stores. For these companies, radio was a promotional device; it helped sell more newspapers or attracted people to the store. Nobody envisioned that it might be possible for a radio station to make money.

In time, however, costs started building up. To compete successfully, stations required reliable equipment, special studios, and technicians and professional talent who had to be paid for their labor. Rising costs forced many stations off the air. Those that were left scurried to find some way to produce revenue.

It was the phone company that came up with the answer. Considering broadcasting an extension of the telephone, AT&T developed a system whereby anyone who had a message to deliver would come to its station, pay money, give the message, and leave (just as people did when they came to a phone booth and made a call to a single person). AT&T called the arrangement "toll broadcasting." It wasn't long before advertisers began to appreciate the potential of this new arrangement. The Queensboro Corporation, a New York real estate company, was the first to buy time on WEAF. Others quickly followed.

Although it may seem odd today, this early experiment in commercial broadcasting was resented by many listeners. There was even talk of a bill in Congress to prohibit it. By 1924, however, enough stations had followed WEAF that it was obvious the public did not object to radio ads. If anything, the audience liked the improved programming that came with advertising. By 1929 advertisers were spending more than $20 million on radio advertising, and the new medium was on solid financial ground.

Radio Networks

There were three main reasons for the development of chain or network broadcasting in the mid-1920s. The first stemmed from the broadcasters themselves and was primarily economic. It was less expensive for one station to produce a program and to have it broadcast simultaneously on three or four stations than it was for each station to produce its own program. The second reason came from the audience. The listeners of local stations in rural areas—far from the talent of New York, Chicago, or Hollywood—wanted better programs. Networking allowed big-name talent to be heard over small-town stations. A third reason was the desire of advertisers to increase the range of their programs beyond the receivers of local stations and thus multiply potential customers. Given the pressure from these three sources, the development of networks was inevitable.

After AT&T pioneered the interconnection of stations using its long-distance phone lines, RCA, headed by David Sarnoff, set up a new company in 1926 to separate the parent company from the broadcasting operation. The National Broadcasting Company (NBC) was to oversee two broadcasting networks. The "Red" network consisted of the stations acquired from AT&T when the phone company left the broadcasting business, and the "Blue" network comprised stations originally owned by RCA, Westinghouse, and GE. By 1933 NBC had 88 stations in its network.

A competitor came on the scene when the Columbia Broadcasting System (CBS) was formed in 1927. Under the direction of William S. Paley, CBS started with 16 stations, but by the end of 1933 the younger network had 91 members. Another network, the Mutual Broadcasting System, began operation in 1934. The radio networks would be the controlling force in broadcasting for the next 20 years.

Radio networks forever changed American society. First they stimulated national advertising. With one phone call, advertisers could procure nationwide exposure for their products. Second, radio networks brought to rural areas entertainment previously provided to urban areas. Now everybody could hear the same comedians, big bands, Hollywood movie stars, and political commentators. Network radio stimulated the beginnings of a truly national popular culture. Finally, the networks changed American politics as campaigns became truly national in scope. Politicians who mastered the new medium, as Franklin Roosevelt did in his fireside chats, had a distinct advantage over their competitors.

Rules

Attempts to regulate the new medium can be traced back to 1903, when a series of international conferences was called to discuss the problem of how to deal with wireless communication. The result of these efforts for the United States was the Wireless Ship Act of 1910, requiring certain passenger vessels to carry wireless sets. Two years later, the pressure for more regulation increased when amateur wireless operators were interfering with official navy communications. In the midst of this, the *Titanic* struck an iceberg and sank. Hundreds were saved because of wireless distress signals, but the interference caused by the many operators who went on the air after knowledge of the disaster spread hampered rescue operations. As a result, the public recognized the need to develop legal guidelines for this new medium. The Radio Act of 1912 required sending stations to be licensed by the Secretary of Commerce, who could assign wavelengths and time limits. Ship, amateur, and government transmissions were to be assigned separate places in the spectrum.

The problem with this law was that it envisioned radio as point-to-point communication and did not anticipate broadcasting. Consequently, as more stations went on the air, broadcasting for long periods, interference became a severe problem.

By 1926 the interference problem had become so bad that it was obvious to all that some form of federal control was needed if radio was to avoid being suffocated in its own growth. In response to requests from the radio industry for legislation, Congress passed the **Radio Act of 1927.** Its key assumptions were the following:

- The radio spectrum was a national resource. Individuals could not own frequencies, but they could be licensed to use them.
- Licensees would have to operate in the public interest.
- Government censorship was forbidden.

In addition, a five-member **Federal Radio Commission (FRC)** was established to enforce the new law. Within five years the FRC had solved the interference problem and laid the groundwork for an orderly system of frequency sharing that would obtain maximum benefit for the public. In 1934, in an attempt by President Franklin Roosevelt to streamline government administration, Congress passed the **Communications Act of 1934,** which replaced the FRC with a seven-member **Federal Communications Commission (FCC).** The basic philosophy of the 1927 law, however, was not changed.

RADIO DAYS, RADIO NIGHTS: 1930–1948

The years from 1930 to 1948 can be termed the radio years. The new medium grew at a phenomenal rate, became an integral part of American life, developed new forms of entertainment and news programs, and ran into a few problems along the way.

Growth

Table 1–1 documents the skyrocketing growth of radio. Other statistics are equally impressive: from $40 million spent on radio advertising in 1930 to $506 million in 1948; from 131 network affiliates in 1930 to 1,104 in 1948. Keep in mind that this growth occurred despite a worldwide depression and another world war.

With growth came new problems. One had to do with questionable radio content. The FRC, with backing from the courts, was able to shut down radio broadcasts by quacks and swindlers, such as John R. Brinkley, who used his station to promote bogus patent medicines, and Norman Baker, who touted his homemade cancer cure over KTNT in Iowa.

Table 1–1	The Growth of Radio		
Year	**Number of Stations**	**Percentage of Homes with Radio**	**Number of Employees**
1930	618	46%	6,000
1950	2,867	95	52,000
1970	6,889	99	71,000
2010	14,420	99+	105,000

Another problem concerned FM (frequency modulation) broadcasting. Invented by Edwin Armstrong (see the boxed material), FM transmission was first publicly demonstrated in 1933. FM had two big advantages over AM (amplitude modulation): FM was less prone to static and had better sound reproduction quality. Armstrong took his invention to his friend David Sarnoff, now chief executive at RCA, who had supported the inventor's work in the past. Unfortunately for Armstrong, the time was not right for FM. Conventional AM radio was doing fine; it didn't need additional competition. In addition, RCA had made a major investment in AM and was more interested in getting a return on this money than in developing a new radio service. Finally, Sarnoff was committed to another developing technology, television, which he saw as more important. Consequently, RCA would not back the new radio technology. Dismayed, Armstrong built his own FM station; but World War II intervened and halted its development. Nonetheless, at the end of the war there were about 50 FM stations in operation. The FCC dealt another blow, however, by moving FM to a different spot in the radio spectrum, thus rendering obsolete about 400,000 FM receiving sets. Although its ultimate future would prove to be bright, FM struggled for the next 20 years.

The last problem concerned NBC's two networks and the FCC. After a lengthy study of monopolistic tendencies in network broadcasting, the FCC ruled that NBC had to divest itself of one of its two networks. NBC sold its Blue network to Edwin Noble, who had become rich by selling Life Savers candy. Noble renamed the network the American Broadcasting Company (ABC).

Impact

By now radio had become part of the country's social fabric. It was the number one source of home entertainment, and the stars of early radio were familiar to the members of virtually every household in America. Radio news reports had a sense of immediacy that set them off from items in the newspaper. People trusted and depended on radio.

The social power of radio was demonstrated several times during this period. Franklin Roosevelt used his informal fireside chats to help push his legislation through Congress. In 1938 Orson Welles used a quasi-newscast style in a radio adaptation of

Profile: Edwin Armstrong

In his early years, Edwin Howard Armstrong was fascinated by two things: radio and heights. In 1910, when he was 20, Armstrong built his own antenna to aid his experiments with radio. Armstrong liked to hoist himself to the top of his 125-foot tower to enjoy the view.

A few years later, while climbing a mountain, Armstrong worked out a method by which De Forest's audion could be modified to amplify incoming radio signals as well as detect them. Armstrong's invention, the regenerative circuit, would become part of almost every piece of radio equipment.

Armstrong's inventions were not overlooked by the radio industry. In 1913 David Sarnoff, chief inspector for the Marconi company, visited Armstrong's labs for a demonstration of his equipment. The two quickly became friends.

Armstrong's success in the laboratory, however, was not matched by success in the courtroom. Beginning in 1914, Armstrong became embroiled in a complicated legal struggle with Lee De Forest over who had actually first discovered the principle of regeneration—a battle Armstrong eventually lost.

Armstrong served in the army during World War I and spent some time flying over France in rickety biplanes. While in the army, Armstrong continued to invent devices that improved the quality of radio transmission and reception.

Armstrong's inventions brought him money and fame. In 1922 David Sarnoff, then head of RCA, signed a deal with Armstrong that brought the inventor more than a quarter-million dollars in cash and stocks. A few months later, Armstrong, perhaps symbolizing his new on-top-of-the-world status, scaled the radio antenna atop the 21-story building owned by RCA. Armstrong even sent photographs of his feat to his friend Sarnoff. Sarnoff was not amused.

In the next few years, however, several events brought Armstrong back to earth. After some initial victories in his court fight with De Forest, Armstrong had a setback. The Supreme Court, operating more from technical legal rules than from scientific evidence, ruled against him in 1928.

For most of the next five years, Armstrong devoted his time to perfecting FM, an invention he hoped would bring him to new heights of fame and prosperity. When Sarnoff refused to back the new technology, their friendship began to evaporate.

Undaunted, Armstrong set up his own FM transmitter for demonstrations. By 1940 Armstrong was on top again. Other radio set manufacturers were impressed and paid Armstrong for the rights to manufacture FM sets. The FCC set aside part of the electromagnetic spectrum for commercial FM broadcasting. Even Sarnoff had changed his mind about FM and offered Armstrong $1 million for a license to his invention. Armstrong, probably remembering the earlier incident with Sarnoff, refused.

Word War II interrupted the development of FM. After the war ended, optimism for the new medium flourished again. This confidence, however, was short-lived. The FCC moved FM out of its former spectrum slot, and Sarnoff announced that RCA had developed its own FM system, one that did not rely on Armstrong's inventions.

The break between the two old friends was now total. Armstrong sued RCA for patent infringement, and RCA martialed its massive financial and legal resources against him. The lawsuit lasted four years and drained Armstrong physically, financially, and emotionally. By 1954 Armstrong was near bankruptcy, depressed, estranged from his wife, and convinced that his creation of FM was destined to be a failure.

More than 50 years in the future, looking back, we, of course, know that Armstrong was wrong. Despite the initial hardships, FM flourished. In early 2006, FM commanded more than two-thirds of the listening time of Americans. The inventor, however, would never see his invention succeed. In 1954 Edwin Armstrong, the man who was fascinated by heights, committed suicide by jumping out the window of his 13th-floor apartment.

War of the Worlds that featured Martians invading the United States. Many people thought the program was real and panicked. Finally, singer Kate Smith stayed on the air for 18 straight hours during a pledge drive for war bonds. She eventually raised more than $39 million.

Moreover, radio took advertising revenue away from the newspaper and magazine industries, and radio newscasts effectively killed the "extra" editions of the newspaper. Radio also had an impact on the sound recording industry. The early radio networks refused to play recorded music, and the recording

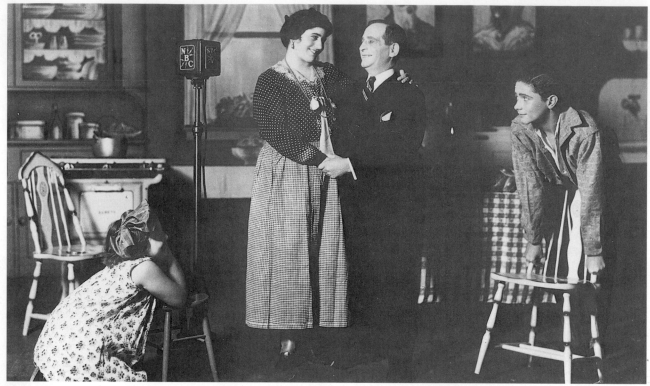

The Goldbergs: Rosalie, Molly, Jake, and Sammy. Gertrude Berg (Molly) was the creative force behind *The Goldbergs*, a radio situation comedy that premiered in the early 1930s and moved to TV in 1949.

industry was reluctant to permit records to be played on radio. As more and more people turned to radio for music, the recording industry nearly died during the economic downturn of the 1930s; it survived thanks to better marketing efforts and the popularity of the juke box, a coin-operated phonograph found in most drugstores, restaurants, and bars. Interestingly, the idea that playing records on the radio would be helpful to both industries had yet to catch on.

Programs

Radio programs during this period were diverse. In fact, almost every program genre now available on contemporary television first appeared on the radio. Situation comedies were numerous; *The Goldbergs* premiered in 1929, as did the biggest comedy hit of the period, *Amos 'n' Andy*. Although it would be considered racist today, almost the entire nation stopped to listen to it during its 7:00 to 7:15 time slot. Other situation comedies, including *Burns and Allen* and *Jack Benny*, quickly followed.

Crime shows, such as *Law and Order* and *CSI*, can trace their ancestry back to 1930s radio programs,

such as *Gangbusters* and *Mr. District Attorney*. The roots of dramatic shows such as *ER* and *West Wing* can be found in *Dr. Christian* (1937) and *Mr. President* (1947). *American Idol* is a more ambitious version of *The Original Amateur Hour* from 1934. *The Hedda Hopper Show* and *Walter Winchell*, both from the 1930s, were earlier versions of *Entertainment Tonight* and *Inside Edition*. And of course modern TV soap operas, such as *The Guiding Light*, owe their heritage to radio soaps, such as *The Guiding Light* (radio version in 1938) and *Ma Perkins* (1933).

Radio news got off to a slow start, but by 1930 the networks were carrying regular newscasts. The events of the 1930s gave radio news a boost as reporters and commentators described and analyzed events leading up to World War II. An impressive array of reporters, including Eric Sevareid, Edward R. Murrow, and William Shirer reported regularly from Europe. Millions of people in the United States would huddle around their radios to hear timely reports on the war's progress. The amount of network time spent on news more than doubled from 1940 to 1945. There were some notable individual achievements, including Murrow's dramatic accounts of the

David Sarnoff standing in front of a TV camera as he opens the RCA pavilion at the 1939 New York World's Fair. This was the first time a major news event was covered by television.

bombing of London. All in all, radio news reached its high point during the war.

After the war, the future for radio never looked brighter. It was America's number one source of news and entertainment. Advertising revenue was increasing, and more and more people were listening. Radio's future, however, was about to change drastically.

TELEVISION

Nine miles from Manhattan, in Flushing Meadows, Queens, a mosquito-infested swamp underwent a magical transformation. At a cost of $156 million, the New York World's Fair opened on that site in April 1939. RCA, NBC's parent company, had chosen this event to make a public demonstration of its latest technological marvel—television. David Sarnoff, the head of RCA, called the invention "a new art so important in its implications that it is bound to affect all society." He was right.

The idea of TV goes back to the 1880s. Early TV pioneers such as Paul Nipkow and Boris Rosing correctly reasoned that if the elements of a visual scene could be scanned and broken down into a series of tiny electrical signals able to be transmitted and reassembled in a receiver, a viewable television picture would result. It took a while, however, to put this principle into practice.

After a series of false starts with mechanical scanning systems, two inventors, Vladimir Zworykin and Philo Farnsworth, were able to perfect a method of electronic scanning that would eventually become the basis for modern television. Working at RCA's research labs, Zworykin developed the "iconoscope," the eye of an electronic TV camera. Farnsworth grew up in Idaho and, working mainly by himself, developed an "image dissector," which, with a different design, accomplished much the same thing as Zworykin's iconoscope. The Depression of the 1930s forced Farnsworth to turn for financial support to the Philco Corporation, a radio set manufacturer and rival of RCA. Even at this early date, it was clear that corporate America would be behind future TV growth. It was also clear that the existing radio industry would be a major force in shaping the new medium. Consequently TV came into being with an organized pattern (networks and local stations) and a support system (commercials) already in place.

Improvements in TV continued during the 1930s. Experimental TV stations went on the air. RCA and Farnsworth settled a patent suit, and RCA was permitted to use Farnsworth's invention to further enhance its TV system. By 1939 the new invention had improved enough to be ready for its public debut at the World's Fair.

The development of a commercial TV system was interrupted by the war. Station construction was halted, and all but a handful of stations went off the air. On another front, however, World War II accelerated the technology behind TV. Scientists involved in perfecting TV went into the military and studied high-frequency electronics. Their work greatly improved the U.S. system of radar and also advanced the technical side of TV. As the war neared its end, it was apparent that TV would be back, stronger than ever.

When the war ended, the broadcasting industry made immediate preparations to shift its emphasis from radio to TV. Assembly lines that had been used to turn out war materials were retooled to produce tubes and TV sets. Returning soldiers, skilled in radar operation, were hired by many stations that were eager to use their electronics knowledge. Set manufacturers made plans to advertise their new, improved products.

Profile: Sarnoff and Paley

The two figures who most dominated the development of American network broadcasting—William S. Paley and David Sarnoff—could not have been more different. Sarnoff, from an emigrant Russian family, began his career as a wireless operator for the Marconi company. Paley came from an affluent family and after his college graduation became an executive in the family-owned Congress Cigar Company. Following his purchase of the struggling radio network, Paley became president of CBS.

Sarnoff gained national attention when he was one of several telegraph operators who relayed messages about the sinking of the *Titanic*. Marconi took note of the young man who was quickly promoted into the managerial ranks of American Marconi and later RCA. Popular history suggests that in 1916 Sarnoff wrote a prophetic memo to his superiors at Marconi, predicting that radio would become a mass medium. Recent research suggests that the memo might have been written some years later, making it less prophetic. In any case, Sarnoff eventually became chief executive officer at RCA and managed the company until 1969. It was Sarnoff who made NBC a force in radio broadcasting and who was a firm believer in the potential of television. Sarnoff also championed color TV.

Paley was more interested in the programming side of the business. He signed Bing Crosby and Kate Smith to contracts at CBS. In 1948 he scored a programming coup when he lured a number of big stars—Jack Benny, Edgar Bergen, and others—from NBC to CBS. Paley's achievements extended into news broadcasting as well. Under his leadership, CBS assembled a crew of reporters that began a tradition of outstanding journalism at CBS. It was Paley who persuaded Edward R. Murrow, the famous war correspondent, to take an executive position at CBS.

Rivals most of their careers, Paley and Sarnoff left their personal marks on American broadcasting.

By 1948 television was clearly on its way; network programming was introduced; popular radio shows made the transition to TV; and the new medium created its own stars. When Milton Berle's program came on Tuesday night at 8 p.m., it seemed the whole country stopped to watch. Ed Sullivan, a newspaper columnist with no discernible TV talent, hosted a variety show that quickly followed Berle's show to the top of the ratings charts.

Freeze

The growth of TV during 1948 was phenomenal. Set manufacturers couldn't keep up with the demand. More stations were going on the air, and many more were seeking to start. It seemed as if every town wanted a TV station. Things got so hectic that the FCC declared a freeze on new TV station applications while it studied the future of TV.

The TV industry, however, was not in a state of suspended animation during the freeze. Stations whose applications were approved before the freeze were allowed to go on the air. By 1950, 105 TV stations were broadcasting. Further, the networks, using AT&T land lines, were able to complete a coast-to-coast hookup, which enabled live network broadcasts to reach 95 percent of the homes then equipped with TV. Despite the freeze, TV had grown to nationwide proportions.

The freeze thawed in 1952 when the FCC produced a document called the **Sixth Report and Order,** which addressed several issues:

- A table of channel assignments was constructed, structuring the provision of TV service to all parts of the United States.

- To accommodate the hundreds of applicants seeking a TV license, the FCC opened up new channels (14–69) in the **ultra-high frequency (UHF)** part of the electromagnetic spectrum to join the channels (2–13) already in use. (Most TV sets couldn't get the UHF channels without a special antenna, so the new channels started off with a technical disadvantage that would slow their development for years to come.)

- Anticipating the future, the commission set standards regarding color TV.

- Finally, thanks to the efforts of Frieda Hennock, the first woman FCC commissioner (see the boxed profile), 242 channels were set aside for noncommercial TV stations.

Television programming developed and flowered during the freeze period. This was the golden era of TV as high-quality plays authored by such notables as Rod Serling and Paddy Chayefsky were key parts of the prime-time schedule. The *Today* show, still going strong at this writing, premiered in 1952. The most significant situation comedy of the era was *I Love Lucy*, starring Lucille Ball, a comedienne who would appear on TV in one form or another in four different decades. *I Love Lucy* was significant not only for its popularity but also because it was filmed in Hollywood, marking the beginning of the Hollywood involvement in TV, a trend that would grow over the next three decades.

RADIO'S PERIOD OF ADJUSTMENT

Faster than most people imagined, TV became the dominant news and entertainment medium. Although some people thought that radio might go the way of the blacksmith and the icebox, it managed to adjust and prosper.

At the risk of oversimplification, the coming of TV had four main effects on radio. First, it completely changed network broadcasting. After the freeze was lifted, mass-market advertising moved to TV. By 1955 network radio was taking a financial beating, with revenues dropping by about 58 percent from 1952. As major radio stars like Jack Benny and Bob Hope shifted to TV, network radio programs lost audiences to the new medium. Pretty soon the once-powerful radio networks were reduced to providing 10-minute newscasts on the hour and some daytime programs. It would take network radio nearly 30 years to recover.

Second, television made radio turn to specialized audiences through the development of particular formats. Local stations, faced with more hours to fill since the networks cut back on their programs, looked for an inexpensive way to fill the time. They found it with the disc jockey (DJ) and recorded music. Abandoning the long-standing antagonism against playing records on the air, stations chose music that would appeal to a specialized audience. Some rural stations concentrated on country-and-western music, while some stations in urban markets developed a rhythm-and-blues format. Many FM stations played classical music. The most influential format developed in this period, however, was called Top 40. Capitalizing on the growing popularity of rock-and-roll and the growth of the "youth" culture, Top 40 appealed to teens by playing a relatively small number of popular songs over and over. By 1960 hundreds of stations had adopted the format.

Lucille Ball and Desi Arnaz starred in *I Love Lucy*. From 1951 to 1957, the show was always among the three most popular TV programs.

Third, the advent of TV brought the radio and record industries closer together. Contrary to past thinking, radio airplay helped sell records. The record companies kept radio's programming costs to a minimum by providing the latest hits free to the stations. In return, the radio stations gave the record industry what amounted to free advertising. Record sales nearly tripled from 1954 to 1959.

Finally, television forced radio to become more dependent on local advertising revenue. Since they were no longer conduits for material produced by the networks, local stations became more responsive to their markets. They could play regional hits; DJs could make special appearances at local events; stations could provide more local news. All of this increased radio's appeal to local advertisers. In short, radio redefined its advertising base. In 1945 less than one-third of radio advertising came from local ads. Ten years later that proportion had nearly doubled.

To sum up, over the course of about a dozen traumatic years, radio made the necessary adjustments that enabled it to prosper in an era that was to be dominated by TV.

Frieda Hennock always valued education. Born in Poland, she moved to the United States when she was 6. After graduating early from high school, she took law classes at night and finished her degree at the age of 19. She was admitted to the bar two years later and, not surprisingly, became the youngest woman lawyer in New York City. During the late 1920s she distinguished herself as a criminal lawyer, but eventually her interest turned to corporate law. Her expertise and ability earned her a position at one of New York's leading law firms.

During the 1940s Hennock became active in politics and raised money to support several prominent Democrats, including Harry Truman. In 1948, when all political experts were predicting a Truman loss in the upcoming election, Truman repaid Hennock for her past support by nominating her to the Federal Communications Commission. This gesture, however, may have been more symbolic than substantive because, at the time, Republicans in Congress were blocking all new presidential appointments until after the election, when, presumably, a Republican would hold the office. Hennock nevertheless displayed impressive political skills and gained support from both Democrats and Republicans. To almost everyone's surprise, her nomination was approved by Congress, making her the first woman on the commission and the only one out of 800 Truman appointees to be confirmed. (Truman, of course, also surprised everybody and won the 1948 election.)

Hennock joined the FCC at the start of "the freeze," the period when the commission refused to consider new applications for TV stations while it worked out technical rules and regulations for the new medium. Her interest in education came to the surface. In the early days of radio, many educational institutions acquired broadcasting licenses only to give them up later after coming under pressure from commercial broadcasters who saw an opportunity for profit. When FM came on the scene, the FCC reserved 15 percent of the frequencies for use by educational institutions. The commercial broadcasters didn't object to this because they didn't think FM would amount to much.

Hennock believed that a similar reservation should be made for educational TV stations—a position that immediately put her at odds with commercial broadcasters who wanted the frequencies for themselves. As they had done during the early days of radio, the broadcasters argued that they were the ones who could best provide educational programming through sustaining, or commercial-free, programs. Hennock's colleagues at the commission favored the broadcasters' position.

Despite the odds against her, Hennock mobilized support from educators, private foundations, and the media. In 1951 she was rewarded with a partial victory when the FCC proposed reserving about 10 percent of available TV channels for noncommercial educational broadcasting. Hennock, however, campaigned for 25 percent. Despite her efforts, when the freeze was lifted in 1952, only 12 percent of the channels available were set aside for noncommercial broadcasting. Hennock voiced her dissatisfaction with the ruling and continued to campaign for greater educational access to television.

Hennock's remaining years on the commission often found her at odds with her colleagues and the establishment. She opposed the proposed merger of ABC with Paramount Theaters. She argued against rate increases for AT&T. Because many of the new educational stations were in the UHF band, she spent her last days on the commission campaigning to make UHF stations more competitive with VHF stations.

Hennock completed her term in 1955, and Republican President Dwight Eisenhower did not reappoint her. She resumed her successful law practice until her death in 1960. Today's noncommercial broadcasters can be thankful that Frieda Hennock's determined efforts gave education a permanent place in the television spectrum.

TV'S GROWTH CURVE: 1953–1962

The next 10 years saw an incredible surge in the fortunes of TV (see Table 1–2). In 1952 some 34 percent of households had TV. Ten years later 90 percent were equipped. There were 108 stations broadcasting in 1952. Ten years later there were 541. In the same period, the amount of money spent on TV advertising quadrupled. By any yardstick, TV was booming.

New Wrinkles

On the technology side, the Ampex Corporation introduced videotape recording in 1956. This invention made it possible to store TV programs in a high-quality format that could be used again and again. Tape also made program production cheaper and would ultimately replace film in the production of many situation comedies. Finally, tape helped kill off

Table 1–2	The Growth of Television		
Year	Number of Stations	Percentage of Homes with Television	Number of Employees
1950	98	9	9,000
1970	862	95	58,400
2010	1,782	99	205,000

live drama on TV. Before long, only news and sports were broadcast live; most other shows were either taped or on film.

RCA introduced color TV sets in 1954, and after a slow start, color TV eventually caught on. By 1962 about a half-million color sets were sold, and RCA announced it was finally making a profit from their sales.

As mentioned earlier, UHF TV stations got off to a slow start because their signals did not go as far as **very high frequency (VHF)** signals, and TV sets were not equipped with the special antenna needed to pick up UHF broadcasts. In 1961 the FCC persuaded Congress to pass the All-Channel Receiver Bill, which required all television sets to be able to receive all TV channels, not just VHF. Even so, UHF grew slowly.

Two other technological milestones occurred during this period that were to prove highly significant for the future of TV. The significance of the first was immediately apparent. A rocket roared off Cape Canaveral in July 1962 carrying *Telstar,* the first active communication satellite capable of relaying signals across the Atlantic Ocean. Only 25 years after Marconi's death, wireless signals were crossing the Atlantic in a way he had never imagined.

The ultimate significance of the second event was overlooked by virtually everybody. A new idea, introduced in the early 1950s, was gaining ground. People who lived in mountainous areas could not get good over-the-air TV reception. Residents of these areas hit on a novel solution. They would put an antenna on top of one of the tall peaks and run wires down to the homes in the valley. The residents would pay a fee to receive their programs over a cable. This system was called **community antenna TV,** or **CATV.** Later CATV would come to stand for cable TV. Conventional broadcasters thought that transmitting signals by cable was a clever idea but that it would have little general application. As the next chapter illustrates, they were mistaken.

Hollywood and New York

Although Hollywood had been a major center in the production of radio programs, it was not a significant force in the development of early television programming. Hollywood's lack of influence is somewhat surprising given that the major motion picture studios had the experience, talent, and facilities that could have easily been adapted for TV. Two factors were mainly responsible for Hollywood's lack of influence. First, the Federal Communications Commission indicated that postfreeze applications for TV stations from movie studios would not be favorably received. This prevented the studios from starting their own networks to compete with the established networks in New York. Moreover, if they couldn't compete directly against the existing TV industry, the studios were not going to cooperate with it by providing content. Hollywood saw television as a threat to its profitability; the more people who stayed home watching TV, the fewer who went to the movies. Consequently the major studios refused to release their current films to the TV networks and prohibited their biggest stars from appearing on TV shows.

Eventually, however, economic conditions brought the two industries closer together. The struggling DuMont Network, lacking stations in many of the major cities, went out of business in 1958. The ABC network was also having financial problems but found a new source of cash when it merged with Hollywood-based United Paramount Theaters in 1953. Thanks to its improved financial condition, ABC became more competitive during the late 1950s.

The merger also marked the beginning of a trend toward closer cooperation between Hollywood and the New York–based TV industry. The major film studios discovered that they could make money by producing series for the new medium. ABC again led the way when it signed a contract with the Walt Disney studios for a one-hour weekly series called *Disneyland.* The show was a big hit, and in short order other mainstream Hollywood companies, such as Warner Brothers and MCA Universal, followed suit. By 1960 about 40 percent of network programming was produced by big movie studios. Hollywood's desire to compete directly with the established TV networks was finally fulfilled in the late 1980s when Twentieth Century Fox established the Fox Network. A few years later Paramount and Warner Brothers debuted their own networks, and Disney got back into the network TV business when it acquired ABC in 1995.

Programming

Big-money quiz shows, such as *The $64,000 Question* and *21,* were popular at the end of the 1950s but quickly died out after a major scandal revealed that some of the shows were rigged. Adult Westerns, such as *Wyatt Earp* and *Gunsmoke,* also became popular; by 1959 there were more than 20 Western series on the air. Television news grew slowly during these years; nightly network newscasts were only 15 minutes long.

STABILITY FOR TV: 1963–1975

The next dozen years or so marked a fairly stable period in the history of broadcast TV. The networks were the dominant force of entertainment and news and enjoyed more or less steady financial growth. In any given minute of prime time, around 90 percent of the sets in use were tuned to network shows. Programming, while sometimes innovative, basically followed the formats from the 1950s. True, some events within the industry ruined the placid mood, but compared with what was to come, these years seem almost tranquil.

Technology

On the technological side, the slow but steady growth of cable TV began to capture the attention of the broadcasting industry. The early developments of this new medium are detailed in the next chapter. For now, the main thing to note is that cable grew slowly during this period, reaching only 10 percent of all TV homes in 1974.

Interestingly, UHF stations got a boost from cable. Cable systems had to carry all of the local stations in a market, including UHF. Once on the cable, the signal strength disadvantage of UHF no longer mattered, putting UHF and VHF stations on an equal footing and helping UHF increase its audience reach.

Finally, communication satellites became more important to TV. Those that followed *Telstar* were placed in a geosynchronous orbit, which meant that the satellites maintained their position relative to a point on earth and could serve as relays for ground stations. Satellites would eventually replace wires as the preferred medium for sending much of the content of broadcast TV.

Public TV

Noncommercial TV progressed slowly during the early 1960s, growing to 100 stations in 1965. A major development occurred in 1967 when a study sponsored by the Carnegie Foundation recommended a plan for what it called "public" TV. The term **public broadcasting** came to include a wide range of station owners: universities, school boards, state governments, school systems, and community organizations. Indeed, some of the problems that were to plague public broadcasting were in part caused by its heterogeneous nature. In any case, one of the important things about this report was a shift in philosophy: Noncommercial TV would no longer be limited to programs stressing formal instruction and education. Instead, it would provide an alternative to commercial programming. With amazing rapidity (just eight months later), Congress passed the **Public Broadcasting Act of 1967,** which created the Corporation for Public Broadcasting (CPB). The main function of CPB was to channel money into programming and station development. Two years later, CPB created the Public Broadcasting Service (PBS) to manage the network interconnection between the public stations.

Unfortunately Congress never provided enough funds for public TV, making it difficult for public TV to establish any long-range plans. Nonetheless, the service presented some award-winning programs: *Masterpiece Theater; Upstairs, Downstairs; Black Journal; Sesame Street;* and *The Electric Company.* By the late 1970s, however, its future was somewhat cloudy.

New Regulations

In 1971, after much debate about the harmful effects of cigarette smoking, Congress passed a law prohibiting the advertising of cigarettes on TV. Despite initial complaints from broadcasters that the new law would cost them more than $200 million in revenue, other advertisers quickly replaced the tobacco companies and TV ad revenues continued to increase.

Around this same time, the FCC was concerned that the networks were dominating TV. Accordingly, the commission announced the **Prime Time Access Rule (PTAR)** in 1970. In effect, this rule gave the 7:30–8:00 p.m. (EST) time period back to the local stations to program. The rule encouraged the growth of syndicated programs, such as *Wheel of Fortune,* and

The cast of *All in the Family*, a show that brought a harsh edge of realism to the situation comedy format.

made the syndication market an important one in TV programming.

Programming

There were several overlapping trends in TV programming during these years. In the early 1960s, programs containing violent content, such as *The Untouchables*, were becoming popular and began a controversy—that continued into the next century—over the effects of TV violence. At the same time, CBS was successful with a number of rural comedies, such as *The Beverly Hillbillies* and *Green Acres*. Escapist programs were also popular; *I Dream of Jeannie* and *Star Trek* both premiered during this period. Another notable trend in programming was the maturation of the situation comedy. *All in the Family* and *M*A*S*H* injected a new style of realism into the situation comedy. Finally, this period also marked the coming of age of TV news. The networks expanded their nightly newscasts from 15 to 30 minutes in 1963. In addition, audiences for local news shows were also increasing. At some stations, revenue

from news programming was the station's most important source of income.

CHANGES FOR TV: 1975–1999

The period from 1975 to 1999 heralded great changes in the TV industry. New technologies emerged to compete with traditional TV, increased competition lessened network domination of audience viewing, and the industry itself was reshaped by changes in the economic and business climate.

Competition

The growing popularity of cable TV, discussed in the next chapter, siphoned viewers away from broadcast TV networks. Premium channels, such as HBO, specialized cable channels, such as ESPN and MTV, and **superstations,** such as WTBS, became increasingly popular. Broadcast audience shares declined as more people opted for other viewing choices. Moreover, videocassette recorders (VCRs) became increasingly common in American households. From only a handful in operation in 1978, VCRs were in more than 80 percent of homes by the end of 1999. Some people used VCRs to tape network shows and play them back at more convenient times, but many others used them to watch rented theatrical movies on tape, which also ate into the broadcast networks' audiences. In addition, a fourth network—the Fox Broadcasting Company—premiered in 1987, dividing the audience into even smaller segments. By the mid-1990s, thanks to its acquisition of the rights to major-league baseball and professional football and some innovative programming such as *The Simpsons*, *Ally McBeal*, and *The X-Files*, Fox had emerged as a major network player. Three other networks, WB (owned by Warner Brothers), UPN (owned by Paramount), and the Pax network, also entered the scene.

In addition, cable channels, the Internet, video games, and prerecorded videocassettes siphoned off more of the audience of broadcast TV. Not surprisingly, the share of the audience that tuned to the four major networks continued to decline, dropping to about 50 percent in 2000.

The **Telecommunications Act of 1996** (see Chapter 10) made the television business even more competitive by allowing telephone companies to offer TV services. As the 21st century began, however, the phone companies were moving cautiously in this area and had yet to make a significant impact on broadcast TV. The 1996 act also relaxed the limits on television station ownership and made it easier for TV stations to own cable systems.

Mergers

From 1975 to the present, mergers and acquisitions have periodically reshaped the broadcasting landscape as companies jockeyed for market superiority and competitive advantage. Two main strategies behind mergers and acquisitions are **diversification** (branching out into other businesses) and **vertical integration** (expanding into related businesses at different points in the production process). In 1985 Capital Cities Broadcasting, a big group owner of TV stations, bought the ABC television network. Over the next few years the new Capital Cities/ABC diversified into cable TV by gaining control of ESPN. Ten years later, in an example of vertical integration, the Walt Disney Company acquired Capital Cities/ABC. The films and TV programs from Disney's production division were guaranteed an outlet over ABC's network of TV stations and cable channels.

Another example of diversification occurred in 1986 when, in an example of history coming full circle, GE, one of RCA's original owners back in 1919, acquired RCA and NBC. GE, one of the nation's biggest companies with interests ranging from defense systems to home appliances, was now firmly entrenched once again in the broadcasting business. A few years later, Westinghouse, another broadcasting pioneer, acquired CBS. In the late 1990s Westinghouse spun CBS off from the rest of the company, and, in another example of vertical integration, the network merged with media conglomerate and content producer Viacom.

The biggest deal of the period, however, was the $166 billion megamerger in 2000 between America Online and media conglomerate Time Warner. The new company had interests in a wide range of media including the Internet, cable TV, publishing, and moviemaking.

The competitive maneuvers continued during the first half of the new decade as Rupert Murdoch's News Corporation—a conglomerate that includes newspapers, a movie company, and a film studio—acquired satellite broadcaster DirecTV, another example of vertical integration. In addition, new business strategies continue to emerge. In an effort to focus its operations and improve its stock price,

Viacom announced in 2005 that it was splitting into two companies: the CBS Corporation, which would include all the broadcasting operations, and Viacom, consisting of the film and cable divisions. Finally, in 2006 Warner Brothers and CBS announced plans to merge the UPN and WB television networks into a single network called CW, and Fox started a new network called, appropriately enough, My Network TV.

Many critics have argued that continued mergers will severely limit the number of diverse social and cultural voices. They suggest that as the number of competitors decreases, so does the number of different viewpoints, types of artistic expression, and alternative information outlets, resulting in a society whose knowledge, tastes, and attitudes are homogenized. On the opposite side are those who say that in the age of the Internet, bloggers, satellite radio, and 500-channel cable systems, it is impossible for any small group of media companies to dominate the public's information and cultural outlets.

Public TV: Searching for a Mission

Public TV's recent history has been marked by two main themes: a general lack of money and a search for a purpose. A second Carnegie Commission Report, dubbed Carnegie II, was released in 1979. The report reviewed the problems that had plagued PBS from its inception: a lack of long-range funding from Congress, the lack of insulation of public TV from political squabbles, a clumsy managerial structure, and a need to define its mission.

Regarding the debate of public broadcasting's basic mission the following questions arose: Should public TV return to its original purpose during its inception in the 1950s and become an educational service? Or should it provide more general-appeal programming as an alternative to commercial broadcasting? But what exactly was an alternative? "High-brow" programming for the culturally elite or programs such as *Austin City Limits*? Should it compete with the major networks or become a service for minority interests? Which minorities? Such questions are still being asked today.

To make matters more complicated, cable networks were providing some of the material that had previously been the province of public TV, and public TV was beginning to look more like a commercial network; The Discovery Channel, the Arts and Entertainment Network, and the Learning Channel

Profile: Robert Adler, Unsung Hero

Most people know that Alexander Graham Bell invented the telephone and Guglielmo Marconi constructed the wireless, but almost no one knows whom to thank for developing one of the most important and ubiquitous devices that totally reshaped the modern television viewing experience: the remote control.

Some early TV sets were equipped with a wired device that changed stations, but the real breakthrough came with development of a wireless remote control. Technicians at the Zenith Radio Company developed an early version that used photo cells and light beams, but the device never gained popularity because a beam of sunlight could strike the TV and set off a flurry of channel switching. Another prototype changed channels using radio waves, but radio waves traveled through walls and might affect TV sets in the next room or apartment. In 1956 a Zenith engineer, Robert Adler, found a method that got around these problems. Adler's remote control, called the Space Command, used ultrasound (sounds at frequencies that were inaudible to the human ear) to change channels and turn the set on and off. The inside of the Space Command contained four aluminum rods (no batteries needed). When the viewer pushed the appropriate button, it struck one of the rods and generated a tone that the TV receiver translated into the appropriate action.

The early remote controls were generally sold with expensive, high-end TV sets, which limited their popularity. Moreover, because only two or three channels were available to most viewers, the remote control was not much help. It was only with the advent of cable and satellite services in the 1970s and 1980s and the drastically increased number of channels available that the remote control became a truly useful device.

Modern devices have made great strides since the Space Command. They use infrared light and UHF radio waves to transmit their signals and can perform dozens of different TV tuning and selection tasks. Today almost every TV set in the United States comes equipped with a remote control device.

As for Robert Adler, he served as director of research for Zenith until 1982 and was eventually awarded a total of 180 U.S. patents for his innovations. Adler received an Emmy in 1998 for his development of the remote control. He also earned the gratitude of millions of couch potatoes.

---

presented educational and prestige programming that siphoned away some PBS viewers. And public TV stations, in an attempt to raise more money, adopted a policy of "enhanced underwriting," announcements from companies that helped underwrite the costs for programming and that sounded suspiciously like commercials.

As of 2010 public television was still struggling. Its prime-time programming averaged a 1.1 rating during the 2008–2009 season, which was about half the rating of USA network's *WWE Raw*. There were, however, some optimistic signs. The Obama administration did not ask for more budget cuts from PBS in 2009, and PBS officials were hopeful that their budget might actually increase in the next few years. In addition, PBS still produced programs that garnered critical praise and loyal fans. Ken Burns's 2009 series *The National Parks* reached a total audience of 33 million viewers. *Sesame Street* has been on the air for more than 40 years, and regularly scheduled news and public affairs programs such as *Frontline* and *PBS NewsHour* score steady if not spectacular ratings.

Programming

One of the biggest programming trends of the late 1970s was the emergence of the prime-time continuing episode series, also called prime-time soaps, such as *Dynasty* and *Dallas*. Another significant trend was the shift back to warm and wholesome family situation comedy as exemplified by *The Cosby Show* and *The Wonder Years*. News programming continued to expand both on cable and on broadcast TV. The Cable News Network (CNN) began in 1980 and prompted the broadcast networks to expand their own news programming by adding late-night and early-morning programs. By the mid-1980s, the networks were providing about 40 hours of news every week.

The 1990s were notable for the growth of the news magazine program, such as *60 Minutes, 48 Hours,* and *Dateline NBC*. In 1995 the networks scheduled eight hours per week of these programs. Part of the reason for their popularity was economic. News magazines cost less to produce than sitcoms and dramas. Despite their production costs, sitcoms were also popular, and NBC led the way with *Seinfeld, Cheers*, and *Friends*.

Television programming in the first decade of the new century was dominated by two genres: "reality" programming, such as *Survivor* and *Amazing Race,* and procedural dramas, such as *CSI* and *Without a Trace.* The fall 2004–2005 prime-time schedule, for example, had 14 hours of reality shows. The reason for this proliferation was simple: Reality shows got good ratings and were relatively cheap to produce.

Technology

In the 1970s TV production equipment became smaller and easy to carry. One of the results of this was the development of **electronic news gathering (ENG),** which revolutionized TV coverage. Using portable cameras and tape recorders, reporters no longer had to wait for film to be developed. In addition, ENG equipment was frequently linked to microwave transmission, which allowed live coverage of breaking news.

The 1980s saw the development of **satellite news gathering (SNG).** Vans equipped with satellite uplinks made it possible for reporters to travel virtually anywhere on earth and to send back a report. Local stations sent their own correspondents to breaking news events in Europe and Asia for live reports. Stations also formed satellite interconnection services that swapped news footage and feeds.

The **direct broadcast satellite (DBS)** made its appearance during the 1990s. DBS uses high-powered communication satellites to send programming to umbrella-sized dishes mounted on rooftops. After a slow start, the DBS services grew in popularity. About 15 million homes were receiving DBS signals as the new century began.

The emergence of the Internet and the growth of the World Wide Web during the 1990s posed both challenges and opportunities for broadcasters. Stations and networks were quick to establish Web sites. These Web sites functioned primarily as promotional devices for their traditional services and as a handy source of audience feedback about programming. Broadcasters were initially concerned that their Web sites might siphon off viewers from their local programs, especially local newscasts. Eventually, however, both the networks and the local stations discovered that their Web sites could complement their programming. Local TV stations, for example, added headlines, community events calendars, and local weather radar to their sites. Networks added episode lists, actor biographies, previews, program clips, and even whole episodes to their sites. Moreover, broadcasters were searching for ways to make their Web sites profitable for their companies. Maintaining a mutually beneficial relationship between the Web site and the traditional broadcast service continued to be a problem into the new century.

RADIO IN THE VIDEO AGE

Since 1960 the TV set has pushed radio from center stage. Television now dominates news and entertainment, and radio has carved out a new niche for itself. This section will examine the more significant trends that have shaped modern radio.

High Tech

Radio became portable during the early 1960s because of the **transistor,** a tiny device that took the place of the vacuum tube. This made it possible to produce small, lightweight, and inexpensive radios. The invention of printed and integrated circuits shrank radio sets even further. Taking advantage of these and other developments, the Sony Corporation marketed the Walkman, a miniature radio–cassette player that produced high-quality sounds through lightweight earphones. Radio had become a truly personal medium. Satellite radio debuted in 2001 with Sirius and XM broadcasting digital signals to specially equipped receivers. A few years later the radio industry introduced HD radio—a high-quality signal that made AM radio sound as good as analog FM radio and FM sound as good as a CD. This innovation, however, was slow to catch on, and sales of HD radio receivers were disappointing.

By 2005 many traditional radio stations began broadcasting their signals on the Internet. They were joined by thousands of Internet-only stations. Many of these online stations played highly specialized music that would not ordinarily be carried by traditional stations.

FM

Perhaps the most significant event in the radio industry since 1960 has been the evolution of FM to being the preferred service among radio listeners. After a slow start, the number of FM stations nearly tripled from 1960 to 1980. The number of FM radios increased from 6.5 million in 1960 to 350 million in 1980. Listening patterns had totally changed: In 1972 FM held only 28 percent of the audience's total listening time

Conservative Glenn Beck's radio program is heard on more than 400 radio stations.

and AM held 72 percent, but by 2000 the figures were reversed—72 percent FM and only 28 percent AM. Why the change?

First, FM was able to broadcast in stereo. This enhanced sound gave it a distinct advantage over AM among the many consumers who valued improved audio quality. Second, AM stations were hard to come by. Those wishing to go into broadcasting during this period were almost forced to start FM stations because all the AM frequencies were taken. Third, the new FM stations developed new formats, such as progressive rock and easy listening, that drew listeners. Faced with declining audiences, AM stations searched for a format that would be successful. Many went to an all-talk format, while others switched to golden oldies.

Radio Networks

The 1960s were dark days for network radio. Advertising revenues dropped, and fewer stations were network affiliates. Looking for some way to rebound, ABC split its original network into four specialized services that complemented the new specialized for-

mats on local stations: entertainment, information, contemporary, and FM. The idea worked, and ABC had doubled the number of its affiliates by 1970. NBC, CBS, and Mutual soon followed suit. Network radio bounced back, and by 1980 there were more than a dozen nets in operation.

This growth was accompanied by changes in network ownership. In 1987 Westwood One took over the NBC network. Consolidation in the radio network business would continue into the 1990s as Infinity Broadcasting took over Westwood One and eventually merged with CBS.

Coupled with this trend was the growth of radio **syndication** companies. Syndication companies, much like networks, send programming to local stations. The growing popularity of syndicated talk shows, such as those of Rush Limbaugh, Sean Hannity, and Glenn Beck, helped build the audiences of many AM stations.

Fine-Tuning Formats

The increased number of radio stations has made radio a highly competitive business. In an effort to attract an audience segment that is of value to advertisers, many radio stations have turned to audience research to make sure that the station's programming reaches its target audience. This research has produced a set of highly refined **formats** that have sliced the radio audience into smaller and smaller segments. For example, there are several subvarieties of the country format; album-oriented rock attracts 18- to 24-year-old males; and news-talk is geared for the over-45 male audience. In 2010 stations were featuring dozens of different formats, ranging from "alternative" to "Vietnamese." In the larger markets, a radio station that attracts only 10 percent of the listening audience will usually rank at or near the top of the ratings.

Consolidation

The 1996 Telecommunications Act lifted the national ownership limits in radio stations, prompting an unprecedented wave of consolidation in the inudstry. By the start of the new century, Clear Channel had emerged as the biggest radio company, owning more than 1,200 stations in 190 markets. Other large group owners included Viacom, Cox, Entercom, and ABC Radio. The top 25 radio companies accounted for about 80 percent of the advertising money spent on radio.

Glee is one of the highest rated shows on the Fox Network.

RECENT TRENDS

The current state of the radio and television industries is discussed in more detail in Chapters 4, 5, and 6. The section briefly lists the major highlights of the past few years that have shaped and will continue to shape the current state of affairs:

1. *Economics:* The recession at the end of the first decade of the new century profoundly affected the electronic media. Advertising dollars dried up, and both networks and local stations saw their revenues decline. As a result, many organizations eliminated jobs. Radio station group owner Clear Channel cut its workforce by 9 percent. Time Warner Cable laid off more than a thousand workers. NBC Universal reduced its staff by 500; ABC cut about 300 employees, and CBS cut about 100 jobs from its news division. Local stations also slashed their payrolls.

   The tough economic times were also reflected in prime-time television programming. As was the case earlier in the decade, rather than investing in expensive comedy and drama series, the major networks turned to relatively inexpensive reality programs. At the start of the 2009–2010 season, ABC, CBS, Fox, and NBC programmed about 25 hours of reality shows per week. NBC made the most drastic move toward reality programming when it moved Jay Leno's late-night talk show into prime time five nights a week. The strategy proved to be unsuccesful as pressure from NBC's affiliates forced the network to move Leno back to his late-night spot.

   Finally, broadcasters tried to develop new revenue streams for their operations. Local stations negotiated new deals with cable and satellite companies that compensated them for the retransmission of their programs. In addition to receiving retransmission fees for their owned and operated stations, the networks were also attempting to get a share of the fees collected by their affiliates. Many radio stations now receive income from nontraditional sources, such as sponsoring concerts and other community-related events; and some stations are exploring ways to use text messaging as an advertising tool.

2. *Technology:* Television broadcasting went to an all-digital system on June 19, 2009. Digital TV allows clearer pictures and better sound quality. In addition, DTV makes it possible to broadcast high-definition television (HDTV). The popularity of HDTV skyrocketed during

the last few years of the new decade. As of 2010 around 50 percent of U.S. homes were equipped with HDTV. Finally, digital signals are compressed and take up less space in the electromagnetic spectrum. Consequently broadcasters can subdivide the digital channel and offer several different programs in the same space. As of 2010 most broadcasters had yet to turn these new channels into a profit-making enterprise.

The DVR (digital video recorder) has changed the way many Americans watch TV. Rather than watching a program when it airs, viewers record the show for viewing at a more convenient time. Nearly 40 percent of homes were equipped with DVRs in 2010. The popularity of the DVR has raised issues for advertisers who fear that viewers are fast-forwarding through commercials during playback.

Broadcasters and cable companies have also turned to new distribution channels in an attempt to increase their audiences. Not surprisingly, the Internet will play a big role in their future plans. Many broadcasters and cable networks let viewers watch full episodes of their shows on their Web sites. NBC and Fox launched Hulu.com in 2008 (ABC joined later) and gave viewers the chance to watch full episodes of current and past television shows for free. As of 2010 Hulu.com was the second most popular video Web site, trailing only video-sharing site YouTube. Local TV stations also upgraded their Web sites, adding video clips, breaking news stories, and information about community events. (For more about Internet audio and video, see Chapter 6.)

Television and radio have also gone mobile. Those who own iPods can download music videos, podcasts, and full-length programs from Apple's iTunes store. Cell phone users can pay a monthly subscription fee and get a line-up of preselected channels from their cell phone provider. MobiTV, for example, is available to Sprint and AT&T subscribers for about $10–$15 a month and carries programming from NBC, CBS, ESPN, Fox, and many other channels. In 2010 some of the nation's biggest broadcasters announced plans for an advertising-supported system that would send live TV programs directly to cell phones. Broadcasters and cable companies were also exploring the potential of

Apple's iPad as a video platform. ABC, for example, developed an application that lets iPad owners watch ABC programs.

Finally, several TV manufacturers unveiled 3-D TV sets. ESPN networks aired some sports events in 3-D in 2010. DirecTV also announced that it would launch an all 3-D channel by the end of the year. Whether viewers will opt for the new system remains to be seen.

3. *Business developments:* The trend toward mergers that began in the early years of the first decade of the new century continued at the decade's end. The two companies providing satellite radio service merged in 2008. The new company, Sirius XM, had nearly 19 million subscribers in 2010. The second merger involved a cable company and a broadcast network. In late 2009 Comcast, the nation's biggest cable company, announced plans to acquire NBC Universal. The new company would control about two dozen cable networks, a broadcast network, several local TV stations, a motion picture production company, and several Web sites and theme parks. In radio, however, the biggest business news was deconsolidation. In 2008 a group of private investors acquired radio giant Clear Channel and sold off more than 400 of its stations.

4. *Legal:* Controversy continued to swell around the issue of broadcast indecency. A 2009 ruling by the Supreme Court upheld the right of the FCC to fine stations for airing certain expletives during a live broadcast but did not address the question of whether the FCC's policy was constitutional. A lower court eventually ruled against the FCC.

In 2010 the FCC announced an ambitious plan to provide 100 million households with a high-speed Internet connection as well as finding more spectrum space for wireless broadband. One proposal called for TV stations to voluntarily hand over spectrum space in return for a portion of the revenue from auctioning off that spectrum space to broadband companies. Some critics question whether the FCC has the legal authority to regulate the Internet. The courts may ultimately decide this issue (see Chapter 10).

5. *Convergence:* The move toward convergence continues to grow. As digital movies on DVD

and digital television programs become more common, they will ultimately combine with video games, Internet video, and digital music to form one standardized stream of digital content. In like manner, the current channels of distribution—cable, satellite, and the Internet—will converge into one high-speed broadband connection. Consumers will ultimately have one big screen in their homes where they will watch TV, play back digital movies, surf the Internet, send e-mail, play video games, and run their usual computer software . . . but we're

getting ahead of ourselves. This chapter is about history, not the future.

Speaking of the past and of the future, remember that Fessenden made his first radio broadcast in 1906. What if Fessenden were alive today? It is doubtful that he or any of the other early inventors could envision how radio and TV would evolve over the next hundred years or so. By the same token, it is unlikely that you or anybody else reading this book will be able to imagine what TV and radio will be like a hundred years from now.

SUMMARY

- Marconi, Fessenden, and De Forest were early inventors who helped radio develop. General Electric, Westinghouse, and AT&T were companies that were interested in early radio. Each company held patents needed by the others, and, as a result, many legal battles hampered radio's early development.

- During World War I, the navy took responsibility for patent infringement, which allowed significant technical improvements in the medium. When the war was over, a new company, RCA, was formed and quickly became the leading company in American radio.

- The 1920s were a significant period for radio. Early stations were experimental, and the notion of broadcasting was discovered more or less by accident. The new fad grew quickly, and soon there were hundreds of stations on the air. Radio networks and radio advertising were developed, and the federal government took charge of radio regulation.

- The period from 1930 to 1948 was the "golden age of radio" when the medium was the prime source of news and entertainment for the nation. This situation changed as television came on the scene in the 1950s.

- Developed by Zworykin and Farnsworth, TV was first unveiled in 1939. After its development was interrupted by World War II, television quickly became popular, and by the mid-1950s it had taken radio's place as the number one medium in the country.

- The FCC froze applications for TV stations from 1948 to 1952 while it determined standards for the new medium. After the freeze was lifted, TV growth skyrocketed. Networks dominated TV until the 1970s when cable emerged as a formidable competitor.

- Radio reacted to TV by becoming a localized medium that depended on formats to attract specific segments of the listening audience.

- Television's Fox network premiered in the 1980s, which caused ABC, CBS, and NBC further audience erosion. The ownership of all three major networks changed hands during the 1980s and 1990s. The Telecommunications Act of 1996 prompted a wave of consolidation in the radio industry.

- The Internet and the shift to digital technology will have an impact on the future of radio and TV broadcasting.

KEY TERMS

crystal set   7
audion   7
Radio Act of 1927   11
Federal Radio Commission
    (FRC)   12
Communications Act of 1934   12
Federal Communications
    Commission (FCC)   12
Sixth Report and Order   16
ultra-high frequency (UHF)   16

very high frequency (VHF)   19
Telstar   19
community antenna TV (CATV)   19
public broadcasting   20
Public Broadcasting Act of 1967   20
Prime Time Access Rule
    (PTAR)   20
superstations   21
Telecommunications Act
    of 1996   21

diversification   22
vertical integration   22
electronic news gathering
    (ENG)   24
satellite news gathering (SNG)   24
direct broadcast satellite (DBS)   24
transistor   24
syndication   25
formats   25

SUGGESTIONS FOR FURTHER READING

Abramson, A. (2003). *The history of television, 1942 to 2000.* Jefferson, NC: McFarland.

Archer, G. (1938). *History of radio to 1926.* New York: American Historical Society.

Barnouw, E. (1966). *A tower in Babel.* New York: Oxford University Press.

———— (1968). *The golden web.* New York: Oxford University Press.

———— (1975). *Tube of plenty.* New York: Oxford University Press.

Brock, P. (2008). *Charlatan.* New York: Crown.

Douglas, S. (1987). *Inventing American broadcasting.* Baltimore, MD: Johns Hopkins University Press.

Eberly, P. (1982). *Music in the air.* New York: Hastings House.

Hilliard, R., & Keith, M. (1992). *The broadcast century.* Stoneham, MA: Focal Press.

Lewis, T. (1991). *Empire of the air.* New York: Harper-Collins.

Stashower, D. (2002). *The boy genius and the mogul: The untold story of television.* New York: Broadway Books.

Sterling, C., & Kittross, J. (2001). *Stay tuned: A concise history of American broadcasting.* Belmont, CA: Wadsworth.

Udelson, J. (1982). *The great television race.* Tuscaloosa, AL: University of Alabama Press.

White, L. (1947). *The American radio.* Chicago: University of Chicago Press.

INTERNET EXERCISES

Visit our Web site at **www.mhhe.com/dominickbib7e** for study-guide exercises to help you learn and apply material in each chapter. You will find ideas for future research as well as useful Web links to provide you with an opportunity to journey through the new electronic media.

2 History of Cable, Home Video, and the Internet

Quick Facts

Cost of monthly cable service, 1950: $3.00

Cost of monthly digital cable service, 2010: $75 (does not include high-speed Internet access)

First satellite TV broadcast: NBC, 1962

Cost of first home satellite dish, 1979: $36,000

Cost of DirecTV satellite system, 2010: $0 (but you have to sign up for a year of service)

First consumer VCR: 1975

Development of the World Wide Web: 1991

Introduction of Facebook: 2004

Cost of downloading an HD movie on iTunes, 2010: $4.99

As we discussed in the last chapter, a sea change occurred in the radio business in 1978, when the majority of radio listening in America shifted from the AM band to FM. In 1998 a similar moment of significance took place when ratings revealed that more Americans were watching cable programming in the evening than were watching the over-the-air broadcast networks. In scarcely a generation, cable has moved from a small-time adjunct to broadcast TV to a huge and influential media business. This chapter traces the growth of cable and other alternatives to broadcast television, including satellites, DVRs, and the "new kid on the block"—the Internet and its network, the World Wide Web (WWW). Like many mass media today, cable's beginnings were modest and its early steps were halting. What follows is a small part of the cable success story.

DEMANDING WIVES AND POWERFUL ALLIES: THE STORY OF CABLE TELEVISION

On Thanksgiving Day, 1949, KRSC in Seattle became the first operating TV station in the Pacific Northwest. In Astoria (near Portland), Oregon, there was at least one family with a television set. Back in 1947 Ed Parsons and his wife, Grace, were at a convention in Chicago, where they first saw TV. Grace wanted one in her home, so Ed bought one by mail order. He tried to tell his wife they were too far from any TV stations to get any channels. "She figured I was an engineer; so there was no reason why she shouldn't have television," he later said. For months the set sat idle. Ed thought it would end up as an interesting-looking table.

But the new station in Seattle kindled Ed's interest and inventiveness. He put together a system of antennas, amplifiers, and converters and tried to pull in a signal from Seattle. He took the rig all around town and even flew it in his own airplane. Ultimately he found he got the best signal from Seattle (where KRSC was testing its tower) from the top of the Astoria Hotel, just across the street from Ed and Grace's apartment.

Working out of his small radio repair shop, he built the antenna array and amplifiers needed to pull in KRSC, and he stretched antenna wire over to his apartment. As the new station signed on, the Parsons—and more than a dozen friends and relatives who crammed into their apartment—were the only people in Astoria who could watch it. Soon, however, Parsons was stringing antenna wire all over town for $125 per household. Grace was happily watching "Uncle Miltie," as were millions of other new TV viewers.

Back east, a big union boss was planning a brief trip. John L. Lewis was a man who usually got what he wanted. As president of the United Mine Workers, one of the nation's most powerful unions, he wielded enormous power. It was difficult to say no to Lewis or to his legion of large, loud, and loyal "friends." One day in 1950, one of those friends—an executive secretary in the union—was expecting a weekend visit from Lewis. There was one major problem, though. The secretary lived out in Lansford, Pennsylvania, about 70 miles from Philadelphia, too far to receive a decent TV signal. And Lewis liked to watch TV, especially the Friday night boxing matches.

On the edge of town, near Summit Hill (the next town over), Bob Tarlton, a young veteran of World War II, was working at the radio and appliance store he and his father owned. Summit Hill was about 500 feet higher than Lansford. Fuzzy pictures from Philadelphia could be seen on the new TV sets the Tarltons had just started to sell. But they wanted to improve the picture (and sell some TV sets as a result). So they strung antenna wire from their store to a radio antenna in Summit Hill. The picture was greatly improved.

One day, a well-dressed but rather swarthy and brusque man appeared in the Tarltons' shop. It was the union secretary from Lansford. He wanted that crisp, clear picture in his home for Lewis. It was an offer the Tarltons couldn't refuse. They ran a cable from a hilltop in Lansford down to the union secretary's home. Lewis and his friend were pleased.

Soon the Tarltons' other customers wanted to get on the antenna to improve their reception, especially those who had just bought a TV set from them. The Tarltons borrowed money from a local bank, improved their antenna system, and replaced common antenna wire with the new coaxial cable the telephone company was using to promote long-distance service. They began charging customers $100 for installation and a monthly fee of $3.

Through the early 1950s, in Astoria, Oregon, Lansford, Pennsylvania, and dozens of other small communities on the fringes of good TV reception, community antenna TV (CATV, or more commonly, **cable TV**) was catching on. By the end of the famous TV freeze in 1952, 70 cable systems were serving about 15,000 homes in the United States. Five years later 500 systems brought improved TV signals to about 350,000 homes. As President Kennedy took office in early 1961, about 650 systems served just under 700,000 subscribers.

Broadcasters weren't sure how to regard the new industry. At first they welcomed the fact that their signals were reaching homes that otherwise couldn't receive them. On the other hand, broadcasters planning on starting up new UHF stations might find that they could not make a profit unless they were carried on the cable. Their prosperity would be under the control of the cable operator, a situation broadcasters did not find appealing.

The FCC was reluctant to get involved. In 1958 the commission decided that it did not have the authority to regulate cable because cable was not broadcasting and used no spectrum space.

Meanwhile the cable industry continued slow but steady growth. By 1964 a thousand cable systems were in operation, mainly serving small to medium-sized communities. Two years later the number grew to more than 1,500. At about this same time, the concept behind cable was changing. In addition to carrying local stations, cable systems began to import the signals of distant stations that previously were not available to the community. This development alarmed the broadcasting community because most communities had only three or four stations. If several new stations were suddenly available in a market, the audience shares and the advertising revenues of the existing stations would decline, perhaps forcing some local broadcasters off the air. Particularly disturbed were the owners of UHF stations, whose operations were not very profitable to begin with. The broadcasting lobby asked the FCC for some protection.

A few years earlier the FCC had committed itself to the development of UHF broadcasting to encourage the expansion of broadcast television. The growth of cable posed a threat to its policy. Accordingly, from 1965 to 1966 the FCC reversed itself by claiming jurisdiction over cable and issued a set of restrictive rules that protected over-the-air broadcasting. (The prevailing philosophy at the FCC at this time envisioned cable as merely an extension of traditional TV signals. Thus it is not surprising that any challenge to broadcasting by cable's development would be curtailed by regulation.) Cable systems had to carry all TV stations within 60 miles and couldn't carry shows from distant stations that duplicated those offered by local stations. In 1968 the commission ruled that CATV systems in the top 100 markets had to get specific approval before they could import the signals of distant stations. Taken together, these rules effectively inhibited the growth of CATV and made sure that any growth would be limited to smaller communities. While all of these rules were being made, CATV systems were quietly improving their technology so that by the late 1960s many systems could carry as many as 20 different channels.

In 1972 the FCC, pressured by both traditional broadcasters and the cable industry, issued yet another set of rules. Among other things, these rules specified the following:

1. Local communities, states, and the FCC were to regulate cable.

2. There would be 20-channel minimums for new systems.

3. All local stations would be carried.

4. More regulations on the importation of distant signals, including the nonduplication provision mentioned earlier, would be implemented.

5. Pay cable services would be approved.

Once again, the major impact of these rules was to discourage the growth of cable in urban areas. Cable was insignificant to city residents, who already received good reception from a number of local stations. Cable system operators were not encouraged to bring service to urban areas because the stringing and installation of cable were expensive in densely populated areas, and once cable were installed the operators would have a big job making sure that no imported signal duplicated local programs. To top things off, a major cable company nearly went bankrupt. Cable did, however, grow in midsized markets, and by 1974 it had penetrated a little more than 10 percent of all TV homes. On balance, its future did not look promising. As we shall see in the next section, however, things changed.

Pay TV: An Idea Ahead of Its Time

Early on, a number of entrepreneurs had the notion that cable could be used to control what programs went into any individual household. Specifically, they thought that one or more channels on a TV set could be used to send movies and sports for a one-time or extra monthly fee. As early as 1953, Paramount Pictures built a cable system in Palm Springs, California, and offered movies like *Forever Female* with Ginger Rogers for $1.35. It also offered the

Notre Dame–USC football game for $1.00. Only about 75 homes signed up for this "pay as you look" service, and it ended—amid strenuous objections from TV broadcasters and fearful theater owners— less than a year later. Though similar pay TV ventures were tried in Oklahoma, Los Angeles, and elsewhere, the idea was tabled for nearly 20 years.

Cable Growth

There were two basic reasons for the explosive growth of cable in the late 1970s—one technological, the other regulatory. In 1975 a then little-known company in the pay TV business, Home Box Office (HBO), rented a transponder on the communications satellite *Satcom I* and announced plans for a satellite-interconnected cable programming network. Cable systems could set up their own receiving dish and HBO would transmit to them first-run movies, which the operators could then sell to their subscribers for an additional fee. Although pay TV was not a new idea, HBO's new arrangement meant wider coverage of cable systems at a lower cost. Further, the new programming service provided a reason for people in urban and suburban areas to subscribe to cable. Now the big attraction was no longer better reception of conventional channels but content that was not available to regular TV viewers, including movies, sports events, and musical specials. In a few years other cable-only channels were also distributed by satellite— Showtime, The Movie Channel, Christian Broadcasting Network—as well as independent local stations, dubbed "superstations," such as WTBS in Atlanta and WGN in Chicago. Other specialized cable networks—ESPN (sports), CNN (news), and MTV (music videos)—soon followed. Cable now had a lot more features to attract customers.

The second reason for growth came from the FCC. By the mid-1970s the commission realized, with some help from the courts, that its 1972 rules were stifling cable's growth. Consequently the FCC postponed or canceled the implementation of many of its earlier pronouncements and changed its philosophy: It would henceforth encourage competition between cable and traditional TV. Eventually, as the Reagan administration advanced its deregulation policies, the FCC dropped most of its rules concerning cable. In 1984 Congress passed the **Cable Communications Policy Act.** The law, which was incorporated into the 1934 Communications Act, endorsed localism and set up a system of community regulation tempered by federal oversight. The FCC was given definite but limited authority over cable. The local community was the major force in cable regulation, which it exercised through the franchising process. The act gave cable operators, among other things, greater freedom in setting their rates and released them from most rules covering their program services.

Together these two factors caused a spurt of cable growth that attracted the interest of large media companies such as Tele-Communications, Inc. (TCI), which in turn invested in cable. This caused cable to grow even faster. In fact, the growth was so great that many cable companies in a rush to get exclusive franchises in particular communities promised too much and had to cut back on the size and sophistication of their systems. Nonetheless, although the growth rate tapered off a bit in the mid-1980s, the statistics are still impressive. From 1975 to 1987, the number of operating cable systems more than tripled. The percentage of homes with cable went from about 14 percent in 1975 to 50 percent in 1987. Even the urban areas shared this growth, and at least parts of many big cities were finally wired for cable.

Ted Turner used cable TV to take a struggling Atlanta UHF station and turn it into superstation WTBS.

Table 2–1	The Growth of Cable TV		
Year	Operating Systems	Subscribers (millions)	TV Homes (%)
1960	640	0.7	1.4%
1965	1,325	1.3	2.4
1970	2,490	4.5	7.6
1975	3,366	9.8	14.3
1980	4,048	15.5	20.5
1985	6,600	37.3	43.7
1990	10,200	54.0	58.0
1995	13,000	60.0	63.0
2000	9,947	73.1	70.0
2005	7,926	73.4	66.0
2010*	7,527	101.0	78.9

*Includes cable, satellite, and telco video subscriptions.

Source: Compiled by the authors from various industry publications.

By 1988 the cable industry had become dominated by large multiple-system operators (MSOs). The era of a locally owned "mom-and-pop" cable system was over. The top 10 MSOs controlled more than 54 percent of the nation's subscribers, and the largest MSO, TCI, alone had more than 10 million subscribers. In this same year, cable passed the "magic number": More than half of all households in the United States were cable subscribers.

The growth of cable (detailed in Table 2–1) continued through the 1990s and 2000s. At mid-decade cable was available to more than 98 percent of American homes. About 66 percent of all TV homes subscribed to some form of cable. Annual revenue from these television services amounted to about $53 billion in 2009. There were signs, however, that the cable boom was cooling off. Subscriber growth has declined in the last few years, with cable losing subscribers to satellite broadcasters such as DirecTV and Dish Network and broadband video. One bright spot was the continued growth of cable advertising revenue, amounting to more than $24 billion in 2009.

ALTERNATIVES TO CABLE

It should come as no surprise that the rise of cable led other innovators and entrepreneurs to get on the multichannel bandwagon. Leading the way were satellite; multichannel, multipoint distribution service (MMDS); and a huge consumer favorite: playback devices such as VCRs, DVDs, and DVRs. (See Table 2–2.)

Profile: From Cottonseed Salesman to Cable King—Bob Magness and TCI

The media world was shaken in 1998 with the announced merger of two of its largest companies: telephone giant AT&T and cable power Tele-Communications, Inc., also known as TCI. The combined company, valued at nearly $50 billion, is a world leader in local and long distance telephone, cable television operations, and entertainment and information programming. It may be hard to believe, but global powerhouse TCI wasn't even founded until 1965. And it probably wouldn't have even existed if a young cottonseed salesman hadn't stopped to pick up a couple of hitchhikers whose truck had broken down one day in Paducah, Texas.

A native of Oklahoma, Bob Magness had served in a rifle platoon under General George Patton in World War II. After the war, he got a business degree from Southwestern State College in Texas and went to work selling seed to farmers and ranchers. One day, after visiting a cattle rancher near Paducah, Magness stopped to help two workmen whose truck was stalled at the side of the road. He was amply rewarded for his Good Samaritan gesture.

It turns out the hitchhikers had been constructing a cable system in Paducah. Over lunch at a hamburger stand, they boasted how good a business cable television was getting to be. Magness was bitten by the cable bug. In 1956, with money he got by mortgaging his ranch, Magness built his first cable system in Memphis, Texas. Two years later, he moved to Bozeman, Montana, to build a system there. In 1965 he took his cable operations to Denver, and he renamed his company TCI in 1968. A short time later, he brought in John Malone to help run his operations. For the next two decades, Magness and Malone grew the company into a cable and media superpower. At the time of his death in 1996, Bob Magness was Colorado's second-richest resident, with a net worth greater than $1 billion.

It makes one rethink the old notion that picking up hitchhikers is a bad idea.

Table 2–2	Growth of Satellite TV
Year	**Number of Subscribing Households**
1995	2,200,000
1998	8,700,000
2001	17,000,000
2004	20,000,000
2010	31,580,000

Source: Compiled by authors from industry sources.

The Satellite Sky

In 1945 science fiction writer Arthur C. Clarke wrote an article in *Wireless World* describing the elements of a satellite communications system. He theorized that global communications could be possible by reflecting signals off three satellites parked in orbit at equal distance from one another. It took a little over 20 years for this dream to become a reality, spurred by the "space race" between the Soviet Union and the United States.

In 1962 the first satellite TV transmission was made using *Telstar I*. Commentator David Brinkley reported from France to eager audiences in the United States that "there was no big news." He was mistaken. Satellite TV was on its way. By the early 1970s Western Union had successfully launched the *Westar I* and *Westar II* satellites. The industry took its first major step into the entertainment field in 1976 when Home Box Office used satellite TV for the "Thrilla in Manila" heavyweight championship fight between Muhammad Ali and Joe Frazier. That same year Ted Turner put his Atlanta station WTBS on satellite, and the Christian Broadcasting Network (later to become The Family Channel) became the first satellite-delivered basic cable network.

Proof that satellite TV had arrived came in 1979 when Neiman Marcus featured a home satellite dish on the cover of its famous Christmas catalog. Price: $36,000. Throughout the 1980s the price began to drop and dishes began to proliferate, aided by crucial decisions in Congress and at the FCC. In 1984 the Cable Communications Policy Act (cited earlier) legalized the private reception of satellite TV programming. Hardware prices dropped below $5,000, and more than half a million home dishes could be seen dotting the American landscape, especially in rural areas unlikely to be served by cable TV due to low population density. The act also permitted program services, like HBO and Showtime, to scramble their signals and to require dish owners to subscribe (like cable customers) to these services.

TVRO: The Big Dish By the late 1980s direct-to-home satellite (DTH, in industry parlance) became a growth industry. The backyard satellite dish was dubbed TVRO (TV receive-only), and sales of the three-meter dish eclipsed first 2 million (1988) and then 3 million (1990) consumer households. But these dishes were too big and cumbersome to supplant cable TV in suburban homes. Some neighborhoods considered them unsightly and developed local codes restricting their use. The antipiracy provisions of the cable act allowed for prosecution of those receiving program services illegally. Sales peaked, then plummeted. By 2005 only about 2 million TVROs could still be seen strewn across the American landscape. To take off, satellite TV would have to become physically smaller and cheaper; that development didn't take long.

Direct Broadcast Satellite A new alternative to cable TV took the nation by storm in the mid-1990s. High-powered **direct broadcast satellite (DBS)** service provided for nationwide distribution of TV programming from a new generation of orbiting satellites to compact (18-inch) home dish receivers. The dishes were aimed at one of three satellites launched by Hughes Communications. With use of digital compression (see Chapter 3), these satellites could beam over 200 channels to subscribing households; the channels were offered in different packages by four competing organizations: DirecTV, United States Satellite Broadcasting (USSB), Echo Star, and the Dish Network. In the 1990s the new dish, mounted on a window ledge or near the chimney, became a new TV status symbol, not unlike the rooftop antennas of the 1950s.

The number of households that subscribed to DBS grew from 2.2 million in 1995 to more than 32 million by 2009. This growth was fueled by two factors: (1) DBS systems dropped in price (see the Quick Facts at the beginning of this chapter) and (2) Congress softened existing regulation governing satellite TV and allowed DBS systems to include local channels in their offerings. Mergers and acquisitions resulted in just two companies, DirecTV and

The event that brought HBO into national prominence was the "Thrilla in Manila," a heavyweight championship match between Muhammad Ali and Joe Frazier that was distributed by satellite and cable.

Dish Network, dominating the field. Clearly cable had a new competitor.

Wireless Cable

As we have seen, because of construction costs, utility problems, and franchise disagreements, cable service lagged in the inner cities. In major urban areas satellite dishes, even the smaller ones now available, remain impractical. There is simply too little space. Yet people in major urban areas also want cable services, especially movies.

One solution is wireless cable, also known as **multichannel, multipoint distribution system,** or **MMDS.** MMDS makes use of short-range microwave transmissions to beam channels of video programming from a central transmitter location, such as the top of a tall office building. Receiving households use a small microwave antenna to pick up the signals and a special decoder called a **downconverter** to turn them into TV channels.

MMDS service never really caught on as a serious competitor to cable. By 2006 there were fewer than a million wireless cable households. Some of the large telecommunications companies have opted to use this part of the radio spectrum to bring wireless broadband services to the growing mobile broadband marketplace.

HOME VIDEO

For nearly half a century, Peter Goldmark was one of the true visionaries in telecommunications. From his laboratory at CBS had come high-fidelity sound recording, the long-playing phonograph record, and some of the basic research that resulted in color TV. Regarding home video, Goldmark made this prediction in 1976 (cited in *Videography,* July 1986, p. 61):

> I doubt that packaged video programs for home entertainment would be economically justifiable. It's speculative in so many ways, and basically a question of cost. Will people pay . . . for a first-rate entertainment program they know they may view only once or twice?

In fairness, Goldmark was talking about buying movies for home viewing. Nobody had yet conceived the idea of video rentals. However, the statement does reveal the speedy germination of a new industry that would have immediate and long-term impact on American TV. In less than 20 years the home video market exploded onto the media scene. Today broadcast, satellite, and cable and Internet TV are just part of a total "home video environment." Wedded to many home screens is a range of attachments and accessories, including VCRs, DVD players, video game consoles, DVRs, and surround sound, that has helped transform the way we watch TV. This revolution began with the introduction of the **videotape recorder (VTR).**

The history of videotape recording is intertwined with the history of television provided in Chapter 1. Before the videotape recorder became a mainstay in the American home, it first had to be perfected in production studios, networks, and TV stations. Few inventions in media history have been as significant. After all, for more than six decades—from early inventors tinkering in the 1880s to the battle between CBS and NBC over color in the early 1950s—TV was *live.* What you saw was what was actually going on—in the studio or in the "great outdoors"—in front of the camera.

The Kinescope Recorder

Until the mid-1950s, there was only one way to record TV programs. The **kinescope recorder** was a film camera especially equipped to shoot an image from a TV screen. The quality of a kinescope recording (or "kinny" as it was colloquially called) was

poor. The images were fuzzy; the picture was too dark; and because the film frame was different from the TV frame, the kinny sometimes cut off heads, feet, and other parts of the picture. After a single replay, the kinescope was generally discarded, which explains why so few of TV's early programs are around today.

The Videotape Recorder (VTR)

On November 30, 1956, the videotape recorder (VTR) made its debut. A short time later, the Ampex Corporation introduced a color VTR. In fact, an impromptu debate between U.S. vice president Richard Nixon and Soviet premier Nikita Kruschev was captured on videotape at an exhibition in Moscow in 1959. One highlight of this encounter (dubbed the "Kitchen Debate" because the exhibit also included a demonstration of a modern U.S. kitchen) had the future U.S. president sheepishly admitting that the Russians were ahead of America on certain things, such as space travel, but that "we are way ahead on other things, like color TV."

Events: Life in the Kinescope Days

Before the videotape recorder, video recording meant kinescope. Because were so many problems with this process, it was no wonder that the networks eagerly welcomed a substitute. In addition to their poor quality, kinnies used expensive film stock. In 1954 American TV operations used more raw film for kinnies than did all the Hollywood film studios combined. NBC alone used more than 1 million feet of film a month to feed programs to stations in the different time zones.

Kinescope recording was also troublesome and a little nerve-racking. At CBS Television City in Hollywood, recording started at 4:30 p.m. to pick up the shows broadcast live at 7:30 in the East. Engineers recorded a 35-millimeter kinescope along with a 16-millimeter backup copy. When the first 34-minute kinny reel was done, a switch was made to a second kinescope machine. Then a courier grabbed the exposed reel and rushed it to a nearby film lab. Meanwhile, another courier took the 16-millimeter copy and, using a different route to minimize the chances that both reels would get caught in a traffic jam, rushed it to the same lab.

As the film came out of the dryers, it was spooled onto reels and packed into cans. The waiting couriers then rushed it back to the CBS projection room. These films were called "hot kinnies" because at airtime they were still warm from the dryer. At the same time, another set of couriers was heading back to the lab with the second kinny reels to be developed. If traffic was bad or if the film lab had problems, things could get tense. Veteran engineers recall several times when they were threading up a reel only a minute or so before airtime, and there were other occasions when they had to use the 16-millimeter backup copy. Despite these hardships, CBS never lost a show because of a kinescope processing problem. Nonetheless, everyone was relieved when magnetic recording was perfected.

For 20 years, however, from its debut in 1956 to the eve of the nation's bicentennial birthday celebration in 1976, the video recorder was a device made for TV stations, networks, and production facilities, not for home viewers. It was too cumbersome, large, and above all expensive.

TV Recording Comes Home: The VCR

The **VCR (videocassette recorder)** revolution began with the introduction of the Betamax VCR by Sony in 1975. Crude by today's standards, the table model machine could record up to one hour of video. However, the machine touched off a fiery court battle between Sony and Universal Pictures. Shockingly (at least to the movie studios and their major clients, the broadcast networks, for whom they produced the majority of programs seen on prime-time TV), Sony was promoting the machine's ability to tape broadcasts off the air! "Piracy!" claimed the studios. After a much-publicized legal battle, which came to be known as the "Betamax case," in 1984 the U.S. Supreme Court ruled that home taping did not violate copyright law. Not that they needed further encouragement, but this ruling essentially gave Americans a green light to tape TV shows.

Sony's Betamax machine did not have the home video market to itself. Another Japanese firm, Matsushita, introduced a competing format, VHS (for video home system), in 1977. The two formats were incompatible; VHS tapes would not play on a Betamax machine and vice versa. Although Betamax produced better picture quality, the VHS format had a longer recording capability. The two formats battled for marketplace superiority during the late 1970s and early 1980s. Eventually VHS won the battle and became the standard home recording medium and playback medium for the next 20 years.

In 1978 there were 175,000 VCRs in use in the United States. By 1982 nearly 5 million units were in use, representing about 9 percent of TV homes; in 1985 some 26 million homes had VCRs—about one-third of all households; and by 1988 the figure had doubled: 52 million VCRs were in use, representing just under 60 percent of homes. Today fewer than 88 million households own a VCR, down from a high of 98 million in 2004. As we shall see, most of these machines are rapidly becoming obsolete thanks to the rising popularity of DVD players and DVRs.

At first all home VCRs were table models, designed mainly to record TV shows off the air for later playback (a phenomenon known as **time-shifting,** the term reportedly coined by Sony executive Akio Morita). However, in a few short years technological development had reduced the size of the VCR and had made home color TV cameras practical realities. A second growth industry was created: home video moviemaking. Weddings, confirmations, bar mitzvahs, and other cultural rites were captured by camcorders (portable combination camera and VCR units), which replaced 8-millimeter film as the medium of record. The proliferation of home camera equipment was almost as spectacular as the rise of the VCR itself. In 1985 about half a million homes had portable video equipment. By 2005 there were over 40 million camcorder units in use, about one in every four homes! Although newer camcorders use digital technology to record their content to a memory stick or thumb drive, the march of technology

Akio Morita, a cofounder of the Sony Corporation, the company that pioneered the development of the VCR.

continues. New mobile devices like smart phones frequently include video capability.

DVDs and DVRs

A significant trend over the past 10 years has been the growth of the acceptance of the **DVD (digital video or versatile digital),** which has replaced videotape as the dominant home video medium. Using the same digital technology as the audio CD, the DVD has several advantages over tape: The DVD contains more content, has better picture and audio quality, and doesn't wear out after repeated plays. In 1998 there were only 1 million DVD households in the United States. By 2001 that number had grown to 18 million. By the end of 2007,

thanks to falling prices, more than 131 million DVD units were sold in the United States.

Hollywood movies that were previously released on videocassettes were replaced by movies on DVDs. In addition, a new revenue stream for production companies emerged with the advent of DVD boxed sets of TV programs. The boxed sets of the first two seasons of *Seinfeld*, for example, generated more than $95 million in revenue.

As the new century opened, digital video recorders (DVRs), such as TiVo, made their debut. These machines record content not on tape or a DVD but on a hard disk drive, similar to what is found inside a computer. They make it possible to record up to 300 hours of programs and pause live TV and resume it at any point in the program. Initial sales

Issues: Format Wars—History Repeating Itself?

As mentioned in the text, when videocassette players were first introduced, there were two competing and incompatible formats: Beta (championed by Sony) and VHS (short for video home system, championed by JVC). Consumers faced a problem because they had to choose one system over the other. Although many experts thought that the picture quality was better on the Beta system, it was VHS that eventually won out in the marketplace. The big deciding factor was recording length. The Beta cassettes could hold only an hour of video; the VHS tapes could hold about three hours. If a consumer wanted to record a two-hour movie, it would take two Beta cassettes but only one VHS. As the film rental business began to blossom in the early 1980s, most of the early stores stocked their shelves with VHS cassettes. Sony eventually gave up the fight and by 1988 began to produce VHS machines.

Another format war began brewing in 2006—this time over the format for high-definition DVDs. Once again two incompatible systems were vying for marketplace domination, and once again the consumer was caught in a dilemma. The two formats were Blu-ray, backed by Dell, Panasonic, Pioneer, and Sony, to name a few, and HD-DVD, backed by Toshiba, NEC, Sanyo, and several big movie studios.

Engineers who have seen the two formats side by side agree that both formats produce excellent high-definition images. Both formats are also what technicians call "backward compatible," which means that both formats can play all old standard-definition DVDs as well as high-definition DVDs with resolutions of up to 1080p.

Blu-ray disks could hold more information, but HD-DVD seemed to possess a significant economic advantage: HD-DVDs could be manufactured with only slight changes to existing machinery that creates the standard DVD. On the other hand, the Blu-ray system required that manufacturers install totally new equipment. Any disk-manufacturing company choosing the Blu-ray format faced a huge expense in retooling. In addition, HD-DVD was the first out of the gate, appearing on the market in mid-2006, whereas Blu-ray made it to retailers' shelves months later.

Two years later the HD-DVD format was dead. This time the SONY-backed format won—so what happened? The key technical factors that seemed to make Blu-ray more attractive were the facts that disks could hold 40 percent more data than HD disks and SONY's Playstation PS3 game machines came with Blu-ray capability. But it also appeared that HD-DVD did not have sufficient movie industry backing. SONY, which lost the tape wars in the 1980s, was determined to have content as well as technology, so it bought Columbia Pictures in the late 1980s. In January 2008, when Warner Brothers announced it was supporting Columbia Pictures and Disney in releasing Blu-ray disks, HD-DVD became a dead format.

were slow, but household penetration grew as cable and DBS companies began packaging DVRs within their set-top boxes. By 2009 DVR penetration had grown to more than 32 percent nationally, with some television markets exceeding 40 percent penetration.

The Video Store at Home and by Mail

In scarcely 10 years a new commercial establishment, the video store, became a fixture at neighborhood strip malls, including many large grocery stores. By 1984 about 20,000 specialty video stores were operating. VHS tapes dominated the sales and rental market until the turn of the century, when they were replaced by the DVD. As of 2004 there were about 25,000 video outlets in operation. Renting and selling DVDs is a big business. In 2005 consumers spent more than $16 billion to buy DVDs and more than $5 billion renting them.

However, technology has created opportunities to download video, and now the outlook for these stores is cloudy. Revenue growth slowed in 2005. Video stores faced increasing competition from pay cable and pay satellite channels that can offer a choice of dozens of movies at a price that is equal to or less than a DVD rental. Cable and satellite providers are also experimenting with video on demand, a system that would allow subscribers to choose from hundreds of movies and to view their choices at their convenience. Faced with this competition, the traditional video store, such as Blockbuster, diversified its offerings and now stocks video games and movie paraphernalia on its shelves.

In 1998 two entrepreneurs started a mail-order business to rent and sell DVDs over the Internet. The company did not do particularly well for the first few years, but then it offered a service called CineMatch, which allowed users to search for videos similar in taste to previous rentals. A couple of years later they changed the company name to Netflix, and the business grew steadily. By 2010 more than 15 million people had membership, and the service provided both DVD rentals and video streaming services. As gaming devices grew in popularity, manufacturers began building in streaming and Blu-ray capabilities, making movie streaming viewable on televisions as well as computers.

Finally, audiences were dividing their time and attention more and more between traditional media (television and radios) and new media such as computers and wireless devices. When the home

computer burst on the scene in the early 1980s, few envisioned that it would become a home entertainment device to rival television or that it would have its own "network": the Internet and the World Wide Web (WWW). We close our brief history of electronic media with the story of the Web and the current revolution in mobile computing.

THE INTERNET AND THE WORLD WIDE WEB

The term **Internet** refers to the global interconnection of computer networks made possible by using common communication protocols. The **World Wide Web** is just one service available on this global network. Other Internet services we use, including e-mail, FTP, and video chat, may function within a Web browser, but they are really separate network technologies. There are others, too, and more are in development. But our book is about sending sounds and pictures, mainly. So our discussion will focus on the development of the Internet and its primary audiovisual component: the World Wide Web.

Cold War and Hot Science: The Birth of the Internet

The Internet, like television, was in development for decades. Like radio, the Internet was developed out of concern for military preparedness and assurance that the military could communicate in times of emergency.

The main impetus behind the Internet's development was the Cold War struggle between the United States and the former Soviet Union, which marked the period from the end of World War II in 1945 until the fall of the Berlin Wall in 1989.

In 1957 the Soviet Union astounded the world by launching *Sputnik,* the earth's first man-made satellite. This event would have a huge impact on U.S. technology, planting the seeds for the Internet. Many people began to question how it was possible for the Soviet Union to completely surprise the United States with a new, possibly threatening technology. President Dwight D. Eisenhower called the nation's top military advisers and scientists to form a new agency called the **Defense Advanced Research Projects Agency (DARPA).** On January 7, 1958, DARPA was created to ensure that America would never again be taken by surprise by new technologies.

When Joseph C.R. Licklider wrote *Man–Computer Symbiosis* in 1960, his work inspired many to seriously consider the relationship between computer science and psychology. In 1962 DARPA's attention turned toward computers, and "Lick," as he was known, was chosen to head up DARPA's behavioral science office. **Cybernetics,** the study of the interrelationship between man and machines, was a new field of study, and Licklider was keenly interested in it. His ideas that a computer could serve as a problem-solving partner to humans, in real time, sounded like science fiction to many. Licklider even talked about creating an "Intergalactic Network" of interconnected computers and of a new concept called **time-sharing.** The notion of connecting computers together to function in some kind of an interconnected network was a radical idea. Though many computers had been interconnected into networks, the process was cumbersome and expensive; usually one communicated with computers using punch cards and "dumb" terminals.

Cold War tensions between the United States and the Soviet Union prompted America to embark on research into many different technologies simultaneously. Computers and communication systems became a priority, and the military's SAGE project inspired Licklider to see computing in a new light. He reasoned that it didn't make sense to have many different computers using different operating systems, all of them unable to communicate with one another. The Intergalactic Computer Network should have a standardized connection, he thought. Soon after, Licklider began pulling together some of the nation's brightest young researchers to work on the project, among them Bob Taylor of Dallas, who by 1963 headed up DARPA's Office of Information Processing Techniques. Taylor had three terminals in his office at the Pentagon. One was connected to the University of California at Berkeley, another to the main computer at the Strategic Air Command in Santa Barbara, and the third to Lincoln Labs at MIT. Unfortunately none of the computers could communicate with the others, and they all required different log-in procedures. Taylor found the lack of interconnection frustrating.

Computers weren't small and they certainly weren't cheap, Taylor thought. Why not fund a networking project that would try to link them together? With networking, researchers at MIT could use resources at UCLA and vice versa. Taylor called on Larry Roberts, a brilliant 29-year-old scientist at MIT, to help make this happen. The rest, as they say, is history. But Licklider's influence on DARPA and network computing in indisputable. "Lick was among the first to perceive the spirit of community created among the users of the first time-sharing systems," said Taylor. "In pointing out the community phenomena created, in part, by the sharing of resources in one time-sharing system, Lick made it easy to think about interconnecting the communities, the interconnection of interactive, online communities of people."

Post–Nuclear War: Would There Still Be a Dial Tone?

In the wake of the Cuban missile crisis in October 1962, when the United States and the Soviet Union stood on the brink of nuclear war, military commanders became convinced that it was going to be necessary to develop a communication system that could survive a missile attack. A lot was already known about building sophisticated voice and video networks. AT&T had interconnected the country with telephones by 1914, and the first coast-to-coast hookup for television was completed in 1951. But computer networks were relatively new and consisted mostly of using modems on a standard phone circuit to make an interconnection. Telephone switching centers were located near major cities, and they were sure to become targets of Soviet missiles. To make the nation's emergency communication system less vulnerable, a new approach to networking was necessary.

The air force hired the Rand Corporation to figure out a way to bolster American communication systems in case of war. Paul Baran of Rand had been pondering some hypothetical questions about the capabilities of different types of computer networks. He reasoned that, in order to make a communication system less vulnerable to attack, that system would need to take many paths to send messages. This concept was similar to the way neural networks work inside the human brain. If one brain cell is damaged, an alternative neural route around the damaged area can be found because of the millions of neural connections that exist. Baran was convinced that a computer network could mimic a neural network, but his ideas were so revolutionary few people in the telecommunications industry believed they were possible. It took Baran nearly five years to convince people that such a network could work. Meanwhile a British physicist named Donald Davies, working independently, came to the same conclusion: A distributed network of information could provide redundancy of information. Davies thought that data should be broken up into small strings of bits that could be enclosed in "electronic packets," which would be able to move quickly within a communications network having many different connections. The notion of **packet switching** was born.

Packet switching provided the ideal solution to the problem of data loss during emergencies. Data packets were small, and if a packet was lost, it could be sent and resent over the networks easily. With many interconnected computers, packets had several possible paths they could travel to reach their final destination. This distributed system could provide survivability in case of a missile attack because, if one part of the network was destroyed, there would be other paths available.

ARPANET: Forerunner of the Internet

Bob Taylor at DARPA decided to build the network that could survive nuclear war. In 1968 the ARPANET project was born.

Twelve different companies bid on the project, but a small engineering firm in Cambridge, Massachusetts (Bolt, Beranek, and Newman—BBN), got the contract to begin development work on the basic network computer called the Interface Message Processor (IMP) machine.

Early work in computer interactivity was going on at several separate geographical locations simultaneously. How could all of the various universities and research labs working on DARPA projects communicate with one another? The solution was to build an interactive computer network that could share data quickly. Engineers realized that to make this happen they would have to devise a way of controlling how the messages were sent. The **Network Control Program (NCP)** was a scheme devised to provide this control. NCP became the forerunner of today's **Transmission Control Protocol (TCP),** the switching system that controls modern communication networks.

In the fall of 1969, the first of many links in this distributed network was tested. Success of the network was not immediate. Researchers at UCLA wanted to connect their new machine with another computer at Stanford. Sitting at a computer terminal at UCLA's computer lab, undergraduate Charlie Klein typed an "L." Stanford called back on a standard telephone and confirmed the computer had received an "L." Then Klein typed an "O," and again the researchers at Stanford confirmed an "O." Feeling more confident, Klein typed a "G," hoping to connect up and gain remote access to the Stanford computer. He hit the carriage return, and both computers crashed—perhaps the first (but definitely not the last) time an attempted log-in failed!

Later that day, the bugs were ironed out of the log-in process and the first computers designed for networking were connected. Soon more nodes (sites) were added to the network. In 1970 the University of California at Santa Barbara and the University of Utah were connected; then MIT, Harvard, Carnegie-Mellon, and other major research universities were added. **ARPANET** became the first fully interconnected nationwide computer network.

Where It's @: The Rise of Electronic Mail

While designers of the ARPANET system had originally envisioned its primary use for the exchange of missile telemetry information and had planned for large database transfers using file transfer protocol (FTP), most users were actually using the network to send personal communications to their colleagues. In 1972 Ray Tomlinson of BBN, the company that designed the network, had invented the first practical network e-mail program. Tomlinson and all ARPANET users had their own specific computer accounts, but each user needed a way to separate his own name from the name of the computer system he was using. Looking at his teletype terminal, Tomlinson saw mostly letters and numbers. However, when he saw the @ sign, Tomlinson thought it could be used to combine one's personal user name with the name of his host computer system. Today the @ has become one of the lasting symbols of our interconnected world.

The 1970s were pivotal for the development of ARPANET. Several public demonstration convinced DARPA to extend packet-switching capability through the use of communications satellites and ground mobile radio transmitters. Also, nodes connecting England and Norway broadened the international scope of the network. By 1976 Web pioneers Vinton Cerf and Robert Kahn had developed Transmission Control Protocol/Internet Protocol (TCP/IP) to replace Network Control Program. Now a file sent over the network could just as easily be a document, a picture, or a set of numbers. This change in protocol made it easier to send photographs, sounds, and other material over the network. With new nodes being added every month, ARPANET grew from its original 2 connections to more than 200 by 1981 and encompassed more than 1.5 million miles of interconnected telephone lines. While ARPANET's success was well known to many, its usage was limited to people with high-level military clearance or researchers in business or at large universities. It was still a medium not available to the masses.

USENET: Bringing Computer Networking to the Masses

In 1976 Steve Bellovin, a graduate student at the University of North Carolina, created **USENET,** a system that enabled groups of computer users to send messages between the UNC campus at Chapel Hill and nearby Duke University in Durham. USENET operated like a bulletin board. A topic area was created, and computer users on the network could post their opinions on the topic. At first most bulletin boards featured postings on computer-related topics. It wasn't long until politics (mostly liberal), music (mostly contemporary), and sex (mostly recreational) became popular topics on the system.

In the late 1970s Matt Glickman, a high school student, and Mark Horton, a graduate student at the University of California at Berkeley, rewrote the USENET program to extend its capacity. Through USENET, faculty and students at dozens of universities, who were not previously authorized for ARPANET accounts, now had access to the network. USENET grew rapidly. Starting from just three sites in 1979, USENET grew into thousands of different newsgroups. As might have been expected, the ARPANET administrators objected to USENET's carrying discussions about drugs, sex, and rock-and-roll over the network's computers (this was a military project, after all). As a result, an alternative routing system was created to route USENET newsgroup messages around the main ARPANET network, carrying messages on almost any conceivable topic—from collectors' Barbie dolls to the latest gossip about popular soap operas. The growth of the net for communication was growing rapidly, but it was still limited mostly to people with access to large computer networks.

The various interconnected computer networks grew as users realized TCP/IP would provide greater flexibility than the many different proprietary systems that existed. There was no single initiative to create a vast, worldwide interconnected network, yet that's exactly what seemed to be happening. One innovation, called **TELNET,** gave users the ability to connect to and control various computers from remote locations, often through telephone dial-up connections. Ethernet allowed an array of computers to be connected into a single **local area network (LAN).** Now it was possible for all kinds of computers to be linked together, both in the same office and literally around the world. These network innovations gave rise to widespread usage of e-mail and electronic bulletin boards, and they provided remote access to unique scientific databases. Government funding allowed more and more universities to join the network. By the early 1980s a flourishing research community was interconnected.

Personal Computing: The New Mass Medium

The contribution of the personal computer to the growth of networking cannot be overestimated. Personal computers made it affordable for businesses to provide workers with individual computers instead of teletypes or "dumb" terminals, and when Apple introduced the Macintosh computer in 1984, the desktop publishing revolution began. This revolution and the growth in networking capability allowed individuals to access networked materials, use e-mail, and develop materials for publication. Many people were beginning to predict a closer relationship between computers, communications, and a social usage for the network with Compuserve, America Online, and other services providing individual accounts.

To meet the growing demand for interconnection, domain name servers such as ".gov" for government, ".edu" for educational institution, and ".mil" for military unit were developed. It was no longer necessary to memorize numerical IP addresses. Now it was possible to send a message to a person's name at a particular institution (<yourname>@hostinstitution.edu.country).

An early Macintosh computer.

With the success of interconnection came a realization that problems associated with speed and bandwidth would eventually grind the network to a halt. A highly influential report, "Towards a National Research Network," issued by the National Research Council, spurred then-Senator Al Gore to sponsor legislation to fund a super high-speed network using fiber optic technology. This set the stage for the development of **NSFNET (National Science Foundation NETwork)** and the **information superhighway** concept, a high-speed backbone that linked government-sponsored supercomputer centers at Cornell, San Diego, Illinois, and Pittsburgh.

The Internet at Last!

The Internet was officially born in 1986, when this new network replaced the aging ARPANET with a faster network providing 30 times more bandwidth. For the first time, faculty at smaller institutions had access to a fast computer network. At the same time, commercial vendors recognized the importance of the developing trends and started work on commercial products that could take advantage of the unique networking characteristics of TCP/IP. As the 1990s arrived, private **Internet service providers (ISPs),** such as America Online (AOL), gave consumers access to the Internet, while large telecommunications corporations, such as MCI and AT&T, provided new backbone capability. Public access to the Internet was occurring at libraries and universities around the country, too.

The Birth of the World Wide Web (WWW)

In March 1989 Tim Berners-Lee, while working at CERN, Europe's high-energy particle physics laboratory, circulated a paper that called for the creation of a program that used a graphical interface (pictures, as opposed to text) for requesting information available on networked databases. After the paper kicked around for more than a year, CERN gave Berners-Lee the job to write the program. He dubbed his concept the "World Wide Web." Here's how his revolutionary concept worked.

The vast majority of information on the Internet consisted of text: words in documents, and lines of letters and numbers. Berners-Lee's idea was to insert a system of **hyperlinks,** packets of computer commands, within the texts. By clicking on a link, the program makes a request to the server that acts like a library directory. The server determines the location of the link through the use of a **URL (uniform resource locator)** address, gets that information, and sends it back to the computer that requested it. Since the data inside the requested packets could be anything (text, video, audio, or the like), the Internet was now capable of displaying text, video, audio, or any combination, and the user did not need to know elaborate computer code to find it.

By the fall of 1991, the World Wide Web began running experimentally on several different computer systems in Europe and the United States. During the next year, various versions of the CERN browser were installed on some 26 different computers around the world for testing. In January 1993 Marc Andreesen, a graduate student, released the first version of Mosaic, the forerunner of Netscape Navigator and Firefox. This revolutionary program made it even easier for computer users to find text, sound, and pictures on the Internet. At this point, World Wide Web traffic was still minuscule, roughly 0.1 percent of all the traffic on the Internet. That would soon change.

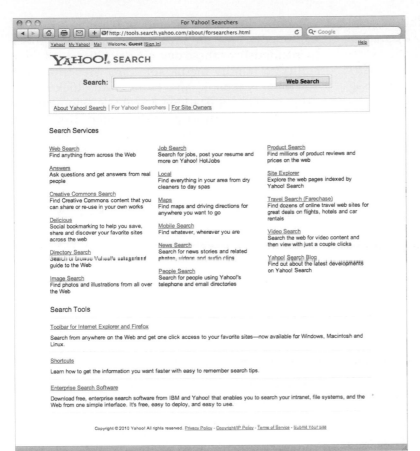

Nearly 60 million people per week visit Yahoo's Web site.

Mosaic and the World Wide Web together formed the two "killer applications" that were needed to make the Internet really take off among all sorts of people. The World Wide Web became an overnight sensation. Within six months the number of Web-based servers jumped from a few to over 200, and traffic increased tenfold as well. People outside the research community began to take a real interest in the WWW. Everywhere newspapers, television, and magazines were talking about the new phenomenon. In 1994 Andreesen left NCSA to form Netscape Communications, and the World Wide Web saw its first commercial applications.

The usage statistics for the Web are staggering. Between 1993 and 1995 the number of Internet users more than tripled, from about 12 million to 40 million worldwide. By 2005 that number had skyrocketed to more than 900 million. Although that is a huge number, it represents only about 15 percent of the total world population.

There are more than 100 million Web sites. The total number of Web pages on the Internet is hard to determine. Yahoo, a widely used search engine, scans about 20 billion pages, but some experts suggest that the total number is probably much higher, maybe around a trillion pages. Internet traffic growth has slowed a bit since the beginning of the decade, but it is still increasing at a rate of about 100 percent a year. As we enter the second decade of the century, some estimates put the number of Internet users at more than 1.9 billion.

Broadcasters and Web-centric companies have developed a wide variety of services that run on today's computers, along with increased bandwidth capability of the Web. YouTube, Facebook, Flickr, and other media services have gained widespread acceptance as alternatives to television and cable.

Blackberries, iPhones, Androids, and Other Wireless Marvels

As we entered the 21st century, technology made it possible to develop portable devices called **personal digital assistants.** Several companies developed a wide variety of these devices that performed calendaring and message services, but in 2002 a Canadian company, Research in Motion (RIM), introduced the first really useful smart phone called the Blackberry. It combined e-mail, mobile telephone, text messaging, and Internet access in a small handheld device. The Blackberry connected through the growing **WiFi** and mobile telephone networks that were rapidly expanding as consumers switched from land to portable cell phones. It was an instant hit, and people could be seen checking their devices everywhere and anywhere. Soon it spawned a major competitor.

In 2006 computer and marketing wizard Steve Jobs announced that Apple was about to introduce a smart phone of its own. In January 2007 the first iPhone was introduced to tens of thousands of expectant fans. It was an audio/video player, Web browser, game unit, telephone, and personal digital device all in one, and it had an easy-to-use touch screen. An interesting aspect of the iPhone was that it used the iTunes Store interface to sell third-party applications. The iPhone soon became the device that all other smart phones were compared with. By 2010 a new generation of iPhones with videoconferencing and high-definition video editing capability was released.

As 2007 came to a close, Google announced that it would develop an open-source smart phone system based on the Linux kernel. These Android phones manufactured by a variety of companies went on sale in 2009 as direct competitors to Apple's iPhone. Functionality of these devices is similar to that of the iPhone, although generally less expensive to purchase.

As the new century began, consumers in large numbers began adopting laptop computers with media and wireless capabilities. Today's laptops often have DVD or Blu-ray playback and fast wireless capability. Some have built-in video cameras and high-definition screens.

Beginning in 2007, smaller portable computers called "netbooks" were introduced by PC computer manufacturers. These devices made use of the growing cloud computing capability of the Web to provide functionality to users but were often limited in their multimedia display capabilities. Apple once again surprised the general public by introducing the iPad, a larger tablet computer that combined many functions of the iPhone with a nine-inch screen capable of providing high-quality video and text viewing. The iPad could be purchased to run solely on WiFi or on a wireless 3G mobile network.

Mobile downloading and uploading of video, multimedia, and audio programming have grown tremendously as these devices have increased their ability to handle media software. Web sites like YouTube, Facebook, and Hulu were quick to develop mobile applications. Local television and radio stations began to provide content directly to the Web. Today many viewers choose to watch their favorite programs on their laptops or mobile devices.

CABLE, SATELLITES, HOME VIDEO, AND THE INTERNET IN THE 21ST CENTURY

As of mid-decade, the following developments had occurred:

- The cable TV industry continued to consolidate. In 2002 Comcast acquired the cable assets of AT&T Broadband. Three years later, Comcast teamed up with Time Warner to announce plans to acquire Adelphia's cable systems.

- Cable continued to draw audiences away from the traditional TV networks. In 2005 about 60 percent of the prime-time audience were watching cable. That number might increase thanks to a 2005 deal that would move *Monday Night Football* from ABC to ESPN.

- Cable companies began using its lines to provide other services to subscribers, including high-speed Internet access, video on demand, and local telephone service.

- Speaking of telephone service, the Telecommunications Act of 1996 paved the way for competition between telephone companies and cable companies. After a slow start, competition heated up in 2005. Thanks to a technology called **Voice over Internet Protocol (VoIP),** cable companies began offering phone service to their subscribers. VoIP was cheaper than traditional phone service and was popular with consumers. By mid-decade, about 75 percent of all cable systems offered telephone service.

  Because many of the subscribers who turned to VoIP canceled their traditional phone service, the phone companies fought back by offering video. The major phone companies announced plans to spend more than $20 billion to upgrade their systems in order to provide TV service.

Verizon, for example, intended to offer 100 channels of TV to its subscribers in 2006 or 2007.

- More and more consumers were turning to high-speed broadband Internet connections, such as DSL telephone lines and cable modems, that make it easier to receive audio and video. At the start of 2010, more than 50 million households had broadband, and more than 75 percent of all households had some access to the Internet.

- The Internet allowed everyone a chance to be a mass communicator. Web logs, or **blogs,** are personal journals that are kept by private individuals and periodically updated. They may discuss politics, art, education, or society, or they may contain introspective comments. Although the exact number is hard to pin down, it was estimated that as of 2006, about 10 million blogs existed on the Web. Another development is **podcasting** (the name is derived from Apple's popular iPod). Podcasting is the production and distribution of audio or video files that are available on the Web. Podcasting allows an individual to put together self-produced radio or TV shows.

SUMMARY

- Cable television began in the late 1940s and early 1950s as viewers in mountainous and rural areas strove to be a part of the "TV craze." At first the FCC was reluctant to regulate the cable business, but under pressure from broadcast TV, a set of restrictive regulations was put in place that stymied the growth of cable for over 20 years.

- Cable's period of explosive growth began in the 1970s, spurred by the adoption of new FCC rules, the spread of satellites for program distribution, and the rise of innovative programming services. Two important program concepts, pay TV (led by Home Box Office) and the "superstation" (developed by Ted Turner), were developed at this time. By the 1980s more new program services appeared, like CNN and MTV, making cable increasingly attractive to TV households. Cable boomed as more than half of all TV homes decided to subscribe to the service. Today cable TV reaches more than 6 in 10 TV households and delivers a range of services to consumers, including video, data, and even telephone service.

- Cable's growth created competition, including direct broadcast satellite and the consumer favorite: the videocassette recorder (VCR). The first home satellite dishes were large, cumbersome, and expensive. Nevertheless, TVROs dotted the landscape in the 1980s. A new generation of smaller and more affordable satellite dishes appeared in the 1990s and have taken the video industry by storm. Other alternatives to cable, including MMDS, or "wireless cable," have been less successful.

- The rise of the VCR and DVD has been spectacular. The home video business exploded on the scene in the 1980s, fueled by a landmark Supreme Court case legalizing home video recording, the arrival of affordable video recorders, and the rise of video rental shops. The video sales and rental business tops $20 billion in annual revenues, but growing use of the Internet for streaming may threaten growth of this industry.

- The newest of the so-called new media is the Internet and its video/audio segment known as the World Wide Web (WWW). The Internet is a by-product of the Cold War between the Soviet Union and the United States, arising from an initiative to link major universities and civil defense sites to avert (or survive) nuclear war. It arose from the creation of the Defense Advanced Research Projects Agency (DARPA) in 1957, following the successful launch by Russia of its *Sputnik* satellite.

- By the 1970s most users of ARPANET were not using the system to exchange missile guidance information. Instead researchers and college professors were using the system to exchange electronic messages. The concept of e-mail was taking shape. By the end of the decade USENET, a simplified bulletin board system, and TELNET, a means of dialing into large computers from remote locations, were growing in popularity.

- Sales of personal computers skyrocketed in the 1980s. The Apple and IBM PC brought a new class of entrepreneurs, experimenters, and enthusiasts to the field of computing. Individual computer users in universities and businesses could now connect to one another to exchange data (and e-mail). In response to the growing demand, the National Science Foundation replaced the aging ARPANET infrastructure with a faster network that had much higher bandwidth. Hundreds, then thousands, of universities and schools soon logged on to the network. They were followed in the early 1990s by millions of home computer enthusiasts, using commercial gateways like Prodigy and America Online (AOL).

- The last piece of the puzzle was provided by Tim Berners-Lee, who coined the term *World Wide Web*. His innovative idea was to connect data on the Web via *hyperlinks:* packages of computer commands that computer users could execute with a simple click of the mouse. As a result, text, sounds, and pictures could be transmitted and received on the Internet virtually anywhere in the world, without the need for sophisticated or technical commands.

- Today the Internet is taking its place alongside radio, broadcast TV, and cable television as a means of send-

ing and receiving media content. Time will tell if the Web replaces such "ancient" networks as CBS, NBC, and ABC.

- Web functionality became wireless as we entered the 21st century. Growing popularity of laptop computers and mobile smart phones made it possible for users to connect to the Internet, upload and download media files, and play games.

KEY TERMS

cable TV   31
Cable Communications Policy
   Act   33
direct broadcast satellite (DBS)   35
multichannel, multipoint
   distribution system
   (MMDS)   36
downconverter   36
videotape recorder (VTR)   37
kinescope recorder   37
VCR (videocassette recorder)   38
time-shifting   38
DVD (digital video or versatile
   digital)   39

Internet   40
World Wide Web   40
Defense Advanced Research
   Projects Agency (DARPA)   40
cybernetics   41
time-sharing   41
packet switching   42
Network Control Program
   (NCP)   42
Transmission Control Protocol
   (TCP)   42
ARPANET   42
USENET   43
TELNET   43

local area network (LAN)   43
information superhighway   44
NSFNET   44
Internet service provider (ISP)   44
hyperlinks   44
URL (uniform resource
   locator)   44
personal digital assistants   45
WiFi   46
Voice over Internet Protocol
   (VoIP)   46
blogs   47
podcasting   47

SUGGESTIONS FOR FURTHER READING

Bartlett, E. R. (2000). *Cable television handbook.* New York: McGraw-Hill.

Hafner, K., & Lyon, M. (1996). *Where wizards stay up late: The origins of the Internet.* New York: Simon & Schuster.

Hillstrom, K. (2005). *The Internet revolution.* Detroit, MI: Omnigraphics.

Ovadia, S. (2001). *Broadband cable TV access networks.* Upper Saddle River, NJ: Prentice Hall.

Lotz, A. (2007). *The television will be revolutionized.* New York: NYU Press.

Lyons, J. & Plunkett, J. (2007). *Multimedia histories: From the magic lantern to the Internet.* Exeter: University of Exeter Press.

Parsons, P. R. (2008). *Blue skies: A history of cable television.* Philadelphia: Temple University Press.

Randall, N. (1997). *The soul of the Internet: Net gods, netizens, and the wiring of the world.* Boston: International Thomson.

Reid, R. H. (1997). *Architects of the Web: 1,000 days that built the future of the Web.* New York: Wiley.

Robichaux, M. (2002). *Cable cowboy: John Malone and the rise of the modern cable business.* Hoboken, NJ: Wiley.

Salus, P. H. (1995). *Casting the net: From ARPANET to the Internet and beyond.* Reading, MA: Addison-Wesley.

Southwick, T. (1999). *Distant signals: How cable TV changed the world of telecommunications.* Denver: The Cable Center.

Sterling, C. J., & Kittross, J. (2001). *Stay tuned: A concise history of American broadcasting.* Belmont, CA: Wadsworth.

Winston, B. (1998). *Media technology and society: A history.* New York: Routledge.

INTERNET EXERCISES

Visit our Web site at **www.mhhe.com/dominickbib7e** for study-guide exercises to help you learn and apply material in each chapter. You will find ideas for future research as well as useful Web links to provide you with an opportunity to journey through the new electronic media.

Audio and Video Technology 3

Quick Facts

Bandwidth of an FM channel: 200 kilohertz

Number of Americans who own cell phones, January 2010: 234 million

Percentage of U.S. households that own a device used specifically for gaming, 2010: 73%

First high-definition TV broadcasts: 1998

Cost of 51-inch digital HDTV projection TV, 1999: $5,000

Cost of 51-inch digital HDTV plasma TV, 2011: $1,169

Percentage of U.S. homes with broadband access, 2009: 63%

Refresh rate of 3D HDTV: 120 HZ

Cost of new 3D interactive glasses, 2010: $114

Percentage of Americans interested in owning a smart phone, 2010: 30%

Watching TV and listening to radio are among the easiest things in the world to do. Just twist that dial, flip that switch, or punch that button and poof: Vivid sounds and picturesque images are yours (unless, of course, you're watching a test pattern). Surfing the Internet requires a bit more interactive work, but not too much. In fact, it's getting easier all the time. New smart phones and cameras can record videos and post them directly to YouTube or send them to your best friend's e-mail account. The ease with which we command modern electronic media hides the incredibly complex technical processes involved in moving sound and pictures from their source to you. This chapter attempts to demystify the magic of modern electronic media related to the mass media. We describe how the process works and, more important, why it matters. In many ways understanding the technology behind electronic media helps you understand their history, legal status, social and political power, and future.

BASIC PRINCIPLES OF MEDIA TECHNOLOGY

It's helpful to begin a discussion of technical aspects of radio, TV, and electronic media with some basic principles.

Facsimile Technology

All modes of mass communication are based on the process of **facsimile** technology. That is, sounds from a speaker and pictures on a TV screen are merely representations, or facsimiles, of their original form. We all learn and practice facsimile technology at an early age. Did you ever use a pencil or crayon to trace the outline of your hand on a sheet of blank paper? That's an example of facsimile technology. Having one's face covered by plaster of Paris for a mask or sculpture is facsimile technology; so are having your picture taken and photocopying a friend's lecture notes.

In general, the more faithful the reproduction or facsimile is to the original, the greater is its **fidelity.** High-fidelity audio, or hi-fi, is a close approximation of the original speech or music it represents. And while DVDs provide very good picture and sound quality, Blu-ray technology is even better. Indeed, much of the technical development of radio and TV has been a search for better fidelity: finding better and better ways to make facsimiles of the original

sounds or images. Some technological innovations are less concerned with the highest-quality audio or video. Often it is just as important or useful to develop a way to scale the fidelity of a product to the needs of the consumer. For example, the video streamed to an Xbox 360 can be higher in quality than the video streamed on a smart phone. Today's developments in digital technology are giving consumers unprecedented choices for audio and video.

The second point about facsimile technology is that in creating their facsimiles, radio and TV are not limited to plaster of Paris, crayon, oils, or even photographic chemicals and film. Instead, unseen elements such as radio waves, beams of light, and digital bits and bytes are used in the process. Although you cannot put your hands on a radio wave as you can a photo in your wallet, it is every bit as real. The history of radio and TV is directly linked to the discovery and use of these invisible "resources," from Marconi's early radio experiments in the 1890s to the newest forms of digital transmissions of today.

In the technical discussion that follows, bear in mind that the engineer's goals in radio, whether it's for TV, cable, or some high-speed information network, are to create the best possible facsimile of an original sound or image, to transport that image without losing too much fidelity (known as signal loss), and to recreate that sound or image as closely as possible to its original form, *given the limitations of the delivery system or the needs of the specific user*. While broadcasters use both analog and digital systems to transport images and sounds, more and more have switched to digital transmission.

We're going to look at some fundamental concepts before we focus on the systems that make electronic media work.

Transduction

Another basic concept is **transduction,** the process of changing one form of energy into another. We use transducers everywhere in ordinary daily life. For example, when you turn a lightbulb on, you're transducing electrical energy to light. Similarly, when you send a text message to your friend in the middle of a dark movie theater, you are transducing—although not all those around you may appreciate it.

Have you ever tried sending a video clip of a concert to your friend using a smart phone? Getting a sound or picture from a concert hall to another person's phone usually involves at least three or four transductions. Broadcasting a concert involves the same processes (although on a larger scale). At each phase loss of fidelity is possible. With any system of broadcasting it is possible that with each phase the whole process may break down into **noise**— unwanted interference—or an interrupted transmission, rendering the communication impossible. Although breakdowns due to transduction rarely occur, they do happen. Technicians were embarrassed when the sound went out during the 1976 presidential debate between Gerald Ford and Jimmy Carter. Closer to home, a scratched DVD can make a Tchaikovsky ballet look jumbled.

Over the past decade the world has gone through an amazing digital revolution. In fact, although the DVD player was the fastest-selling consumer electronics device of the decade, many Americans now watch movies on a PS3, Xbox, or computer laptop. And television stations have converted their signals to a digital television (DTV) system that includes both high-definition and multiple-channel transmission. New HD radio systems provide greatly improved fidelity with reduced noise, but more and more Americans are listening to Internet radio services such as Pandora and Slacker.com every day. Even as new technologies give us greater choice, old technologies often remain useful to us.

Television and radio signals begin as physical energy, commonly referred to as light waves or sound waves. When you hear a blue bird chirping in a tree, your brain directly perceives the event by processing the sound waves that enter your ears and vibrate your eardrums. Simultaneously you see the bird as your brain processes the reflections of light that have entered the eye and fallen on the retina. This is direct experience: no transduction, no signal loss; true high fidelity. To experience electronically, however, the following translations or transductions occur.

Suppose you are standing near the tree and you decide to record this bird with a smart phone, like an iPhone or something similar. Several systems within the phone are going to act like a television studio to record the event. First the bird's song will be changed into mechanical energy in the phone's tiny microphone. The various sound wave pressures cause a small electrically charged metal plate to vibrate back and forth. This sets up a weak electrical current that mirrors the pattern of the original sound waves. Next this current is fed into a special device that samples the changes in electrical current and converts them into a series of digital bits. Thus the

bird's song is translated into patterns of zeros and ones as the sound is converted into a series of digital samples. How well the transduction occurs is based on the ability of the phone to create an accurate facsimile. In other words, the higher the sample rate, the better the quality of the recording.

While the bird's song is being converted into a series of electronic pulses, the lens in the phone's camera is focusing the light reflected off the bluebird onto a tiny electronic wafer that transforms light into electronic current. The wafer is light-sensitive and actually has three layers (one red, one blue, and one green). When the light reflected off the bluebird's feathers is focused on this device, electrons in the blue-sensitive layer are excited, creating a pixel charge at that spot on the wafer. Green leaves in the tree will cause the green layer to create a charge, and the other colors in the picture will also affect parts of the light-sensitive wafer. (If you were to think of this light-sensitive wafer as a grid, the image of the bird in the tree would form a series of pixels that would be a facsimile of the original picture.) The electronic currents of this wafer go to a special circuit that accumulates this information and converts them into data bits of light and dark areas.

Now we have two different facsimiles: one of the sound of the bird chirping and another of the image of the bird. In the process, the sound and light images have been converted into on–and-off pulses (**binary digits or bits**) that are mixed together into long strings of digital information and sent to the phone's transmitter.

Next we transduce the digital information into electromagnetic energy. Here the signal is superimposed onto the radio waves assigned to the phone in a process called _modulation_ (examined in detail later). The fidelity of the signal is based on the phone's capabilities (such as the number of pixels in the camera and its ability to convert audio into accurate complex samples), your location, the phone's channel, the bandwidth of your phone carrier, and other factors. The service provider takes the data message (your video recording) and routes it through a series of computer radio networks and cell towers, ultimately reaching the destination of the person you called.

Your friend's telephone senses an incoming call and goes from a sleep state to an awake state. This happens because the antenna in the phone receives the electromagnetic energy, detects the signal, and begins to record the data into the phone's memory module. When your friend sees that you've sent a message and presses the video play button, the reverse of the encoding process occurs. The message that was stored in your friend's phone memory as a series of bits will be decoded and split into separate video and audio data channels and then sent to digital decoders that recreate the picture of the bird and the sound of the bluebird's song. As the video is decoded, the fluctuating current is sent to a display that turns on blue, green, and red pixels, which in turn recreate the video of the bird that you recorded. At the same time the audio data is transduced back into a sound waveform that is analogous to the bird's song. These waveforms are amplified and played through the phone's speaker. This is a complex process, but note the many transductions.

What's the point of all this? Why does the transduction process matter?

Digital: The Good, the Bad, and the Ugly

First the recording example we discussed took video and sound and converted the two components into a digital file. Digital technology has many advantages over older analog recording techniques. Assuming that the original sound was faithfully sampled and properly stored, the quality of the sound will always be the same as long as the integrity of the digital file is kept intact. So once you've made a good digital recording, you can make many copies of an audio or video program that will all be as good as the original. This is one of the real benefits of digital technology.

However, this is not the whole story regarding the difference between analog and digital media. When an analog recording is made, it becomes complete unit that has specific parameters. For example, a 30-second TV commercial will take 30 seconds to play back; it takes up a certain amount of videotape; and it has specific attributes. These parameters are not easily changed. Digital files can be more easily manipulated. As digital technology became more prevalent, producers found that it was easier to scale the messages created for different devices. For example, digital television pictures can be made rectangular or widescreen for large-screen TVs or small for mobile devices or a couple of different sizes for computers with different network connection speeds. Similarly, digital audio files can be made to have limited fidelity or extremely high fidelity depending on sampling size and bit rate. **Compression** is the term for making larger video and audio files smaller. By using compression techniques it is possible to increase the speed of a video download on a computer network or to increase the number of different programs that can be placed on one digital television channel. Once a program is digitized, it can be reused in many different forms; the same program can be played for a small phone or for the biggest home theater system.

There are potential problems too. A digitized program can be more easily copied and distributed illegally. Files can be placed on a computer network without the producer's permission and distributed around the world in a matter of minutes. Another person can add or subtract video and audio with a computer, altering the program beyond the intentions of the original producer. The digital file can be stored on any number of hard disks, moved about on a flash drive, transferred easily to a DVD, or stored on a network (like YouTube) where many people can see the product. So the attributes that can be considered benefits of the digital process can also be problematic in some situations.

Oscillation and the Waveform

Another principle basic to both audio and video signal processing is the concept of **oscillation.** Recall that we hear sounds and see images as variations, fluctuations, or vibrations detected by our ears and eyes and interpreted by our brain. Remember too that every vibration has a unique signature or "footprint"; every sound and image has its own characteristics. How well we see, how acutely we hear, and how well we can recreate these signals as sounds and pictures depend on our ability to identify, store, and recreate those vibrations. In electronic terms, the vibration of air produced by our mouths, the instruments we play, and objects in our natural environment, as well as the vibration of light that accounts for every color and image our eyes can see, is known as oscillation. The footprint or image of an oscillation we use to visualize the presence of the invisible is known as its **waveform.** Figure 3–1 demonstrates the phenomenon of oscillation and the common waveform.

The most common way we can visualize oscillation is by dropping a small rock into a pool of water. You know that the result will be a series of circles or waves, radiating outward from the spot where the rock fell, until dissipating some distance from the center (depending on the size of the pool and the height from which we drop the rock). All audio and video signals produce a pattern like this, except that they are invisible to the naked eye. However,

Figure 3–1

Principle of Oscillation and the Common Waveform

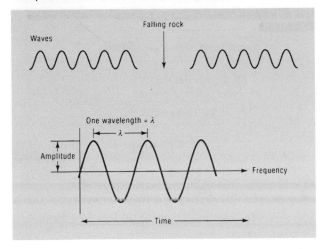

while we can't see the patterns with the naked eye, by using the appropriate electronic equipment (such as an oscilloscope and a waveform monitor), we can detect them, use them, and even create them ourselves.

Frequency and Amplitude

A major way in which we describe a wave is by its **frequency,** the number of waves that pass a given point in a given time. Originally measured in cycles per second (cps), frequency is more commonly measured now in **hertz (Hz)** in homage to early radio pioneer Heinrich Hertz.

In our example with the rock, depicted in Figure 3–1, the frequency is simply the number of waves that pass a given point in a single second. Note also from the bottom of Figure 3–1 that the distance between two corresponding points on a wave is called the **wavelength.** Also note that frequency and wavelength are inversely related. High frequency means a short wavelength; low frequency means a long wavelength. In the early days of radio, U.S. stations were classified by their wavelengths. Today we identify them by their frequencies (microwaves are very small, for example).

A wave may also be described by its height or depth, from its normal position before the rock is dropped to the crest created by the splash. This is known as its **amplitude.** When choosing a section of beach to swim in, families with small children are likely to select those with slow, low, undulating waves—

waves of low amplitude or, to use a radio term, long waves. Surfers will select a wild stretch of shoreline with frequent, mammoth (high-amplitude) waves capable of picking the swimmer up and depositing her anywhere on the beach. In radio terms, these are the high-frequency short waves.

What's the significance of all this? For one thing, this is precisely how radio and TV work. As we examine in detail later, local radio stations wish to blanket their area with a strong local or regional signal. That's why AM signals use medium-length waves. International broadcasters like the BBC and Radio Moscow seek to spread the word about their countries around the globe. Hence they use short waves to hopscotch around the world. Even digital technology has not transcended the way in which we use channel assignments to carry information and entertainment on radio waves.

Frequency Response and Bandwidth

Consider a final point about oscillation and the waveform. How well we can record and play back music depends on the range of frequencies that a radio is capable of receiving or reproducing. This is known as the unit's **frequency response.** Let's think about a broadcast of your favorite band on your local FM station. An inexpensive portable radio that can reproduce only a limited set of frequencies, say between 500 and 5,000 cycles, will simply exclude very low and very high sounds. This radio will make your favorite band sound tinny; it will not have great *fidelity.* But if you own a fancy receiver with the best speakers capable of reproducing the entire spectrum of sound (from 20 to 20,000 hertz), it will be able to reproduce all the sounds the human ear can hear. The difference is dramatic. You may not have given it much thought before, but this is critical because the history of the popular arts is directly linked to the frequency response of the prevailing methods of signal processing.

In the recording industry the early success of banjo-playing minstrel-type performers, who frequently whistled in their acts, was in large part due to their audibility on 78-rpm records of limited, mainly high-frequency capability. Early recording stars such as Al Jolson, Rudy Vallee, and Eddie Cantor fall into this class. Similarly, in retrospect, Elvis Presley's early hits had limited tonal range that seems to have directly fit the limitations of the cheaply produced 45-rpm record popular in the 1950s, which was meant to be heard on a teenager's much-abused "personal" record player (certainly not on dad's hi-fi in the den). In fact, early rock-and-roll record producers frequently listened to the final mix of a song on small car speakers instead of big studio monitors! So is it any surprise that the orchestrations, sound collages, and other experimentations ushered in by the Beatles' *Sergeant Pepper's Lonely Hearts Club Band*, the Beach Boys' *Pet Sounds,* and other groups in the late 1960s were aided by the developments of high-fidelity studio recording and FM stereo broadcasting? Today the complexities and acoustic calisthenics of modern pop and hip-hop performers (such as Lady Gaga, Eminem, or the Black Eyed Peas) are made possible by the extended range of frequencies available with new audio components, such as digital recording consoles and CD players.

Just as radio receivers may have large or limited frequency response, broadcast stations have specific limitations in their bandwidth. AM radio sounds somewhat tinny compared with FM because AM has a much smaller bandwidth. As a result AM stations cannot reproduce all the frequencies the human ear is capable of hearing. The FCC determines a station's bandwidth when it determines what frequencies that station can use. We call this allocation a station's *channel assignment*.

Digital television (DTV) lets the broadcaster decide how much bandwidth to use for various different kinds of programming. A sporting event with lots of action in high definition may require all the bandwidth available, whereas a news show, with mostly talking heads, may be perfectly acceptable using less bandwidth.

STEPS IN THE MEDIA DISTRIBUTION PROCESS

Earlier we described the steps involved in the creation of an audio and video signal when we talked about how you could record a bluebird singing in a tree. Although that might make an interesting personal video that you could send to a friend, it is not likely to be of sufficient quality to broadcast the event to a large audience. So we're going to extend our discussion to include more detail about the creation and distribution process. Some of the technology is cutting-edge and some is a bit difficult to think about; but our goal here is not to teach either production or engineering, so we're going to keep the discussion to the basics. Although many people use these tech-

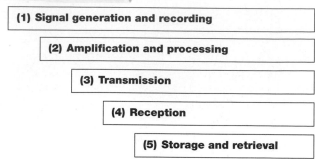

Figure 3–2

Steps in Signal Processing

(1) **Signal generation and recording**

(2) **Amplification and processing**

(3) **Transmission**

(4) **Reception**

(5) **Storage and retrieval**

nologies without knowing how they work, we think your education will be richer with this knowledge.

Signal Generation and Recording: Mechanical and Digital Technologies

Sound signals are generated by two main transduction processes: mechanical and electronic. Mechanical methods, like microphones, phonograph records, and tape recorders, were in use for many years. They have been replaced by digital electronics, such as CDs, DVDs, and computer files.

Let's briefly review how mechanical methods work because they are still useful to us. Mechanical methods uses facsimile technology to create an **analog** of the original signals—that is, mechanical means are used to translate sound waves into a physical form. The most common analog transducer used today in broadcasting is the microphone. There are three basic types of microphones: dynamic, velocity, and condenser. Each produces the electrical waveforms required for transmission in a different manner; but while the operations of the different types of microphones vary, they all change sound pressure generated by the actual sound waves into a tiny electrical signals that mirror the original sounds in frequency and relative loudness.

In a dynamic microphone a diaphragm is suspended over an electromagnet. In the center of the microphone is a coil of electrical wire called a *voice coil.* Sound pressure vibrates the diaphragm, which moves the voice coil up and down between the magnetic poles. This movement induces an electrical pattern in the mike's wire analogous to the frequency of the entering sound. (To visualize this process think about moving a powerful magnet over a pile of pins. As you move the magnet, the pins underneath will

If you play Nintendo's Game Boy, you're probably familiar with Pokémon, a popular series of games also known as Pocket Monsters. It seems that one of the monsters terrorized Japan, sending hundreds of kids to doctors and hospitals with symptoms of convulsions, including nausea, dizziness, diarrhea, and vomiting.

This situation occurred near the end of a half-hour episode of Pokémon in 1997, the cartoon that is based on the video game and that is aired on TV Tokyo, Japan's channel 12. An animated attack and explosion caused the TV screen to flicker in rapid, bright red and blue flashes produced by the animation studio by using special digital video effects. Soon ambulance sirens could be heard across the country. A 5-year-old girl in Osaka stopped breathing (she recovered). Children began vomiting. Thousands reported feeling nauseated; more than 600 showed up at hospitals throughout the evening. Near midnight a 30-year-old woman became ill; she had just watched a tape of the show on her VCR. One account claims that more than 12,000 Japanese children had various signs and symptoms of illness. Immediately after the incident, the TV show was shut down for several months, with some parents expressing concern that Pokémon should not be screened again.

What happened? The Japanese Health and Welfare Ministry set up a study team. Numerous explanations were offered. One psychologist suggested the cause was photosensitive epilepsy, an epileptic effect induced by flashing lights that seemed to be more common in teenagers and children than adults. Another suggested that the problem was a kind of group hysteria—kids across Japan were "too engrossed" in the country's most popular animated series. For its part, Nintendo blamed the TV station and said its video games were completely harmless. Later, however, a report in the *Southern Medical Journal* reported that only a small fraction of the 618 children who were treated were actually diagnosed with photosensitive epilepsy.

Fast-forward to 2007, when a movie clip on the official London 2012 Olympic Games Web site showing a person diving into a pool that had flickering, multicolored ripple effects caused similar seizures in at least 30 viewers. According to BBC reports, when the clip was shown on television it also triggered seizures. The British group Epilepsy Action claimed the images could have affected thousands who have photosensitive epilepsy. One research at Epilepsy Research UK said he found it incredible that the piece of animation was approved because there are specific television guidelines on broadcasting patterns of flashing lights because of this medical problem.

Although quite a bit of medical research has been done, it is not really understood why certain patterns, colors, and light combinations falling on the retina can trigger these seizures, although it is known to be more common in girls than boys. Interestingly, this may be a syndrome destined to extinction. Researchers have discovered that the new generation of LCD and LED televisions do not induce seizures because they do not flicker at the slower rates of old analog television; their screen refresh rate is much higher, and this eliminates flickering.

move in concert with the force of the magnet.) Thanks to durable and rugged design similar to a sturdy kettle drum and good frequency response with voices and most music, dynamic mikes are frequently used in radio and TV productions, especially in remote broadcasts such as sports and news.

Velocity microphones (also known as ribbon microphones) and condenser microphones work on slightly different mechanical principles, but they perform the same function. Each type of microphone has benefits and specific uses that make it useful in broadcasting and recording.

Other than microphones, most audio used today in broadcasting comes from recorded sources such as **Compact Discs (CDs)**, digital files stored on computers, or some kind of distribution network like a satellite or an intranet (a specialized or closed computer network). Digital audio was made possible by the development of a means of signal generation known as **pulse code modulation** (PCM). This and other modulation methods are seen in Figure 3–3. At the top of the figure is the original waveform: the shape of the original sound we seek to record and reproduce. Let's say it's the sound of a guitar solo. In that original waveform we see the frequency (pitch of the guitar string) varying in amplitude over time. Below the waveform is its shape, transduced into an AM signal. Like a surfer on a wave, its new shape is a series of peaks and valleys, or changes in amplitude. Below that is the same waveform transduced into an FM signal. Now the message is in the form of a series of changes in the number of times the signal occurs in one second—

Figure 3–3

Modulation Methods

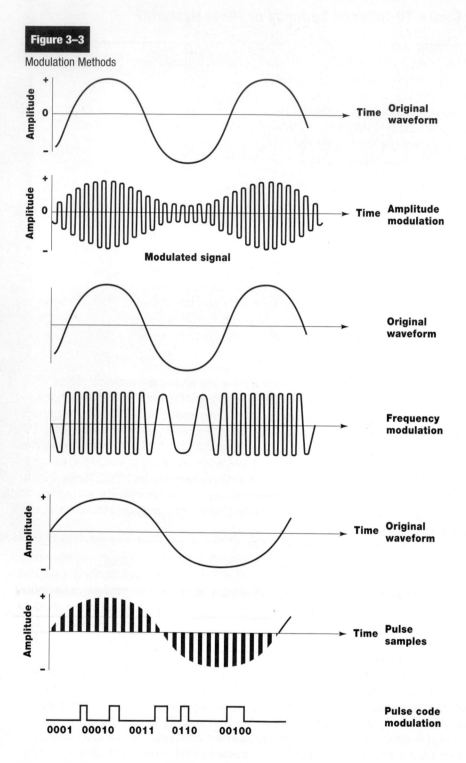

that is, its frequency. At the bottom is the waveform translated into a digital signal. By sampling the amplitude of the wave at varying intervals, turning a laser beam on and off (pulsing and measuring the length of the light beam at each interval), we can pro-

duce a digital version of the wave via pulse code modulation. Developed in 1937, PCM was first used to encode classified messages during World War II, but in the 1980s it was adapted for use in home audio with the introduction of the CD (compact disk).

The tiny electret condenser is the preferred microphone in TV news due to its small size and rugged design.

What are the benefits of digital encoding? As we have mentioned, a digital wave file is a virtual constant—it has the identical shape on recording, on transmission, going into the amplifier, and coming out of the speakers. In addition, digital devices preserve the original sounds in a noise-free environment. Let's examine how this works in digital devices.

Digital Recording Technology   As we have just noted, pulse code modulation made **digital recording and transmission** possible. As shown in Figure 3–4, once a sound has been transduced into electrical current (through a microphone, for example), it can be sent to a device that converts that signal into a series of samples that represent both the frequencies of the sound and its loudness (amplitude). Once it is in digital form, the information is coded and stored in a process called **quantization.** For quality audio recording, the sampling occurs frequently, more than 40,000 times per second. The higher the sampling rate, the higher the quality of the audio file. How these data are stored often determines the type of device we use. They may be stored as a computer file such as a .WAV file or some other file type. Digital file formats provide extremely high-quality representations of audio files because they are generally recorded without compression and can provide the user with sophisticated editing and postproduction capability. Media files used in standard CD playback are not compatible with .WAV and other recording formats. These files can be fairly large, so they are sometimes hard to transport across data networks. MP3 files are much smaller because the audio is **compressed** and becomes more easily transportable. (Compression can take many forms, but essentially it shrinks the size of the audio file.) Music players like the iTunes Player and Windows Media Player can play back a variety of different formats, including those just mentioned.

CDs and DVDs   The information on a DVD or CD is carried beneath the protective acrylic coating in a polycarbonate base. In the base is a series of pits and flats. The pits vary in length in precise correspondence to the waveforms they represent. The flats represent no waveforms: utter silence. As the disk rotates, a laser beam is focused on it. Like a mirror, when the beam "sees" a pit, it reflects back a light wave that contains data about the original sound wave. Those data are accumulated into a memory register. Now, using a digital-to-analog converter and other electronics, it is a simple matter to transduce the data into an electrical signal through amplifiers and into speakers. The result is a clean, nearly perfect sound. In technical terms, the frequency response for CDs ranges from 20 to 20,000 hertz (remember, that's a wider set of frequencies than most people can hear), and CDs have a signal-to-noise ratio of 90 decibels (compared with about 60 decibels for analog systems

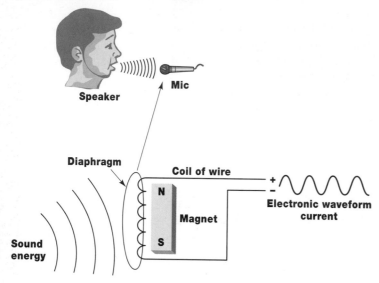

Figure 3–4

As the speaker talks, sound energy causes small movements in the microphone's diaphragm. These variations in sound pressure cause electrical energy to flow in the microphone.

like records and tapes)—the common measure of the intensity of sound.

Disks are comparatively immune from damage in routine handling and storage, but they can be scratched. With proper care, they should never warp or scratch or jam in the player, and they cannot be accidentally erased.

Writable compact disks (CD-RWs) are standard features today on home computers and have the added ability to record audio and video signals. As peer-to-peer file sharing became popular on the Internet, CD-RWs came into their own. CD-RWs have popularized the MP3 format, which we'll discuss in a moment.

Digital Versatile Disks   DVDs have become remarkably popular since their introduction in 1997, practically replacing the older VHS standard as the consumer standard. Most people use DVDs for home video playback of movie rentals or prerecorded entertainment, but others use them for home recording as well (DVD-R). DVDs are capable of reproducing multiple channels of audio, such as Dolby 5.1 surround sound—something CDs cannot do. This makes it possible to view movies encoded with Digital Theater Sound (DTS). In addition, a different audio format, DVD-A, which was introduced in 2001, allows multichannel audio playback and fidelity

greater than the current CD format. Some audiophiles claim that CDs are incapable of producing harmonics above the limit of human hearing and that the sampling rate for CDs is inadequate, imparting a coarse, almost clinical sound. The DVD-A format allows a wider band of frequencies to be recorded with greater fidelity (24-bit recording as opposed to 16 bits for CDs), but these disks have not gained wide consumer acceptance at this point.

DVDs use a recording and playback format called MPEG 2 (Motion Picture Expert Group 2) that was specifically devised to record video. Because of the large amount of data needed to store video information, the MPEG 2 format compresses the digital file to make storage, transmission, and playback easier. High-definition television broadcasts also use the MPEG 2 format. New Blu-ray DVD players allow 3D playback utilizing a separate picture synchronized for each eye; special glasses are needed to see the 3D image.

Digital Audio Formats   Several different audio formats are used to record and play back digital audio files. The most common, **MP3** (Motion Picture Expert Group—audio layer 3), is the name for files that use recording compression technology that was developed for file sharing and exchange on the Internet. It

Sampling has been around since the beginning of the digital revolution. Digital sampling techniques allow virtually any sound or image to be reproduced and rerecorded, thereby raising a critical ethical dilemma. Is it ethical to borrow musical phrases from one song and then combine them with pieces of other songs? Most performers and musicians argue that their work should be protected from such digital manipulation. Others argue that this technology has created a new art form. Composers should be free to use sounds and images from other works to create new ones, especially those that use the expropriated images for comedic or satirical purposes.

Negativland is one of those groups. The "band," if you can call it that, exists by purloining the work of other artists and turning compilations of those bits of work into their own songs. Their albums use hundreds of digital samples—from familiar rock guitar riffs to snippets of conversations from TV talk shows to slogans and jingles from radio and TV advertisements. The results are mixed (pun intended), but when it works, the effect can be insightful and interesting.

A few years ago the Irish group U2 sued Negativland when it released an album titled *U2,* which included a vicious parody of the supergroup's "I Still Haven't Found What I'm Looking For." Then their *Dispepsi* CD made use of samples of dozens of soft drink ads to satirize the leading cola companies. Apparently too busy with their "cola wars," thus far Coke and Pepsi have failed to file suit.

Negativland caused quite a stir in late 1998 with the release of its new CD with the not-so-clever title *Over the Edge Volume 3—The Weatherman's Dumb Stupid Come-Out Line.* According to the band's co-leader Mark Hosler, five CD-pressing plants refused to manufacture the disk, apparently under pressure from the Recording Industry Association of America. Disctronics, a plant in Texas, said it was refusing to make the CD because it might contain unauthorized sound clips.

Negativland immediately went on the offensive. The band wrote a protest letter to the RIAA, posted the letter on the Internet, and called for free speech advocates everywhere to rally to the group's side. For its part, RIAA's president and CEO Hilary Rosen called the group's concerns "misplaced" and said RIAA has had "absolutely no involvement with Negativland or its new release."

Negativland gained national attention when *Newsweek* cited one of its projects: a CD and matching photobook containing scavenged junk (shopping lists, letters, sheet music, and so on) from wrecked cars. (According to the *Newsweek* article, the band may have found a correlation between people whose cars get wrecked and bad spelling.) Critics claim the CD sounds a lot like a car crash. Privacy issues aside, however, there appears to be no copyright issues with the latest offering.

While maybe not a household name, Negativland celebrated its 30th anniversary in 2010 with its newest release *It's All In Your Head FM Version 2.0.* This is a two-hour live performance probing human belief in celestial deities. If you want to catch what the group is all about, there are several clips on YouTube.

quickly spread from college campuses to home audio systems to broadcasters. MP3 files are smaller than CD audio files because they eliminate inaudible frequencies as a way of shrinking the file size of an audio recording. This compression scheme, which made it possible to share audio files via the Internet quickly, has grown to become a preferred method of listening to music on portable players (such as iPods) and other devices. One distinct advantage of the MP3 system is that CD-Rs can store many hours of music on one disk as opposed to only 74 minutes on a standard CD. Today many DVD players and personal CDs also play back the MP3 format. MP3 files come in a variety of bit rates that affect the playback quality standards; but while the highest-quality MP3s nearly equal the sound of CDs, some experts claim that the format is inferior to other recording formats.

Some broadcasting stations have encoded music on computer drives using MP3 technology, although many use a format similar to the .WAV audio file, which provides higher audio quality. Over the past few years the cost of digital storage has declined. The result is that it is possible to store hundreds of hours of music on a large computer hard drive. Today most stations use computers for music playback because special programs allow the program director to order music selections in accordance with the station's format. Using computers to store audio files has made it easier to automate radio station programming.

Video Signal Generation

Television's ability to transmit images is based on the technology of **scanning.** You can think of scanning as the visual equivalent of audio sampling. The TV camera has a pickup device that is essentially a grid of lines with light-sensitive capability. The more dense the grid, the greater the resolution of the picture. In making a television picture, the camera scans each element of a picture line by line; the LCD or plasma screen in your TV set retraces the same scene in the same order once the picture is transmitted. Earlier in the chapter we said tracing the outline of your hand is a way to create a facsimile representation on the sheet of paper, like the illustration in Figure 3–5(a). Let's change the game a little bit. Instead of drawing one continuous line, suppose we trace the hand by using a series of five parallel lines, as depicted in Figure 3–5(b). We move the crayon straight across. We lift it when it encounters the hand and return it to the paper when it passes by a "hand" area. The result is the rough facsimile of the hand in Figure 3–5(b). Now let's use 10 lines instead of 5. This tracing will provide a fairly good representation of the hand, as in Figure 3–5(c). Just for fun, let's alternate the tracing by doing every odd-numbered line first, then each even-numbered line. After two passes, top to bottom, the result is Figure 3–5(d). In this exercise we have actually demonstrated the workings of TV technology.

When done invisibly by the TV camera, the tracing process is called **scanning.** The process of alternating lines is known as **interlace scanning.** And the process of replicating the scan on the picture tube to produce the image at home is known as **retracing.** The process originates in the TV camera and is recreated at home on the television screen.

The Importance of Scanning

At this point you may feel saturated by a hefty amount of technical information. Actually there are excellent reasons why this information is critical to understanding modern telecommunications. High-definition TV, using flat-screen TVs for Internet access, and three-dimensional television all are capabilities that rely on the set's capability to scan and display images. We're going to look at the most important aspects of television technology here.

Standardization

First is the issue of standards. Although it is true that broadcasters have switched to digital transmission, tens of millions of analog TVs are still out there. The old analog system used a 525-line system adopted in 1941 by a group known as the **NTSC (National Television Systems Committee).** A complete picture consists of two separate scans or **fields,** each consisting of 262½ horizontal scanning lines. Because specific blank lines were used to synchronize the television transmission with the home set, an old television actually reproduced about 480 lines of resolution. The two fields combine to form a single picture, called the **frame.** In the United States, the AC power system oscillates at 60 hertz. Thus our TV system uses a 60-hertz scanning rate. Because two fields are needed to produce one frame, 30 complete pictures are produced every second.

Other countries use different systems. Much of European TV, for example, uses a system known as PAL, adopted several years after the U.S. system. Based on the AC power available there, European TV uses a shorter scanning rate (50 hertz) with more scanning lines (625). Most countries with highly developed broadcast systems are converting to digital television, but again several different standards will be adopted.

Bandwidth

This term refers to how much space a radio (or television) channel occupies on the electromagnetic spectrum. We can make a generalization here. The greater the bandwidth, the greater the fidelity or capability of the station. Television stations each have 6 MHz of bandwidth allocated to them. That's quite a bit of capability; so while TV signals are complex, digital technology allows a substantial amount of flexibility.

Digital Television and High-Definition Television

High-definition television uses digital technology, but not all digital television is high-definition. The scanning process is directly involved in many current technical innovations in the TV medium, and the level of scanning defines the quality of the picture. **High-definition television (HDTV)** is the moniker for digital television utilizing up to 1,080 scanning lines, producing an image rivaling 35-millimeter film in quality. But the **digital television** transmits a scalable picture—which means the transmission can be varied from 480 lines to 1,080 lines of resolution depending on the television station transmitting the signal. DTV also allows changes in the aspect ratio (the ratio of screen width to screen height) of conventional TV. In standard TV the screen is 4 units wide and 3 units high. In DTV the ratio is 16:9 (16 units wide and 9 units high), much like the frames of

Figure 3–5

Examples of Scanning

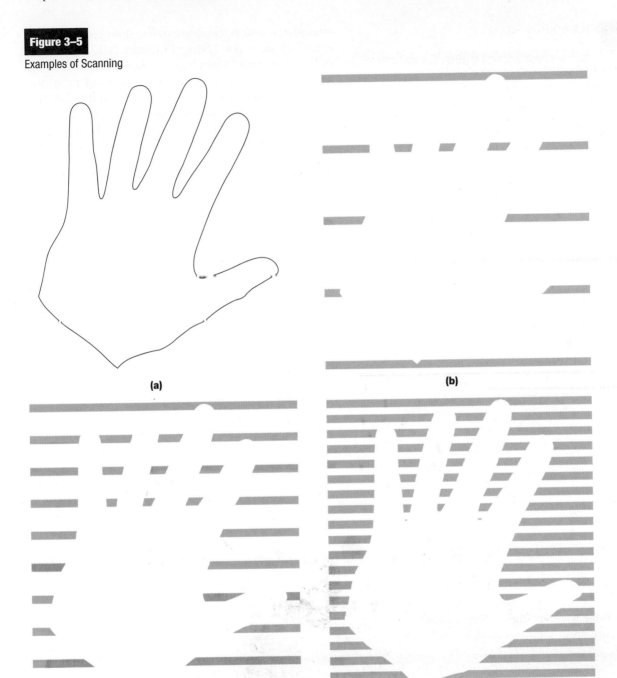

(a)

(b)

(c)

(d)

a motion picture (see Figure 3–6). Television stations can change the resolution of the picture to meet the needs of the programs transmitted.

While we're on the subject of scanning, the switch to DTV actually involved three sets of lines and two scanning methods. DTV sets can tune in TV signals using 480, 720, and 1,080 lines, all of which have much higher fidelity than the old 525 NTSC signal (because there's less noise in the picture). And DTV signals can be sent every other line (the traditional interlace method) or line by line—an alternative scanning method known as **progressive scan**.

Wide-screen TV sets have an aspect ratio of 16:9 compared with an aspect ratio of 4:3 for traditional sets. The new aspect ratio is closer to the dimensions of a theater screen.

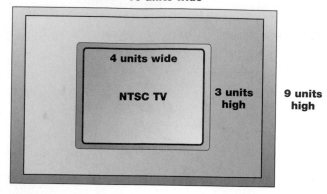

stream, television stations can use their bandwidth in a variety of ways. Using 480 lines (which requires only a portion of the channel allocation) allows TV stations to send more than one version of programming (like NBC1 or CBS2) over their channel allocation. One station might actually transmit as many as four different programs on one 6 MHz television channel. Broadcast TV is touting this feature so it can compete more successfully with its cable competitors, which have made multiple versions of their channels available for some years (like ESPN, ESPN2, and ESPNews). A local television station could start its own all-local news program service, for instance, and still broadcast the network program feed on the same channel. A digital tuner can recognize these as different programs and display them separately.

In addition, digital television sets that use the progressive scan method bring TV much closer to the computer business, which has used progressive scan on its monitors for years. Some large, flat-screen displays can now be used for both progressive scan television and computer images and even have built-in network connections for watching streamed programming from Netflix or Hulu.

Another feature of digital television systems is that they can scan an image at a much higher rate than old standard TVs. Modern televisions can scan images at 120 frames per second. Because this is essentially double our regular visual scanning rate, it is possible to transmit separate left- and right-eye pictures, creating the opportunity for three-dimensional television.

One thing that often confuses people is the fact that a scanned line is made up of various pixels. Each line will have pixels turned on or off to give the picture brightness and contrast. Standard-definition pictures (480 lines) usually paint 640 pixels across one scanned line. This gives the viewer a 4×3 aspect ratio. By contrast, a high-definition picture will have 1,920 pixels painted across one scan line. With 1,080 lines painted across 1,920 pixels the viewer gets a wide-screen 16×9 aspect ratio.

So what difference does this make? Plenty. Because broadcasting now is transmitted as a digital

The conversion to digital television spurred tremendous growth in high definition, flat-screen televisions.

Figure 3–7

Inside the TV Camera

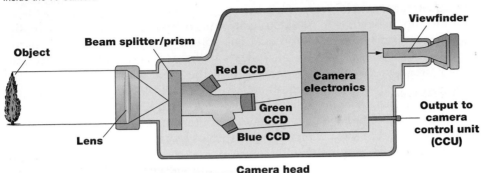

Camera head

Inside the Camera: Pickup Device   The purpose of scanning is to transduce physical light into electronic signals. The process occurs inside the TV camera, as depicted in Figure 3–7. While there are different types of cameras available, they work on roughly the same principles.

The first step in creating TV is the collection of an image by a lens. Light reflecting off objects in the desired picture is converged by the lens onto a diachronic filter that acts like a prism. The filter breaks down the image into the primary colors of red, green, and blue. The three primary color images are then focused onto light-sensitive wafers called **charge-coupled devices (CCDs).** Each of the light-sensitive chips can sample over hundreds of thousands of picture elements in a manner not unlike the way a printing press uses dots to produce a color newspaper photo. The CCDs rasterize the red, green, and blue components of the picture by turning them into rows of individual dots that we call *pixels.* These signals are extremely weak and need to be amplified by the camera electronics. (Later each row of pixels will be combined to form a scanned line of information.) A black line is added after each horizontal line and after each complete scan to allow the image to burn into our retina. These are known as the **blanking pulses.** The signal that exits the camera thus contains two sets of information: picture plus blanking. At the camera control unit (CCU) or in the switcher, a third signal is added. The **synchronization pulse** enables the output of two or more cameras and other video sources to be mixed together and allows all the scanning processes to take place at the same time, from camera to receiver.

CCD cameras have a number of advantages that make them useful in broadcasting. First, the chips are small, allowing for smaller, lighter cameras. Second, because the CCD is flat, picture distortion is reduced. In addition, CCD cameras are rugged and durable. Today these so-called chip cameras have become the preferred acquisition medium for much TV news. Inexpensive, small, lightweight, and durable, they have proved their worth under fire: first in the Persian Gulf War, and later in such global hot spots as the Middle East, Bosnia, and Somalia. It is not uncommon today for news organizations (such as CNN) to send dozens of consumer-grade chip cameras into areas of crisis in hopes that a few will be smuggled out with usable pictures. Unlike high-paid correspondents, the relatively inexpensive CCD cameras are considered expendable.

In NTSC television, the complete TV picture of red, green, and blue scan lines, picture plus blanking plus sync, is known as the **composite video signal.** Digital television and DVDs frequently provide separate outputs of the color channel signals, known as **component video.** This provides better picture fidelity.

The Concepts of Amplification and Processing

Audio Amplification   An **amplifier** is a device that boosts an electrical signal. Typically in electrical circuitry the voltage or current of an input is increased by drawing on an external power source (such as a battery or an AC or DC transformer) to produce a more powerful output signal. Devices to perform this function range from the original vacuum tube created by DeForest (whose development made radio and sound movies practical in the 1920s) to transistors (which emerged in the 1950s to enable manufacturers to reduce the size of radios and TVs) and finally to integrated circuits in the 1970s permitted the creation of extremely small devices like an iPod Shuffle or a Bluetooth earpiece).

Modern amplifiers perform a couple of functions. They may increase power in a circuit and that may increase output, such as when you turn up the volume control on your television. They may perform modifications to the original signal, such as when you turn up the bass on your stereo; or they may do a combination of things that change the waveform, such as when a distortion device puts a fuzz tone on a guitar. This is called signal processing. Other examples are phasers (not the kind used by Kirk and Spock) that manipulate the phase relationship between frequencies to create the illusion of stereo from mono signals, pitch changers can turn an out-of-tune musician into an accomplished soloist, and computers that can be manipulated to record sounds backward and to speed up or slow down recordings.

Mixing Consoles and Control Boards and Computer Programs

Radio and television stations use mixing boards that combine signals. These devices use amplifiers and special circuitry to allow the announcer to mix her voice with music and other signal sources to create programming.

Many radio executives have converted their stations into "tapeless" radio stations, where the announcing, music, amplification, and mixing are done on desktop computers. Once a source is recorded as a computer file, it can be stored and called up at will. This has spawned many programs that have automated the broadcasting process.

Desktop Audio   As you might expect, the rush to digital media has spread to the amplifier and control board. Today's high-memory, fast desktop computers can perform the same audio tricks as can the largest, most sophisticated mixing consoles. With a microphone, a sound card, and a fast hard drive, many home computers can be turned into fully functional sound studios.

One company, Radio Computing Services (RCS) of Scarsdale, New York, calls its desktop system Master Control and touts it as the "paperless, cartless, all-digital studio." In its system, all audio signals—jingles, ads, commercials, musical selections, even telephone calls from listeners—are stored on computer hard drives. There are no tape machines, turntables, or microphones. In essence, an entire radio station is converted into a network of desktop computers. The jock doesn't even have to be in the same city as the radio station because the system can send the voice tracks as sound files over the Internet.

Video Amplification and Processing

You're watching a live newscast, but before the TV signal travels from the camera to the transmitter,

Modren radio control board. Radio stations use a variety of computers systems and advanced audio technology to create live radio programming.

several things happen. First, the electrical signal is amplified—increased in electrical intensity—and carried along a wire to a monitor within a video control room, where it is viewed by the director and other production personnel. In most TV programs the cameras and other video input sources (tape machines and computers, the graphics generator, and so on) are mixed together before they are transmitted. The **switcher,** a device used for mixing TV signals, is probably the first thing a visitor to a TV control room notices. Advanced models are impressive-looking devices that **mix** together amplification with computer technology to create many special effects we take for granted today. A television director uses a switcher to put the desired picture on the air. If camera 3 shows what the director wants to see, then pushing the appropriate button on the switcher puts camera 3 on the air. If a segment of the program had been prerecorded, pushing another button will start a video server playing back that program segment.

The switcher also lets the director choose the appropriate transition from one video source to another. Simply punching another button generates what's known as a **cut**—an instantaneous switch from one picture to another. By using a **fader** bar the director can dissolve from one picture to another or fade an image to or from black. A special-effects generator can add a host of other transitions. One picture can wipe out another horizontally, vertically, or in many other patterns. In addition, a split screen with two or more people sharing the screen at the same time is possible, as is **keying,** an effect in which one video signal is electronically cut out or keyed into another. The most common use of this process is **chromakey.** Weathercasters, for example, use a chromakey process and usually perform in front of a blue background, which is replaced by keyed-in weather maps or other graphics. (Performers must be careful not to wear clothing that is the same color as the chromakey blue, or they will appear transparent on screen.)

Digital Video Effects   As might be expected, digital technology has had an immense impact on video processing. Each TV signal can be converted into a series of binary code numbers that can be manipulated and then reconverted back into a TV signal. There are numerous types of digital video effects, or **DVE,** in industry parlance. They include freeze-framing, shrinking images in size and positioning them anywhere on the screen (as happens when an anchor talks to a field reporter and both pictures are kept on screen), stretching or rotating a video picture, producing a mirror image, and wrapping the picture into a cylindrical shape. These effects are now common, and the audience is used to a multitude of graphics in news and sports programs.

Video inputs are mixed together in the television control room.

Desktop Video   Until the late 1980s, generating video special effects required large, expensive processing equipment. Only a few big-city TV stations and production centers had the capability to produce digital video (DV).

In the early 1990s the Commodore and Apple computer companies merged the video signal with the personal computer. Windows for IBM-compatible computers soon made video manipulation possible on the typical desktop PC, too.

Today digital video can be produced on an inexpensive personal computer. Apple Computer's Final Cut Pro and AVID's Media Composer software provide professional video editing capabilities in systems that interact with digital camcorders and other production devices. These systems are nondestructive, meaning that the original footage is never really edited. It is preserved and can be reused or re-edited over and over again. Advances in high-speed DVD and hard drives allow storage and retrieval of photographic and television images. As a result, the kind of spectacular visuals once reserved for music videos with huge budgets, or for the promotional messages of the major networks, can now be produced by anyone with a broadcast-quality camcorder linked to a computer. As if to underscore the low cost and simplicity of the new digital machines, one common setup is known in the industry as the "video toaster."

TRANSMISSION: GETTING THE SIGNALS OUT THERE

We've now succeeded in selecting sounds and pictures, changing them from physical energy into electronic signals, and amplifying and mixing them. The next step is to take them from point A to point B, the process of signal transmission. As we read in the history chapter, the modern age of broadcasting began when scientists and inventors became able to do this over the air, without wires. Ironically, as the new century dawns, we are now trying to do it all over again by wire (over the Internet) and by wireless (using wireless local area networks). But let's not get ahead of the story.

Signal Transmission

As Chapter 1 described in detail, the radio pioneers found that electrical signals created by human beings could be transported across space so that buttons pushed here could cause a buzz over there. They soon replaced signals and buzzes with a voice at both ends.

The Electromagnetic Spectrum   This magical process was made possible by the discovery and use of the **electromagnetic spectrum,** the electromagnetic radiation present throughout the universe. Figure 3–8 is a chart of the spectrum. A fundamental component of our physical environment, electromagnetic radiation is traveling around and through us at all times. We can see some of it (the narrow band of frequencies corresponding to visible light and color, or the "heat waves" that radiate off a parking lot in the summertime). But most of the spectrum is invisible to the naked eye and must be detected by human-made devices (like radio and TV receivers).

Over the last century we learned how to superimpose, or "piggyback," our own electronic signals on the electromagnetic waves that exist in the environment, a process known as **modulation.** This is done by generating a signal that is a replica of the natural wave. This signal, produced by a radio station on its assigned frequency, is called a **carrier wave.** It is "heard" on our radios as the silence that comes just before the station signs on in the morning, or after the national anthem at signoff. The radio signal is created by varying the carrier wave slightly, in correspondence with the frequencies of the signals we mean to transmit. Our radio, tuned to the precise middle of the carrier, interprets these oscillations and reproduces them as sounds in the speaker system. If this process seems hopelessly complex, consider this metaphor. Suppose there is a natural rock formation in the shape of a bridge. Adding a bed of concrete atop the formation, we have propagated a carrier wave. When we ride a car across the bridge, we have superimposed a signal, or modulated the carrier wave.

Radio Frequencies   Only a small part of the electromagnetic spectrum is used for AM and FM broadcasting and related transmissions. This range spans from long waves of very low frequency to extremely short waves of relatively high frequency. In general, the higher one goes in the spectrum, the more sophisticated electronics are needed in the modulation process. Unlike AM and FM, new satellite radios use very high frequencies beamed from a geostationary satellite to your car or home. Mobile smart phones use microtransmitting and receiving technology that hands the user off from one small geographical locale (called a cell) to another as the user travels down the highway.

Each new development in electronic media has taken us higher in the spectrum. Radio broadcasting

Events: Apple and Google—Battle of the Giants

Every time Apple introduces a new product it seems to cause a media frenzy of such proportion that the major media feel compelled to dispatch reporters to take a look at the technological and sociological impact the product will have on American life. The iPod, iTunes, and iPhone have literally revolutionized the way Americans listen to music and use mobile devices. Maybe Apple has superior PR in addition to producing highly useful products.

Everybody already knows Google, too. It's become such a part of our daily life that the word has become a verb that we use to mean "to search for." We discuss Google's power as a search giant, services powerhouse, and owner of YouTube in other chapters in the text. But now Google and Apple seem to be on a trajectory that will cause sparks to fly and giants to compete. In 2009 Google introduced an operating system that allowed mobile phone competitors like Motorola, Samsung, and LG to market phones that effectively compete with Apple's iPhone. Based on the company's Android operating system, many of these smart phones have been runaway best sellers, effectively competing with Apple's phone for dominance in that market.

In turn, Apple entered the mobile phone advertising business when it purchased Quattro Wireless and quickly became a competitor in the advertising marketplace where Google had been the undisputed leader.

Recently the spotlight has had to make room for new innovations from both Apple and Google. Who will win the race to dominate the home entertainment market? That may ultimately be the question that needs to be answered before we can predict what will be the next big innovation in television entertainment. In 2010 a new tiny Apple TV product was released that some claimed could help revolutionize the home television market. The new device would stream HD movies from Netflix and television shows that consumers could rent or buy, could play music from the home computer's iTunes collection, and allowed iPhone and iPad users to stream information from their mobile devices to their televisions. The device cost less than $100.00.

GoogleTV is a new network device that is similar to Apple TV but will also allow users to combine the power of Google search with the television interface. So consumers can use Google applications to get sports scores while watching a sporting event in a portion of the television screen. When this book went to press, the price point for this new device was three time more than Apple TV. But there was speculation that satellite providers might offer the device with a price reduction.

Although there are some similarities in capabilities, the two systems are different. The Google device runs "apps" that are developed for the Android system and allows the user to interact directly with the Internet. Apple TV boasts the sleek, easy-to-use interface that makes Apple products so popular, and it is much cheaper. And some speculate that an apps store for Apple TV is on the way.

It's too early to tell which device consumers will prefer; but if these devices sell well, they may signal a new rivalry between the two companies. And more importantly, acceptance of these devices will signal a new way we use the television in our daily lives.

began toward the low end of the spectrum, in the area ranging from 0.3 to 3 megahertz (mega = million), a region known as the medium waves. Included in this region is the range of 550 to 1,605 kilohertz (kilo = thousand), which is the range of the AM radio dial. In fact, in many countries AM is still referred to as the medium-wave (MW) band.

The high frequencies (which, with satellite and infrared communications, actually aren't so high anymore) range from 3 to 30 megahertz. These waves are used for long-range military communications, CB, and ham radio. Because high-frequency waves can be used to transmit signals over greater distances than can medium waves, this part of the spectrum has been used for over 50 years by international shortwave stations such as the BBC and the Voice of America. The shortwave band on a radio is sometimes labeled HF for high frequencies.

The very high frequency, or VHF, band ranges from 30 to 300 megahertz. Television stations operating on channels 2 to 13, FM radio stations, police radios, and airline navigation systems are located in this band.

Above this are the ultra-high frequencies, or the UHF band, spanning the region from 300 to 3,000 megahertz. This part of the spectrum is used for TV stations 14 to 83, including most of the new digital TV stations, police and taxi mobile radios, radar, and weather satellites. In addition, it is UHF radiation that is modulated to cook our food in microwave ovens.

Figure 3–8

The Electromagnetic Spectrum

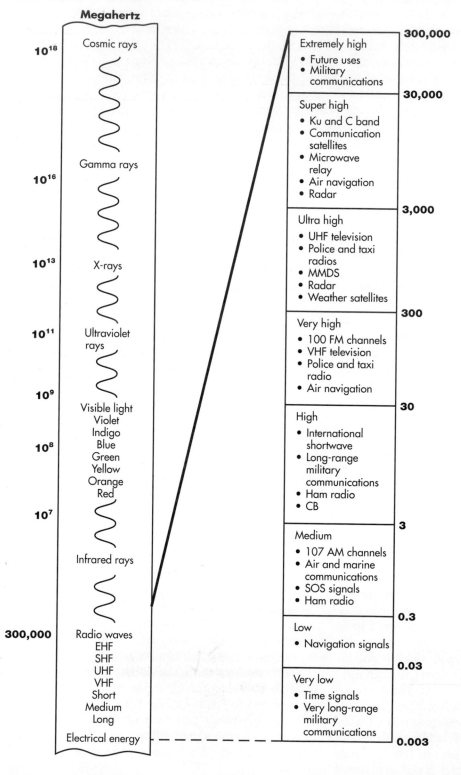

Much of recent telecommunications development has occurred in the next two radio bands: super-high frequencies (SHF) and extremely high frequencies (EHF). SHF spans from 3,000 to 30,000 megahertz and EHF from 30,000 to 300,000 megahertz. Commercial satellites—which deliver pay cable channels, superstations, and satellite news—emanate from these bands, as do new developments in digital audio broadcasting, military radar, and air navigation.

Spectrum Management Keeping track of all these uses of the electromagnetic spectrum is difficult and requires substantial domestic and international coordination and regulation, a process known as **spectrum management.** In the United States, decisions regarding which services operate in which regions of the spectrum, and at what operating power, are handled primarily by the Federal Communications Commission (FCC). Here's how radio and TV service is administered in the United States.

Radio Channel Classifications At the latest count more than 14,500 radio stations were on the air in the United States. Yet there are only 107 AM channels and 100 FM channels. How is this possible? The answer is spectrum management. By controlling operating hours, power, antenna height and design, and other

factors, the FCC squeezes all these stations into the 207 channels. If you can imagine 14,000 cars competing for 200 parking spaces (kind of like the first day of classes), you have a sense of the task at hand.

- *AM channels and classifications.* The 107 AM channels are divided into three main types: 60 are called **clear channels,** 41 are **regional channels,** and the remaining 6 are **local channels.** Here's how the system works: The clear channels are frequencies that have been designated by international agreements for primary use by high-powered stations. Such stations use ground waves in daytime and sky waves at night to reach a wide geographic area, often thousands of miles, see Fig. 3–9. Though we share those frequencies with Mexico and Canada, the United States has priority on 45 clear channels. Stations on these frequencies include some of our oldest and strongest. Class A stations, like WABC in New York at 770 kilohertz, WJR in Detroit at 610 kilohertz, and KMOX (1120 kilohertz) in St. Louis, have the exclusive right to the clear channel after sunset. They operate at high power, from 10,000 to 50,000 watts. Class B AM stations use the clear channels but must operate at reduced power at night to avoid interference. Their power

Figure 3–9

Radio wave propagation.

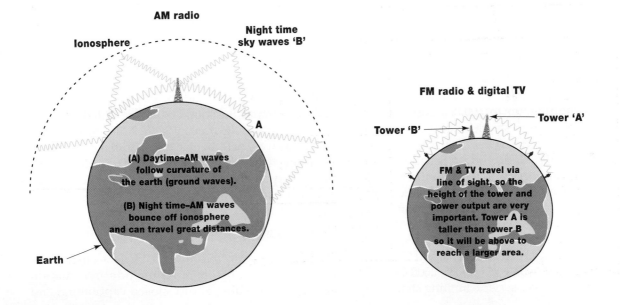

outputs range from 5 to 25 kilowatts. Class C stations are designated as regional stations. Ranging in power from 500 to 5,000 watts, they must share channels with numerous other stations. To do this they generally use directional antennas and strategic placement to blanket their main population areas. Over 2,000 Class C stations share the 41 regional channels. Other Class C stations operate on local channels. These stations are mostly at the right or top end of the dial (above 1,230 kilohertz) and are limited in power, usually between 250 and 1,000 watts.

- *FM channels and classifications.* In 1945 the FCC set aside the region from 88 to 108 megahertz in the VHF band for FM. This allowed room for 100 channels, each 200 kilohertz wide. This means that when your FM radio is tuned to 97.3 the station is actually radiating a signal oscillating from 97.2 to 97.4 megahertz (remember that we called the space occupied the station's bandwidth). Of the 100 channels, 80 are for commercial use. The remaining 20 channels, located from 88 to 92 megahertz, are reserved for educational and noncommercial stations.

To facilitate the development of commercial FM, the FCC divided the United States into three regions. Zone I includes the most densely populated area of the United States: the Northeast. Zone I-A covers the southern California region. The rest of the country composes Zone II. FM stations also use A, B, and C designations. Class A FM stations operate in all zones, Class B's in Zone I, and Class C's only in Zone II.

This is a bit confusing, but each class of FM station is defined by its **effective radiated power (ERP),** the amount of power it is permitted to use, and its antenna height. That's because FM transmission is based on line of sight, see Fig. 3–9. The higher the tower, the farther a signal can transmit. Class C FMs are the most powerful, transmitting up to 100,000 watts (ERP). They may erect transmitters with a maximum **height above average terrain (HAAT)** of 2,000 feet. Class B's can generate up to 50,000 watts ERP at 500 feet HAAT, and Class A's are authorized to a maximum of 3,000 watts ERP at 300 feet HAAT. The height of the transmitter above average terrain is an important consideration for how far the signal will travel. At maximum power and antenna height, Class C's can cover about 60 miles, Class B's about 30, and Class A's up to 15. As we noted earlier, in January 2000 the FCC created a new low-power service, limiting stations to a maximum of 100 watts ERP with an antenna height of 100 feet HAAT. These new low-power stations have a coverage radius of approximately 3.5 miles and are available only as a noncommercial service.

Sidebands and HD Signals   The bandwidth of FM (200 kilohertz) allows these stations to transmit more than one signal on their channel. Such signals use the area above and below the station's carrier frequency, known as the **sideband.** The most common use of the sideband is to disseminate separate signals for the left and right channel to broadcast stereo. This is called **multiplexing.** If you have an old FM stereo receiver, it may be labeled "FM multiplex."

FM station operators may use additional spectrum space to send multiplex signals, which can be tuned only by specially designed receivers. To do this, stations apply to the FCC for a **subsidiary communications authorization (SCA).** Such services include the "background" music one hears in malls and elevators, a Talking Book service for the blind, telephone paging, data transmission, and special radio services for doctors, lawyers, and some others.

HD is the newest wrinkle in the radio world. The FCC allows radio stations to transmit a portion of their signal as a digitally encoded program. But HD radio will not replace traditional broadcasting. When a station transmits an HD signal, it converts the signal into a digital stream that is piggybacked on the station's carrier wave. The HD radio senses the signal and decodes it. Stations can actually encode and transmit more than one channel. So it is possible to have multiple formats transmitted simultaneously. HD sound quality for FM stations is improved because the digital encoding eliminates some of the multipath distortion possible when the FM signal bounces off several buildings. Just like MP3 players that use compression to reduce file size, the higher the bit rate, the better the sound quality. HD sound on FM can approach CD quality or mimic the sound of analog FM, depending on the bit rate of the transmission. AM signals are improved as well, with higher transmission bit rates approaching the quality of analog FM. The technology is proprietary; that is, stations must pay an annual licensing fee to transmit HD signals.

Video Transmission

As might be expected, digital TV is a fairly complex signal because it must include information about picture, color, audio, closed captioning, and synchronization for the home TB to reproduce the transmitted signal.

The Television Channel   Each TV station licensed in the United States is given a bandwidth of 6 megahertz. This is equivalent to enough space for 30 FM radio stations and 600 AM stations!

Our old analog TV, the NTSC system, was perfected in the 1930s and 1940s when amplitude modulation (AM) techniques were considered state-of-the-art. For this reason it was decided to transmit the TV picture information via AM. Engineers calculated that 6 MHZ was the appropriate bandwidth for the system they envisioned.

TV Allocations   The complexity of the TV signal and its vast need for space caused the FCC in the 1940s and 1950s to assign it a place higher in the electro magnetic spectrum than any that had been used in prior years.

Channels 2 to 13 are located in the **very high frequency (VHF)** portion of the spectrum, the area ranging from 54 to 216 megahertz. Interestingly, a sizable portion of the VHF band is not used for TV purposes. The area between channels 6 and 7 includes the space for all FM radio stations as well as aircraft–control tower communication, amateur or "ham" radio, and business and government applications.

Channels 14 to 83 lie in the **ultra-high frequency (UHF)** portion of the band, the region between 470 and 890 megahertz. There is another gap, this time between channels 13 and 14, which is reserved for government communications. When the FCC mandated a conversion to digital broadcasting, it was able to recapture part of this spectrum in 2009.

Historically, VHF stations have tended to travel "first class" in the TV business, while UHF properties have typically been relegated to the "coach" section, and that's because it required much more power for UHF stations to cover the same area as their VHF counterparts. Today these differences are relatively meaningless because most digital stations are on the UHF spectrum.

ATSC: Digital TV Channels   In 2009 analog broadcasting for full-power TV stations ended. A set of transmissions standards set by an industry group—the **Advanced Television Standards Committee (ATSC)**—had been adopted by the FCC in the 1990s. The standard uses a form of video compression and a different modulation system than our analog standard.

Today's digital television picture is really a series of sequential digital images that are displayed so quickly that the eye sees them as a moving image. As we have already noted, for HDTV a television needs to paint 1,920 pixels across each scan line. And it will scan 1,080 lines across the TV screen 60 times per second. To fit all the details about shape, color, brightness, and contrast, the engineers developed a digital video signal encoding scheme called MPEG-2 (Motion Picture Expert Group level 2) that reduces the size of the digital file without degrading picture information so the eye can reconstruct an image with high enough quality to be called high definition. For technically inclined readers, the transmission data rate is about 19 MB per second, which is about two and a half times the amount of data that most home broadband systems currently provide for users.

Once the encoding process is complete, the encoded video, audio, and related information channels are sent to a television transmitter that synchronizes the data packets and adds a sophisticated error correction scheme to the signal; then a pilot signal is placed in the signal and it is sent into the air. The purpose of the pilot is to allow the home television to locate and decode the transmitted signal.

The U.S. system is one of several digital transmission systems used throughout the world, so just as the earlier NTSC system was different from the PAL system. The ATSC system differs from the systems used in Japan and Europe.

Satellite Transmission

A common sight on lawns, homes, and businesses is the satellite dish, which has become an important means of radio and television transmission. These dishes are all pointed at the sky toward one or more of the dozens of communications satellites in orbit about 22,000 miles above the earth. These satellites are launched into an orbit that moves at the same rate as the earth rotates, a technique known as **geosynchronous orbit.** While the technology is complex, the concept is simple. For all intents and purposes, the satellites are "parked" in their unique orbital slots.

Satellites operate in the **super-high frequency (SHF) portion of the electromagnetic spectrum.** Just as new developments led radio and TV to move up the spectrum, the same has happened in satellite communications. The first geosynchronous satellites were assigned to the area ranging roughly from 4 to 6 gigahertz (gHz, or billions of cycles) in an area

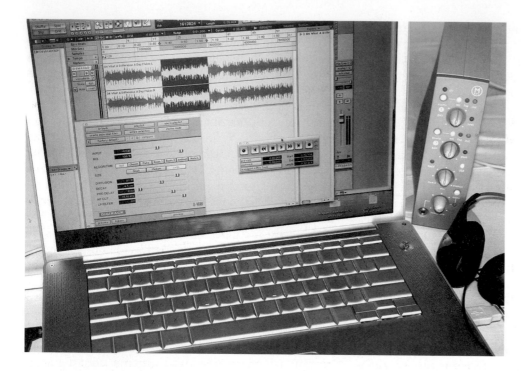

Modern computers can function as digital workstations.

known as the **C band.** Newer, more powerful satellites operate from 12 to 14 gigahertz, a region known as the **Ku band.** Satellites are called transceivers because they have two functions. First they receive signals from earth stations; then they amplify the signals and retransmit them back to earth.

Direct Broadcast Satellite   The year 1994 saw the launch of a new form of communications, known as **direct broadcast satellite (DBS).** DBS makes use of higher-powered satellites with a much larger footprint than traditional C- and Ku-band "birds" (as satellites are sometimes called). In addition, rather than needing a three-meter dish (the size you see in some backyards), DBS receivers are only 18 inches wide. They can be made to work successfully on a rooftop or window ledge, much like the TV aerials of yesteryear.

Marketed by such firms as DirecTV and The Dish Network, DBS has enjoyed widespread consumer acceptance. Today DBS reaches one in four TV households.

Digital Audio Broadcasting   If we can get direct satellite-to-home TV, why can't we also get direct satellite-to-car radio? Well, we can. **Digital audio broadcasting (DAB)** combines the technique of pulse code modulation (PCM), which made CD audio practical and popular, with super-high-frequency transmission (such as that used for satellites and microwaves). The result is CD-quality sound from a home or car radio without the need for records, tapes, disks, or your local radio station.

In 1997 the FCC auctioned off part of the spectrum to two companies—American Mobile Radio (now called XM Satellite Radio) and CD Radio (now Sirius)—that promised to deliver CD-quality radio service to the United States. In 2002 they began beaming digital audio to cars and homes. Both services transmit all-digital radio services to subscribers across America, and both services offer nearly 100 channels of unique programming. XM beams its signals to customers from two geosynchronous satellites (appropriately named Rock and Roll), while Sirius uses three satellites that rotate in an elliptical orbit. The satellites transmit in the 2.3 gigahertz digital audio radio service (DARS) band. Today the services have merged but still use the two different systems to provide programming. A small car-phone-sized antenna that fits unobtrusively on the roof of an automobile is used to receive the services.

Back to the Future: The Return to Wired Communications

As we traced in Chapter 1, the modern era of broadcasting began with the liberation of the telegraph by

Marconi's wireless. Ironically, a century later, much of the change in contemporary telecommunications was due to the return to prominence of wired communications. This trend was led by the phenomenal growth of cable television and the rise of the Internet.

Cable Transmission   Shortly after World War II a new type of cable, called *coaxial cable*, was developed to support the burgeoning telephone industry. In addition to handling thousands of simultaneous telephone conversations, this cable was soon found to be an excellent conduit for disseminating TV signals. Since then cable TV has become an increasingly widespread and important means of TV signal propagation.

Coaxial cable, or "coax" for short, consists of two electronic conductors. At the center is a copper wire shielded by a protective insulator called the *dielectric*. Outside the dielectric is a wire mesh, typically made of copper or aluminum. This conductor is shielded by a durable plastic coating, the outer body of the cable. This design gives the cable some special properties. The shielding keeps the signals within a confined space, reducing the electrical interference common in normal wiring (like that in household appliances). Coaxial cable can also carry its own DC power source, which allows for expanding the service area of the cable operator. In addition, good shielding allows the coax to last many years without contamination by water or other invasive materials.

Over the years, as the materials used to make coaxial cable improved, the number of TV signals transmittable by cable increased. In the 1950s cable TV systems could carry only three to five TV signals. In the 1960s transistorized components and new cable materials raised cable channel capacity to 12 channels. An explosion of services in the 1970s came about as further technical refinements allowed cable systems to carry as many as 60 TV channels, as well as a range of other services (FM radio to data, text, and so on).

As you can see, local cable operators can exert a kind of media power that broadcasters cannot. Within certain limits (see Chapter 5), they—not the FCC—can control where a given TV station is placed on the cable. In addition, during the 1990s cable systems began deploying **fiber optic** cables as the backbone to their "truck" or main delivery system in place of coaxial cable. Fiber optic cable is a kind of "wireless wire." Instead of the copper and aluminum elements found in coaxial cable, fiber optic cable contains strands of flexible glass. The electrical signals normally transmitted through conventional wire are replaced by light pulses transmitted by a laser light source. These on–off (binary) pulses are decoded at the receiving source by a photodiode—a small, light-sensitive device. The process is similar to the way CDs produce high-quality sound.

This innovation plus compression technology enabled cable operators to develop very high channel capacity. Moreover, cable operators converted their systems to allow communication to be sent from the home receiver to the head end, enabling two-way, or interactive, communication. These technologies created the opportunity for new services such as movies on demand, pay TV options, and multiple programming sources (HBO1, ESPN2, and the like). Some digital cable systems boast more than 500-channel capacity.

Another capability of cable is **addressability**, which is the ability of a cable system to send a program to some houses that request it and to not send it to those that don't; this is possible because the video signals are encrypted. The cable operator can send a key to your home cable set-top box to unlock services. This addressability was important in the development of pay-per-view TV, where only a portion of subscribers are willing to pay extra to watch a recent movie or sports event. Since 2000 **digital video recorders (DVR)** have been available. Cable companies, taking a cue from their direct broadcast satellite competitors, began offering home DVRs built into the addressable cable set-top boxes. Modern cable systems provide customers with a huge number of options, all for progressively larger monthly fees.

This flexibility accounts for cable's great expansion in recent years, detailed in Chapter 2. Originally a source of improved reception of only three or four nearby TV stations, the cable has become a broadband source of local and regional broadcast stations, distant superstations, and sports, movies, and other special-interest channels to more than two-thirds of the nation. And the introduction of high-speed cable modems allows cable to offer high-bandwidth Internet service and digital telephone services in addition to cable programming.

For nearly half a century, two different wires connected most homes for communications. The common "twisted pair" brought telephone calls to the home. The "coax" connected subscribing households to a cable television company. However, telephone companies are now installing a newer technology that allows them to provide video service and broadband Internet (called digital subscriber line or DSL) service into the home, effectively competing with

A fiber optic bundle. Eventually fiber optics will replace the copper wires that now carry TV and telephone signals.

old telephone wire (often called twisted pair). Unlike cable these systems do not push out many channels to the home subscriber, waiting for a set-top box or cable-ready TV to be tuned to the specific channel. Instead these systems use **IPTV (Internet protocol TV**—a technology similar to TCP/IP), which asks for a specific address, much as your computer asks for a URL when connecting to a specific Internet location. This streaming service moves television and Internet services closer together.

The pure, noise-free digital signal passing through a fiber connection into a home can be a telephone call, a radio show, a broadband connection to the Internet, games, or a TV program. It should not surprise the reader, then, that radio, TV, cable, and telephone companies are in the process of entering one another's businesses to one degree or another.

Back to the Future II: The Growth of New Wireless Services

You may remember in the movie *Back to the Future II* Marty and Doc have to go back in time to undo something that was completely unforeseen. Today the communications revolution seems to face a similar situation. Just when it seemed clear that we'd be living in a wired world, things changed. People seem more connected now than ever, but wirelessly. Cellular telephones, laptops, and other handheld wireless devices are essentially **transceivers:** They can both transmit and receive.

Over the past few years costs of laptop computers and wireless home routers declined dramatically, making them much more affordable. Some families began opting for wireless laptops instead of desktop computers that could be used in only one location in the house. The merging of computer and telephone networks have created an alternative to the wired world.

But while the smart functions of a mobile device and those of a wireless computer are the same, their technology is somewhat different. Let's look at phone service first.

cable TV. Battle lines are forming due to this new means of video signal distribution.

FIOS and Telephone Fiber Optics Systems   Fiber optic technology is at the center of the struggle now emerging between the telephone and cable industries. Large regional telephone companies like Verizon and AT&T are replacing their copper wire trunk lines with fiber optics. As just noted, most cable companies have also converted their systems to fiber. The benefits of fiber optics over traditional copper cable are significant: clearer video and audio, low maintenance costs, and a virtually unlimited capacity for video and Internet services.

Telephone systems are different from cable systems. FIOS and similar systems bring the fiber connection directly to the home, where a converter box turns the light waves into digital signals. Another system uses fiber optic connections to a neighborhood hub where signals are then distributed by plain

Cellular Services   Cellular telephone service has exploded around the globe during the past 10 years; and with each new generation of cell phone have come new capabilities. Texting, tweeting, and staying connected are the new normal. As we noted at the start of this chapter, cell phones can capture video and transmit it to other phones or Facebook pages.

In 2010 more than 70 percent of Americans had access to broadband services in the home and nearly 90 percent used a cell phone, more than half for e-mail and other nonvoice activities. In fact, CTIA, the International Wireless Association, claimed that Americans traded an astounding 822 billion text messages in 2009. And if you have a smart phone you can surf the Internet, watch videos on YouTube, or check your friends' vacation pictures on Flickr. That means that within its circuitry is a microcomputer processor that controls data functions and other smart applications. Smart phones can perform many tasks of a computer but are small enough to fit into the palm of your hand. With these numbers growing rapidly, cell phone carriers had to build a network that would support alternative media delivery systems.

Most mobile broadband networks are either 3G (third generation) or 4G (fourth generation) cellular systems. Two different systems, the Global System Mobile (GSM) and Code Divison Multiple Access (CDMA), are common in the United States. While these systems use somewhat different technology, the concept of separating out voice from data services on your smart phone or wireless card maximizes the use of the network. But as you may have already discovered using your smart phone, as you move away from larger metropolitan areas, the speed of the service decreases. When you hear someone's voice or receive a text message, the phone is acting like a receiver, essentially like any radio. When you speak into the phone, tweet, or send a picture, your phone acts like a transmitter; a nearby cellular tower receives that signal and relays it to a network for transmission that ultimately delivers it to the call destination. The destination phone has a SIM card that provides the network with identification.

Wireless Services Wireless computer networks (WiFi) work exactly the same way as wired broadband networks. Computers use a MAC (media access code) address, which becomes a unique identifier to other devices on the network But wireless networks are two-way systems that receive and transmit on different frequencies. Often these networks transmit on 2.4 gHz or 5 gHz, depending on the wireless card your computer uses. Usually range is limited to a given area, called a **hot spot.** Many businesses set up free hot spots for their customers as a way to increase foot traffic.

However, there are a variety of possible networks, and using a higher frequency allows more informa-

tion to be transmitted. The standard used for wireless was developed by the Institute of Electrical and Electronics Engineers (IEEE) and is referred to as the 802.11 standard. There are various levels of service (802.11b, 802.11g, and so on) that provide faster services. *Bluetooth* devices use a similar standard known as *WPAN or wireless personal area networks*, and these devices work over a very short range.

Newer, long-range high-speed networks called WiMax are being deployed on a trial basis in a number of metropolitan areas. WiMax networks work just like WiFi but can provide services over a larger geographical area. Many experts predict that WiMax networks will become common in cities, allowing people to use tablet computers such as Apple's iPad anywhere. Many automotive experts predict that cars with integrated hot spot and GPS capabilities will use such networks.

RECEIVING: FROM WIRES OR WIRELESS

We've now modulated, amplified, mixed, and transmitted an audio or video signal. The next step is reception: capturing that signal on a receiving device, such as a radio or TV set. As you might expect, the once-simple task of tuning a radio or dialing in a TV station has become complex. Just think of how many different remote control devices you own, or how many different boxes are connected to your TV set. Let's trace trends in some common audiovisual reception devices.

Radio Receivers

AM (Medium Wave) Band Receivers The location of AM radio in the medium-wave part of the spectrum has several advantages. Long telescopic antennas are normally not needed, and a good signal may be received even when the radio is in motion. This makes AM ideal for car radios. AM radios can take almost any form, from microscopic transistor versions to large tabletop models. Normally good reception is only a matter of moving the receiver slightly for best tuning. At night AM signals can travel hundreds of miles.

However, consider some of the disadvantages: A check of the spectrum chart shows that the MW band is precariously close to the bandwidth of electrical energy. Thus AM radios are prone to interference and noise, heard mostly as static. In cars, energy produced by engines and electrical systems can often be heard on AM. At home, one can "hear" vacuum cleaners, lights turned on and off, and so on. Buzzing and whining are often present as a result of carrier wave interactions with other AM stations. These distractions make AM difficult for serious listening.

Another limitation of AM reception has to do with its limited frequency response. As you know, AM stations generate signals in a bandwidth only 10,000 hertz wide. Recall that the human ear can hear a bandwidth about twice that. As a result, you may have noticed that AM sounds somewhat thinner or tinnier than FM (with a 15,000-hertz response). AM is best suited to speech and music of limited orchestration. Hence news/talk and sports tend to be popular AM formats.

HD AM stations can improve the sound quality of the transmission, but because AM is subject to skip interference, HD transmissions are limited at night.

FM Receivers   The evolution of the FM receiver has followed an interesting path. From the beginning, the noise-free dynamic range of FM made it a natural element for the hi-fi enthusiast's home audio system. Thus many early FM tuners were plugged into Dad's hi-fi system in the den. However, when FM stereo boomed in the late 1960s, consumers demanded FM in forms they had become familiar with in AM: in cars, transistor radios, table models, and so on. Thus most radios manufactured after 1970 were capable of both AM and FM reception. As a result, FM moved from an "add-on accessory" to the most important part of the radio receiver.

Because the FM signal requires a line of sight from transmitter to receiver, there are some potential pitfalls in signal reception. First, FM normally requires a long antenna, in the shape of a telescoping rod or a wire. The antenna needs to be directed for best results. FM signals tend to be blocked by buildings or moving objects with signals fading in and out in rural areas or in dense city environments. Reception can also be improved by attaching the radio antenna to a TV antenna and in some areas by hooking the receiver to the cable TV system.

Moreover, multipath distortion is commonly experienced in cars when a station's signal is reflected off buildings or tall objects. Unlike the AM signal, this type of signal distortion is seldom heard as static. Instead the distortion manifests itself as a blurring of the sound, sibilance, or a brittle sound. To solve this problem, the FM antenna needs to be redirected to minimize multipath. HD radios for FM

do not suffer from this reflection problem, and that fact may speed acceptance of HD radios.

Some car manufacturers provide hard drives in their radios, allowing owners to download the contents of their MP3 device into the car. Others are using storage memory features to allow drivers to rewind and replay live radio.

"Smart Radios"—Radio Broadcast Data Systems   Digital technology makes possible a new generation of "smart" FM radio receivers. Using their subcarrier frequencies, FM stations can send information signals to the receivers. On such radio sets, a small display can provide a readout of the station's dial location, call letters, format, and even the title and artist of the song being played. Weather forecasts can display a map; news and sports reports can show stock tickers, scoreboards, and so on.

These new smart radios are known as **radio broadcast data systems (RBDS).** Many stations now provide call letters and information about the song titles and artists on the radio's display. One of the problems with the RBDS technology is that only a few words can be broadcast and the refresh time is slow. HD radio provides much better data service, and eventually this may become a selling point for the adoption of HD radios.

Satellite Radios   Satellite tuners capable of receiving one of the two satellite radio systems went on sale in 2003. Automotive manufacturers such as General Motors, Hyundai, and Honda began offering XM Radio receivers in many of their 2003 model cars, while Ford and Chrysler began offering Sirius receivers. Home and car adapters are also available for consumers who want to convert their current radios to receive satellite programming. Today many new cars come equipped with one of the two types of receivers built into the standard AM/FM car radio. Satellite radios can display both singer and song title along with other informational services. Some of the newer radios allow you to pause, rewind, and replay up to 60 minutes of radio and get alerts when your favorite song or artist is being played on one of the channels.

TV Receivers

Improvements in our media devices usually are confined to making the items either grossly large or incredibly minute. For example, consider the contrast in radios between nearly piano-size boom boxes and personal stereos custom-fit to the human ear canal. Changes in size and shape head the list of new developments in TV as the industry prepares for HDTV.

Large-Screen TV   In the early 1970s wall-sized TV screens began appearing in bars, nightclubs, and conference facilities. Today they can be seen filling the walls of restaurants and homes alike. And in the home, a relatively new phenomena has developed as we move the television from the den to the media center. Large-screen televisions are connected to multichannel sound systems, video games, Blu-ray players, and now the Web itself.

Large-screen TVs come in two main types. The first is the projection TV systems that beam the red, green, and blue elements that compose the color signal through special tubes to a reflecting screen suspended at a distance from the video unit. This is the type of system most commonly seen in sports bars, conference rooms, and classrooms.

At home we are seeing large, flat display televisions that produce high-definition images with startling realism. These receivers make use of new developments in computer imaging, such as the charge-coupled device (CCD) discussed earlier, liquid crystal devices (LCD), and light-emitting diodes (LED). The picture tube is made up of a matrix of over 200,000 red, blue, and green light-emitting elements. Excellent color, crispness, and detail are achieved. In addition, the screen is flat, free from the type of distortion common in standard curved vacuum-tube systems. Although expensive, these solid-state, large-screen systems are beginning to move from sports stadiums to the home video market. Some sets feature letter-box screen dimensions and are ready to receive standard or HDTV signals from external tuners.

Multifunctional Digital TV Sets   How many times have you tried to watch two or three TV programs simultaneously? Using a remote control or nimble fingers, you flip continuously from one to the other—playing a sort of TV musical chairs—and end up missing the important parts of all programs. Well, if you're an inveterate flipper (like the authors), the digital receiver is for you. The integrated microchips that make tubeless cameras and micro-TVs practical have made it possible for the TV screen to display more than one channel at a time. The technique is known as **picture-in-picture (PIP).**

Some digital TVs also perform other electronic tricks. Suppose, when watching a baseball game,

you decide to try to see the catcher's signs to the pitcher. **Zoom** allows you to fill the entire picture with just one small detail you would like to see, in this case the catcher's hands. To really get the sign, you can stop the picture momentarily, a technique known as **freeze frame.**

Major TV set manufacturers, led by Sony, Samsung, LG, and Panasonic, have introduced large-screen, digital television sets capable of receiving standard television and the new 480-, 720-, and 1,080-line progressive video signals. These sets are capable of displaying high-definition television pictures, connecting to the Internet via wireless broadband connections and allowing users to stream movies from the Web and auxiliary inputs for connection to Blu-ray, games, and other peripheral devices. Prices are vary for plasma TVs, but because they tend to be larger displays, they are still in the range of $500 to $3,000; however, their prices have been dropping every year.

LCD and LED screens are making an impact as well. These sets can be used for computers or as televisions and produce great pictures in all lighting conditions. Perhaps one of the most striking aspects of LCDs and LEDs is that they're only a few inches wide and can be easily mounted on your wall. They usually come tailored for the 16-by-9 format, meaning you can watch TV or DVD movies in the widescreen format, as they were meant to be viewed. New sets by Sharp and Samsung come in many sizes and can actually display a split screen, half television and half computer. LCD prices have dropped dramatically in the last two years. Their prices have dropped dramatically over the past few years, and they are now available in all sizes and price ranges.

STORAGE AND RETRIEVAL

The final step in audio and video technology is the storage and retrieval of sounds and moving images. As we all know, old programs never die: They live on forever in reruns. Some of the great growth industries in mass media in recent years are based on improved means of storing and accessing images, including the video store, nostalgic TV networks like Nick at Night, TV Land, and, yes, the Nostalgia Network. In fact, one benefit of the World Wide Web is that the content of all the memory of all the computers connected to the Internet is accessible to any single user. Increasingly, that content includes sounds and pictures, not merely text. Yet not too long ago (in the 1940s and 1950s) radio and TV programs were produced "live" because recording methods were noisy and inefficient.

Even today the complex signals involved in high-quality speech, music, motion pictures, and TV put demands on the current Web standards requiring large storage spaces and lots of network capacity. That's because streaming uncompressed video still taxes the storage and processing capacity of even the fastest microcomputers, so we're still a bit away from dialing up on our PC any movie ever made. Let's see where things stand with respect to radio and TV storage and retrieval.

Audio Storage

Phonograph Recording   The old standby, the phonograph record, has been around since the turn of the century. From that time, the sizes and speeds have been changed, but the basic design has remained consistent. Today the most common record format is the 33⅓ revolutions per minute (rpm), 12-inch, high-fidelity recording. Few new records are issued each year, but many people still have large record libraries. New USB turntables have become popular over the past few years. These turntables convert the analog signal directly into a digital signal recordable on your home computer. Software available can eliminate some of the scratches and surface noise found on older LPs.

Magnetic Tape and Hard Disk Recording   The development of magnetic tape recording was revolutionary for both radio and TV. Unlike earlier recording methods, such as disk and wire recordings, magnetic tape was of very high fidelity. For all intents and purposes, radio and TV programs recorded on magnetic tape sounded just like they were "live." Tape recorders became the heart and soul of radio and TV stations.

Most commercials and other short program materials are usually recorded on a digital cart. These devices are a bit of a misnomer. They usually use a hard disk to record and store information, but many of us forget that hard disk recording is a form of magnetic recording. Hard drives use very dense, highly polished magnetic surfaces to record, store, and retrieve the digital pulses in computer programs and related files. Some radio stations still rely on high-quality cassette recorders for keeping a record of programs, and some are used by radio reporters to record meetings and to do interviews in the field.

A few manufacturers still make analog tape recorders, but fewer and fewer are made and sold each year. Some musicians and audio engineers prefer their rich, full sound compared with the crisp, clean sound of digital recordings. Tape manufacturers, including Sony, BASF, 3M, Ampex, and others, continue to make better and better products of these types. Thus, because there is a huge library of reel-to-reel and cassette material recorded over the past 50 years, audio recorders promise to remain in limited use for some time to come.

Video Storage

Magnetic Video Recording   The **videotape recorder (VTR)** made its network debut with *The CBS Evening News with Douglas Edwards* on November 30, 1956. But it hardly resembled today's tabletop VCR. For nearly 20 years, TV's tape machines were the size of a refrigerator–freezer and required four hands (two people) to operate them. The reels of tape, as big as 35-mm film canisters, were 2 inches across (thus these were called 2-inch recordings). But they produced excellent, long-lasting copies of TV programs. Most television networks still keep one or two of these machines available so they can play back archived material.

The next revolution in videotape recording was started by the Japanese. At the forefront of the emerging field of microelectronics, Sony technicians, in the late 1960s, perfected a means of storing the complex video signal on narrower tape moving at slower speeds.

The idea was to stretch the magnetic tape around the revolving recording head so there was virtually continuous contact between the tape and the recording head. For an analogy, imagine that instead of taking a single piece of chalk to one blackboard at the head of the class, your instructor had a piece of chalk in each hand and foot and was surrounded by a huge cylindrical blackboard. This technique became known as **helical-scan tape recording** because the heads are positioned obliquely to the tape and the lines of picture information produced on the tape form the shape of a helix.

The Birth of a Standard: ¾-Inch VTR   The helical-scan recorder had many advantages. Tape width shrank from 2 inches to ¾ inch, which had financial as well as technical advantages. The tape could be packaged in a protective case; thus the videocassette became popular. Most important, the size of the tape recorder shrank. In the early 1970s it became practical to send cameras and recorders into the field for coverage of breaking news and live sporting events. Although a number of helical-scan recorders had been introduced, by 1975 the industry had standardized. The 2-inch machine gave way to the ¾-inch VTR.

The VTR was soon a fixture in TV production. After its introduction, recorders became small, portable, and usually dependable. Editing from one machine to another became easy, especially with the development of computer-assisted editing equipment. And the entire field of broadcast news changed: The era of electronic news gathering, or ENG, was launched.

Home Video In 1976 Sony introduced its first Betamax **videocassette recorder** (priced at $1,200); by the early 1990s the use of VHS machines to record and play back video at home had become fairly widespread. As we noted earlier, the home movie rental business was based on this technology.

Essentially, the ½-inch machines sacrificed some picture quality for smaller, lighter, and cheaper recorders with longer recording times. Clearly the compromise was worth it: By 2002 more than 93 million U.S. homes (about 90 percent of all households) had acquired VCRs. They were cheap and generally reliable, and the quality was acceptable.

Initially there were two competing varieties of ½-inch helical-scan VCRs. Machines produced by Sony and its licensees used the Beta format; machines produced by other manufacturers used VHS tape and electrical components. However, in the interim the American consumer had decided on the standard. Since more prerecorded tapes were available in the VHS format, by the mid-1980s the home market had more or less standardized in the VHS format. Beta videotape didn't die off, however. A high-fidelity version, Beta-SP, became a vital part of professional TV production. At home, ½-inch tape was shrunk even further, into a compact version of VHS (VHS-C) and another popular Sony format only 8 millimeters wide.

Digital Video Recording It should come as no surprise that the digital revolution sweeping the audio industry soon spread to television recording. The first wave of digital video recording was the appearance in the early 1990s of **digital videotape.** Today many TV studios boast camera and editing systems that use digital videotape. Sony's system is easy to spot: Its equipment uses the DV prefix to denote digital videotape. DVC-Pro is the line of machines in widest distribution.

In a way, digital videotape is a hybrid recording system, combining the analog system of putting images on magnetic tape with the new digital sampling techniques. With the increasing processing and storage capacity of today's computers, it's possible to go all-digital. Why have tape at all? Why not store all the TV sounds and images on a computer server or a DVD recorder? More and more TV facilities, from CNN International to large-station newsrooms, have no VCRs in sight. Systems like Apple's Final Cut Pro and AVID are moving TV news and entertainment programming production from linear editing suites to desktop computer consoles.

Digital Versatile Disc (DVD) and DVD Recording The DVD playback format has become enormously popular since its introduction. In fact, in 2002 the DVD became the hottest-selling consumer electronics device, with penetration reaching nearly 90 percent by the end of 2006. Movie studios put extra features on DVDs and frequently release new movies on DVDs first because DVDs cost less to produce than videotape. The recording devices are capable of much higher picture resolution than VCRs and provide a stable storage environment. In addition, DVD recorders are common in both home computers and laptops, so it is no wonder that stand-alone DVD recorders were created for the home market. Many of these machine also "up–convert" standard DVDs to play back on wide-screen HDTV screens.

Small DVD camcorders are widely used by consumers to record sporting events, dance recitals, and other personal moments. These camcorders can be connected to home TVs for general viewing. Newer devices use a relatively new compression scheme that makes it possible to record high-definition video on the existing DVD media.

Digital Video Recorder (DVR) The DVR is a video recorder that uses a computer hard drive as the main

Modern smart phones have the ability to play and record video and audio.

storage device. The recorder, marketed under such trade names as TiVo, Replay, and others, connects to your cable box and telephone. It has the ability to record and play back television shows via a remote control, but its ability does not stop there. The TiVo is essentially a set-top computer that collects information about what television shows are on and when. You can tell the device what you like, and it will record programs for you. For example, you could program the TiVo to record every episode of *Modern Family* for an entire season. And because the machine allows instant record and playback access, you could skip through the commercials on a program or pause live TV. Both cable and DBS service providers frequently bundle these devices with different levels of video services they provide. Widespread adoption of DVRs has actually had an impact on the way television networks measure viewing habits, mostly among the 18 to 49 demographic.

WEBCASTING: AUDIO AND VIDEO STREAMING

We close this section on audio and video technology with a technology that is transforming the way Americans consume and use media. The technique, called **streaming,** allows sounds and moving pictures to be transmitted on the World Wide Web and other computer networks. It allows these complex, high-memory transmissions to travel on high-speed cable modems or digital subscriber line (DSL) connections on broadband WiFi networks and mobile 3G and 4G networks.

The early days of streaming were highlighted by frustrating starts and stops because networks were not fast enough and large enough to provide fairly continuous streams of data. Streaming audio and video makes use of two nifty shortcuts called **buffering** and **compression.** To put a complex radio or TV signal on the Web, the signal is first "shrunk" and then transmitted in a much simpler form, using techniques of digital compression. Essentially, the complex signal is sampled, and redundant, nonessential information is stripped away, to be added back later (in decompression).

There are a variety of different standards for playing back media: QuickTime (.mov), Windows Media Player formats (.wma and .wmv), Advanced Streaming formats (.asf), and Adobe Flash (.flv) files. A browser plug-in controls the playback of the media based on the coded information provided in the stream. And unless the event is live, usually consumers can start or stop, rewind, or forward through the playback.

Recent studies indicate that more than three of every four Internet users in the United States were using streaming technology to listen to or view programs on computer networks regularly. YouTube, Hulu, Fox Interactive, Yahoo!, and iTunes are among the most popular sites. MP3 audio streams such as SHOUTcast.com and RealAudio streams from NPR.org are a few of the many programmers to provide real-time feeds. All the major news outlets, most television stations, and numerous other media organizations provide updated video programming on their Web sites.

The software display controls are similar to a radio or TV set (with tuning buttons and volume controls). Two types of streaming are typical. The first is in real time. As you watch or listen to a stream, the program player discards the data, so you can't save it on your hard disk. The second is a form of progressive scan that downloads part of a file before it starts playing and then allows you to view part of the program as the rest of the download occurs. Some formats allow you to save the data on your hard disk or smart phone after it has completed downloading.

To make video and audio streams work, computer systems use a **codec** (compression/decompression technology) scheme to reduce the size of the media file. By using standards, it is possible to play back material on devices other than the one that made the recording. Home videos are as popular as full-length television shows and movies. YouTube and many other sites allow viewers to post their home videos online. New digital cameras record video using standard compression technology.

Viewing sizes can vary greatly depending on whether you are playing back video on a high-definition, wide-screen large monitor, a laptop computer, or a small smart phone. Therefore scalability is an important factor. In the past few years, as streaming technology, computer capability, and network bandwidth have improved, more and more people have turned to the Web to hear audio and view videos and movies. Hulu and iTunes provide many of the same programs now available on broadcast television and cable. Netflix can stream current movie releases in high definition through game devices such as Wii and PS3s or on home computers.

During the recession some people stopped subscribing to cable and began to watch television exclusively on the Web. Also, in 2010 new network devices from AppleTV and Google were released. These devices provide streaming capabilities from the Internet directly to televisions. Finally, as we noted earlier, some new televisions have Internet connections and will allow people to surf and stream Web programming.

SUMMARY

- Broadcasting, cable, and new media use facsimile technology, reproducing sound and sight in other forms. The better the correspondence between the facsimile and the original, the higher the fidelity.

- Transduction involves changing energy from one form to another; it is at the heart of audio and video technology. Transduction can be analog—the transformed energy resembles the original—or digital—the original is transformed into a series of numbers.

- Audio and video signal processing follow five main steps: signal generation, amplification and processing, transmission, reception, and storage/retrieval.

- *Signal generation.* Audio signals are generated mechanically, by using microphones and turntables; electromagnetically, by using tape recorders; and digitally, by using laser optics. Television signal generation involves the electronic line-by-line scanning of an image. An electron beam scans each element of a picture, and the image is then retraced in the TV receiver.

- *Amplification and processing.* Audio and video signals are amplified and mixed by using audio consoles and video switchers. Today's digital technology enables sophisticated signal processing and a variety of special effects.

- *Transmission.* Radio waves occupy a portion of the electromagnetic spectrum. AM radio channels are classified into clear, regional, and local channels. FM stations are classified according to power and antenna height. The wide bandwidth of an FM channel allows stereo broadcasting and other nonbroadcast services. There are two types of digital radio: satellite-based and HD terrestrial services that are broadcast in-band,

on-channel. The traditional systems of transmitting a TV signal are (1) over-the-air broadcasting utilizing electromagnetic radiation on channels located in the VHF and UHF portions of the spectrum and (2) by wire through a cable system using coaxial cable that can carry more than 100 channels of programming. New distribution technologies include fiber optics, satellite transmissions, and digital distribution.

Television and radio are moving to new forms of digital distribution. On the TV side, the FCC mandated switch to digital high-definition television took place in 2009. Coupled with large sales of HD televisions, high-definition television programs have become plentiful.

- *Signal reception.* Radio receivers pull in AM, FM, and satellite signals, in monaural or stereo. New digital multiband receivers are becoming more prevalent. In TV, large-screen receivers have attained record sales in recent years, abetted by new digital capabilities and "smart" remote control devices.

- *Storage and retrieval.* New technology is reshaping audio and video storage and retrieval. Phonograph records, compact disks, and videotapes are being supplemented and may ultimately be replaced by digital storage media, such as recordable CDs, digital versatile disks (DVDs), and high-capacity disk drives on computers.

A comparatively new phenomenon, audio and video streaming, permits radio and TV stations to send their complex signals onto the Internet. Today more than three-quarters of Americans watch videos online, and services are expanding rapidly.

KEY TERMS

facsimile   50
fidelity   50
transduction   50
noise   51
analog signals   54
quantization   57
digital recording and
    transmission   57
oscillation   52
waveform   52
frequency   53

hertz (Hz)   53
wavelength   53
amplitude   53
frequency response   53
pulse code modulation   55
compact disc (CD)   57
digital versatile disc (DVD)   57
MP3   58
scanning   60
interlace method   60
retracing   60

NTSC (National Television Systems
    Committee)   60
fields   60
frame   60
digital television   60
high-definition television
    (HDTV)   60
progressive scan   61
charge-coupled devices
    (CCDs)   63
blanking pulses   63

SUGGESTIONS FOR FURTHER READING

Austerberry, D., & Starks. G. (2002). *The technology of video and audio streaming.* Tempe, AZ: Dimension Books.

Baldwin, T. F., & McVoy, D. S. (1987). *Cable communication.* Englewood Cliffs, NJ: Prentice-Hall.

Bertram, H. N. (1994). *Theory of magnetic recording.* New York: Cambridge University Press.

DeSonne, M., ed. (1996). *International DTH/DBS.* Washington, DC: National Association of Broadcasters.

Horn, D. T. (1991). *DAT: The complete guide to digital audio tape.* Blue Ridge Summit, PA: Tab Books.

Luther, A. (1997). *Principles of digital audio & video.* Norwood, NJ: Artech House.

Marlow, E. (1991). *Shifting time and space: The story of videotape.* New York: Praeger.

Menin, E. (2002). *The streaming media handbook.* Englewood Cliffs, NJ: Prentice Hall.

Mott, R. L. (1990). *Sound effects: Radio, TV, and film.* Boston: Focal Press.

Hausman, C., O'Donnell, D., Messere, F., & Benoit, P. (2009). *Modern radio production* (8th ed.). Belmont, CA: Wadsworth.

McCregor, M., Driscoll, P., & MCDowell, W. (2010). *Head's broadcasting in America: A survey of electronic media* (10th ed.). Boston: Allyn and Bacon.

Paulsen, K. (1998). *Video & media servers: Technology and applications.* Woburn, UK: Butterworth-Heinemann.

Persson, C. (1999). *Guide to HDTV systems.* Clifton Park, NY: Delmar.

Pohlmann, K. C. (1992). *The compact disc: Handbook of theory and use* (2nd ed.). Madison, WI: A-R Editions.

Robin, M., & Poulin, M. (2000). *Digital television fundamentals.* New York: McGraw-Hill.

Todorovic, A. (2006). *Television technology demystified.* Boston: Allyn and Bacon.

Soderberg, A. (1995). *Desktop video studio.* New York: Random House.

Whitaker, J. (2001). *DTV: The revolution in digital video.* New York: McGraw-Hill.

Zettl, H. (2003). *Video basics 4.* Belmont, CA: Wadsworth.

INTERNET EXERCISES

Visit our Web site at **www.mhhe.com/dominickbib7e** for study-guide exercises to help you learn and apply material in each chapter. You will find ideas for future research as well as useful Web links to provide you with an opportunity to journey through the new electronic media.

Part Two   How It Is

Radio Today | 4

Quick Facts

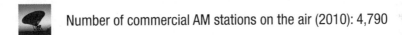 Number of commercial AM stations on the air (2010): 4,790

Number of AM and FM stations licensed in the United States (2010): 14,503

Leading radio format by share of audience, 2009: News/talk/information (12.6% share)

Average number of radio stations available in most U.S. markets: 25

Number of commercial stations in the United States playing a polka format: 4

Percentage of classical music listeners who are 65 or older, 2010: 47%

Top radio market in United States (by revenue): Los Angeles

Number of songs under license to Broadcast Music Incorporated (BMI) (2010): 6.5 million titles

More wondrous far than legends' figments wrought
By the ingenious bards of long ago. . . .
I feel like a spirit medium that can bring
The listener what'er he wishes from the void.
Do you want multitudes of thoughts, all types?
Full measure comes with the revolving dial;
The masters wait to pour out symphonies
That rock the world and set your soul on fire. . . .

Robert West, "My Name Is Radio!" (1941)

We'll be looking for caller number 10 but first you've got a lock
on a 30-minute block of rock direct from stereo compact disc on
the hot new Z-93 . . . Hot . . . hot . . . hot . . . hot.

DJ on large-market FM station (1999)

200 stations that span more than 25 genres of music plus 150+
CBS RADIO stations from across the United States all avail-
able on your iPhone and iPod Touch. The application is free and
you can download it now.

AOL Radio apps for mobile devices (2010)

Mobile radio apps! Satellite radio! or HD radio? Video downloads! High-definition TV! Podcasting! . . . Amid the furor of today's communications explosion it's easy to overlook persistent, enterprising, unassuming radio. If nothing else, radio is resilient. It has withstood frontal attacks from an array of new media services, each promising to sound the death knell of the radio business. But in every instance, from the introduction of sound pictures in the late 1920s to the arrival of TV in the 1940s, from the birth of music TV in the 1980s to the surprising growth of music applications on mobile devices, radio has rebounded, reformulated, and, most important, remained.

Radio today is as vital as ever. It is chameleonlike in form: from the FM tuner in the supertiny iPod nano to the new high-definition digital radios. It is omnipresent: Most households have five radios or more. It fills the air: There are more than 14,500 stations on the air in the United States alone, not counting new low-power FMs. And it seems to meet our needs: Somewhere on that dial there can be found many different forms of music, all kinds of advice, scathing political commentary, hundreds of ball games, and special music events. Perhaps most important of all, in the face of an unprecedented flow of competition from within and outside the industry, radio remains economically viable.

Why do we continue to tune in to radio? As we pointed out in Chapter 1, radio has been around longer than any other electronic medium. Like baseball, hot dogs, and apple pie (to borrow an old commercial slogan), radio has become a part of our culture and tradition.

Radio has always been the most intimate of the mass media. It's portable—and personal. For many years, Walkmans provided youth with portable means to listen to their latest tunes, but now we are seeing a growing number of youth listening to iPods or mobile phones that increasingly provide multiple choices of entertainment for their owners. What does that mean for the future of radio?

Even as the communications sphere grows more global, radio continues to be an individualized service medium. In the aftermath of the terrible earthquake in Haiti, Radio Caraibe's journalists broadcast live reports about relief efforts to victims from the streets of Port-Au-Prince. But radio's changing too. Now we can drive across the country and listen to Radio Margaritaville from Sirius XM radio, choose from regular or HD programming on many stations, and even pause or replay live broadcasts on newer cars equipped with hard drives built into their radios.

Sometimes in our rush to credit TV for almost everything good or ill in our culture, there is a tendency to overlook radio. Let's not make that mistake. To borrow from some of its supporters, let's remember: Radio is red hot! In fact, "heat" is the appropriate metaphor. Everything about radio—from its competitive policies to its flamboyant personalities to increasingly large indecency fines—tends to be intense. Let's don our insulated gloves and delve into the radio business.

THE "THREE C'S" OF RADIO TODAY: COMPETITION, CONSOLIDATION, AND CONTROL

During the first years of the new century the radio business could be characterized by the three "C"s: **competition, consolidation,** and **control.** With many thousands of stations on the air, and consumers faced with many attractive alternatives to radio (like TV, MP3 players and DVD players, VCRs, and computers), radio competes vigorously for listeners. With radio deregulation (discussed more fully in Chapter 10) came radio consolidation: the ownership of more and more stations by fewer and fewer large corporations. The combination of competition and consolidation has led to enormous control in the radio business, including the development of narrower, intensively researched radio formats, voice tracking, and the rise of satellites and computers in radio operations, the meat of the material in Chapter 8. While these trends have not fully abated, some of the large radio corporations found business difficult, partly because the many stations purchased during the consolidation process pushed debt beyond the profit margins for many stations.

Competition in Today's Radio Business

Any discussion of the radio business must begin with one word: competition. Radio is arguably the most competitive of contemporary media. By almost every criterion there is more "radio" than anything else. There are more radios than there are TVs (about three times as many). There are five times as many radio stations as there are daily newspapers and nearly six times as many radio stations as TV stations. And radio on the Internet provides listeners with many specialized music formats. About the only thing there is less of in radio is advertising revenue. To understand commercial radio today, we must begin with its economics.

For some reason many people have difficulty with economic terminology, but few fail to understand the intricacies of pizza. So imagine you and a group of friends have just been served two pizzas at your favorite restaurant. As usual, the pies have been sliced. Let's see where the cuts are.

Advertising Revenue   Pie 1 (Figure 4–1) is apportioned on the basis of advertising revenue. It is estimated that annually advertisers will spend about $164 billion trying to convince the American public to buy their products. The bulk of that spending, nearly $68 billion or about 36 percent, went to the television and cable. Newspapers and magazines got the second biggest slice with about $48 billion, or about 26 percent of all advertising dollars. A lot went to custom publishing ($16.9 billion); about 20 percent went to other media, like online media, yellow pages, product placement, and branded advertising.

Look at the paltry radio slice: about 8 percent of total advertising expenditures, representing about $14.3 billion in 2010 (down from more than $16 billion in 2008). Lesson number one, then, for radio, is that if this pizza party were given in honor of America's leading advertising vehicles, you would leave comparatively hungry. What's even more worrisome is

Estimated Advertising Expenditures for 2010

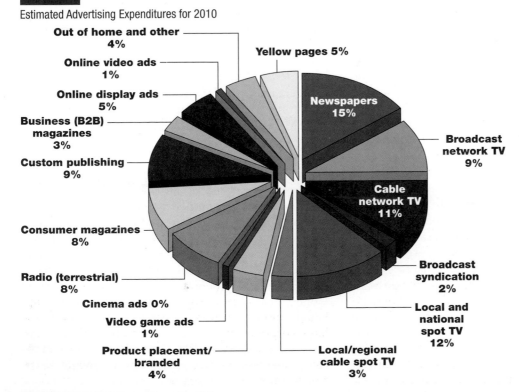

Source: Jack Meyers Media Business Report, May 2010.

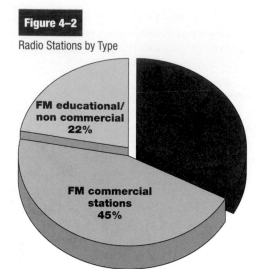

Figure 4–2

Radio Stations by Type

FM educational/
non commercial
22%

FM commercial
stations
45%

that radio revenue as a share of total advertising expenditure seems stagnant.

The Station Universe   Pie 2 (Figure 4–2) is divided on the basis of radio station type. There are about 14,500 commercial radio stations on the air. About 3 in 10 stations (33 percent) are commercial AM stations. Although many of these are powerful stations emanating from large cities, the majority of AM stations are relatively low-powered, local operations serving the small and midsized communities that constitute the essence of "middle America." A larger proportion of radio stations (6,483) are commercial FM operations. Because of their relatively late arrival on the scene and their technical requirements the majority of the FMs started out being allocated to midsized and large cities. In recent years, however, the Federal Communications Commission (FCC) allocated new FM stations to small communities.

The remainder of radio stations, about 3,180, or 22 percent, are designated as noncommercial stations. Almost all are noncommercial stations are FMs.

The point of this pie is that radio today is largely a locally based medium. Many stations are commercial AMs, trying to operate on the advertising revenue available from local advertisers in the smaller markets or they are trying to compete with FM stations that control the majority of listeners. Large cities are often dominated by one or two large AM news/talk stations and four or five very large FM commercial stations, where major advertisers call the shots. Within the noncommercial environment the pressure is on to find funding: from the federal government, from religious organizations, from foundations, from university administrations or student fees, or from individual listeners.

Share of Audience   The point of both pies becomes clearer with one more statistic in view: share of audience. Today almost 82 percent of all radio listening is to FM stations. In some cities, like Terre Haute, Indiana; Tallahassee, Florida; and Johnstown, Pennsylvania, FM share of audience is above 90 percent. In fact, many radio listeners, especially younger ones, rarely, if ever, tune to the AM band. According to FCC surveys, the median age of the AM listener is 57 years old. Few young teens listen to AM, mostly for talk or sports programming.

To sum up the competitive battleground, commercial radio is a business where more than 11,270 commercial stations compete for a comparatively small percentage of national advertising expenditures. More than half of all stations serve the largest 300 cities in the United States (about three-fourths of the population lives in these cities).

While approximately 4,800 AM and 6,500 FM commercial stations compete for listenership most radio listeners prefer the FM band. It should not be surprising, then, that the most profitable radio stations are the big FM music stations in the major cities and the powerhouse AM stations that cater to older listeners focusing on news/talk stations. Many smaller stations, both AM and FM, report modest profit at best or are in a constant struggle to survive.

Added to this mix are nearly 20 million satellite listeners and new HD digital services (see the box) becoming standard equipment in car radios along with MP3 player inputs, so it's easy to see competition to survive is fierce.

Consolidation: The Big Radio Groups

The increasingly competitive nature of the radio business is reflected in the kinds of companies now involved in the medium. For nearly one-half century, radio was generally a small business. Owners were also operators and lifelong residents of the community in which the station operated. Many owned other businesses in the area, such as automobile dealerships, restaurants, and even local newspapers. Reflecting this ownership pattern and the "homespun" environment in which they operated, such stations were commonly referred to as "mom-and-pop" stations.

Issues: Racist Radio? Consolidation versus Diversity

One of the burning issues in radio today is the impact of consolidation and industry concentration on diversity in ownership, management, and the operation of America's radio stations. As we have seen, women and members of ethnic minority groups represent key audiences for radio stations. Members of minority groups—especially African Americans and listeners of Hispanic descent—listen to radio more than other audiences.

At the same time, evidence suggests that the number of minorities and women who own or manage radio stations is shrinking. As the industry consolidates, ownership is more and more concentrated in the hands of fewer and fewer people, most of whom happen to be middle-aged white males. According to FCC minority ownership reports published in 2004, only 438 women were listed as majority owners in radio and television stations. Minorities owned 389 facilities. In other words, fewer than 3.4 percent of all commercial broadcast stations in the United States are licensed to a minority.

These dry statistics were brought to life with the publication of a 2005 survey released by the Radio and Television News Directors Association. While the percentages of minorities working in television newsrooms are on the rise, the number of women and minorities working in radio news is on the decline. In radio the percentage of minorities dropped to 6.4 percent, and the percentage of women working in radio news declined to 24.8 percent, down from 27.5 percent the year before.

Perhaps the new low-power, noncommercial FM radio services started recently by the FCC will encourage minority community groups to apply for some of the licenses, but these stations will be so small they certainly will have a difficult time attracting listeners and underwriters. Is this an indicator that minorities will be relegated to second-class status in broadcasting?

What do you think? Should the government intervene on behalf of women and minorities in the realms of ownership and management of radio stations? Or do such initiatives amount to illegal quotas, restrict the free enterprise system, and give preferences to people just because of their gender and skin color?

Today mom-and-pop radio has largely disappeared. Why? The competitive situation traced in the previous section was not lost on the radio business. Led by the National Association of Broadcasters—the industry's largest lobby group and trade association (see Chapter 11)—throughout the 1990s the radio business successfully lobbied Congress for regulatory relief. Their argument was that radio had become so competitive, with so many stations competing for such a small advertising segment and with so many stations losing money, that radio group owners should be able to own more stations. In addition, the argument went, a single owner should be able to operate multiple stations (several AMs and FMs) in the geographical service area typically called the "market."

Significant ownership restrictions were lifted with the passage of the **Telecommunications Act of 1996.** Instead of being limited to a small number of AM and FM stations, group owners could consolidate stations; and almost overnight the ownership landscape literally changed the rules of the radio business. The new rules allow a single radio group to own as many stations as it wants. Today there are no national ownership caps. Even within markets, groups can amass multiple stations. For example, in large markets with more than 44 stations, one company can own up to 8 stations (no more than 5 AM or FM). In cities with 30 to 44 stations, a single company can own 7 stations (up to 4 AM or FM). In midsized communities (15 to 30 stations) a single company can control 6 stations. Even in smaller towns (with up to 15 commercial stations), a single group can control 5 stations (up to 3 AM or FM).

These new rules have changed the radio business radically, at least in ownership. As the 1990s ended, local ownership gave way to the rise of the radio **supergroup.** By this we do not mean rock-and-roll bands like Maroon 5, Green Day, or Red Hot Chili Peppers. The supergroups we refer to are radio's largest companies, which control most of the listening—and therefore most of the revenue—in radio today.

Table 4–1 lists the largest radio groups by overall revenue. Leading the pack is Clear Channel Radio, with over 800 stations in 89 of the largest 100 radio markets and total sales of more than $3.3 billion. Like the big fish gobbling a school of smaller ones, Clear Channel emerged as a comprehensive radio corporation managing its huge number of stations but also providing syndicated programming like Rush Limbaugh, Ryan Seacrest, and Fox Sports Radio. In addition, Katz Media Group, the largest media represen-

Broadcasters are developing applications for new mobile devices like the iPad as a way to retain listenership. The AOL Radio app allows users to tune into favorite CBS radio stations anywhere there's a WiFi connection.

Table 4–1	Largest Group Owners by Stations, Revenue, and Potential Audience 2009			
Ranking	Company	Number of Stations	Radio Revenue 2009 in Millions	Potential Audience
1	Clear Channel Communications	844	723.62	143.9 million
2	Cumulus Broadcasting	303	256.05	8.4 million
3	Citadel Broadcasting	205	723.62	11.6 million
4	CBS Radio	130	1,220.00	77.7 million
5	Entercom	112	372.4	17.9 million

Sources: CBS Annual Report, StateoftheMedia.org, Entercom Annual Report.

As the chart shows, the power of radio groups is not measured solely by the number of stations owned by the group; how much advertising the group amasses is also significant. For example, number one

tation firm in the United States (see Chapter 7), is also part of this radio division.

Based in Atlanta, Cumulus Broadcasting owns about 300 stations in 59 markets around the United States and is the second largest group owner. Citadel Communications comes next with stations in more than 50 radio markets. Citadel entered a joint agreement with Disney to operate the ABC Radio Network in 2006. The economic downturn and large debt from mergers and acquisitions caused Citadel to declare bankrupcy in 2009. Today Citadel has emerged from bankruptcy and operates 205 stations in addition to providing programming to more than 4,400 ABC affiliates in North America. It is followed by CBS Radio with 130 stations, with almost all of its stations operating in the top 50 radio markets. Rounding out the top five is Entercom, which owns 110 stations in 23 large and medium-sized markets.

The number of stations is not the only way to gauge the size and scope of some group operations. Table 4–1 also shows the largest groups by revenue. When you look at the chart for revenue it tells a somewhat different picture.

Mel Karmazin, one of the most influential people in radio, is CEO of SiriusXM Radio. Sirius shook up the radio world in fall 2004 by hiring Howard Stern; Mel joined Sirius in late fall 2004.

Ethics: Outrageous Radio and Congress's Response

When Howard Stern was on terrestrial radio he was perhaps the most infamous and controversial radio personality—but he's certainly not the only one who has stretched the boundaries of good taste. That distinction may now belong to Opie and Anthony. Increasing competition for advertising, especially in the nation's largest markets, has led to an unprecedented series of incidents that have stretched the bounds, some observers say, of good taste and fair play. Outrageous radio is also known as "raunch radio," and its air personalities are often called "shock jocks."

In 2002, when Greg Hughes (known as Opie) and his sidekick, Anthony Cumia, were fired by Infinity Broadcasting after the duo broadcast a live account of a couple having sex in the entrance of St. Patrick's Cathedral in Manhattan, many thought that outrageous radio would be reined in. The incident wasn't the only time Opie and Anthony were in trouble. Two years earlier the duo was fired from their Boston gig for a hoax in which they claimed the mayor of Boston had died in a car crash.

However, it appears that the desire for ratings and to shock the audience may sometimes be too much for radio personalities to resist. In St. Louis a radio station aired phone messages from a well-known TV weatherman talking about a love affair and played an interview with a woman who claimed the weatherman was harassing her. The next day the weathercaster died in a fiery plane crash that appeared to be a suicide.

In Denver a station ran a contest asking people "What Would You Do for $10,000?" but the promotion went badly awry when paramedics had to revive one contestant who suffered hyperthermia as a result of towing a boatload of pigs across a reservoir. "It just doesn't look good to kill your listeners," commented the station's promotion director.

A Nashville station got into trouble for defacing American currency after it put 100,000 one-dollar bills in a swimming pool and had listeners coat themselves with honey, rolling around the pool for free money. More than $90,000 didn't stick to the listeners. The Federal Reserve stuck to its guns, however, and refused to take back the money until it was washed! And evidently winning something can help people in the afterlife: Many listeners at a Tenessee radio station entered a contest for a chance to win a funeral.

Today things may become more subdued. That's due in part to the new fines that the FCC can now assess when it finds that a broadcasting station has been egregiously indecent. In 2006 Congress gave the FCC the authority to raise indecency fines to $325,000 per incident, and the president signed the measure, making it law (see Chapter 10). Tom Taylor, editor of *Inside Radio*, said the effect of the new law will definitely be to change the way stations behave. Back in Columbus, Ohio, the morning host for WBZX was quoted as saying that the rules would end the Holiday Hooters contest in which the morning crew gave away plastic surgery for Christmas.

ranked Clear Channel, which owns about 9 percent of all commercial stations, takes in substantially less money than CBS Radio, which is ranked fourth in terms of the number of stations. Simple arithmetic reveals that the typical CBS stations earn much more in annual advertising revenue than almost all other radio stations. In fact, CBS owns many of the nation's highest-billing radio stations, including all-news powerhouses WCBS-AM and WINS in New York, KNX-AM and KFWB-AM in Los Angeles, and WBBM and WMAQ in Chicago. One estimate is that the CBS all-news stations earn nearly seven times more per station than Clear Channel all-news stations, which tend to be located in smaller markets than the CBS stations. It's clear to see that the profitability of a station is frequently tied to the size of the market.

Radio Revenue Changes Revenues have been depressed since the economic downturn. Total revenue for 2009, for example, was 18 percent lower than the previous year, and industry analysts predict that revenues will continue to be soft through 2013. While radio stations have seen a decline in traditional local spot sales, their profits from online and mobile services have begun to increase. Yet while these revenue streams are increasing rapidly, they are tiny compared with traditional local spot sales. (See Figure 4–3.)

A New Kind of "Doo-wop": Duopoly and LMAs It is ironic (or at least coincidental) that the medium of radio, built in part on early rock-and-roll music known as "doo-wop," has given new meaning to that shopworn bit of slang. Where as once doo-wop referred to the sound produced by harmonizing street-corner singers (Dion and the Belmonts, the Coasters, and the Drifters, for example), today its homonym "duop" refers to the in-market control of radio listening and revenue by a few large group owners.

Figure 4–3

Digital Revenue Breakout Began in 2009.

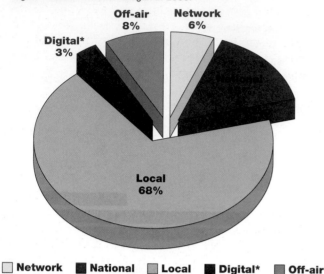

Off-air
8%

Network
6%

Digital*
3%

Local
68%

☐ **Network**   ■ **National**   ☐ **Local**   ■ **Digital***   ■ **Off-air**

*Source: RAB analysis-Miller, Kaplan, Arase & Co. data

As we have seen, the FCC now permits a single company to own as many as eight stations in a single radio market. In addition, the FCC permits one company to manage the assets of another in the same market without being in violation of ownership rules. Known as a **lease management agreement** or **local market agreement (LMA),** the arrangement permits one station or group to control the programming, operations, and sales of additional radio stations in the same marketplace.

A review of the industry shows a pattern of consolidation since 1996. For example, since 1996 the average number of radio owners in each market has dropped from about 13.5 to 10, and consolidation continues in both large and small radio markets. In the top 50 markets, including New York, Boston, Los Angeles, and Miami, the top group owner controls approximately 36 percent of the market revenue, and the next largest firm controls 25 percent of radio station revenue. The four largest group owners generally control more than 75 percent of the revenue in these markets. In the smallest 100 markets the top two firms control more than 75 percent of the radio revenue in those markets. Duopoly is big business.

Is ownership consolidation in radio a good thing? Advocates of this trend maintain that group ownership allows economies of scale (more efficient programming, better news gathering) to keep big-city radio exciting and interesting. Critics charge that group owners lack the sensitivity to community concerns that mom-and-pops have and that combining operations has caused stations to share resources. For example, a 2009 study conducted for the Radio and Television New Directors Association found that more than 43 percent of news directors had to supervise two or three radio stations, and 18 percent oversaw four stations. These numbers suggest that as programming oversight for radio stations is consolidated into fewer hands, programmers will have less time to devote to each programming service. If you're planning a radio career and favor local independent ownership, you may wish to consider small-market radio (although as we've seen, small markets have group owners too). If you're heading for New York, Chicago, Los Angeles, or other large markets, the corporate culture is no doubt in your future.

Control: Radio Programming and Promotion

The last "C" of radio today is *control*. With increasing competition and consolidation has come a desire on the part of radio managers to gain more and more control of the programming, promotions, and marketing of their stations. Radio today is marked by the kind of rigorous product and consumer research used to sell all kinds of consumer products, such as soap, automobiles, and cheese. Like all consumer items, the process begins with a full understanding of the attributes of the product. In the case of radio, the product is its programming. Let's examine the major trends in radio programming today.

RADIO PROGRAMMING TODAY

While it was possible to develop a stereotypical chart of radio listening 10 years ago, it is not possible today. Mobile devices and the growth of the Internet have begun to suggest fundamental shifts in listening behavior. A 2010 study by Bridge Ratings suggests that teens are listening less to terrestrial radio and more to Internet radio services, some local and some not. The aging baby boomer population is moving toward more news/talk and sports content. What can we learn from the latest trends in listenership?

With more than 13,700 stations on the air and more than 25 local stations typically available for most listeners, and while competing for audiences against smart phones, MP3 players, TV, Internet radio, movies, and even live entertainment like concerts and theater, radio has become a focused and highly targeted medium. That is, rather than programming to meet the broadest tastes of the largest numbers of people in their listening areas, most stations today cater to a fairly narrow market segment, the core of listeners who prefer a certain type of programming. The two key components of this trend are **target audience** and **format.**

The concept of target audience emerges from advertising research, which shows that the majority of purchases of a given product are made by a minority of the public: the primary group for which that product is designed. For example, the overwhelming majority of beer is purchased by men between the ages of 21 and 49, teenagers account for most movies attended, and adults over 45 take the most European trips and antacids (although we're not saying they're related). In developing their campaigns, advertisers try to identify the target market for a product and then to develop appeals that meet the needs of this group.

Commercial radio today, particularly in the largest cities, is programmed in precisely the same fashion. Reflecting this trend, in fact, cities themselves are known in the business as "markets." For example, Baltimore-Towson, Maryland, the **metropolitan statistical area (MSA)** that encompasses the counties immediately surrounding those two cities, is called the Baltimore market. Within that MSA station management identifies a target audience by its age, gender, music preferences, lifestyle, ethnicity, and other information, and it develops a program strategy to satisfy that group. The program strategy is known as the radio station's format. A successful radio station consistently delivers its intended target audience, in both aggregate size (quantity) and lifestyle preferences (quality). Its listeners are an identifiable subgroup, largely similar in age, gender, income, habits, leisure pursuits, and other characteristics. This makes the station attractive to advertisers: the name of the game in commercial radio.

Arbitron, the company that collects market data for radio, lists 300 metropolitan markets, from the largest, New York, with more than 15 million potential listeners, to the smallest, Casper, Wyoming, with a little more than 60,000 potential listeners. Much of the discussion about formats is drawn from the multiyear studies that Arbitron publishes; and the company's Web site provides much useful information for students interested in programming.

Table 4–3 list the top 10 radio formats in terms of number of stations, and Table 4–4 shows the top

formats by listenership, demographic characteristics of the formats, and regional popularity. By looking at these two tables it is easy to compare the popularity of each top format and its intended audience. Chapter 8 details how a format evolves from conception to execution. Until then, let's identify and highlight some aspects of the major formats today and their typical target audiences.

News/Talk and Sports

News and talk, a broad radio format on nearly 1,600 commercial stations, currently tops all other formats, possibly due to the increased intensity of political debate in the United States since 2008. At one end of the scale are all-news operations, usually AM stations in major metropolitan areas that program 24 hours a day of news, sports, weather, and traffic information. Examples are WCBS in New York, WBBM in Chicago, and KNX and KFWB in Los Angeles. At the other end of the scale are all-talk stations, which rotate hosts and invite listeners to call in on a range of topics—current affairs, auto mechanics, and counseling in every area, even sex. Examples are KABC in Los Angeles and KSTP-AM in Minneapolis. Between these extremes there are many news/talk/information stations, some of which mix play-by-play sports and occasional musical segments into the format. However, even the "hybrids" center their programming on news or information services.

More than half of all AM listening today is to news/talk and sports stations. The news format attracts males in "big numbers," particularly during

Table 4–3	Top Full-Time Commercial Formats (July 2009–July 2010)	
Rank	**Format**	**Station Total**
1	Country	1,997
2	News/talk	1,437
3	Spanish	665
4	Sports	637
5	Oldies	806
6	Classic hits	481
7	Adult contemporary	637
8	Top 40	634
9	Classic rock	495
10	Hot AC	417

Source: Insideradio.com.

Table 4–4	Radio Formats by Popularity, Listenership, and Demographics					
Rank	Format Name/ % of Population Listening	Demographics	Male/Female Listenership	Derivations	Additional Info/ Listenership Away from Home	Leading Markets
1	News/Talk (12.6%)	35+ with 65+ largest group	M 57.1%, F 42.9%	All news, talk, personality talk and all sports	#1 format in morning drive, equal listenership at home and away	L.A., Chicago, San Francisco, Washington, DC
2	Country (12.5%)	18–54, primarily 25+	M 46.9%, F 53.1%	Classic country, new Country	Often tied with news as #1 format, 66% listen away from home	Dallas-Ft. Worth, Atlanta, Minneapolis, Baltimore
3	Adult Contemporary (8.2%)	25–64, primarily 25+	M 36.5%, F 63.5%	Christmas at holiday season	Most popular format, in Mid-Atlantic states, 69% listening away from home	New York, Long Island, Philadephia, Phenoix, St. Louis
4	Pop/Contemporary Hit Radio (5.9%)	12–54, primarily 12–44	M 37.4%, F 62.6%	Top 40, Hot Hits	Highly rated in New England and Mid-Atlantic states, 67% listen away from home	Wide popularity across the U.S. except very largest radio markets
5	Classic Rock (3.9%)	18–64, primarily 35–54	M 69.7%, F 30.3%	—	Strong listenership in Midwest and South Atlantic states	Philadelphia, Minneapolis
6	Classic Hits (3.9%)	35–64, primarily 25+	M 52.9%, F 47.1%	—	Growning listenership trends, 71% listen away from home	New York, Chicago, L.A., and Miami
7	Rhythmic Contemporary Hit Radio (3.7%)	12–44, primarily 18–34	M 47.4%, F 52.6%	—	Listenership growing in 25+ but 50% of listeners are under 25; 60.8% listen away from home	Boston, Tampa-St. Pete, Denver, San Francisco, San Jose
8	Urban Adult Contemporary (3.6%)	25–64, primarily 35–64	M 43.9%, F 56.1%	—	Strong in South-Atlantic stats, 57.8% listen away from home	Miami-Ft. Lauderdale, Charlotte, Baltimore
9	Hot Adult Contemporary (3.5%)	18–54, primarily 25–54	M36.7%, F63.3%	—	Strong in New England and Midwest overall, 74.6% listen away from home	Detroit, Dallas-Ft. Worth
10	Urban Contemporary (3.3%)	12–54, primarily 12–44	M 45.5%, F 54.5%	—	Strong South-Atlantic States, 54% listen away from home	Atlanta, Detroit

Source: Aribitron Study-Radio Today 2009.

the important drive time in the morning and afternoon. It follows that people who listen for news, traffic, and weather information are on their way to jobs. Nearly 90 percent of all listeners are at least 35 years old, and this format frequently ranks at the top of many major markets.

Nationally syndicated personalities like Rush Limbaugh, Don Imus, Michael Savage, Dr. Joy Browne, and Dr. Laura Schlessinger are reaching millions of listeners each day. At the local level, news, talk, sports, and information stations are rife with acerbic commentators, smart-talking "jocks," computer gurus, social media mavens, car aficionados, and gabbers of all political stripes.

In the talk category about 600 stations are all-sports operations, mostly in large cities that boast teams in the four major professional sports leagues. All-sports stations typically frame play-by-play action of these professional teams and major college games with nonstop discussion, analysis, and debate about sports teams, athletes, and coaches. The demographic for sports is overwhelmingly male. While the format is popular with males 25 and older, the majority of listeners are actually 45+. As you would expect, listenership rises during key games and during playoff season.

Country

Today country radio is king of music formats with more than 1,600 stations across the country delivering to 56 million listeners each week. While people of all ages listen to country, its highest listenership is in the 25- to 49-year-old range. Listenership is predominantly white, and like most music formats, it delivers more women than men, with some stations targeting female listeners. Country fans are loyal, tending to listen to a single favorite station for long periods of time; this makes many country stations a prime delivery vehicle for advertisers.

The growth in popularity of country music in the 1980s and 1990s led to the development of various derivatives. "Traditional" or "classic" country stations consider themselves the purest players of the format playing standards of 20 or 30 years ago.

"Contemporary" or "modern" country stations concentrate on current hits on the country charts, particularly the most up-tempo or upbeat tunes. Strong airplay is usually given to the "superstars" of country, like Carrie Underwood, Tim McGraw, Brad Paisley, and Keith Urban. Up-and-coming country stars such as Taylor Swift and Rascal Flatts have gained broad exposure, bringing younger listeners in the 18 to 24 demographic to the format.

Most country stations are "full-service" operations with friendly and helpful announcers who are directly involved in community events. Many stations provide news, weather, and other information to their listeners, unlike many other music formats. Remote broadcasts are common, from concerts and fairs to shopping malls and drive-ins.

Country is the number one FM format and number two on the AM band, where other types of music are hard to find in substantive numbers. Like rock-and-roll, country radio is here to stay.

While country radio represents 15 percent of commercial stations, its strength is concentrated in medium and smaller markets in the midwest like Indianapolis and Bismark and southern markets like

Singer Faith Hill had hits on both country and adult contemporary radio stations.

Little Rock and Augusta, Georgia. Though popular, country stations do not lead listening in the nation's most populous markets. For example, in 2010 New York City did not have a country station in the top 25 stations, and in Los Angeles, country format KKGO-FM was ranked 26th in the market.

Adult Contemporary

Adult contemporary (AC) is a major force in radio with more than 700 adult contemporary stations running along a continuum from "lite hits" to "mix FM" while another 400 "hot AC" stations play to more uptempo audiences. AC/soft stations emphasize current music with lyrical songs and melodic beats. In addition to Sheryl Crow and Sara Bareilles, you're likely to hear 3 Doors Down, David Cook, Uncle Kracker, Daughtry, and Rob Thomas. Hot AC stations have a stronger mix of rhythmic hits included in the playlist.

Some AC stations that take the "oldies" route play soft, nonmetallic rock-and-roll hits. These stations

Podcasting provides broadcasters with new opportunities to connect with listeners.

focus on music of the 1960s, 1970s, and early 1980s and frequently label themselves something like "Oldies 97." The songs played were usually big hits in their day by the best-known bands of their time. The Beach Boys, the Beatles, the Supremes, and the Stones are mixed with other mainstays of the pop and rock charts such as the Eagles, Styx, Foreigner, and Fleetwood Mac. Other stations play a wide range of oldies but are more contemporary in their playlists (such as "music of the 80s, and 90s, and today") and may call themselves "mix FM" or some other moniker; but you're just as likely to hear The Counting Crows and Naked Eyes doing covers of 1960s hits.

In AC announcers are generally pleasant, friendly, and often noncontroversial. In fact, many listeners would be hard put to name the announcers at their favorite AC station. In some larger markets the morning show uses well-known hosts, but then the station focuses on music for the rest of the day because the main reason audiences listen is for the music (such as the "9 a.m. At-Work" music hour).

Women between the ages of 25 and 64 listen most to this format, and Arbitron's data show that "lite" stations peak with nearly 25 percent of the listenership between the ages of 45 and 54 while hot AC skews younger in the 35 to 44 age group. The appeal of AC is wide: from urban areas to rural, from college-educated to grade school, from upper income to the poverty line. AC is particularly strong "where it counts" to many advertisers: among middle- and upper-income housewives and working women in urban and suburban areas.

AC's strength in the bigger markets and attractive suburbs accounts for its large listenership. Today about 14 percent of all radio listening is to some of the many forms of AC stations, but the number of AC stations has been declining lately thanks to a rebound in news/talk and the growth of Hispanic and urban format stations. The target audience is also attracted to other formats, especially contemporary hit radio and black urban contemporary (discussed in a later section). While some older audiences prefer oldies to the more contemporary AC, it remains a well-known and highly profitable radio format.

Contemporary Hit Radio

Targeting a younger listener is the contemporary hit radio (CHR) format. CHR and Top 40 stations act like a jukebox. The emphasis is placed on the music leading the charts in record sales (and downloads),

Profile: The Growth of Hispanic Listenership

For the past few years revenue for radio has been flat, with little prospect of increasing given the growth of competitive services such as satellite radio, mobile devices, and podcasting. In some market sectors, however, this is not the case. Abritron's Hispanic *Radio Today* study for 2009 suggested that there was growth of the Hispanic-targeted formats. Overall reach for the Hispanic audience remained strong at between 94 and 96 percent. According to this study, Hispanics aged 12 or older listened almost 16 hours per week. That's more than the national average for all listeners.

The rise in Hispanic radio probably comes as little surprise because the Hispanic population in the United States has exploded and now constitutes the largest single minority group in the United States. Current census estimates peg the population at nearly 40 million, or roughly 14 percent of the total population. Of that number, roughly 29 million are Spanish-speaking.

It's no wonder then that radio has turned to serving this growing population. Since the mid-1990s there has been a huge increase in Hispanic radio. With more than 650 stations in the United States programming one of the three primary Hispanic formats, it is among the most popular formats in the United States by numbers of stations. Formats run the gamut from reggaeton to Mexican regional to Latin urban to Spanish religious. At the moment Mexican regional represents nearly one out of every four Hispanic stations in the United States. While the vast majority of stations are along the corridor bordering Mexico, you can also find the format doing well in Chicago, Denver, and Phoenix.

In 2007 ESPN launched Deportes Radio, the only 24/7 national Spanish-language sports radio network in the United States. Currently its programming is carried on 46 U.S. radio stations. Some experts indicate that Spanish-only programming trends are likely to continue as Hispanic listenership grows.

Demographics show that the audience composition is young, mostly in the 18- to 44-year-old range, with more female (55 percent) listeners generally; some research data show that one-quarter of all Hispanic listeners label radio as an "essential medium," which compares with just 17 percent of the general population calling radio essential. Some broadcasters think that the market for Hispanic radio is growing so quickly that there's an actual lag between listenership and revenues. If that's true, look for Hispanic radio revenue to keep outpacing the radio industry generally.

---

up-and-coming hits, and recurrent hits that are still popular. The music played is almost always bright or up-tempo. With a strict format, slow songs, long songs, and oldies (even those only a few months old) are avoided. Songs play again quickly (a program strategy known as **fast rotation**) and are removed from the playlist as soon as there is evidence that their popularity is declining.

Disc jockeys (DJs) are often assertive, high-energy personalities who sprinkle their shifts with humor, sound effects, and gimmickry. These stations sound "busy" compared with ACs. The air is filled with commercials, contests, jingles, jokes, and, above all, hits. Currently about 10 percent of all listening is to this format; the majority of stations using the format are FM stations in large markets. Listeners are in the under-25 age group who are avid Web surfers looking at radio stations, movie sites, and other entertainment venues. They range from preteens to young adult women. This is the group in recent years that has made mammoth stars of Justin Bieber, Lady Gaga, Maroon 5, and Gwen Stefani.

Once thought to be a format in decline, CHR has rebounded remarkably in recent years. There are numerous reasons for this turnaround. First, a spate of new artists appeared on the scene. Many were solo female performers, whose songs of independence, emotional turmoil, and love found and lost resonated with the core audience of young adult women. Such artists include Katy Perry and Ke$ha, as well as long-time torchbearers Mariah Carey and Madonna. In addition, a different form of CHR called "hot adult contemporary" (hot AC) found success with a fairly broad demographic of women (ages 25–54), moving these women away from their allegiance to oldies and soft rock standards. Some singers like Jason Mraz and Gavin Rossdale got their first exposure on hot AC formats. Groups such as Daughtry, Fuel, and Lifehouse appealed to this segment with melodic tunes, solid hooks, and good lyrics. Some CHRs in large cities are slanting their playlists toward specific music genres such as rock. In some instances, contemporary radio also has begun to merge with the sounds of America's inner cities, giving rise to two important formats: Hispanic and black/urban contemporary.

Ethnic Formats: Hispanic and Black/Urban Contemporary

Next in share of listening are the so-called ethnic formats, those radio stations that target minorities in major cities. The leading ethnic formats are Hispanic and black/urban contemporary. Together these formats can be heard on hundreds of stations, and they account for about 8 percent of all radio listening. In fact, "ethnic" may be a misnomer: Their growing popularity indicates that people of many cultures enjoy these stations, mostly because of the attractive beat and rhythms of their music.

Hispanic Radio   Hispanic radio is the growth format of the day, with the number of stations more than doubling as we entered the 21st century. There are a variety of different Hispanic formats, but Mexican Regional is most popular in the Southwest and in large urban centers such as Los Angeles and Denver. Spanish Contemporary is growing in acceptance, particularly in the Mid-Atlantic states, and attracts an increasingly upscale audience, particularly in the 25 to 44 demographic. Ballads form the backbone of this format, with artists like Luis Miguel and Chayanne sharing the spotlight with more pop-based sounds of Shakira and Maná.

The rise of Hispanic radio is due to two factors. The first is the growing population and economic clout of the Hispanic community. Today the Hispanics represent more than 13 percent of the U.S. population. Advertisers spend more than $1 billion each year to reach this important group, with more than $300 million in radio advertising.

Various formats such as rhythmic contemporary hit radio and Spanish adult hits also benefit from the rising popularity of its music. Subgenres within Hispanic formats include reggaeton (a mixture of Latin and urban dance beats, sometimes with very explicit lyrics), Mexican, and salsa each attracting large and loyal followings. Some of these formats have made stars of such artists as DJ Flex, Shakira, Enrique Iglesias, Primavera, Intocable, Marc Anthony, and Grupo Innovacion. Many of these subgenres tend to do well in urban settings on both coasts. Arbitron reported that contemporary formats within these subgenres have been gaining listener share over the last few years.

Black/Urban Contemporary   The black or urban contemporary (UC) format refers to the percussive, up-tempo sounds of the stations in America's major cities. While people of all racial and ethnic backgrounds enjoy the music, the music skews toward listeners under 35, and the format appeals more to women than men. Urban contemporary arose out of the disco craze of the mid-1970s, when a young, gyrating John Travolta captivated the culture and sent a new generation to the dance floors. By the 1990s, rap music had emerged with a new sound. Today variations of the format range from rap, hip-hop, and "house" music to more traditional rhythm-and-blues and soul music stylings. Hot urban contemporary artists in recent years include Eminem and Black Eyed Peas, along with newer artists like T-Pain and Jazmine Sullivan. Like Hispanic radio, the urban format is played on stations in major cities with large African-American populations and garners about 3 percent of the listening audience.

Urban AC and urban oldies are the most mature of the ethnic formats and they tend to skew to an older listener (35–54). Station playlists include artists like Alicia Keys and Jennifer Hudson are often mixed with hits from the past. Stations playing Urban AC garner another 3.5% of the listening audience.

Adult Hits   Popularized by the Jack format and other variations, this type of station is sometimes said to be the radio equivalent of an iPod on shuffle. A fairly broad variety of pop hits from the 1970s through the 1990s are played, often creating an interesting mix of music. This format differs from classic hits somewhat because it often includes a fairly deep playlist with more obscure hits and with a longer rotation between repeating songs and artists. The format has worked well in many major markets and can be found in more than 20 of the top 30 markets. Huey Lewis and the News, Tina Turner, and Def Leppard will be found interspersed between typical Eagles, Billy Joel, and Fleetwood Mac hits from that era.

While the majority of listeners fall within the 35- to 54-year-old demographic, listenership among adults aged 55+ has been gaining in recent years, growing by nearly 30 percent since 2008.

Active and Album-Oriented Rock

If you're looking for one of the few formats where men outnumber women in the listening audience (by nearly three to one), active rock fulfills that mission. This format ranks high among teens and millenials, peaking in the 25- to 34-year-old age group, but strong among men aged 18 to 44.

Active rock stations often do well in areas where there is a lively new music scene, such as Seattle–Tacoma and Minneapolis–St. Paul. The format is likely to play artists like Disturbed, Godsmack, Smashing Pumpkins, and Linkin Park along with 1990s stalwarts Soundgarden and Stone Temple Pilots and 1980s rockers like Guns N' Roses, AC/DC, and the ever-popular Aerosmith. Even Ozzy Osbourne made the active rock charts in 2010!

Typically active rock is not a market leader, but listeners are loyal; and the high proportion of male listeners makes this an attractive format for many advertisers.

Album-oriented rock is a subset of both classic hits and active rock, growing out of the long-lasting legacy of the progressive rock movement of the late 1960s and early 1970s. At this time, rock artists began to experiment with the form, producing theme albums (such as the Beatles' *Sergeant Pepper,* the Who's *Tommy, and Dark Side of the Moon* by Pink Floyd). The length of songs played on the radio began to increase, from two minutes to five minutes or more. Like jazz before it, album rock developed a core of informed, dedicated, loyal listeners—most of them young adult males. In fact, like classic hits and active rock, album rock is most heavily skewed to male listeners. Over 60 percent of the album rock audience is male, and 90 percent of its listenership is Caucasian.

Those stations seeking aging male baby boomers (like the authors of this text) are known as classic rock stations. Their core audience of 25- to 54-year-old listeners is loyal to the music of the supergroups of the 1960s, 1970s, and early 1980s, including the Rolling Stones, the Doors, the Eagles, U2, the Allman Brothers, Led Zeppelin, and others. Proof of the enduring appeal of older rock artists to both older and younger males is the fact that the most successful tours in recent years have been mounted by such aging rockers as the Stones, Pink Floyd, Aerosmith, Kiss, the Eagles, and Black Sabbath, giving new meaning to the phrase "long live rock."

Other Formats

Together, the formats just described account for a large percentage of radio listening in the United States. The remainder is filled out by a number of other formats.

Religious stations appeal to a variety of faiths, but Christian stations are most plentiful. In addition to delivering inspirational talks, many religious stations include music in their format. Those targeting the black audience are generally known as gospel stations. Religious stations tend to be most popular among women aged 45 and up. They are often found on the FM dial, with contemporary Christian stations being among the most popular formats. Contemporary Christian stations feature upbeat Christian rock artists like MercyMe, Jeremy Camp, and Amy Grant, and their audiences skew younger than most other religious stations.

In 2009 there were more than 1,700 commercial and noncommercial stations playing some form of religious format. Despite their proliferation, religious stations lag in listenership, with generally less than 3 percent of the listening audience. At any given point in time, fewer than 2 in 50 radio listeners are tuned to religion; but those listeners are loyal and tend to listen for a longer time.

While classical music and jazz are the backbone of public radio stations (see the discussion that follows), some 260 or so commercial operations play each of these formats. Classical stations attract a very upscale listener in the 55+ demographic, typically college-educated and professional. Like religious stations, classical stations enjoy higher ratings in home listening than most other formats. The jazz enthusiast reflects a younger profile with listenership in the 35-and-above age groups. Although the number of classical and jazz aficionados is small (compared, say, with the audience for adult contemporary), the "high quality" of their listeners makes these stations potentially attractive advertising vehicles. On noncommercial stations, underwriters frequently like jazz and classical listeners because they represent a highly educated, more upscale listener.

It sometimes appears that there are almost as many other formats as there are radio stations. Filling out the dial, a variety of foreign-language stations have substantial multicultural populations. Many stations play dance music or a variety of world music formats.

Noncommercial Radio

The bulk of America's radio stations seek profits through advertising sales, but about one in six stations does not. Into this class fall more than 2,100 noncommercial radio stations. There are three main types of noncommercial stations: community, college, and public.

Community stations are those that are licensed to civic groups, nonprofit foundations, local school boards, or religious organizations. There are about 500 of these stations, which operate in the FM band (between 88 and 92 megahertz), providing a range of services including coverage of local issues, study-at-home classes in conjunction with local schools, religious services, niche music programming, local talk shows, and other "home-based" activities.

WMNF-FM is a good example of one of the many successful community stations operating in the United States. The Tampa Bay station has been on the air since 1979 and programs an eclectic variety of music throughout the day that reflects the interests of its many volunteers and station members. For example, stripped across the weekday schedule you'll find blues and rock in the afternoons, but weekends switch to alternative and international music. Some evenings feature jam bands whereas other nights feature punk, electronic, and club music. Many volunteers share the mic to bring an amazing assortment of specialty shows to listeners.

The station is supported by donations and the annual Tropical Heatwave festival, which features 45 bands over multiple venues and has become one of the most popular annual concerts in the Tampa Bay area. Over the years the famous and not so famous have played in support of the station.

College radio is a broad category comprising about 800 stations licensed to universities and some secondary schools. About 650 of these stations are members of the Intercollegiate Broadcasting Society (IBS).

KULT-LP (licensed to the University of North Iowa) is a good example of college radio stations. It started out in the 1950s as KYTC, an AM carrier current station. In the early 1990s the station moved to Channel 5 of the college's cable television system. In 2001, after the FCC approved low-power broadcasting (see the Low-Power FM section), the faculty adviser and the student board applied for a 100-watt permit; and in 2003 KULT-LP took to the FM airwaves. The station has a rich 50-year broadcasting history even though it's been an FM station only for a short time. Today KULT and hundreds of other college stations continue to entertain and inform their listeners.

College stations are a diverse group. However, most of them share a similar programming pattern. The musical mix is eclectic and "progressive," featuring program blocks of new wave, new age, reggae, metal, jazz, and other alternatives to standard formats. Many college stations operate as training sites for students planning broadcast careers. Thus, in addition to announcing, staffers gain experience in news, play-by-play sports, public affairs, programming, and promotions. As broadband access has increased, a large number of college stations have begun streaming their services on the Web. Some colleges have created Web-based college stations or have begun podcasting.

Public radio stations are also known as CPB-qualified stations. These stations meet criteria established by the Corporation for Public Broadcasting (CPB), enabling them to qualify for federal funds and to receive programs from National Public Radio (NPR). Today there are approximately 800 stations affiliated with NPR or carrying its programming.

In 1998 standards for CPB-qualified stations were tightened. Today's public radio stations must have a professional staff of at least five full-time members; must operate at least 18 hours per day, 7 days a week; must operate at full power (250 watts AM and 100 watts FM); and must demonstrate sufficient local financial and listening support to justify federal grant monies. NPR listenership has been growing over the past two decades, and while federal appropriations seem secure for the foreseeable future, there are critics who claim that public radio should not receive federal tax dollars to support radio programming.

As one might expect, the audiences for public radio tend to be comparatively smaller than those for commercial stations, but that does not mean the numbers are insignificant. Nationwide, public radio averages about a 2 percent share of audience at any given time. This compares with shares of 6 to 15 percent for highly ranked commercial radio outlets. However, in some cities public radio attracts sizable audiences. For example, KQED (San Francisco) and WRVO (Oswego–Syracuse, New York) are regularly ranked among the top 10 stations in the market and garner a 5 to 8 percent audience share. Sometimes it's useful to point out that while the numbers seem low, in reality, almost 20 million people listen to NPR programming every week.

Public radio listeners are very desirable to underwriters. Education level (almost 70 percent are college grads) and household income are above average. Male listenership is slightly higher than female, and while it has listenership in all demographic groups 25 and up, on average 70 percent of public radio listeners are at least 45 years old.

Among the most popular programs in public radio are NPR's leading news programs *Morning Edition* and *All Things Considered;* the entertaining call-in program *Car Talk;* and the entertaining news quiz *Wait, Wait, Don't Tell Me.* In addition to NPR programming, most public radio stations carry programs from other suppliers, including American Public Media and Public Radio International. Popular shows such as *A Prairie Home Companion,* hosted by Garrison Keillor, attract a large and loyal following.

Some public stations have formed regional networks and program consortiums to develop programming that serves the needs of the region. Wisconsin Public Radio and Alabama Public Radio are examples of regional networks that develop programs for their specific listening audiences.

Public Radio Formats   Arbitron points out that stations qualifying as NPR stations tend to cover a broad cross-section of news, entertainment, and cultural genres. Formats tend to be quite different from commercial counterpoints because of the nature of the noncommercial formats. Nearly half of all public radio listening is captured by news/talk

stations, often mirroring the popularity of the commercial format, but differing from commercial stations with substantially more long-form reports. News/classical is a format that appears to be unique to public radio and stations; this format may broadcast *Morning Edition* and *All Things Considered* but switch to classical genres for afternoon and evening listening.

Classical music has gained public radio listenership as more commercial stations drop classical to adopt a format that attracts a younger demographic. Listenership is overwhelmingly in the 65+ demographic. A number of public radio stations also program an eclectic format known as AAA (adult album alternative) or jazz, which rounds out the most popular formats. Like active rock and AOR formats, AAA tends to appeal to males and provides NPR stations with a substantial number of listeners in younger demographics (25–34). Jazz listenership is getting progressively older (55 and up), although NPR stations programming news/jazz tend to skew to younger listeners (45+).

Low-Power FM   In 2000 the Federal Communications Commission approved **low-power FM** (LPFM) services. These news stations have power levels from 10 to 100 watts and serve small listening areas (approximately a four-mile radius or less). The FCC requires low-power stations to program a minimum of 36 hours per week, and they must be noncommercial. Entities such as governments, colleges, religious groups, and nonprofit groups serving their local community are eligible to apply for a LPFM license. As of 2010, the FCC had granted more than 850 licenses for this new service.

Small community stations like Portsmouth Community Radio, WSCA-FM, and Radio Sausalito (which has no call sign) provide small communities with new opportunities for developing local content. Sausalito's station is all jazz and uses microrepeaters on the FM band along with a more powerful AM station. Portsmouth has a much more diversified format including an obscure oldies show called *Metaphysical Circus.* The station has operated on a volunteer basis since 2004 and is entirely listener supported.

In 2009, the House of Representatives passed the Local Community Radio Act, which could clear the way for many new low-power stations. As of this edition the Senate has not passed a version of the bill. Whether these stations will flourish over the next several years will likely determine whether more communities apply for low-power stations.

KULT, like many other stations, provides listeners with different opportunities to stay connected by streaming programming on the Web, using Facebook and Twitter.

SATELLITE RADIO TODAY

In the 1990s two companies bet that there were a substantial number of Americans willing to pay extra for radio service that surpassed what you could get on AM and FM. But were they right?

XM Radio and Sirius won licenses from the FCC to build satellite radio services capable of reaching the entire continental United States. In November 2001 both companies began providing programming services to customers who purchased specially equipped radio receivers capable of downloading the satellite radio signal.

Initially the future of satellite radio appeared to be skyrocketing, with some experts projecting that the two services would have more than 45 million subscribers and annual revenues of nearly $8 billion by 2014. However, in early 2006 satellite radio subscriptions began to slow, and by the end of the year both XM and Sirius had revised their projected listenership goals downward. Some experts speculated that the amazing growth of iPod usage and mobile telephones made satellite radio services less attractive.

Both services began adding specialized programming and sports programming in an effort to boost subscriptions. In January 2006 radio personality Howard Stern began broadcasting on Sirius, and in that year XM started special programming with Oprah Winfrey. However, mounting programming costs and slowing consumer interest in the service forced the companies into merger talks in 2007; and in 2008 SiriusXM was born.

Programming on the two services is niche-oriented. While some of the programming easily fits within the mold of the formats we discussed earlier in this chapter, much of satellite radio's offerings are simply beyond the scope of what a commercial radio station could program. Full-time reggae, blues, movie soundtracks, Broadway standards, and underground dance are just a few of the specialized channels available. News, sports, and talk programming cover just about any political or social spectrum imaginable. Just as cable television began to grow as it offered a diverse array of programming, satellite radio is betting that it can offer programming that appeals to specific audiences that, while small from one market to another, will become large enough in the aggregate at the national level. This gamble is expensive; both XM and Sirius have lost nearly a billion dollars in their first decade of operations.

In 2010 SiriusXM announced a small profit for the first time; and as the decade came to a close, the number of subscribers surpassed 20 million—but that means fewer than 12 percent of Americans have access to satellite radio. **Churn,** which is the term used for a customer giving up a service, has been problematic because new car buyers with satellite radios often get a free subscription and then discontinue the service after the free period. Studies show that the average subscriber is 45 or older and that there appears to be a reluctance on the part of younger Americans to pay for radio and music.

SiriusXM now offers radio services on the Web on a subscription basis. Whether this will attract a large audience is not known, but the cost of the service is in addition to the regular monthly subscription while many Internet-only radio services are free. What online services cannot offer is the multiple choices of sports programming and news channels.

Growth of Internet and Mobile Broadcasting   The widespread adoption of broadband in the home and the tremendous growth in mobile computing has made Web-based media services important content for audience attention. Arbitron estimated that more than 80 percent of Americans have access to a broadband connection and nearly 50 percent of all homes have at least two working computers. Over the past several years new services have emerged to provide popular genre-specific programming for broadband users. In addition to the huge base of computers that have access to the Web, mobile broadband users are increasingly using their devices for entertainment. In 2010 ComScore.com reported that 14 percent of smart phone usage was to listen to music. A look at these services illustrates the diversity available to users.

Pandora Radio was started in 2000 by struggling musician Tim Westergren as the Music Genome Project. Pandora builds radio stations around a "seed" of music that the customer inputs at the beginning of each session. It struggled for many years, but in 2010 it boasted 60 million registered users; while that number is large, only about 13 million users access Pandora each month. Also, the cost of operating an online music service is high because unlike terrestrial radio, Internet music services have to pay a fee to the **Copyright Royalty Board (CRB)** for performance rights to the music.

Westergren was quoted as saying that he wants to build a radio business that looks a lot like the tradi-

Events: Is There Too Much Radio?

In 2003 the FCC authorized all radio stations in the United States to broadcast in HD (high-definition digital) in addition to the stations' current analog channel. Then in 2004 the FCC authorized low-power FM. Currently more than 11,000 commercial radio stations compete for listeners every day, and now that number could double. Each radio station in the country could immediately start broadcasting a second channel in high-definition sound. As of 2010, more than 2,000 AM and FM stations had made the conversion and started broadcasting in HD.

There are some real issues. Few digital radios can receive the new signal, and the digital radios that are on the market are fairly high-priced (usually at least $150). But if previous technology adoption is any indicator of what is likely to happen, within a few years HD radios will be cheap, and they will be built into cars by auto manufacturers. At the moment many cars are already equipped with AM/FM and satellite receivers, which brings us to an interesting question: Is there too much radio in the United States?

Mobile users can now download apps like IHeartRadio and AOL Radio, which gives listeners many more choices beyond the local market stations.

At the beginning of this chapter, we discussed the fact that radio advertising revenues were likely to remain constant at less than 10 percent of all advertising expenditures. If there is no real increase in the amount of money spent on radio advertising, how will radio stations make money on HD radio?

The obvious answer is that as more and more listeners switch from analog to digital, advertising dollars will shift as well. But that would mean AM and FM analog services would see a decline in revenue as listeners and advertisers switched over to HD. Also, some people complain that the digital signal is not as robust as the analog signal, limiting the distance a station can broadcast. However, fewer commercials and the greater diversity of programming could be strong attractions for some listeners. Then, too, 50 million Americans own iPods, and these devices are capable of downloading podcasts, representing another level of programming that is not subject to FCC rules about indecency (or any other rules for that matter).

While terrestrial broadcasting and the National Association of Broadcasters have been touting HD radio as the next great innovation, the facts suggest that as the number of stations increases, it will be difficult going in an increasingly competitive market for listeners.

tional radio business, selling both national and local advertising; but to do this he would need to grow monthly listenership substantially. The music service saw a huge increase in users after it developed applications for mobile phone and Apple's iPad. Now it wants to bring Pandora to the automobile. Most auto manufacturers are currently testing a variety of systems that would allow users to stream Web-based programming in the car.

Currently Pandora offers dozens of genre stations based on 20 categories of music from pop to songwriters to classical to alternative choices. Advertising on the Web site and an interface that allows users to buy selections played provides current revenues.

Live365 is a mixture of independent programmers and radio stations that are categorized by genre. Unlike Pandora, the programming is not generated by Live365. Programmers can purchase a broadcaster membership, allowing them to mount programming services. The service boasts more than 250 genres of music and thousands of individual stations, but Live365 varies from programmer to programmer. Some services stream low-quality audio while others are higher in quality. Some services are limited to a specific number of streams, depending on the contracts developed with the CRB. This service is supported through Web site advertising.

Jango is another radio music site that allows the user to request music, playing music of similar artists alongside the choices made by the user. It bills itself as a social music service that lets the user create a shared custom radio station (much like sharing a favorite playlist) by choosing the artist or song. The Web page provides users with videos, information about the artist, fan comments, and suggestions for similar music.

AOL Radio is a large music service boasting 350 sports, talk, and music services that provide listeners with a huge variety of genre-specific radio stations and access to many of the highly rated CBS radio stations around the United States. Commercials are interspersed through the music service for the genre service, and the CBS stations broadcast their regular programming. The service is linked with the AOL Radio Web site that provides the user with information about favorite music and many customizable features.

These services are a few of the many available via broadband links, whether on a computer network or through a mobile service provider. Increasingly Americans between the ages of 12 and 34 are turning to the Internet to find out about new music and to get information. As music and news services gain widespread use, terrestrial radio will have to ensure that it remains an important, vital service to listeners.

RADIO STATION ORGANIZATION

Regardless of their size, radio stations tend to share an organizational pattern. Over the past decade, groups with multiple stations in a market or a region have frequently consolidated some common activities with the organization. Figures 4–4 and 4–5 illustrate typical organizational structures for single and group radio stations. Figure 4–4 diagrams the personnel structure at one station while 4–5 shows the flow of managerial control that might be seen within a group at midsized to large station. Let's assume for

our discussion that this radio group owns four or five stations in a midsized market.

Overseeing the general operations for all stations is the **regional market manager.** This person oversees all the different managers for the different stations and ensures that local policies are consistent with those of the corporate office. Under the RM we would likely have an organizational structure with an operations manager, director of sales, a promotions and marketing manager, a business manager, and an engineering/IT department.

The **operational manager** will oversee the work of the **program directors.** For large stations within the group there may be a separate program director for each station; or if the group owns one or two news/talk or talk/sports stations, one PD will oversee the programming for these stations. Another PD may handle all the AC and hot hits stations, and another may handle country. The program director has overall responsibility for the sound of the station(s) including music, news, and public affairs. Stations with a music format may also employ a music director to oversee the development and implementation of the format; news/talk stations may appoint a news director to handle the logistics of news and public affairs coverage. Frequently the PD pulls an air shift on the station as part of the position's responsibility.

The **director of sales** is very important. This person oversees sales personnel, who are fond of point-

Figure 4–4

A Radio Station Table of Organization: Single Station Ownership

Multiple station ownership within a regional market reflects a much more complex personnel operation

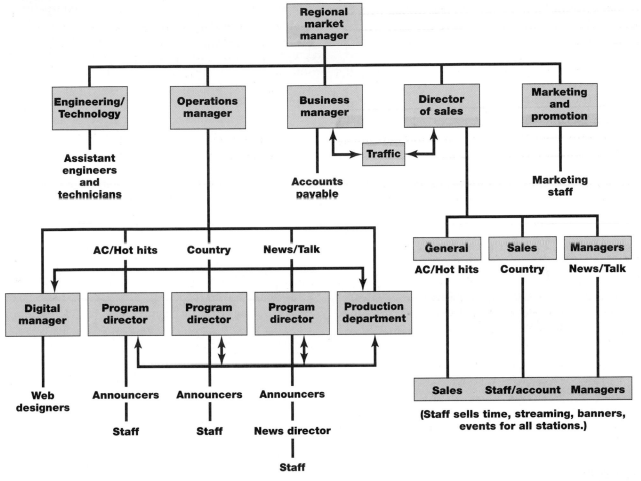

(Digital and promotion works for all stations.)

ing out that theirs is the only department that makes money; all the others spend it. There may be separate sales managers for the larger stations, or that person may be assigned to oversee several stations. Below the sales manager, account executives are responsible for selling commercial time to local, regional, and national advertisers. Depending on the size of the station (and the size of its commercial client list), stations may employ both a local sales manager to oversee local sales and a national sales manager to handle spot advertising accounts. Usually public radio stations, such as NPR stations, will have an **underwriting manager** whose job is similar to that of a director of sales.

The **promotion and marketing manager** will oversee the general image or branding for the different stations and will coordinate events, live remotes, contests, and other promotional activities with the different station program directors. Today's commitment to branding and promotion makes these important functions of this department, prompting many stations to value highly a promotions director and research manager. More and more today, a new position called **Web master** is charged with keeping the Web site current, reaching out to listeners using a variety of social networking techniques, and placing banner ads or other sales pieces into the station Web sites.

The **engineering department,** headed by the chief engineer, basically has two functions: to keep the station on the air with the best signal possible and to implement information technology (IT) that serves the station's needs, including its online and mobile operations. (Smaller station operations often retain the services of a consulting engineer, who works part-time, as needed, to keep the station in prime operating condition.)

A **business manager** keeps track of station financial operations. Usually this person will work closely with someone in **traffic,** who is responsible for getting commercials plugged into the different station schedules (an account executive may sell more than one station to a large client, like a local automotive dealership). The business manager is responsible for business and financial matters, including station revenues and expenses, short- and long-term planning, budgeting, forecasting, and profitability.

While the regional manager must run the stations in accord with local, state, and federal regulations, usually the program directors are responsible for maintaining and representing the different stations' images in the community. The people who work for the program directors include the announcers, newscasters, or talk show hosts—the people who are closest to the listeners. Usually these staff members become the face of the station by appearing at local events such as state fairs, store openings, community service events, and the like.

Traditionally, the route up the corporate ladder into the management of radio stations starts in sales; most radio GMs have backgrounds as account executives, promotion directors, or research managers. However, it is not unheard of for GMs—even station group owners—to come from the music or announcing ranks. At a radio management meeting one will hear many well-modulated announcer voices; a very high percentage of owners and operators are former DJs.

As noted above, radio consolidation is leading to new management structures. In most markets, groups operating multiple stations have consolidated sales by using one sales staff to sell commercials on as many as eight stations. The engineering and promotions departments have been similarly streamlined. However, most duopolies prefer to keep programming decentralized. Because radio is still primarily a local service medium, it makes sense to maintain local control of what the station sounds like, as well as what it's like to work there.

GETTING A JOB: RADIO EMPLOYMENT TODAY

The consolidation of radio due to rising competition, increasing group ownership, duopolies, and LMAs has had a measurable effect on radio employment. Employment has dropped since duopoly rules went into effect, and the Bureau of Labor Statistics predicts the decline in employment will continue through 2012 and beyond.

With consolidation continuing, voice-tracking has become a popular option at group-owned radio stations. Modern technology makes it is possible to prerecord an entire four-hour airshift and have a board operator or computer software correctly insert all the voice tracks in their appropriate places within the show. Some jocks do shows in different cities this way. While this practice allows group owners to more effectively use their highly paid talent, others see it as taking the spontaneity out of radio.

The news is not all bad. Opportunities for women and members of ethnic minority groups have been increasing in radio in recent years. For example, in 1977 the percentage of women in radio jobs was 28, and ethnic minorities accounted for only 10 percent of employees. By 1990 almost 40 percent of the radio workforce was female, and the percentage of ethnic minorities had risen to 15. Today the radio workforce is about 17 percent ethnic minority and more than 40 percent female.

Most of the new opportunities for ethnic minorities and women have occurred in sales and announcing positions. Twenty years ago black and Hispanic announcers were virtually unheard of (and unheard) outside of "ethnic" stations, but radio today has an increasingly multiethnic and multicultural sound.

The FCC estimates that about 70,000 people work in the radio business. The majority work at commercial radio stations. Noncommercial radio employs about 4,000 people. The remainder of radio jobs are at corporate headquarters and networks. For people looking to start out in radio, smaller community stations are more likely to hire people with limited experience for on-air work. Many people work part-time or are self-employed. Because broadcasting is a 24/7 business, hours can be long, including nights and weekends. Being able to talk knowledgeably about a variety of subjects (theater, music, sports, politics, and so on) can improve one's chances of getting past the front door.

Radio Salaries

Salaries in the radio business are largely a function of the size of the market. Overall, the average radio salary is low—only about $25,000 per year. In smaller markets most people, especially announcers, earn at or slightly above minimum wage. A salary of less than $20,000 is typical for most small-market air personalities. However, in larger markets, top personalities—particularly the popular DJs in the lucrative early-morning time period—can earn seven-figure salaries.

In radio, the better-paying jobs are in sales. Account executives in large markets exceed $150,000 in annual income. The nationwide average is over $110,000 per year for radio sales managers. This trend is also apparent in smaller markets. For example, a general sales manager averages about $97,000 per year in earnings, nearly $25,000 more than the average salary for the program director. In fact, in some markets a successful sales manager might even make more than the station's general manager.

Talent is still sought after and rewarded in radio. The morning personality in a large market will command more than $150,000 per year; a highly rated morning team can earn as much as a million dollars.

SUMMARY

- Judging by the number of radio stations on the air and by the number of radios in homes, there is no doubt that the medium has survived the threat of TV. However, radio receives less than 10 percent of total advertising expenditures. This means that radio is arguably the most competitive of the electronic media businesses. Increasingly difficult economic conditions have generally depressed the radio market since 2008.

- Radio stations, once family-owned operations, now are merged into groups of stations owned by corporations. Fueled by relaxed ownership regulations, these corporations have consolidated the radio business. Duopolies allow a single owner to operate as many as eight stations in a single community.

- Because of intense competition, most stations have turned to highly structured formats, targeting their programming toward specific factions of society. Some fear these trends are resulting in the franchising and depersonalization of the medium.

- Country, news/talk, contemporary hit radio, and album rock tend to monopolize commercial radio. Talk formats frequently rely on syndicated programming, such as Joy Browne and Rush Limbaugh. Black and Hispanic radio stations are growing in popularity.

- Three kinds of noncommercial radio stations— community, college, and CPB-qualified—compete for audiences with their commercial counterparts. Affiliates of National Public Radio (NPR) are the most influential in this group, though they are subject to the uncertainty of federal funding and face increasing technical, employment, and programming requirements.

- SiriusXM radio provides a subscription radio service with many niche programming choices. However, a decade after its introduction, satellite radio is still struggling to find enough subscribers to make the services profitable.

- Online music services provide programming to broadband computer and mobile listeners. Increasingly, younger demographics seem comfortable in using online programming services instead of terrestrial radio broadcasters.

- Most radio stations have several major departments: operations, (which handles programming), sales, and engineering. The GM is responsible for all the executive decisions at a station, and group stations my have a regional manager overseeing all of the different operations.

- Radio consolidation has caused considerable shrinkage of the workforce. However, opportunities continue for women and minorities, and positions in sales, promotion, and programming can lead to lucrative careers in senior management.

KEY TERMS

competition   86
consolidation   86
control   86
Telecommunications Act of
   1996   89
supergroup   89
lease management agreement   92
local market agreement
   (LMA)   92
target audience   93
format   93
metropolitan statistical area
   (MSA)   93
fast rotation   97
community stations   100

SUGGESTIONS FOR FURTHER READING

Adams, M., & Massey, K. (1995). *Introduction to radio: Production and programming.* Madison, WI: Brown & Benchmark.

Dempsey, J. (2006). *Sports-talk radio in America: Its context and culture.* Binghamton, NY: Haworth Half-Court Press.

DiTingo, V. (1995). *The remaking of radio.* Boston: Focal Press.

Engleman, R. (1996). *Public radio and television in America: A political history.* Thousand Oaks, CA: Sage.

Gross, L., Gross, B., & Perebinossoff, P. (2005). *Programming for TV, radio, & the Internet* (2nd ed.). Boston: Focal Press.

Hausman, C., Benoit, P., Messere, F, & O'Donnell, L. (2007). *Modern radio production* (7th ed.). Belmont, CA: Wadsworth.

Keith, M. (2000). *The radio station* (5th ed.). Boston: Focal Press.

Laufer, P. (1995). *Inside talk radio.* Secaucus, NJ: Carol Publishing Group.

Looker, T. (1995). *The sound and the story: NPR and the art of radio.* Boston: Houghton Mifflin.

Lynch, J. (1998). *Process and practice of radio programming.* Lanham, MA: University Press of America.

MacFarland, D. (1997). *Future radio programming strategies* (2nd ed.). Mahwah, NJ: Erlbaum.

McCoy, Q., & Crouch, S. (2002). *No static: A guide to creative radio programming.* San Francisco, CA: Backbeat Books.

Norberg, E. (1996). *Radio programming: Tactics and strategy.* Boston: Focal Press.

Perebinossoff, P., Gross, B., & Gross, L. (2005). *Programming for TV, radio, and the Internet.* Boston: Focal Press.

Pringle, P., & Starr, M. (2006). *Electronic media management* (5th ed.). Boston: Focal Press.

INTERNET EXERCISES

Visit our Web site at **www.mhhe.com/dominickbib7e** for study-guide exercises to help you learn and apply material in each chapter. You will find ideas for future research as well as useful Web links to provide you with an opportunity to journey through the new electronic media.

Broadcast and Cable/Satellite TV Today | 5

Quick Facts

- Network share of prime-time audience (1975): 90 percent

- Network share of prime-time audience (2009): 27 percent

- Share of households watching prime-time pay cable (2009): 2.8 percent

- Number of TV networks (1975): 3

- Number of TV networks (2010): 7

- Number of digital converter coupons redeemed (2009): 34,879,001

- Percentage of TV homes with DVD players (2010): 88%

- U.S. homes that are HD capable (2010): 47.4 million

- Average cost of cable or satellite service (2010): $71 per month

It would be hard to come up with one word that sums up the television industry today. It might be "transformed." Traditional broadcast television stations spent millions of dollars upgrading to digital TV, and in 2009 HD televisions began selling like hotcakes. Broadcasters can now transmit high-definition signals or multiple standard-definition signals. Cable has expanded its digital offerings, and these additional choices continue to gain viewership at broadcast TV's expense. Another word that comes to mind is "converged." Viewers are watching television on a variety of different platforms—whether on the local channel, on a fiber optic cable system, or streaming on a mobile smart phone. The content is still most important, but the delivery systems have converged.

There are other changes, too. In 2006, CBS and Warner Brothers shuttered the WB and UPN TV networks and formed the CW network. As if local stations did not have sufficient competition already, DVRs have gained in popularity and now take their place next to DVDs, video games, and YouTube and WiFi applications Networks distribute their programming via iTunes, Hulu, YouTube, and other new media technologies. This chapter takes a brief look at the dynamics of industry today, particularly the broadcast and cable businesses. The next chapter presents a snapshot of the new media, especially the World Wide Web.

TELEVISION NOW

Watching TV is one of America's favorite pastimes. More than 98 percent of the homes in America—nearly 115 million homes—have at least one TV. Of the homes with TV sets, 98 percent have a color set. Eighty percent of the homes in the United States have more than one set. More than a decade ago the census reported that American homes had more TVs than indoor toilets; that disparity continues to grow.

According to the ACNielsen ratings company, the average American home watches TV for 31.5 hours each week. Those viewers have a lot of choices. About 90 percent of all homes subscribe to either cable or satellite, and the typical TV household today receives more than 100 different channels of programming. And in just 15 years, 33 million Americans have subscribed to a DBS service.

TYPES OF TELEVISION STATIONS

There are over 1,750 TV stations in operation today. The various types of stations are depicted in Figure 5–1.

Commercial and Noncommercial Stations

The stations depicted in Figure 5–1 can be divided into two categories: commercial and noncommercial. The primary distinction between the two is the way in which each type of station acquires the funds to stay on the air. Commercial stations—78 percent of the total number of TV stations—make their money by selling time on their stations to advertisers. Noncommercial stations are not allowed to sell advertising. These stations, which were set aside by the FCC for educational, civic, and religious groups, must adhere to the FCC mandate not to sell advertising time. They survive strictly through donations from individuals, businesses, and the government.

There are about 1,750 stations on the air across the United States. Approximately 380 of these stations are noncommercial, meaning that they must rely on underwriting, viewer donations, or funding by their owners like a church or university. Of course, like the situation in radio today, the commercial stations do not share equally in TV revenues. And noncommercial TV faces the same funding problems that public radio faces: Funding sources tend to be more difficult to secure during times of economic downturn, and viewers are sometimes frustrated by the annual fund-raising drives that interrupt the regular broadcast schedule.

The broadcast TV business is actually two businesses in one. There is the local television business,

Figure 5–1

TV Stations by Type

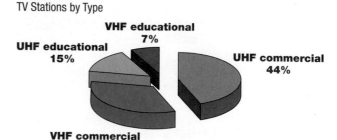

which revolves around scheduling programs and selling advertising in the many cities and towns in which TV stations can be found. Managers of these stations earn their revenue primarily through the sale of advertising in their community and region.

Then there is **network television,** a system in which ABC, CBS, NBC, FOX, CW, and some smaller networks develop program schedules for their affiliate stations. The networks sell most of the advertising in those programs (a process traced in detail in Chapter 7), which is how they make most of their money.

Let's first take a look at the network TV business.

NETWORK TELEVISION

For many years the TV business (like the U.S. automobile business) was dominated by three giant companies. At the peak of their power in the 1960s and 1970s ABC, CBS, and NBC dominated the viewing habits of the nation. That dominance was especially acute in prime time: the evening hours during which the overwhelming majority of American households were watching TV. On the East Coast and in the far West, prime time ran from 7:00 p.m. to 11:00 p.m.; in the Midwest and certain parts of the Rocky Mountain region, prime time spanned 6:00 p.m. to 10:00 p.m.

At the height of their prime-time power the three major networks commanded more than 9 in 10 of all TV homes with TV sets on. With competition from new sources—most notably Fox, cable, and home video (see Chapter 2), the 1980s saw the beginning of a significant decline in the networks' audience share. For example, the three networks drew 91 percent of U.S. TV households in prime time in 1978. By 1986 their share had slipped to 75 percent. By 1992 the network share for ABC, CBS, and NBC had slipped to 60 percent. The 2005–2006 TV season saw ratings for the networks fall below 30 percent.

Today the viewing shares for the major four networks (ABC, CBS, NBC, and FOX) hover around the 27 percent range.

As we discussed in Chapter 1, NBC, CBS, and ABC all started as radio networks and made the switch to television in the earliest days of television. For nearly four decades they were unchallenged. However, when the FCC changed ownership rules in 1985, a new competitor saw an opportunity.

Fox Broadcasting Company

The Fox Broadcasting Company (FBC) was launched in 1986 by Australian media magnate Rupert Murdoch. Murdoch had purchased the former Metromedia stations and was interested in using his newly acquired TV studio (Twentieth Century Fox) to produce programs for these stations. The decision was made to introduce programming slowly—first, one day of the week (Sunday), then gradually extending it throughout the week.

Today Fox network programming is available seven nights per week. Many successful shows now attract audiences and advertisers to Fox, including *American Idol, Glee, The Simpsons, Family Guy,* and *House.*

New Century and Networks Come . . . and Go

Motivated by the success of Fox and the revenue potential of the network TV business, two big players entered the network game in the mid-1990s.

The United Paramount Network (UPN), owned by media conglomerate Viacom/CBS, debuted in January 1995, anchored by *Star Trek: Voyager.* Like Fox, UPN began with two evenings of programming, with plans to expand beyond prime time to other days and other day parts. By 1999 UPN was broadcasting five nights per week. However, its ratings were low compared with Fox and the Big Three networks. *WWE Smackdown!* led the ratings for the network.

Another network called the WB was backed by multimedia conglomerate Time Warner. WB Network launched in 1995 with comedies at its core, including *Father Knows Nothing* and *Unhappily Ever After.* If these programs seem suggestive of Fox series, perhaps this is because the WB Network was led at launch by two of Fox's founders: Jamie Kellner and Garth Ancier. WB found some success with shows like *7th Heaven* and *Smallville;* and as the 1990s came to an end, WB seemed to be outpacing UPN, propelled primarily by the success of two shows with followings (especially among teenagers)—*Buffy the Vampire Slayer* and *Dawson's Creek.* However, neither network attracted more than 5 percent of the prime-time TV audience overall, and both reported to their shareholders that they were losing money. But that wasn't enough to keep another competitor from entering the fray.

Pax TV, founded by longtime TV station owner Lowell "Bud" Paxson, launched in fall 1998. Unlike WB and UPN, which aggressively courted the teenage,

For many years, various groups critical of the television ownership policies by the FCC have pointed to the fact that women and minorities do not control broadcasting in the same proportion as the general population. A study titled "Out of the Picture 2007: Minority and Female TV Station Ownership in the U.S." provided some troubling statistics about who owns American broadcasting properties:

- Women make up 51 percent of the U.S. population but own only 5.87 percent of all full-power commercial television stations.

- Minorities make up 34 percent of the population but own only 43 stations. That works out to less than 4 percent of all full-power stations.

- Blacks make up 13 percent of the entire population but own only 8 stations (less than 1 percent of all stations).

- Hispanics and Latinos make up 15 percent of the population but own only 1.25 percent of stations (17 stations).

- Asians make up 4.5 percent of the population but own only 13 stations (less than 1 percent).

- Non-Hispanic white owners control 81.9 percent of all full-time television stations in the United States.

This disparity is even more striking when it is compared with other sectors in the U.S. economy. For example, minorities own 18 percent of all nonfarm U.S. businesses but only 3 percent of commercial broadcast stations.

In the past two decades there has been considerable pressure for media companies to consolidate. The Telecommunications Act of 1996 lifted caps on the number of stations that a group can own. Since then there has been a 40 percent decline in the number of stations owned by minorities.

Many programming executives say ownership is less important than the types of programs that are aired by the stations. They say television programs are created for the intended audience, and that includes women and minorities. So, in theory, any market with a substantial minority population will have programs reflecting their interests. But several studies have shown that minority-owned stations emphasize issues of presumed interest to those populations more than do group-owned stations; and minority-owned stations air more minority-related news programming than do comparable white-controlled stations.

Do you think Congress should direct the FCC to find ways to encourage more diversity in broadcast station ownership?

inner-city crowd, Pax TV targeted older, more conservative audiences (perhaps because Paxson was an evangelical Christian and proponent of "family values"). The anchor programs for Pax TV were reruns of the popular CBS shows *Dr. Quinn, Medicine Woman; Diagnosis Murder;* and *Touched by an Angel.* Early ratings for the new network were meeting their projections. That's the good news; the bad was that these projections called for only 1 in 100 TV households (a rating of 1). In 2007 the network became ION television, and soon after changed its strategy, refocusing the network to the 18–49 demographic. ION now repackages syndicated more youthful programming such as *My Name Is Earl, Criminal Minds,* and *Without a Trace.* In 2009 the network introduced original programming with an unscripted show starring Emeril Lagasse. It also negotiated deals with major studio networks to air recent movie releases.

In early 2006, CBS and Time Warner announced that they were pulling the plugs on the two money-losing ventures and decided to jointly create CW (C for CBS and W for Warner Brothers). The new CW targeted the 18 to 34 demographic, pulling some ratings with shows like *90210, America's Next Top Model,* and *The Vampire Diaries.*

Both UPN and WB had a large number of affiliated stations, and combining the two left some stations, many owned by News Corp and Sinclair, without a network affiliation. Then Rupert Murdoch stepped forward and announced the creation of MyNetworkTV (MNTV), a companion network to Fox. MyNetwork debuted in the fall 2006 season, programming 2 hours a night, Monday through Saturday. Currently MyNetwork is more like a syndicated programming service showing reruns of *Law and Order: Criminal Intent, Monk,* and *Deal or No Deal.* The only deviation from this strategy seems to

American Idol: American Idol has been a ratings powerhouse for FOX. Even though the show starts in the spring season, strong ratings help both the network and local stations during spring sweeps.

be the continued broadcast of *WWE Friday Night Smackdown*. Rating for 2009 improved when MyNet's lineup switched from new to syndicated programming.

The End of Network Television?

With seven networks competing for audiences (especially in prime time) and with growing attention paid by viewers to cable, home video, and the Internet, some observers have speculated that network television is a dinosaur business. Through the 2000s, audiences shrank, program costs rose, and advertising revenues have been lackluster. The result is that a TV network is no longer the steady source of corporate profits it used to be. For example, the Television Advertising Bureau says that the combined revenue of the big four networks was about $22 billion in 2009, down from $25 billion in 2005. But profits are a different story. The four major networks sold about $16.8 billion in spots for 2005 but generated few profits. Fox, the number one network in the key 18–49 demographic in 2009, reported a mere $18 million in revenue despite several billion in ad sales. CBS said that network revenue declined 40 percent despite the fact that it had 12 of the top 20 shows for the season. With the economic recession of 2008 the average cost for a 30-second prime-time spot de-

clined 15 percent to about $122,000. Because much of broadcast television's revenue is from advertising, ratings and the overall economic health of the economy heavily influence revenue. The television network business is complicated and fickle.

Will network TV go away? Unlikely. Even at their worst, network programs still attract larger audiences than do most cable networks, DVD rentals, and the Internet. Think of the size of the audience for the Super Bowl—or for an episode of *American Idol, Grey's Anatomy,* or *CSI.* It's many times larger (usually by a factor of 10 or more) than the number of people watching wrestling on cable or watching videos on YouTube. But with escalating production costs and talent fees, reducing overhead as a way of maximizing revenue has become a way of life at the TV networks. Jeff Zucker, chief at NBC Universal, was quoted in *The New York Times* saying, "Broadcast television is in a time of tremendous transition, and if we don't attempt to change the model now, we could be in danger of becoming the automobile industry or the newspaper industry."

LOCAL TELEVISION

The major networks seem to get all the attention in the TV business, even though they account for only half of all the advertising revenue spent on the

Figure 5–2

Rating the TV Stations

	VHF	UHF
Network O&Os	★★★★★	★★★★
Big Four network affiliates	★★★★	★★★
CW/Pax affiliates	★★★	★★
Independents	★	★
Low-power TV	½★	½★

medium. This section looks at where the rest of the dollars go—to about 1,300 commercial TV stations.

Figure 5–2 rates the various types of TV stations in economic terms. The rankings range from "five-star" stations, which traditionally have been the most profitable, to "one-star" stations, which have faced considerable financial hardship and even apathy among America's TV households.

Television's Biggest Winners: Network Owned-and-Operated Stations

At the top of the rankings of commercial TV stations there are those that are owned outright by the corporate parents of the four established TV networks—ABC, Fox, CBS, and NBC. In industry parlance, these are owned-and-operated stations, or O&Os for short. These are the five-star stations in Figure 5–2.

Network O&Os have traditionally been the most profitable of all TV stations and are considered the flagship stations of their networks. Situated in the largest TV markets, they often boast the call letters of their networks. As a result of the recent merger, Comcast is the new owner of NBC-Universal as well as being the parent of WNBC and WNJU in New York and KNBC in Los Angeles, plus stations in Chicago, Philadelphia, Boston, Miami, and Washington, DC. CBS owns WCBS in New York and KCBS and KCAL in Los Angeles, as well as other stations in Boston, Minneapolis, Chicago, and Miami. Disney/ABC O&Os include WABC (New York), KABC (Los Angeles), plus TV stations in Chicago, San Francisco, Philadelphia, and Houston. Purchasing its own stations has been a cornerstone of the Fox strategy to achieve parity with the other major networks.

It has invested hundreds of millions of dollars to purchase such stations as WNYW in New York, KTTV and KCOP in Los Angeles, WTTG in Washington, KRIV in Houston, and WFLD in Chicago. Most of the networks own more than one station in New York, Los Angeles, and Chicago, the three largest television markets in the country.

Ownership by a major network guarantees a steady supply of programming to these stations and a high profile for potential advertisers. Owned-and-operated stations are typically local news leaders in their marketplace. The fact that they emanate from the corporate or regional headquarters of their networks permits economies of scale and access to programming and personalities that other stations can't match. Traditionally, extended local news shows will generate quite a bit of cash for these stations.

For these reasons network O&Os have been the most profitable of all TV stations. When there were only three networks a annual profit margins above 50 percent were commonplace. Given the modern marketplace, with so many different forms of media, profit margins are much lower. But, even as the ratings of their parent networks decline, O&Os remain cash cows for their companies, returning, on average, more than 30 cents in profit for each dollar of sales economic downturns notwithstanding. So while NBC, CBS, ABC, and Fox may lose money producing programs for the networks, they make money showing them on their O&O stations.

Second Place Finishers: Major Network Affiliates

The second most profitable class of TV facilities consists of those stations affiliated with a major network but owned by a different entity. In industry parlance, such stations are network-affiliated stations, or **affiliates** for short. Traditionally, the best affiliation to have was with one of the three "old guard" networks, ABC, CBS, and NBC. Like O&Os, most of these affiliates have been leaders in local news and public service in their communities. Many have been in operation since the dawn of TV (the early 1950s), and over the years they have cultivated enormous goodwill among their viewers.

But the world of TV affiliation has changed dramatically in recent years. Since 2000, ad revenues for affiliated stations have declined more than 30 percent. In addition, stations often are asked to pony up money to cover the cost of certain high-profile sports programs.

In the wake of the changing media landscape, many stations that once boasted strong, independent news organizations have partnered with former competitors to jointly produce newscasts. Today the FCC allows one company to own stations and manage competing stations in the same market. Some stations are trying new ways to supplement spot advertising by enhancing their Web sites and developing mobile applications that can enhance their audience size.

Today about 200 stations each are aligned with CBS, NBC, ABC, and Fox. Many group owners such as Gannett, Hearst-Argyle, and Cox Broadcasting own large numbers of network-affiliated stations.

CW, MyNetwork, and ION Affiliates

Affiliates of these newer networks are next in our hierarchy of TV station profitability. CW has more than 100 stations that carry its programming; some of these stations are low-power stations, and some outlets are channels on the local cable franchise. Ion TV, which launched as PAX in late 1998, covers about 75 percent of U.S. TV households with about 95 affiliates.

In Figure 5–2 we grant two stars to those that are full-service stations broadcasting on the DTV band. Some stations, such as CW's legendary KTLA in Los Angeles and WPIX in New York, are large, full-service operations that can generate substantial revenues for their owners. However, the overwhelming majority of CW, ION, and MyNetwork affiliates tend to be smaller stations that rely on cable to extend their reach. But viewers will find their shows regardless of where they are.

Independents: A Vanishing Breed

An **independent TV station** is one that does not align itself with a major network. With seven networks from which to choose, independent TV stations appear to be a vanishing breed. With each new edition of this book fewer and fewer stations have been relying on their libraries of movies, syndicated programs, and local professional sports to fill their program schedules. In 2005 fewer than 50 stations were not affiliated with ABC, CBS, NBC, Fox, or one of the newer networks; however, that figure changes as the network scene shifts.

Unlike affiliated stations, independent stations have to develop programming for the entire broadcast day, seven days a week. Also, while affiliates get a boost from shows with high network ratings (*CSI*, for example), indies have to do much more promotion in the local market. For this reason, we assign one star to independents. In major markets, an independent station can be a strong competitor. Los Angeles's KCAL (channel 9), with strong news programming, was a very profitable station. In recent years many independents have been purchased by large broadcast companies and share resources with their sister stations. In some markets an indie is the home broadcaster of a local baseball or basketball team, so revenues can be quite good. However, in smaller markets, where the stations are likely to have fewer resources, the remaining independents struggle for viewers and advertising support.

Low Power to the People: LPTV

The FCC authorized **low-power television** service in 1982. There are three types of stations. LPTV stations are low-power outlets that may rebroadcast TV signals from other stations or originate their own programming. Class A stations fall under the Community Broadcast Protection Act and must generate at least three hours of locally produced programming per week. TV translators rebroadcast a full-service station, usually to a community that cannot receive the original signal.

Originally LPTV was created to increase opportunities for minority ownership of TV stations and to increase the number of broadcast offerings in a community. To promote minority investing in these stations, the FCC promulgated rules that would show preference for minority applicants. The FCC hoped that if it increased the number of TV stations that served those communities, niche programming services to small communities that cannot sustain a full-power TV station would develop.

An LPTV station may operate as long as its signal does not interfere with that of another station on the same channel, but those stations that qualify as Class A receive interference protection under FCC rules. And while there are fewer program-related regulations, the FCC still enforces a ban on obscene material.

Today nearly 3,000 LPTV stations are in operation. While most are located mainly in rural areas (Alaska has the most LPTV stations), many large cities boast a number of LPTV stations. Many have faced financial hardship to date. In most cases LPTV operations have been unable to compete with affiliates and full-power independents for attractive programming, although there are LPTV affilates for all the television networks. Their limited broadcast range sometimes makes it difficult for a station to interest advertisers in the medium. This is why we place LPTV at the bottom of our rankings of TV stations, with only one-half star.

However, LPTV still holds promise as a venue for special-interest and minority programs, and there are no limits to the number of LPTV stations that an entity can own. Spanish-language services like Univision and GEM have aligned with LPTV stations. Not all LPTV stations have converted to digital transmission. The FCC did not require LPTV stations to meet the 2009 conversion deadline, so many are still analog.

Table 5–1	Television Station Penetration, 2007
CBS Corp.	35.65%
ION Media Networks	31.86
Fox Media Stations	31.36
NBC	30.41
Tribune	27.53
ABC TV Stations	23.17
Univision Communications	22.97
Trinity Broadcasting	17.89
Gannett	16.44
Hearst-Argyle	15.28

Source: *Broadcasting & Cable*, April 14, 2008, p. 20.

From *The Market Share Reporter*—2010.

Note that new figures reflecting the change to DTV have not been released. Stations are ranked by the percentages of television homes that they reach.

TV STATION OWNERSHIP

Generally, one wouldn't ask "who" owns a TV station but would ask "what." Television stations are so expensive that few individuals can afford to own them. Instead most TV stations are owned by companies that own other stations and networks or by investment groups.

For many years, TV station ownership was strictly regulated, with the number of stations a group could own limited to 12, to prevent concentration. Recent years have seen significant streamlining of TV station ownership. Today a single TV group can own as many TV stations as it likes, as long as the total number of U.S. TV homes reached by those stations does not exceed 39 percent of the population. However, even that restriction may be relaxed in coming years. The leading TV group owners are listed in Table 5–1.

Today CBS is the largest station owner, with 27 stations reaching 35.65 percent of TV households. The leading CBS-owned stations include New York's WCBS, Los Angeles's KCBS and KCAL, and Chicago's WBMM. CBS also owns stations in Philadelphia, Boston, Dallas, Atlanta, Detroit, and even Green Bay, Wisconsin, and Austin, Texas.

ION Media Networks is the second largest station owner, with 53 stations reaching 31.86 percent of TV households. However, none of these stations has a dial position lower than 14 (WPXA in Atlanta). Paxson has UHF channel positions in New York, Los Angeles, Chicago, and Philadelphia, but many Pax-owned sta-

tions are in smaller cities, like San Antonio, Texas; Knoxville, Tennessee; and Cedar Rapids, Iowa.

Fox Media comes in third with 27 stations that reach 31.36 percent of the nation's population. The leading Fox-owned stations include New York's WYNY and WWOR, Los Angeles's KTTV and KCOP, and Chicago's WFLD. Fox also owns stations in Philadelphia, Boston, Dallas, Atlanta, Houston, and even Birmingham, Alabama, and Austin, Texas.

Other leading TV group owners include Tribune NBC, Tribune ABC, Univisions Communication, and Trinity Broadcasting. These companies, and the others in Table 5–2, also hold other diversified media interests, including networks, newspapers, and cable systems.

It should be noted that station penetration may have been affected by the 2009 switch to DTV. As of this edition, 2010 figures were not available.

PUBLIC TELEVISION

Not all TV stations are in it for the money (at least not overtly). More than 380 TV stations are considered noncommercial operations. These stations, owned primarily by governmental organizations, universities and school boards, and religious organizations, form the backbone of an often-struggling but ongoing alternative to commercial TV and cable, the public television service. Most of these stations are affiliated with the Public Broadcasting Service (PBS) network.

Table 5–2	Top Cable and DBS Operators	
Rank	**MSO**	**Basic Video Subscribers**
1	Comcast Corporation	23,447,000
2	DirecTV	18,660,000
3	Dish Network Corporation	14,337,000
4	Time Warner Cable, Inc.	12,817,000
5	Cox Communications, Inc.*	5,100,000
6	Charter Communications, Inc.	4,801,000
7	Cablevision Systems Corporation	3,064,000
8	Verizon Communications, Inc.	3,029,000
9	AT&T, Inc.	2,295,000
10	Bright House Networks LLC*	2,257,000
11	Suddenlink Communications*	1,244,000
12	Mediacom Communications Corporation	1,234,000
13	Insight Communications Company, Inc.	723,000
14	CableOne, Inc.	667,000
15	WideOpenWest Networks, LLC*	396,000
16	RCN Corp.	361,000
17	Bresnan Communications*	303,000
18	Atlantic Broadband Group, LLC	275,000
19	Armstrong Cable Services	245,000
20	Knology Holdings	236,000
21	Service Electric Cable TV Incorporated*	225,000
22	Midcontinent Communications	212,000
23	MetroCast Cablevision	182,000
24	Blue Ridge Communications*	174,000
25	General Communications	149,000

Source: NCTA Top 25 Multichannel Video Programming Distributors as of March 2010, 1–25.
*contains estimates from SNL Kagan

In 2009, PBS celebrated its 40th anniversary. There was much to celebrate. Founded in 1970, PBS took over the functions of the old National Educational Television service. Today it provides programming to 169 licensees operating 348 member stations serving the United States, Puerto Rico, the Virgin Islands, Guam, and Samoa. Nearly 90 million people in the United States watch PBS in a typical week, including about 35 million children. The fiscal year 2005 budget for PBS was $340 million. Approximately 75 percent of the budget goes to programming and promotion, while another 7 percent is spent on satellite distribution.

In some ways PBS operates as commercial networks do. It provides a means of national distribution of programs (its satellite distribution network was operational in 1978, before those of NBC, CBS, and ABC). Its national programs attract a loyal following, from *Sesame Street* to *Nova* and *Masterpiece Theater*. But PBS differs from the commercial networks in some important ways. Generally programs are produced by one or more large PBS stations such as WNET in Newark–New York, WGBH in Boston, and KCET in Los Angeles. These larger producing stations hold a great deal of power in determining which programs will be produced. Some long-running series like *Masterpiece Theater* and *Nova* are frequently coproductions with the BBC or another international broadcasting entity.

Public TV programs rarely try to match the ratings of those on commercial TV. In fact, the PBS audience is typically 2 percent of the homes in the United States; however, while that seems small, remember that 2 percent equals the size of the audiences for TLC, Bravo, MSNBC, PAX, and CNBC combined! The highest-rated PBS series of all time, Ken Burns's *The Civil War*, attracted an average of just under 9 percent of U.S. homes, a figure that would probably have led to its quick cancellation were it a series on ABC, CBS, or NBC. To put this into perspective remember that 9 percent of more than 115 million households represents a large number of viewers. Its national programs attract a loyal following, from *Sesame Street* to *Nova* and *Masterpiece Theater*.

The audience for public TV reflects the overall U.S. population demographically. PBS viewers tend to be important opinion leaders in their communities. A high proportion have college and advanced degrees and hold key leadership positions in government, business, education, and the arts in their communities.

Surveys find that the viewing audience has come to rely on public television for some of its programs, particularly its news reports (especially the highly regarded *The Nightly NewsHour*) and children's programs (*Sesame Street, Between the Lions,* and the like). That the public supports public television is borne out by the fact that viewers pledge nearly $500 million each year to local public TV stations. That equates to about 55 percent of all revenues for the stations.

Public television was an early advocate of digital television, and in some large cities, the PBS stations were broadcasting in high definition before local commercial stations. In addition to high-definition programming, PBS has been expanding services online and on multiple platforms.

PBS kids' series *Between the Lions* is one of many educational shows on public television.

CABLE TELEVISION

As we all know, there is a lot more to TV than can be tuned in with a pair of rabbit-ear antennas atop the TV set. In fact, for most television viewers, the set-top or rooftop antenna has become a relic of the past. With its impressive roster of program services; its multiplicity of channels; and its promise of better pictures, better sound, and even Internet access and other services, cable TV today has overtaken the traditional TV networks as having the most viewers during prime time (and most other times).

Over the years, cable has grown in gross revenues, from small mom-and-pop operations carrying local channels to a huge business in its own right. In 1980, for example, cable was a $3 billion business—about a fourth the size of the TV business. Today cable revenues hover around $89 billion annually. Advertising revenue for cable channels exceeds the total revenues of all over-the-air TV networks.

At one time virtually all cable systems were 12-channel operations. Attaching the TV set to the cable generally filled most of the channels from 2 to 13. In the mid-1970s new cable systems offered 35 channels, requiring most TV homes to have a converter box. By the 1980s many older systems were upgraded, and new franchises were awarded to companies pro-

viding 54 or more channels. New technologies like fiber optics and digital compression enabled many cable systems in the 1990s to boast well over 100 channels as the number of cable networks exploded. By 2003 there were nearly 280 nationally distributed cable networks available to cable operators. Today digital cable and pay-per-view offerings have made the cable universe even larger.

Nationwide, more than two-thirds of the cable systems, representing three-fourths of all cable viewers, provide over 100 different channels of programming. The average subscriber can view 80 or more cable channels. That's an increase of almost 70 percent since 2000. However, studies indicate that the majority of households generally watch fewer than 20 channels regularly.

Clearly cable provides more viewing alternatives. Whether more TV is better TV is an important question that we address in some detail in a later chapter.

Cable Programming

The cable business today is something like a shopping mall. There may be room for 100 retail stores in a new mall, but how many will actually sign a lease? Which stores will be most popular with shoppers and thereby take the lion's share of the profits? While

Profile: Chief Faces Many Challenges to Ensure PBS Survival

The president of the nation's Public Broadcasting Service, Paula Kerger, has many obstacles to conquer over the next few years to ensure that PBS survives. Kerger, a veteran of one of the nation's largest PBS stations, WNET in New York, took the reins of PBS in 2006 amid a scandal that rocked CPB (the Corporation for Public Broadcasting) and PBS (see Chapter 9).

Finding funding for public television has always been a struggle. During the Bush years, a more conservative Congress questioned its investment in a TV service whose output has been accused of being decidedly liberal. Despite studies that indicated that PBS was balanced in programming, the Bush administration continued to push for cuts, proposing a 56 percent cut for the 2010 year. Interestingly, the timing of the proposal to cut funding for PBS coincided with the airing of a *Frontline* documentary titled *Bush's War. Frontline*, the award-winning documentary series, examined the Iraq war over the previous five years. Kerger dismissed the notion that PBS would bow to political pressure, saying it was unrealistic "to expect that every single program will represent all points of view."

Corporate underwriting for public television programs has similarly faced a decline. Large corporate sponsors General Motors, IBM, and others have faced rounds of belt-tightening, mergers, and acquisitions. Support for the arts is often a casualty of such events under the banner of "downsizing." Like Congress, large corporations are not fond of funding programs they sometimes find are at cross-purposes with their lobbying activities or their corporate agendas.

Keeping PBS free from outside political influences while maintaining a sufficient budget to develop important new programs is part of Kerger's responsibilities. New media, the growth of alternative cable programming, and a traditional struggle from PBS stations for more say in decision making have posed significant challenges as well.

For her part, Kerger has said that she wants to strengthen public TV's offerings on new media platforms but acknowledges that PBS doesn't have the same deep pockets as the media conglomerates, which control most of the broadcasting and cable networks. Experts think that PBS will have to push past "survival mentality" mode and into establishing an interactive relationship with its audience.

Mending relations with Congress will be important for PBS, but Kerger is no stranger to Washington. She earned her degree from the University of Maryland and got her first job at UNICEF headquarters in Washington. In her first few years at PBS she worked to grow PBS's online presence and to make children's programming accessible across multiple platforms. Whether PBS can thrive in the new digital environment is perhaps the issue that will determine Paula Kerger's success.

---

some stores will be mass merchandisers, attempting to bring in lots of customers with discounting practices and volume sales, others will be specialty stores or boutiques, aiming at a narrowly selected clientele (like teens for Old Navy, college students for Abercrombie, young adults for the Gap, and professional males for Brooks Brothers). The same situation applies in the quest for cable audiences.

There are well over 300 national and 80 regional program services available to cable, with more in the planning stages. Some are mass marketers appealing to a diverse audience, like Sears or Macy's; others are boutiques, like Banana Republic or the Sharper Image.

For convenience, cable programming can be divided into three broad classifications: basic cable services, pay cable services, and specialty services. Let's examine each in detail.

Basic Cable Services   The backbone of cable is its lineup of basic services. These are the program ser-

vices available for the lowest subscription charge. There are two main types of programming found in basic services: local and regional broadcast signals and advertiser-supported cable services. Certain federal requirements mandate that local channels must be carried on the basic service.

From "Must Carry" to "Retransmission Consent": Local/Regional Broadcast Signals
For years cable systems were obligated to provide space on their systems to retransmit local TV stations within their communities. These rules prevented the cable company from substituting a distant signal for the local station. Such rules, known as "must carry," were declared unconstitutional in 1985. Local broadcasters fought diligently in the ensuing years to reinstate the rules and to receive some form of compensation for cable carriage of their services. In 1993 new regulations were implemented by the FCC to resolve this dispute after Congress passed the Cable Television

Political debate is no longer relegated to Sunday morning news programming. Many politicians, including Vice-President Biden, have made appearances on the Daly show and other entertainment venues.

Consumer Protection and Competition Act of 1992. Broadcasters were instructed to choose either "must carry" or "retransmission consent." With a selection of must carry, the cable company was required to air the local TV station's program schedule in its entirety, but the broadcaster was not entitled to compensation. Broadcasters choosing retransmission consent were required to negotiate some form of compensation from the cable system in return for their signals being carried on the cable.

In the wake of the new rules, the leading station groups generally made their stations available free to local cable operators. In return, as compensation, many were provided channel space on cable systems for new services, such as regional news channels (see Chapter 9). Networks negotiated for retransmission consent and received new space on cable systems. They created secondary services like ESPN2, the FX network, ABC Family, and MSNBC.

The net effect of the rules is that most cable systems continue to carry the programming of most TV stations in their service area. Even today, local and regional broadcast channels remain the backbone of basic cable programming despite growing ratings for cable network programming.

In the last few years, local stations and networks have pressed cable companies for a larger share of compensation in return for the rights to rebroadcast programs. Cable and television companies have been waging public campaigns, each side saying the other is being unreasonable. This situation came to an ugly head in 2010 when WABC decided to withhold coverage of the Academy Awards from Cablevision customers. Disney, the parent company of ABC, pulled the signal at 12:01 a.m. on the day of the broadcast. Three million viewers in the New York City area were blacked out as the awards ceremony began; but 40 minutes into the program an agreement was reached, and the program was restored.

As programming costs increase, broadcasters will push for larger revenues from retransmission consent agreements.

Advertiser-Supported Basic Cable Services   The second classification of basic cable services is advertiser-supported cable networks, which are program services specifically designed to reach cable audiences. Like the broadcast networks (ABC, CBS, NBC, and Fox), they carry national advertising. They also provide opportunities for local cable systems to place their own advertising spots.

Topping the list of the leading ad-supported cable networks are USA and TNT. Also highly rated are ABC Family, TBS, Fox News, ESPN, CNN, Cartoon Network, the Arts and Entertainment Network (A&E), Nickelodeon, and the Lifetime Channel. Some basic services are dedicated to women (Lifetime and Oxygen), while others are geared toward sports fans (ESPN), some to education and information (Discovery and The Learning Channel), and some to genres of music (Country Music Television).

The Home and Garden Channel (HGTV), Food Network, Versus (formerly OLN), CNBC, The Weather Channel, Court TV, and many others succeed in reaching niche audiences by providing specialized fare to the cable viewer.

The Disney Channel is frequently rated among the top cable nets, although it is not ad-supported. However, it is usually included in the extended basic tier on most cable systems.

Digital Services As cable companies ramped up for providing high-definition services, many companies added capacity to transmit digital signals to their customers. Often the digital tier is priced as an add-on to the enhanced basic service. With digital cable, customers can frequently access 150 or more channels, many in high definition. In 2010 the National Cable and Telecommunications Association claimed that digital cable had grown from fewer than 10 million customers in 2000 to more than 42 million customers in 2010.

A growing trend in digital cable is to broadly offer more channels for a higher monthly fee. One trend is to add international channels, like RAI Italia (Italian TV), ART (Arab Radio and Television), and Russian TV, along with Spanish versions of ESPN, History, CNN, and other advertiser-supported networks.

Pay Services Pay services became popular in cable in the 1970s as a source of home viewing of theatrical motion pictures, major sports events, and entertainment specials. They are called pay services because subscribers must pay an additional fee to receive the service. Their selling feature is original programming that is not available on broadcast TV, most typically commercial-free movies and home-team sports.

The giant of pay cable is Time Warner's Home Box Office. HBO boasts 28 million households, a little more than one in three TV homes in the United States. It easily leads all pay services in the number of subscribers. Time Warner also owns Cinemax and counts the two services together when talking about number of subscribers. Viacom's two services, Showtime and The Movie Channel, are chief competitors to HBO and Cinemax. These services are seen in 16.5 million homes. Starz has seen tremendous growth in recent years and boasts 17 million subscribers. Other pay services with a movie emphasis include Encore with 2.9 million subscribers, The Sundance Channel, MGM HD, and Universal HD; These are usually packaged in special tiers, sometimes with other services. Many subscribers have movie "packages" that may provide more than one pay movie service.

Regional sports services represent a strong and growing segment of pay cable programming. Fox scion Rupert Murdoch has made a specialty in recent years of acquiring regional sports channels around the country (as well as owning teams, like the L.A. Dodgers and the Manchester United soccer club). Viewers pay an extra fee each month to watch the exploits of their favorite teams on Fox Sports Chicago or Fox Sports New York and more than a dozen other regional Fox outlets. However, Fox hasn't bought them all (at least not yet). New York sports fans can subscribe to Yankees Entertainment and Sports (YES) Network, unless they're Mets fans, of course, and people in the Boston area can see their beloved Red Sox, Celtics, and Bruins on New England Sports Network (NESN). Those more interested in other teams can choose the Big Ten Network, CBS College Sports, and other services like ESPN GamePlan, NBA League Pass, and NHL Center Ice. These pay-per-view sports packages are gaining in popularity.

Not all the battles are played on the field, however; a number of skirmishes over who will control the rights to broadcast high-profile teams seem to be brewing. The ruckus off the field was most intense in large cities like New York, Philadelphia, Washington, and Los Angeles. Comcast, which runs regional sports channels on its cable systems, had refused to share regional programming with satellite providers; it has the cable franchises in many of the top 25 markets, giving it special access to sports in these cities. In January 2010 the FCC ruled that distributors who did not make their networks available to competitors on reasonable terms would be in violation of its program access rules.

Specialty Services Some additional services available from cable include public service channels like C-SPAN, regional news channels, electronic program guides (EPGs), local governmental channels, jukebox-style music channels (like Music Choice), many shopping channels, even a channel devoted to state lotteries (The Lottery Channel), and local weather.

One way to categorize stations is by the channels on which they broadcast. Prior to the conversion, stations that broadcast on channels 2 to 13 were called **VHF,** or **very high frequency,** stations. Those stations that broadcast on channel 14 and above were called **UHF,** or **ultra-high frequency,** stations.

VHF frequencies had been the preferred channels for broadcasters. During the 1950s and most of the 1960s, TV sets often did not have the capability to receive UHF signals. The quality of the UHF signal was also judged to be inferior to that of a VHF signal. Because of the lower frequencies used in the VHF band, these stations tended to provide better reception for viewers than their UHF counterparts.

In 2009, when analog TV channels were replaced by digital channels, the distinctions disappeared because most DTV channel assignments were in the UHF band. The question in the mind of many VHF station managers was whether the public would find the new higher-numbered channels. Since the beginning of television service, stations had spent millions promoting themselves and their channel assignments. (New Yorkers, for example, always thought of channel 2 being CBS.)

Fortunately, with digital technology came the ability to "virtualize" the channel assignment. What this meant was that even though the new digital signal was most likely on a different channel assignment than the original, the converter box displayed the old number. So even though good old WCBS-TV in New York was assigned the UHF DTV channel 33, digital converter boxes saw it as the old VHF channel 2. The cable system in New York kept the station on channel 2, so for the majority of viewers there was no change, except the station was now capable of broadcasting in high definition, whereas the old channel 2 was strictly an analog station.

The reassignment and virtualization had an impact on cable too. Cable systems had reassigned many local UHF stations to lower channel numbers; and in the conversion, they simply kept that assignment. In Syracuse the FOX affiliate WSYT was originally assigned by the FCC to UHF channel 68, but it appeared on the local cable system as channel 8. So the station advertised itself as "WSYT FOX—Channel 68 and Cable 8." When the DTV reassignment occurred, WSYT's reassignment became channel 19. However, the station still calls itself channel 68, and it still appears on cable channel 8. Confused yet?

Over the last five years noncable services have really taken off. Today cable is the largest supplier of broadband Internet services and is beginning to provide full telephone services (VoIP). While most people pick cable because of its television implications of more channels, broadband services are rapidly expanding (see Chapter 6) by providing video downloads to mobile devices and home computers. Before we look at the Internet, let's look at how the cable industry prices and packages its program offerings.

Packaging Cable Services: The Trail of "Tiers"

Cable is marketed to attract different types of customer households. The monthly charge for basic service has been regulated by the FCC to keep cable affordable to most homes in the United States and to guarantee carriage of most popular services (including local broadcast services and some of the ad-supported basic services discussed earlier). These regulations were eliminated in 1999 amid a loud outcry from consumer groups concerned about escalating cable rates.

While the majority of revenue to cable companies is provided by basic subscribers, profitability in the cable business is often based on the number of homes that upgrade to higher levels of service. To create different service levels, cable operators package their offerings in groups, with each succeeding level costing more per month. This process is known as **tiering.** Let's trace the trail of "tiers," from initial wiring of a home for cable to attracting the most lucrative cable households.

Types of Cable Households   In the cable business not all homes are created equal. Cable companies make clear distinctions between the types of households in their service areas, on the basis of which program options they elect. The various types of TV homes in the United States can be viewed as a pyramid, as illustrated in Figure 5–3.

Homes Passed   The base of the pyramid consists of those households in the United States that are in an area served by cable TV. This statistic is known as

Figure 5–3

The Cable Subscriber Pyramid

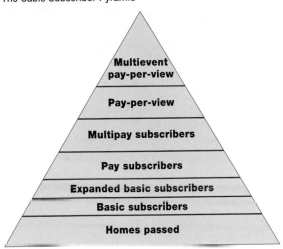

Multievent pay-per-view

Pay-per-view

Multipay subscribers

Pay subscribers

Expanded basic subscribers

Basic subscribers

Homes passed

Total U.S. TV households

homes passed (HP). Homes passed are all households that could subscribe to a cable system if they wanted to. The cable literally passes by these households.

In real numbers, there are about 115 million homes with TVs in the United States. About 112 million homes are located in an area served by cable, for an HP figure of about 97 percent.

Cable Households   The next level of the pyramid includes those HPs that decide to subscribe to cable TV. This figure can be calculated as the ratio of subscriber households to HPs. The resulting percentage is sometimes called the cable system's **basic penetration.** For example, if a cable system passes 100 homes and 85 take the cable, the basic penetration rate is 85 percent. Obviously a cable operator would like all HPs to take cable service—that is, a penetration rate of 100 percent. This ideal world does not exist. The percentage of households that elect to subscribe varies widely in cable areas. Some suburban systems have enough "upscale" consumer households to boast over 90 percent basic penetration. Other systems, including many in poor inner-city and rural areas, report penetration rates below 50 percent. Industrywide, about 48 percent of all HPs are cable subscribers, about 61 million homes.

Digital cable uses compression technology, and it can provide many more channels than standard analog cable. Some digital basic systems provide special

services and demand services, such as start over and pause, along with the basic channels.

Pay Households   Those cable homes that pay an additional fee for the pay services listed earlier (such as HBO or Showtime) are known as **pay households.** Through the period of cable's massive growth—from the mid-1970s to the mid-1980s—as many as 90 percent of all cable subscribers also took a pay service. Faced with competition from new media outlets (mainly video stores, DVDs, and the Internet), the percentage of pay units began to drop in the late 1990s. Today about 52 million homes have some sort of premium cable service, representing about three-quarters of cable homes and about 45 percent of all TV households in the United States.

Multipay Households   There are two types of pay cable households: those that elect just one pay service and those that subscribe to more than one. The homes that take more than one service are known as **multipay households.**

Multipay subscribers pay the biggest cable bills—$75–$100 per month or more—much of which is additional profit for the cable company because it can negotiate reduced rates from pay services to "bundle" its program offerings and because pay tiers are not regulated by the FCC.

Pay-per-View   Near the top of the subscriber pyramid are those households that can choose their pay programming selectively by ordering it as desired from the cable company. This is known as **pay-per-view (PPV).**

PPV requires special cable technology. Pay-per-view homes require cable boxes that can be isolated by the cable company and separately programmed (so that only the home that orders the event will receive it). Such devices are known as **addressable converters.** Addressable converters are available in most cable homes.

New digital technology gives subscribers many more options to choose which services they would like. These services may include premium movie channels and regional sports networks, as well as specialty program services (such as BBC America, high-definition channels, Music Choice, and on-demand services). Digital on-demand services require addressability at the cable headend but offer consumers new options. HBO On-demand, for example, allows the viewer to choose the start time for any movie currently playing on the channel.

At the top of the cable pyramid is **multievent PPV,** also known as *impulse PPV*. As digital cable channel capacity increases and addressability spreads, cable executives have begun delivering a wider choice of movies and special programs. Some cable systems are now offering movie releases that coincide with the release of the DVD home video version. Their hope is to have consumers purchase many different events each month on a PPV basis. Movies on demand provide the cable company with about a dollar in revenue for each rental.

Cable and MSO Ownership

Cable TV is different from broadcasting in one important respect. Whereas there is a history of federal caps on the number of broadcast stations that can be owned by a single entity, no such limits have been imposed on cable ownership. In other words, a cable entrepreneur can own as many systems and boast as many subscribers as can be amassed, subject to antitrust law and a rarely enforced cap of 30 percent of national households. Consequently the cable business is marked by a concentration of ownership by a large number of **multiple-system operators (MSOs).** Owners of only one system are known as **single-system operators (SSOs)** or simply **cable system operators (CSOs).** The MSOs dominate the business, as depicted in Table 5–2.

The largest cable MSO is Comcast with more than 23 million subscriber households. Next we find the two DBS providers, DirecTV and Dish Network.

(While they're not cable, you get a sense of the size of DBS.) The second largest cable MSO is Time Warner Cable, a subsidiary of the entertainment giant, which also owns HBO and Cinemax. Time Warner's cable systems amount to nearly 13 million homes. Comcast and Time Warner account for roughly 36 million subscriber households. This means that roughly 45 percent of all cable bills in the country are paid to one of these two huge companies. Other major MSOs include Charter, Cox, Cablevision Systems (the owner of the MSG Network, as well as the New York Knicks and the New York Rangers), Mediacom, and CableOne. Adelphia, which suffered from corporate scandals and bankruptcy in 2002, is in the process of being absorbed by Comcast and Time Warner.

The largest individual cable systems are located in major suburban areas and range from about 250,000 to about 3 million subscriber households. The largest systems are Cablevision's sprawling operation for the Greater New York area; followed by Comcast in Boston; Time Warner in Los Angeles; and Comcast's operations in Philadephia and Chicago. Table 5–3 shows the largest systems.

Cable Economics

Unfortunately it is difficult to evaluate cable systems using a five-star rating system as we did for the various types of television stations. But some industry rules of thumb can apply.

With high up-front capitalization and operations costs, it might appear that making money in cable is

Rank	Designated Market Area	Cable Penetration (%)	Cable Households
Table 5–3	**Top 10 Cable Markets in the United States**		
1	New York	79	5,869,550
2	Los Angeles	50	2,834,240
3	Philadelphia	75	2,208,540
4	Chicago	61	2,111,450
5	Boston (Manchester)	83	1,976,550
6	San Francisco–Oakland–San Jose	66	1,594,910
7	Washington, DC (Hagerstown)	64	1,467,570
8	Atlanta	59	1,370,720
9	Tampa–St. Petersburg–Sarasota	74	1,319,420
10	Detroit	65	1,244,480

Source: *Broadcasting and Cable Yearbook 2009.*

difficult, if not impossible. But the truth is that cable can be an enormously profitable enterprise. After all, few businesses find subscribers writing a check to them every month, year after year, "just for TV." While there will be an increase in revenues from advertising, the rise of PPV, and DVRs, many cable executives think that the largest share of additional revenue will come from broadband Internet and telephone services.

Despite enormous construction costs, cable systems can come quickly to profitability. Once systems pass the construction phase, expenses tend to become controllable, if not constant. For example, adding a new broadband or telephone service to an existing household might bring in $25 per month in fees but might cost only $5 to provide the service. Simple arithmetic indicates an 80 percent profit margin!

For these reasons cable operations have received good reports from financial analysts. The increasing value of cable systems is driven home by a key industry indicator: cost per subscriber. When a cable system is sold, cable investors and industry observers divide the sales price by the number of subscriber households to arrive at this figure. It is a good measure of how much a cable system is truly worth.

In 1977 the typical cable system sold for under $400 per subscriber. By 1980 the figure had risen to about $650. By 2005 Time Warner offered $3,500 per subscriber to take over Adelphia customers! Few industries can match the pace of this economic growth.

Not all is rosy for cable entities, though. In 2010 most cable companies saw a decrease in the number of subscribers. Some have gone to satellite TV, but a growing number of families are turning toward the Internet and mobile downloads for their television. In the last two years, Comcast, the nation's largest cable operator, lost about 500,000 subscribers.

DIRECT BROADCAST SATELLITES (DBS)

In less than a decade, direct broadcast satellite television service has grown to become an important competitor to cable television. Most people originally expected DBS to be a premium service for the video aficionado or a delivery vehicle for rural viewers who are unable to get cable. But since its inception in 1994, DBS has grown at a remarkable pace to serve nearly one of every four subscription television families in the United States. That translates into 33 million television homes.

Two DBS companies provide satellite television service in the United States. One provider is DirecTV, whose controlling interest is Fox Broadcasting's Rupert Murdoch; and the second service, Dish

DirecTV: Satellite television's subscription base continues to grow principally at the expense of rival cable systems.

Network, is owned by EchoStar Communications. Both DBS services provide a wide variety of programming from high-powered Ku-band satellites in geostationary orbits.

DBS Programming

DBS provides subscribers with a wide range of programming and pricing options. The number of channels available to the subscriber is tied to a monthly subscription fee, and satellite packages resemble cable tiers in the way program selection is accomplished. In addition, premium services like STARZ and HBO can be ordered to enhance the regular tier offering. At the low end, a subscriber will receive approximately 30 channels of service, with higher-priced services delivering up to more than 220 channels of programming.

One of the things that differentiated cable from satellite service was the carriage of local television channels. Advances in technology and changes in FCC rules made it possible for DBS to offer viewers local television channels in addition to the national programming services. At the moment satellite service provides local television channels to about 90 percent of all television households. For those who do not live in those markets, subscribers must use an outside television antenna and an A/B switch to receive local television service (including over-the-air network channels such as NBC and Fox). It should come as no surprise that an FCC study shows that where DBS provides local television service, satellite service penetration is much greater than in those markets that don't offer local channels.

Importantly, DBS tends to be priced less than cable for comparable services. This price advantage has helped entice some cable subscribers to switch to satellite service in recent years. In the last few years both DirecTV and Dish Network have been adding local television stations and DVRs to their systems. These services and aggressive pricing propelled sizable growth, but DBS providers are worried that bundled broadband and VoIP services will entice many consumers to stay with cable instead of switching to satellite.

DBS Today and Beyond

Satellite television has been a leader at using innovative technology. Currently DBS transmission standards are already digital, meaning that satellite pictures are pristinely clear. In addition, satellite television was an early provider of HD programming for subscribers with the televisions capable of displaying HD pictures.

Some of the other innovative services that direct broadcast satellite has introduced include digital video recorders (DVRs) that allow users to record programming directly to a computer hard disk and innovative satellite-to-home broadband Internet services like HughesNet. DBS can provide television signals where it is not profitable for cable to wire; and, unlike cable, DBS providers sell their hardware directly to customers at retail operations such as Best Buy, Radio Shack, and Wal mart or via the Internet.

Looking for new ways to compete with cable, Dish Network has introduced an online video portal that will allow viewers to watch live and recorded TV shows and movies via broadband connections.

Satellite television's outlook is not entirely without problems. During the economic recession many Americans began looking to broadband video as a replacement for both cable and satellite. While satellite packages tend to be slightly lower in price than cable, customers are often put off by poor customer service, and weather can be a factor in certain parts of the country.

Telco Fiber Optic Services

Verizon and AT&T have introduced fiber optic television services in certain geographical parts of the United States. In 2010 service was limited, but where the service has been introduced it has made some inroads as competition to both cable and satellite providers.

Like cable, this service can provide the customer with an integrated package of video, broadband, and telephone services. Picture quality for customers is very high because fiber systems can provide large bandwidth and the telephone companies have made a point of providing excellent customer service. In customer satisfaction surveys in areas where fiber systems were available, customers ranked quality as very high. Given the high cost of wiring neighborhoods, it is difficult to assess whether telecommunications companies will choose to implement fiber optic services on a broad, national level.

WORKING IN TELEVISION

We close this chapter with a look at television stations and cable operations as places to work and build careers. First, we look at how television facilities are organized and staffed. Second, we take a look at salaries. In short, where are the jobs and how much do they pay?

TV Station Organization

The organizational structure of a TV station varies according to the size of the organization. There is no specific way in which all stations are organized, but there are some general areas common to most TV stations. Figure 5–4 presents a typical organizational structure for a station in a large community.

At the top of the organizational ladder is the general manager (GM), or station manager—two different names for the same job. This person is ultimately responsible for the operation of the station. If the station is part of a group of stations, the GM usually is a vice president in the parent organization.

TV stations are generally divided into five divisions, each division having its own head who reports directly to the station manager. The five areas are sales, engineering, business, programming, and news. Each of these areas is vital for the efficient operation of a TV station.

Sales   Sales is the most important part of the TV station—at least according to anyone in the sales department. This division of the TV station is headed by a general sales manager. It is her or his job to oversee the sales staff—both local and national. The salespeople for the station are called account executives or sales representatives.

The sales department is also in charge of **traffic** and **continuity.** Traffic is not the helicopter reports but that part of the station that schedules commercials and verifies that scheduled commercials are aired properly. Traffic departments are responsible for the program logs that tell the people in the control room when each video event is to occur. The continuity department makes sure the station's schedules have no interruptions between commercials and programs.

The verification that an advertisement was played is just as important as scheduling it. If the scheduled commercial doesn't air or only partially airs (say, because of an equipment malfunction), then the sponsor is entitled to a **make-good**—a free commercial in the same time category—to replace the commercial that didn't air. Make-goods are given in lieu of returning the advertiser's money.

Engineering   The second major division in a TV station is engineering. Engineering is the most important part of the TV station—just ask any engineer.

The engineering department is responsible for the maintenance of the equipment, including the transmitter. If there is an equipment failure, it is up to a member of the engineering department to find the problem and correct it.

In sufficiently large or unionized stations, engineers run the audio/video equipment. People who load the video machines, edit, run the audio board, and push the buttons on the switchers are from the engineering department. Camera operators are also usually from this department. In smaller stations or nonunion shops there may be no hard-and-fast rules about who uses what equipment.

Business   The third area of the TV station, is the business division. The business division is usually headed by the business manager. Most business managers feel that they run the most important division of the station. Accounts payable (money owed by the station) and accounts receivable (money owed to the station) are handled in this division. Everyone who is owed money by the station and everyone who owes money to the station has his or her paperwork go through this division. Receptionists and secretaries are also a part of the business division.

Programming   The fourth and, according to the people who work there, the most important area of a TV station is programming. The program director, often abbreviated PD, oversees a number of subdivisions and, in consultation with the station manager, is responsible for the purchase of all new programming for the station and the scheduling of the programming during the broadcast day.

Under the program director, three subdivisions can be identified at most stations. Usually the largest subdivision is run by the production manager, who oversees studio workers such as floor managers and lighting directors, art directors and videographers, producers, directors, and production assistants. In small markets the crew may double up on many activities. In recent years, some group stations have combined operations between stations.

The second subdivision is headed by the community relations director and her or his staff. This division is usually in charge of public service announcements. The community relations director may also

Figure 5–4

The Organizational Structure for a TV Station

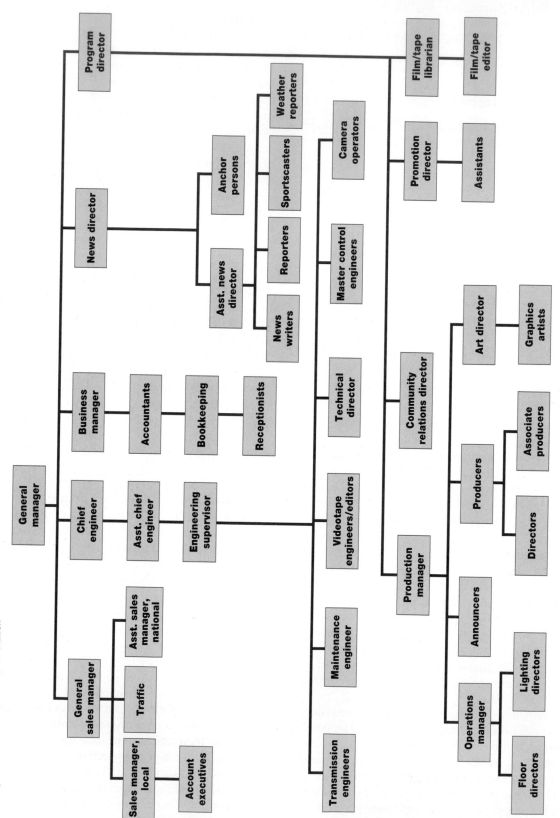

Events: After Hurricane Katrina

Television covered Hurrican Katrina brilliantly. It provided a sense of the calamity and the tragic failures of the state and federal governments to respond in a meaningful way. However, one common criticism of the news media is that we see only what the networks decide to show us. Since that disaster, a devastating 7.0 earthquake in Haiti demonstrated the power and importance of the new social media networks. Reports live from Hiati brought important information to the world, and new media technology played an important role in the earliest coverage of the disaster.

Unlike in Katrina, social media played a pivotal role, with some experts saying that it reshaped media as we know it. Consider the following:

- Twitter provided the fastest and best time-sensitive vehicle delivering information.
- Bloggers provided needed details about the needs of the survivors.
- The local telephone service was destroyed, but aid organizations used Skype to communicate a sense of the devastation and to locate volunteers.
- Footage from cell phones appeared instanteously on YouTube and Facebook.

Broadcast news organizations offered substantial coverage themselves as they searched out and reported human interest stories in Port Au Prince, where water and food were desperately needed; and as they did after Katrina, the news media continued to report on many facets of the story for weeks after the initial qualro. But ao ono roportor put it, gone are the days when the networks choose what to provide the public with footage and accounts.

be in charge of TV programs examining minority interests at the station or may be the official spokesperson for the station at community events.

The third subdivision is run by the promotion director, who typically has three duties. First, the promotion director oversees the creation and placement of messages that promote programs, movies, specials, and the station's image. Second, she or he plans and runs activities designed to gain publicity—such as sponsoring a local charity road race. Third, the promotion director is responsible for the purchase of advertising in other media. This person is in charge of the commercial aspects of promoting the station, whereas the community relations director is usually seen as being in charge of the altruistic side of the station.

News The fifth division is news, which, as any newsperson will tell you, is the most important part of the station. The news division is headed by the news director, who is in charge of the reporters, news writers, anchors, sportscasters, and weather forecasters. The news division of a station is supposed to operate independently of influences from the other divisions and so is separate from all other divisions. The smaller the station is, the harder it is to maintain this independence. As with the other division heads, the news director reports directly to the station manager.

News has a special place in broadcasting. Stations with active news departments become more important to—and are viewed more favorably by—the communities they serve. The overall quality of a station is often judged by how good its news department is. The value of a station during a sale can be affected by the reputation of the news department; a good news department is considered an asset to a station.

Today with the number of duopolies of stations increasing in major markets (a duopoly is where one company owns more than one station), the news department in the larger station may produce a news show for the smaller station. Thus some stations may not have news departments.

Departmental Evaluation As indicated, each department thinks it is the most important department at the station. Which department is really the most important? Are the sales executives right that the station would close its doors if they were not finding sponsors? Are the programming and production people right when they argue that without them there would be nothing to sponsor? Or do the engineers, who insist that without them there wouldn't be any signal, have the better claim?

Cable System Organization

Cable systems have an organizational structure similar to that of TV stations, but use slightly different names to denote the major functions. Figure 5–5 provides an organizational chart for a typical cable television system.

First, in cable, the manager of the cable system may be known as the general manager, as in broadcast TV, or as the system manager. At one time these executives were called "sysops" (short for "system operators"). Today that designation is more common to computer networks.

The technical side of the cable business is handled by the chief technician (chief tech, in cable parlance). Roughly equivalent to the chief engineer on the broadcast side, the chief tech supervises cable plant as well as installation and maintenance. The chief tech has the additional burden of coordinating and dispatching field crews to maintain and improve cable service throughout the system.

Figure 5–5

Cable System Organizational Chart

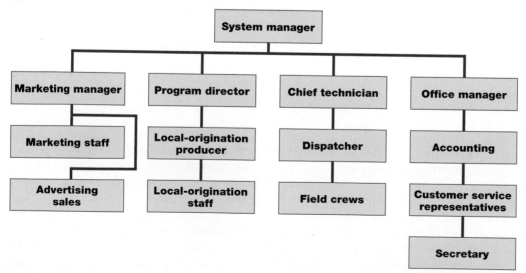

The sales function in cable includes advertising sales, but it also involves the important task of recruiting and retaining subscribers. Thus the promotion function in cable is a bit broader than on the broadcast side. For this reason, cable promotion executives tend to be called **marketing managers** (rather than promotion directors). Similarly, office management requires more people than is common in broadcast TV. Cable systems often have more than one retail location, at which numerous **customer service representatives (CSRs)** process bills, hand out converters, and take complaints from subscribers.

Finally, the programming department in cable is slightly different from its counterpart in broadcast TV. In cable, the program director is the liaison between the various program services and the local system. Locally produced programs (such as home shopping and local call-in programs) typically fall under the aegis of the **local-origination (LO) producer,** the rough equivalent of the community affairs director in broadcasting. Cable systems with full-fledged local news operations (see Chapter 9) may also boast a separate news director and production staff. Some cable operations have sophisticated remote production capability and do a fair amount of regional sports programming, too.

All told, however, cable systems and TV stations are staffed and managed in similar ways. Critical departments include general operations, programming, sales, and engineering.

THE JOB OUTLOOK

Before we look at the job picture, remember that broadcast and cable television are part of the larger information industry sector, and some general observations can be made. While the U.S. Bureau of Labor is predicting some growth in information sectors of the economy, the first line of this chapter stated that TV is an industry going through a transformation. That means that the jobs (and salaries) described here are frequently changing—as are technology, ownership, programming, and distribution. So one kernel of good advice is to keep an open mind about your career choice. The job you seek today may not exist when you graduate. If it does, it's apt to require a set of skills other than those you acquired in the classroom or on an internship.

A second thing is true about a career in television—whether broadcast or cable: Both are "cottage industries"—that is to say, despite the power and influence of their programming, the industries are in fact quite small. All told, the combined television and cable workforce represents about 316,000 people, including all employees of both commercial and nonprofit TV stations and networks and of cable systems and headquarters; and nearly 40 percent of these companies employ fewer than five people. As in other small industries, a move up the career ladder requires skill, dedication, and perseverance. Employers frequently look for someone with a good work ethic and a large dose of creativity. Too, much like the popular game "six degrees of Kevin Bacon," you'll find it quite easy to find a link between your current employer or coworkers and other managers and employees from other stations, networks, or organizations. Thus it is good advice to maintain positive relationships as you move along the career path and not to "burn bridges" by exhibiting the kind of workplace behaviors apt to catch up with you later on. As the old saying goes, it's not what you know, but whom you know (and what they think of you as a coworker or boss).

Finally, the trend toward industry concentration and automation traced throughout this text has had great impact on the media workforce. Generally speaking, there are fewer jobs in areas like television production and news; also, the power of trade associations, unions, and guilds has diminished. At the same time, the competition for audiences and from new media has led to job growth in other areas, like Web site development, sales, marketing, and promotion. Workforce growth in the online areas has also occurred, as more and more TV stations and cable systems look to providing local content on mobile applications as a means of driving viewer interest and attention.

Broadcast TV Job Trends

Fewer than 120,000 people work in one of the broadcast TV professions (e.g., camera, editors, reporters, engineers)—nearly 80 percent work in commercial TV, with the remainder in public TV. Nonsupervisory salaries tend to average about $41,000 annually. The highest earnings tend to be in the northeastern and northern states; the lowest are in the South. Salaries depend on a number of factors: the size of the community in which the station is located, whether the workers at the station are unionized, the dominance of a station in its market, and so on.

Sales executives are usually paid on a commission basis. To survive, they must sell time. If they are not

Though employment opportunities for women and minorities have improved in broadcasting over the past two decades, reporting jobs are among the most competitive.

good at selling time, they rarely make enough to live on and so move on to a different field. If they can sell, then TV can be very lucrative. There is always a strong demand for good salespeople in broadcasting, and TV is no exception.

Production crews and those who appear on the air are represented by unions at some stations. Organized (that is, unionized) stations almost without exception pay their employees better than nonunion stations in the same area. There are several different unions representing workers at a station. Generally performers are represented by AFTRA, the American Federation of Television and Radio Artists. Engineers and production people are usually represented by NABET, the National Association of Broadcast Engineers and Technicians; IATSE, the International Alliance of Theatre and Screen Employees; and/or IBEW, the International Brotherhood of Electrical Workers.

Unions usually represent the workers at contract renewal time, when management and union come to agreement on compensation and work responsibilities.

Reflecting national trends, unions have been in decline in TV. Whereas nationwide the number of employees belonging to a union was once as high as one in three, today fewer than one in six workers belongs to a union. This trend has also been felt in TV: The

power of NABET, IATSE, and other organizations is much less today than it was in the 1960s and 1970s.

Pay in TV is determined largely by the size of the market you work in. Simply put, the larger the city, the more money you will earn. In addition, on average, larger-market stations, and network affiliates pay better than do independents. Commercial TV tends to pay better than public television, although public broadcasters tend to have higher job security than their counterparts at commercial stations.

As is true for most businesses, managers make the most money in TV. Nationwide, the typical GM earns over $100,000 per year, over $177,000 in the nation's top 50 TV markets. As in radio, sales managers make the most money. In fact, you would be hard-pressed to find a sales executive in a top 10 TV market earning less than $150,000 per year.

Next to sales, salaries in the news department are the highest in TV. In the top 10 markets, anchors and reporters can earn six-figure salaries. The downside is that salaries slip significantly in smaller markets.

Engineering and programming positions, from the video editor to the camera operator, tend to provide steady employment at stable but lower salaries than high-profile sales and news jobs offer. For example, the National Association of Broadcasters says

Chapter 5   Broadcast and Cable/Satellite TV Today

133

the average annual salary for camera operators was $30,000 in 2005. There is less volatility from market to market in salaries and employee benefits.

Cable TV Job Trends

During the era of cable's great expansion, from the late 1970s to the mid-1980s, it was estimated that the cable industry was expanding by an average of 1,000 new jobs per month. This was an astonishingly high figure, particularly since this expansion coincided with an era of high national unemployment and a serious economic recession.

Cable employment slowed in the late 1980s and early 1990s as most systems completed their construction, and many cable networks faced cost-cutting due to increasing competition. Today there are nearly 10,000 cable systems in the United States employing 130,000 people. About 1 in 10 cable employees is found at network or MSO headquarters; the remainder are at local cable systems around the country.

Whereas the size of the staff in a radio or TV station is usually based on the size of the station's home city, in cable, the number of employees is based on the number of subscriber households. That is, systems with more homes hire more people. This makes sense: Large systems are more likely to sell advertising and to program their own channels. They also need more customer service representatives, installers, and technicians. A large system (more than 300,000 subscriber households) is about the size of a large TV station, with 75 or more full-time employees. Midsized systems (100,000 to 300,000 subscribers) are more like large radio stations, with 30 to 50 people on staff. Small cable systems (under 100,000 households) are run like small-market broadcast stations, both radio and TV, with fewer than 30 total employees.

Unlike broadcasting, cable is a decidedly blue-collar industry. Most jobs fall into the technical or office/clerical category. Technical jobs generally require training in fields like electronics and engineering. Cable recruits its technicians from trade schools, community college electronics programs, and vocational-technical (vo-tech) schools. Job applicants are also sought from related communications fields, including the telephone and data-processing industries, and the Society of Cable Telecommunications Engineers (SCTE) offers certification programs for a number of technician positions.

Because of its history and tradition as a service business (and not "show business"), cable salaries have typically lagged behind those in broadcasting. One reason for lower salaries and wages is the relative lack of union membership in the cable business. Whereas most telephone employees and many broadcast technicians belong to unions, less than 10 percent of the cable workforce is unionized. However, as cable operations become more profitable, they are also becoming more like broadcast stations. As we have seen, many cable systems are actively seeking advertising dollars.

Nationwide, the typical general manager of a cable system earns about $80,000. Other high-paid positions in cable include treasurer or finance director ($70,000), human resources director ($55,000), program manager ($58,000), and marketing director ($60,000). Lower-paying positions include office manager ($32,000) and cable service and technical operators ($40,000).

Women and Minorities in TV

Like many other industries in the United States, TV has been, historically, primarily a white, male-dominated industry. Steps were taken in the late 1960s and early 1970s to begin to rectify the imbalance, but changes have been slow in coming.

Overall, women hold about 4 in 10 jobs in television today, and members of minority groups (including African Americans, Hispanic Americans, Asian Americans, and Native Americans) represent nearly 30 percent of TV employees. The good news is that those percentages have been on a slow and steady increase in recent years.

On the negative side, women still tend to find themselves in office positions. More than 87 percent of office and secretarial staffs remain female. Ethnic minorities tend to find themselves in technical and operations positions. However, gains for both women and members of minority groups have been seen in recent years in the more lucrative areas of sales and news. Today, slightly more than half the broadcast news anchors in the United States are women, and behind the scenes about 50 percent of the sales workforce, and 45 percent of the cable sales force, are female. One in five TV newspersons is a member of a minority group. However, entry into management is another matter. Fewer than one in five TV news directors are woman, and only 1 in 10 TV news department heads are minorities.

As in much of American industry, there remains a large gender gap. Men make more than women in both broadcast and cable TV. All told, women's salaries lag about 10 percent behind those for men in similar positions. Some good news for women is that they have tended to get larger pay increases than men in recent years. However, the gender gap re-mains real and persistent. According to the National Organization for Women, this is most visibly demon-strated in prime-time cable news programs, where 67 percent of the guests are men and 84 percent of them are white.

SUMMARY

- The popularity of television with American viewers has made it an important and highly profitable busi-ness. However, it is also a business in transition, fac-ing new competition for viewers and from new technologies.

- More than 1,700 TV stations compete for audiences. Commercial stations earn their revenue primarily from advertising sales. Noncommercial stations rely on government funds, grants, and donations from viewers. In 2009 all full-time TV stations were con-verted to digital (DTV).

- Network television is a segment of the TV business in which local TV stations agree to carry programs from a major network in return for a share of their advertis-ing slots. In recent years, compensation paid by the network has declined for network affiliates. The net-work business was dominated for many years by ABC, CBS, and NBC. Newer networks are now on the scene, including Fox, CW, and ION TV.

- The local television business relies on sales to local and regional advertisers. The most successful local TV stations are those owned and operated by a major network, or those owned and managed by a large TV station group owner. Weaker TV stations include independents and low-power operations. About 380 stations are public television operations. PBS provides programming to most of these stations, and its children's shows, news, and documentaries have attracted viewers and continuing government support.

- Cable television has grown in recent years to become an important component of the television landscape. Cable is in more than two-thirds of America's TV homes, and more than 300 different na-tional program services compete for space on the ca-ble. The cable business makes its money by marketing and selling to different levels of customer homes. Rev-enues are enhanced by moving customers from basic service to pay, multipay, and new services, including Internet access and local telephone service. The cable business is dominated by large, multiple-system oper-ators, most of which also have ownership interest in cable programming services, telephone services, and broadcast TV services. In recent years satellite televi-sion has grown dramatically.

- Both broadcast and cable television facilities are orga-nized into separate staffs, which typically include gen-eral management; programming; sales, marketing and promotion; and engineering. Job growth has been noted in the marketing and sales areas, as well as in local news, as cable systems and local TV stations aggressively court viewers faced with more and more options.

- In general, the best salaries are earned by employees of large TV stations and cable systems, and by em-ployees in sales or general management. While oppor-tunities for women and members of ethnic minority groups have risen in recent years, the television indus-try still lags behind other industries in employment and salary equity.

KEY TERMS

local television   110
network television   111
network O&Os   114
affiliates   114
independent TV station   115
low-power television (LPTV)   115
VHF; very high frequency   122
UHF; ultra-high frequency   111
tiering   122
homes passed (HP)   123

basic penetration   123
pay households   123
multipay households   123
pay-per-view (PPV)   123
addressable converters   123
multievent PPV   124
multiple-system operators
   (MSOs)   124
single-system operators
   (SSOs)   124

cable system operators
   (CSOs)   124
traffic   127
continuity   127
make-good   127
marketing managers   131
customer service representatives
   (CSRs)   131
local-origination (LO)
   producer   131

SUGGESTIONS FOR FURTHER READING

Arango, T. (2009). "Broadcast TV faces struggle to stay viable." *The New York Times*, February 27.

Berestaunu, A., & Ellickson, P. (2007). "Minority and female ownership in media enterprises." *A report to the FCC*, June 7.

Blumenthal, H., & Goodenough, O. (2006). *This business of television* (2nd ed.). New York: Billboard Books.

Day, J. (1995). *The vanishing vision: The inside story of public television*. Berkeley: University of California Press.

Ellis, E. (2004). *Opportunities in broadcasting careers*. New York: McGraw-Hill.

Engleman, R. (1996). *Public radio & television in America: A political history*. Thousand Oaks, CA: Sage.

Jessell, H. (2006). *Broadcasting and cable yearbook 2006*. New Providence, NJ: R.R. Bowker.

Parsons, P., & Frieden, R. (1998). *The cable and satellite television industries*. Boston: Allyn & Bacon.

Sherman, B. (1995). *Telecommunications management* (2nd ed.). New York: McGraw-Hill.

———. (1999). *The television industry standard*. New York: Gerson-Lehrman.

Vogel, H. (2001). *Entertainment industry: A guide for financial analysis*. Cambridge, UK: Cambridge University Press.

Walker, J., & Ferguson, D. (1998). *The broadcast television industry*. Boston: Allyn & Bacon.

Waterman, D., & Weiss, A. (1997). *Vertical integration in cable television*. Cambridge, MA: MIT Press.

Weaver, D. (1998). *Breaking into television: Proven advice from veterans and interns*. Princeton, NJ: Peterson's.

INTERNET EXERCISES

Visit our Web site at **www.mhhe.com/dominickbib7e** for study-guide exercises to help you learn and apply material in each chapter. You will find ideas for future research as well as useful Web links to provide you with an opportunity to journey through the new electronic media.

6 | The Internet, Web Audio, and Web Video

Quick Facts

Number of Internet users worldwide (2010): 1,800,000,000 (estimated)

Most popular Web site worldwide (2009): Google

Number of Americans with broadband Web access (2010 estimated): 210,000,000

Number of iPods sold since being introduced in October 2001 (2009): 220,000,000

Number of YouTube videos streamed per month (2009): 5,000,000,000

Percentage of Americans who cite the Internet as their main source for news (2009): 40

As Microsoft founder Bill Gates once wrote, "… [T]he Internet changes everything." Gates was referring to business in general when he wrote those words, but they apply with equal force to almost every area of life. The Internet has influenced politics, the economy, science, education, and culture. On a more personal level, the Internet has changed how people shop, communicate, socialize, pay bills, get their news and entertainment, and spend their free time. Of more relevance to this book is the fact that the Internet has become a significant mass communication medium and has changed what we expect from traditional broadcasting and cable/satellite services. Rather than trying to describe all the details, consequences, and implications of this new medium, this chapter will take a narrower focus. We will first take a broad look at the Internet as a communication medium and then concentrate on audio and video on the Web.

THE INTERNET

Basics

The Internet is a global system of millions of interconnected computers in more than a hundred countries. A common set of operating procedures is necessary for all these computers to communicate with one another. Under the general direction of the Internet Society, a set of Internet standards and protocols (a set of rules) was created that made it possible for computers, applications, and services to operate across many different computer networks. A **transmission control protocol (TCP)** breaks a message into smaller packets and recombines them at the message's destination. An **Internet protocol (IP)** puts an address on each packet and makes sure the packets get to their destination.

Locating a specific destination on the Internet is handled via a **uniform resource locator (URL).** Each URL has an exact format. The specific protocol comes first (such as www for the World Wide Web). Next comes a secondary domain name (usually the name of a company or institution), followed by a primary domain name (such as .edu, .com, or .org). Thus the Web address for *The New York Times* is www.nytimes.com.

With the basics out of the way, let's look at some specific uses of the Internet.

The Internet as a Communication Medium

The biggest use of the Internet is for interpersonal communication. Experts estimate that more than 200 billion e-mails and about 50 billion instant messages are sent every day. Those are impressive numbers; but more relevant to our discussion is the way the Internet has become a mass medium.

The Internet functions as a mass communication medium thanks to several developments in computer science. The first was the development of the **World Wide Web** by Tim Berners-Lee in the early 1990s (see Chapter 2). Other advances that helped the Web become a mass medium included these:

- **HTML (hypertext markup language)** is a tool used to create Web pages. HTML structures text and multimedia documents and also allows the creation of hypertext links between documents.

- **Browsers** are programs that people use to access the Web. Browsers allow users to communicate with various Web sites anywhere in the world by interpreting and displaying the contents of HTML documents. The most popular browser is Microsoft's Internet Explorer, followed by Mozilla's Firefox, Google's Chrome, and Apple's Safari.

- **Plug-ins** are software programs that expand the abilities of browsers. Plug-ins are used to play sound or video clips, decompress files, or process images. Some popular plug-ins are Adobe's Flash Player, Quicktime, RealPlayer, and Java.

Both organizations and private citizens were quick to see the communication potential in this new medium. Before long, the Internet took its place

Microsoft's Internet Explorer is the most popular Web browser.

Profile: Steve Jobs—Media Mogul

Steve Jobs altered the media business forever. Jobs, the adopted son of Paul and Clara Jobs, grew up in the nascent Silicon Valley, a region filled with apricot orchards surrounding tech companies such as Hewlett-Packard. As a teen he hooked up with an engineering wizard, Steve Wozniak, and the two of them developed a small computer in Jobs's garage that soon evolved into the Apple II.

The Apple II may have been the product that made the home computer industry take off, but it was really the Macintosh's introduction in 1984 that changed what we thought about computers. With its sleek design and an amazing, intuitive graphical interface (soon copied by Microsoft), the Mac ignited the desktop publishing industry. Interestingly, although Jobs brought the innovative computer to the market, he lost control of his own company because investors thought him too young to be CEO of Apple. In 1985, at the age of 30, Jobs was both a millionaire and unemployed.

Jobs kicked around for a new project and founded another computer company called NeXT. This computer was praised by engineers but was too expensive for most companies and thus was not a success. Jobs, looking for other ventures, purchased a small animation studio called Pixar from George Lucas in 1991. Within the next few years *Toy Story* had developed into the first computer-animated feature film to become a huge breakthrough success.

Ironically, Apple Computer, losing market share and money, was looking for a new operating system for the aging Macintosh platform. It chose NeXT, and in 2000 Jobs found himself back at the helm of his former company.

Back at Apple, Jobs looked for new directions for a company that had lost its way. One year later the iPod was born, soon followed by iPhoto, iMovie, and iTunes. Many also credit Jobs with persuading the languishing music industry to take a chance on selling music downloads by creating the iTunes Music Store. The iPod and its music store have become huge successes for Apple, burnishing its tarnished image.

Pixar's unbroken string of hit film successes like *Toy Story 2, Finding Nemo,* and *The Incredibles* gave Jobs the muscle to negotiate a sale of the animation studio to Disney, and in 2005 Jobs was given a seat on the Disney board. The Disney–Pixar operation has turned out such hits as *Cars, Wall-E, Up,* and *Toy Story 3.*

Jobs helped convince ABC (a Disney subsidiary) to sell downloads of popular television shows like *Lost* in the iTunes store, stimulating the video downloading craze. Movie downloads soon followed.

In 2007 Jobs shook things up again when Apple introduced the iPhone, a combination cell phone, iPod, digital camera, and Internet-enabled device. As of 2010 consumers had purchased more than 40 million iPhones, and developers were turning out thousands of applications that owners could download to their phones. "There's an app for that" became a new national catchphrase. Not all of Job's innovations, however, have been successful. Apple TV, a device that let users buy or rent movies and TV shows and watch them on their HDTV sets, did not enjoy high sales numbers.

Not content to stand pat, in 2010 Jobs and Apple revealed the iPad, a tablet computer with a touch screen. Apple sold a million of these devices in the first month.

Sometimes criticized for his lack of patience and his driving nature, Jobs is also seen as a visionary. In Jobs's own words, "Don't let the noise of others' opinions drown out your own inner voice."

alongside radio, broadcast TV, and cable/satellite TV as a means of sending and receiving media content. Now let's examine some of the consequences of the emergence of this new mass communication channel.

Effects on Other Electronic Media

The Internet has totally changed the music industry. File-sharing programs such as Napster revolutionized the way that people sought and acquired music. Rather than buying CDs, Napster users could simply type in a title of a song and receive a list of servers where they could download the music. Under legal pressure from the music industry, the original Napster was shut down in 2001 (it later reemerged as a site where people could pay to download tunes).

Around that same time, Apple introduced the iPod, an iconic new MP3 player, and the iTunes store, where people could purchase individual songs for as little as 99 cents. The iPod and its later versions were a huge success. It was apparent that consumers did not want to pay for a CD with 14 or 15 songs when they wanted to hear only one or two of them. By 2010 the iTunes store had sold more than 6 billion songs, and many other downloading services had sprung up: Rhapsody, Target, eMusic, Amazon, and many others.

Sales of CDs dropped about 35 percent from 2007 to 2010 while digital downloads increased by 46 percent for the same period. This shift has prompted the music business to search for new business models and marketing techniques.

The motion picture industry is also concerned about the Internet's effect on its business. First, the Internet has made it easier for people to download pirated copies of movies. The Motion Picture Association of America estimates that the industry is losing more than $5 billion a year because of pirated movies. Second, many companies such as Netflix and Blockbuster now stream movies directly to a consumer's TV set. In 2010 Netflix reported that 55 percent of its 14 million subscribers were watching movies via the Internet compared with just 36 percent a year earlier. This trend has not yet hurt the theatrical box office because people still enjoy going out to see a movie; but it has cut into revenues from DVD sales, a significant source of Hollywood's income. From 2008 to 2009 DVD sales dropped more than 13 percent.

The Internet has both hurt and helped the traditional television industry. People who spend time on the Internet spend less time watching TV. Of course some, but not a lot, of that time online is spent watching episodes of TV programs that originally aired over cable or broadcast TV. One survey noted that about 8 percent of its sample regularly watched at least one TV episode online every week.

As for radio, because most radio listening is done in cars, the Internet has had only a minor impact on listening time. The one area where the Internet does take some time away from traditional radio listening is at the office because some people tune in Web-only stations rather than broadcast radio. One 2009 study found that respondents spent about 1.5 hours per day listening to Internet-only stations.

Effects on Entertainment: Video Sharing, Gaming, Social Networks

It may have started off as "the information superhighway," but it didn't take long for the Internet to turn into an entertainment medium. A recent survey asked respondents, "What sources of entertainment do you turn to most often?" The Internet came in second, behind only television.

As is obvious, the Internet has expanded the entertainment options available to the consumer. Less obvious is how the Internet has changed the definition of entertainment. In the survey just mentioned, about 60 percent considered social networking sites to be a form of entertainment. Among 18- to 24-year-olds the percentage was even higher: more than 70 percent. This finding suggests that Americans are relying more on their friends, particularly their friends on social networking sites, for diversion and less on the entertainment industry.

"Surfing the Web" has become a national pastime; Americans spend on average about three to four hours a day on the Internet, with much of that time spent on activities that fall in the entertainment category. In addition to visiting social networking sites, Americans are uploading and watching video, playing games, reading blogs, checking sports scores, listening to music, and looking at pictures.

Video-sharing sites, such as YouTube, reinforce the point made earlier: Our friends and neighbors are supplying a significant amount of our entertainment. New digital cameras and powerful editing software has made it easy for consumers to shoot and edit video and post the final product on the Web. YouTube has more than 120 million videos, and about 80 percent of them were produced by amateurs. (We discuss video sharing in more depth later in this chapter.)

Video games have become a popular form of entertainment. Sales of gaming platforms, software, and accessories amounted to nearly $20 billion in 2009—about double Hollywood's box office revenue. New video game consoles, including the Xbox 360, PlayStation 3, and the Wii, have built-in hard drives, advanced graphics, and wireless connectivity that allows for interactive gaming over the Internet. Although numbers are hard to come by, experts estimate that about 30 to 40 million people play online games using the Xbox or the PlayStation.

Table 6–1	Growth of the Internet—Number of Internet Hosts	
Year	**Number of Internet Hosts (Approximate)**	
1995	4 million	
2000	100 million	
2005	300 million	
2010	700 million	

The scope of online gaming is impressive. MM-PORGs (massive multiplayer online role-playing games) have attracted a huge following. The science fiction game *Halo 3* has sold about 6 million copies in the United States. As of 2009, *World of Warcraft* had nearly 12 million subscribers. About 15 million people have played the war game *Call of Duty 4* online.

More video games are using motion sensors, such as those found in Nintendo's Wii. This means many games are easier to play and do not require users to read a thick instruction manual or memorize button configurations. As a result, many older people have joined the video game audience, and the average age of a video gamer is now just past 30.

As already noted, social networking sites such as Facebook, Twitter, and MySpace represent yet another form of entertainment made possible by the Internet. Social networking sites have become enormously popular. As of 2010, Facebook had nearly 500 million

A typical visit to Facebook lasts about 10–15 minutes.

members. (If Facebook were a country, it would be the third largest in the world, behind only India and China.) MySpace boasted about 120 million users, while Twitter reported about 75 million members. Facebook and MySpace members use these sites to socialize with friends; share music, photos, and videos; join networks based on occupation, interest, or college; post links to blogs and other content; and play games. Facebook users spend an average of seven hours per month on the site.

Social networking sites siphon some people away from their TV sets, but quite a few are multitasking—watching TV while they are on Facebook, MySpace, or Twitter. One 2009 survey found that 59 percent of Americans reported surfing the Web while watching TV at least once during a typical month. Moreover, it appears that people watching TV while online are not passive viewers because they post messages commenting on what they are watching. During the 2010 Academy Awards telecast, about 13 percent of viewers were also online, most of them on Facebook or Twitter, trading messages with friends.

Social networking sites have a downside. Sharing too much personal information such as phone numbers and addresses can be dangerous. Embarrassing or revealing photos can come back to haunt people. Parents have complained that social networking sites have been used for bullying, and there have been reports of sexual predators enticing minors into meeting for sexual encounters.

Effects on News

The Internet has become a significant competitor to traditional news media. According to the Pew Research Center's report, *The State of the News Media 2010*, on a typical day more than 60 percent of Americans get their news online, putting the Internet in second place, behind television but ahead of newspapers. Those who rely most on the Internet for their news tend to be younger, better educated, and more affluent than the general population.

This increased competition is one of the reasons behind the declining audiences of traditional news sources. The audience for the networks' evening news programs declined by 30 percent from 2000 to 2009. The audience for local station newscasts shrank as well. Only cable TV networks, thanks primarily to Fox News, have seen their audiences grow.

In response to this competition, traditional news outlets have devoted more resources to their Web sites.

In 2009, according to the Nielsen rating service, MSNBC.com, CNN.com, FOXnews.com, and ABCnews.com all ranked in the top 10 most visited Web sites. MSNBC and CNN averaged about 39 million unique visitors in a month.

Social media have also become part of the news reporting landscape. Postings on such sites as Twitter and Facebook are sometimes the main source of information about a breaking news event. Firsthand accounts of the earthquake that struck Chile in 2010 were available within minutes on Twitter. Demonstrators in Iran made heavy use of YouTube, Twitter, and Facebook.

Traditional news organizations are also relying more on "citizen reporters." Thanks to the proliferation of inexpensive digital video cameras and video-equipped smart phones, everybody can be a reporter. CNN's iReport contains stories, photos, and video provided by private citizens. MSNBC has a similar arrangement called FirstPerson. Many other sites, including The Weather Channel, Reuters, Fox News, and the BBC, also rely on user-generated content.

Citizen participation in the news process is also illustrated by the growing importance of **blogs.** Blogs are Web journals that display information in reverse chronological order. There are literally millions of blogs on the Web covering a staggeringly wide range of topics. Most relevant to this chapter are blogs that concentrate on current events. Blogs influence news in several ways. First, blogs provide a check on the mainstream press. This was vividly illustrated during the 2004 presidential election campaign when bloggers called into question documents in a *60 Minutes* report about President George W. Bush's military service record. Second, blogs turn private citizens into reporters. Bloggers provide eyewitness accounts of many news events, such as the 2010 earthquake in Chile. Third, blogs can affect what is covered by the mainstream press. CNN.com, for example, tracks trends in the "blogosphere" and reports on the topics that are most discussed. In 2010, when Apple unveiled the iPad, CNN.com posted excerpts of reviews from the leading technology blogs. Many reporters regularly scan blogs to find new story ideas.

Effects on Promotion and Marketing

Cross-promotion is now a common advertising tool. Program producers coordinate programming both on television and on their Web sites. Fans of *Glee* can find a wealth of information on the show's Web site, including photos, video clips and full episodes, discussion groups, games, and information about cast members. Also included are links that allow fans to buy *Glee* merchandise such as DVDs and CDs. CBS.com offers full episodes of CBS programs, previews, and special features, such as how to build the perfect sandwich to accompany your favorite CBS show. Showtime offers sample programming, such as the pilot episode of an original series, in an attempt to attract new subscribers. The pilot for *The United States of Tara* received more than 1.5 million online views.

Cross-promotion is not limited to entertainment. If you want more details about a story you've seen on ABC, you can go to ABCnews.com, where more information is available. Similarly, Web users expect services they can't get from traditional media. For example, fans of NPR's *All Things Considered* can go to the NPR Web site to download a segment they missed. Podcasts (discussed soon) also provide a convenient way to download audio and video content and transfer it to a portable device.

In addition, new concepts in coordinated promotions between traditional media and the Internet are developing rapidly as more people access the Internet with mobile devices. *Glee* has an app for the iPhone that lets users record their own voices while they sing songs from the program and share their efforts with their Facebook friends. Game shows *Wheel of Fortune* and *Are You Smarter Than a 5th Grader?* have versions that can be downloaded on the iPhone. In short, the mobile Internet promises to open up new possibilities for traditional media.

The Mobile Internet

There were more than 20 million laptop computers with wireless net access in 2010; and thanks to the iPhone and other smart phones, more than 50 million people used their cell phone to connect to the Internet. The number of mobile Internet users will also increase as Apple's iPad becomes popular. (A million iPads were sold in the first month of its availability.) The Pew Research Center has predicted that by 2020 mobile devices will be the primary tool worldwide for connecting to the Internet.

What do people do when they log on to the mobile Web? They look for news and information, play games, watch videos, check their Facebook, My Space, and Twitter accounts, trade stocks or

Apple expects to sell nearly 30 million iPads worldwide in 2011.

access other financial information, and check out movie times—pretty much the same things they do on their home computers. In short, mobile Internet usage is becoming mainstream.

It is a good bet that more and more people will be watching TV on their cell phones or iPads. MobiTV, for example, is available to iPhone subscribers for about $10 to 15 a month and carries programming from NBC, CBS, ESPN, Fox, and many other channels. Mobile phone chip maker Qualcomm offers FLO TV with news and entertainment programs from ABC, CBS, Comedy Central, and CNN among others. ABC has an iPad app that lets people watch full episodes of their programs. NPR's iPad application lets users download stories, access live NPR programs, and save favorite stories to a playlist for future listening.

In 2010 a consortium of the nation's biggest broadcasters, including Fox, NBC Universal, and Gannett, announced plans to develop programming for mobile devices such as cell phones and the iPad. When in full operation such an arrangement could offer mobile content to more than 150 million people.

In sum, the Internet will become an increasingly attractive place to deliver audio and video directly to the consumer. Obviously this development has significant implications for the traditional television and radio industry. Consequently, the rest of this chapter examines the fast-growing and ever-evolving world of Internet audio and video.

AUDIO AND VIDEO ON THE WEB

Today's college student might find it difficult to believe that only a dozen or so years ago video on the Internet was hard to find. Slow connection speeds, hard-to-use software, and a lack of content providers meant that even short video clips rarely appeared on Web sites. Thanks to music file-sharing programs, audio on the Internet was more common, and a few radio stations were streaming their station's signals on the Web—but traditional AM and FM dominated listening time.

Just a little more than a decade later video and audio have exploded on the Web. Now it's rare to find a Web site of a major corporation or organization that doesn't include video. YouTube and other video-sharing sites have made television producers of anyone who owns a digital video camera. Internet video has created stars of formerly unknown performers. Full-length episodes of TV shows and movies are widely available, and many Americans are canceling their subscriptions to cable companies and watching all their video on the Web. More than a thousand Web-only radio stations are now in operation.

Bringing Audio and Video to the Web

Early attempts to set up electronic information-sharing systems depended on the telephone system, such as Minitel in France, or used the home TV, such as

CEEFAX in Great Britain and newspaper company Knight-Ridder's videotext system in the United States. All these efforts were text-based and slow and had limited graphics capability.

More successful attempts used the home computer as a communication device. An early Internet service called CompuServe became the first home computer network. In 1985 Prodigy, a venture that involved Sears Roebuck and IBM, began operation. Prodigy was quickly followed by America Online (AOL), a service that offered special services such as e-mail, chat rooms, and forums. These early services did not catch on right away. Most were still text-based; users depended on slow dial-up modems to connect to the network; and telephone charges could mount quickly.

More powerful computers with color monitors and faster modems soon appeared, and the breakup of AT&T resulted in lower phone rates for many consumers. As a result, online services became more popular. AOL embarked on a massive marketing campaign, sending out millions of free software packages. Graphics were greatly improved. By the mid-1990s about 18 million people in the United States were using the Internet.

The creation of the World Wide Web allowed documents, graphics, and audiovisual files to be linked together and accessed simply by a click of the mouse. The Web gave a huge boost to the popularity of the Internet. As mentioned earlier, displaying information on the Web became much easier with the emergence of Web browsers such as Internet Explorer; and the creation of search engines, such as Google and Yahoo!, made it simple to find information quickly. By 2000 the number of U.S. Internet users had grown to more than 150 million. More and more Internet service providers, including some cable and telephone companies, came on the scene. All these developments meant that the Internet was becoming a popular entertainment and information medium.

Not surprisingly, business executives looked for ways to make money from this new channel. Newspapers, TV and cable networks, and many other companies started Web sites in the hope of attracting advertising money or promoting their products. One way to make a Web site more attractive is to add multimedia, such as audio and video. Unfortunately, in the late 1990s and early 2000s, connection speeds were much slower than they are today. As a result, downloading audio and video files required huge amounts of patience. Even a five-minute video file might require hours to download.

Table 6-2	Top 10 Internet Sites, May 2010	
Rank	**Property**	**Unique Visitors (in Millions)**
1	Google sites	179
2	Yahoo! sites	167
3	Microsoft sites	160
4	Facebook.com	130
5	AOL LLC	112
6	Ask network	92
7	Fox interactive media	88
8	Turner network	86
9	Glam media	81
10	CBS interactive	70

That situation changed with the development of new data-encoding formats, such as MP3 for audio files, and the growing availability of high-speed broadband connections, such as DSL phone lines. Progressive Networks released Real Audio, a free, easy-to-use audio player, and Microsoft offered its version shortly thereafter. As a result, audio files could be downloaded more quickly.

College radio stations were the first to recognize that faster downloads enhanced the broadcasting potential of the Internet. In 1994 WXYC (University of North Carolina) and WREK (Georgia Tech) began sending radio programs over the Internet. A few commercial stations also experimented with online programs. By 1996 about a million people were listening to Internet radio.

By 1998 there were about 1,700 radio stations on the Web, many operated by established broadcasters and others started by amateurs dissatisfied by the lack of diversity on commercial AM and FM stations. Other sites aggregated a large number of audio channels. Investors poured money into Internet radio operations during the dot-com "boom" of the late 1990s as Yahoo! acquired Broadcast.com for more than $5 billion and AOL bought up Spinner for around $400 million.

The introduction of Apple's iPod and its iTunes store in 2001 opened up new channels of delivery for audio. Adam Curry, a former MTV VeeJay in the 1980s, hit on the idea of syndicating audio programs that could be downloaded directly to a person's iPod. This started a technique known as **podcasting**—distributing an audio file that can be downloaded for later listening. Podcasting quickly

Events: Podcasting—New Pathway to Fame

There was virtually no warning when popular Los Angeles talk station 97.1 FM suddenly changed formats from the home of syndicated gab to a Top 40 jukebox station. CBS Radio, owner of 97.1 FM, had been the home of the self-proclaimed King of All Media, Howard Stern, for over a decade. The station had a full lineup of comedy and political teams to fill every hour with either thought-provoking or side-splitting entertainment.

In 2009, however, the plummeting demand for radio advertising meant the largest talk station in the western United States could no longer afford its costly original talent, including radio and television personality Adam Carolla. The station gave listeners just three days' notice before pulling the plug on talk radio.

Still under contract, Carolla would continue to be paid by CBS Radio for a full year despite the fact that he was no longer on the air. Desperate to be heard, Carolla decided to venture into the barely known world of Internet podcasting. He had heard stories of how fellow comedian Ricky Gervais and tech guru Leo Laporte created loyal online followings through this new medium and thought he could bring his listeners on board as well.

Podcasting is a distribution method that allows audio and video files to be automatically downloaded from a Web site using a protocol called Really Simple Syndication (RSS). With the advent of iTunes, the new *Adam Carolla Show* was available with just a single mouse click, completely free of charge.

Fast-forward to a year later, when Adam Carolla had the most popular podcast on iTunes with over half a million daily downloads. Carolla was now free to do the show he had always wanted without much filtering. The Internet had provided a relatively inexpensive medium for him to produce and distribute his own uncensored content. By December, when no longer under contract with CBS Radio, Carolla added his first advertiser. With the power of podcasting, this creative personality was able to function as the gatekeeper of his own content.

Adding a podcast to iTunes is a simple process. Anyone can become a popular broadcaster with thousands of loyal listeners. For example, *The Kevin Pollak Chat Show* is a weekly video podcast in which the host, veteran actor Kevin Pollak (he's been in dozens of movies and TV shows, including *The Drew Carey Show* and *Shark*), can have a totally unscripted conversation with his celebrity pals. Shows have ranged from 30 minutes to well over two hours in length. Pollak has complete control and can take a break at any point he feels the conversation is waning or wants to cut to a video clip. Compare this with the tightly scripted five-minute segments on NBC's *The Tonight Show*. I'm sure television producers squirm when they learn that Pollak's show features a recurring bit in which Pollak stares at the camera lifelessly for up to 30 seconds of dead air. Why? No reason—just because…he can. "Creepy, isn't it?" he'll finally ask the camera. That's not the sort of thing you're apt to see on traditional TV.

Written by Robby Millsap

became a hit, and podcasts spread over the Internet. In addition, many Internet radio stations began streaming live talk and music over the Web. The number of listeners to Internet radio jumped from 4 million in 2000 to more than 20 million in 2005.

Streaming was also key to the growth of Internet video. Streaming means a Web user does not have to wait to download a file to play it. Instead media are sent in a continuous stream of data and are played as they arrive. The data can be stored or buffered so a person can watch the beginning of the video while the remainder is still downloading. By the mid-2000s new software, such as Flash video, helped Internet TV explode.

In 2004 Rocketboom, the first online daily newscast, premiered; as of this writing it is still in opera-

tion. Later that same year, the "Numa Numa" video was viewed more than 2 million times in just three months, making it the first video to go "viral"—a term used to describe a video that becomes widely popular after being mentioned in blogs, e-mail, instant messages, and media-sharing Web sites. Advertisers quickly recognized that viral videos were an inexpensive way to generate awareness for their products, adding even more momentum to the video boom.

The next year the video-sharing site YouTube premiered. Amateur video enthusiasts embraced the site, and YouTube was soon streaming millions of videos every day. Similar to the situation when motion pictures were first invented, early Web videos were short and usually portrayed the unusual or the humorous. Early content consisted of magic tricks, short comedy clips, concert excerpts, and segments of copyrighted TV shows—a situation that would cause later problems for the site. New digital video cameras and software made it even easier for a person to shoot video footage, edit it on a personal computer, and post the resulting video on the Internet. YouTube was soon joined by many other video-sharing sites, including Joost, Grouper, and Revver.

Established media companies quickly recognized the potential of Web video. CNN started Pipeline, featuring live video feeds of breaking news events. In 2006 ABC offered free episodes of its programs the day after they were shown on the network. ESPN added video to its site, as did many other cable networks such as HGTV and the Discovery Channel. Also in 2006, Web search engine giant Google acquired YouTube in a $1.65 billion deal.

That same year *Lonelygirl15*, a series based on the life of a teenage girl, premiered on YouTube and proved that a Web-based series ostensibly produced by an amateur could generate huge interest. *Lonelygirl15* eventually wound up with more than 110 million views. (It was later disclosed that the series was actually produced by aspiring filmmakers in an attempt to generate interest in their future projects.)

The years 2007–2008 saw the growth of video sites devoted to content original to the Web. Comedian Will Ferrell started funnyordie.com, which featured new comedy routines and sketches. NBC offered the original Web series *Gemini Division* along with several others. A strike in Hollywood prompted several writers to turn their talents to creating video for the Web. Josh Whedon and his *Dr. Horrible's Sing-Along Blog* is one example. Programs that air on the Internet are called *webisodes*, and Webisodes.org contains dozens of links to this type of content.

The next year saw the beginning of Hulu.com, a cooperative venture between Fox and NBC (ABC would join later). Hulu carried full-length episodes of current and vintage television series from both broadcast and cable networks. In addition, YouTube announced that it would also carry full-length episodes of TV series.

As of 2010 online video and audio were firmly established as major media channels. Podcasts were available on many sites, and more than 10,000 radio stations were on the Internet. In 2010 it was estimated that more than 60 million people listened to online radio. YouTube was the most popular online video site, while Hulu was in second place. New software made it simple for people to embed videos in social networking sites such as MySpace and Facebook. Advertisers and marketers have made online video a key part of their campaigns. About $1.5 billion was spent on Web video ads in 2010. The Online Video Guide provides one measure of Web video's popularity. The site lists two dozen categories of online video, ranging from anime to travel. For example, those interested in fitness can choose videos in several subcategories such as yoga, where links are provided to nine sites that feature yoga videos. Many TV sets can now connect to the Internet, making it even easier to access Web programs. Clearly online audio and video are here to stay.

Let's take a closer look at Web radio and television. We'll start with radio.

Types of Online Radio Stations

Given the great number of stations online, it is difficult to construct a comprehensive category system for Internet radio. Nonetheless, there appear to be four main types of stations:

- Online stations that are affiliated with a broadcast station.
- Aggregators.
- Choice-based sites.
- Format-specific, Internet-only stations.

Let's look at each in turn.

There are thousands of broadcast radio stations that provide online content. Some simply simulcast their over-the-air signals on their Web sites; others offer different choices. KIIS FM, for example, offers NewRadio where listeners can sample new releases not yet on the station's broadcast playlist. Chicago's rock station WBBM-FM gives online visitors the chance to sample a dance music format.

Aggregators are sites that provide access to a large number of radio stations. Radiotower.com, for instance, has links to more than 6,000 stations with formats ranging from blues to tropical. Some broadcast radio networks are leading aggregators. CBS is in charge of AOL's Internet radio service. Visitors to the AOL music site can listen to about 150 CBS stations or about 200 channels offered by AOL. CBS Radio also made a similar arrangement with Yahoo!'s Music Launchcast Radio, making CBS, one of the first terrestrial broadcasters, a major player online. Big station group owner Clear Channel started erockster,

Web music site Pandora lets listeners program their own radio stations by suggesting music that is similar to what listeners report they enjoy. As of 2010, Pandora had about 48 million users.

where listeners can listen to a nationwide service or tune in to one of Clear Channel's local stations.

Choice-based sites let listeners program their own unique station. Users choose their favorite artists and types of music, and the site suggests other musical selections that are similar. Listeners can vote on whether they liked the site's recommendations, and the site takes the votes into account when generating future selections. The two main choice-based sites, Pandora and Lastfm, claim to have millions of subscribers.

Format-specific Internet stations play narrowly focused genres of music. There are hundreds of these stations online, some owned by large corporations while others are one-person operations. Examples include Weirdsville.com, specializing in strange and obscure music; Radio Free Kansas, specializing in progressive rock; and Batanga.com, which plays music by Weird Al Yankovic and similar artists.

Monetizing Online Radio

Online radio sites make money from selling advertising space, from user subscription fees, from a combination of ads and subscriptions, or from direct selling. They may also compile e-mail lists of their subscribers and sell the lists to third parties. Most sites

that are affiliated with a terrestrial station generally rely on advertising. The Web site for WSB-FM in Atlanta, for instance, contains banner ads for local businesses as well as promotional announcements for WSB-TV. A common practice is for Web site advertising to be sold along with commercials on the broadcast station.

Aggregators such as Yahoo!'s Launchcast or AOL Radio might show a commercial before allowing a user to access their stations. RadioTower sells premium upgrade software and sells radio-related items in the online store. Live365 sells banner ads on its site.

Subscribers to choice-based station Pandora can listen free to a number of songs but eventually must pay a fee if they wish to hear more. In addition, Pandora sells banner ads on its home page. Lastfm sells banner ads and sells a premium version for listeners who want additional features.

The biggest financial problem facing Internet radio stations is a legal one. When they play music, online stations have to pay royalties to performers, songwriters, and composers. (As of mid-2010, terrestrial broadcast stations did not have to pay these costs, but that situation may change.) An increase in these royalty rates threatened to put many online stations out of business. A 2009 compromise allowed stations to pay either a fee based on the number of songs they stream or a percentage of their revenues. This deal allowed Internet radio stations to stay solvent, at least in the short term.

Audiences and Content

More than 60 million people listen to Internet radio every week. About 80 percent listen to the streaming programming of traditional AM/FM stations while the rest listen to online-only stations. Those who listen to AM/FM streams listen for about 2.5 hours a day compared with 1.4 hours a day for those who choose online-only stations. Much of the online listening is done at work. As of early 2010, CBS Radio claimed the largest online audience, followed by Clear Channel.

The thousands of Internet radio stations provide a hugely diverse lineup of content. In addition to the traditional music formats of rock, urban, country, and adult contemporary, an online listener can sample such formats as techno, reggae, free-form, and tribal. Those who favor talk over music can listen to 116 talk radio stations, 68 sports radio stations, and a dozen comedy stations.

Now let's take a look at Internet video.

Types of Online Video

Similar to the situation in radio, constructing a category system for online video is a difficult task because so many different types of sites exist and feature an array of diverse content. Nonetheless, at the risk of oversimplification, it appears that most online sites fall into four main categories:

- Commercial video sites.
- Video-sharing sites.
- Corporate video sites.
- Microcasting sites.

Of course this organization is not perfect because it doesn't include all sites and because some sites might fit into more than one category; but this arrangement is useful as a starting point.

Commercial Video Sites   When Web video first appeared, most experts thought that only short clips would be viewed online because the quality was not up to broadcast standards and because viewing on a computer was not as enjoyable as watching on a big-screen TV. The birth of sites such as Hulu and CBS.com, however, showed that viewers would sit still for full-length programs.

Commercial video sites are generally owned by broadcasters and cablecasters and feature professionally produced full episodes of current or past TV series. Most of their content is repurposed; the programs have already aired on broadcast or cable TV and have been converted into online form. Episodes can be watched for free, but commercials might appear before, during, or after an episode. (Hulu gives viewers the option of seeing commercials at the beginning of a program or with several commercial breaks.) The amount of time devoted to ads is far less than the amount during a broadcast program. In addition, banner ads might appear next to the video player that is included in the site.

Some sites, such as Hulu, Fancast, and TV.Com, are aggregators, making available programs from various sources. Hulu's site contains programs or clips that originally aired on NBC, Fox, ABC, and other networks. As of early 2010, popular series such as *Grey's Anatomy, The Office,* and *30 Rock* were available on Hulu. Other sites, such as USAnetwork.com and Discovery.com, contain only shows that appeared on the parent network. Sony Pictures Television offers Crackle.com, a site with original Web series as well as TV shows and older movies, and

clips from *The Dr. Oz Show,* which is syndicated by Sony.

Most of these sites allow viewers to embed clips or programs in their personal Web sites or post them to their Facebook or MySpace pages. In addition, these sites usually let viewers post comments about what they have seen; and the sites' video players allow for pause, rewind, and fast forward and can be expanded to fill the screen.

Many companies are producing original Web video for their brands as marketing tools. Breyer's Ice Cream, for example, featured *30 Rock's* Jane Krakowski in two webisodes to promote its "Smooth and Dreamy" ad campaign. I Can't Believe It's Not Butter produced a Web video featuring Megan Mullally, and Bertolli Pasta produced videos starring Marissa Tomei around the theme "Into the Heart of Italy."

Netflix, primarily known for renting movies to consumers, has also become a major player in the online video arena. In addition to computers, subscribers can receive online video via Web-to-TV player Roku and video game systems including the X-Box 360 and Play Station 3. In 2010 about half of the company's more than 12 million subscribers watched at least 15 minutes of streaming video. This may not seem impressive, but much of the content available for streaming included only old TV shows and B-list movies. If Netflix is able to arrange deals with TV content providers allowing it to stream current episodes, it would become a formidable competitor in the market.

As of mid-2010 Hulu has been the most successful of the commercial video sites. Hulu has contracts with more than 200 content providers, including PBS, the NFL, and A&E. In December 2009 viewers watched about 1 billion videos on the site. However, as noted soon, despite its popularity, Hulu has not been a financial success.

Video-Sharing Sites   As of 2010 there were more than 100 video-sharing Web sites where amateur producers could post their videos. YouTube was the most popular of these sites, receiving more than 9,000 hours of uploaded video every day. Other popular sites include Metacafe, Vimeo, Revver, Yahoo! Video, and Google Video. Many of these sites, including YouTube, also contain episodes of TV shows and other professionally produced repurposed content along with large amounts of corporate video (discussed next). Nonetheless the main thing these sites are known for is user-generated amateur video.

Events: Webisodes: Ready for Prime Time?

When online video first started to gain popularity, most of the viewing was done during the daytime, usually between noon and 3 p.m., when much of America was at work. Online viewing during the workday was common because Internet connections were probably faster at work and because the shorter video clips that made up much of early online video were perfect for viewing during a lunch or coffee break. The clips could not compete with network-produced programs, so prime-time viewing was still devoted mainly to traditional TV series.

That situation seems to be changing as more people are turning to online video during the evening hours. In mid-2010 Blip.tv, a service that distributes more than 50,000 independently produced Web shows, reported that its peak viewing time was 8 p.m. to 11 p.m. across all time zones. Other online viewing sites, such as Revision 3 and Break.com, also report growth in prime-time online viewing.

Why the increase? First, more people get broadband Internet access at home, making it easier to watch online video. Second, some of the increase is due to people visiting Web sites that offer full-length TV shows online, such as Hulu; but a significant portion of the growth comes from viewers watching original programming on the Web. In addition, as their audience grows, webisodes' quality and production values improve.

Blip.tv distributes *Anyone But Me,* an original Web series about the lives of teenagers in and around New York City that has been airing since 2008 and has received critical praise. Its writing, acting, and production are on a par with many series on traditional TV. Crackle TV hosts 50 episodes of *The Rascal,* a James Bond spoof that has acquired a loyal following. Even traditional TV producers are getting into the webisode arena. ABC.com presents *Seattle Grace: On Call,* a mock documentary about the *Grey's Anatomy* doctors at their favorite after-work bar.

This trend has several implications. First, it offers new outlets for those interested in TV production. Online video gives content creators a chance to have traditional media executives sample their efforts, which might lead to employment opportunities. Second, online video might siphon off viewers from traditional prime-time TV series—a trend that could become more significant when TV sets are routinely equipped with high-speed Internet access. Such a development would further fractionalize TV audiences. Third, advertisers now have a cheaper alternative to expensive prime-time commercial costs. AT&T recently launched a campaign on Blip.tv with many of its ads slated for prime time. Of course more advertising money means that Blip.tv can funnel more money back to program creators who, in turn, could use it to increase the quality of their shows even more.

The volume of video uploaded to YouTube is staggering. In 2009 every minute saw 20 hours of video uploaded to the site—the equivalent of releasing more than 60,000 Hollywood movies a week. It is physically impossible for one person to watch every video on YouTube in a lifetime. In a month YouTube videos get about 30 billion views worldwide.

As noted previously, video-sharing sites have introduced a new set of problems. Illegally posted copyrighted material continues to be a vexing issue for YouTube. For example, Viacom has filed a $1 billion lawsuit against Google, YouTube's parent company, claiming that the video-sharing service made available more than 160,000 unauthorized clips on its Web site. In mid-2010 a federal judge ruled in favor of Google, but Viacom announced it would appeal the decision.

A second problem involves privacy. Small, affordable digital cameras are in the hands of many people who think nothing of uploading video to YouTube and other sites without permission of those who were recorded. Many professors have been surprised to find clips of their lectures on YouTube with titles such as "World's Most Boring Class" or "Boring Professor" or worse.

In just five years YouTube has become part of the fabric of American life. For example, the 2008 presidential election campaign included debates where candidates answered video questions submitted through YouTube. President Barack Obama had his own YouTube channel. A search of the site in mid-2010 revealed nearly 100 channels devoted to music. Many of the videos on these channels had been viewed more than a million times.

In entertainment, YouTube has helped a number of performers, including Esmee Denters (21 million views), Susan Boyle (88 million views), and VenetianPrincess (180 million views), achieve fame. Dave Chappelle's career was helped by his YouTube videos, which were viewed more than 10 million

YouTube has helped launch the careers of many recording artists, including Esmee Denters. Her videos were viewed more than 20 million times during her first nine months on the site.

attacks? It's available on YouTube. Looking for Pee Wee Herman's 1986 interview on *The Joan Rivers Show*? It's there too.

Many sites, such as YouTube, accept video for any and all topics. Other sites are more selective. The Weather Channel, for example, has a site (uservideo.weather.com) that contains user-generated video dealing with weather-related topics. Our Media specializes in amateur clips about social issues, while Drop Shots features family-oriented videos.

A number of sites specialize in "lifecasting," which is broadcasting the details of one's life online using a Web cam or other portable cameras. Justin.TV is probably the best known lifecasting site. Other sites include Selfcast TV and Ustream, where users simply leave their Web cams running all the time.

Not surprisingly, not every video-sharing site has been a success. Veoh, partly funded by Time Warner and Goldman Sachs, went under in 2010. Other sites that didn't make it include Soapbox and Stage6.com.

Corporate Video   Corporate video is a catch-all term for video that serves the particular needs of a company, corporation, or other organization. Historically corporate video was distributed through channels that were not available to the general public, such as viewing programs in the workplace or providing workers with tapes or disks to be viewed at home. The emergence of the Internet, however, has opened up new communication channels for corporate video and has made it available, theoretically at least, to a mass audience. Today much corporate video can be found on company Web sites or posted on video-sharing sites such as YouTube.

At the risk of oversimplification, there are three main uses of corporate video:

* Training and orientation.
* Sales and marketing.
* Public relations.

Let's take a brief look at each.

Perhaps no activity lends itself better to video than employee training. Many companies use video to teach basic operational skills and to train employees in sales, management, and interpersonal dynamics. In the past, much of this training took place on site with groups of employees watching videos in conference rooms or work rooms. Although this method is still common, much training and orientation activity has moved online. A brief search of the

times. Viewers who choose not to stay awake for *Saturday Night Live* can catch clips of their favorite segments the next day. YouTube and other sites offer original series produced by amateurs.

Advertisers have embraced Web video. Ad campaigns typically contain a YouTube version that the advertiser hopes will "go viral." Bottled-water maker Evian, for example, was delighted when its "Roller Babies" video got nearly 20 million views. The trailer for the vampire movie *New Moon* topped 29 million views.

Moreover, YouTube has become a video archive of both historical and trivial events. Richard Nixon's television address in which he resigned the presidency is on YouTube, as is the opening sequence for *Klondike*, a TV Western that lasted for 17 episodes in 1960–1961. Looking for video from the 9/11/2001

Web will turn up numerous examples. Mastery.com offers employers the option of setting up their own online safety training courses for their employees. Possible topics include electrical safety, fire prevention, and dealing with hazardous materials. For those interested in hairstyling, myhairdressers.com has more than a hundred training videos with topics ranging from basic to advanced haircutting. Those interested in video editing can access several training videos at Lynda.com.

There are several general sales and marketing areas where corporate video is commonly used. Companies that need to show potential consumers how their product works can produce a demonstration video and post it on the company Web site or on a video-sharing site. This technique can be particularly useful for companies whose products are too large for salespeople to carry around or if the service or product needs a visual dimension to fully show off its benefits. Eagle Technologies, for example, posted a three-minute video on its Web site that demonstrated how its lower-cost card-printer ribbons provided results on a par with more expensive brands. Caterpillar's Web site has a short video demonstrating the virtues of its backhoe loader.

The Web sites of most major companies now contain videos on their home pages that advertise a featured product or service. Many of these are online versions of broadcast ads; others are constructed specifically for the Web. The Web site of Macy's department store, for example, includes Macy's TV, where viewers can get a preview of upcoming Macy's ads. Some companies, such as GoDaddy.com, use broadcast videos as teasers for racier ads that are available on their Web sites.

Introducing a new product to distributors, dealers, and potential customers scattered across the country is a difficult task that is made easier by corporate video on the Web. When BMW introduced its new electric-powered car in 2010, it produced a four-minute video for its Web site that featured the new model. In late 2009 Marantz America used its YouTube Channel to introduce its new Universal Disk Player. Instant feedback is one of the benefits of using the Web for this purpose because companies can track how many times their videos have been viewed.

Corporate video is frequently used for public relations activities that include communicating with the general public, shareholders, and government leaders. Some common uses include these:

- *VNRs:* A **video news release (VNR)** is a recorded presentation of company news that is distributed to TV stations or other outlets in the hope that it will be used during local TV newscasts or aired online. The purpose of a VNR is to promote a product or to shape public opinion. Most VNRs take a subtle approach, and it is sometimes difficult to distinguish them from a typical news report. A reporter introduces a recorded segment and then does a recap at the end.

In the past VNRs were distributed to local TV stations. The more recent trend is to post them on YouTube or other social media sites such as Facebook or MySpace. For example, to launch its new voice communication software, the Nuance Company posted a "Man vs. Machine" texting competition on YouTube. The three-minute video was viewed more than 300,000 times. The U.S. Federal Housing administration posted a video on its Facebook page designed to educate Hispanic families about their housing rights.

- *Company image:* More and more organizations are including video in their corporate Web Sites that portrays the company in a positive light. To name just two, a 2010 visitor to the McDonalds's Web site would find a video that shows how local McDonald's business owners play a vital and positive role serving the communities they operate in. Burger King's Web site contains several videos detailing the company's commitment to the environment and to its employees.

- *Communicating with shareholders:* Most people who own stock in a company usually don't attend the annual meeting of shareholders. Video gives companies a chance to reach more of their stockholders in order to make this yearly ritual more meaningful. In the past some companies might make a DVD with an edited summary of the event and offer to send it to interested parties. More recently the highlights of shareholder meetings have been posted online. For instance, shareholder.com provides video equipment and technical help so that companies can webcast their annual meetings.

Microcasting   Microcasting, transmitting a message to a small group of interested people, was made possible by the widespread availability of Web cams and broadband Internet connections. Examples of microcasting are plentiful. Viva Las Vegas Weddings streams live webcasts of weddings for friends and family who can't get to Las Vegas for the ceremony. Daycarewebwatch.com lets parents and grandparents view the activities of their children and grandchildren live from various day care centers. St. Paul's Episcopal Church in San Francisco webcasts its Sunday services for congregation members who can't attend. More than 60 U.S. funeral parlors offer live webcasts of services. Perhaps Vidder.com, a company that specializes in microcasting, best sums up the situation with this statement on its Web site: "In this multimedia age, why shouldn't every public meeting, public entertainment event, and family occasion be webcast . . . ?"

Microcasting will become even more popular when Internet-capable cell phones are routinely equipped with high-definition video cameras that can send live signals through the Web. Parents could microcast children's football games to grandparents; birthday parties could be webcast to friends in other states or countries; and every piano student's recital could be available online.

Monetizing Online Video

Sites such as YouTube and Hulu are business ventures; as such, they expect to make a profit. There are a limited number of ways in which an online video site can make money: advertising, subscription fees, or a combination of the two.

The subscription model is relatively simple: A viewer pays a fee and in return is allowed to see a video program. This is the model used by Netflix, where a subscriber pays a monthly fee to download movies. It is also the model for Apple's iTunes store: Episodes of TV shows can be purchased for $2.99 or music videos for $1.99. For about $100, baseball fans can subscribe to MLB.TV and watch more than 2,000 games. Finally, the subscription model is used by a large number of pornography sites.

Let's take a look at advertising support. Although online video is extremely popular, that popularity does not necessarily translate into profitability for ad-based Web video sites. Watching online video is now a mainstream activity with about 80 percent of

U.S. Internet users reporting they watch videos on the Web at least once a month. In addition, the average time spent online per week is only slightly less than the average time per week spent watching TV. Despite this potentially large audience, advertising dollars have been slow to materialize. In 2008 more than $300 billion was spent on advertising. Television received 22 percent of that money while online advertising got only 6 percent. In short, although more people seem to be watching video on the Web, advertising dollars have not followed.

Why the lag in advertising revenue? First, there are thousands and thousands of Web sites where an advertiser can place an ad. In such a situation, the laws of economics prevail. When advertising demand is constant (or even decreases as it did during the recession at the end of the decade) and supply is abundant (as it is on the Web), the price of an ad goes down. As a result, the revenue from online advertising is much less than that from traditional sources.

Second, it is difficult for an advertiser to know how many people actually see an ad that appears on an online video Web site. Ads can be 10, 15, or 30 seconds long and can appear before, after, or during the video program; or they can appear next to the video player as banner or floating ads. Although an advertiser can count the number of "views" for a video, there is no agreement on what exactly constitutes a view. For some measurement organizations, a view is counted after only three seconds of viewing. Other sites count a "play start" as a view even if the viewer watches for only a fraction of a second. If the same viewer stops and restarts a video (maybe because of buffering problems), it is counted as another view. (More information about how online viewing is measured can be found in Chapter 12).

Third, in commercial TV, advertisers have some control over when and where their ads appear. They buy time in programs that will reach potential customers and that are compatible with their products. Thus a golf club manufacturer would advertise during a televised golf tourney. On the Web, however, there is less control, particularly when the site depends on material submitted by amateurs, such as YouTube. Although YouTube offers advertisers some selectivity over ad placement, there is still some uncertainty where the ads will actually show up. For example, an ad for a frozen fish dinner recently cropped up before a video on outsourcing of U.S.

jobs, and a commercial for a Web site that let people turn themselves into cartoons ran during a video about birds of prey. Moreover, sites such as YouTube reverse the general rule of advertising: The bigger the audience, the higher the cost of an ad. The most viewed videos on YouTube tend to be the ones that many advertisers would avoid. For example, during early 2010 among the most viewed user-submitted videos was one titled "Does Size Matter?" Another was titled "Hot Chick Gets Ogled," and a third was news video of the fatal accident at the 2010 Winter Olympics.

A site such as Hulu, which depends primarily on professionally produced programs, has less of a problem in this regard; but it too has not seen its popularity translate into significant profit. In 2009 it was estimated that Hulu sold only 60 percent of its available advertising time. Advertisers seem cautious about buying spots on the site because they have no way of precisely determining who will be exposed to their ads. Further, the cost of reaching a thousand people tends to be more expensive on sites such as Hulu or NBC.com than on broadcast television, making advertisers even more cautious about buying time on these sites.

Although precise numbers are difficult to find, it has been estimated that in the past few years, YouTube has lost hundreds of millions of dollars and Hulu has yet to become profitable. Not surprisingly, both sites are looking for ways to increase their income. In early 2010 articles in the trade press suggested that Hulu would adopt a subscription model for at least part of its content. YouTube announced plans to separate its "premium content," including TV shows, movies, and music, from its amateur-produced videos in the hope of becoming more advertiser-friendly.

Audiences and Content

There is no doubt that the audience for online video has grown over the past several years. According to the Nielsen Company, in January 2010 there were about 143 million unique viewers of Web video compared with about 50 million in 2003. Surveys done by the Pew Research Center suggest that the typical viewer of online video tends to be male and under 30, with some college education and a household income above $75,000 annually.

In 2009 the average online viewer watched about 450 minutes of video per month, or about 15 minutes

per day. As the numbers suggest, much of online viewing consists of short clips. A recent survey found that jokes, bloopers, and comedy clips were the most watched type of online video mentioned by 50 percent of respondents. News clips ranked next, followed by movie trailers and music videos. Only 27 percent reported that they had watched a full episode of a TV show. Women are more likely to watch full episodes of TV shows while men are more likely to watch short, user-generated clips. The most popular time for watching network TV series on the Web is from noon to 2 p.m. (People apparently catch up on shows they missed the night before during their lunch hour.) Table 6–3 shows the top five online video destinations in early 2010. Note that YouTube dominates in total streams but Hulu viewers spend more time on its site.

Online Video: Promise and Problems

Online video has been a plus for most Web sites. The ability to air short news clips has made sites such as CNN.com and MSNBC more effective in reporting the news. Movie companies and TV networks promote their upcoming shows by presenting previews on their sites. As discussed earlier, many companies use video to promote their products or services. The U.S. government has also embraced video. Social Security, the Census Bureau, the White House, and many other agencies all have online video. The Department of Education even has its own YouTube channel.

The creation of video-sharing sites, where visitors upload their own amateur videos, has prompted an outlet for user-generated video that didn't exist 10 years ago (and has made the founders of YouTube rich). New software lets members embellish their Facebook or MySpace pages with video.

Table 6–3	Top Video Streaming Sites, December 2009	
Source	**Total Streams (Approximate)**	**Time per Viewer (Minutes/Month)**
YouTube	6,400,000	119
Hulu	634,880	247
Yahoo! Video	244,000	13
Turner Sports	142,000	56
MSN/Windows Live	141,000	25

Ethics: Technology's Dirty Little Secret—Porn

Sex sells. It is undeniable that the porn industry is a big entertainment (many would say exploitation) industry. Just how big a business is it? Not surprisingly, it is difficult to pin down exact numbers because many companies do not want to talk about their connection to the "adult" industry. Estimates range from $13 billion to $14 billion in 2009.

The pornography industry adopted the Internet very early as a technology, as it did with the VCR and DVD. Adult entertainment companies were among the first to use online payments, Web cams, streaming video, and other Web technologies that we now take for granted. Their work paid handsomely. Today the term "sex" is usually among the most frequently used search terms at the various Web search sites.

Big companies don't like to admit it, but many have been in the porn business for years. Comcast, DirecTV, and the Dish Network, among others, offer pay-per-view porn channels to their subscribers. Big hotel chains, such as Marriott and Westin, provide in-room X-rated movies.

Porn is also available on cell phones. Adult content providers such as Mobile Phone Porn and Xobile have targeted mobile services. Why? New telephones have better video capabilities, making them better instruments for displaying porn. Many early adopters are willing to pay a premium to receive pornography on personal devices, such as cell phones, leaving the family's computer in the den untouched.

Recently, however, technology has turned against the porn industry. Revenue from DVDs and online pay sites has plummeted because of what are labeled "tube sites"—Internet sites that provide free porn. There are more than a thousand tube sites, many of which feature pirated porn clips along with amateur videos. Adult entertainment companies now constantly patrol the Web and send out take-down requests when they find pirated video. This tactic has limited success because the pirated content soon shows up on another tube site. Things have gotten so bad that in 2009 leaders of the porn industry requested $5 billion in government stimulus funds to bail out the beleaguered industry. As stated by Joe Francis, producer of the *Girls Gone Wild* series, "The U.S. government should actively support the adult industry's survival and growth, just as it feels the need to support any other industry cherished by the American people." As of this writing, Congress has turned a deaf ear to the proposal.

Not every development, however, has been positive. Copyrighted material posted without permission on video-sharing sites has caused legal problems. Sites such as YouTube have had to start policing to eliminate material posted illegally as well as racist and offensive clips.

The advent of Hulu and other online sites that contained full episodes of programs raised another set of problems. Broadcast networks were in favor of these sites because they could sell advertising space and create an additional revenue stream from programs that had already aired—not as much revenue as they received from originally airing them, but some revenue nonetheless. Local TV stations affiliated with a network, however, saw this development as a threat because people who watched a show on Hulu were no longer watching it on a local station, thus reducing the station's audience size and advertising rate. To help offset this possibility, many stations offered access to full episodes of network programs from the local station's Web site.

Moreover, cable networks faced a loss of revenue if consumers started watching their favorite shows online and canceled their cable subscription. Consequently cable networks searched for ways to make sure online access to their shows was available only to subscribers. Time Warner, for example, introduced a "TV Anywhere" plan whereby subscribers could watch TV shows on their computers or even their cell phones. Nonsubscribers presumable would not be granted access or would be offered a chance for a Web-only option. The next few years will probably show whether this model catches on.

THE FUTURE OF ONLINE AUDIO AND VIDEO

Predicting the future of something as dynamic as the Internet is risky, but experts suggest the following developments for Internet video. First, there will be more of it. One of the founders of YouTube has predicted that Internet video will become the most ubiquitous and accessible form of communication. As video cameras become smaller and simpler to operate and video editing software becomes even more user-friendly, more and more people and organizations will shoot video and post it on Web sites.

Second, it will become easier to find. Today's video search engines search by genre, source, length, or key words that are associated with the video. Tomorrow's search engines will scan all the spoken words within a video and perhaps even some of the images, making it much easier to locate a specific piece of content.

Third, much Internet video will come with a price tag. Viewers will probably have to pay for professionally produced content, such as episodes of TV shows. The specific arrangements might include micropayments (for example, paying 25 cents to watch an episode of *The Office*), subscriptions (paying a monthly fee to a site such as Hulu.com to watch an unlimited amount of programs), or something similar to the TV Everywhere system, where current cable or

satellite subscribers can watch what they want online provided they are current cable or satellite customers.

Finally, much of television viewing will be done over the Internet. It won't be long before all new TV sets will be Internet ready. It may take longer for the picture quality of Internet TV to equal that of cable or satellite, but it will get there. When that happens, the whole model of TV viewing will change. People will no longer watch stations or networks; they will watch particular programs using a system much like the video-on-demand arrangement that now exists at many cable companies.

As for Internet radio, it should become more reliable now that its royalty dilemma has been settled. Expect even more choices on the Web as Internet radio becomes the preferred way of listening in the workplace. Traditional radio will still be around and will dominate in-car listening.

SUMMARY

- The Internet is a global system of millions of interconnected computers in more than a hundred countries. Internet protocols make it possible for computers, applications, and services to operate across many different computer networks. Locating a specific destination on the Internet is handled via a uniform resource locator (URL).

- The Internet can be used for mass communication thanks to several advances in computer science, including the development of the World Wide Web, hypertext markup language, browsers, and plug-ins.

- The Internet has had an impact on other media. Downloading forced the recording industry to explore new business models. The motion picture industry is concerned about the Internet's effect on its business. The Internet has hurt and helped the traditional television industry, while radio listening has been mostly unaffected.

- The Internet has expanded the entertainment options available to consumers through video sharing, gaming, and social networks.

- The Internet has become a significant competitor to traditional news media. Social media and blogs have become part of the news reporting landscape.

- More people are connecting to the Internet through cell phones and other wireless devices.

- CompuServe, Prodigy, and America Online were early online services. Slow connection speeds impaired the development of Web audio and video.

- Broadband connections and the development of streaming helped the growth of online audio and video. As of 2010, online video and audio were firmly established as major media channels.

- There are four types of online radio stations: those affiliated with a broadcast station, aggregators, choice-based sites, and Internet-only stations.

- There are four types of online video sites: commercial, sharing, corporate, and microcasting. Hulu.com was a popular commercial site. YouTube was the most popular video-sharing site, receiving more than 9,000 hours of uploaded video every day.

- Making a profit remains a problem for many online video sites.

KEY TERMS

SUGGESTIONS FOR FURTHER READING

Farkas, B. (2006). *Secrets of podcasting*. Berkeley, CA: Peachpit Press.

Gralla, P. (2006). *How the Internet works*. Indianapolis, IN: Que Publishing.

Negroponte, N. (1995). *Being digital*. New York: Vintage Books.

Palfrey, J. (2010). *Born digital: Understanding the first generation of digital natives*. New York: Basic Books.

Ryan, J. (2010). *A history of the Internet and the digital future*. London: Reaktion Books.

Strangelove, M. (2010). *Watching YouTube: Extraordinary videos by ordinary people*. Toronto: University of Toronto Press.

INTERNET EXERCISES

Visit our Web site at **www.mhhe.com/dominickbib7e** for study-guide exercises to help you learn and apply material in each chapter. You will find ideas for future research as well as useful Web links to provide you with an opportunity to journey through the new electronic media.

Part Three How It's Done

The Business of Broadcasting, Cable, and New Media

7

Quick Facts

Average cost of 30-second Super Bowl spot (1976): $125,000

Average cost of 30-second Super Bowl spot (2009): $3 million

Total amount spend on online ads in the United States (2009): $22.7 billion

Total sponsorship revenue for National Public Radio (2005): $37.7 million

Cost of a 30-second spot on CBS's *The Amazing Race,* 8 p.m. (Fall 2009): $109,736

Cost of a 30-second spot on NBC's *Sunday Night Football,* 8 p.m. (Fall 2009): $339,700

Total spot TV advertising in Los Angeles TV market (2008): $2.75 billion

100th largest radio market in the United States (2009): Boise, ID, 474,900 people aged 12+

It's time for a short quiz. One question: What is the primary product that a radio or television station has to sell? Here are the choices:

a.   Entertainment.
b.   Advertising time.
c.   Listeners to advertisers.
d.   Weather updates.

If you answered *c*, you're right. All the other answers are less correct.

Let's dwell on this for just a minute. Commercial mass media have a unique dual nature. Mass-media technology is designed to link audiences with program suppliers and with sponsors. Broadcasting and cable operations need to provide listeners and viewers with programs that meet their tastes and needs. Stations transmit programs to attract an audience. Internet sites develop information and entertainment on their sites for the same reason. A commercial radio station, for example, doesn't make any money unless it has an audience that some advertiser pays money to reach. Television stations that broadcast network programs make some money because an advertiser is paying the station for the time adjacent to network programming.

So while it's true that stations are attracting audiences because of their programming, it is the advertising revenue generated as a result of having a desirable audience that really pays for the programming. Banner and other ads on Web sites provide revenue for the Web producer in much the same way. Mass-media technology provides a means of reaching a large number of people simultaneously, and as a result it is an economical way of linking audiences with advertisers via television and radio programming. Essentially you and your friends are the product a broadcasting station is selling to an advertiser.

In all electronic media there is this kind of interplay among the technology, the consumer, and economics. For example, there is an interplay for the cable industry, but it works just a little differently from broadcasting. Obviously cable has advertising, and thus cable, too, must be selling the audience's attention to advertisers (unless a consumer is willing to pay extra money to receive noncommercial channels such as HBO or Showtime). But there is a difference between over-the-air broadcasting and cablecasting. Cable companies also charge viewers a monthly subscription fee for the privilege of receiving cable programming. In fact, the majority of cable's revenue is

generated by the monthly subscription fee that consumers pay to receive the service. Cable thus has a dual income: Cable operators sell advertising, and in addition they collect revenues from a monthly subscription service. Some cable companies such as Comcast and Time Warner are also offering high-speed Internet access and telephone (VoIP) as services, which act as additional sources of income for these companies. Of course cable operators also have a different cost structure because cable is a different technology from over-the-air broadcasting: Cable franchisers have a large video distribution network to maintain, while broadcasters just have a transmitter and studios. The business model for radio and television is thus different from that for cable; both cable and broadcasting must be technology-dependent. Web sites make money through ad placement, much like a newspaper or magazine, or by selling goods or services like the iTunes store.

This chapter will address the economics of broadcasting, cable, and the Internet; but while economics is sometimes referred to as a dismal science, advertising revenues for electronic media are anything but dismal. They've grown steadily since broadcasting's beginnings. We need to understand how a station generates revenue and spends money. Broadcasting, cable, and the Web are big businesses, after all. Without profits, there would be no money for program development and thus no programming. Exploring the relationships that exist among broadcasters and other electronic media and advertisers and within the industry will give us some insight into how the business works.

COMPETITION AND ELECTRONIC MEDIA

Radio, television, cable, and satellite broadcasters all face competition from other services. Web services compete against many similar pages with similar information. The amount of competition often helps the government determine how closely it will monitor and control the mass-media facility. Chapter 10 goes into regulation in detail, but let's discuss a few basic principles here. Generally the amount of government oversight of the electronic media is tied to how competitive those media are. If there is more competition, there is less regulation.

Radio is less heavily regulated than television, for example. There are more than 11,000 commercial radio stations compared with about 1,370 commercial television stations. Guess which medium has fewer regulations regarding ownership? With cable television there are different rules too. For example, few places in the United States have more than one cable operator in a franchise area. As a result, the cable operator can be mandated to provide government and public access channels for the local municipality. How about the Internet? Isn't it more like a magazine stand with thousands of different choices and lots of competition? The point we are trying to make is simply this: The different electronic media have different levels of competition and face different amounts of government oversight as a result.

If a medium faces no competition, there is a **monopoly.** It's hard to find a place in the United States today that receives only one local radio station and no other distant radio or television signals. If there were such a town, the station in that town would have a monopoly on advertising for electronic media. If there are a limited number of competitors—say, only three national commercial television networks—we would call that an **oligopoly.** Here the limited number of competitors means that each of the networks will probably gain a share of available advertising revenue. If a market faces complete competition—say, a large radio market with 25 or more radio signals available—it is possible to let the listeners decide which stations will become popular and thereby gain a large share of the advertising dollars. We call this a "marketplace" solution, or **pure competition,** because the competitive forces within the market make each commercial station try hard to gain a share of the advertising revenue. Within this last category, it is possible for weak stations to actually go out of business or get purchased by larger group owners when they do not succeed in gaining a sufficient audience.

Competition among Different Media Types

This may seem obvious to you, but let's state it anyway. People use the various forms of media differently. To some extent competition is defined by how people use a specific medium and what competition it faces from all other competitors. For example, the competition for specific listeners among radio stations must be different from the competition for viewers on television. As we noted in Chapter 4, radio is the most intimate of the mass media. It is a highly portable and personal medium. It is more likely to compete against other portable devices such as MP3 players and smartphones for your attention than against cable or television. Radio programming centers around music, news, and talk. There is practically no drama. Comedy on radio is more like stand-up than situational. And radio is omnipresent. People can listen in places where watching television would be difficult. While someone jogging or driving a car could listen to radio, he or she could just as easily be listening to an iPod but could not watch television. Workers in an office are likely to listen to the radio in the background; in fact, some have started listening on their computers via the Internet.

Television is used differently. Many people get home, kick off their shoes, and sit down to watch a little TV. The term *couch potato* engenders thoughts of someone at rest, but the term is rarely applied to radio listeners! Television is more likely to compete with cable and movie rentals for its viewers. We can compare other media too. Obviously billboards must compete with radio somewhat, but newspapers have the potential to compete with both radio and television, depending on where and when people read their papers. Today wireless broadband allows Internet services to compete with all other forms of electronic media. You get the point.

Advertisers will frequently buy different media to reach as many customers as possible. They will also frequently spread their messages over different times in the broadcast day to ensure the broadest dissemination of their message. A look at Figure 7–1 shows that time spent listening to the radio and watching television is greater than time spent with any other media; thus advertisers are particularly concerned with these two media.

Determining a Medium to Buy and Figuring Out Its Cost

There is a triangular relationship in the media business between programmers, media sellers, and media buyers. How does the advertiser actually decide to buy time from one radio station over another, or why does an appliance store use television as opposed to the local newspaper for advertising? Obviously many factors can influence the media purchase (called a "buy"). Some factors may be strictly *internal*, such as the budget allocated to a particular product line, and some may be *external*, such as the usage of new media by potential customers.

As we learned in Chapters 4 and 5, broadcasters need to develop successful programs that certain

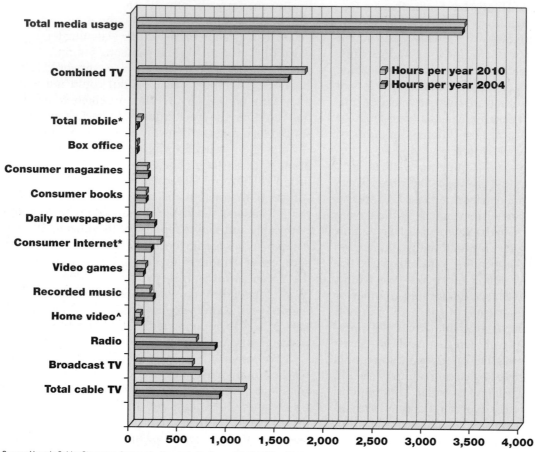

Source: Veronis Suhler Stevenson Communications Industry Forecast 24th Edition (2010).

*Consumer Internet and Total Mobile includes at home and school, not business uses.

^Home video also includes in-flight video entertainment.

people will want to listen to or watch. To determine just how successful a TV program is, a station needs to evaluate how many viewers watch the program. Finding out about the age, gender, and income of viewers (demographics) is important too. Stations can use that information to attract certain advertisers. Chapter 12 covers audience measurement, so this chapter will focus on how the advertiser decides to allocate advertising dollars.

Marketers and advertisers generally put together a buying plan developed on three basic elements: (1) population or market size and other demographic information, (2) **effective buying income (EBI),** which is often a reflection of the "disposable"

income of the average family, and (3) retail sales for each geographical area where they sell their products. If the product is a national or regional product, advertising agencies and marketing firms collect data relevant to that product and may develop a **buying power index (BPI)** for the specific markets they're interested in. The higher the BPI, the greater buying power for that market or region. If the media plan is sizable—that is, if there is a substantial amount of money allocated for advertising the product—the advertiser may use the services of a company that provides information regarding the amount of money that competing national advertisers spend on various media. Research companies break down advertising expenditures according to specific classifications of products, such as nonprescription drugs. This information provides the advertiser with a way of gauging what the competition is spending on media.

After data collection, the advertiser will develop media plans for the product. Of course, today there are many different types of advertising outlets, so radio and television will probably be used in conjunction with print, the Internet, and some out-of-the-house advertising (such as billboards and transit ads). Frequently, sophisticated analysis will be used for allocating advertising funds to buy time on broadcasting stations. For example, a national restaurant chain may target the Durham, North Carolina, market for spending because the chain is expanding the number of restaurants in that area. A brand manager will want to purchase airtime on television stations for several weeks prior to the opening of each new store. The time segments available for commercials in radio and TV are called *spots*, and this term is also used to refer to the commercials themselves.

Media buyers use various formulas for determining the effectiveness of ad placement. One such measure, called **gross rating points (GRPs),** gives the buyer a way to evaluate a run of x number of commercials over the specific time period (*frequency*) that has a consistent rating for the target audience (*reach*). **Gross impressions,** another measure, reflect the total of all persons reached by each commercial in the advertising campaign. Using this kind of information to determine audiences and effectiveness, advertisers will calculate how much money they want to spend to achieve their marketing goals.

Nationally advertised brands such as Coke or McDonald's may decide to purchase broadcasting time on national television and cable networks, or they could choose to buy time on network affiliates or independent stations on a market-by-market basis. Frequently, nationally advertised brands will also help out the local retailer through cooperative advertising. (We discuss these differences in greater detail a bit later in this chapter.)

Occasionally an advertiser will select or not select specific media based solely on cost; for example, Pepsi decided not to advertise during the Super Bowl in 2010 largely because of the cost of each spot. And some advertisers have found that certain media work better for their products than others. Coupons work well for grocery products but are not easily used in electronic media.

Placing the Ad

Once advertisers determine the kind of media they want to buy (radio only or television only, for instance) and when (such as morning drive time on radio or prime time on TV), they can begin to evaluate the benefits of purchasing time on one or more specific media outlets. Generally advertising time is sold for a specific number of spots called a *package* and covers a specific period (called *flight dates*). For example, a nursery wouldn't want its "Spring Gardening Sale" spots aired at the end of July or beginning of August. So the media buyer will specify beginning and ending dates for the advertisement to run. Time buyers want to be able to compare the cost of doing business at station A with another media facility (station B) down the road. For this example we're going to use radio, but both radio and television stations use rate cards (see Figure 7–2) to help time sellers and buyers evaluate the cost of advertising. The next step is to find out how many potential listeners you can reach for your money.

Frequently rate cards will reflect charges based on different numbers of spots. As an advertiser purchases more time, the cost per spot decreases.

CPM: Measuring the Cost of Advertising on Two Stations

Media buyers use a standard formula to figure out the actual cost of a commercial spot. The unit cost is expressed as the cost to reach 1,000 audience members. **Cost per thousand** is abbreviated CPM, where M is the roman numeral for 1,000. To calculate the CPM of a radio station, you need to know the cost of the spot and the size of the audience. For example, if a shoe store owner wanted to advertise on station WXXX, which charged $240 per spot and had a listening audience of 20,000 people, the CPM formula would look like this:

$$CPM_{WXXX} = \frac{\text{Cost of spot}}{\text{Audience (000s)}} = \frac{240}{20} = \$12.00$$

Thus the CPM, or cost of reaching 1,000 listeners, would be $12.00 on WXXX. Now compare this CPM with that of station WZZZ, a station that has a similar listenership in terms of demographics. While the cost of advertising on WZZZ is slightly higher, it also

Figure 7–2

Multiweek ratecards give the account executive a breakdown of costs for each radio daypart. Placing a commercial at a specific time (P) is slightly more expensive than simply buying time (T) within each daypart.

WKKZ-FM
Multiweek Rate Card

SD	SL	MON		TUE		WED		THU		FRI		SAT		SUN		MON–FRI		SAT–SUN		MON–SUN	
		P	T	P	T	P	T	P	T	P	T	P	T	P	T	P	T	P	T	P	T
AMD	:60	$74	$67	$74	$68	$59	$54	$55	$50	$55	$50	$31	$28	$32	$29	$63	$58	$32	$28	$54	$49
	:30	44	40	46	42	40	36	39	35	37	34	23	21	22	20	41	37	22	20	36	33
	:15	19	17	19	18	16	15	15	14	15	14	9	9	11	10	17	16	10	10	15	14
MID	:60	51	46	56	51	57	52	67	61	60	55	36	32	34	31	58	53	35	32	52	47
	:30	37	34	37	34	40	36	46	42	44	40	28	26	27	24	41	37	28	25	37	34
	:15	14	13	14	13	16	14	18	16	18	16	13	12	13	12	16	14	13	12	15	14
PMD	:60	69	63	66	60	64	58	61	55	61	55	35	32	31	28	64	58	33	30	55	50
	:30	45	41	43	39	44	40	42	38	44	40	27	25	26	23	44	40	26	24	39	35
	:15	18	16	17	16	18	16	17	15	18	16	13	12	13	12	18	16	13	12	16	15
EVE	:60	26	23	24	22	22	20	23	#21	23	21	17	15	17	15	24	21	17	15	22	20
	:30	20	18	18	16	18	16	16	15	17	15	15	14	12	11	18	16	14	12	17	15
	:15	8	7	7	7	8	7	8	7	9	8	8	7	6	6	8	7	7	6	8	7
ON	:60	8	7	5	4	7	6	9	8	6	5	14	12	14	12	7	6	14	12	9	8
	:30	5	5	4	3	4	4	5	5	3	3	9	8	9	8	4	4	9	8	6	5
	:15	10	9	6	6	1	1	1	1	1	1	4	3	4	3	4	4	4	3	4	3
AMD-PMD	:60	65	59	65	60	60	55	61	55	59	53	34	31	32	29	62	56	33	30	54	49
	:30	42	38	42	38	41	37	42	38	42	38	26	24	25	22	42	38	26	23	37	34
	:15	17	15	17	16	17	15	17	15	17	15	12	11	12	11	17	15	12	11	15	14
AMD-EVE	:60	55	50	55	50	50	46	52	47	50	45	30	27	28	26	52	48	29	26	46	42
	:30	36	33	36	33	36	32	36	32	36	32	23	22	22	20	36	33	22	20	32	29
	:15	15	13	14	14	14	13	14	13	15	14	11	10	11	10	15	13	11	10	14	12
AMD-ON	:60	46	41	45	41	42	38	43	39	41	37	27	24	26	23	43	39	26	23	38	35
	:30	30	28	30	27	29	26	30	27	29	26	20	19	19	17	30	27	20	18	27	24
	:15	14	12	13	12	12	11	12	11	12	11	9	9	9	9	12	11	9	9	12	11

Selected weeks (week beginning): 9/27/2010, 10/4/2010, 10/11/2010, 10/18/2010, 10/25/2010.

has a slightly larger audience. The cost of advertising on WZZZ is $270 per spot for reaching 30,000 listeners, so its cost per 1,000 is only $9.00:

$$\text{CPM}_{\text{WZZZ}} = \frac{\text{Cost of spot}}{\text{Audience (000s)}} = \frac{270}{30} = \$9.00$$

If the media buyer were to compare the costs per thousand for the two stations, WZZZ would be a better buy. Even though WZZZ charges slightly more

per spot, the CPM is lower because it has a larger listening audience.

CPM is a good way of expressing efficiency—that is, the cost of reaching a thousand potential buyers of the product. For advertisers, the goal is generally to reach the largest potential audience for the smallest dollar investment; however, sometimes it is useful to spend more money to reach audiences with specific demographic characteristics. For example, a luxury car dealership may choose a show with a smaller audience, if the audience for that show is more affluent and likely to purchase luxury cars. **Cost per point (CPP)** is another good way of measuring efficiency and is similar to CPM except that it measures a specific demographic. Let's take our luxury car dealership again. If the cost of the advertising unit (such as a 30-second spot) was divided by the average rating of males 35 years and older listening to the station, you could figure the CPP for reaching males likely to buy your automobile. Marketers frequently try to determine **reach,** which is the number of different audience members exposed to an ad at least once during the period an advertisement is run.

Local Markets

Obviously the scenario we described for developing a media buy doesn't apply to all situations. Many advertisers are just not large enough to hire an advertising agency or a media buyer. In many smaller markets, a station sales representative will work directly with a store owner to develop a commercial package. Once the commercial is written and approved, it will be turned over to the station's production manager to execute. The sales representative will then schedule the spot in the station's commercial rotation for play.

The sales representative and the store owner might develop a long-term contract that reflects a discount for sponsoring a specific time slot—say, the 8 a.m. news. The sales rep will place a **standing order** for the shoe store's commercial to run over a specific period (several weeks or months, for example). Now no other advertiser will be able to sponsor the morning newscast for the duration of the standing order. This is known as a *nonpreemptible spot* because it cannot be bumped by another advertiser. In this example, the station's sales rep is acting like an account executive by fulfilling the needs of the local shoe store. Because the time period is reserved for weeks or perhaps months, the sales representative will need to see the shoe store owner regularly to develop new ideas for the commercials that air during the news sponsorship.

Small market radio stations frequently don't subscribe to a ratings service. As a result it may not be possible to calculate the CPM on small market stations. In rural America, where some towns have only a weekly newspaper, one or two local radio stations,

and the cable franchise, a store owner may simply work out the best deal possible with some or all of the local media available.

BROADCASTING SALES PRACTICES

Radio Sales

There are more than 13,000 radio stations in the United States. Five out of every six are commercial stations. Radio stations derive their revenues by selling listeners to potential advertisers who have products or services they want to promote. In Chapter 4 we stated that the goal of a radio station is to gain a large number of a certain type of listener. Radio sales are closely tied with demographic analysis and program planning. An all-news format radio station does not expect to have a large number of adolescents in its listening audience. An analysis of listening habits for people ages 12 to 18 would show that adolescents and young adults tend to listen to radio stations that concentrate on playing music appropriate to their age group.

The all-news radio listeners, according to research, however, will tend to be older and more affluent than listeners of most other radio formats. So while the all-news format station might actually have many fewer listeners than a station that caters to the young adults (say an urban contemporary format), it may actually charge the advertiser more for those listeners. A look at the type of sponsors might reveal that those clients interested in buying time on the all-news station are likely to be more upscale than the advertisers on a station trying to reach a much younger audience. Luxury cars, travel cruises, and commercials for brokerage houses or insurance are likely to be advertised on all-news radio. The station's charge for time may be day dependent (weekends are often cheaper than weekdays) and time dependent; morning drive will be more expensive than other times of the day because commuters are in the audience.

The Search for Spots   As we mentioned earlier, there are three types of advertising purchases made in broadcasting. The term *local sales* refers to the sale of commercial advertising by stations to advertisers in their immediate service area. Auto dealers, appliance stores, and restaurants are frequent local advertisers. As we noted, salespeople will call on local businesses and attempt to sell them ad time on the station. Today radio and television stations would try to combine their spot ads with banner ads on their Web sites. For example, a Buick dealer may buy radio spots and highlight pictures of a specific model on the radio station's Web page.

Station ad rates are pegged to the share of the audience that is listening to the station at a given time. Shares are determined by Arbitron (see Chapter 12), which publishes radio ratings reports (Nielsen publishes television reports). The larger the share, the more money a station can charge for its commercial spots. Most stations give discounts if an advertiser buys a large number of spots (called a package) and if the advertiser commits to buying spots that will run over an extended time, such as two **broadcast months.** Broadcasters use a special calendar where every month ends on the last Sunday of the month. These calendars make it easier to air spots on a Monday through Friday or Monday through Sunday schedule.

Ads cost more or less depending on the time period in which they air. The rate card for the radio day is broken down into **dayparts.** The most expensive daypart in which to advertise is generally morning drive time, and afternoon drive time is the second most expensive. The largest numbers of listeners are found in the audience during morning and evening drives. Commuters are frequent targets of advertising; tire and battery sales, insurance, and convenience stores are frequently advertised during these periods. Special sections of a ratings book will usually highlight average commute times for each radio market. The time between morning and evening drive is called *midday.* It is also an important advertising time. Evening is the next daypart, followed by late night or overnight. When an advertiser buys a package that will run on a station throughout the broadcast day, the term *run of schedule (ROS)* is used to designate that the spots are played during all the dayparts. Advertisers may buy time throughout the day or for specific dayparts. They will also buy time across the week or over several weeks or months, depending on the advertiser's needs.

Radio stations also use **cooperative advertising,** or simply co-op. Many local retail stores sell items made by national manufacturers. In a co-op arrangement, the national firm will share the cost of advertising with the local business. Thus the Maytag Company might pay part of the cost of local radio time purchased by Green's Appliance Store. Local retailers like co-ops because, in addition to helping Green's pay for the ads, the spots are often produced

by national ad agencies and are high in production value. Co-ops allow local retailers to tie their businesses in with a national campaign. Stations need to provide affidavits showing how many times the co-ops run. In fact, at some stations one or more members of the sales staff are assigned exclusively to deal with co-op plans.

The term *national spot sales* refers to the sale of commercial radio time to major national and regional advertisers. For example, Ford and General Motors buy national spots so that their commercials are heard all over the country but at different times and on different stations. The local dealer will participate in buying local spot sales with the manufacturer (for example, "Your Chevy dealers have great deals on end-of-year clearance models"). Frequently, national brands have regional managers to handle the ad campaigns, which can vary greatly from one region of the country to the next. For example, Goodyear probably won't run snow tire commercials in the South or the Southwest. The brand manager will buy time on northern stations where snow is most likely.

National spot sales are normally made on behalf of local stations by station representation firms, or reps. Reps maintain offices in the nation's biggest cities, like New York, Los Angeles, Dallas, and Atlanta, which are also home to the nation's leading advertisers and their agencies. Suppose Coke's media buyers want to buy spots on classic rock stations all over the United States. They will contact rep firms that may handle many different stations in markets around the country. The Coke media buyer places one order but buys airtime for many different individual stations in many different markets using this technique.

The third type of radio advertising is *network sales,* which is the sale of commercial advertising by regular networks, such as ABC or CBS, or special radio networks that carry specific programs such as a regional college football game. Network commercials are aired within the programs and carried on each station in the network. Although local stations receive no revenue for carrying the program, there may be some available time within the programs allocated for local spot sales. Network programs and sporting events can usually be sold locally at a premium, making carriage of the game a lucrative event for the local station. Some specialized programs, such as *American Top 40,* are distributed via CD or satellites to local stations with national spots embedded within

Table 7–1	Radio Advertising Volume, 1965–2009 (in $ millions)				
Year	**Network**	**National Spot**	**Local**	**Digital**	**Total***
1965	$ 60	$ 275	$ 582		$ 917
1970	56	371	881		1,308
1975	83	436	1,461		1,980
1980	183	779	2,740		3,702
1985	365	1,335	4,790		6,490
1990	433	1,626	6,780		8,839
1995	512	1,741	7,987		10,240
2001	893	3,036	13,932		17,861
2005	1,050	3,380	15,509		19,939
2009	1,048	2,361	10,842	480^	14,731

*Does not include off air sales.
^Breakout for digital began in 2009.
Source: Universal McCann and Radio Advertising Bureau analysis (Miller, Kaplan, Arase & Co., February 2010).

the program. Local spots may be inserted at the top or bottom of the hour for these weekly specials.

The Future of Radio Sales   Take a look at Table 7–1. It displays radio revenues reaped by advertising agencies since 1965; the revenues are broken down by type of expenditure. In 1970 about 30 percent of all radio buys were national spot sales. Local sales accounted for about two-thirds of all revenue. Network radio was in substantial decline at this time (before satellite distribution), with advertisers spending less than 4 percent of their radio budgets on network programs. Today nearly 75 percent of all radio sales are local. National spot sales account for only $1 out of every $13 of radio advertising. The majority of these sales go to the top-rated stations in the largest markets carrying popular talk shows such as Rush Limbaugh, Dave Ramsey, Mike, and Dr. Joy Browne. We will trace this trend in more detail in Chapter 8.

How does advertising affect radio's future? Radio, along with other advertising media, was hurt by the economic failures of 2008, and home sales declined in their aftermath. However, radio is poised to grow slightly over the next few years. During the previous two decades, radio garnered only about 7 percent of all advertising dollars. Some radio group owners have started consolidating with Internet and off-air sales (such as billboard advertisers), making the radio–new media–billboard combinations more attractive places for ad dollars; but while online, billboard, and out-of-home advertising are growing,

radio has largely stagnated. National spot advertising has declined since 2006. High-definition (HD) radio may offer some new opportunities for radio groups, but it will be several years before there are enough receivers in the field.

As in the TV business, national spot advertising is usually sold on the basis of station popularity, as measured by ratings. Almost without exception the highest-rated stations will get the majority of advertising expenditures. Media buyers usually go with these higher-ranking stations, leaving the other stations out of the huge advertising expenditure. Stations with higher rankings in market share thus outbill and outearn their competition, usually by a wider margin than their ratings advantage. Consequently, a station's share of the audience is an extremely important sales tool for a media rep. The higher-ranking stations are much easier to sell to media buyers.

Public Radio Stations   Public, educational, and noncommercial radio stations are difficult to categorize. Many noncommercial radio stations operate on tiny budgets, frequently as part of a high school or college communications program. Some of these stations operate part-time, while others are full-service stations. It is possible for the FCC to require a part-time, noncommercial station to share its frequency with other noncommercial entities in an urban area.

Public radio stations are affiliated with NPR (National Public Radio). These stations carry network and syndicated programs reflecting the entire range of programming from news to classical music, from *Car Talk* to *Prairie Home Companion* to *Talk of the Nation* and *Wait Wait . . . Don't Tell Me!* Many stations are well financed by local educational or community entities while others rely heavily on listener support. Unlike PBS, which acts as a television program distributor and syndicator, National Public Radio is a program producer and supplier. NPR uses underwriting to help defray the cost of programming, but it also receives money from its affiliated stations, which purchase programming, and from the Corporation for Public Broadcasting (CPB). NPR has embraced some new technologies as a way of expanding programming and revenue. It has developed a wide variety of offerings online, has two satellite channels on Sirius XM Satellite Radio, and provides a wide range of podcasts on iTunes Music Store, which are sponsored. Like the rest of the industry, the economic turndown forced the network to cut positions and trim budgets in 2009 in the face of a $23 million deficit. NPR's budget was approximately $165 million in 2009.

Many NPR stations ask for listener support as part of their way to raise the funds necessary to buy programming. Some local and state governments support public radio stations through grants, although grant monies have been in decline since the mid-1990s. Because educational and noncommercial radio stations run the gamut from extremely small to very large, it is difficult to generalize about personnel and budgets. Noncommercial stations can solicit corporate or advertiser support through underwriting. Unlike commercial advertising, underwriting cannot make a call to action, such as "To order yours call 202-555-XXXX now."

Television

America's 1,750 full-time television stations are much more complex structurally than radio stations. Television stations have a greater reliance on outside programming sources than radio. Radio stations rely either on local talent for playing music for a local audience or satellite programming that is demographically targeted to that audience. Television network programming is primarily based on shows of a fixed length that are meant to reach very large audiences. While some cable television is geared toward more demographically specific audiences, like network television the majority of its programming is based on fixed-length programs. It makes sense, therefore, that television programming is acquired, aired, and sold rather differently from most radio programming.

In small to medium-size television markets, almost all the stations are affiliated with one of the four big television networks, or with one of the smaller networks like Ion or CW. Affiliates downlink the network feed off a geostationary satellite. During those times when the network is supplying programs, the television station is responsible for retransmission of the network programs for that market and for station breaks at designated times. Station breaks between network programs allow the local stations to sell advertisers **adjacencies,** lucrative local spots that are aired next to prime-time, daytime, late-night, and weekend network programming. Those few minutes adjacent to network programs usually command a premium and are very lucrative for affiliated stations.

The amount of money that a particular station or network can charge sponsors is influenced by several factors, such as the number of people predicted to watch a given program or to watch during a given time period and the number of commercials the advertiser wishes to place with the station or network. In general, the cost charged to the advertiser is based on the estimated number of people viewing a program. The larger the ratings estimate, the more a station or network will charge for the spot.

Several economic factors affect the way the industry works, but competitive programming is the primary factor (see Chapter 9). Networks are important producers of programming. They develop different kinds of shows to cover many time slots throughout the broadcast day, including the crucial prime-time hours between the evening news and late news. But when there is no network feed, television stations turn to the **syndication** market for programs. Shows that were once successful on the network are frequently syndicated to local stations. These former prime-time rerun shows like *The Office* and *CSI* compete with other syndicated programming produced exclusively for local distribution, such as the popular game show *Jeopardy,* talk shows like *The View,* or magazines such as *Entertainment Tonight;* these are examples of first-run syndication. All these shows compete with locally produced programming. Local news and information shows are also important programs for television stations. As you can see, television programming is quite different from that of radio.

Profile: *Wheel of Fortune* and *Jeopardy*—The Grand Daddies of Quiz Shows

The 1950s had game show scandals with programs like *Twenty-One* and the *$64,000 Question*. Since then game shows have come and gone: *Concentration*, *$20,000 Pyramid*, and *Family Feud*. Some new shows like *Deal or No Deal* do very well for several seasons, but *Wheel of Fortune* and *Jeopardy* continue to reign supreme in the hotly contested first-run syndication market. Both shows are produced by King World Productions.

Even though *Wheel* and *Jeopardy* have distinctive sets, you may have noticed that both shows go "on the road" every season. Harry Friedman, executive producer for the two shows, took *Jeopardy* on the road for the first time in November 1997. Since then the shows have traveled extensively. Friedman says that even though producing a game show on location is expensive, taking the shows around the country creates a buzz in the local markets where the shows stop, and this frequently causes ratings to jump in those regions of the country. Special shows, such as *Jeopardy's* college contests, also provide ratings boosts through important sweeps periods.

Both shows, despite having been on the air for many years, still rank high in syndicated ratings, though *Wheel* consistently ranks higher than *Jeopardy*, particularly in the important women 25 to 54 audience.

Wheel and *Jeopardy* have been the top-rated game shows since they premiered in 1983. Perhaps one of the reasons that *Wheel* attracts such a large audience year after year is that the show's two stars seem real and down to earth. Pat Sajak, the host, says the show's neither hip nor too young. "It's a diverting half-hour, and that's all it's supposed to be."

Every season brings something new to the shows. In its 20th season, *Wheel* fine-tuned its format by adding a "mystery round." The change adds two mystery wedges to the wheel; if the player lands on one, he or she needs to decide whether to take the money or choose the mystery prize on the back of the wedge. Just one hitch, though. The back of the wedge could be either a prize or a bankrupt, forfeiting the winnings up to that point.

Jeopardy has seen some revamping, too. All the dollar amounts of the questions have been doubled, and contestants can stay on the show as long as they win. In 2005 *Jeopardy's* ratings skyrocketed when Ken Jennings won for 74 consecutive days. Whew!

Both shows have been renewed through the 2013 to 2014 season. Friedman says, "It's okay to change the show, but we never change the game." He must know what he's talking about. Friedman's worked on 30 game shows during his career.

Network Sales—Getting Things Upfront Even though audiences for the television networks have slipped well below the 50 percent mark, network television is still a cost-effective way to reach large numbers of Americans at one time. Advertisers buy time slots within individual programs on the networks to reach the large mass audience. Television viewing is heaviest during the fall and spring; it's lightest during the summer rerun season. Media buyers purchase network time to meet the specific needs of their client's products, frequently paying more for special times of the year, such as the pre-Christmas selling season, or special occasions such as the Olympics, or special events like the Academy Awards.

The television advertising year is broken down into a number of different sales periods, but most networks like to see **upfront** revenue. This sales period begins in late spring and ends in the summer before the fall television season begins. National advertisers buy time on the new season before it starts because this assures advertisers that they control time slots within the popular program time periods or program nights and during important selling seasons, like the holiday season between Thanksgiving and New Years. Upfront is an important time. Network sales produce the revenue stream that they use to pay for the cost of programming, to pay the costs of distribution, and to pay the creative talent to develop new programs. In other words, when a network sells more inventory before the season starts, it is better able to gauge revenues for the upcoming season, something Wall Street seems to appreciate. Cable networks sell upfront inventory for their programs too.

National advertisers also use **scatter buying,** which involves buying time in prime-time and other slots during the broadcast day, to purchase network time. The four quarters in the scatter buying market correspond to the seasons of the year. Buying time this way can be very cost-effective for advertisers. If the actual audience share does not meet preseason estimates, the cost for buying that time slot will decrease in the scatter market. The reverse can be true, too. For example, if analysis of a new television show's audience reveals a greater viewership, particularly strong among females aged 25 to 45 (a very attractive demographic), advertising agencies may decide to buy time during that show in the scatter market even though the rates increase. Buying time in the scatter market allows an advertiser to use a planning cycle more effectively, and some networks give ratings guarantees for these purchases since hard numbers can be ascertained from overnight ratings. But broadcast networks also offer guaranteed audience targets in the upfront market to protect the incentive to buy time early. This strategy seems to be working less well in recent years; upfront sales for the 2010 television season were estimated to net $8.7 billion, down slightly from the highs of 2006. Some networks sell as much as 60 percent of their available time in the upfront market.

Networks collect large sums of money from advertisers because they offer buyers the promise of reaching large audiences, but they must rely on affiliates to carry their programming to make good on delivering the numbers. Fox sells time to Chevy and promises that the ad can be seen by 95 percent of the total U.S. population. However, the guarantee for 95 percent of the population is based on all Fox affiliates carrying the specific program where the ad is placed. The relationship is symbiotic both for advertiser and programmer. For example, Fox and its affiliates agreed to share the costs for NFL programming when it started broadcasting NFL games. In return, Fox and its affiliates both get a program that targets a desirable population (males) that's hard to reach with regular programming.

Some networks use **compensation** as an incentive for affiliates to carry their programs. Networks and affiliates negotiate for the rights to sell additional local inventory in return for carrying programs. Usually this means that affiliates can make additional revenue since CPMs in prime time are much higher than other parts of the broadcast day. This usually turns out to be very lucrative for five-star and four-star stations that are actually owned and operated by the networks or strong affiliates. In essence, networks help themselves when they carry their own programs, along with all the other group owners who have affiliated stations. Networks sometimes make very little money on their network operations;

but they make a tremendous amount of cash flow (money) on their owned-and-operated stations. KNBC in Los Angeles and WNBC in New York are among the most profitable stations in the country. They're owned by NBC Universal.

The Economics of Networking The finances of network television programming are very complex. In the 1970s, when the networks were at the peak of their power, the government barred them from owning financial interests in their programs (financial syndication rules). These government regulations, which allowed independent producers to develop, were relaxed in recent years as more competitors have entered the television marketplace. Today television networks own or coproduce a great deal of their own programming, and they can develop new programming with the intention of profiting from the show when it is placed into the syndication marketplace (reruns) or when it is sold to international audiences. Conversely there are instances when a network's parent company may produce programs for competitors. For example, *Big Bang Theory* is produced by Warner Brothers in association with CBS, which airs the program.

Television programs, particularly dramas and high-profile situation comedies, are very expensive to produce. The per-episode cost for a drama can be in the millions of dollars. Much of the cost is personnel, but the cost of production has escalated over the years. Programs that survive the first few weeks of a television season sometimes go on to become hits and run for years. Programs such as *Friends* and *24* are prime examples. However, it is not unusual for networks to lose money the first season that a program airs, and sometimes the network never makes enough in advertising to break even. That's because the cost of production, promotion, and compensation can exceed the revenue the networks derive from the sale of time. Some expensive shows never make enough advertising revenue to pay for production either because they don't receive a high enough rating to merit higher advertising rates or they cost too much to produce.

To make network television profitable, networks charge a large amount of money for a 30-second spot during the most popular programs. Table 7–2 shows the costs to advertise on some popular network programs. Even though costs are high, particularly for *American Idol* and *CSI*, the CPM for these shows is only about $27.00 because the shows garner such

Table 7–2	Cost of 30-Second Time Slot for Prime-Time Programs (2009 Season)		
American Idol (end-of-season shows)	$490,000	FOX
Sunday Night Football	339,700	NBC
Grey's Anatomy	240,462	ABC
Desperate Housewives	228,000	ABC
Two and a Half Men	226,635	CBS
The Office	191,236	NBC

Source: *Advertising Age*, October 26, 2009.

high ratings. The CPM for advertising on a network television is actually in line with many national brands' advertising budgets and generally lower than buying time on local television stations individually. Network television still provides a truly mass audience, even though audiences are getting smaller.

Networks usually negotiate to broadcast the program at least twice: once in either the fall or spring 11-week season and one rerun in the summer or in the holiday season. So a highly rated prime-time show might generate between $2 million and $3 million in ad revenue for the first showing; that's not enough to offset the $3 to 4 million a show costs to produce. The rerun allows the network to recoup some of that loss. Also, television producers will frequently share the costs with the network. Producers, too, may actually lose money in the first showing of a hit series, but they tend to make money in the *back-end* market. This means that when a program gets sold for distribution in syndication, the show can make a tremendous amount of money for the producers because it is sold to a cable network or to television stations on a market-by-market basis or to a cable network on a per-episode basis. Syndicated shows that are sold with exclusivity to a cable network will garner a higher per-episode cost than shows that may be sold to several cable outlets.

Sports provide a real dilemma for television networks. Televised professional sporting events are becoming increasingly expensive as the salaries for sports stars rise to astronomical levels. Sports leagues demand increasing revenue for broadcast rights for a number of reasons. (CBS, NBC and FOX are paying the NFL $11.6 billion to broadcast games through the 2011 season.) Some sports teams do not make sufficient revenues from gate sales to pay the athletes' salaries. Team owners rely on royalties from the broadcast of games and merchandising to sup-

plement the gate receipts. Since sporting events have less potential as reruns, there are few ways for networks to recoup the cost for the rights to air the event (especially with declining viewership). When costs exceed the ability to charge advertisers for the product, they lose money. Networks continue to ante up for large sporting events to capture male viewers aged 18 to 49. In recent years, some networks have lost money broadcasting certain professional sports. Industry analysts pegged ABC's losses on *Monday Night Football* at $150 million during the 2006 season. When asked to pony up more, ABC and its affiliates, which had helped pay for NFL rights, passed. As a result, *Monday Night Football* moved to ESPN, which has two revenue streams: advertising and subscription fees. ESPN is paying $8.8 billion for the multi-year contract through 2013.

Syndications and Local Sales   Stations will fill non-network time with TV shows that have been purchased in the syndication market. Syndicated programming may be composed of *off-network syndications* (reruns) such as *Seinfeld, Everybody Loves Raymond,* and *CSI,* or the shows could be developed specifically as *first-run syndication*. First-run syndications such as *Jeopardy, Entertainment Tonight,* and *Access Hollywood* are shown directly on local television stations, usually in *early fringe* (the hour before prime time).

When a television station licenses a syndicated show package, it obtains the exclusive rights to show each episode a certain number of times in the local market. For example, suppose WEEE-TV decided to pay $10,000 per episode for the rights to show 150 episodes of *CSI: Crime Scene Investigation* three times each. (Striped across the 5-day week, 150 times 3 is 450 daily showings; this will provide approximately 1½ years of local programming for the station.) This deal, worth $1.5 million for the program producer, would be based (1) on the size of the market and (2) on how much other TV stations in that market might be willing to bid for the rights to the show. If the producers were able to strike similar deals in just 50 of the largest 240 television markets in the United States, they would be very happy and very rich. To carry this example to a conclusion, WEEE-TV sells the number of commercial minutes available within each *CSI* episode locally or in national spot sales. The station must make back the cost of syndication plus enough money to cover station overhead, station commissions, and still meet a profit target. You can

Issues: Changing the Way Networks Do Business

In earlier chapters, you read about the growth of the networks and how this growth made both David Sarnoff and William Paley wealthy, famous, and powerful. Today the economic situation is different from the heady days when networks commanded 90 percent of the viewing audience. In 2006 network audience shares combined were less than 45 percent, and only two of the four major television networks reported profits for the year (ABC and CBS). In 2010 network shares fell even further.

The reality of the business today is that making money in network television has never been harder. Cable is an increasingly competitive player, introducing new shows that seem to be attracting significant attention in the press and significant viewership. This new reality has prompted some within the industry to change the way the networks do business.

NBC, struggling to find a hit drama in the important 10 p.m. slot, developed a new strategy. After years of being the ratings king in the late-night spot, Jay Leno was moved into prime time. NBC reasoned that it could use Leno's popularity to gain enough audience share to make money without necessarily winning the time period. The real advantage from NBC's point of view was that a talk show would cost much less to produce than a drama, even with Leno making a huge $30 million salary.

According to reports in the industry, the cost differential between producing a talk show versus a drama, averaging about $3 million per episode, would save NBC millions of dollars every week. Some estimated that the *Tonight Show* could be produced for less than $500,000 per show.

NBC also thought that Conan O'Brien would bring his loyal base into the 11:30 p.m. time slot, giving the network some younger demographics for the earlier time. NBC had already promised the *Tonight Show* slot to O'Brien when Leno was ready to vacate the spot.

What NBC didn't count on was a virtual revolt from its affiliates from across the country. Lower ratings for Leno meant that there was no strong lead-in for the late news that most affiliates produced. Because news is the most profitable time for affiliates, this was seen as a make-or-break issue for many stations already reeling from significant revenue reductions during the recession.

The interesting experiment was pulled after about 6 months on the air, and NBC used the Winter Olympics to fill the 10:00 hole. Although Leno went back to the 11:30 slot, Conan fared less well, choosing to take a large buyout for his trouble.

see that the amount of money needed to support showing network reruns, particularly big hits, on the local station can be very high. Because costs for quality programming can be so high, many shows are offered as barter syndication.

Syndicated programming runs the gamut from sophisticated coproductions to quiz shows to dramas to fairly vulgar talk shows. Some programs don't cost any money at all, while some are expensive; barter syndication programs may be provided to television stations for little or no money, but if the station uses barter, it offers the distributor a certain amount of its commercial time to sell within the program. As we noted with radio, stations are obliged to carry the spots if they carry the programs. Frequently these shows will include a couple of 30-second "holes" in which local spots can be inserted by the local station. On some quiz shows, viewers will see product placements (that is, where the items are given

away as prizes). These products are given by sponsors as consideration for the promotional value of having them seen on the show, making quiz shows relatively inexpensive to produce. Next time you watch *Wheel of Fortune*, note how many automobiles are on the floor as grand prizes.

News and informational programs are extremely important local products for the station to sell. Many stations operate large and sophisticated news departments capable of programming several hours per day on the station. Time sold during and adjacent to highly rated local news programming often generates large percentages of the TV station's revenue. Some studies indicate that time sales during local news programming generate as much as 40 percent of a station's total revenue. Networks encourage affiliates to have strong local news because they often run directly before the network news. A good local newscast can provide a strong lead-in for the net-

Some commercial advertisers use a person to represent the company. "Flo" has become a spokesperson for Progressive insurance. Other insurance companies have used ducks and reptiles, adding humor to the commercial message.

work newscast. With the higher ratings numbers, higher spot prices can be charged.

Spot Advertising   Spot advertising consists of commercials that national advertisers place on selected stations across the nation. For example, makers of harvesting equipment might wish to purchase ads in a large number of rural markets. Buying time on the network would be inefficient for them because it would be unlikely that many people in New York City or Los Angeles would be shopping for harvesters, although that same company may buy network time to advertise its lawn mowers. Local advertising consists of commercials that are shown on the broadcast

Wheel of Fortune is the most popular game show on television.

station in your area and that feature products and services in the local community served by the TV station.

Most spot buying is handled by a local station's national representative (or simply rep) firm. The rep represents local stations to national and regional buyers. National reps make it easier for buyers to purchase time by being a central contact point for a given station. A national rep may represent only one station in a given market or all the stations of a group owner. Some rep firms sell spot advertising outside the station's local market because a station often has its own in-house sales team selling time for the local market. This prevents a conflict of interest.

Reps will also offer programming advice and market research to help the station increase its viewership. This advice is not altruistic, however; an increase in viewer numbers means better ratings. Reps have an easier time selling time at higher rates to national advertisers for stations that have the highest ratings in their areas. More time sold at a higher CPM means more profit for the rep (whose fee is a percentage of sales) as well as for the station. Because the goal of the rep is to sell commercials on each of the many stations he or she represents in a

Figure 7–3

TV Advertising Sales 2010 (in Billions)

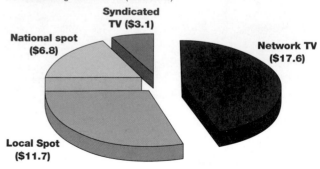

Source: Jack Myers Business Reports and industry sources.

given market or region, this kind of advertising is usually known as the spot business.

As Figure 7–3 indicates, the local and national spot business today is a sizable advertising segment, totaling about $17.6 ($11.7 is local) billion annually in billings for 2010. National and local spot advertising is the lifeblood of many TV stations, especially those in major markets. Automotive retailers, national restaurant chains, movie studios and entertainment enterprises,

QVC is one of the most profitable cable networks, generating billions in revenue each year.

Events: Gillette, Sports Networks, and Super Events

In 1939 the Gillette razor company paid $200,000 for the rights to broadcast the World Series by radio. Paying this sum of money, large for 1939, established the facts that sponsoring sports was both costly and profitable. This event triggered the beginning of a relationship among sports teams, players, and the product sponsors that like to be associated with them. The target was to reach males in the audience. Over the years, costs and technology have changed the way the game is played.

Networks quickly realized there was money to be made by selling advertising within these mega-events. Today Rupert Murdoch, Disney, and Comcast all want to exercise control over sports broadcasting. By 2000, Murdoch's News Corporation, the parent company of Fox, purchased a financial stake in 19 of the 23 networks that broadcast regional sporting events. These deals did not include teams in the National Football League that already play games seen over the Fox television network. Murdoch wanted to offer advertisers the convenience of one-stop spot shopping. Buyers can go to one organization and make buys on most teams in the three primary professional sports. News Corporation became the first real competition to ABC/ESPN, which has long dominated professional sports. However, there is a difference. While advertisers buy network time on ESPN, spots shown on News Corporation are primarily purchased regionally as spot sales. There's more flexibility.

Comcast, the nation's largest cable company, created the Outdoor Life Network (OLN) to compete with ESPN and other sports venues in 1995 with a mere 4.8 million subscribers. OLN started life a few years earlier as the Outdoor Channel, an offshoot of a successful infomercial called *The Gold Prospecting Show.* In its early days the network's offers were limited to smaller sports venues. The growing popularity of events like the National Hockey League games, the Tour de France, and the Boston Marathon have helped the network grow. OLN became Versus in 2006.

Regional and specialized sports networks have also developed for cable viewers. Comcast started four regional sports networks to compete with Fox. Comcast offers different regions Sports West, Philadephia, Baltimore–Washingon, and Chicago. All provide regional games to Comcast viewers. These regional venues are joined by networks like YES and the New England Sports Network.

Today the NFL dominates the sports scene. In the 2010 football season, CBS, NBC, ESPN, Fox, and DirecTV all carried NFL action and aired thousands of spots promoting various NFL games. Media experts say that all the various deals will yield revenues of $20 billion for the NFL during the 2011 and 2012 seasons. But of all sporting events, the Super Bowl is king. Each year a handful of advertisers ante up a royal sum for 30 seconds of time in the most coveted of advertising time periods.

The 2010 Super Bowl's advertising time raked in between $2.5 million and $3 million for CBS and yielded 106 million viewers for advertisers. Viewers wait eagerly to see the commercials. High-profile advertising has become a tradition during the Super Bowl since Apple Computer ran a now-famous commercial introducing the Macintosh in 1984. Consumers wait to see what ad agencies have cooked up for the show.

As a new twist, the NFL provided multimedia distribution for just the TV commercials, allowing viewers to see them again on cable video-on-demand, on the Web, or by having them downloaded to cell phones.

Multiplatform programming is becoming more popular. Shown here is the SportsCenter 360 XBOX Live screen display.

and computer/office equipment suppliers tend to use national spot sales heavily. Election years provide substantive advertising dollars for local TV as candidates vie for viewers' attention. Firms with a particularly impressive track record for their clients include Katz and Telerep.

Local Sales   Today an increasing amount of the advertising revenue of a local station comes from the sale of advertising time to local merchants. Local car dealerships, appliance stores, lawyers, laser hair removal services, and others seek to tell people about their services and products through advertising on the local station.

Stations employ salespeople called *account executives* to visit potential advertisers and to demonstrate how advertising on their TV station will increase business. As we noted earlier, a good account executive will help the client develop an advertising strategy based on the amount of money the advertiser has to spend. Like the radio example we used earlier, the account executive should help the client plan the time of the year and the broadcast day during which to advertise and may, particularly in smaller markets, help write commercials. Account executives are usually paid a commission, a percentage of the value of advertising they sell.

The primary tools of the account executive are the ratings and the list of prices for advertising, which are on the rate card. The cost of advertising is based on the show the client chooses to advertise in.

In terms of advertising revenues, local businesses are increasingly important to local stations. In the last 30 years, local advertising from local merchants and service providers has increased substantially until the economic downturn. Local spot sales totaled more than $11 billion in 2010. The recession caused significant reductions in the automotive sector (almost 30 percent in some markets) and other typical spot ads.

Cable Television Sales   National cable television sales are similar to that of network television, and it is becoming an increasingly important venue for advertisers (see Table 7–3). National advertisers buy time both upfront and in the scatter markets. In recent years, cable upfront sales have increased substantially, reaching about $8 billion in 2010; but the CPM is lower than broadcast TV. That's because cable is still very much a niche medium and there are many cable channels, even though cable's largest

Table 7–3	Top 15 Cable Advertisers: 2009	
Rank	**Parent Company**	**2009—$$$ (000)**
1	Procter & Gamble	877,999.9
2	U.S. government	435,042.6
3	Johnson & Johnson	297,140.7
4	General Mills	266,629.6
5	Walmart Stores	259,928.3
6	YUM! Brands	258,071.5
7	Pfizer	247,691.9
8	Berkshire Hathaway	241,412.5
9	Time Warner	239,411.3
10	General Electric	224,939.9
11	Progressive Corp	221,987.3
12	Verizon Communications	209,793.5
13	Walt Disney	208,135.4
14	AT&T	200,420.9
15	Sony	190,061.6

Source: CAB analysis of AdViews.

networks have made substantial gains in ratings over the past few years.

The Cable Advertising Bureau projected that the growth of advertising for cable will remain strong. Basic cable network advertising was estimated to be about $19.7 billion in 2010, with total cable ad revenue estimated at $24.4 billion. Automotive and telecommunications are among cable's largest advertisers (see Table 7–4). Cable's ability to target specific audiences is a real plus, but some cable networks that target broad audiences are doing well. Today some cable network ratings exceed the lower-rated broadcast networks. In addition, cable has a strong children's television audience. These factors point to the prospect of steady growth in national cable sales. Comparatively speaking, cable sales have grown more rapidly than those of over-the-air television.

Table 7–4	Top Product Categories
1	Automotive, auto accessories, and equipment
2	Telecommunications
3	Local Services
4	Financial
5	Miscellaneous Retail

Source: Kantar Media Reports - January 2011.

Ethics: Radio Promotion—Chaos Out of Control?

While promotion is increasingly important in the hotly competitive environment of radio today, there are indications that some stations are going overboard in their efforts to lure audiences. Some examples:

- A morning DJ for a Phoenix station pogo-sticked the entire 26-mile route of the Boston Marathon—it took him two days—and he wound up with severe knee damage.

- An Abilene, Texas, DJ tried to raise money for the United Way by spending 81 straight hours on a Ferris wheel. One night, while adjusting his sleeping bag, he fell off. Luckily for him, he was at the bottom of the wheel at the time. The Ferris wheel attendant who immediately rushed to his aid, however, was not so lucky; he was hit by the wheel and suffered a concussion.

- In Jacksonville, North Carolina, Fat Boy, the morning shock jock, sent his sidekick Waffleman covered in mud to ring the doorbells at people's homes, asking if he could take a shower at their homes. Numerous residents called the cops and complained. The shock jock resigned, but we don't have any details of what became of the sidekick and whether he came clean on the promotion.

- Two DJs in Miami almost caused an international incident when they telephoned Fidel Castro and pretended to be Venezuelan president Hugo Chavez. Castro was not amused.

Listeners are well aware of the treasures to be had in radio promotion. Sometimes they listen just for a chance to win. Sometimes the promotion goes wrong. T-Bone of Kansas City's *The Rock* taped 100 Powerball lottery tickets to his naked body and then stood on a median strip at an intersection of the Shawnee Mission Parkway, encouraging listeners to drive by and take tickets off him. T-Bone, using his cell phone, described his exploits to his listeners until the police picked him up for public nudity and disorderly conduct. Evidently none of the tickets was a winner for the lottery, which was worth $250 million that week.

Local cable television spots air across many different basic ad-supported cable networks simultaneously. Today, many different cable systems have interconnected, allowing cable ads to be sold over entire geographic regions. Cable spot advertising firms provide clients with the ability to buy nationally, regionally (called multimarket), locally, or even in a portion of a market. By coordinating the station break times on different cable networks, local franchisers are able to show commercial **pods** of local spot sales. In addition, many larger cable franchises now cover large urban and metropolitan areas of major U.S. cities. Local cable revenue is expected to become much more important in the next few years.

Public Television Public television stations can be small or large, depending on the markets they serve. Funding for a public station comes from a variety of sources. Fewer federal and state dollars are available for public stations than in the past, and as a result underwriting rules for television were relaxed in the mid-1980s. They cannot "sell" time as commercial stations do, so public stations generally rely on underwritings and local revenue-raising promotions for a portion of their budget. Underwritings for public television are much more commercial-like than they were 10 years ago, using logos and other identifers.

Corporate underwriting is not a large portion of public television's revenue, amounting to 20 percent of the overall production budget for PBS nationally programming. According to PBS, national underwriting had been flat prior to 2008 and decreased in the following recession. One of the problematic areas for public television is that it is difficult for PBS to respond to underwriters' need for shorter on-air messages. Some new thinking is being applied to these problems, including adding banner and skyscraper ads to companion online sites and uplinking underwriting messages in separate modules that can be changed easily.

At the local station level, corporate underwriting usually means that a local company will help pay for the cost of the specific programming. Shows such as *The Antiques Roadshow* will have both a national and local underwriter. The show's production costs are partially underwritten by the national sponsor, while the local PBS affiliate may use a local retail store to pay for the rights to air the program or costs associated with local station operations. Membership drives usually occur twice each year; their goal is to resubscribe current station members and add new ones to the roster. During these membership periods the station will run a heavy schedule of specials and promotions.

Promotions tend to center around art auctions, community fund-raising events, and similar activities that raise revenue for the station. PBS also makes substantial use of its image as the place for quality programming in order to raise funds. During special membership drives, local stations will broadcast concerts and specials by noted performers as a way of generating new station members. Concert specials will often be followed by the star herself or himself asking for your pledge of support. In the same vein, PBS stations use their children's television stars, such as Big Bird, to help raise funds for the station.

Over the past few years, federal funding for public television programming has risen modestly to slightly more than $400 million in 2010. PBS and others have criticized the low government funding levels, but Congress has not seemed especially interested in increasing levels for noncommercial television programming, especially during times of looming federal debt. PBS officials are quick to point out that despite modest increases over the years, funding levels have not kept pace with the rate of inflation.

OTHER ASPECTS OF BROADCAST SALES

Station Identification and Promotion

Station identification is extremely important because the sale of time is directly related to the number of listeners the station has, and generally, the greater the listenership, the greater the potential number of sponsors. So stations try to make themselves identifiable to their listeners and sponsors through the use of slogans and promotional contests.

Radio stations use a combination of call letters and their frequency (location on the radio dial) as a means of promoting themselves. Number and letter combinations like "95X" often connote music preference in the same way that "Lite 102" has meaning for the listener. Other stations use slogans like "the River" as a way to make themselves more identifiable. These combinations are recorded in diaries at "sweeps" times, and a rating for the station is determined. Stations will adopt slogans that help identify them to their listeners. For example, stations that call themselves "your news leader" will place heavy emphasis on their information and news services. You

can guess what the programming will be like when a station calls itself the "Sports Authority."

Promotions are very important for a station, especially before or during a sweeps period. Frequently a radio station will trade out commercial time for products or services that the station can give away. For example, a station may give away a luxury car and trade the equivalent value of the car for air time that the dealership can use. Contests are used as a way to build listenership and loyalty. Promotions vary greatly based on the size of the market and the station.

Good ratings are vital. Just one ratings point can translate into thousands of dollars in extra sales for a station. In the last few years, many stations have increased the value of the prizes given away during sweeps in an effort to raise the diary numbers and ultimately their ratings. Expensive sports cars and cash prizes in excess of $10,000 or $20,000 are not unusual prizes.

Radio stations also use another type of promotion to raise listenership: Commercial-free rides encourage extended listening. Commercials are then clustered together at the end of, say, "20 minutes of nonstop music." When the 20-minute ride extends past the 15-, 30-, or 45-minute mark, that listener is counted in the ratings for that average quarter hour. (See Chapter 12.)

When a station changes its overall format, it may change just prior to a ratings period. After an advertising blitz, stations might begin a "commercial-free" month during that period. The commercial-free month may boost ratings, and the station's sales for the next quarter or half of year will be set by the numbers garnered during that ratings period. Frequently listeners are drawn to the station during the commercial-free month but often revert back to old listening habits when commercials resume. Most stations realize that they need good numbers all year long, so promotion tends to be an ongoing process. Other promotional vehicles may include station events within the community.

Television has a great need for promoting programs and personalities. Television promotion tends to be somewhat different from that of radio. You'll see few contests and even fewer opportunities to win the sports car of your dreams. Instead, television promotion tends to be divided into two specific categories: the promotion of specific shows or the copromotion of events in coordination with a sales event.

Promotional announcements, or promos, are short announcements that publicize a program on the station. These messages remind you of the content of a show—"Tomorrow on *Maury:* Satanic transvestite drug-abusing prostitutes who want to adopt"—or they may just remind the viewer of an upcoming program—"Eleven top stories tonight at 11." The process of promoting a television show is important and costly for broadcasters. Remember that every 10- or 20-second promotion is time that a television station cannot sell. Obviously a station must make a commitment to promote itself and its shows. Viewers won't immediately know when they can watch *Judge Judy* unless the station tells them (although some viewers do use the TV listings!).

Local television news is another area in which stations need to promote themselves. Does the station have a particular focus on local government? A special investigative team? Or special "family health-casts" or a "Your Stories" feature? Does the station specialize in covering a particular local sports team? Viewers will need to know what distinguishes one station's news programming from that of the competition. (One station in Southern California touts the fact that it is the only station in the market with Doppler radar even though it rarely rains in that part of the country!) Solid promotions are necessary to build audience and, as a result, revenue through high-priced advertising. Usually television stations will need to use cross-promotion (such as billboards) to reach potential viewers who normally don't watch that newscast.

Station Web sites are increasingly important to building strong ties to listeners or viewers in the

Advertising is often keyed to content. On this web page a GMC car ad (right box) came up when the term "SUV" was search on the JDPower.com website.

community. As a result Web sites are important promotional vehicles for broadcast stations. A good broadcast Web site provides important linkages to the station's programming and news departments. Many stations are providing extended coverage for local news stories on the Web. Frequently there are resources linking people to community service organizations, expanded weather and sports coverage, particularly for television stations that have significant news organizations.

Web sites are usually linked to the station's public service initiatives and can provide important information for members of the community. In the aftermath of the Hurricane Katrina disaster, many broadcast stations in southern states provided information on their Web sites about how to get help, look for missing persons, and apply for disaster relief. Stations along the Gulf Coast produced many special reports for viewers about the ecological and economic problems that developed as a result of the BP oil spill. Many stations set up special sections of their Web pages to keep residents informed about the disaster. The outreach programs that broadcasters provide build important linkages between the stations and their listeners.

Other Announcements

The second type of announcement aired on broadcast stations is the *public service announcement (PSA)*. These announcements, as the term implies, are unpaid. Every year broadcasters perform millions of dollars' worth of public service by offering timely announcements to their audience without charge. At the national level, PSA campaigns are organized and managed by the National Association of Broadcasters and the Advertising Bureau.

Local radio and television stations frequently donate airtime and talent to produce or cosponsor local events that raise millions of dollars for local charities and people in need. In the aftermath of the 2010 floods in Nashville, broadcast stations stayed on the air with extended coverage and began collecting donations for the relief effort, putting relief information on their Web sites and publicizing events to help people who were devastated by the disaster. Television stations across the Great American Country network aired a national telethon featuring some of the biggest names in country music. Later in the year Cumulus Nashville's five stations did a day-long commercial-free fund-raiser to help the Nashville Area Habitat for Humanity group turn

renters into home owners. These are a few examples of events that broadcasters around the country organized as part of their public service efforts.

WEB ADVERTISING AND ONLINE AND NEW MEDIA OPPORTUNITIES

Internet Sales Basics

Today it's all about *coordination*. Broadcasters, networks, and program producers are vitally interested in making sure their audiences online experience provides the right complement to its programming. Whether it's a radio or television station, a cable network or an online media service, such as Hulu, the user experience must support the mission of the programmer. Figure 7–4 shows the increasing importance of online advertising.

Unlike the traditional media, online services are interactive; thus customers are really in control of what messages and content they are exposed to. A television station that has strong news programming in the community will want to reinforce that local video programming with a strong online news presence. Stations now encourage local viewers to upload amateur video related to local stories, often with labels such as "Your Stories." Web sites that constantly update local news, weather, and sports are likely to attract users with a strong desire to follow local events. Radio stations may stream their programming and provide additional features that give information about the artists played, synchronized album art or song notes, upcoming area concert info, or links to favorite videos. Because many station groups own more than one station in a community, they may choose to aggregate Web programming in a communal site.

Selling the Web becomes a logical, coordinated opportunity that the station provides for the advertiser. For example, the local HMO may regularly sponsor part of the 6 p.m. newscast and buy a coordinated skyscraper ad (sort of a vertical banner) that displays whenever the viewer clicks on the "health news" link on the station's Web site.

Networks are providing their shows in part or full episodes for viewers. Regular ads or sponsorship may be attached to the show as it streams to the viewer's computer or mobile device. Internet networks like Hulu provide complete programs with limited commercial interruption as a form of advertising sponsor-

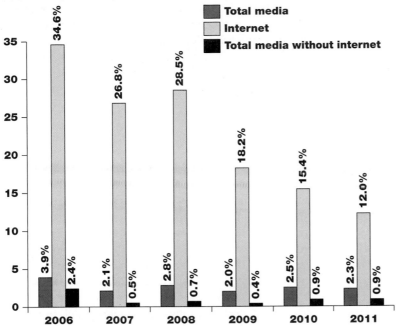

Figure 7–4

Online Advertising Spending to Continue Growth

Note: eMarketer benchmarks its U.S. online advertising spending projections against the Interactive Advertising Bureau (IAB)/PricewaterhouseCoopers (PwC) data, for which the last full year measured was 2004; online ad data includes categories as defined by IAB/PwC benchmark—display ads (such as banners), paid search ads (including contextual text links), rich media (including video), classified ads, sponsorships, referrals (lead generation), and e-mail (embedded ads only); excludes mobile ad spending; eMarketer benchmarks its US total media advertising spending projections against the Universal McCann data, for which the last full year measured was 2006; includes television (broadcast and cable), radio, newspapers, magazines, Internet (excludes mobile), outdoor, direct mail, yellow pages and other.

Source: eMarketer, October 2007.

ship. Thus, while the show plays, the sponsor's banner is displayed across the top of the page along with commercials that accompany the program.

Web sites have a variety of ways to sell inventory—that is, space on the Web sites. **Banner ads** may be displayed across the top of a page or vertically as a side panel or skyscraper. They represent the most common form of Internet advertising. **Contextual ads** are banners that will be coordinated with the display of the page. For example, you would expect to see banners from Lowe's or Home Depot on the HGTV channel. **Behavioral targeting,** based on monitoring a consumer's surfing behavior, provides a way of tailoring ads to viewers' needs. A television station will track the clicks of the user and provide information related to the specific surfing pattern. For example, when a

viewer clicks on news from a particular geographic area within a large metropolitan area, that surfing history will be remembered by **cookies** that are placed on the user's computer. The cookie will send back to the server information detailing the history of the user's previous visit. When the user returns to the station's Web page at some point in the future, local news related to that geographic region can be displayed along with ads from local merchants located in that region. Such behavioral targeting allows real-time marketing opportunities.

Pop-ups are another popular advertising form. They can vary in size and shape but are usually smaller than the page display. *Pop-unders* are a variation in which the ad is displayed under the page and is revealed when the page is closed. Some companies like Google won't accept pop-unders, and the effectiveness of both forms has been reduced with the increasing use of pop-up blockers.

Webcasting uses **push technology** to send messages to customers rather than waiting for the consumers to find them. Frequently Web users will subscribe to RSS (really simple syndication) feeds that update news headlines, blog entries, stock prices, or sports scores. New mobile applications for local TV stations will provide weather, news, or sports updates to smart phones, usually with a commercial message preceeding the information stream.

Links provide opportunities to let viewers find out more about some aspect of the service provided. A television station may provide complete weathercast streams from the morning, noon, or evening newscast. Usually clicking on the weather link is an opportunity to expose the viewer to additional banners or **interstitial ads** while the content is downloading. Interstitials may be a shortened commercial or a simple display ad. They can be blocked, however.

The model for selling coordinated Web advertising is different from that of traditional media sales. Media organizations selling such advertising for their online sites would have a difficult time paring a visitor's Web usage with traditional broadcast CPMs, reach, or frequency figures.

Broadcast properties make Web sites attractive to users who may or may not be viewing station programming; so while you could coordinate the sales message from an ad placed within the local news broadcast at 6 p.m., it is not necessary to do so. For messages that do move across different platforms, such as television and the Web, the advertiser would look at ways to optimize the placement of those ads, a process known as **cross-media optimization.** This is more likely to be used with advertisers on cable and broadcast networks, which are likely to use **online commercials** that play when the viewer goes to the site initially. For example, when a visitor goes to Oxygen.com a small 10- or 15-second video commercial message plays before the video player continues with a preview of one of the Oxygen channel programs. Messages may be randomized so that, for example, a hair care product plays one time but a car message plays another time. Banners and skyscrapers are also likely to be placed on splash pages.

A cable network like TNT, which focuses on drama, does not sell time on its splash page. Its primary interest is **institutional advertising** that essentially promotes the shows carried by the network and

allowing viewers to watch previews or full episodes or link through to other services the online site is meant to deliver. Discovery.com provides linkage between its programming and DiscoveryStore.com, where viewers can buy DVDs of popular series or products related to programming.

Measuring the success of online advertising occurs in a number of different ways. Clicks or click conversions are some of the ways media properties can tie together sales from both media properties.

Mobile Apps

The iPhone spawned a craze that illustrated that smart phone users are willing to use these devices in new and interesting ways. Clearly the phone and texting capabilities existed before the Apple device was introduced, but applications (apps) were quickly introduced that allowed users to surf the Internet, play games, and do a wide variety of other things. With the introduction of the iPad, it became clear that Internet and wireless usage was becoming more mobile. Some advertisers and marketing firms were quick to realize that these devices represented a new distribution channel—a special link to users that had direct value.

Broadcasters and media companies realized that special, easy-to-use applications could bring up-to-the-minute content to smart phone users, and this would be a way to create a new connection with the viewer on the go. Advertising for mobile applications can be differentiated from the general Internet in that usually there is one ad per page of information. Lots of banners and special links work less well on small smart phone screens; but because the user really has to connect with the site by interacting with the application, there are more opportunities for measuring per-user metrics. So broadcasters and advertisers are getting a level of engagement that may not be possible elsewhere.

THE FUTURE OF BROADCASTING AND CABLE/SATELLITE SALES AND BEYOND

Good is an appropriate word. It describes the current general outlook for electronic media. The economic recession of 2008 caused many advertisers to pull back, and advertising revenues shrank to pre-2000 levels, leaving the overall advertising environment in 2009 in a fairly gloomy state. However, media research analysts from a number of firms point to slow but annual growth in the single digits between 2011 and 2014. That's good news for readers hoping to get a job in one of the electronic media fields after graduation.

Sales managers for television and radio stations usually like to point out that sales are among the top-paying jobs in the field. Further, they insist that as sales managers, they hold the most important jobs in broadcasting. If the salespeople didn't do their job well, there would be little money for programming. We think there's something to what they say.

According to Nielsenwire, a number of advertising trends are emerging as we enter the second decade of the 21st century. Advertisers are looking to optimize the convergence of media, as we have noted. To do that, understanding consumer behavior will be critical. But this convergence suggests that cross-media advertising campaigns on different media platforms will become more important over the next few years. Sales still look promising as a way to venture into the electronic media.

SUMMARY

- Electronic media outlets such as radio, television, and cable and online sell audiences to advertisers. The audience gains entertainment or information, and media outlets sell the audience's attention to advertising agencies.

- Different media outlets compete for audience attention. For example, television competes against video outlets such as cable and video rentals. Radio competes against audio competitors and outdoor advertising. Cable gets revenue through advertising but makes the majority of its income charging subscribers access fees.

- The amount of competition in the marketplace frequently defines the kind of regulation that is appropriate for that medium. In a monopoly there is no effective competition, and government regulation is likely to be greater. When there is a great amount of competition, ratings define the leading media outlets.

- Advertising effectiveness is measure in cost per thousand (CPM). Advertisers usually look to buy at the lowest CPM.

- In comparing the various outlets to place an advertisement, media buyers look at the cost of advertising on the different media. Cost per thousand is a way to compare the cost of advertising on different media.

- Both radio and television have different ways of selling time to advertisers. Local, spot, and network sales provide venues for advertisers to focus in on specific audiences or to advertise broadly. Television networks are complicated media outlets. Networks develop compensation agreements with affiliates for carrying their programs or give affiliates time in which to advertise.

- Stations fill their broadcast times with syndication and local programming when networks do not provide programming.

- There are several types of announcements on radio and television. Promotions help to provide excitement for the station or its programming. Public service announcements (PSAs) provide free announcements and publicity to nonprofit organizations or to help with appropriate charity causes.

- Internet advertising is becoming an important secondary source of revenue for many media outlets. A variety of sales techniques such as banners, contextual ads, pop-ups, and interstitials are used.

- Mobile device applications are providing media companies with new ways to connect with potential listeners and viewers.

KEY TERMS

monopoly   159
oligopoly   159
pure competition   159
effective buying income (EBI)   160
buying power index (BPI)   160
gross rating points (GRPs)   161
gross impressions   161
banner ads   179
contextual ads   179
behavioral targeting   179
cookies   179

pop-ups   179
webcasting   180
push technology   180
interstitial ads   180
cross-media optimization   180
online commercials   180
institutional advertising   180
cost per thousand (CPM)   161
cost per point (CPP)   163
reach   163
standing order   163

broadcast month   164
dayparts   164
cooperative advertising   164
adjacencies   166
syndication   166
upfront (sales)   167
scatter buying   167
compensation   168
pods   175
station identification   176

SUGGESTIONS FOR FURTHER READING

Alexander, A., Owers, J., Carveth, R., & Hollifield, C. A., eds. (2003). *Media economics: Theory and practice.* Hillsdale, NJ: Lawrence Erlbaum.

Belch, G., & Belch, M. (2009). *Advertising and promotion: An integrated marketing communication* (8th ed.). Boston: McGraw-Hill.

Cave, M., ed. (2002). *Handbook of telecommunications economics.* Amsterdam: North-Holland.

Dizard, W. (1994). *Old media/new media.* White Plains, NY: Longman.

Gross, L., Gross, B., & Perebinossoff, P. (2005). *Programming for TV, radio & the Internet* (2nd ed.). Boston: Focal Press.

Hoskins, C., McFadyen, S., & Finn, A. (2004). *Media economics: Applying economics to new and traditional media.* Thousand Oaks, CA: Sage.

Jessell, H. (2006). *Broadcasting and cable yearbook 2006.* New Providence, NJ: R.R. Bowker.

Parsons, P., & Frieden, R. M. (1998). *The cable and satellite television industries.* Needham Heights, MA: Allyn & Bacon.

Shane, Ed. (1999). *Selling electronic media.* Boston: Focal Press.

Sherman, B. L. (1995). *Telecommunications management* (2nd ed.). New York: McGraw-Hill.

Goodrich, W. B., & Sissors, J. (2001). *Media planning workbook* (3rd ed.). New York: McGraw-Hill.

Tapscott, D. (1996). *The digital economy: Promise and peril in the age of networked intelligence.* New York: McGraw-Hill.

Vogel, H. (2007). *Entertainment industry economics: A guide for financial analysis* (7th ed.). New York: Cambridge University Press.

Walker, J., & Ferguson, D. (1998). *The broadcast television industry.* Needham Heights, MA: Allyn & Bacon.

Wimmer, R., & Dominick, J. R. (2010). *Mass media research* (9th ed.). Belmont, CA: Wadsworth.

INTERNET EXERCISES

Visit our Web site at **www.mhhe.com/dominickbib7e** for study-guide exercises to help you learn and apply material in each chapter. You will find ideas for future research as well as useful Web links to provide you with an opportunity to journey through the new electronic media.

Radio Programming   8

Quick Facts

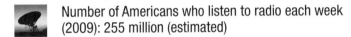
Number of Americans who listen to radio each week
(2009): 255 million (estimated)

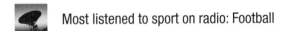
Most listened to sport on radio: Football

Number of hours per week listeners 55+ spend listening to
radio (2010): 23

Number of hours per week listeners 12–17 spend listening to
radio (2010): 14

Radio's most important time of day: 6–10 a.m. (morning drive)

Number of direct broadcast radio satellites in U.S. orbit: 5

Estimated number of Americans who regularly listen to
Internet radio streams on both computers and mobile devices
(2010): 77 million

To unlock the secret of radio programming today, it's helpful to turn to the biological sciences. Biologists define *symbiosis* as "the living together in intimate association or close union of two organisms," especially if mutually beneficial—like silverfish and army ants or coral and sea creatures.

Symbiosis is also an especially good term to use to describe radio programming today. Radio enjoys a close and mutually beneficial relationship with a variety of other "organisms." The popularity of music from feature films (from *Saturday Night Fever* in 1975 to *Dirty Dancing* in 1987 to *Pulp Fiction* in 1994 to *He's Just Not That Into You* in 2010) illustrates how radio is intertwined today with the movie business. The success of TV shows like *Glee* and MTV's *10 On Top* and the numerous stars who have graduated from *American Idol* to become successful pop stars point to radio's interrelationship with TV. But radio's most symbiotic relationship is with the popular music business: the world of iTunes, CDs, and DVDs.

Radio is in flux today. As younger listeners mix local radio and Web stations and music services, change is in the wind. But radio, whether on the Web or terrestrial, is more than just an electronic jukebox, we will also examine the dynamics of information programming—the nature of news radio and talk radio.

RADIO REGULATION AND FORMAT DESIGN

For this symbiotic relationship to work, it's necessary for stations to have the freedom to choose the programming they want to provide to their communities. Section 326 of the Communications Act, the law that empowered the FCC to govern broadcast operations, states,

> Nothing in this Act shall be understood or construed to give the Commission the power of censorship over the radio communications or signals transmitted by any radio station, and no regulation or condition shall be promulgated or fixed by the Commission which shall interfere with the right of free speech by means of radio communication.

In short, the FCC has neither the right nor the power to control radio programming. Radio stations are free to program their airtime however they may. In certain specific areas, such as political advertising, obscenity, and indecency, Congress has directed the FCC to promulgate programming rules (see Chapter 10). However, the bulk of radio programming—music, news, and information—is largely free of governmental intrusion. In fact, this characteristic is one of the fundamental distinctions between the sound of American radio and that of the rest of the world. Basically, American radio is programmed to satisfy listener tastes and not, as in government-owned systems, to serve political or bureaucratic interests.

We call this situation "format freedom." Faced with the task of filling 24 hours per day, 365 days a year, radio programmers are on their own. Their task is simple: to provide attractive programming to meet the informational and/or entertainment needs of an audience. In commercial radio, the audience must be large or important enough to be of interest to advertisers. Public stations must entertain and inform their listeners to an extent that justifies financial support from government agencies, foundations, business underwriters, and the listeners themselves. If the task seems especially formidable, generally programmers don't have to worry about direct governmental intrusion.

Internet Stations and Formats

Web-based stations that do not use the public's airwaves are exempt from program restrictions, but most services still need to meet the needs of their audience to gain listenership. Our discussion in this chapter applies to most radio, regardless of the technology used to delivery it.

A MATRIX OF RADIO PROGRAMMING

Figure 8–1 maps the types of radio programming today. Across the top of the matrix of radio programming are the sources of radio programming. **Local programming** is original programming produced by

Figure 8–1

Types of Radio Programming

Type	Source		
	Local	Prerecorded/ Syndicated	Network
Music	1	2	3
News/Talk	4	5	6

the radio station in its studios or from locations in its immediate service area. **Prerecorded or syndicated programming** is programming obtained by the station from a commercial supplier, advertiser, or program producer from outside the station. Common sources of this type of programming are from record companies or program distributors. Prerecorded programs may also be received by stations as MP3 downloads through an Internet connection or by microwave relay, and very commonly from a satellite or distributed via CD. Stations that belong to a network such as ABC, CBS, or National Public Radio are permanently interconnected via an Internet conection or satellite transponders. Unlike syndication, **network programming** is regularly scheduled, that is, with few exceptions, network programs run the same time each day at every station on the network.

Top to bottom in Figure 8–1 are the two main types of radio programming. Most plentiful in radio today is music programming, from opera to hip hop to country, from "adult standards" to progressive jazz. News/talk covers the broad spectrum from news, sports, and traffic reports to sexual advice, from stand-up comedy to stock tips.

Music

Now let's examine the kinds of radio programs that fall into each box of Figure 8–1. In box 1 is locally produced music programming. Once a staple of radio programming, when many stations employed their own orchestras, original music emanating from studios or area concert halls is heard today on only a few stations (mostly noncommercial). Some rock

---

Profile: Unvarnished Advice from the Queen of Talk Radio

America's most popular female radio talk show host, Dr. Laura Schlessinger, recently announced that she was retiring from talk radio. Currently heard from coast to coast by an estimated 9 million listeners, Dr. Laura's show isn't all love and roses. She's made a name for herself dispensing unvarnished moral advice to her listeners. In fact, one critic has labeled her "the Village Scold" of talk radio. For Dr. Laura, that has been both a problem and a virtue.

Talkers magazine, a trade publication in the radio industry, estimated Schlessinger's audience at around 8 million listeners but shrinking. While that's enough to put Dr. Laura in the top five after talk leaders Rush Limbaugh and Sean Hannity, over the past few years she has lost several million listeners as her show was dropped by big stations in New York, Boston, Chicago, and elsewhere. A number of stations dropped or bumped Dr. Laura after the 9/11 attack, putting on programs that were more news oriented.

Schlessinger built a large and loyal audience as her sharp-tongued lectures were something of a novelty. Dr. Laura's voice resonates with sternly worded strong medicine. During the mid-1990s, she was radio's hottest property, but problems began when she became embroiled in a public dispute with the gay community by calling homosexuality "a biological mistake." Gay advocacy groups started a nationwide advertising boycott campaign against her, and then her newly launched syndicated TV show quickly went sour.

After the TV show failed, she claimed that TV has more froufrou and celebrity but is not as meaningful as radio. Even though she's made millions from radio, Schlessinger has said that she thinks radio has become too narrow and that it needs to move back to becoming more full service. In 2010 she created another controversy when she told a black woman with a white husband, "If you're that hypersensitive about color and don't have a sense of humor, don't marry out of your race." These remarks came after Schlessinger said that there was a double standard for language and used the N-word a number of times. After a wave of outrage, Schlessinger apologized to the woman and her listening audience.

A native New Yorker, Schlessinger made her name as an alternative to the frequently male-dominated world of talk radio. While Dr. Laura holds a PhD, it's not in either psychology or psychiatry. Her graduate degree is actually in physiology, but her advice is followed by millions of listeners. At her peak, she was heard on nearly 400 stations and claimed nearly 15 million listeners.

stations have had success promoting the music of local bands. For example, KEXP (90.3), a public radio station in Seattle, has an amazing set of live performances that listeners can hear on their Web site; WNNX (99X) in Atlanta, a modern rock station, features a popular late-night show called *Locals Only.* The *Locals Only* Web site features both music and interviews with featured artists. Since 1979, Classic Rocker WTKW (TK99) in Syracuse has featured the latest releases of local bands along with interviews every Sunday night on *Soundcheck. Soundcheck's* MySpace page features videos and info about the local groups. Some programs heard nationally today began as local productions. American Public Radio's *Prairie Home Companion,* hosted by affable Garrison Keillor, started in this fashion at Macalester College in 1974. However, locally produced music is becoming increasingly rare and is thus the smallest segment of the matrix.

The biggest element of radio programming today is box 2, prerecorded and syndicated music. Nearly 9 of 10 radio stations rely on some kind of music as the backbone of their schedule, and that music is most likely coming from a CD, a computer hard drive, or a satellite transponder. This is the high-intensity world of format radio, described in detail later.

Pronounced dead and buried by industry observers just a few years ago, network music programming (box 3) has undergone a renaissance in recent years. Joining the long-running serious orchestral and opera broadcasts (such as the Metropolitan Opera, which celebrated 80 years of broadcasts in 2010, New York Philharmonic, Philadelphia Orchestra, and Chicago Symphony broadcasts) have been the live broadcasts of popular music formats from Westwood One, the Los Angeles–based radio network. Rock-and-roll music has been the network's strong suit, featuring live national broadcasts of concerts by the Rolling Stones, Eric Clapton, the Red Hot Chili Peppers, and the Dixie Chicks. More recently, Westwood One's *Absolutely Live,* is a new series of hour-long concerts featuring premier rock artists like Linkin Park, Foo Fighters, Dave Matthews Band, and Radiohead and distributes the well-known Los Angeles alternative music program *The Kevin and Bean Show,* which mixes music, news, comedy bits, and celebrity interviews.

Citadel Media distributes numerous daily and weekly shows that can be integrated into the station's broadcast day. The daily or weekly programming offered to stations includes Tom Kent Radio

Network, ABC News Radio, ESPN radio, and Radio Perez. These program services can be fully automated so that the local station can run with a minimum of personnel or they can be integrated into local operations.

News/Talk

Locally produced news/talk programming (box 4) includes the many news, sports, weather, and traffic reporters at work in radio today, as well as a range of local hosts of political, civic, medical, and financial information shows. As we saw in Chapter 4, news and talk stations have the largest staffs in radio, including hosts, anchors, reporters, producers, and technicians.

As a morning radio personality, Howard Stern made a name by being controversial and pushing the limits. Since moving to SiriusXM Radio Stern has not had to worry about language usage, but his audience is now limited to those wishing to subscribe to the pay service.

You will note from Figure 8–1 that there is a dashed line between boxes 5 and 6: syndicated and network radio. This is because the two forms are combining into similar services.

For example, many popular talk personalities who have been successful in one market are now being syndicated via satellite to many other markets. Howard Stern of WXRK in New York was aired in about 20 markets until he moved to satellite radio in 2006. A popular syndicated talker now on WABC (New York) is personality Don Imus, who left WFAN after making derogatory remarks about Rutgers University women's basketball team. Imus is heard on stations around the nation, including WDCG-AM in Tampa and KTMS-AM in Santa Barbara.

Other leading syndicated radio talkers are Jim Bohannon, Sean Hannity, Bill O'Reilly, Laura Ingraham, Lou Dobbs, and Dr. Laura Schlessinger, the most listened-to woman on American radio. Even if you are not familiar with these personalities, you've probably heard of the reigning king of talk radio: Rush Limbaugh.

Limbaugh, a conservative commentator, is heard on hundreds of stations, with a weekly cumulative audience of more than 15 million Americans. While many listeners disagree with his politics, there is no denying his contribution to the radio business. When his program began to attract attention 22 years ago, AM radio was in decline. Most AM stations were bankrupt or near bankrupt. The AM listening audience was shrinking. Thanks to the popularity of Limbaugh, his legion of imitators, and his ideological opposites (like progressive Thom Hartmann). By 1998 talk radio was the leading format in many of the top 25 metropolitan areas, reaching a daily audience of more than 10.5 million adults, most on their way to or from high-paying jobs. Today we are seeing talk formats spill over onto the FM band to attract younger audiences.

MODES OF RADIO PRODUCTION

Just as radio programmers have a full menu of types and sources of programming, they likewise have a range of ways to produce programs for their audiences. This is just one example of the many decisions that have to be made by radio managers. We call these choices modes of radio production. Figure 8–2 depicts the various modes.

At the left end of the continuum is local, live production. When radio stations employ their own

Figure 8–2

Modes of Radio Production

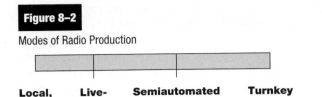

| Local, live | Live-assist | Semiautomated | Turnkey automation |

Source: FCC, 2001.

announcers or newscasters locally and play music that they themselves own, they are using this mode of production.

Live-assist production occurs when radio managers use limited automation or syndicated programming, such as satellite-delivered music services, but retain local announcers and DJs as the backbone of their program schedule. In this case the live air personality may be playing music preselected by a supervisor but announces and does voice-overs live, in real time. In other instances the announcer may assist in the implementation of the syndicated schedule, where the program is developed at some distant location but live local breaks are programmed in—hence the term *live-assist*. Often morning news programs may mix syndicated features with live local reporting in this way.

Figure 8–3 is an example of an hour of semiautomated programming called The Tom Kent Radio Network. Semiautomation refers to the reliance of the local station on the services of the syndicated program producer. For example, the music typically comes in via satellite. When a break point for a commercial or program announcement is reached, a digital

Figure 8–3

Even though the program is distributed nationally via satellite, local stations can put their own announcements or IDs in during stop sets. This can be done live or with an automation program.

Schedule QuickPrint   **Music Master**   TKRN-FM
9/6/2010 7PM through 9/6/2010 11P

s: AirTime	s: Runtime	Schedule: Description
07:00:00p	00:00	Monday, September 06, 2010 7PM
07:00:00p	02:28	LOOKIN' OUT MY BACK DOOR / CREEDENCE CLEARWATER REVIVAL
07:02:28p	03:49	DRIVE / CARS
07:06:17p	03:20	BRICK HOUSE / COMMODORES
07:09:37p	03:52	FEELING ALRIGHT / JOE COCKER
07:13:41p	06:30	STOP-SET
07:26:53p	03:33	LIDO SHUFFLE / BOZ SCAGGS
07:30:26p	03:29	LITTLE LIES / FLEETWOOD MAC
07:33:55p	03:06	RIGHT BACK WHERE WE STARTED FROM / MAXINE NIGHTINGALE
07:37:01p	03:38	(I CAN'T GET NO) SATISFACTION / ROLLING STONES
07:40:39p	02:56	HOT BLOODED / FOREIGNER
07:43:35p	03:44	AMERICAN WOMAN / GUESS WHO
07:47:19p	06:34	SOMEONE SAVED MY LIFE TONIGHT / ELTON JOHN
07:53:53p	04:22	HEARTACHE TONIGHT / EAGLES
07:58:15p	03:17	MONDAY MONDAY / MAMAS & THE PAPAS
07:61:32p	06:30	STOP-SET
08:00:00p	00:00	Monday, September 06, 2010 8PM
08:00:00p	04:49	RAMBLIN' MAN / ALLMAN BROTHERS BAND
08:04:49p	03:34	CENTERFOLD / J. GEILS BAND

cart machine or a computer is triggered to play an announcement by a subaudible cue tone triggered in the satellite transmission. In a semiautomated system the station inserts local programming, perhaps in the morning drive program or for news, sports, and local weather breaks at designated times in the schedule. The local announcer may update information quickly, but the backbone of the programming is the syndicated music schedule.

At the far end of the radio production continuum is **full studio automation.** This refers to fully automated radio stations that take one of two main forms. Some automated stations consist largely of a satellite dish and a control board. The satellite dish downlinks a radio program service, such as country, rock, or beautiful music. ABC Radio, for example, offers 11 different formats from Jack FM to traditional country to oldies. These formats are programmed 24/7 and require very little local talent. In some cases the service has been made to sound so localized that time, weather, and news information are sent by satellite or computer to the program producer in time for the announcers thousands of miles away to prepare the inserts.

Other full studio automation systems rely on hard drives and digital cart machines that interface with a computer console. The program director uses a com-

puter program to prepare the logs and schedule all the music, information, and commercial elements, including their order, length, and frequency. Once the manager has approved the logs, the same or another computer at the station controls the program schedule, playing the music, commercials, and sound files with news and weather from a number of computer hard drives or other recording media.

Voice-tracking surfaced several years ago as computers offered program directors the option to take local talent and build a station that sounds virtually live. With automation software, a jock can record all the "intros" and "outros" to songs, along with additional banter for an entire airshift, in less than an hour. The computer can integrate the voice and music portions of the show to provide the listener with a seamless show. While automation makes it possible for a station group owner to hire one jock to do the voice tracks for several different stations around the country, it reduces the spontaneity of live radio.

The task facing radio program managers is formidable. They must decide whether to emphasize talk or music or strive to operate a full-service station. Having made that decision, they must determine where the programming should come from. Will it all emanate locally? Should the station

Dr. Laura Schlessinger is moving from radio to YouTube; new media are presenting new opportunities for talkers like Schlessinger.

acquire a music library? If not, which program sources should be used? Should the station purchase a satellite dish? For what services? Should it affiliate with a network? If so, which one(s)? And to what degree of commitment? In addition, the programmer must decide how the programs will be produced for the audience. Will format freedom reign, giving local control to program directors and disc jockeys? Will outside consultants make many program decisions, with the goal of assisting local announcers and personalities? Will the station use programming from afar via satellite, with only occasional local break-ins? Or will the station be essentially a radio music box, completely automated and controlled by management personnel and their desktop computers?

CREATING THE RADIO FORMAT

The myriad options facing radio management regarding programming can be answered by the process of creating and refining a format. In radio terminology, the format is the overall sound and image of the radio station: its comprehensive approach to its talk, music, advertisements, promotional strategies, community relations, personalities, and other factors. There are three keys to a successful format:

1. To identify and serve a predetermined set of listeners.
2. To serve those listeners better than the competition.
3. To reward those listeners both on and off the air so they become consistent customers for the products and services advertised on the station.

In radio today, the format reigns supreme. It is both an art and a science, combining such artistic expressions as the musical talents of singers and groups and the diverse personalities of DJs and talk show hosts with the social and behavioral sciences, including polls, surveys, and focus groups.

RADIO MUSIC FORMATTING

Today more than 8 of 10 radio stations overall, and 9 of 10 on FM, choose some form of music as the backbone of their programming. Figure 8–4 details the process of developing a radio music format.

THE "FORMAT HOLE"

Whether placing a new station on the air, acquiring an established station, or reevaluating the programming of an existing station, programmers have two main choices about how to fill their airtime. They may try to outdo the competition in a given service by programming the same format—most of the nation's largest markets boast at least two of radio's major formats, from contemporary hit radio, to urban, country, and rock—or the station may decide instead to inventory and analyze radio programming in the market in search of an unfulfilled programming need. Managers may decide to try ethnic, modern rock, progressive jazz, or other formats in areas where these services were previously not heard.

Successful radio programming enables the station to carve a unique niche, one that will deliver a large enough audience to attract advertising revenues to that station. In the radio business the phrase used is "find the format hole." The process is dependent on two sets of factors: internal and external.

Internal factors affecting the analysis include the ownership of the station, its dial location, power, technical facilities, and management philosophy. For example, it would not make much sense for a small-market station at 99.5 on the FM dial to play contemporary music if a competitor is already playing this format at 101 FM. It would not be wise for a 5,000-watt AM station at 1570 on the dial, with a full-service country format, to compete against a 50,000-watt powerhouse in that format at 720 on the dial. The more powerful station with better dial position will win. Another internal consideration may be whether the station has several HD streams and, if so, how that impacts the decision to implement a format. Web stations may consider whether they acts like a station or more like a program service, whether they have high-quality streams, and so on.

The process of external analysis begins with a competitive market study, which examines the existing stations, including their technical properties, their ownership, their financial performance, their ratings, and of course their current formats. If there are competitors, are they strong? Or do they have program weaknesses (bad musical selection, poor announcers, weak promotions, bad dial location, too much clutter, and so on) that make them vulnerable to competitive attack? Unlike terrestrial stations that do not pay performance royalties, Web stations must consider such external pressures on their programming.

Figure 8–4

Developing the Music Format

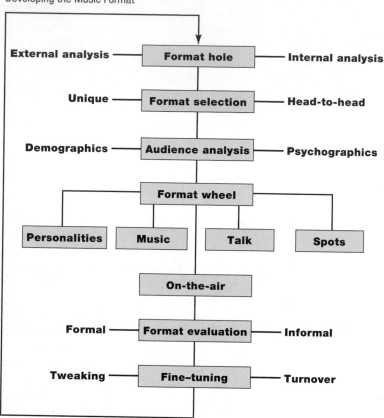

Other external factors include geography and population characteristics (country/western in Wichita, laid-back new age in Los Angeles, urban contemporary for Baltimore, or nostalgia for the aging population of West Palm Beach, for instance).

The search for the format hole yields one of two outcomes: The station selects a new or different format that is unavailable in the market, or it decides to compete in the same format with one or more existing stations. The former choice makes the station unique; the latter we refer to as becoming a head-to-head competitor.

Audience Analysis

The goal of radio programming is to attract and maintain an audience. So it makes sense that one of the primary steps in creating a music format is audience identification. In format radio, every station must ascertain its **target audience,** the primary group of people sought by the station's programming. As we traced in Chapter 4, the target audience is usually de-

fined by its principal **demographics,** including age, gender, racial/ethnic background, income, and other descriptors. In examining formats we discovered that several formats frequently had overlapping demographic characteristics.

The radio audience can also defined by listeners' attitudes, beliefs, values, hobbies, lifestyle choices, and motivations for listening. These kinds of audience attributes are known collectively as **psychographics.** Following are some industry rules of thumb regarding demographics and psychographics.

Listener Demographics   One reason radio has remained and even rebounded in the TV, cable, and Internet eras is its phenomenal reach. As we have seen, radio is an intensely personal medium that reaches almost all Americans daily. All told, radio reaches over 255 million people each week. Just under half of all Americans over the age of 12 listen to radio between 6 and 10 a.m. on weekdays. From 6 a.m. to 6 p.m., radio reaches more people than TV, cable,

Issues: Are People Turning Radio Off? Here's a Definite Answer: Maybe

Satellite radio, podcasting, MP3 players, HD radio, and even good old technologies like compact disks are having an effect on radio listenership. There are two issues that need to be addressed regarding this phenomenon: Is the trend significant? And if listenership is really in decline, what should radio do about it?

Bridge Ratings has been conducting a multiyear study regarding radio audiences, and the results are both instructive and alarming for radio people. For the 2006 study, 6,000 people in six national markets were interviewed on their listening behavior weekly over a period of time. AM/FM listening among the very important 18- to 34-year-old group was significantly off the 2005 mark. What was the cause of the decrease? The report cites some reasons: Alternative entertainment venues seem to be growing in popularity, particularly among young listeners. Podcasting seems to be attracting new listeners. People who get MP3 players may spend less time with radio, particularly during the first three months of ownership.

When asked what accounted for the decrease in radio listening, some responded an increase in cell phone use (14 percent) and more MP3 use (18 percent), but perhaps just as interesting was the response that radio was really "same-old, same-old" programming. Listeners for rock were most likely to use MP3 players instead of radio, but urban format listeners were less likely. People who spend a majority of their time listening to news/talk radio were more likely to download podcasts of their favorite personalities.

A study released in 2010 focused on the impact that social media marketing was having on radio and other traditional media. Bridge Ratings interviewed nearly 250 managers in 150 key markets around the United States. The goal was to understand what was transpiring at the station level during this transitional period in digital media. Two responses seemed to be universally echoed by station management: money, know-how and staffing. Many expressed an interest to move in new directions but lacked the resources to do so.

In the same study, more than 2,500 people aged 12+ were interviewed to determine how they used radio and competing new media. They found that between 2006 and 2010 use of MP3 players was up nearly 20 percent, Internet radio usage was up 30 percent, and social networking site usage was up nearly 40 percent. The study found that radio was left out of the social networking equation, with nearly 80 percent of the respondents saying they had never read a communication from a radio station via any social network. Whether stations need to Tweet or send out skyrockets, this study suggests that radio needs to connect with younger audiences and get into the new social media.

---

newspapers, magazines, and computers and online services. In short, radio has excellent demographics.

Radio managers divide the U.S. population into standard demographic categories. Gender is demographically defined in terms of men and women (naturally enough). Combined, men and women over age 12 are considered "persons." Those 18 and above are "adults" in a radio ratings book. The standard age cutoffs (known as "age breakouts," or simply "breaks," in the radio business) are tots (ages 2–11), teens (12–17), 18 to 24, 18 to 34, 18 to 49, 25 to 34, 35 to 54, and 55 and above (the growing audience of "senior adults"). Demographic research indicates that radio is primarily a "young" medium (even though radio is over 100 years old): Nearly 55 percent of the radio audience is under the age of 45; more than a third of the radio audience falls into the 25 to 44 age range, and the largest groups of female listeners (who make most consumer purchases) are in the 18 to 54 age range. This changes as the population ages.

Currently the ideal radio format appeals to women, especially those in their mid-30s—hence the popularity of country, oldies, and adult contemporary, three of the leading radio formats. Radio stations attracting males would be wise to seek an older, professional audience (oldies/news), aging baby boomers (news/talk or classic rock), or younger (18–24) music aficionados (active or classic rock).

Nationally, the black and Hispanic audience together represent about 26 percent of all listeners—a large and growing group. Thus there has been the rapid rise of Hispanic, black/urban/contemporary, hot AC, and other radio formats described back in Chapter 4.

You may recall that radio programming begins with an analysis of these demographics and other characteristics as they occur in a station's local market. Younger demographics might send a program director toward a younger format; older, to an older sound. But at best, demographics provide only a

Chris Martin: "Cross-promotion is very important in entertainment. Coldplay made use of the Internet to give away free downloads of a live CD that was available in the physical CD format only if you attended a concert."

partial picture of the radio audience. Thousands of stations stream today, but most terrestrial stations that provide an Internet service are trying to extend the listening opportunities for their regular listeners.

Internet-only stations will use demographic considerations when programming unless the service is more like Pandora, which chooses music genres based on listener-designated preferences.

Listener Psychographics   With about 15 distinct format categories (and several subcategories within specific formats) competing for a share of the radio audience, and with more than one station and as many as five or six programming similar formats in many cities, stations have tried to develop more detailed methods of identifying their audiences. The current rage in radio research is listener psychographics (see Chapter 12), also known as *values and lifestyle* or *qualitative research*. *Psychographic research* is an attempt to understand radio listeners according to their attitudes, values, beliefs, leisure pursuits, political interests, and other fac-

tors. For many radio programmers today, the age and gender of the audience are insufficient data: They need to know how their listeners view the world (and how their selected radio stations fit into that world).

Since the late 1980s radio stations have amassed volumes of research about what works and what doesn't. But as consumer tastes and behaviors change, lifestyles and attitudes research frequently gives radio program directors better insights into trends than simply playing the demographic numbers game.

America's tastes and interests are constantly changing, and psychographic studies try to get at these changes in taste. Consider the growth in popularity of the iPod and the iTunes store. (One study claims 280 million Americans owns an MP3 player.) Has the growth in MP3 players occurred because listeners were tired of hearing the same songs on the radio? To answer these questions, program directors needed more sophisticated research than simple demographic information. Psychographic information about consumer behavior and attitudes provides program directors with insights about how to arrange music and program segments to please the listening audience.

A senior executive for Edison Research notes that by properly using focus groups station managers can develop an understanding of consumer viewpoints that is difficult to get elsewhere. Previous qualitative studies have provided data that have helped provide differentiation among formats. Let's take a look at the results for one format.

Contemporary Hit Radio (CHR)   Research has revealed that listeners to CHR or Top 40 stations tend to fall into two main psychographic groups. One group listens primarily to hear new music with an up-tempo beat and a lot of urban rhythms (the kind of music heard blaring from cars with their windows rolled down). Radio W.A.R.S., a classic series of studies done for the National Association of Broadcasters, called these listeners "new music trendies" and "get-me-up rockers." Another subset of the format seemed attracted to CHR, however, because it returned them to the format's heyday in the late 1950s and early 1960s. For them, listening to CHR was motivated by the desire to be put into a romantic, nostalgic mood. Songs about young love, funny DJs, and lots of oldies are what they want.

As the 1990s ended, this research seemed quite predictive. Studies concluded in 2010 reinforced these findings: multiple forms of CHR are very popular. Top hits are the most prevalent choice among

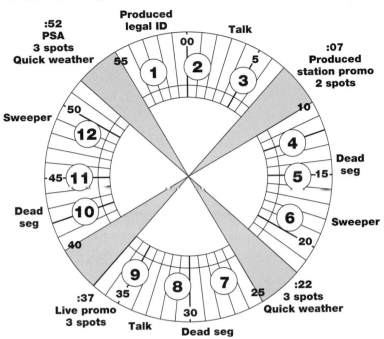

According to Arbitron research, women who listen to country music don't want the DJ to waste their time. Talk is kept to a minimum with an emphasis on music.

teens, but there are many different variations on the format. In addition, CHR listeners are also more likely to listen to Spanish, alternative, urban, and modern rock stations than are listeners to other formats like country, adult standards, and news/talk. Depending on the target audience, the program manager would manipulate the station's playlist to reflect the tastes of the listeners.

The Hot Clock

The next step in radio music programming involves the implementation of the schedule: the planning and execution of the station's sound. Most radio programmers today employ a version of a useful chart known as the **hot clock,** "format wheel," or "sound hour." Figures 8–5 and 8–6 are sample hot clocks.

Radio Dayparts   The format wheel looks like the face of a clock, with each element of the station's on-air sound—music, commercials, news, sports, promotions, and so on—scheduled at its precise interval in the programming hour. The hot clock performs two main functions. First, it enables programmers to get a visual image of an otherwise invisible concept, their

"sound." Second, it enables programmers to compare their program proposals with the competition. In this way programmers make sure that at the time they air music, the other station plays its commercials; that the news does not air on both stations at the same time; that it is unlikely that the same song will air simultaneously on both stations; and so on.

Normally programmers use a different clock for each important scheduling period. Figure 8–7 illustrates how radio use varies throughout the day from Monday to Friday and on weekends. Find the peaks on each chart, and you have discovered the medium's key **dayparts** (important time periods).

Morning Drive   Let's examine the Monday-to-Friday graph first. The highest point on the graph is radio's most important time period: Monday to Friday in the early morning. For convenience, programmers usually identify the boundaries of this time period as 6 to 10 a.m. Because most listeners are preparing to commute or are commuting to work and school, this is known as morning drive time. In most radio markets this is *prime time.* This is where radio managers in the major markets commit their greatest program resources. The highest-paid radio personalities toil

Figure 8–6

Hot clock for a Music Station

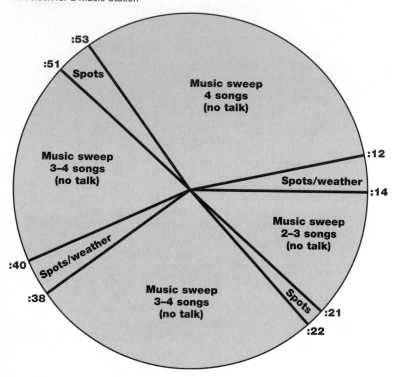

Figure 8–7

Radio Listening Throughout the Day

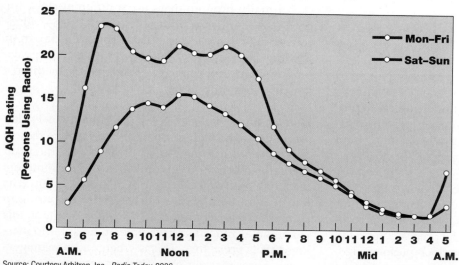

Source: Courtesy Arbitron, Inc., *Radio Today*, 2006.

Ethics: Paid to Play—Payola

In the late 1950s the DJ became "king" of the radio business. Big-name DJs in major markets, like Allen Freed in Cleveland, Howard Miller in Chicago, and Murray the K in New York, had become well known to thousands of loyal listeners, and they exerted considerable influence in the record business. Simply put, if they liked a song and played it over the air, the song had a good chance of success.

This fact did not go unnoticed by the record industry, which showered DJs and music directors with gifts and gratuities, known as *payola.* Lucky "jocks" received cars, golf clubs, vacation trips—you name it. But the gravy train ground to a halt in 1960, when, following a series of highly publicized hearings, Congress enacted legislation making the acceptance of payola a criminal offense, punishable by a $10,000 fine. Since then, many stations have had their DJs and PDs (program directors) sign affidavits guaranteeing compliance with the payola statutes.

However, payola has never really vanished. In 2005 New York Attorney General Elliot Spitzer took the music industry to task for misconduct. Succeeding where federal prosecutors had failed previously, Spitzer sued Sony, Universal, EMI, and Warner Music Group for pay-for-play activities, including bribing station personnel and providing benefits for listeners in exchange for airplay. But payola can take several forms. Spitzer was also concerned about the practice that pays independent promoters who are hired to promote specific songs. These "indies" then approach radio stations to get them to play certain releases. They're paid by the record company when a song is added to the station's playlist, but here's where the problem develops: The indie may then turn around and pay the radio station for promotional expenses such as concerts or provide trips for the disc jockeys and music directors for promotional tours. Opponents of this practice say it shuts out recording artists who aren't paying the independent promoter or other spokespersons.

While none of the record companies admitted to wrongdoing, the four paid nearly $28 million in settlements. But this does not mean all is well in radio land. In another investigation into major radio broadcasters Entercom, Clear Channel, and Citadel, the practice of repeatedly playing certain songs in the graveyard shifts so the songs would get counted by charting agencies was being investigated. Record companies have been doing this by sponsoring the overnight programs. Even though the programs contain sponsorship announcements that comply with federal law, sometimes the practices mislead the listening audience. Some marketing experts have said that the music charts are easily manipulated with social media. What do you think?

in this time period, frequently earning salaries in the mid- to high-six-figure range. Stations go to great expense and effort to have the top-rated morning show. Beginning in the 1990s the competitive battle had taken outrageous turns, leading to the rise of "shock jocks." Today the trend is for more moderate hosts for music stations, while many talk stations use popular syndicated hosts.

Another recent trend in morning drive is based on trends in the population. One study in 2009 concluded that 44 percent of all radio listening occurs during the daily commute. In addition, Americans are working longer hours. As you've probably noticed, traffic is generally worse than ever before. Thus, morning drive has begun earlier with top radio talents beginning their shifts at 5 a.m. Some still work until 10 a.m. (often repeating elements from their earliest hours); others make way for the midday team at 8:30 or 9:00 a.m.

Evening Drive The next "hump" in the Monday-to-Friday graph is seen in the late afternoon, radio's second-most-important time slot: 3 p.m. to 7 p.m.

The audience for evening drive is only about two-thirds the size of that for morning drive. This is because not everyone who commutes to work goes directly home. Also, the attractiveness of late-afternoon TV (Oprah Winfrey and Jerry Springer, for example) and early TV newscasts captures much of the audience at this time. People at home are more likely to watch these shows than listen to radio.

One programming element above all tends to dominate this daypart: traffic. Take a look skyward the next time you find yourself in afternoon city traffic. Chances are you'll spot multiple helicopters and a few light airplanes with radio station logos on them, each promising the best traffic reports for their stations.

Ratings books can help programmers develop the optimal hot clock for the drive time periods because

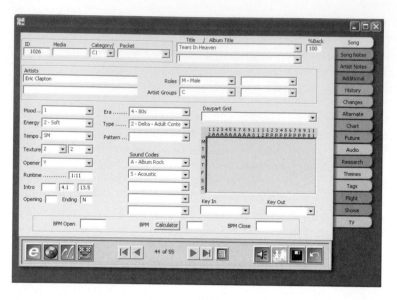

RCS: Music scheduling programs allow the program director to create a uniform sound for the station and make notes about songs, themes, and other program elements that create the overall station format.

the book will show listener trends, including information about the time spent listening (TSL) and the time spent commuting in the specific market.

Daytime   There is a nice plateau in the weekday chart where radio listening holds steady at this time. This is the fast-growing daytime period, from 10:00 a.m. to 3:00 p.m. The popularity of portable radios in the home and workplace makes this one of radio's most important time periods.

The noon hour is especially critical to radio programmers in daytime. This is because of the popularity of listening to radio on lunch breaks. Many music stations air special programs designed for their target audiences at this time. AC stations may feature an "oldies café"; CHR stations may feature a "danceteria"; and an album rock station may run a "metallic lunchbox."

Evening and Late Night   Note how radio listening slides in the early evening (as America turns on its TV sets and PCs) and continues to plummet through the night until dawn. Thus two less important Monday-to-Friday dayparts for programmers are evening (7:00 p.m. to midnight) and overnight, or graveyard, from midnight to 6:00 a.m.

Most stations to format in the evening and late-night hours. That is, they play long, extended versions of the preferred programming for their most dedicated listeners. Since it is harder to sell commercials in these dayparts (because of the comparatively small audience), the loyal listener is rewarded with

longer musical programs, specials, and other extended programming.

Weekend Radio   Looking at the weekend plots on Figure 8–7 immediately reveals the most important time period to programmers and advertisers: Saturday and Sunday in the late morning and early afternoon. This is when we are most likely to turn the radio on, as we clean the house, wash the car (or the dog), and head to the park or beach. There is a slow and steady decline from about 2 p.m. on through the rest of the day on weekends as we turn our attention elsewhere.

Note that at no time on the weekend does radio listening exceed levels achieved on Monday to Friday. The best weekend time seems to be between 10 a.m. and 2 p.m. But with many listeners attending church, shopping at the mall, or sleeping late, this time slot is usually not a prime programming period.

Filling the Clock: Radio Programming Terminology

At minimum, stations will use a hot clock for their Monday-through-Friday schedule in the morning drive time period, the midday time slot, the afternoon drive slot, and the evening schedule. Stations may also employ a weekend clock for the daytime slots comprising late morning through the early afternoon.

Of course these days radio hot clocks are rarely constructed with a compass or by outlining a paper pie plate, as was common "back in the day." Instead program directors plot their show elements on their desktop PCs using software that tracks music rotation and schedules breaks and fine-tunes the station's sound. Still, the process is the same, as is the terminology. Here's how the hot clock is put together.

There are three main types of information depicted in the hot clock: commercial and promotional matter, music, and news/talk segments. The number and location of the commercial positions normally are set first by the general manager in consultation with the sales and program managers. Their job is to decide how many commercials will run and in which parts of the hour. While some adult contemporary or "lite" music stations run as few as 8 or 9 commercial minutes per hour, some rock stations run as many as 15 or 16, and up to 20 or more in peak seasons such as the Christmas rush. The FCC has no strict limit on the number of commercial minutes per hour, but many stations hold the line at 16. The decision on number and placement of commercials is crucial. Although commercials pay for everything else on the station, too many spots—a situation called advertising **clutter**—may cause listeners to tune out or, worse, to tune elsewhere. (In 2005 one of the largest group station owners cut commercial minutes by 20 percent in an attempt to reduce clutter on its stations.)

In addition to scheduling commercial matter, stations will also use the format wheel to schedule their promotional announcements, including contests and giveaways. The commercial and promotional segments of the hot clock are normally known as *spot sets*. Somewhat confusingly, they may also be called *stop sets* because the music stops during these breaks.

The musical segments of the hot clocks are typically broken down into two or three subcategories, such as current hits (given the most airplay); recurrents, recent hits that are still popular; and gold, for golden oldies. Sometimes programmers use keywords to denote the various song categories, such as "power cuts" or "prime cuts" for the most popular current songs, "stash" or "closet classics" for obscure oldies, and "image cuts" for songs that seem to match the format perfectly, such as Billy Joel songs for adult contemporary. Some programmers use color-coding schemes. Red typically denotes power cuts, green may identify a new song in heavy rotation, and gold is used to signify an oldies set. Some stations like to mix up the order of female to male to group songs, and this can be reflected in a hot clock as well.

The area of overlap on the format wheel, where one program element ends and another begins, is known as a **segue,** pronounced "segway." The purest segue is one in which the musical segments blend from one song into another, without DJ interruption. But there are other options. The transition may be made by naming the artists and saying something about the previous song, a procedure known as a "liner." The station identification (ID) may be made. The announcer might give the time and temperature (T&T). She might promote an upcoming feature ("teaser") or highlight a list of program and promotional activities ("billboard"). A promotional announcement ("promo") might be made. The air personality might promote the next artist or album ("front-sell") or announce the performers of the last set of songs ("back-announce" or "back-sell"). Or the DJ might cover the time to the next musical set ("sweep") with comedy, ad libs, or listener call-ins ("fill"). With this glossary in mind, see if you can determine the program "sound" of the stations depicted in 8–6.

Once the hot clock has been set, the format is in motion and the station is on the air! But the programming process is far from over.

Format Evaluation

Music programming is a particularly dynamic task. Audience tastes are constantly changing. A new pop star is always appearing on the charts. Television programs like *Saturday Night Live, American Idol,* and *Glee* and Web sites like YouTube and Facebook can make a new song (or a cover of an oldie) immediately popular. Listeners tire quickly of some songs. Others remain in our ears and minds seemingly forever. So how does the music programmer select the songs for the wheel? When does a song get pulled? This is the difficult process of format evaluation, the next step in radio programming.

One good way to start is by keeping track of song popularity by using Web services like iTunes Music Store or by reading influential industry publications like *Billboard*.com. Many stations have software that automatically publishes their playlists on their Web sites. The major record labels use these report cards to make sure their artists are receiving airplay and can gauge their appeal because each music download is tracked. Student radio stations find the *CMJnetwork (cmj.com)* an indispensable guide to breaking musical acts.

Events: You Don't Know Jack

Calling a radio station Jack or Mike or Bob or Dave may not sound like a really great promotional scheme, but it began happening all over the country in 2005. When venerable WCBS-FM in New York City, long the nation's premier oldies station, changed to the iPod-inspired Jack FM format, things got interesting. The station immediately fell from 8 to 22 in the ratings, and WCBS had to give advertisers additional airtime to make up for losses in ratings. Former Monkees rock-and-roll star turned disc jockey Mickey Dolenz and other highly paid radio legends were sent packing. But ratings did not improve in the next ratings period; evidently, Jack was having a difficult time making friends in the Big Apple.

What would convince highly paid program executives at WCBS-FM, part of the Infinity broadcasting empire, to desert a popular format with well-liked, established personalities for a brand-new format? One word: age. WCBS-FM listeners (like your authors) had grown up on 1960s rock-and-roll and were approaching 60 themselves. Radio managers and advertisers seem to covet youth or, more specifically, younger audiences, and WCBS's managers were no exception. Over the years, WCBS listeners had begun to drop out of that core of 25- to 54-year-old listeners.

All over the country Jack FM format stations (generally classified as adult hits) have been sprouting. To put it simply, adult hits is a radio format that disdains the conventional wisdom that most listeners respond well to lots of repetition and station self-promotion. Research seems to support this notion. In examining the psychographic characteristics of listeners, Bridge Ratings concluded that younger listeners were more prone to listen to Internet radio and MP3 players, where the diversity of the music was greater than terrestrial radio.

The Jack FM format, which started in Canada, plays a wider range of adult hits than tightly formatted radio stations. According to Arbitron there's a much broader playlist and the frequency of rotation songs drops from 7 to 10 plays per week to 4 or fewer, while the playlist may double in size. While the format appeals to 25–54, the largest part of the audience (60 percent) leans toward the younger part of the demographic. In addition, gains in the listening audience appear without regard to station personalities, and that makes the format cheaper to produce. Where the format had been tried, it had gained market share for listeners 12+ and 25–54. In addition, these adult hits format stations tend to hold on to listeners, meaning listeners stay with the station longer.

Jack FM didn't work out as expected for WCBS-FM. New York has reclassified itself as adult hits, essentially playing the same music but reintroducing some standard programming practices. Arbitron's 2009 study says that adult hits are currently on about 180 FM stations across the country, racking up 17 million listeners per week. Importantly, the format is attractive to both men and women.

Most stations also keep track of what their listeners are telling them about their format. **Call-ins,** telephone calls to the station, are logged to determine how listeners feel about the songs, artists, and personalities on the station. Stations use lists of contest entrants and telephone directories to conduct **call-outs:** Short (5- to 10-second) selections of the music, known as *hooks,* are played over the phone, and listeners are typically asked to rate the song as one they like a little, are unsure about, or like a lot.

Stations also assemble groups of their listeners in large rooms and conduct **auditorium tests.** In this forum up to 200 or 300 songs can be "hook-tested." Or stations may select a small group of listeners (from 3 to 15) and conduct in-depth interviews about their musical preferences; this is a **focus group study.**

If the task of evaluating the format sounds complex, that's because it is. Many different elements go into choosing the music played on a station. Consider the importance of each of the following:

- The popularity of the artist(s) and success of previous releases.
- The promotional thrust (new concert tour, appearances on TV, new Web site).
- Connection with a popular show, movie, or other pop venue.
- Rising or falling popularity of the musical genre.
- Seasonal elements of the lyrics.
- Timeliness of the lyrics. (Do they relate to a major event?)
- Major YouTube video release.
- significance of the artist's Facebook and MySpace presence.

As you can see, many things go into determining what will become a pop song for a format, so for this reason many stations hire outside experts to help select their music, conduct their audience research, train their DJs, organize their promotions, and perform similar programming tasks. Such services are provided by program and research consultants.

There are essentially two main types of radio consultants. *Specialized consultants* provide expertise in one particular area, such as research, music selection, promotion, or financial management. *Full-service consultants* provide "soup-to-nuts" services, from how to decorate the radio station to how to deal with crank phone callers. Some industry leaders are the Randy Lane Company; Media Strategies; Shane Media of Houston, headed by program guru Ed Shane; and Wimmer Research, based in Denver.

Fine-Tuning the Format

The final phase of radio format evolution is fine-tuning. Using data based on listener reaction—as indicated by audience ratings, station research, phone calls, and other means—the program manager makes changes in the schedule. The changes can range from minor to drastic. Minor changes involve substitutions in the musical mix, reformatting the various time periods, moving personalities around throughout the day, and so on. Major adjustments include replacing air personalities (most typically in morning drive); developing new promotional campaigns, including occasional call-letter changes; and firing music directors (a relatively common occurrence). The most drastic change is to abandon the format altogether and to try a new type of music, targeted to a different audience demographic. In recent years "format turnover" has been increasing at a spectacular rate. In the late 1990s some estimates indicated that as many as 20 percent of radio stations change formats in a given year.

Despite the apparent complexity of the process of radio music formatting, it remains popular and rewarding work. Major-market program and music directors can look forward to high incomes, great visibility in the high-gloss world of popular music, and excellent "perks," like backstage passes to concerts and limo rides with the stars.

NEWS/TALK AND SPORTS FORMATTING

On the surface it might appear that programming a radio station without music is a simpler task than formatting the latest in rock-and-roll or figuring out who

will be the next country legend. The format strategies of talk radio, however, are just as complex as those in the various music formats. How much news? How much telephone interview? What types of personalities? Sports? Which and how much? And like the music formats, how many commercials? When?

The first consideration for a station planning a spoken-word service is to determine the type and amount of talk. While there are really four common programming elements (news, talk, business, and sports), there are two extremes in the format. At one end is the all-news operation, providing summaries and spot news reports around the clock. Leading the way in this format are such classic all-news operations as WINS in New York, WBBM in Chicago, KNX in Los Angeles, and KYW in Philadelphia. At the other extreme are all-talk stations, which lean heavily on the concept of the telephone call-in as the basis for their programming schedule. On this list are such stalwarts

One of a group of conservative commentators, Bill O'Reilly's Radio Factor is available on syndication and at BillOReilly.com.

as New York's WOR and Los Angeles's KABC. Of course, some stations like WBEN in Buffalo and WBAP in Dallas combine news and talk in their market.

Just like their musical counterparts, most news/talk radio stations use a format wheel to schedule their programming. Examine the clocks for an all-news station and an all-talk station in Figures 8–8 and 8–9.

All News

First let's look at the all-news wheel. There are three basic elements in the sound hour: news segments, feature segments, and commercial matter. Typically news stations provide network news at or near the top of the hour. This provides the audience broad national and international coverage, which the station can interpret or "localize" for its audience in other news segments. Some all-news stations break for network news reports at other times, typically at the 30-minute mark (the "bottom of the hour"). Other stations use a different cycle. For example, WINS has

made a slogan of its cyclical format: "You give us 22 minutes, we'll give you the world."

Credible announcers are a critical ingredient to the success of the all-news operation. Announcers must sound confident and authoritative. For this reason many all-news operations prohibit announcers from delivering commercial "pitches." This is to avoid hurting the newscaster's credibility, which might result from the announcer's reporting a natural disaster, for example, and then segueing to a used-car spot.

Feature programming at an all-news station runs the gamut from the expected (weather, sports, and traffic) to the more specialized (political, economic, and health reports). These reports usually are presented in a streamlined fashion—in units of three minutes or less.

By definition, all-news stations need to be bright, brisk, and dependable. News listeners tend to be "no-nonsense" information seekers. When they tune in to an all-news station, they expect to become well informed quickly. For this reason the format wheel in all-news tends to spin rapidly; time checks are frequent; and program elements are repeated regularly throughout the day. Phrases such as "around the globe in 15 minutes" and "traffic and weather next" give evidence of this speedy rotation, especially in key dayparts like morning and evening drive. In this regard, the programming pace at an all-news station is similar to that at a Top 40 station.

News/Talk

Compared with all-news stations, those emphasizing talk tend to be "laid back." News segments are common, particularly at the top and bottom of the hour, with the remainder of the program hour filled by features, interviews, and telephone call-in segments. As an example, inspect the hot clock for an all-talk station (Figure 8–9).

Note the more leisurely pace of the talk format. Talk segments of five to seven uninterrupted minutes are commonplace, like the "music sweeps" in adult contemporary and adult standards. These are presided over by talk-show hosts. Unlike the announcers on all-news stations, who tend to be interchangeable (credibility, rather than individuality, is the key for them), talk hosts are distinct personalities. Some boast political beliefs on the left of the political spectrum; others are at the far right.

Feature elements are more commonplace in the talk format. Many stations have "resident experts" in such fields as medicine, psychiatry, finance, law, economics, and politics.

Figure 8–8

Hot Clock for an All-News Station

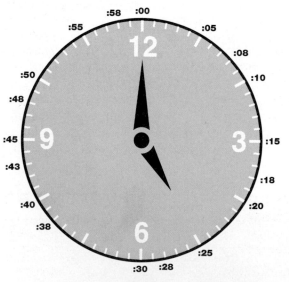

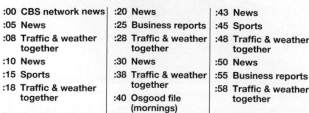

:00 CBS network news	:20 News	:43 News
:05 News	:25 Business reports	:45 Sports
:08 Traffic & weather together	:28 Traffic & weather together	:48 Traffic & weather together
:10 News	:30 News	:50 News
:15 Sports	:38 Traffic & weather together	:55 Business reports
:18 Traffic & weather together	:40 Osgood file (mornings)	:58 Traffic & weather together

Source: Courtesy CBS Radio.

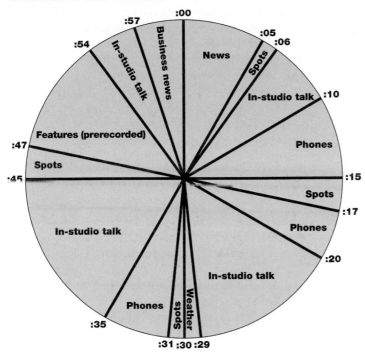

Figure 8–9

Format Wheel for an All-Talk Station

The prohibition of the reading of commercials by the announcer in the all-news format rarely extends to talk radio. In fact, talk-show hosts tend to be expert "pitchmen" (and women) who frequently give broad testimonials for their sponsors' products, sometimes longer than the 30 or 60 seconds the sponsor paid for.

Both news and talk tend to carry play-by-play sports on their schedule. In large markets there is considerable competition to land the broadcast rights to professional and major college sports in those cities. Smaller news and talk operations sign on to carry regional professional teams, as part of a network. Many also carry local college and high school games.

Talk radio is one of the top two formats, fueled by the war on terror, sensational scandals, and politically charged news events. Research on the audience, conducted in 2009 by the trade magazine *Talkers*, is informative. The talk radio garners about 17 percent of the total radio audience. Listeners are mostly male (56 percent, compared with 45 percent female); mostly mature (56 percent are aged 45 or older); mostly white (21 percent African American and 10 percent Hispanic American); and mostly smart (70 percent with more than a high school education). Republi-

cans outnumber Democrats (27 to 16 percent), while the majority of talk radio listeners describe themselves as independents (52 percent). For what it's worth, Internet-only Web sites have replaced Fox as their most watched TV news source, while few claim to read either *Time* or *Newsweek*. Football (35 percent) and baseball (31 percent) are their favorite sports, and their music formats of choice are country (22 percent) and oldies (18 percent each). Table 8–1 shows the top 7 syndicated talk shows.

Table 8–1	Top 7 Syndicated Talk Shows
Talk Show Host	**Weekly Cume (in millions)**
1 Rush Limbaugh	15.00+
2 Sean Hannity	14.00+
3 Glenn Beck	10.00+
4 Mark Levin	8.50+
5 Michael Savage	8.00+
6 Dr. Laura Schlessinger	
7 Dave Ramsey	

Source: *Talkers Magazine*, 9/10/2010.

NONCOMMERCIAL RADIO PROGRAMMING

As we traced briefly in Chapter 4, noncommercial radio programming can offer different formats and program services depending largely on the type of facility. Recall that there are three main classes of noncommercial facilities: public, university, and community.

Public Radio Stations

Public radio stations are those that meet guidelines for federal grant assistance through the Corporation for Public Broadcasting. CPB-qualified stations must employ at least five full-time employees, must broadcast at least 18 hours per day, and must develop good quality programming to serve a demonstrated need in the community. These CPB-qualified stations and organizations, numbering about 260, operate 784 stations nationwide, forming the backbone of the National Public Radio network. Since its inception in 1971, NPR has built a reputation for quality, long-form news broadcasting, often providing extended coverage of congressional hearings and breaking news. NPR is often seen as the place for in-depth reporting, and listenership to news programming has grown more than 48 percent since 1998. Today more than 27 million people listen to NPR every week. Well-known programs *All Things Considered, Morning Edition,* and *Performance Today* are produced by the network. Large member stations like WAMU produce *The Diane Rehm Show; World Café* is produced at WXPN Philadephia, and *Wait, Wait, Don't Tell Me* is produced by Chicago Public Radio.

While NPR is part of the Corporation for Public Broadcasting, most stations generate the majority of their operating revenue from individuals and business underwriting.

CPB-qualified stations may also feature the programs offered by a smaller competing networks such as Public Radio International (PRI) and American Public Media. PRI produces programming and distributes programs produced by other organizations. Some of its most popular shows include *This American Life,* produced by Chicago Public Radio, and *BBC World Service.* American Public Media distributes programs such as *Marketplace* and CBC's long-running *As It Happens,* but it is probably best known for distributing *A Prairie Home Companion,* the venerable variety show hosted by Garrison

Keillor. Today *Prairie Home Companion* is heard on more than 500 radio stations by an estimated 4 million listeners weekly.

Typically CPB-qualified stations rely on NPR, PRI, and American Public Media for about a quarter of their daily schedule. The remainder of the schedule is filled with locally originated music and public affairs programs. The overwhelming majority of classical music stations in the United States today are CPB-qualified. Other forms of music receiving airplay include jazz, opera, folk, and show tunes.

In addition to news programming, NPR offers a variety of music programs from classical to jazz to world music. Stations determine the format and programs that best serve their local audiences. As the audience for classical music has aged, many commercial stations have given up this format, so public stations make up the largest sector of this format. Currently the trend in public radio is to move toward a fully integrated format and away from a **checkerboard** schedule.

NPR has been diversifying its programs and distribution networks over the past five years. With the advent of new technologies, public radio has been eager to make programs and show segments available to the listening audience via Web sites and through podcasting technology. As the first decade of the 21st century came to a close, more than 14 million listeners were downloading podcasts every month. NPR was quick to provide special apps for

The long-running, live musical variety show starring Garrison Keillor harkens back to the Golden Age of radio when much of the programming occurred before a live studio audience. *Prairie Home Companion* is one of the most popular programs on public radio stations.

smart phones. Research indicates that more than 2.5 million Twitter followers and a million Facebook fans use these services.

But it's not all wine and roses for public radio. NPR receives no direct federal funding and generates two-thirds of its revenue from station programming fees and program sponsorships. For individual member stations, funding continues to be an important concern as government representatives look for ways to cut looming federal and state deficits. During the economic downturn, both network and station operations have been pared, and some colleges and community license holders have considered selling their licenses to Christian broadcasting organizations.

College Radio

College radio is another form of noncommercial broadcasting, but these stations are not NPR affiliates. Instead we are referring to about 800 stations licensed to American colleges (and some high schools) that do not meet the CPB criteria. Many are operated as student activities or training centers; most feature "alternative" programming schedules to both NPR and commercial radio. The musical mix at most college stations is eclectic and mostly progressive. College stations often program a wide variety of music, depending on the interests of the station personnel, which frequently changes from year to year. Their schedules illustrate both block and strip

Figure 8–10

Many community and college stations are known for promoting local, live music. KEXP in Seattle slogan "Where the music matters" reflects the focus of the station's programming.

programming techniques. Progressive rock is striped across most of the weekday, with special blocks of programming interspersed through the day and in the evenings.

As we have seen, commercial radio formatting is tightly structured and controlled. For this reason, college radio has served both as a place where new music is likely to be played first and where there is likely to be less structured programming. During the 1980s and 1990s college radio pioneered what is now commonly called *alternative rock,* and it's always served as a place where many new performers received their initial airplay. Venerable rockers like U2, the Police, and R.E.M. started out on college radio, and more recently the Shins, Death Cab for Cutie, the White Stripes, and the Decemberists have made the transition from indie bands to major artists.

Many college stations are active in news and public affairs programming. Again, the structure and approach of these services is an amalgam. Stations affiliated with journalism and mass communications programs may have news and public affairs schedules that emulate those at a commercial operation. Others rely for news programming on volunteer efforts by their staffers. In such cases schedules tend to be sporadic and content varied, to say the least.

Community Station Programming

If *diversity* is the word to describe college radio, the term is equally suited to the broad category of community radio stations. Community stations are operated by civic associations, school boards, charitable foundations, and, increasingly, religious organizations.

Most community stations use a **block programming** approach. Unlike commercial formats, where

Profile: Muzak—It Isn't Just for Elevators Anymore!

Most people associate the name *Muzak* with lush stringed instrumental versions of pop standards. You may remember when you were growing up, standing in line at a bank, wondering why the store piped in a bland instrumental version of a great Beatles song.

Muzak was founded by George Squier in 1922. The company, called Wired Radio, delivered music and news to homes in Staten Island through telegraph wires. Needless to say, broadcasting quickly supplanted the need for a wired programming service in the home, so Squier's company began concentrating on delivering background music to restaurants, hotels, and other businesses.

In 1934 Wired Radio became Muzak, and the programming we fondly called "elevator music" was piped into buildings in and around New York City. The company pioneered a concept called "stimulus progression," 15-minute music cycles gradually increasing and decreasing in intensity. The concept worked pretty well through the mid-1960s, but then a musical revolution began. Muzak's playlist and rock music began to diverge; people began to use the name derisively to refer to anything bland. Muzak updated its concepts some in the 1970s and 1980s, but it wasn't until the 1990s that things really changed.

VP for programming Alvin Collis, a former sound engineer and self-proclaimed musician and storyteller, had a revelation. Modern stores are like theatrical sets (think Old Navy or Banana Republic). Music needs to meet the expectations of the customer, and that means programming specifically to the store's demographics and psychographics. Music played for British Airways will be different from the music chosen for the Charlotte Russe or Gold's Gym.

Today Muzak employs program designers, mostly musicians or people with deep musical background. Muzak provides more than 100 core programming services to thousands of different customers throughout North America. They develop programs for customers from a fairly vast library of digital recordings including every popular genre from jazz to heavy metal to country. Today Muzak is as likely to program a cut by Velvet Revolver as by Kenny G. There might be a broad playlist or a fast rotation of top 40 songs, depending on the client. (Some clients actually specify which artists they want on their programs.) Muzak programs to meet the tastes of the customers whose clients choose the programming service. When you think about it, it's a lot like programming a radio station.

the music, talk, and commercial elements are generally consistent throughout the day, in the block scheme, programming is divided into two- or three-hour blocks appealing to different audiences at different times. Educational outlets, for example, may begin the day with a two-hour block appealing to elementary-age students. Midday might be used for in-home college-level instruction, and the afternoon dedicated to social studies programming for secondary schoolers.

The trend toward diversity in programming at noncommercial stations extends to the religious stations. While virtually all religious operations make live broadcasts of church sermons and activities a vital part of their programming day, beyond that there is great variation. Among Christian stations, for example, at various times one can hear old-time gospel (like "The Old Gospel Ship"), solemn hymns, or "contemporary Christian" rock. And within the religious radio milieu, there are "networks." For example, the Salem Radio Network programs three full-service different Christian music formats for stations as well as specialty programs. Its programs are heard on more than 1,500 stations around the country each week.

Micro-Broadcasting and Low-Power FM   In the 1960s and 1970s, the FCC allocated low-power licenses to educational institutions and community groups. However, in 1978, the commission stopped the practice and required all 10-watt stations to increase power to a minimum of 100 watts. In January 2000 the FCC began authorizing new, very low power FM stations again. Former FCC chairman William Kennard began this new service as a way of providing options for small community organizations that were not being served by current commercial and public services. These new stations are typically 100 watts or less, and have an average listening radius of about only four miles. These stations are only available for noncommercial entities including public safety organizations and public transportation facilities.

As noted in Chapter 4, the FCC has granted more than 850 licenses for this new service, and a number of stations have signed on. Similarly to some college radio, these stations often run on a shoestring budget. Programming can be anything from an eclectic mix of music to a fully formatted all-jazz station. Because the service is new, it is difficult to predict the impact it will have on radio generally.

SUMMARY

- There are strong ties between radio and the music business: It is evident that airplay means higher record sales. The advent of alternate program outlets and new technologies has also reinforced the interdependence of these businesses with radio.

- Radio programming can derive from local, prerecorded or syndicated, and network sources. Radio shows can be produced in four ways: local live, live-assist, semiautomation, and full studio automation.

- Stations strive to make their formats unique. One way of achieving this is to analyze the market of a particular city and to find a format hole or a niche that is not being well served.

- When a station attempts to choose a format, internal factors that are considered include ownership, dial location, power, technical facilities, and management philosophy. External factors such as strength of competitors, geography, and demographics also need to be analyzed. The new trend is toward psychographic research, which tells programmers the type of listener each musical category attracts.

- Station managers plan their programs on a hot clock. This helps them visualize the sound of a station. A program schedule is divided into dayparts, including morning drive, daytime, evening drive, evening, and overnight.

- Talk radio has seen spectacular growth in recent years, resuscitating the AM band and providing its listeners a range of services, from all-news to sports, financial advice, and psychological counseling.

- On the nonprofit side, public radio stations receive programming from three major network sources: National Public Radio (NPR), Public Radio International (PRI), and American Public Media. College stations tend to emphasize diversity and block programming; religious and community stations offer everything from chapel broadcasts to Christian rock-and-roll. Low-power FM stations will provide programming opportunities for community groups in the future.

KEY TERMS

local programming   184
prerecorded or syndicated
   programming   185
network programming   185
full studio automation   188
voice-tracking   188
target audience   190

demographics   190
psychographics   190
hot clock   193
dayparts   193
clutter   197
segue   197
call-ins   198

call-outs   198
auditorium tests   198
focus group study   198
checkerboard   202
block programming   204

SUGGESTIONS FOR FURTHER READING

Clark, L. (1998). *Shock radio*. New York: Forge.

Eastman, S., & Ferguson, D. (2005). *Media programming: Strategies and practices* (7th ed.). Belmont, CA: Wadsworth.

Glass, Ira, & Able, J. (1999). *Radio: An illustrated guide*. Chicago: WBEZ Alliance.

Gross, L., Gross, B., & Perebinossoff, P. (2005). *Programming for TV, radio & the Internet* (2nd ed.). Boston: Focal Press.

Hausman, D., Benoit, P., Messere, F., & O'Donnell, L. (2007). *Modern radio production* (7th ed.). Belmont, CA: Wadsworth.

Hillard, R., & Keith, M. (2003). *Dirty discourse: Sex and indecency on American radio*. Ames: Iowa State University Press.

Keith, M. (2003). *The radio station* (6th ed.). Boston: Focal Press.

Laufer, P. (1995). *Inside talk radio: America's voice or just hot air?* Secaucus, NJ: Carol Publishing Group.

Looker, T. (1995). *The sound and the story: NPR and the art of radio*. Boston: Houghton Mifflin.

Lynch, J. (1998). *Process and practice of radio programming*. Lanham, MD: University Press of America.

MacFarland, D. T. (1997). *Future radio programming strategies: Cultivating leadership in the digital age* (2nd ed.). Mahwah, NJ: Erlbaum.

Perebinossoff, P., Gross, B., and Gross, L. (2005). *Programming for TV, radio, and the Internet* (2nd ed.). Boston: Elsevier.

Warren, S. (2006). *Radio the book* (4th ed.) Boston: Elsevier.

INTERNET EXERCISES

Visit our Web site at **www.mhhe.com/dominickbib7e** for study-guide exercises to help you learn and apply material in each chapter. You will find ideas for future research as well as useful Web links to provide you with an opportunity to journey through the new electronic media.

TV Programming 9

Quick Facts

Percentage of Americans who cite network TV as biased politically (2009): 60

Percentage of Americans who say they would pay for news online (2010): 19

Number of prime-time broadcast and cable shows canceled in the 2009–2010 season: 84

Percentage of Americans who use TV as their primary source of local news (2009): 64

Cost per episode of *Seinfeld* in cable syndication: $1 million

Number of new program ideas pitched to TV networks each year: 5,000 (est.)

Number of successful new TV series each year: 1–3 (average)

Average number of Americans who watch the nightly news on one of the three broadcast networks (2010): 22.3 million

"When television is good, nothing—not the theater, not magazines or newspaper—nothing is better. But when television is bad, nothing is worse."

Newton Minow—"The Vast Wasteland" speech, 1961

We study television for a lot of reasons: its social impact; its effect on politics; its influence on modes of conversation, fashion, and relationships; and on and on. Throughout this book, we've looked at its ownership, its financial structure, its employment patterns, and the like. But for the majority of the public, television is really about only one thing: programming. And that programming, whether it's found on the broadcast networks, local TV stations, cable, satellite, or the Internet, has only two main functions: information and entertainment. Simply put, people watch TV programs for either news or entertainment. In this chapter we examine how television programming is made. First, we look at information programming—the often-controversial topic of television news. Second, we examine the field of entertainment television—how TV manufactures "stars and stories" for the entertainment of a large, loyal, and eager public. But first we bring you the news.

A BRIEF HISTORY OF TV NEWS

Although we have provided a history of broadcast, cable, and the Internet in earlier chapters, it is important to put television news into a historical perspective.

The Kennedy Assassination: The Death of Camelot, the Growth of Conspiracy Theories, and the Birth of Television News

Was there a government cover-up? Did Oswald act alone?

Nearly 50 years after JFK's death the majority of Americans are skeptical of the official conclusions about his death. Despite countless government investigations and television documentaries, the majority of Americans seem convinced that Lee Harvey Oswald had help assassinating the young president. Did television have something to do with reinforcing this persistent belief?

President John F. Kennedy had been warned by his advisers not to go to Dallas. Like many places in the South, the city was torn by political and racial unrest. The press hinted that there might be trouble

Television coverage of the Kennedy assassination and the events that followed, including the shooting of Lee Harvey Oswald, was watched by more than 500 million people worldwide during November 1963.

when a president perceived as a liberal traveled to a staunchly conservative city, but Kennedy could not be dissuaded from going. A large contingent of the media was on hand as the president's motorcade passed the Texas School Book Depository. Shots rang out. The president was mortally wounded.

Within 5 minutes, news of the shooting moved on the United Press wire service. Within 10 minutes the three TV networks had interrupted their afternoon lineups of game shows and soap operas. Receiving the news from a young Dallas reporter named Dan Rather, an emotional Walter Cronkite told the nation on CBS that its president had been slain. Incredibly, within hours, a suspect was apprehended at a nearby theater.

Assassinations in other nations often lead to governmental chaos and public violence, but in the United States it turned people to their TV sets for news, for comfort, and most importantly for explanations. For four days all regular programming was suspended and people sat, seemingly transfixed by the story unfolding on TV. The full resources of the TV medium were turned to this one event. Television was there when President Kennedy's widow, Jacqueline, returned with the coffin to Washington and when the accused assassin, Lee Harvey Oswald, was himself gunned down by a Dallas nightclub owner, Jack Ruby. And TV permitted the nation to attend the funeral, as world leaders came to pay their respects. In hindsight, Ruby seemed to have unfettered access to killing Oswald before the assailant could explain himself and before authorities could be certain he was the only shooter. How could this happen? Many asked questions, but there were few answers.

We claim no special knowledge, nor do we subscribe to any of the various theories about the events; but while the unfolding story during the four days in November provided compelling television, there were few answers. Many Americans became convinced that events were carefully orchestrated and that Oswald did not act alone. A conspiracy theory was born.

Like the events of 9/11/2001, more than 9 in 10 Americans were said to have watched the TV coverage that fateful weekend. Watching, too, were over 500 million people in 23 countries, as the coverage was fed to a new device that had recently been launched: the communications satellite. More importantly, however, the events surrounding the assassination began the era of television news supremacy.

Both local and network news had been expanding from 15 to 30 minutes, but TV news was still relatively primitive. Previously, a few stories were shot on film and mostly voiced over by the anchor, but the norm was a news reader. With the coverage of the assassination, TV news seized the public consciousness. Things would never be the same.

No longer was TV news the stepchild of print or of its progenitor, radio. As 1963 drew to a close, both NBC (with the formidable team of Chet Huntley and David Brinkley) and CBS (with the "most trusted man in America," Walter Cronkite) were telecasting 30 minutes of nightly news with pictures from the field. By 1965 the national news was in color. This became important as events both at home and abroad began to capture and command the TV news eye.

Television News Comes of Age

Today there is a certain nostalgia for the era of the 1960s and early 1970s, a period in history bounded by the Kennedy assassination in 1963 and the Watergate scandal, which ended in 1974 with the resignation of President Richard Nixon. Aging baby boomers (people born after World War II and who reached adolescence in the 1960s) tend to recall the time as a period of playful experimentation, blue jeans, Woodstock, and "flower power." There certainly were moments of fun, but the decade was marked by violent confrontations, social upheavals, and cultural change. And for the first time in history it all happened in front of TV cameras. Three major events occurred in this period. Each event became forever intertwined with the growth of TV journalism.

Television and Civil Rights   In 1962 Dr. Martin Luther King, Jr., outlined a new strategy:

> We are here today to say to the white men that we will no longer let them use their clubs in dark corners. We are going to make them do it in the glaring light of television.[1]

And it worked—TV was there in Little Rock in 1957 to capture the violence following the integration of Central High School. It was in Montgomery, Birmingham, and other southern cities to witness sit-ins at lunch counters and bus stations. American society was changing and TV was there to cover it.

[1]In David J. Garrow, *Protest at Selma* (New Haven, CT: Yale University Press, 1978), p. 111.

It was in Washington when Dr. King proclaimed "I have a dream" to more than two hundred thousand who rallied for civil rights in 1963. In darker days television was in Detroit, Watts, and Newark to cover civil disorders, presenting searing images of white police chiefs turning dogs and fire hoses onto defenseless demonstrators. It revealed the hatred of white supremacists, including the Ku Klux Klan, as throngs of peaceful protesters filed through their towns. Later it demonstrated black anger and frustration, as TV turned its cameras on arsonists and looters in the summer riots of 1965 and 1967 and following the assassination of Dr. King in 1968.

Television in Vietnam   A second major news event of the 1960s took place thousands of miles away. But it too harnessed the power of TV—particularly its ability to bring distant events into America's living rooms. The event was the war in Vietnam. Although Vietnam has been called "the first television war," TV had gone to Korea in the early 1950s. This early coverage, however, lacked the immediacy that would characterize Vietnam reporting. The years in which the war was actively fought by Americans (1961–1975) were indeed the "television years." During this period, TV news made virtually all its major advances: portable cameras, satellite relay systems, color, videotape replay, and on and on. This was the era when TV's first generation of reporters (Eric Sevareid, Chet Huntley, Charles Collingwood, and others), who had been trained in radio or print journalism, gave way to a new wave of youthful reporters who had grown up in the age of TV. In this group were Ed Bradley, Tom Brokaw, Steve Bell, and Liz Trotta, the first woman to cover war for television.

Vietnam provided a training ground for the new people and techniques coming to TV. As a result, the public was deluged with daily reports, with illustrations of American and enemy dead, and with dramatic "point-of-view" shots from cameras mounted on helicopter gun ships and later in the bellies of evacuation aircraft.

For many who lived through those years, the war is remembered as a series of indelible TV images: the whirr of engines as choppers evacuated wounded soldiers; GIs "torching" a village with their Zippo lighters (reported first by Morley Safer on CBS in 1965); antiwar demonstrators chanting "the whole world is watching" as they clashed with police during the 1968 Democratic National Convention in Chicago; the execution of a prisoner by Saigon police chief Lo An (aired on NBC in 1968); panic-stricken South Vietnamese clutching the landing gear of evacuation aircraft in 1975; and flotillas of rafts and fishing boats crammed with refugees as the "boat people" fled their country in the late 1970s.

One Small Step   Starting in 1957 the United States and the former Soviet Union were locked in a fierce battle to control the new frontier: space. During the early days it wasn't clear who would win; but beginning with Alan Shepard's space flight in 1961, "space shots" became a major focus on TV news, leading up to the lunar landing of *Apollo 11*.

In the summer of 1969 Neil Armstrong set foot on the moon, an event witnessed by the largest global TV audience up to that time, an estimated 600 million people on six of the seven continents. NASA had carefully orchestrated the event as a TV program, having mounted a small camera (provided by RCA) on the steps of the landing craft, in front of which astronauts Armstrong and Edwin "Buzz" Aldrin would cavort. The two unfurled and planted an American flag, stiffened by an aluminum rod to give the appearance that it was fluttering in some imaginary lunar breeze. Within minutes President Nixon was on a split screen to talk to the astronauts by telephone. Two hours later the world audience watched as the astronauts blasted off for the return trip to earth. The astronauts had provided for this unique TV angle (the first point-of-view shot from outer space) by setting up another RCA camera in the lunar soil.

TV News Becomes Big Business

Civil rights; Vietnam; the space race; and subsequent events like the Watergate scandal (in 1974 and 1975), the hostage crisis in Iran (in 1980), the disasters involving space shuttles *Challenger* (1986) and *Columbia* (2003), the unthinkable collapse of the World Trade Center towers, the aftermath of Hurricane Katrina (2005), and the oil spill in the Gulf (2010) brought TV news to the forefront. The major networks expanded their news coverage (ABC's *Nightline*, for example, began as a nightly update of the hostage situation in 1979). Local television news also grew. And for good reason. It had become a profit center for television stations, accounting for as much as one-third to one-half of all advertising revenues. Following are some major trends in TV news in its growth period of the 1970s and 1980s.

"Happy Talk"   TV news has been identified with its anchors and reporters. Newscasters, at both the national networks and local stations, tended to appear strong, serious, some would say staid, and conservative. The faces of Walter Cronkite, Eric Sevareid, John Chancellor, David Brinkley, Nancy Dickerson, and many others were seen night after night in homes across the country. In every major city there were established figures in news too, each with impeccable credentials and an aura of journalistic integrity and self-assurance.

In the late 1970s a new breed of newscaster began to appear. Men were younger, more daring, and even dashing, frequently dressed in the most modern clothing styles, many with facial hair (previously avoided— except for the stately mustache sported by Cronkite).

For the first time women began to appear in the anchor position. Like the new breed of male newscasters, they were young and attractive. On-camera looks, charisma, charm, and sex appeal became at least as important as journalistic training and ability.

Not only did this new breed look different, but they also acted different from their predecessors.

They talked to each other on the air. Sometimes they talked about the news reports they had just seen; sometimes they just seemed to be engaging in the kind of gossip and repartee found in most offices. TV news was lambasted by the print media, which called it "happy talk." There was concern that TV news was moving away from issues toward personalities, away from information to entertainment, and away from serious news to "sleaze." Research seemed to support these claims. Studies found that stations with the happy-talk format featured more sensational and violent content than did traditional newscasts. They also had higher ratings.

ENG and SNG   Another new trend in TV news was its dependence on new communications technologies. The trend can be summed up in two three-letter abbreviations: ENG and SNG.

Electronic news gathering (ENG) emerged in the mid-1970s, when portable video cameras and recorders became commercially available. Lightweight, portable TV cameras and small videotape recorders revolutionized news coverage.

Edwin 'Buzz' Aldrin walking on the moon.

Sports has always played an important part in television. Early coverage of baseball and football filled weekend schedules when prime-time dramas and comedies were not appropriate. Olympics coverage has always provided a ratings boost for the network that carried the games.

In 1979 Getty Oil provided funding for a new venture that became Entertainment and Sports Programming Network or ESPN for short. Like other cable television networks, it benefited from the tremendous growth of cable subscribership during the early 1980s.

Early ESPN programming ran the gamut from darts to slow-pitch softball to coverage of the Canadian Football League, but the most important show from those early days was *SportsCenter* hosted by Lee Leonard and George Grande. In 1992 the show hired Linda Cohn, who made history in the 1980s by becoming the first full-time U.S. female sports anchor on national radio.

In 1982 ESPN was bought by ABC and benefited from the contracts and experience of the network and its history of covering sports. During the 1980s the network partnered with the National Basketball Association and the National Football League. The league agreed to allow ESPN to simulcast the games carried over local television, and *Sunday Night Football* was born. During this time the NCAA tournament, National Hockey Night, NASCAR, and tennis were added to the lineup. By 1990 Major League baseball was added, and ESPN was transformed into a programming powerhouse.

Over the years, the rights to carry sporting events have increased as player salaries forced owners to look for greater revenue. In 2010 Turner Broadcasting snagged a majority of NCAA March Madness coverage as part of a $10.8 billion pact with CBS to cover the playoffs.

Sports has become a major programming force on cable television. Industry experts say that ESPN is paid the highest per-subscriber fee of any of the advertising-supported cable channels. The Golf Channel, The Tennis Channel, HBO Boxing, Versus, Turner Sports, and many regional programming services offer viewers the opportunity to spend more time watching and less time actively engaged in sporting activities.

With ENG, cameras and recorders could go anywhere. Events could be recorded in full, with natural sound, and the most important parts could be edited together electronically in a speedy and cost-efficient manner.

Several years later, the dawn of **satellite news gathering (SNG)** had arrived. Satellite news gathering refers to the use of mobile trucks mounted with satellite communications equipment to report local, national, and international events. SNG trucks and vans could transmit up to communications satellites the pictures and sounds gathered by ENG. The satellites sent the signal back down to local stations and networks to use in their news programs. It was thus possible to obtain live news pictures from virtually anywhere in the world.

Large stations bought their own "flyaway uplink" vans, capable of transmitting events live to a satellite and back to earth, to the studio. CNN and the major networks have access to satellite uplink equipment small enough to cram into a suitcase.

Today new networking capabilities like satellite phones, Skype, and other innovations make it even easier to cover events.

The News as Showbiz With increasing profitability inevitably came the "ratings war." News directors began to follow ratings with at least as much concern as their counterparts in the sales and programming departments. At local stations the competition for audiences was most intense during the periods when the Nielsen ratings company conducted surveys of local TV viewing (see Chapter 12). These periods are known as **sweeps.**

In TV the sweep periods occur four times a year—in February, May, July, and November. In a quest for "number one" status, many local news operations took to programming series of short documentaries, known as **minidocs,** during these times. Many minidocs aired during the sweeps focused on sensational topics, including teenage prostitution, spousal and child abuse, and religious cults. They were accompanied by extensive advertising campaigns on the air and in print, on billboards and buses. In many ways the hoopla surrounding news was not unlike that which accompanied the premiere of a new motion picture. In fact, TV news became the stuff of movies and TV shows—*Broadcast News, Switching Channels, Max Headroom, Murphy*

Brown—suggesting that the TV newsperson had become a modern icon.

A number of **news consultants** emerged to provide the expertise required of news managers in this competitive environment. Leading news consultants included such firms as Frank Magid, Reymer and Gersin, and Audience Research and Development, Inc. Consultants provided advice to stations to use in selecting their talent, designing their sets, using graphics, devising sweeps-weeks promotions, and other areas. Their research techniques, ranging from focus group tests to viewer surveys, are analyzed in Chapter 12.

All News, All the Time   The cable industry began C-SPAN in 1979. The public service operation provides gavel-to-gavel coverage of congressional hearings, political party conventions, and other public affairs programming. However, on June 1, 1980, brash cable TV entrepreneur Ted Turner started CNN, a 24-hour news service. *CNN Headline News* started 18 months later, and both services struggled for several years before attaining widespread coverage on cable systems. But the Persian Gulf War in 1991 changed CNN's fortunes and its stature as a major news provider. Within minutes of the beginning of the war, CNN cameras in Baghdad showed the nighttime air raid and Iraqi antiaircraft fire. During the next 24 hours, CNN correspondents Peter Arnett and Bernard Shaw provided continuous coverage of the early days of the war. The first Gulf War marked a turning point for cable news, as research showed that during the early days of the war CNN had more viewers than any of the three television networks.

Other cable information services sprang up during this period. In 1991 CNBC was forged by NBC when it acquired Financial News Network, and Bloomberg Information Television was inaugurated in 1995. However, the creation of Fox News Channel and MSNBC, both started in 1996, demonstrated that news had become an important source of programming for cable providers. Since 2009 Fox News has led cable services with the highest ratings. In the past few years, programming that espousing particular editorial opinions, like *The Glen Beck Program*, have become important parts of the cable news business.

TV NEWS ECONOMICS TODAY

As television stations, networks, and cable systems face increasing competition—from one another, from the Internet, from radio, from magazines, and from apps that run on smart mobile phones—news has become increasingly important and expensive. The recession of 2008 precipitated some trends. According to the 2010 study by the Pew Research Center, the structure of the news business is changing dramatically. Consider the following:

- Local television ad revenue fell 22 percent in 2009; this had a significant impact on the revenue most newscasts generated for their stations.

- Some analysts think that even after the economy rebounds, newspapers, radio, and magazine revenues will be more than one-third less than in 2006.

- One expert estimated that local television news has shed more than 1,600 jobs since 2008.

- In 2010 ABC announced it would eliminate 25 percent of its news workforce.

Unbundling the News

According to the Pew Research Center, the old model of journalism involved taking revenue from advertising and using it to cover local civic news. News editors aggregated news into sections of a newspaper or segments on a local newscast.

With online sources, this model is becoming outmoded as consumers are less likely to turn to just one source for their news. Users often hunt for news by topic and often graze among a number of news sites.

This new behavior pattern changes the traditional revenue mechanism supporting news; and this, in turn, may impact what news is reported. According to the 2010 study, more than two-thirds of the top Internet news sites are largely tied to TV and newspaper financed operations whose resources are shrinking. That means cutbacks in traditional media may significantly affect online content in the future.

Coventuring

One important trend has been the development of cooperative ventures by television news outlets with other stations in their market, with their arch-rival cable systems, and even with their oldest competitors, the local newspapers. As the costs of gathering TV news mount, and as new means of delivering information become increasingly available to consumers (such as online services, news apps for mobile devices and interactive cable), news managers have recognized that coventuring makes good business sense.

News operations can be excellent sources of revenue for many local stations, although recent trends have seen some consolidation of operations in certain markets. Stations with strong news organizations can help build an image in the local community.

Coventuring with other TV stations in the market usually occurs between a local news leader at a network affiliate and an independent or smaller station. Today many station groups own more than one station in the same market. Often the news organization from the larger station will provide a separate service to the second station. In other instances, the news leader buys time on the independent station to program an alternative version of its local news.

Television news outlets are also coventuring with news/talk radio stations. For example, in Washington, DC, ABC's WJLA-TV and all-news station WTOP-FM (a Bonneville station) have entered a news partnership. Now WJLA's weathercast are broadcast on WTOP and Websites are linked to the WTOP Web site.

Some markets are shrinking. In 2009 Syracuse television pioneer WTVH announced that it had entered a management partnership with WSTM-TV and WSTQ-TV. WSTM immediately assumed control of the WTVH operations, firing 40 news staff members and merging the three television operations. WSTM also operates Weather Plus on the Time-Warner cable system along with local portal cnycentral.com. According to one report, viewership of local news in the market had declined more than 20 percent over the past 25 years.

At the corporate level, coventuring has become commonplace. CNN reporters are frequently seen on CBS, and Anderson Cooper, who does the *AC360* program on CNN, also does segments for CBS *60 Minutes*. CNN and *Sports Illustrated* (both owned by Time Warner) have partnered to develop SI.com, a sports Web site.

Regional and Local Cable News

Another significant trend has been the rise of regional cable news channels. Unlike local newscasts at 6 and 11 or news headlines, which offers quick cut-ins or news summaries to viewers, **regional cable news services** are 24-hour localized versions of CNN.

The pioneer in regional cable news is News12 Long Island, created by Cablevision to serve subscribers in Nassau and Suffolk counties, suburbs of New York City. Today News12 is part of a regional interactive service run by Comcast. Different news services provide local news for suburban New Yorkers in the Long Island, Westchester, Connecticut, New Jersey, and Hudson Valley regions. Inside the city limits, Time Warner's NY1 provides news around the clock to cable viewers in Brooklyn, Queens, the Bronx, Manhattan, and Staten Island. Similarly, Chicagoland Television (CLTV) uses the resources of the *Chicago Tribune* to provide regional cable news to the second city and nearly 2 million regional subscribers, while Cable Pulse (CP 24) provides Toronto with a 24-hour service.

Smaller regional news channels have emerged in the last few years. YNN-Your News Now serves the Central New York region, including the cities of Syracuse, Ithaca, and Watertown. Six New Now serves Sarasota, Florida. More than 40 regional cable news services are operating in all parts of the United States.

Events: Networks scramble to cover Egyptian uprising

Non-stop coverage of breaking world events is not unusual for television and cable news operations. In the last few years, news networks have been helped by the ability of citizen journalists to provide video updates using mobile devices and the new social media. The West started seeing pictures as the "Jasmine Revolution" that started in Tunisia quickly spilled over to neighboring Egypt. Throngs gathered in Cairo to demand that President Mubarak resign. Over the next few days the world watched as crowd sizes increased a thousand-fold.

Egypt, which had been slowly liberalizing its media over the past few years, quickly acted to repress information. State journalists were ordered to downplay the seriousness of the protests. When several seasoned journalists refused, they were promptly put on 'vacation' until further notice. Internet access was cut by the government as protesters started using Facebook and Twitter to gather support for the protests. CBS news chief Sean McManus said that this complicated reporting greatly since networks use the Internet heavily to communicate with reporters and sources.

American networks were caught off guard as the uprising gained momentum. Surprisingly, the clearest, most complete reporting was Al Jazeera TV, an Arab news network that kept up a continuous, live feed despite Egyptian attempts to block broadcasts. When Secretary of State Clinton urged Egypt to stop blocking the flow of information, Al Jazeera broadcast her remarks live with simultaneous Arabic translation on a split screen showing the situation in Cairo, where protesters were violating government curfew. Egyptian officials claimed that Al Jazeera unfairly portrayed the situation, but many experienced journalists from around the world took notice.

Reporting on political unrest is always dangerous, but a turning point occurred when journalists themselves became the targets of combat. Usually protesters and governments alike use the media to get their side of the story out. But things got ugly. Reporters from Fox and CNN were beaten and ABC's venerable Christiane Amanpour was surrounded by unfriendly crowds shouting their hate for America. David Verdi, NBC VP of worldwide newsgathering, was quoted in *Broadcasting and Cable Magazine* saying, "This one caught us by surprise because it went from a demonstration to a riot to roving gangs targeting journalists in 24 hours."

Global News

Ironically, at the same time TV news delivery becomes more and more localized through regional cable and news-on-demand, it is also moving in an opposite direction. The success of Cable News Network has generated competition in serving the global news audience.

BBC World competes worldwide with CNN and broadcasts to more than 200 countries and territories around the world. In fact, the service became available in the United States in February 1995, as BBC America, and is found on many U.S. cable channels. News Corporation's Sky News offers an alternative to CNN in Europe, in parts of Southeast Asia on Star TV, in Australia, and other regions of Rupert Murdoch's considerable reach.

International news channels are not limited to the English language. France's TF-1 and France Television have teamed to create an all-news service for the French-speaking world. Not to be outdone, Televisora de Costa Rica created Telenoticias, a Latin American service entirely in Spanish. The Arab news service, Al-Jazeera, also began a world news service. Operating out of Qutar and other major capitals, the Arab news service in available in about 40 million homes worldwide; and RT (formerly Russia Today) operates a worldwide service with different versions in Arabic, English, and Spanish.

So television news remains an important part of the media landscape. For local TV stations, it is a profit center and a critical source of viewer attention, identification, and loyalty. For networks, like CNN, ABC, NBC, CBS, and Fox, news is more than a necessary evil. It helps them earn and retain credibility, especially in the eyes of those viewers who tend to distrust what they hear on talk radio or read on the Internet. Speaking of the Internet, reliable and credible news helps Web surfers separate the few grains of wheat from the tons of chaff available on the World Wide Web. News-based pages help the new medium earn the trust (and the business) of many consumers put off by the vitriolic—and often downright scurrilous—content of many Web pages. The news for TV news is mostly good. Now let's see how TV news gets made.

THE TV NEWS TEAM

TV News Command Structure

Television news is a collaborative craft. It is not unusual for a large market station to boast more than 100 people in the news department. The major networks still maintain hundreds of news personnel, but staff layoffs at all the broadcast networks in the last three years were geared toward making operations leaner. CNN alone employs over 3,000 people at its Atlanta headquarters and nearly 4,000 people worldwide, so payroll is a huge expense in gathering news. Coordinating the efforts of these small armies is no easy task, especially with the pressures of both the deadline and the bottom line. Thus TV news organizations tend to follow certain command structures, such as the one outlined in Figure 9–1. Because many stations now integrate online reporting and stories with the broadcast portions, some positions in the newsroom are undergoing change.

The News Director Overall responsibility for the news department falls to the news director. News directors tend to have a solid background in TV news, many as former reporters or anchors. The news director hires news personnel, establishes news and editorial policy, and evaluates the newscast in post-mortem screenings with the staff of the news department. Today's news directors are increasingly concerned with budgets, making sure the news is produced at a profit. The exciting, high-pressure nature of the job has led to a typical job tenure in the range of about three years.

News Producer If the news director is the boss of the day-to-day news operation, the executive producer is in charge of planning and coordinating the activities of on-air and production staff and other team members for various programs, such as the "11 o'clock Report" or "The Noon News." The producers maintain editorial control over the stories that make up their individual TV newscasts. Line producers prepare the story lineup, determine the stories' lengths, and decide how they will be handled. The producer of each newscast will proofread all copy, select the graphics, and be present in the control room to make last-minute changes during the newscast. Field producers travel with the reporters and crew and take charge of covering all aspects of covering the story on location. Today field

Figure 9–1

TV News Command Structure

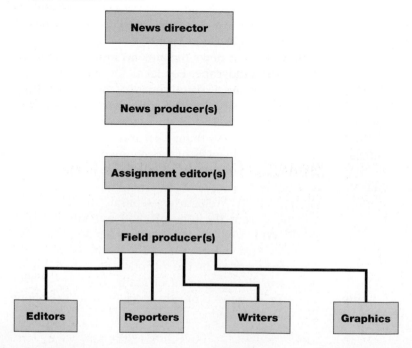

producers work mostly for network operations or the largest stations.

Most news operations have special segments, or "beats," such as consumer affairs, health, arts and entertainment, and of course sports and weather. These beats may be headed by unit producers, who assume overall responsibility for these segments.

Assignment Editor   The main job of the assignment editor is to dispatch reporters and photographers to cover news stories. The job requires great organizational skills. At a local station, as many as five different crews may be out in the field at one time. At a network, literally dozens of crews need to be dispatched and returned to the studio for editing and other production tasks. To assist in this complex task, assignment editors maintain a **future file.** This is an annotated listing of upcoming news stories, scheduled as many as 30 or 60 days in advance. For example, an editor working for a financial network would keep track of when the government will announce economic reports and figures on unemployment and on job creation. Of course the future file is useless when breaking news occurs: A bank failure, a sudden announcement of bankruptcy, or physical events like the Gulf oil spill will have tremendous impact on financial reporting and can really tax the skills of the assignment editor and the entire staff.

Reporters, Correspondents, and Analysts   Reporters receive their orders from the assignment desk and begin their research, usually on the telephone. They set up interviews and determine shooting locations. Typically, the reporter has been teamed with a photographer. At many stations and regional news channels, the reporter may be a one-person band, responsible for shooting her own stories. The reporter proceeds to the scene, obtains interviews and other video, does the report in front of the camera, and returns to the studio to supervise the editing, writes and announces the voice-over and lead-in copy, and, if part of the newscast, gets dressed and made up for the newscast. Correspondents are reporters who are working for larger news entities, such as a broadcast or cable network, and may cover a beat such as the White House or may do substantive reporting on large stories, such as unexpected natural disasters or investigative reports.

Analysts are reporters who have specialized knowledge about a particular field. Political analysts often host the Sunday morning talk shows on the various networks.

Writers   It is a sad fact that many of today's reporters may be selected for their on-camera appearance rather than their journalistic skills. For this reason some stations and networks employ newswriters to help script the newscast. Writers may prepare some material for reporters and anchors (although most anchors like to write their own material). They frequently prepare the clever lines used to introduce the newscast (teasers) or to attract the audience to return after commercial breaks (bumpers). Sometimes they do research with the reporter in developing complex stories.

Photographers and Editors   Most newscasts consist of separate stories, called *packages,* linked by the anchors and reporters. Each package is a complete story requiring shooting video and interviews and then editing together the various pieces with its own voice-over and graphic material. The photographer naturally shoots the material, and the editor is the person who puts the package together. Typically the reporter returns from the field with too much material, all of it shot out of sequence. He may have done the introduction to the story six or seven times; there may be dozens of separate pieces to an interview. The reporter (and sometimes the field producers, unit producer, producer, or news director as well) retreats with the editor to a small editing room to make sense of the mayhem of the typical field report. In many news operations, reporters edit their own packages.

TV news has benefited greatly in recent years by the development of digital editing systems, such as Apple's Final Cut Pro (see Chapter 3).

BROADCAST JOURNALISM IN FLUX

In the issues box we address the state of news credibility, but there is a shift in viewing going on as we write this edition of the book. Certainly broadcast journalism is not going away, but there have been some substantive changes in the way news is produced. In 2009 local television news fell 22 percent, causing many stations to cut back on staff and reporting initatives. One estimate reported by the Pew Research Center in 2010 put local station news losses at about 1,600 jobs over the past two years.

Events: The Demise of the Evening News Anchor?

For more than two decades, the majority of Americans heard about the day's events by tuning in Rather, Brokaw, or Jennings. All three anchors spent years honing their journalistic skills covering everything from the civil rights movement of the 1960s to the Arab-Israeli Six-Day War to the fall of the Berlin Wall to the attacks on the World Trade Center. Rather, Brokaw, and Jennings inherited their seats from notables: Cronkite, Chancellor, and Reynolds. In taking over their seats, the anchors inherited the power to shape opinion by insisting on the coverage of certain stories. They spoke with almost God-like authority.

But now many media experts say that their departures signal a change in the news business and the way news is digested in America. In 1970 the combined ratings for the three newscasts stood at approximately 48.* Today those ratings stand at 18 percent of the population, and they're falling.

News choice has exploded since 1995. Americans are as likely to tune into Fox News or CNN as to watch ABC. Younger Americans are comfortable choosing Internet news sources for a quick look at world events, and many college students frequently say they get their news from shows like the *Daily Show.* But isn't that really a comedy show? Some media experts think that this change in viewing represents a sea change in the news business. For example, during the 1970s and 1980s, the evening news was appointment television for many families. The news came on during the dinner hour and gave us a digest of the important stories of the day. According to the Pew Center for Research, 46 percent of those who responded in the annual news survey described themselves as news "grazers."

There may be other changes as well. Former CBS News president Andrew Heyward said that the anchors "used their extraordinary power to fight for serious and important stories." Heyward wonders if the next set of anchors will have the clout to battle corporate executives for coverage of serious issues. Other journalists share Heyward's concerns. In a poll conducted by Public Perspective, half the journalists responding to a survey said that the most important problems facing journalism were quality, standards of reporting, and journalistic ethics.

The face of the evening news has changed. Brian Williams, Diane Sawyer, and Katie Couric now represent the faces of the evening news. Will audience share continue to dwindle, or will a new generation of Americans consume the daily digest as part of the evening entrée?

*Each rating point equals approximately 1 percent of the total U.S. population.

Some industry estimates suggest that declining revenues for radio and television will continue into the future, although cable networks have held steady. For local TV, audiences continue to fall across all timeslots.

Social media sites such as Twitter and others have emerged as powerful tools for disseminating information quickly; we saw this with events in Haiti after the devasting earthquake. However, immediacy can have drawbacks. Some experts worry that efficiency of reporting is replacing the traditional skeptical fact-checking that provided broadcast news organizations with high credibility in the past (see Table 9–1).

It is still difficult to predict how stations will integrate their broadcast and online operations. Clearly there is a substantial relationship among the various electronic technologies today. Telling a compelling news story, whether from NewsCenter 4 in New York or an online news Web site in Lima, Ohio, still requires shooting video and creating an audio track that provides context for what we see. Also, technology is shifting our focus, allowing broadcasters to cover more breaking news. This, in turn, gives stations

Table 9–1	Decline in News Credibility since 1996*				
Network	**1996**	**2000**	**2002**	**2004**	**2008**
NBC News	29%	29%	25%	24%	24%
CBS News	32	29	26	24	22
ABC News	31	30	24	24	24
CNN	38	39	37	32	30
NPR	—	25	23	23	27

*For respondents who could rate each news source.

Source: The Pew Research Center for the People and the Press, 2008.

more opportunity to influence public persceptions about the story.

The majority of Americans still get their news from television (58 percent) and radio (34 percent), but online sources have gained in the past five years, now beating newspapers as the place people turn for news. Today 34 percent of those surveyed say they regularly go online for news. While radio percentages declined about 6 points in the past five years, online sources increased about 10 points in the same period. (The percentages here don't add up to 100 percent because many respondents said they got news from more than one source.) And in the latest surveys more people are admitting that they get news at different times throughout the day as opposed to watching a specific television newscast. The impact of these changing trends will make broadcast news more competitive in the future.

TV ENTERTAINMENT PROGRAMMING

Most of us use the mass media for relaxation, escape, and diversion—in a word, entertainment. Entertainment does not come cheap in TV and cable. A major TV network might spend more than $25 million a week on nonnews programming. The entertainment programming business is an integral part of modern broadcasting and cable.

There are three basic ways in which a TV station or cable company can acquire programs: network, syndication, and local origination. First, we provide brief definitions of these terms. Then we examine each major program source in detail.

As you might expect, **network programming** refers to original programming funded by, produced for, and distributed by the major TV and cable networks. Recent popular broadcast network programs include *NCIS* and *The Big Bang Theory* on CBS and *Grey's Anatomy* on ABC, *Law and Order-SVU* and *The Office* on NBC, and *House* and *Family Guy* on Fox. In the past few seasons, reflecting America's diverse nature, *Soy tu Duena* on Uni has also made it into the top 25 ratings.

Cable works differently because its programming originates via the network directly to cable franchises around the country. There are no affiliates, and clearance is not an issue. In recent years cable has offered more competitive original programming such as *Entourage* on HBO or *Mad Men* on AMC, *The Closer* on TNT, and *Jersey Shore* on MTV; but some insights into how much ground cable has gained in the last few years can be realized by looking at original cable programming. *Nip/Tuck* on FX, *Project Runway* on Bravo, and *Monk* on USA all gained national viewing audiences in their first season.

Syndication refers to TV programming sold by distribution companies to local TV stations and cable services. As we noted in Chapter 7, syndication

Hawaii Five-0 is a remake of a popular crime show from the late 60s, both produced and telecast by CBS Television. The theme song, composed by Morton Stevens, has become among the most recognized themes on television. The name *Hawaii Five-0* was originally conceived in honor of Hawaii's status as the 50th state.

companies sell two kinds of shows: off-network (series that have appeared first on the networks and are being rerun by local stations or cable systems) and first-run (shows expressly produced for syndication). Some off-net successes in syndication include comedies like *Two and a Half Men*, *Everybody Loves Raymond*, *South Park*, and dramas from the *Law and Order* and *CSI* franchises.

First-run powerhouses are mostly talk and game shows, like *Ellen*, *Wheel of Fortune*, and *Entertainment Tonight*. Some other shows like *Judge Judy* and *Family Court* have been consistent winners, too; but first-run dramatic programs often have a difficult time. The exceptions have been MGM's *Stargate SGI* and *Star Trek: The Next Generation*.

In past few years, syndication has become a success stream of programming for cable TV, which uses its own series and off-network shows in a fairly heavy rotation.

Local origination refers to programs produced by local TV stations (or cable companies) for viewers in their own communities. The most common forms of local origination programs are the local news and talk shows that most TV stations and cable systems carry daily. Larger market television stations tend to develop more local programming than medium and small market stations. In the 1950s and 1960s many stations also featured cartoon programs for kids hosted by "talent" from the station (typically a cameraman or technician frustrated in an earlier career in vaudeville or theater). If you don't remember these local shows from your youth, your parents probably do.

NETWORK TELEVISION: THE BIG FOUR, PLUS THREE

From the beginnings of TV in the late 1940s to the late 1970s, TV programming was dominated by three commercial networks: CBS, NBC, and ABC. For more than a generation these networks were America's great entertainers. Their programs, ranging from variety shows like Ed Sullivan's *Toast of the Town* to comedies like *I Love Lucy* and *Mork and Mindy*, dramas like *The Fugitive* and sports programs like the Super Bowl, attracted millions of viewers. In the 1980s, a new service emerged as a fourth network: Rupert Murdoch's Fox Broadcasting Corporation. In the mid-1990s, two newer networks struggled for a share of television's huge audience:

Paramount (UPN) and Warner Brothers (WB). They were joined in 1998 by broadcaster Lowell "Bud" Paxson's Pax TV (now Ion). WB and UPN merged into CW, but it appears that over-the-air television has had a difficult time sustaining more than four full-time networks.

Affiliation

The backbone of any network is the group of stations that carries its programs. Stations that receive network programming are known as **affiliates.** Traditionally, roughly 200 stations were affiliated with each of the Big Three of ABC, CBS, and NBC. Following its major expansion in 1994 (with the acquisition of New World and its investment in other properties), the Fox lineup approached parity with ABC, CBS, and NBC.

With roughly 200 stations each, the major networks cover nearly all the U.S. homes with TV. This is critical because national coverage enables them to sell the nation's leading advertisers commercials within their programs. Just as local broadcasters do, networks charge advertisers based on viewership, measured in CPM.

The newer networks are at a comparative disadvantage, each launching with about 100 affiliated stations, often covering fewer than 9 in 10 U.S. households. These services also distributed their programs on local cable channels in some areas to boost their coverage.

To become an affiliate, the local TV station signs a contract, known as an **affiliation agreement,** with the network. Historically, the major networks paid stations a fee for broadcasting network programs. This fee is known as **network compensation.** The fee could range from under $500 to more than $10,000 per hour, depending on the station's coverage area, market size, and popularity; however, with the rise in the cost of programming, this practice began changing as we entered the 21st century.

The high costs of original programming (like $13 million per episode for *ER*) and rights to sports events caused the major networks to rethink their affiliation agreements. By 2010 all of the networks were asking their affiliates to help pay for programming. Over the past few years, network affiliates have seen their payments from retransmission consent rise, and networks have asked affiliates to shoulder more costs for programming. Today compensation occurs when networks provide affiliates with more time within network programs for local sales. Local affiliates can charge higher CPMs in prime-time programs because the audience is fairly large.

Affiliates may elect to carry the network shows, or they may refuse them however, contracts usually require stations to carry the majority of the network schedule. Programs that are carried by the station are said to have **cleared;** those that are refused are known as **preemptions.**

In return for their investment in programming and their affiliation agreements, the networks gain access to the mass audience. Through their system of local affiliates, the networks have the potential to pull together a huge simultaneous audience, which they can sell to a national advertiser for a concomitantly large price. The name of the game is the audience. Networks try to attract either a large, undifferentiated audience, as is the case with *American Idol,* or a relatively smaller audience that has the demographic profile that advertisers find attractive, as is the case with *How I Met Your Mother,* with its 18- to 34-year-old audience. It's a high-stakes game. The network with the most successful programs will make the most money (or lose the least money). The one with fewer viewers or the wrong kind of viewers will have bad news for its shareholders, and its suffering affiliates will respond appropriately. When a network does poorly, the adjacent spots bring in less money, and the lead-in for local news can hurt local ratings.

The Network Programming Process

Network programming is cyclical: Like baseball, it has its own seasons, pennant races, winners, and losers. First, let's examine the ground rules.

Financial Interest and Syndication Rules

With the exception of news, sports, and a limited number of other programs, historically the networks did not own the shows that filled their nightly schedules. Fearing monopoly in entertainment production by the Big Three, in the early 1970s the FCC adopted a set of regulations known as the **financial interest and syndication rules.** In showbiz jargon the regulations were known as "fin-syn." In a nutshell, the rules limited network participation in the ownership of programs produced for them and in subsequent syndication. Rather than paying outright for their shows, the networks paid **license fees** to production companies for the rights to show them. After the

work-run programs were sold into syndication, not by the networks but by the program owners. After nearly two decades of legal wrangling, the fin-syn rules were substantially modified by the FCC in 1993 and were abandoned entirely by the end of 1995. By 1995 cable had gained enough viewers to ensure that the four networks couldn't dominate both the production and distribution markets.

The net effect was that after 1995 networks were allowed to own their own shows and to sell them in syndication following the completion of their network runs.

By the late 1990s, the networks were actively involved in the production of their own programs. CBS was a partner in *King of Queens* and *Everybody Loves Raymond.* NBC Universal owns the *Law and Order* franchise along with shows like *Will & Grace* and *Las Vegas.* As owners of studios (see the section on studios that appears a bit later in the chapter), ABC (Disney), Fox (Twentieth Century), NBC (Universal), and WB (Warner Brothers) are likewise directly involved in program development as well as ownership.

Prime-Time Access Rule

The FCC implemented the **prime-time access rule (PTAR)** in 1971. The rule restricted the amount of time an affiliate could accept from the network, in effect allowing networks to control no more than three hours of the four-hour prime-time nightly schedule (with some exceptions). Because TV viewing increases through the evening, naturally the networks maintained control of the three hours from 8:00 to 11:00 p.m. (7:00–10:00 p.m. in the central time zone). This created *early fringe,* a one-hour segment for local affiliated stations to fill by themselves. The top 50 markets were prohibited from using this time (known today as "local access") with off-network syndicated programs (reruns of shows they already owned).

Although the intent of the rule was to encourage production by non-Hollywood companies and maybe even stimulate local production, the reality is that most stations turned to first-run syndication in this time period. Evening game shows, especially *Wheel of Fortune* and *Jeopardy,* became very popular as did shows like *Entertainment Tonight* and *Access Hollywood.*

PTAR had another lasting effect: It enabled independent stations to compete on more equal terrain with network affiliates in the very important hour when people were sampling the TV schedule to make their nightly viewing choices. By programming their best shows here (ironically, a lot of popular old network shows that could not be shown on some network stations), many new independent stations were able to siphon viewers from affiliates to themselves. Today most of those independents are affiliated with CW, Ion, or MyNetworkTV.

As with fin-syn, there was great pressure to modify or abandon PTAR. The FCC scrapped most of the PTAR requirements at the end of 1996. Still, "access" survives as an important lead-in to network prime-time programming as it is very lucrative for local affiliates.

Network Seasons   Network programming is organized around two seasons. The fall premiere season begins in late September and runs through the middle of December. This is when new programs are launched and returning programs begin showing new episodes. The so-called second season runs from the end of January through the beginning of May. This is when the networks replace low-rated programs with specials and new series.

At one time the two seasons were distinct. The three networks premiered their new shows in one week around late September; the second season almost always occurred in early February. Today, however, there seems to be more variability. Some shows will take a hiatus midseason in the fall and return in the spring. Some important network shows, such as *American Idol*, didn't have a fall season at all.

Fox was especially instrumental in this trend. Fox staggered the introduction of its new programs, sprinkling premieres throughout the year. A particularly effective strategy included running new episodes of hit shows, like *The Simpsons* and *American Idol*, in the summer, when ABC, NBC, and CBS were in reruns. The same strategy has been pursued by ABC with *Dancing with the Stars*.

In past years the network season lasted 39 weeks. As many as 32 episodes of a new show would be ordered, with the remaining 20 weeks occupied by specials and reruns. Today escalating production costs, competition, and a declining success rate have led the networks to order as few as 8, 10, or 11 new episodes of a series, with an option to repeat at least two. This is one reason the season has shrunk (or expanded to year-round, depending on one's point of view).

Who gets the orders? Production of TV series is dominated by a few large studios, increasingly,

owned by the huge communications conglomerates that also own many of the television networks. These are the major studios, or "the majors," for short. However, some hit shows come from outside these huge conglomerates. A small number of independent producers ("independents" for short) exert important influence over the network programs we see. Let's start with the majors.

The Major Studios   The major studios in TV production are familiar names, although their ownership may be less familiar. Longtime television heavyweight SONY Television, which produced such shows as *The King of Queens* for CBS, *Rescue Me* for FX, and *Seinfeld* for NBC, is part of the Columbia Pictures/SONY conglomerate. Today Sony produces first-run syndicated shows like *Jeopardy* and *Wheel of Fortune* along with daytime favorite *Days of Our Lives*.

Another foreign-owned major is Twentieth Television, part of Rupert Murdoch's News Corporation empire. While Twentieth produces some programs for its own Fox network (*Glee* and *The Simpsons*), it also provides programming to its competitors such as *Modern Family* for ABC and *Burn Notice* for USA.

Not all the programming majors are foreign-owned. Warner Brothers, owned by Time Warner, is the home studio of such recent hit shows as *Without a Trace, Two and a Half Men* for CBS, and *The Closer* for TNT (a network owned by the parent company Time Warner). WB also produces *The Ellen Degeneres Show* in syndication. Paramount, a part of the Viacom conglomerate, is the source of such shows as *NCIS: Naval Criminal Investigative Service* and CBS's *Medium*, plus its own enormously successful *Star Trek* series.

Another firm with major studio status in Hollywood is NBC Universal. In 2010 Comcast purchased a controlling interest in NBC Universal, gaining access to thousands of movie and television titles. Recent TV shows produced by Universal include all the different variations of *Law and Order, CSI* for CBS, and the FOX hit *House*. NBC Universal also produces *Access Hollywood* and *Deal or No Deal* for syndication.

The TV programming arm of the Disney media empire is its Hollywood-based Walt Disney Studios, Touchstone Pictures, and Buena Vista Television divisions. Such shows as *Desperate Housewives* and *Dancing with the Stars* as well as current hits *Scrubs* for NBC and the syndication *Who Wants to Be a Millionaire* come from Disney, which has also partnered in other series like the animated *PJs* on Fox and the WB youth drama *Felicity*.

It is clear that Hollywood studios and television fortunes are linked. These programs provide thousands of jobs for producers, directors, writers, and production personnel.

Independent Producers   The networks also order programs from a small number of independent producers that have had a series of network successes. Perhaps the hottest producer in Hollywood at the moment is Chuck Lorre, who has had phenomenal success with *Two and a Half Men* and *The Big Bang Theory*. Lorre also produced *Dharma & Greg* and *Cybill*.

Law and Order is produced by Dick Wolf, who started the franchise in New York in 1990 where it became one of television's longest-running dramatic series with 455 episodes. Along the way *Criminal Intent* and *Special Victims Unit* made him a top television producer.

Jerry Bruckheimer is a Hollywood producer known for creating megahits on both the big and small screen. Bruckheimer produces *The Amazing Race* along with *CSI* and *CSI: Miami* and *New York* for CBS.

Dreamworks, the film studio created by Steven Spielberg, David Geffen, and Jeffrey Katzenberg, entered television in a big way. With former ABC programmer Ted Harbert at the helm, Dreamworks has produced the ABC comedy *Spin City* and the less successful *Undeclared* for Fox. Dreamworks also produced *Band of Brothers* for HBO and its 2002 project *Taken*, which aired on the Sci-Fi channel. In 2006 the studio was purchased by Paramount and has produced another HBO series, *The Pacific*.

Older producers include Stephen Bochco, an influential independent, with a track record on network TV, including *Hill Street Blues, Doogie Houser, M.D.*, and series creator of *L.A. Law*. Bochco's megahit *NYPD Blue* is one of the most respected shows ever produced for television. The late Aaron Spelling, another famous independent producer, died in 2006. His two monster hits *Dynasty* and *Hotel* were preceded by *Love Boat* and *Beverly Hills 90210, Melrose Place*, and *7th Heaven*.

The independent television market is now a relatively small community because the major studios essentially control all the major prime-time television shows.

The significance of the sale of television programming on Hollywood is vital to understand. In 2004 the major studios collected more than $17 billion in revenues and royalties for the sale of TV productions. Ironically, some industry analysts claim Hollywood makes a bigger share of its profits from television than from the feature film industry because the costs of promotion and distribution of films are so high. In television, these costs are borne by the networks. Thus it is little wonder that the relationship between major studios and the television networks has become more important in recent years.

Pitching a Program   Programs get on the air through two primary means. Some are commissioned by the network, whose research and development discovers public interest in a particular program concept. It is said that the late NBC program executive Brandon Tartikoff ordered *Miami Vice* by telling producer Michael Mann to "give me MTV with cops!" Similarly, after meeting Mr. T at a Hollywood party, Tartikoff is reported to have handed Stephen J. Cannell a piece of paper reading, " 'The A-Team,' 'Mission Impossible,' 'The Dirty Dozen,' and 'The Magnificent Seven,' all rolled into one, and Mr. T drives the car!"

More commonly, new program ideas are introduced, or "pitched," to the networks by their producers. The pitch may be a briefly written synopsis—a short description of the idea meant to engage the interest of the evaluator—or it might be a **concept,** a short story narrative, also known as a story or **treatment,** or it might be a fully developed sample script. It is estimated that the networks are presented with as many as 5,000 new program ideas each year in one form or another. About 500 are chosen for further development.

At this point a development executive begins working with others in the producing field. Lawyers, accountants, and agents get involved in the **development process.** Producers spell out their rights, and the parties often agree on the options (who owns what rights) available. Most commonly, the program (by now known as a "property") is developed under the terms of a **step deal**—an arrangement by which the property is put together in a series of distinct phases spelled out step by step in a contract. Usually the first step is to get a producer to hold an option to develop the program. Options may last for a year and may be renewed. The second step is when a network or studio accepts the project for development. Each party needs to agree to the terms of the arrangement, and this is often done through a set of deal memos. For example, under the terms the network may get **right of first**

refusal, the contractual right to prohibit the production company from producing the program for another client. In some instances, the deal also enables the network to appoint additional writers to develop the concept or "punch up" the script. When the story idea is finalized, a brief summation of the plot, called a log line, will be used to describe it to studio heads, reviewers, and the like.

At this time fewer than one-half of the optioned ideas lead to a deal or fully scripted stage. According to surveys done by the FilmL.A., the broadcast and cable networks will order between 80 and 100 **pilots,** or sample episodes, each costing in the range of $3 and $5 million to produce. Just because the network has ordered a sample episode, this does not guarantee that the show will find a place in a network's schedule. Usually the networks will show the pilot to test audiences and program executives for their reactions. More changes may be ordered, or the development may be canceled. By early spring about a dozen of these pilots will result in series orders. The shows that did make it through the step-by-step process are placed in the networks' schedules and will be shown to advertising executives during the upfront selling season. (See Chapter 7.) Ten of these twelve are likely to be canceled before the second season. Often, in the late spring or summer, networks will run pilots that didn't make it in an effort to recover some of their production costs.

Network Program Costs
While the concept of a show, its location, and its stars are certainly important, for TV executives, perhaps most important is its cost. The network business is highly speculative because it's difficult to predict which shows will succeed; nevertheless, a network needs to develop a cost target for each show it produces and for each episode. Table 9–2 presents typical production costs for various program types.

The most expensive program type is the lavish, multipart network miniseries, which can cost more than $7 to $12 million per hour to produce. With profits declining and competition increasing, HBO and Showtime have been at the front of the line producing multipart miniseries for their viewers. The HBO 10-part series *The Pacific* had a reported budget of $250 million. The success of such expensive projects often require repeated showings in the U.S. market, international distribution, and sales of DVDs.

Table 9–2	Typical Costs for Network Programs
Program Type	**Cost per Episode ($ millions)**
Major miniseries	$4–7
Movie of the week	3–5
Adventure/mystery/drama	2–4
Situation comedy	0.9–2.0
Reality/newsmagazine	0.75–1.5

The next most expensive program type is movies made for TV. In industry parlance, these are referred to as *movies of the week* (MOWs), "made-for-cable," or more cynically "disease of the week" shows. Typically these shows are contemporary dramas revolving around personal relationships, tragedy, domestic strife, or recent criminal cases. The budget is typically in the $5–8 million range. Today very few movies of the week are produced for television; most made-for-television movies are aired on cable channels like Lifetime, USA Networks, and the Hallmark Channel or are made for one of the pay-cable channels. In 2010 *Temple Grandin* scored big for HBO winning seven Emmys and a Golden Globe, including best performance for actress Claire Danes.

Adventure, mystery, and drama series are the next most expensive, costing, on average, between $2.5 and $4 million on a weekly basis. Action shows like *24,* which have a large number of remote locations week after week, can be very expensive to shoot. The cash-strapped networks have responded as you might think: by seeking less expensive shows to offset the high cost of miniseries, made-for-cable, and action hours.

Fortunately for the networks, the most popular program type is also one of the least costly. Situation comedies cost between $1.5 and $3 million per episode. Sitcoms can hold the line on cost since most are shot in a studio as opposed to an expensive location; they are recorded in real time before an audience, which keeps the need for editing and special effects to a minimum; and today some are shot on videotape, which is cheaper than using film. Many dramas, on the other hand, continue to use film, and many are shot in wide-screen high definition.

If a situation comedy becomes a true hit and lasts several seasons, its costs can increase dramatically, mainly in the area of star salaries. In the 2009–2010 season, Charlie Sheen's salary was a cool $1.25 million per episode for *Two and a Half Men* while Jim Parsons of *The Big Bang Theory* was only making $40,000. (*TV Guide* reported that with *Big Bang's* success, salaries were about to take a large jump when the show was renewed.) The bargain basement of network TV are so-called reality shows, including game shows, news documentaries, and "infotainment" series. For example, CBS's highly rated *60 Minutes*, ABC's *20/20*, and *Dateline NBC* are all bargains for their networks, usually costing 60 percent less than their dramatic counterparts. The low cost of reality shows is one reason for their proliferation in recent years. However, not all reality shows are inexpensive. Both *Survivor* and *The Amazing Race* are fairly expensive (for reality shows) because of the costs associated with shooting on location.

Cable Network Programming

Dramatic Production   Over the past few years, cable has begun mounting its own unique dramatic and comedic shows. The economics of cable and broadcast production are fairly similar, except that costs per episode are usually lower for an equivalent cable series.

Cable programming such as *The Closer*, which holds the record as being cable TV's highest-rated scripted show, *Burn Notice*, and *Royal Pains* all have the same dramatic characteristics as their broadcast counterparts. Steve Koonin, the president of Turner Entertainment Networks, which includes TBS, TNT, and Turner Classic Movies, points out that cable and broadcast schedule programming differently. Cable is likely to show a program at 10 p.m. and again at 2 a.m. and might have a weekend marathon, but the actual programs are similar. Despite this difference, however, Koonin thinks that the average viewer no longer distinguishes between broadcasting and cable outlets.

Theatrical Motion Pictures   As we have seen, the bulk of the program schedule (over 80 percent of airtime) on the major pay-cable services, including HBO/Cinemax and Showtime/The Movie Channel, consists of theatrical motion pictures. Most of these are licensed to the pay services by the "majors," Hollywood's largest studios.

The studios normally make their films (known as "titles" in the trade) available to pay cable a year after their first theatrical release. There is a narrower release window for pay per view (PPV) of six months or less. Sometimes studios will delay the DVD or PPV

The Big Bang Theory pokes fun at society by using stereotypical images of scientists in humorous situations.

According to two studies conducted by the Pew Research Center for the People and The Press, almost two-thirds of Americans think the news they receive is frequently inaccurate, reflecting the highest level of skepticism expressed since 1985 when the Center began doing this survey.

Some of the numbers are difficult to interpret because the poll does not distinguish among television, newspapers, and bloggers. Nevertheless, of the more than 1,000 people surveyed, 63 percent thought that the media were often wrong. Only 26 percent of those who responded in the poll said that the press was careful to avoid bias in reporting. That figure is down from 36 percent when the poll was started. CNN continued to top the list as the most trusted name in news, with 30 percent of the respondents saying they believe most of what that network broadcasts. That's down from 39 percent in 2000. And believability for all the major broadcast networks has declined over the past few years. Of the broadcast outlets, only NPR gained in the survey.

Not surprisingly, more Democrats trusted CNN than did Republicans, who are more likely to give Fox News the highest scores for credibility.

Some news professionals point to the growing number of programs that feature shouting matches on radio and TV programs where partisans are free to disagree, often without a moderator checking facts and assertions. Others think junk blogs and gossip sheets also contribute to the growing public weariness.

The poll indicated that television was still the prime source for news, with 64 percent saying they relied on TV as their primary source.

---

release of major box office hits to continue to reap profits at the box office. Occasionally a theatrical release may be so disappointing that the studio will release the film to cable and home video within weeks of its theatrical debut.

Some distributors make their films available to multiple pay services simultaneously. However, to offset viewer dissatisfaction with pay services ("they all play the same movies"), there has been a trend toward studios' signing **exclusivity deals** with pay services. Such contracts guarantee first cable release to one pay service.

Theatrical motion pictures are also the backbone of a number of the advertiser-supported cable networks, including the USA Network, TBS Superstation, and Lifetime. These films are normally sold in packages, series of titles made available by a distribution company for sale to cable networks and local TV stations. In fact, it was Ted Turner's acquisition of virtually the entire MGM film library (including *Gone with the Wind*) that enabled his launch of Turner Network Television (TNT) and Turner Classic Movies (TCM). American Movie Classics (AMC) has also carved its niche by acquiring distribution rights to large packages of film titles.

Cable-Original Movies In their quest to keep pay cable attractive to consumers despite competition from video stores and other sources, cable program-

mers are producing their own movies. Some have been released for theatrical distribution first, to be followed by a pay-cable run. Others have been produced for a premiere on the cable network, to be followed by theatrical or home video release.

The typical made-for-cable movie today has a budget in the range of $4 million to $8 million. This is less than a third of the typical budget of a feature film but about a third higher than the cost of a "movie of the week" on one of the broadcast networks. For the extra cost, the cable "made-for" can typically attract a better-known cast and high production values and take on more delicate or controversial subject matter than is the norm on broadcast TV.

HBO has been a leader in the production of cable original movies, producing between 10 and 15 each year, many based on real-life stories. In 2010 HBO led the Emmys with more nominations than all other networks. Included in the programs nominated were three made-for-cable movies, including *You Don't Know Jack*, a film about Dr. Jack Kevorkian, directed by Barry Levinson; *The Special Relationship*, a film about President Bill Clinton starring Dennis Quaid; and *Temple Grandin*, which scored more than a dozen Emmy nominations.

Cable Series In their early days, cable and pay cable relied almost exclusively on movies, sports, and concerts for their programming. The few cable series that did run tended to be the low-budget, easy-to-film variety (Las Vegas acts, stand-up comedy, show-biz chatter, and so on). One sign of the maturity of the cable business is the emergence of regularly scheduled high-profile series from many cable networks. In fact, more TV programming is produced today for cable networks than for the traditional broadcast networks.

Some recent cable-original series of note were *True Blood, Entourage,* and *In Treatment* on HBO; *Californication* and *Weeds* on Showtime; VH-1's *Behind the Music*; and MTV's *Jersey Shore*. Dozens of others like *Mad Men, Burn Notice, Psych, In Plain Sight,* and *The Shield* (to mention a few) have sprung up on advertiser-supported cable networks.

Generally cable services produce their original programs at lower cost than do the commercial TV networks. This cost savings is achieved in a variety of ways. First, smaller independent production companies are often used instead of the costly major studios. To cut overhead expenses that pile up while shooting in a big studio lot, many series are shot on location or in major cities outside the United States, where the dollar is stronger than local currency. Canada and England have become very popular production sites, with Toronto and London standing in for Los Angeles and New York.

In addition, cable networks often engage in coproduction ventures with foreign networks and production companies, many of which have had trouble getting their programs into the lucrative American market. For example, the HBO miniseries *Elizabeth I* was a coproduction with England's Channel 4.

Public Television Programming

Although the dominant networks (in terms of audience size and budget) are the major commercial broadcast and cable firms, public TV remains a vital source of national programming. PBS reaches nearly 118 million Americans each week through its on-air programming and through an expanding online presence. Today some 350 full-power noncommercial TV stations have the same needs as their commercial counterparts: to fill their schedule with programming attractive to audiences. To do so, these stations rely on the Public Broadcasting Service (PBS). Generally public television strives for high-quality programming that is often unavailable on either broadcast or advertiser-supported cable channels. Public television stations frequently try to

identify underserved audiences and develop specific programs for those audiences, but is quick to point out that its prime-time audience is often larger than those of HBO, History Channel, Discovery Channel, CNN, and TLC.

PBS operates in reverse fashion from the commercial networks. Whereas NBC, CBS, ABC, and Fox funnel money to production companies and pay stations to carry their programs, PBS charges membership dues to its affiliates (over 90 percent of all public TV stations). In return, PBS provides programs funded by pooled station funds, the CPB, foundations, individual contributions, and other sources. PBS itself produces no programs. Instead, through its National Program Service (NPS), it serves as a conduit to program producers, usually avoiding the suppliers common to network scheduling.

A key difference between the commercial networks and PBS is that the stations (not the network) decide when to carry national programs. The most popular programs on PBS form the "core schedule," which is designated for same-night carriage. PBS recommends but cannot require stations to air these shows the same night that they are fed by satellite to member stations. Same-night carriage helps PBS promote its shows nationally. Although most PBS affiliates air the core schedule the same day, many PBS shows are taped and delayed for days or weeks. And within limits, which vary from show to show, stations frequently rerun PBS shows. Thus, unlike CBS or NBC, a PBS show may or may not air nationally in a given day, and when it finally does run, a show may be rerun long before the summer. Like cable shows, however, rerunning programming can build the cumulative audience.

On average, PBS today distributes about 1,500 hours of programming per year to its member stations (about 4 hours per day). The bulk of PBS programming consists of news and public affairs (about 40 percent). This includes programs like *Frontline, NOVA, Nightly Business Report,* and *The News Hour.* Next most common are cultural programs, such as *Masterpiece Theater* and *The American Experience.* Children's programs make up just over 1 in 10 PBS shows, from *Sesame Street* to *Between the Lions.* How-to shows and special-interest programs are nearly as common, from *Motorweek* to *This Old House* to *Antiques Roadshow.* Filling out the PBS schedule are shows that are strictly educational (like *Sid the Science Kid* and *The Cat in the Hat Knows a Lot About That*) and a very small sprinkling of sports.

Most cable networks aim for niche audiences, such as this program about Thomas Edison on the History Channel.

PBS strives to avoid the producers that are common to commercial TV. Nearly 40 percent of producers for public TV consider themselves independent. Just over one in four programs on the network come from one of its member stations, and about 7 percent emanate from international producers. The remaining shows are developed and funded by unique consortiums of stations, philanthropic groups, corporations, foundations—you name it! The idea of providing the public with an independent point of view is sometimes controversial.

Because part of PBS funding emanates out of the Corporation for Public Broadcasting, a government-funded entity, PBS has always had to walk a line that avoids taking a partisan viewpoint, something commercial networks are free to do. During the early part of 2005, PBS was criticized by government officials as being liberal and biased in its programming and coverage. An internal audit held that year disputed that claim, and a research poll conducted by PBS in 2009 found that most Americans named PBS the most trusted of all national media organizations.

Locally PBS-affiliated stations provide a wide range of local programming from talk to sports to cultural events. Local programs are usually funded by underwriters from the community of license.

To fill out the local schedule, public television stations frequently rely on British-imported comedy and drama series, produced by the BBC or Independent Television (see Chapter 14).

THE WORLD OF TV SYNDICATION

After the networks (broadcast, cable, and PBS), the largest purveyors of programming are the **syndicators:** the companies that sell programs directly to TV stations and cable services. The growth in the number of TV stations, the arrival of cable and new broadcast networks, and the growth of the home video market have created tremendous new demands. Where once syndication meant only two things—movies and network reruns—the syndication universe today ranges from films to talk shows, music videos, and adventure yarns, to how-to shows on everything from exercise to hunting water buffalo. Today TV syndication is about a $9 billion annual business.

The Syndication Market

There are two primary buyers or markets for syndicated programming. The traditional market for syndication is local TV. Today nearly 1,400 local TV stations obtain syndicated programming to fill their program schedules during time periods without network programs or local programs (mainly news).

The second market for syndicated programming is the cable networks. The chief cable buyers of syndication are the advertiser-supported services, like TBS, the USA network, Lifetime, TNT, Bravo and others. Syndicators also sell their product to international broadcasters, but the revenue for this market is much smaller than for domestic syndication.

The Syndication Bazaar

In 1963 a small group of TV programmers got together with an equally small group of syndicators to pool their resources and streamline their efforts. From those humble beginnings has come an annual showbiz extravaganza known as NATPE International. (NATPE stands for National Association of Television Program Executives.)

In 2001 a total of 20,000 TV executives—including programmers, syndicators, and even some stars—attended NATPE International. Part Hollywood hype and part consumer trade show, the convention is the place where new syndicated programs are unveiled and, most of all, plugged. Syndication programmers lure buyers to screening rooms. Liquor flows. Premiums—like cowboy hats from producers of Westerns—abound. And sometimes deals are made. Local television stations can pick and choose programming to fill the time between local programming and network programs.

Fast-forward to 2009, and we find that the syndication market has evolved. Many of the people who attend NATPE now are international customers who are shopping around for American programming to fill their schedules. By 2009, attendance had shrunk to 7,000 and most Hollywood studios had moved their screening rooms off the convention floor to hotel suites. But syndication is a viable competitor to prime time for advertisers. With more than 132 weekly shows being offered, the syndication market is important to broadcast and cable.

Over the past few years increased competition for viewers and quality programming has changed the face of syndication. Now syndicated shows are considering the impact of mobile video devices as an additional way to screen syndicated programming, hoping that this new market could add to the traditional financial model.

Types of Syndicated Programming

What does one see at NATPE? Despite the vast array of programming available, it is possible to classify syndicated programming into three main types: motion pictures that have completed their theatrical run, whose home video and pay-cable releases are sold to stations in movie packages; programming originally produced for one of the major TV networks, sold to stations as off-net syndication; and original programming produced expressly for syndication, known as first-run. Each type of syndication is distributed in a unique way.

Movie Packages Movies are a mainstay of the program schedule for the pay-cable networks (from HBO and Showtime to Encore and Starz), many TV stations, and many basic cable networks (including USA, Lifetime, American Movie Classics, Turner Classic Movies and the Sci-Fi channel). Even network affiliates need movies for parts of their daytime, late-night, and weekend programming. There are lots of movies out there: It is estimated that since the sound era began in 1927, over half a million films have been produced in the United States alone. Keep that figure in mind when you're scanning the offerings from Netflix and you get the feeling that you have seen everything.

From the earliest days of TV, movies have been the backbone of syndication. The new TV stations needed something to show; facing declining attendance, the motion picture business needed a new revenue source. The venture was a match made in heaven (if not Hollywood). Early on, it became unwieldy to sell movies one at a time. Thus the distribution companies (originally subsidiaries of the major studios) began to package the movies as a collection of titles. Today, with the exception of a very few blockbusters, movies sold in syndication are packaged.

Stations acquire the rights to movies under license agreements. The agreements generally run from three to six years and allow the station to show a movie up to six times or more during the period covered. Typically packages of recent box office successes (known as A movies) cost stations more than older and less popular films (known as B movies). In a market like New York City, *Happy Gilmore* may license for as much as $500,000, whereas *I Was a Teenage Werewolf* can run for as little as $50.

Off-Net Syndication Say what you will about the commercial broadcast networks—their imitative

Judge Judy is an example of first-run syndicated programming that would be sold to television stations at the NATPE convention each year.

schedules, their lowest-common-denominator programs, and their so-called demise in recent years. The fact remains that network programs enjoy great popularity, which sustains over time. In the jargon of syndication, network shows have "staying power" and "legs." Old network programs never die: They are sold to stations and cable services as **off-net syndication.** In 2005 the 1950s sitcom *I Love Lucy* still generated millions of dollars for CBS.

Off-net series are packaged for syndication in a manner similar to motion-picture packaging. The station or cable service pays for a certain number of episodes in the series and gets the right to show each title a number of times. Six runs over a period of six years is commonplace. The price per episode for off-net programs varies widely. It depends on the size of the TV market, the popularity of the show in its first run, the number of programs available, and so on.

Normally at least 100 episodes of a network show are needed to launch it in off-net syndication. The ideal number of episodes is 130. Why? Because there are 260 weekdays in a year, an off-net episode can run exactly twice annually when programmed in a time period each Monday to Friday. This process of scheduling a show to run in the same daypart each weekday is known as **stripping.**

Shows that have recently eclipsed the magic number and scored a hit in off-net syndication include *Seinfeld, Two and a Half Men, Everybody Loves Raymond,* and *The Simpsons.*

Even as the 100-episode rule works for broadcast television, the syndicated market is evolving. Some experts regard video-on-demand and downloading off sites like Apple's iTunes as an opportunity to market programs that don't make the 100-episode mark. Interestingly, providing these download opportunities may provide ratings bumps for shows, extending the possibility of making it to 100 shows. Ratings for *Lost* and *Desperate Housewives* actually increased slightly after they became available on iTunes.

First-Run Syndication   Programs that make their debut in syndication, without a prior network life, are known as **first-run syndication.** Traditionally, first-run syndication has been characterized by cheap, easy-to-produce programs designed to be strip-programmed.

Game shows and talk programs have fit the bill perfectly over the years and have been the bulk of first-run syndication. Today's dominating syndicated quiz programs are *Jeopardy* and *Wheel of Fortune.* The queen of syndicated talk, Oprah Winfrey, retired from daytime talk in 2011; and at the time of this edition a new queen of the talk shows had yet to emerge, but Oprah has been joined in first-run syndication by Ellen DeGeneres, Jerry Springer, Dr. Oz, Maury, and a host of others. As we started the second decade of 2000, the court TV show *Judge Judy* displaced Oprah as the highest-rated daytime show. Other court shows include *People's Court* and *Divorce Court.* Syndication executives point out that it is important to have user-friendly programming that invites advertisers to use the program for brand integration. *Rachael Ray* and other cooking shows offer such opportunities. Some group owners like Scripps Television, Raycom, and Post-Newsweek are experimenting with locally produced programming as a way to reduce costs and service local needs. After all, Oprah herself started as a local origination in Chicago more than 20 years ago.

Not all syndicated originals are quiz and talk programs. Off-network drama such as *CSI: Crime Scene Investigation, Law and Order, 24,* and *Smallville* have all worked successfully. And buoyed by Paramount's success with *Star Trek: The Next Generation* and *Deep Space Nine,* as well as the worldwide appeal of *Baywatch,* first-run action/adventure proliferated in the late 1990s. Some of these shows were long on action, short on dialogue, and skimpy on costuming. This category included such first-run epics as *Xena* and *Hercules.*

Cable Syndication   Cable networks have entered the off-network syndication market in a substantial way. High-profile programs are being purchased by cable networks to provide a unique flavor to their offerings, making cable the largest single buyer of syndicated programming. As the viewer shift from network television to cable continues, cable has a stronger base to build advertising revenues. (Remember that local cable franchises pay a monthly subscription fee per subscriber that makes up the bulk of cable's revenue.) Not surprisingly, the cost-per-episode fees are much higher than usual for cable programming.

Barter Syndication

At one time, TV stations would purchase syndicated programming on a cash-and-carry basis. However, for a number of reasons cash sales of syndicated programming have declined in recent years. For one thing, the bottom-line consciousness of the TV industry has made station managers reluctant to take million-dollar gambles on syndicated programs. Station mergers and buyouts along with increased competition from cable have left little cash to speculate in program investment. And syndicators have had difficulty extracting payments from stations on installment plans. In the past some stations have been late in paying their bills; some (especially UHF stations with huge inventories) had defaulted altogether.

Thus high prices have combined with low cash flows to create a new form of syndication finance. Just as the term was used in the days of fur trappers and Indian agents, barter refers to the trading of one commodity for another of similar value. In TV, the valuable commodity offered by the syndicator is programming; the item of value at the station is its airtime. In **barter syndication** the syndicator provides the program to the station free or at a substantially reduced cost per episode (cash plus barter). In return, the station sacrifices some of the advertising slots in the show. The syndicator can integrate its own ads into the show, or the syndicator can act like a TV network, calling on major advertisers to place ads in each of the markets in which the program plays. Recently many stations have negotiated barter arrangements for syndicated programming.

In barter syndication, the key to the syndicator is market clearance. The more markets the program plays in, the larger is the national audience that can be offered to advertisers. Clearing 80 percent of the nation's TV markets is considered good; over 90 percent clearance is excellent.

The economic downturn has left many stations without the deep pockets to pay for programming, and media experts expect barter to increase as the costs associated with off-network programs continues to rise.

LOCAL TELEVISION PROGRAMMING

The last piece of the programming puzzle is provided by individual TV stations and cable systems through their original, locally produced programs.

Local programming has been a growth area in recent years as TV stations and cable systems have sought a unique identity when faced with new competitors like satellite DBS and the Internet.

Local Television Stations

Faced with escalating syndication costs, lagging network performances, and the loss of local advertising dollars to barter, TV stations are placing increasing emphasis on their own local programming. As we saw in a previous section, the bulk of the local TV budget goes to local news and talk.

Many TV stations have expanded their local news "hole" from early fringe and late night to include morning, which is at the forefront of expanding local production. Studies indicate that commuting times are increasing and Americans are rising earlier. Many stations are now programming earlier hours before network morning magazine shows in attempts to reach these commuters. According to a Gallup poll conducted in 1999, 58 percent of American adults say they watch local news in the morning for information, traffic, and weather reports. Overall, viewership for morning news programs reflects a younger audience than the evening news, an attractive demographic for advertisers.

But local news is not the only programming produced by local stations. In virtually all large cities, there are locally produced alternatives to *Today* and *Good Morning, America.* Some local stations are moving from news and talk to comedy, drama, and music programming. Diversity is the key word in local TV production. Surveys of general managers and program directors suggest that local production of everything from situation comedies to dramas will increase in larger television markets.

Local Cable Programming

Just as the future of TV stations may lie in their ability to develop local programming, the cable industry is making similar forecasts.

As we documented earlier in this chapter, cable systems have been especially vigorous in developing news and sports programs as an alternative to local affiliates in their service areas. The rise of regional cable news has been a boon to local cable channels.

Other community channel services on the rise include on-screen TV program guides, electronic bulletin boards that feature classified and personal advertising, regional weather services, and electronic "tours of homes" offered by area realtors.

PROGRAMMING STRATEGIES

Now that we understand the various types and sources of TV programming today, we close this chapter by providing a taste of the techniques of TV programming. Space precludes a full discussion of how TV programmers determine their schedules. This process fills entire books and full-semester courses at many institutions. The books listed at the end of the chapter provide a good beginning point to an understanding of TV programming in practice. Now, on to the "taste test."

There is an old saying in television: "People don't watch stations; they watch programs." This means we select the station to watch based on programming rather than selecting the program because of the station that transmits it. It is also a reminder of the importance of programming to the success of TV.

The first step in programming is to define the potential audience. Cartoons shown while children are in school or a football broadcast while men are at work may attract small audiences, but not the numbers possible if the cartoons are run after school or the football games are shown on Sundays when most men aren't working.

Programmers must also have some idea about which groups prefer the shows that are available to be used. *Murder She Wrote* generally attracted women and older men as its main group of viewers. To have optimum viewership it was necessary to schedule *Murder She Wrote* at a time when these people would be in front of their TV sets. Sunday evenings following *60 Minutes* seemed like a good idea to CBS. The show was a mainstay in that time period for over a decade. The time period was inherited by shows with appeal to a similar demographic: first *Touched by an Angel* and then *Cold Case.*

Some regional cable systems have begun carrying local sporting events as a way to bolster viewing for local channels.

Obviously programming must entail more than merely placing a program that appeals to a particular audience at a time when that audience may view it. There are a number of techniques that programmers use to maximize viewership. Once you have viewers, you want to hang on to them.

Audience Flow

Audiences will tend to stay with the TV station they are watching until something they dislike shows up on the screen. In some ways audiences exhibit inertia, viewing the same station until forced to change. The proliferation of remote controls has changed this tendency because viewers no longer are required to get out of their chairs to change the channel, but inertia still influences viewing. The movement of audiences from one program to another is called **audience flow.**

The successful programmer will build and hold an audience from show to show. This means putting together programs that generally attract the same audience.

One reason for the continuing success of issues-based talk programs like *Oprah* is that they provide the perfect lead-in to local news. At the network level, programmers try to build their evenings around a core audience. CBS's powerful Monday evening block was designed to keep and attract women 25–49, flowing nicely from *How I Met Your Mother* to *Two and a Half Men* in 2010. Fox tried to do the same thing on Mondays with House, but hasn't been successful finding a second program that can compete against the CBS line-up.

Counterprogramming

Counterprogramming is a technique wherein the programmer decides to go for an audience different from the audience that competing stations or networks are trying to attract.

Recently NBC tried this strategy in the 10 p.m. slot by moving talk show leader Jay Leno into prime time. NBC reasoned that with lower costs for production it could make money without winning the time period. After a few months, affiliates balked because Leno turned out to be a poor lead-in for the 11 p.m. local news.

Independent TV stations have long counterprogrammed network affiliates in their market by programming children's programs when their competitors carried local news, or male-oriented local sports when affiliates were in the female-oriented prime-time blocks. Cable networks have also been master counterprogrammers. One example is the success of ESPN's *Sportscenter,* which comes on at 11 p.m., when many local TV stations go to their news programming. CNN carried its most popular talk program, *Larry King Live,* when the major networks go to their dramas and situation comedies. Two more examples: CBS programs Monday nights with comedies like *Two and a Half Men* and *How I Met Your Mother.* It should come as no surprise that this was a counterprogram strategy to *Monday Night Football.* Finally, NBC counter-programs CSI on CBS with the highly popular comedy 30 Rock.

Challenge Programming

Challenge programming is the opposite of counter-programming. In **challenge programming,** the TV network or station goes head to head with the same type of programming as a major competitor, or goes after the same demographic with a different program with similar audience appeal. Local stations often go head to head with their afternoon talk shows, such as *Oprah* against *Jerry Springer.* They do this in local news and may also compete with morning talk and noontime information shows.

One famous example of challenge programming concerned the decision by CBS and NBC in 1994 to go head to head with high-profile medical dramas. CBS sought to win Thursday evenings at 10 (9 central) with *Chicago Hope.* NBC set its sights on the same time period with *ER.* ABC was happy to stay on the sidelines by counterprogramming with *Prime Time Live.* When the smoke cleared, NBC had won the battle; by winter 1995 CBS had moved *Chicago Hope* to Monday nights. By 1999 *ER* was a staple of NBC's Thursday schedule and frequently in the Top 10 programs. The 2010–2011 season saw another example of challenge programming when FOX's two dramas *Bones* and *Fringe* went against CBS comedy hit *The Big Bang Theory* and NBC's *The Office.*

A FINAL WORD

Programming is the fun part of TV. It is what attracts viewers so the station or network can sell time to advertisers to make money. A great deal of thought and effort is put into deciding which programs fit where. The reason for this concern in programming is not primarily that the station or network cares whether viewers are entertained or informed but that this is how they make their money.

SUMMARY

- TV programming takes two major forms: news and entertainment.
- Television news is the nation's primary source of news and is regarded as credible by a large portion of the public.

- Television news reached maturity when President Kennedy was assassinated. The 1960s events such as the civil rights movement, the Vietnam War, and Neil Armstrong's first step on the moon came to life in people's living rooms.

- The 1970s and 1980s were marked by money and machines. Television news became a significant profit center for local TV stations and cable. Anchor salaries rose. Electronic news gathering and satellite news came on the scene.

- The 1990s saw growth in TV news due to new networks, regional cable news, and more global competition.

- Many people are involved in the preproduction stage of the newscast. They are the news director, news producer, assignment editor, field producer, reporter, writers, and editors.

- Television stations can obtain entertainment programming through networks, syndication, and local origination. The commercial networks—ABC, CBS, NBC, and Fox—provide broad, mass-appeal programming.

- Historically networks have relied on outside sources for their programs—in particular, the major Hollywood studios and a cluster of well-known independent producers. Recently the networks have expanded the scope of their own in-house productions and in some cases have merged with studios. The networks receive a great number of suggested storylines. Because the number is so large, there is only a slight chance that any one idea will be accepted.

- Miniseries and made-for-TV and cable movies are the most expensive types of programming. Situation comedies and reality programs, on the other hand, are the cheapest to produce.

- As cable matures, it has directly affected the networks. Cable has been producing higher-quality shows, and the effects can be seen in the ratings.

- Syndication has become a popular source of programming. To understand fully the syndication business, one must be aware of NATPE trade shows and types of syndication.

- Cable syndication is growing as the audience watching cable continues to expand.

- Local TV stations achieve an identity by producing local shows; therefore, many community and cable stations are trying this technique. Because they will be saving money and providing original programming, these stations are likely to survive in the future.

- TV programming strategies include audience flow, counterprogramming, and challenge programming.

KEY TERMS

electronic news gathering
   (ENG)   211
satellite news gathering
   (SNG)   212
sweeps   212
minidocs   212
news consultants   213
coventuring   214
regional cable news services   214
future file   217
network programming   219
syndication   219
local origination   220

affiliates   220
affiliation agreement   220
network compensation   220
cleared   221
preemptions   221
financial interest and
   syndication rules   221
license fees   221
prime-time access
   rules (PTAR)   221
concept   223
treatment   223
development process   223

step deal   223
right of first refusal   223
pilots   224
exclusivity deals   226
syndicators   228
off-net syndication   230
stripping   230
first-run syndication   230
barter syndication   231
audience flow   232
counterprogramming   233
challenge programming   233

SUGGESTIONS FOR FURTHER READING

Auletta, K. (1998). *The Highwaymen.* Wilmington, CA: Harvest Press.

Barkin, S. (2002). *American television news: The media marketplace and the public interest.* Armonk, NY: M. E. Sharpe.

Benedetti, R. (2002). *From concept to screen: An overview of film and television programming.* Boston: Allyn and Bacon.

Block, A. B. (1990). *Outfoxed: Marvin Davis, Barry Diller, Rupert Murdoch and the inside story of America's fourth television network.* New York: St. Martin's.

Blumenthal, H., & Goodenough, O. (2006). *This business of television* (2nd ed.). New York: Billboard Books.

Boyd, A. (1997). *Broadcast journalism: Techniques of radio and TV news* (4th ed.). Oxford; Boston: Focal Press.

Clements, S. (2004). *Show runner: Producing variety and talk shows for television*. Los Angeles: Silman–James.

Eastman, S., & Ferguson, D. (2008). *Media programming: Strategies and practices* (8th ed.). Boston: Wadsworth.

McGregor, M., Driscoll, P., & McDowell, W. (2010). *Head's broadcasting in America*. Boston: Allyn & Bacon.

Medoff, N., & Kaye, B. (2005). *Electronic Media: Then, now and later*. Boston: Pearson.

Walker, J., & Ferguson, D. (1997). *Broadcast television industry*. Boston: Allyn & Bacon.

INTERNET EXERCISES

Visit our Web site at **www.mhhe.com/dominickbib7e** for study-guide exercises to help you learn and apply material in each chapter. You will find ideas for future research as well as useful Web links to provide you with an opportunity to journey through the new electronic media.

Part Four | How It's Controlled

Rules and Regulations 10

Quick Facts

 License terms for TV and radio stations: 8 years

 FCC has five commissioners, 7 bureaus, and about 2,000 employees

 Number of states that permit cameras in the courtroom: 50

 Number of indecency and obscenity complaints received by FCC (July–September 2009): 1,827

 Amount spent by National Association of Broadcasters on lobbying efforts (January–March 2010): $3.56 million

The electronic media are regulated by federal and state laws, by rules enacted by the FCC and other regulatory agencies, and by a system of self-regulation. This chapter looks at the formal system of rules and regulations that have an impact on broadcasting, satellites, cable, and the Internet; the next chapter examines self-regulation.

RATIONALE

Unlike many other industries, broadcasting has always had special requirements and special responsibilities placed on it by government. What makes it different? There have been two main rationales for treating broadcasting as a special case: (1) the scarcity theory and (2) the pervasive presence theory.

The **scarcity theory** notes that the electromagnetic spectrum is limited. Only a finite number of broadcast stations can exist in a certain place in a certain time; too many stations can interfere with one another. This means that only a limited number of aspiring broadcasters can be served and that the government must choose from among the potential applicants.

In addition, the scarcity theory holds that the spectrum is such a valuable resource that it should not be privately owned. Instead it is treated like a public resource, owned by all, like a national park. The government treats those fortunate enough to broadcast as trustees of the public and imposes special obligations on them, such as requiring that they provide candidates for public office equal opportunities to use their stations.

Recent technological advances such as cable TV, which offer would-be broadcasters a large number of channels, have prompted a reevaluation of the scarcity theory. Many critics would argue that it is outmoded. Others, however, point out that as long as the number of people wishing to broadcast exceeds the available facilities, scarcity still exists.

The **pervasive presence theory** is of more recent origin. It holds that broadcasting is available to virtually all of the population and, once the TV or radio set is turned on, offensive messages can enter the home without warning, reaching both adults and children. This situation is fundamentally different from encountering an offensive message in a public forum. If you're out in public, you're on your own.

You might encounter things that offend your sensibilities. Should you meet someone wearing a T-shirt with an offensive word printed on it, your only recourse would be to turn away. The home, however, is not the same as a public place; you should not expect to encounter unwanted offensive messages there. Consequently, the pervasive presence theory holds that you're entitled to some protection. Thus the basic intrusiveness of broadcasting allows the government to regulate it.

HISTORY

How did the government get involved with broadcasting regulation in the first place? In 1910 Congress passed the Wireless Ship Act. Only four paragraphs long, it basically mandated that large oceangoing passenger ships must be equipped with wireless sets. It had little relevance to broadcasting, primarily because broadcasting as we know it did not yet exist. Two years later the Radio Act of 1912 was passed. Spurred by the sinking of the *Titanic* and the need to ratify international treaties, the 1912 act required those wishing to engage in broadcasting to obtain a license from the secretary of commerce. Further, to prevent interference among maritime stations, it provided for the use of call letters and established the assignment of frequencies and hours of operation. The law also strengthened the regulations concerning the use of wireless by ships. As was the case with the earlier law, the 1912 act still envisioned radio as point-to-point communication, like the telegraph, which uses the spectrum only sporadically, and did not anticipate broadcasting, which uses the spectrum continuously. Consequently, for the next eight years or so, when most wireless communication was of the point-to-point variety, the law worked reasonably well. As the 1920s dawned, however, and radio turned into broadcasting, the 1912 act quickly broke down.

As related in Chapter 1, the number of broadcast stations greatly increased, and available spectrum space could not accommodate them. Interference quickly became a serious problem. By 1926 the interference problem had gotten so bad that many parts of the country could no longer get a consistently clear broadcast signal. Consequently, after prodding from President Calvin Coolidge, Congress finally passed a new law—the Radio Act of 1927.

The 1927 Radio Act

Although more than 80 years old, the **Radio Act of 1927** still demonstrates the basic principles that underlie broadcast regulation. Embracing the scarcity argument, the key provisions of the act were the following:

1. The recognition that the public owned the electromagnetic spectrum, thereby eliminating private ownership of radio frequencies.

2. The notion that radio stations had to operate in the "public interest, convenience or necessity."

3. A prohibition against censorship of broadcast programs by the government.

4. The creation of a five-member **Federal Radio Commission (FRC),** which would grant licenses, make rules to prevent interference, and establish coverage areas with its decisions subject to judicial review.

Over the next few years, the FRC enacted technical standards that eliminated the interference problem and further elaborated the concept of the public interest. In one case, the FRC denied the license of a station in Kansas because it broadcast prescriptions for bogus patent medicines (see the box on page 241). The federal court system affirmed this decision, thus demonstrating that the FRC was not restricted to an examination of solely technical matters and could indeed look at content.

The Communications Act of 1934

The 1927 act was superseded seven years later when President Franklin Roosevelt streamlined the government's regulatory operations concerning communication. In response to Roosevelt's recommendations, Congress passed a new communications act **(The Communications Act of 1934),** which expanded the membership of the FRC from five to seven members and gave the organization a new name—the **Federal Communications Commission (FCC).** The powers of the new commission were broadened to include all wireless and wire forms of communication (including the telephone), except for those used by the military and the government. The 1927 law was regarded so highly that much of it was rewritten into the new legislation and the key provisions previously outlined were left unchanged.

The Communications Act of 1934 and related pieces of legislation are found in Title 47 of the U.S.

Code. Title 47 is divided into chapters. The chapter most pertinent for our purposes is Chapter 5, "Wire and Radio Communication." Chapter 5 is further divided into subchapters that incorporate the 1934 act. Subchapter 3 contains provisions relating to radio and TV, and this part of the act has the most relevance for broadcasters. Some of the key sections most often mentioned in the trade press are

- *Section 301.* Users of the electromagnetic spectrum must be licensed by the FCC.

- *Section 312.* Candidates for federal office must be given reasonable access to broadcast facilities.

- *Section 315.* Use of broadcast facilities by candidates for public office is outlined. (This provision is so important that an entire section is devoted to it later in this chapter.)

- *Section 326.* The FCC is forbidden to censor the content of radio and TV programming.

Like most laws, the 1934 Communications Act has been amended and reshaped, usually in response to a current problem or to changing technology. For example, in 1959 Congress amended the act to make it illegal for people to rig quiz shows. Three years later, Congress passed the **Communications Satellite Act,** which expanded the regulatory powers of the FCC. With all of its various revisions, the 1934 law remained the nation's most influential broadcasting law for six decades until extensively amended by the Telecommunication Act of 1996.

Cable Regulation

The history of cable regulation has been marked by major changes of direction. When cable first came on the scene in the 1950s, the FCC refused to regulate it because cable didn't use over-the-air frequencies. By the 1960s, however, cable became a viable competitor to broadcast stations, and the FCC responded to pressure from broadcasters and enacted regulations that effectively hampered cable's growth in large markets. By the 1970s cable operators were exerting their own pressure on the commission, which eventually issued a new set of rules that were somewhat more favorable to cable.

While all of this was going on at the federal level, cable systems were also bound by regulations at the state and local levels. Thus a company that owned cable systems in 20 communities might face 20 different sets of local rules. The most important local rule established exclusivity. Local governments awarded an exclusive franchise to a single cable company to serve a community or neighborhood in exchange for the provision of specialized community channels, payment of a franchise fee, and maintenance of low rates. Many companies, in their zeal to obtain a franchise, overpromised and had to scale down their systems, creating some bad feelings between them and the local governments.

Reexamination

The 1980s saw a general trend toward deregulation. The FCC abolished many regulations that pertained to radio, simplified license renewal applications, and eased operating regulations for TV stations. Congress got into the spirit by extending the license terms for both radio and TV stations and by passing the **Cable Communications Policy Act of 1984,** which allowed cable systems the freedom to set their own rates.

By the 1990s, advances in technology and changes in the business arena prompted Congress to take another look at regulation. New communication technologies such as direct-to-home broadcasting via satellite and the Internet presented new opportunities and challenges. Telephone companies were interested in providing video programming, and some cable companies were actively exploring the possibility of offering phone services. In response to these and other forces, Congress passed the **Telecommunications Act of 1996,** which had a major impact on all areas of electronic media.

The Telecommunications Act of 1996 was the most significant piece of electronic media legislation in more than 60 years. One of the main goals of the act was to foster competition between cable companies and phone companies by allowing phone companies to provide cable TV services and by allowing cable companies to offer local phone service. This competition, it was hoped, would result in more consumer choices, better service, and lower bills.

The act was slow to produce its desired results, but by 2010 competition between phone companies and cable systems was intense. Several phone companies feature video services. AT&T offers U-verse, a video service with more than 390 channels that also includes a DVR. Verizon has FiOS TV, a fiber optic service with 350 channels and thousands of video-on-demand programs. Cable giants Comcast and Charter offer digital phone service. Most phone and cable companies offer local and long-distance phone service, high-speed Internet access, and digital TV service for about $80–100 a month.

Evolving technology and a changing business climate prompted Congress in 2010 to reexamine the 1996 act. One key issue lawmakers will consider is network neutrality, a provision that would block Internet service providers from favoring one Web company over another.

The act also had a significant impact in several other areas, as discussed in Chapters 4, 5, and 6. It removed the cap on the number of radio stations that one person or organization could own. It also liberalized the rules concerning local ownership. In large markets, one organization can own as many as eight radio stations. These changes prompted a wave of consolidation in the radio industry. Concerning television, one person or organization can now own as many stations as she wants as long as the combined reach of the stations does not exceed 39 percent of the nation's homes (the old law set a 25 percent cap). The law also extended the license renewal term to eight years for both radio (seven years under the old law) and television stations (five years under the old law). The law further gave cable systems more leeway in setting the rates they charge their subscribers, a change that resulted in higher bills for cable subscribers. Finally, the act required new TV sets to be equipped with a **V-chip,** a device that enables parents to control access to programs that they consider objectionable. We discuss the V-chip in the next chapter.

REGULATORY FORCES

Broadcast and cable policy results from the interaction of several factors. Legislative, administrative, judicial, political, and economic forces are all important determiners of regulation. Drawing on the model used by Krasnow, Longley, and Terry in *The Politics of Broadcast Regulation*, this section examines eight key components in the process: the FCC, Congress, the courts, the White House, industry lobbyists, the public, state and local governments, and the marketplace.

The Federal Communications Commission

The FCC currently consists of five commissioners, one of whom serves as chair, appointed by the president and confirmed by the Senate, for staggered

Profile: Dr. Brinkley and His Goats

One of the key cases decided by the new Federal Radio Commission concerned station KFKB ("Kansas Folks Know Best") in tiny Milford, Kansas. Licensed to Dr. John R. Brinkley, KFKB ("The Sunshine Station in the Heart of the Nation") became one of the most popular stations in America during the 1920s, primarily because of the notoriety surrounding its owner. John Romulus Brinkley was the son of a medical doctor. At an early age he decided to follow in his father's footsteps and entered medicine. Young Brinkley graduated, if that's the right word, from the Eclectic Medical University of Kansas City. (He apparently finished his course of study in a few weeks, paid $100, and received a diploma.) Forty states did not recognize degrees from his college, but that left "Dr." Brinkley eight others he could practice in. He eventually wound up in Milford and opened a modest hospital, which he immodestly named after himself. If that wasn't enough, he also set up the Brinkley Research Laboratories and the Brinkley Training School for Nurses.

Brinkley had studied a little bit about the workings of human glands. He also was a shrewd judge of human nature. Consequently, he began to advertise his rejuvenation operations over KFKB. Designed to restore sexual drive in middle-aged men, the actual operation consisted of grafting or injecting material from the sexual organs of male goats into his human patients. The operation was done under local anesthesia and took only 15 minutes. The cost was a rather significant sum in those days—$750. (The goats, of course, paid a much higher price.) One interesting touch introduced by the doctor: Patients could pick their own goat in advance from the doctor's private herd, sort of like picking out a lobster for your dinner from a tank at a seafood restaurant. As time passed, Brinkley was touting his operation as a cure-all for skin diseases, high blood pressure, insanity, and paralysis.

KFKB was the perfect medium for Brinkley's advertising. At the time, thanks to the doctor's investment, it was one of the most powerful stations in North America. Twice a day, people from Saskatchewan to Panama could hear the doctor's own radio talk show, in which he promoted his operation, gave precise instructions on how to get to Milford, and even advised prospective patients on how to transport the $750 safely.

People flocked to Milford, and Brinkley became a rich man. In an era when legitimate doctors were making an annual salary of about $5,000, Brinkley was pulling in about $125,000 a year. He owned his own airplane, his own yacht, and a fleet of cars, and usually wore a couple of 12-carat diamond rings.

In addition to his gland operations, Brinkley also started selling his own prescription drugs. On a show called *The Medical Question Box* Brinkley would read letters people had written him about their ailments. He would then prescribe his medicines by number. Pharmacists all over the region were supplied with the Brinkley formulas, which usually consisted of ingredients such as alcohol and castor oil. For each bottle that was sold, the pharmacist would give a cut to Brinkley.

Not all was rosy, however. Kansas City newspapers attacked the doctor's methods, the American Medical Association exposed Brinkley's quackery, and the Federal Radio Commission eventually revoked his broadcast license and further defined the principle that programming must be in the public interest. Undaunted, Brinkley ran for governor of Kansas as a write-in candidate and nearly won. Since KFKB was no longer open to him, Brinkley bought a station in Mexico, XER, 500,000 watts strong, and kept his messages blanketing North America. Eventually the doctor moved to Del Rio, Texas, across the border from XER, and continued his medical practice there, this time specializing in cures for enlarged prostate glands. When a competing doctor opened up a similar practice in Del Rio, Brinkley moved to Little Rock, Arkansas.

Once in Arkansas, Brinkley's troubles began. Malpractice awards to discontented patients, back taxes, legal fees, the costs of running his Mexican station, and his extravagant lifestyle soon exhausted even Brinkley's sizable bank account. The doctor had to declare bankruptcy. As if that wasn't bad enough, the U.S. government finally persuaded Mexico to ease international radio interference problems by shutting down XER and similar stations. Less than a year later, at 56, J. R. Brinkley succumbed to a heart attack, thus ending the career of one of early radio's unsavory but colorful broadcasters. (Pope Brock's book, *Charlatan: America's Most Dangerous Huckster, the Man Who Pursued Him and the Age of Flimflam,* presents an intriguing portrait of Dr. Brinkley.)

Figure 10–1

Structure of the Federal Communications Commission

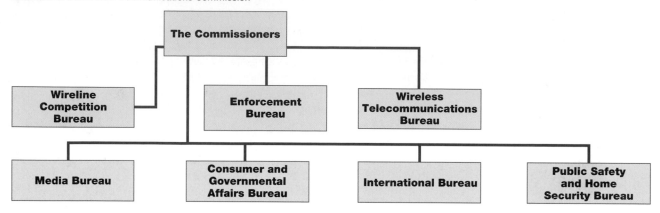

five-year terms. Political balance is achieved by requiring that no more than three members be from one political party.

Serving the commissioners are seven bureaus, as shown in Figure 10–1.

1. The Consumer and Government Affairs Bureau informs consumers about telecommunications goods and services and coordinates policy efforts with other governmental agencies.

2. As the name suggests, the Enforcement Bureau is responsible for upholding FCC rules and regulations.

3. The International Bureau represents the FCC in satellite and other matters that involve the United States and other countries.

4. The Wireless Telecommunications Bureau regulates cellular phones, pagers, two-way radios, and similar devices.

5. The Wireline Competition Bureau regulates telephone companies.

6. The Public Safety and Homeland Security Bureau is responsible for the agency's policies pertaining to public safety communication issues.

7. Of most importance to broadcasting and cable is the Media Bureau, which oversees AM and FM radio, broadcast TV, cable, and satellite services.

The FCC uses a variety of methods to regulate broadcasting and cable, and satellites. These methods are examined in detail next. For now, keep in mind that the FCC is a major force in the development and application of electronic media policy.

Congress

The FCC regulates broadcasting with Congress looking over its shoulder. The FCC is a creature of Congress. Congress created the FCC, and, if it wished, Congress could abolish the FCC. (In fact, in 1982 Congress changed the status of the FCC from a permanent agency to one that had to be reauthorized every two years.) The U.S. Congress is an important part of broadcasting and cable regulation because of its power to enact and amend laws. It was Congress that passed the Communications Act of 1934 and the Telecommunications Act of 1996.

In addition to these two essential communication laws, Congress has enacted other legislation that has had an impact on broadcasting and cable. For example, in 1969 it prohibited cigarette advertising on TV and radio, and in 1990 it passed a law that concerned children's television programming.

Moreover, although it sounds odd, Congress can affect regulatory policy by doing nothing. If it so chooses, Congress can terminate pending legislation or postpone it indefinitely by tabling it.

Congress can also exert pressure in nonlegislative ways. First, Congress controls the budget of the FCC. If the FCC has acted in a way that displeases the Congress, the commission may find its budget reduced. Further, all presidential appointments to the FCC must be approved by Congress. This gives Congress the opportunity to delay or block a particularly sensitive appointment. Finally, Congress can hold public hearings that highlight, at least in general terms, how Congress feels about a topic. The FCC, in turn, may get the message and shape its policies accordingly.

The Courts

If Congress looks over one shoulder of the FCC, the federal court system looks over the other. If a broadcaster, cable operator, or a citizen disagrees with an FCC decision, he or she appeals it to the federal courts. Most cases concerning broadcasting are decided by the U.S. Court of Appeals for the District of Columbia, whose decisions are subject to review by the Supreme Court only. Courts, however, do not act on their own. They wait for others to initiate actions. If a complaint is raised, courts do not normally reverse an agency's decision if the agency acted in a fair, nonarbitrary way and if the FCC actually has jurisdiction over the matter in question.

Although it does not get involved in many of the decisions of the FCC, when the judicial system does get a chance to speak, it has shown itself to be an important factor in determining broadcast policy. It was a court decision that articulated the pervasive presence rationale behind broadcasting regulation and affirmed the FCC's right to regulate indecent programming. Another court decision totally revamped the renewal hearing process. Before 1966, only those who would be affected by technical interference or economic hardship caused by the renewal or granting of a station's license could appear and offer evidence and testimony at a hearing. Then, in the WLBT case, the Court of Appeals ruled that private citizens had the right to participate in the process and citizen involvement grew rapidly in succeeding years. Deregulation has somewhat diminished citizen involvement, but the WLBT case established the right of citizens to intervene.

Of course courts do not exist in a vacuum; they interact with many of the other forces active in regulating broadcasting. Federal judges are appointed by the president with the approval of the Senate. Congress writes and rewrites the laws that the courts interpret. Court decisions, as with WLBT, alter, for some groups, the ease of access into the regulatory process. Broadcasters and citizens can bring lawsuits to attract judicial attention. All in all, courts play a pivotal role in the regulatory process.

The White House

If it were possible for the FCC to have a third shoulder, the White House would be watching over it. The influence of the executive branch may not be as visible as that exerted by the Congress and the courts, but it is nonetheless potent.

In the first place, the president has the power of appointment over both FCC commissioners and judges. With regard to the FCC, since many members do not serve out their full terms, the president can fairly quickly establish a slate of congenial commissioners. President Barack Obama, for example, was able to appoint three FCC commissioners during the first 20 months of his term. Although the Communications Act limits the number of commissioners from one political party to no more than three, most presidents are able to find people who express the administration's prevailing political philosophy. Furthermore, the president can designate any of the sitting commissioners as chair at any time, without congressional intervention or approval. As a result, the president can set the regulatory tone of the FCC.

Second, the White House has its own agency that specializes in the broad field of telecommunications—the **National Telecommunications and Information Administration (NTIA).** Housed in the Commerce Department, the NTIA allocates radio frequencies that are used by the federal government, makes grants to public telecommunications facilities, advises the administration on telecommunications matters, and represents the administration's interests before the FCC and the Congress. The NTIA is one of those organizations that will play as big a role in broadcasting and cable policymaking as the president desires.

Third, the various cabinet offices can also influence broadcasting and cable policy. The Department of Justice can prevent mergers that might result in antitrust problems, and the State Department represents the United States in international matters dealing with satellite orbital slots and mass communication–related businesses. The State Department's role will become more important in the future thanks to the growth of international communication systems.

Finally, the White House can influence policy by initiating communication legislation. Although the president cannot introduce bills in Congress, the White House can draft a bill and usually find a friendly member of Congress to propose it. In that same connection, the president also has the power to veto any unfavorable communication laws passed by Congress. Of course Congress can also override a presidential veto.

Industry Lobbyists

A lobbyist is a person who represents a special interest and tries to influence legislators' voting behavior.

Julius Genachowski, a graduate of Harvard Law School, was appointed chair of the FCC in 2009 by President Barack Obama.

Some people regard lobbyists as a negative force in policymaking, but it should be pointed out that they serve a necessary information function. Many lawmakers regard lobbyists as an asset; they help the lawmaker learn about the impact of pending bills on various segments of society. Lobbying has gone on in Washington for more than 200 years and is a deeply ingrained part of the political process. It comes as no surprise, then, that the broadcasting and cable industries maintain extensive lobbying organizations whose task is to make the industry's wishes known to the FCC, Congress, the courts, and the president.

Each of the major networks maintains its own lobbyists, as do a host of trade associations: the National Association of Broadcasters (traditionally the most influential for the broadcasting industry), the National Cable Television Association (the NCTA—the NAB's rival in the cable industry), the Association of Independent TV Stations, the National Association of Public TV Stations, the National Religious Broadcasters Association, and the National Association of Farm Broadcasters—to name just a few.

Lobbying tends to work best in a negative sense. It seems easier for lobbyists to stop something they consider bad from happening than it is for them to get something good to happen. Some of the biggest lobbying successes stem from the blockage of proposed legislation. In 2010, for example, the NAB was lobbying to prevent Congress from ending the radio industry's exemption from paying performance royalties to artists and record labels. The NCTA was arguing against any attempt to eliminate cable's method of bundling channels into basic and premium tiers and replacing it with an option in which channels would be purchased individually.

Finally, the expense and energy that must be expended to support lobbying groups mean that one key player in the policy arena is underrepresented—the general public. Most citizens' groups lack the expertise, time, and money to maintain full-time lobbyists. As a result, policymaking tends to be influenced far more by the industry than by the average citizen. There are, however, a few ways in which citizens get involved in the process, and this is the focus of the next section.

The Public

Citizen involvement in broadcasting policy was at its high point in the 1970s. Citizen interest or media reform groups were active in more than 30 states in 1974 and had filed almost 300 petitions to deny the licenses of stations coming up for renewal. By the early 1980s, however, dwindling financial support, longer license terms, and a general emphasis on deregulation combined to weaken the power of these groups.

This decline does not mean that members of the public are shut out of the regulatory process. Some public interest groups still remain, most notably the Media Access Project and Parents Television Council. These groups generally try to put pressure on Congress and the broadcasters by generating favorable public opinion for their causes. Finally, the public influences policy in a more general manner through its election of both the president and members of Congress, who in turn help shape communications policy.

State and Local Governments

Federal laws supersede state and local regulations, but many states have legislation that covers areas not specifically touched on in federal communications law. For example, almost every state has a law dealing with defamation (injuring a person's reputation) and/or reporters' rights to keep sources confidential. Many states have their own laws covering lotteries (the conduct of contests and promotions) and statutes covering fraudulent or misleading ads. Public broadcasting, moreover, is regulated by many states through acts that spell out the ownership, operation, and funding of educational radio and TV stations. And, of course, broadcasters must comply with local law governing taxation and working conditions.

States and cities can also enact laws that protect the privacy of subscribers to local stations. Information about personal viewing habits cannot be released to unauthorized persons or organizations (this prevents, for example, a political candidate from obtaining from a cable company the information that his rival subscribes to an adult movie channel). Communities can also collect a franchise fee, subject to limitations, from a cable operator and determine the duration of the franchise agreement.

The Marketplace

In its move toward deregulation the FCC has often used the phrase "let the marketplace decide." It follows, then, that the marketplace has become an im-portant factor in determining broadcasting policy. But what exactly is "the marketplace"? Broadly speaking, it's a place where buyers and sellers freely come together to exchange goods or services. Obviously, with regard to broadcasting and cable, there is no single place where buyer and seller are physically present. In this circumstance the marketplace notion refers to general economic forces, like supply, demand, competition, and price, that shape the broadcasting and cable industries.

The attitude of the FCC toward the marketplace varies with different administrations and with different commissioners. Over the years, however, the general trend has been for the FCC to rely more on the marketplace as an important determinant of the public interest. The philosophy underlying this position views the electromagnetic spectrum as an economic asset that is used best when the government steps back and lets the laws of economics take over. In short, it is hoped that the marketplace will encourage those services that the public wants.

The Parents Television Council was influential in persuading the FCC to take a stronger stand against indecency.

The marketplace has its advantages. It can promote efficiency, encourage the creation of new services, and encourage diversity. On the downside, the marketplace is only responsive to economic forces and is not sensitive to social needs. Moreover, the real marketplace seldom approaches the ideal model posited by economic textbooks. Once they enter the market, for example, big companies exert far more clout than smaller companies.

In some instances the marketplace notion was abandoned in favor of regulation. For example, Congress passed legislation in 2006 that set a final date when television broadcasting switched from analog to digital transmission. In other areas, such as the competition between phone companies and cable operators, the impetus seems to be in the other direction. In any case, it seems likely that the marketplace will continue to be an important factor in broadcasting and cable in the years to come.

Now that the general forces that influence broadcasting and cable regulation have been introduced, the remainder of this chapter focuses on more specific regulatory issues: (1) the FCC's regulatory responsibilities; (2) political broadcasting; (3) other federal laws that apply to the area; (4) laws affecting electronic journalism; and (5) advertising regulations. A note of caution: This is a turbulent area; by the time you read this section, things may have changed. Like industry professionals, students, publishers, and textbook authors face the task of keeping up with this dynamic area. Check the book's Web site for recent developments.

THE ROLE OF THE FCC

Licensing is the primary function of the FCC and the most important method of regulation. The FCC grants new licenses and renews existing ones. Let's first examine how the FCC makes decisions about granting a license. Note that the FCC grants licenses only to stations; it does not license networks. Each of the networks, however, owns local stations that must have their licenses renewed.

License Granting

Applying for a license to operate a new station is a fairly complicated process. (In fact, since there are so few radio and TV frequencies available that would not cause interference problems with existing stations, most persons who get into broadcasting do so

by purchasing an existing facility. Many rules mentioned here would also apply to this situation.) After finding a suitable radio frequency or TV channel, all applicants must meet some minimum qualifications.

Personal Qualifications   First, the applicant must be a U.S. citizen or an organization that is free from significant foreign control. Next, the applicant must meet certain character qualifications, but the law is vague on what exactly constitutes a "good" or "bad" character. In practice, the FCC usually looks at things that are directly relevant to the potential future conduct of a potential broadcaster, although recent developments suggest that the commission has begun to look more closely at general character qualifications as well. In 1990 the FCC required broadcasters to report all convictions for felonies, all convictions for serious misdemeanors, any adverse civil judgments involving antitrust or anticompetitive activity, and any cases of misrepresentation to government agencies. Such activity, said the commission, could jeopardize the broadcaster's ability to hold or acquire a license.

Financial and Technical Considerations   The new applicant must assert the financial capability to build and operate a new station. In addition, as might be expected, all applicants must demonstrate that they can meet all of the technical requirements set forth in commission rules concerning equipment operation. The applicant must also propose an affirmative action employment plan to ensure the hiring of minority group members and women.

Diversity of Ownership

Throughout its history of granting licenses, the FCC has generally endorsed the philosophy that diversity of ownership was a desirable social goal. Recently, however, under pressure from the courts and Congress, the commission has relaxed many of its rules limiting ownership.

As mentioned earlier, the 1996 Telecommunications Act permitted one organization to own an unlimited number of radio stations nationwide and as many as eight radio stations in a single market. In 1999 the FCC loosened its rules to permit under certain conditions one company to own two TV stations in the same market (a duopoly). Further, the Telecommunications Act provided that any organization could own an unlimited number of TV stations

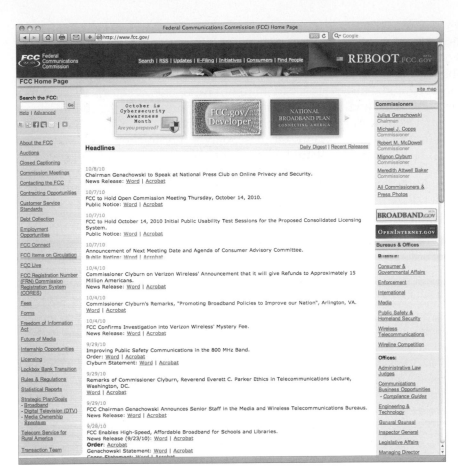

The Web site of the FCC contains current news releases, facts about the commissioners, and consumer information, as well as reports on numerous other topics.

provided that the total audience reach of the station does not exceed 35 percent of U.S. TV households. After much controversy, Congress raised the cap to 39 percent in 2004. In light of the growth of the Internet and its impact on traditional media, the FCC launched a review of its media ownership rules in mid-2010.

License Renewal

In addition to approving applications for new stations' licenses and requests for transfer of ownership to a new license, the FCC must approve license renewals.

Each radio and TV station must apply for a license renewal every eight years. When a license comes up for renewal, the FCC must determine whether the station has operated in the public interest. In past years, the FCC required stations to submit sizable amounts of information along with their renewal applications. The current renewal application for most stations is only a few pages long (some supporting

documentation, however, is also required). Cable TV systems are not licensed by the FCC. Instead this is the responsibility of the local governments that grant the franchise.

Renewal Forms What does the FCC look for in a license renewal? The renewal form gives a pretty good idea. The form makes sure that the station's most recent Ownership Report, which lists owners and shareholders, is on file with the commission. The form also makes sure the licensee is an American citizen, checks for the extent of foreign control, and asks if the station has maintained for public inspection a file that contains those documents required by commission rules. Commercial TV stations must also report their programs that address the educational needs of children.

Competing Applications

What happens when there is more than one applicant for a license? This situation commonly occurs when a license for an existing station is contested by one or more competitors. On the one hand, giving preference to the current license holder might close out newcomers who could do a better job. On the other hand, ignoring past performance could be unfair to a station that had served the public well and ought not be replaced by an untested newcomer. After wrestling with this question for many years, the FCC settled on a method called **renewal expectancy.** If an incumbent station had provided substantially sound and favorable past service, it would be difficult for a challenger to be granted the license over the established station. The Telecommunications Act strengthened this philosophy so that currently a station can expect to have its license renewed unless it has committed some serious violation.

License Denials   What must a station do to have its request for license renewal denied? One big reason for denial is lying to the FCC. If a licensee knowingly gives false information to the commission (such as concealing the actual owners of the station), the license is in jeopardy. Unauthorized transfer of control

is another serious offense. Programming violations alone, such as violating the indecency rules, have rarely led to nonrenewal. Moreover, the FCC is unlikely to deny a license renewal on its own initiative. Cases that are not routinely passed (perhaps 2 to 3 percent of the total) are brought to the commission's attention by private citizens who file a petition to deny. Of these, only a tiny fraction of licenses (less than 1 percent of the total) are not approved at renewal time. Nonetheless, the threat of nonrenewal is perceived as real by many broadcasters and is a potent weapon in the FCC's enforcement arsenal.

Enforcement   The FCC has several different methods it can use to enforce its decisions, ranging from a slap on the wrist to a virtual death sentence. At the mildest level, the FCC can issue a letter of reprimand that scolds a station for some practice that is not in the public interest. Usually, unless the station persists in provoking the FCC, that ends the matter. Other legal remedies include a cease-and-desist order (which makes a station halt a certain practice) or a fine (called a forfeiture). For example, in 2009 the

Events: The FCC and Fines

Some appreciation of all the FCC rules and regulations that broadcasters have to follow can be gained by taking a look at the recent transgressions of some stations that resulted in fines from the FCC:

- FCC rules state that a broadcast station must have at least one employee at its main studio during normal business hours. Failure to do so cost one station $8,000.

- Another rule requires stations that run contests to award prizes to the winners within 30 days. One radio station took seven months to pay off a lucky listener. The FCC fined the station $4,000.

- The lights on a broadcast tower have to be checked daily, according to another FCC rule. Violating this rule cost one station $4,000.

- Noncommercial stations are not immune from fines. Stations must keep in their public file a quarterly list of programs relevant to community issues. A college radio station was fined $7,200 for failure to follow this FCC rule.

- Noncommercial stations, of course, cannot air advertisements. They can, however, accept underwriting, and the FCC has detailed rules that apply to underwriting. Statements that contain price information, calls to action, or inducements to buy or sell are prohibited. Thus when one noncommercial station ran a message by an underwriter that contained the phrase "no down payment required," the FCC ruled that the announcement violated its rule against including price information and fined the station $12,500.

- The FCC has strict rules on the amount of commercial time permitted in children's programming (12 minutes per hour on weekdays, and 10.5 minutes per hour on weekends). The commission proposed a $70,000 fine for one station that violated this rule.

FCC fined radio station KLSU $10,000 for failure to keep its public files up-to-date and levied a $6,000 fine against KDKA-AM for a talk show prank.

The FCC, in effect, can put a station on probation by failing to renew a license for its full term. This is called short-term renewal and usually ranges from six months to two years. The idea behind short-term renewal is to give the commission a chance to take an early look at a station to determine if past deficiencies have been corrected. Infractions likely to bring short-term licenses involve deceptive promotions, lack of supervision of station facilities, and violation of equal employment practices.

The FCC can sound a death knell for stations by refusing to renew a license or revoking one currently in force. Although this action is used sparingly, it does occur. Since 1990 the FCC has denied the renewals of TV stations in Chicago and San Francisco and a radio station in Ohio for misrepresentation.

Policymaking   Another regulatory tool is policymaking. Under the public interest guidelines, the FCC can enact rules governing some aspect of broadcasting and/or cable. To enact a rule, the commission must announce a proposal and allow for public comments. Moreover, the FCC can't put most new rules and regulations into effect until it publishes a summary, usually in a publication called the *Federal Register*.

Another component of the policy process involves planning for the future. The FCC maintains an Office of Strategic Planning and Policy Analysis, which analyzes trends and attempts to anticipate future policy problems. A recent paper, for example, examined procedures for allocating portions of the electromagnetic spectrum for licensed and unlicensed use.

The FCC, Cable TV, Satellite TV, and the Internet

The FCC does not license cable TV systems. Instead state and local governments grant franchises. The length of the franchise period is also set at the local level, usually at some period between 10 and 15 years. When a franchise comes up for renewal, the local franchising authority examines the cable system's performance. Unless the cable system has failed to live up to the franchise terms or has provided unacceptable service, there is a strong presumption that the franchise will be renewed.

The local franchise authority has the power to regulate the rates charged for basic cable service, the lowest level of service that a subscriber can buy. Aside from that, cable systems set their own rates for other tiers of service. Pay-per-view rates and rates charged per channel or per program service (such as HBO) are not regulated by the FCC or by the local franchise authority.

Although the FCC does not license cable systems, it is responsible for enforcing a number of laws and regulations. For example, the Cable Television Consumer Protection and Competition Act of 1992 required that cable systems must carry the signals of broadcast stations that served the cable system's market. The commission would also examine complaints about violations of the Equal Employment Opportunities regulations. In addition, cable operators are required to keep certain documents in a file that is open to the public.

The Communications Satellite Act of 1962 gave the FCC the power to regulate technical issues concerning satellite TV. More recently, the 1999 **Satellite Home Viewer Improvement Act (SHVI)** permitted satellite carriers, such as the Dish Network, to transmit local broadcast TV signals into local markets (sometimes referred to as "local into local"). It also allowed satellite services to provide distant stations (stations not in the subscriber's local market). The SHVI mandated that the FCC establish rules for mandatory carriage of broadcast signals and to determine which consumers are eligible to receive distant stations. In general, the law attempts to put satellite carriers on an equal footing with cable companies, thus increasing competition and giving more choices to consumers.

The FCC's role with regard to regulating the Internet is still evolving. Starting in 2002, the FCC issued a series of decisions that classified broadband Internet access as an information service rather than a transmission service such as a telephone line. This is an important distinction because the FCC has more power to regulate transmission services. In 2005 the FCC issued its Internet Policy Statement that endorsed the principles of an open Internet, a policy that became known as **network neutrality.** In short, network neutrality blocks Internet service providers from favoring one Web company over another. Under network neutrality, an Internet service provider could not charge Google an additional fee so that Google Video would download faster than its competitors.

In 2008 the FCC sanctioned cable giant Comcast because the company violated its Internet principles by interfering with customers' ability to download files from file-sharing services such as BitTorrent. Comcast appealed the decision arguing that the FCC overstepped its regulatory authority and that the commission's net neutrality principles weren't enforceable. In 2010 a U.S. Court of Appeals sided with Comcast, saying that the FCC exceeded its authority and dealing a setback to the notion of net neutrality.

In response to the court ruling, the FCC announced that it would try to reclassify broadband as a transmission service, reversing its earlier position. If this move is successful, the FCC would have the power to enforce network neutrality and implement many of the features of its National Broadband Plan, a proposal that would eventually bring high-speed Internet service to most Americans. In December 2010 the FCC voted to adopt a policy of net neutrality.

The FCC's move to reclassify broadband will likely set off a protracted lobbying and legal battle with Internet providers such as Comcast, AT&T, and Verizon arguing against the plan and Internet companies such as Amazon.com and Google and various consumer groups arguing for it. It is also possible that Congress might preempt the whole issue by passing a new communications act. In any event, it is likely that this predicament may take some time to sort out.

Equal Opportunities: Section 315

From radio's earliest beginnings Congress recognized that broadcasting had tremendous potential as a political tool. A candidate for political office who was a skilled demagogue might use the medium to sway public opinion. By the time the 1927 Radio Act was written, Congress had already seen how some skilled communicators could use the medium for their own advantage. Consequently, what would eventually be known as **section 315** was incorporated into the 1927 act.

Issues: Fairness Doctrine: To Be or Not to Be

Although the **fairness doctrine** no longer officially exists, from time to time someone in Congress talks about resurrecting it. Consequently, it's helpful to know something about its history and constitutional implications.

In the late 1940s, the fairness doctrine was born when the FCC encouraged broadcasters to comment on controversial issues of public importance, provided they covered all sides of the issues. Broadcasters thought the doctrine was unconstitutional, and a case eventually reached the Supreme Court. In response, the Court relied on the scarcity principle to justify more regulation for broadcasting than for newspapers and ruled that the right of the public to receive information was paramount and took precedence over the rights of the broadcasters. Thus the fairness doctrine was constitutional.

The controversy didn't end there, however, and broadcasters continued to pressure the FCC to clarify or modify the doctrine. For its part, the FCC was never an enthusiastic supporter of the doctrine, and in 1981 the commission asked Congress to repeal it. Many members of Congress, however, favored the doctrine and refused to act. In 1985 the FCC released a study concluding that the fairness doctrine was not serving the public interest and once again asked Congress to abolish it. Once again, Congress refused.

Finally, after a federal court ruled that the fairness doctrine was not part of statutory law but was simply a regulation of the FCC, the commission went ahead and abolished the doctrine on its own. Several efforts by Congress during the 1980s and 1990s to write the doctrine into federal law were unsuccessful. After the 2008 election, several Democratic senators along with Speaker of the House Nancy Pelosi voiced their support for bringing back the fairness doctrine, but no new legislation to that effect was introduced in Congress. In fact, since 2006 the only new legislation items dealing with the doctrine were measures designed to prevent the fairness doctrine from being reimposed. As of this writing, none of these efforts was successful. There is, of course, a political subtext to this legislative maneuvering. Critics of the fairness doctrine argue that liberal politicians want to reintroduce the doctrine to counteract the power of conservative talk radio hosts.

When it was in force, the doctrine imposed a duty on broadcasters to identify controversial public issues and present balanced programming to address those issues. Broadcasters were under special obligation to seek out opposing viewpoints. Note that, unlike section 315, the fairness doctrine never said that opposing views were entitled to equal time; the doctrine simply stated that some reasonable amount of time should be devoted to these views.

The crux of section 315 in the current act is the following:

> If any licensee shall permit any person who is a legally qualified candidate for any public office to use a broadcasting station, he shall afford equal opportunities to all other such candidates for that office in the use of such broadcasting station.

Sounds simple enough, but, in operation, section 315 can prove complicated. Note that section 315 talks about equal *opportunities* as opposed to equal *time*. If a station provides a candidate with 30 minutes of prime time, it cannot offer an opponent 30 minutes at 3:00 a.m., nor can it offer the second candidate 30 one-minute spots throughout the day. The station would have to provide 30 minutes in prime time. Note further that section 315 does not obligate a station to provide free time to a candidate unless free time was first offered to an opponent.

Also note that the section is not self-triggering. A station is under no obligation to tell opponents that a candidate has used its facilities. The station is required to keep political files, however, and a candidate can easily examine these to see whether any of the other candidates had made use of the station. The opponent must request equal time within a specified time interval. Also keep in mind that section 312 of the Communications Act requires broadcasters to provide reasonable access for candidates for federal office. They can, however, require candidates to pay for this time.

In addition, there are rules governing how much stations can charge candidates for purchased time. Broadcasters are prohibited from charging more for political time than they do for other kinds of commercials. The rules also make sure that a station doesn't charge candidate A $1,000 for a spot while charging candidate B $5,000 for an equivalent spot.

Other complications also arise. Who is a legally qualified candidate? According to the commission, there are three criteria:

1. The candidate must have announced publicly an intention to run for office.

2. The candidate must be legally qualified for the office (to run for president, you must be a U.S. citizen and at least 35 years old).

3. The candidate must have taken the steps spelled out by law to qualify for a place on the ballot or have publicly announced a write-in candidacy.

This means that if a highly popular president nearing the end of a first term in office, generally expected to seek reelection, appears on TV and harshly criticizes a likely opponent, section 315 will not be triggered because, technically speaking, the president has not announced publicly for the office. Similarly, suppose the 30-year-old leader of the Vegetarian Party announced plans to run for the presidency. The law would not apply since a 30-year-old is not legally qualified for the office.

Section 315 applies only among those candidates actually opposing each other at that moment. This means that it works differently during a primary than it works during a general election. During a primary, an appearance by a candidate for the Democratic nomination to an office would not create equal opportunity rights among those running for the Republican nomination. Once the primaries are over, however, an appearance by the Democratic nominee would mean the Republican nominee would probably be entitled to an equal opportunity to appear.

Section 315 raises a question regarding the definition of "use" of a broadcasting facility. Broadly speaking, a use occurs when the candidate's voice or picture is included in a program or commercial spot. A program or commercial about a candidate in which the candidate does not appear would not qualify. Most of the time, a use is fairly easy to recognize. Sometimes, however, it's trickier. What happens if the candidate appears in a role that is totally different from that of candidate? How about the candidate who makes a guest appearance in a skit on *Saturday Night Live*? Or what about a candidate for the U.S. Senate who appears on a wildlife program and discusses his love for fishing? Could his opponents claim equal time under section 315? The commission has ruled that a candidate's appearance is a use even if the candidate is appearing for a completely unrelated purpose and never mentions his or her candidacy. Thus if the host of a children's show on a local station becomes a legally qualified candidate, each time he or she appears on the kiddie show the opposition is entitled to a comparable amount of time for free.

But what about the situation where an incumbent president who has already announced for reelection holds a press conference? Does this mean that all the other candidates are entitled to equal time? A similar situation occurred in 1959 when a minority party candidate for mayor of Chicago requested equal time because the current mayor who was running for reelection was shown in a series of film clips used on the evening news. Congress reacted by amending section 315 and providing these exceptions. Section 315 does *not* apply to the following:

1. Bona fide newscasts.

2. Bona fide news interviews.

3. Bona fide news documentaries in which the appearance of the candidate is incidental to the subject of the documentary.

4. On-the-spot coverage of bona fide news.

Questions can also be raised about exactly how much time an opponent is entitled to. Usually if the candidate appears or the audience hears the candidate's voice in a 30- or 60-second spot, opponents are entitled to 30 or 60 seconds, even if the candidate was on screen for a few seconds only. But if the candidate was on screen or on mike for only a portion of an interview show, opponents are entitled to an amount of time equal only to that featuring the candidate. For example, if a candidate appears for 15 minutes on an hour-long *Late Show with David Letterman*, opponents are entitled to 15 minutes, not a whole hour.

Note that as of 2010, section 315 regulations apply to both broadcast stations and cable systems that originate their own programming. The situation with regard to cable networks (such as A&E and USA) is less clear, but the FCC has yet to assert that cable networks fall under the provision of section 315. The law does not apply to appearances by candidates in videos on Web sites.

OTHER FEDERAL LAWS COVERING BROADCASTING AND CABLE

In addition to the provisions of the Communications Act of 1934 and the Telecommunications Act of 1996, broadcasters and cable operators must abide by other relevant statutes that relate to their operations. This section discusses five topics to which such laws apply: children's TV, copyright, obscenity, equal employment opportunities, and antitrust.

Children's Television

The **Children's Television Act of 1990** imposed an obligation on TV stations to serve the informational and educational needs of children through programming designed especially to serve those needs. The legislation also put a cap on the number of commercial minutes allowed in children's programs (10½ minutes

per hour on weekends and 12 minutes per hour on weekdays) and established a multimillion-dollar endowment for the funding of children's educational programs. The FCC also ruled that, starting in 1997, TV stations had to present a minimum of three hours per week of educational programs. Failure to provide such programming would result in additional scrutiny by the FCC when the station's license came up for renewal. The commission has taken an active role in enforcing these provisions, and many stations have received fines for exceeding the commercial minute guidelines.

Copyright: Trying to Keep Up

Copyright law protects intellectual property; it allows creative people, such as writers, photographers, and painters, to control the commercial copying and use of intellectual property they create, such as books, films, phonograph records, audio- and videotapes, and sculptures.

In its simplest terms, the current copyright law protects works that are "fixed in any tangible means of expression." This includes CDs and DVDs, dramatic works, motion pictures, TV programs, computer programs, and sculpture. Ideas and news events are not copyrightable (you could, however, copyright your particular written or recorded version of a news story). For a work created during or after 1978, copyright protection lasts for the life of the author plus 70 years. For works created before that date, the period of copyright protection will vary. Frequently the creator of a work transfers the copyright so that in some cases the owner is not necessarily the creator. To be *fully* protected a work must contain notice of the copyright (usually consisting of the letter *C* in a circle, the copyright owner's name, and the date of origination) and must be registered and deposited with the Copyright Office in Washington, DC. Nonetheless, any fixed form of an idea is now granted some protection from the moment that it is fixed in a tangible form.

Once a work is copyrighted, the owner has the right to authorize works derived from the original (for example, a novelist could authorize a movie script based on the book), to distribute copies of the work, and to display and/or perform the work publicly. Even though a work has been copyrighted, others can borrow limited amounts from the material under the doctrine of *fair use*. Critics, for example, can quote from a work without needing permission.

Let's take a closer look at how copyright laws apply to broadcasting and cable, starting first with performance rights. An author is entitled to a royalty payment when his or her work is performed publicly. When a copyrighted work is broadcast over the air—that is, when a radio station plays a recording, that constitutes public performance. The broadcasters pay royalties for such performances. The audience for the material pays nothing.

Music Licensing   There are more than 13,000 radio stations and 1,700 TV stations in the United States, and it would obviously be difficult for composers and song writers to negotiate a royalty agreement each time their songs were played on the air. Accordingly, private music licensing organizations were established to grant the appropriate rights and to collect and distribute royalty payments. In this country, performing rights are handled by the **American Society of Composers, Authors and Publishers (ASCAP), Broadcast Music Incorporated (BMI),** and **Society of European Stage Authors and Composers (SESAC).**

The major licensing firms grant what is known as **blanket rights,** whereby media firms pay a single fee to the licensing agency. In return the stations get performance rights to the agency's entire music catalog. These rights do not come cheaply. To illustrate, in 2004 the radio industry agreed to pay ASCAP $1.7 billion over six years for performance rights. The licensing agencies distribute this money to composers and publishers.

Note that while satellite radio and Internet radio stations pay performance royalties to artists or record labels, terrestrial radio stations do not thanks to an exemption granted by Congress. The rationale for the exemption holds that radio stations are giving performers free advertising and promotion by playing their songs. After hearing a song they like, many consumers will buy a CD or a digital copy of the music, and part of the purchase price goes to the performer and label. Thus the more radio play, the more money for the artist and label. This arrangement wasn't a problem while both radio stations and record companies were making money. As the recording industry fell on hard times during the first decade of the new century, it began to pressure lawmakers to end the exemption enjoyed by terrestrial radio. In 2009 such a bill was introduced in Congress, prompting intense lobbying activity by the radio stations and the recording industry. As this book went to press, the legislation was still pending.

Copyright and the Internet   The key piece of legislation in this area is the **Digital Millennium Copyright Act (DMCA).** The DMCA

- Makes it unlawful to circumvent measures used to control access to copyrighted works.
- Protects Internet service providers against copyright infringement liability for simply transmitting information over the Internet.
- Obligates Internet service providers to remove materials that appear to violate a copyright when such an infringement is brought to their attention.
- Requires that Internet radio stations pay licensing fees to record companies.

The recording industry has made most use of this law. In 1999 the Recording Industry Association of America filed suit against Napster, a file sharing service that allowed subscribers to download free music from the Internet. The court sided with the RIAA and put Napster out of business in 2002 (Napster was later resurrected as a pay-for-download service.) The RIAA subsequently sued several hundred individuals who had illegally downloaded thousands of songs. In 2005 the recording industry successfully sued Grokster, charging that it encouraged its members to violate copyright law and could be held liable for the copyright infringement of its customers. The recording industry was also successful in a lawsuit against file-sharing service Limewire. A 2010 decision found that Limewire was inducing its users to violate copyrights. It is unclear if these legal victories have had a significant effect on illegal file sharing.

Copyright issues have also vexed video-sharing site YouTube. In 2007 YouTube was sued by Viacom for $1 billion for making available more than 160,000 unauthorized clips of Viacom's entertainment programming. Google, YouTube's parent company, argued that the site had fully complied with DMCA requirements. Viacom argued that YouTube had not done enough to stop copyright infringement and that its lack of enthusiasm in this area actually prompted more copyright violations. In mid-2010 a judge ruled in favor of Google, but Viacom was considering an appeal.

Obscenity, Indecency, and Profanity

Section 1464 of the U.S. Criminal Code states that anybody who utters profane, indecent, or obscene

Four-letter words uttered by Nicole Richie and other celebrities on live TV prompted the FCC to fine broadcasters for airing "fleeting expletives." The case ultimately wound up before the Supreme Court.

language over radio or TV is liable to fine or imprisonment. Both the FCC and the Department of Justice can prosecute under this section. If found guilty, violators face a fine of up to $10,000, possible loss of license, or even jail. This seems clear enough. A couple of problems, however, quickly surface. First, remember that the FCC is prohibited from censoring broadcast content. Second, how exactly do you define obscenity, indecency, and profanity?

Let's consider profanity first. *Profanity* is technically defined as the irreverent or blasphemous use of the name of God. In the past the FCC has been reluctant to punish stations that have accidentally aired the occasional profanity. That position is subject to change, however, depending on the political philosophy of the current administration and the FCC membership.

Obscenity is another matter. The struggle to come up with a workable definition of obscenity has been long and tortuous and will not be repeated here. The definition that currently applies to broadcasting is the definition spelled out by the Supreme Court in the *Miller v. California* (1973) case. To be obscene, a program, considered as a whole, must (1) contain material that depicts or describes in a patently offensive way certain sexual acts defined in state law; (2) appeal to the prurient interest of the average person applying

contemporary local community standards (*prurient* is one of those legal words the courts are fond of using; it means tending to excite lust); and (3) lack serious artistic, literary, political, or scientific value. Obviously, most radio and TV stations would be wary of presenting programs that come anywhere near these criteria for fear of alienating much of their audience. Consequently, the FCC tends not to issue many decisions based on the obscenity criterion alone.

But what about cable and the Internet? In the past few years, many cable and satellite systems have been offering explicit X-rated movies on pay-per-view or video-on-demand channels. There are hundreds of Internet sites that offer downloadable adult movies. Don't these movies meet the three criteria for obscenity described in the *Miller* decision? Maybe, but society has become more tolerant of sexually explicit material, and people are reluctant to interfere with what individuals do in the privacy of their homes. If a test case does reach the Supreme Court, a key issue will be community standards. When it comes to the Internet, what community standards apply? The standards of the local community or a national standard set by the Internet community? Moreover, why should the community decide what an adult can watch in private at home?

This leaves the area of indecent programming—the area in which the FCC has chosen to exercise vigilance. Indecent content refers to content that is not obscene under the *Miller* standards but still contains potentially offensive elements. To be more specific, here's the common legal definition of broadcast indecency:

> Something broadcast is indecent if it depicts or describes sexual or excretory activities or organs in a fashion that's patently offensive according to contemporary community standards for the broadcast media at a time of day when there is a reasonable risk that children may be in the audience.

For example, a program that simply contains nudity is not obscene, although some people might be offended. Further, four-letter words that describe sexual or excretory acts are not, by themselves, obscene. They may, however, be classified as indecent.

The Seven Dirty Words Case   George Carlin is probably the only comedian ever to have his act reviewed by the Supreme Court. Here's how it happened. On the afternoon of October 30, 1973, WBAI-FM, New York City, a listener-sponsored station licensed to the Pacifica Foundation, announced that it was about to broadcast a program that would contain sensitive language that some might find offensive. The WBAI DJ then played all 12 minutes of a George Carlin routine titled "Filthy Words." Recorded live before a theater audience, the routine analyzed the words that "you couldn't say on the public airwaves." Carlin then listed seven such words and used them repeatedly throughout the rest of his monologue.

A man and his teenage son heard the broadcast while driving in their car and complained to the FCC; it was the only complaint the commission received about the monologue. The FCC decreed that the station had violated the rules against airing indecent content and put the station on notice that subsequent complaints about its programming might lead to severe penalties. Pacifica appealed the ruling, and an appeals court sided with WBAI and chastised the FCC for violating section 326 of the Communications Act, which prohibits censorship. Several years later, however, the case made its way to the Supreme Court, and the original FCC decision was reaffirmed. The Court said, among other things, that the commission's actions did not constitute censorship since they had not edited the monologue in advance. Further, the program could be regulated because the monologue was broadcast at a time when children were probably in the audience. Special treatment of broadcasting was justified because of its uniquely pervasive presence and because it is easily accessible to children. Thus the FCC could regulate indecent programming.

In the years following the *Pacifica* decision, many radio broadcasters pushed the limits by developing a new format called "raunch radio" or "shock radio." The FCC warned stations of possible fines for this content and suggested it might be more appropriate if presented after midnight when fewer children were in the audience. Congress got into the act in 1988 when it ordered the FCC to enforce a 24-hour ban on indecency, but this ban was overturned by a court decision. After several years of political and legal wrangling, the FCC and the courts agreed to a "safe harbor" provision that protects indecent material aired between 10 p.m. and 6 a.m.

The issue gained even more attention thanks to Janet Jackson's famous wardrobe malfunction during the 2004 Super Bowl halftime show. The FCC received more than 1.4 million complaints in the year following Jackson's overexposure and eventually wound up fining CBS more than a half million dollars for airing the event.

An appeals court threw out that fine, but the Supreme Court ordered the appeals court to reconsider its decision. In mid-2010, six years after the incident, the case was still unresolved.

Congress joined the campaign against indecency by passing new legislation that significantly increased the FCC's clout when dealing with indecent content. Under the 2006 law, a broadcaster could be fined up to a maximum of $325,000 for airing indecency, 10 times the previous maximum. Although many big city stations could probably absorb such a fine, many stations in smaller communities might be put out of business.

Also in 2006, with the FCC under pressure from conservative groups, the commission announced it was taking a harder line against indecency. It fined CBS and its affiliates more than $3 million for carrying an episode of *Without a Trace* that the FCC labeled as indecent. In addition, the commission altered its policy toward "fleeting expletives"—four-letter words that slip out during a live broadcast. In the past the FCC was reluctant to fine stations for such transgressions; but after a couple of celebrities uttered four-letter words during live awards programs, the commission declared that even an inadvertent, one-time expletive would trigger a fine. Broadcasters appealed the FCC's regulations, and an appeals court ruled them null and void. The lower court's decision, however, was overturned in 2009 by the Supreme Court. Although the Court ruled that the FCC's policy change was appropriate, it did not decide if the policy violated the First Amendment and sent the case back to a lower court for consideration of the free speech issue. In 2010 an appeals court ruled that the FCC's indecency policy was unconstitutional. As is probably clear from all this, indecent content continues to be a vexing issue for some members of the public, the courts, and broadcasters.

Indecent Content and Cable   Cable channels generally have a much wider latitude with programming that might be considered indecent. In fact, the 1984 cable act did not authorize the regulation of indecent material. The act differentiated between obscene and indecent material and permitted regulation of the former only. In addition, federal and state courts have found that the FCC's *Pacifica* ruling does not apply to cable. (George Carlin was able to perform his "Filthy Words" routine on HBO without incident.) The courts argue that cable is not as pervasive as broadcasting (you have to order it and pay additional fees for it) or as easily accessible to children (subscribers could buy and use lock boxes to limit viewing).

Nonetheless, the middecade controversy over indecency spilled over to the cable and satellite industries. Citizens' groups such as the Parents Television Council argued that for the average viewer, there is little difference between broadcast and cable/satellite channels, so provisions against indecency should affect all content providers. This view found some support among members of Congress, and there was talk of legislation that would hold cable and satellite networks to the same standards as broadcasters. In response, the cable/satellite industry made it clear that any such attempt would trigger a court battle over First Amendment rights. As of mid-2010 no such legislation had been enacted.

Indecency and the Internet There are probably more than 10,000 sites on the Internet that contain sexually oriented material. The ubiquity of this material and the ease with which it could be accessed by minors prompted Congress to include the Communications Decency Act as part of the Telecommunications Act of 1996. Basically the law made it a crime to transmit indecent and obscene material over the Internet to anybody under 18 years of age.

The constitutionality of this act was immediately called into question, and the case went to the Supreme Court. The Court ruled that the Internet was entitled to the highest degree of First Amendment protection, similar to that afforded books and magazines, and ruled the act unconstitutional. Congress responded with the 1998 Child Online Protection Act, which required commercial Web sites to secure a credit card number or other proof of age before allowing Internet users to view sites with adult content. The law would impose a $50,000 fine and a jail term on operators of Web sites that publish content harmful to children. Portions of this law were immediately appealed, and the appeals set off a 10-year legal battle. In 2009 the Supreme Court refused to review a lower court's decision to block enforcement of the act, thus effectively killing the measure.

In 2000 Congress passed the Children's Internet Protection Act, requiring public libraries to install filters on their computers to block access to adult sites. A federal court ruled against this law, but the Supreme Court ruled in 2003 that the act was constitutional and that filters could be installed in those libraries that accept federal funding. As is obvious, Congress has yet to find a way to protect children from Internet obscenity that also protects the free speech rights of adults.

Equal Employment Opportunities

Broadcasters and cablecasters are bound by federal law prohibiting job discrimination based on race, color, sex, religion, or national origin. Further, they must adhere to regulations set down by the Equal Employment Opportunity Commission. Although not directly responsible for enforcing all equal employment opportunity (EEO) provisions, the FCC has made it clear that it will assert jurisdiction over this area in broadcasting and cable.

THE LAW AND BROADCAST JOURNALISM

Several areas of law are relevant to the news-gathering and reporting duties of broadcast and cable channels. Some of these laws cover topics that are common to both print and electronic journalists (such as libel and invasion of privacy). Other laws are more relevant to video reporters (such as the restrictions on cameras in the courtroom). Further, many of these laws vary from state to state, but some have raised constitutional issues that have been addressed by the Supreme Court.

This section covers four areas that are highly relevant to the broadcast press: (1) defamation, (2) privacy, (3) protection of confidential sources, and (4) use of cameras and microphones in the courtroom.

Defamation

The law regarding **defamation** is concerned with the protection of a person's reputation. A defamatory statement injures the good name of an individual (or organization) and lowers his or her standing in the community. The law of defamation makes sure that the press does not act in an irresponsible and malicious manner. As we shall see, erroneous stories that damage the reputations of others can bring serious consequences.

There are two kinds of defamation: libel and slander. **Slander** comes from spoken words; in other words, slander is oral defamation. **Libel** is defamation stated in a tangible medium, such as a printed story or a photograph, or in some other form that has a capacity to endure. Because libel exists in a medium that can be widely circulated, the courts treat it more seriously than slander, which evaporates after it is uttered. Broadcast defamation is usually regarded as libel rather than slander.

Broadcast journalists have become particularly wary of suits alleging libel because they can carry sizable cash awards to the victims if the media are found at fault.

Elements of Libel If someone brings a libel suit, he or she must prove five different things to win. First, the statement(s) in question must have actually defamed the person and caused some harm. The material must have diminished the person's good name or reputation or held the person up to ridicule, hatred, or contempt. Harm can be such things as lost wages or physical discomfort or impairment in doing one's job. A prime example of a defamatory statement would be falsely reporting that a person has been convicted of a crime. The second element is publication. This usually presents no ambiguities; if a story was broadcast, it fulfills the publication criterion. The third element is identification. A person must prove that he or she was identified in a story. Identification does not necessarily have to be by name. A nickname, a cartoon, a description, or anything else that pinpoints someone's identity would suffice.

The fourth element is fault or error. To win a libel suit, a party must show some degree of fault or carelessness on the part of the media organization. The degree of fault that must be established depends on who's suing, what they are suing about, and which state's laws are being applied. As we shall see, certain individuals have to prove greater degrees of fault than others. Finally, in most instances the individual has to prove the falsity of what was published or broadcast.

Defenses against Libel When a libel suit is filed against a broadcast reporter and/or station, several defenses are available. The first of these is truth. If the reporter can prove that what was broadcast was true, then there is no libel. This sounds a lot easier than it is because the burden of proving truth, which can be an expensive and time-consuming process, falls on the reporter. Moreover, when the alleged libel is vague and doesn't deal with specific events, proving truth may be difficult. Finally, recent court decisions suggest that in many circumstances people who bring libel suits against the media must bear the burden of proving the defamatory statement false. All of these factors diminish the appeal of truth as a defense.

Note that libel suits concern defamatory statements of fact only. There is no such thing as libelous *opinion* because no one can prove that an opinion is true or false. In 1990, however, the Supreme Court ruled that expressions of opinion can be held libelous if they imply an assertion of fact that can

Issues: The Decline of Libel?

The Media Law Resource Center is an organization that monitors, among other things, trends in libel law. For many years the center conducted an annual survey of the number of libel suits in litigation in the United States. As of 2010, however, the center decided to do its survey only once every two years. Why the change? The number of libel suits had dropped so much that it wasn't worth doing a yearly survey. During the 1980s the center noted 266 libel trials. In the 1990s that number dropped to 192. At the end of the 2000s it was down to 124.

Why the decline? First, as noted in the text, it's hard for person, particularly a public figure, to win a libel suit. In addition, lawsuits are expensive and take a long time, and the media tend to prevail in most cases.

Second, individuals are wary of filing defamation lawsuits because of the "Streisand effect," named for entertainer Barbara Streisand, whose attempts to suppress photographs of her residence actually backfired and caused the photographs to receive even more media attention. Filing a libel suit might have the same effect and give the alleged defamation more publicity.

Third, in the age of the Internet, media can post corrections quickly, stopping a potential libel suit before it starts. In addition, those who were defamed now have access to Web sites, blogs, and social media where they can present their side of the story.

Fourth, the decline of libel suits coincides with the decline of media revenue. In the past, many libel suits grew out of the media's investigative reporting. In hard financial times, many media organizations have cut back on expensive investigative reports, and those that are done are carefully scrutinized to avoid a potentially expensive libel suit.

be proved false. Labeling a statement as an opinion does not necessarily make it immune from a libel suit.

A second defense is privilege. Used in its legal sense, privilege means immunity. There are certain situations in which the courts have held that the public's right to know is more important than a person's reputation. Courtroom proceedings, legislative debates, and public city council sessions are examples of areas that are generally conceded to be privileged. If a broadcast reporter gives a fair and accurate report of these events, the reporter will be immune to a libel suit even if what was reported contained a defamatory remark. Keep in mind, however, that accurately quoting someone else's libelous remarks outside an official public meeting or official public record is not a surefire defense against libel.

The third defense is fair comment and criticism. People who thrust themselves into the public arena are fair game for criticism. The performance of public officials, pro sports figures, artists, singers, columnists, and others who invite public scrutiny is open to the fair comment defense. This defense, however, applies to opinion and criticism; it does not entitle the press to report factual matters erroneously. A movie critic, for example, could probably say that a certain actor's performance was amateurish and wooden without fearing a libel suit. If, however, the critic went on and falsely reported that the bad acting was the result of drug addiction, that would be a different story.

In 1964, in the pivotal *New York Times v. Sullivan* case, the Supreme Court greatly expanded the opportunity for comment on the actions of public officials. The Court ruled that public officials must prove that false and defamatory statements were made with "actual malice" before a libel suit could be won. The Court went on to state that actual malice meant publishing or broadcasting something with the knowledge that it was false or with "reckless disregard" of whether it was false. In later years the Court ruled that public figures also must prove actual malice to win a libel suit.

In effect, two different degrees of fault are used as standards in libel cases. In many states a private citizen must simply prove that the media acted with negligence. For some states negligence means that accepted professional standards were not followed. Other states take negligence to mean that a reporter did not exercise reasonable care in determining whether a story was true or false. A few states define

negligence in relation to whether the reporter had reason to believe that material that was published or broadcast was true. Public figures and public officials are held to a higher standard; they must also prove actual malice. (Note that the really big financial awards in libel cases come from what are called "punitive damages"—awards levied by juries to punish the offending media outlet. To win punitive damages, even a private citizen must prove actual malice.)

Invasion of Privacy

The right to privacy is a relatively new area of media law. Stated simply, it means that the individual has a right to be left alone—not to be subjected to intrusions or unwarranted publicity. The right to privacy is not specifically found in the Constitution, although many have argued that the right is implied in several amendments. Like defamation, laws concerning privacy differ from state to state.

Not surprisingly, invasion of privacy is a complicated topic. In fact, legal experts suggest that it actually covers four different areas. The right of privacy protects against (1) unwarranted publication of private facts, (2) intrusion on a person's solitude or seclusion, (3) publicity that creates a false impression about a person (called "false light"), and (4) unauthorized commercial exploitation of a person's name or likeness.

Private Facts Disclosure of private facts occurs when a broadcast station or cable channel reports personal information that the individual did not want to make public. Disclosure resembles libel in that the individual must be identifiable and the facts must cause the individual humiliation or shame. Unlike libel, however, the facts revealed are true and may not necessarily damage a person's reputation. For example, suppose that a TV station shot footage of you in a hospital bed after cosmetic surgery when your face was swollen, black and blue, and generally ugly-looking. The station then ran the tape without your consent on the six-o'clock news with your name prominently mentioned as part of a series it was doing on the hospital. It's possible you might have a case for invasion of privacy. To qualify as the basis for a suit, private facts must be highly offensive to a person of "reasonable sensibilities."

When faced with an invasion-of-privacy suit, the media have several defenses. The reporter might argue that consent was obtained before the information was released. Information obtained from a public record is generally immune to invasion-of-privacy actions. Last, the reporter could argue that the information was released in connection with a newsworthy event.

Intrusion and Trespass **Intrusion** is an invasion of a person's solitude or seclusion without consent. The intrusion may or may not include **trespass,** which is defined as physical presence on private property without the consent or approval of the property's owner. Thus using a telephoto lens to secretly take pictures through a person's bedroom window could constitute intrusion. Secretly sneaking through the yard to take pictures through the bedroom window with a regular lens would probably constitute trespass and intrusion. Problems with intrusion and trespass generally crop up in the news-gathering stage. In fact, a reporter can be sued for trespass or intrusion even if he or she never broadcasts the information that was gathered.

Whether some news-gathering technique violates a person's right of privacy depends on how much privacy a person should normally expect in the particular situation involved. For example, people in their living rooms have a right to expect that they will not be secretly photographed or have their words recorded. People walking down a public street have less expectation of privacy.

Broadcast journalists can generally avoid charges of trespass by securing the consent of the owner of private property before entering it. In some limited instances during fires and natural disasters police or fire officials might control property and can grant consent to reporters to enter. Reporters, however, do not have the right to follow an unruly crowd onto private property without the consent of the owner or the police. In addition, TV reporters might be guilty of trespass if they enter, with cameras rolling, private property that is open to the public—like a place of business.

The concept of trespass assumed greater importance in a 1996 case involving the Food Lion grocery store chain and the ABC newsmagazine *Prime Time Live* over a report that Food Lion was violating health standards. Rather than sue for defamation, Food Lion charged that ABC had committed trespass when it gained access to nonpublic areas of a grocery store under false pretenses and taped employees with a concealed camera. The jury agreed with Food Lion and brought back a $5.5 million judgment

against the network for committing fraud and trespass. A judge later reduced the amount for the fraud offense to $315,000. The jury awarded Food Lion only $1 for the trespass offense. In 1999 a U.S. Court of Appeals threw out the $315,000 fraud award. Even though the trespass verdict did not amount to much, it set a precedent and made investigative reporters reexamine some of their journalistic techniques.

False Light A reporter can cast a person in a **false light** in several ways: omitting pertinent facts, distorting certain information, falsely implying that a person is other than what he or she is, or using a photograph out of context. A suit that alleges invasion of privacy through false light is similar to one brought for defamation (in fact, the two are often brought at the same time). A person can't be put in false light by the truth. Thus, like libel, there must be a false assertion of fact. In addition, the misinformation must be publicized. Finally, to win a false light suit, some people might have to prove actual malice on the part of the media. Unlike libel, in false light suits the false assertion is not defamatory. In fact, suits alleging false light have been brought over the publicizing of incorrect information that was flattering to the person. People who bring false light suits seek compensation not for harm to their reputation—how others feel about them—but for the shame, humiliation, and suffering they *feel* because of the false portrayal.

Commercial Exploitation This area tends to be more of a problem area for advertisers, promoters, agents, and public relations practitioners. Basically, it prohibits the unauthorized use of a person's name or likeness in some commercial venture. Thus it would be an invasion of privacy if you walked into a supermarket and found that a pickle manufacturer had, without your permission, put your face on a whole shelf of pickle jars. The best way for broadcasters to avoid privacy invasion suits based on unauthorized exploitation is to obtain written consent from subjects.

Well-known individuals, of course, can have more of a stake in these matters. In fact, over the last several years an offshoot of the commercial appropriation area known as the "right of publicity" has been articulated by the courts. In contrast with the traditional privacy area, which is based on the right to be left alone, the right of publicity is concerned with who gets the financial rewards when the notoriety surrounding a famous person is used for commercial purposes. In this regard, the right of publicity resembles a property right rather than a personal right and bears a little resemblance to copyright. In essence, the courts have ruled that famous people are protected against the unlawful appropriation of their fame. For example, model Christy Brinkley was successful in her suit against stores that were selling posters of her without her permission.

Protecting Sources

Since 1950 a conflict has developed between courts and reporters over the protection of news sources, notes, and news footage. Some background will be useful before we discuss the specifics.

There are two basic types of litigation. In a criminal trial the government seeks to punish someone for illegal behavior. Murder, rape, and robbery are examples of proceedings that would be covered by criminal law. Civil law involves a dispute between two individuals for harm that one has allegedly caused the other. Breach of contract, claims of overbilling, disputes between neighbors over property rights, defamation, and invasion of privacy are examples of civil suits. In a criminal or civil trial it is necessary for the court to have at its disposal any and all evidence that bears directly on the outcome of the trial in order to ensure a fair decision.

Courts have the power to issue subpoenas, official orders summoning witnesses to appear and testify, to make sure all who have information come forth and present what they know. There are only a few exceptions to this principle, called *privileges*. No person is forced to testify against himself or herself. Husband–wife communication is also considered privileged. Other common areas of privilege are lawyer–client communication and doctor–patient conversations. For many years journalists have argued that their relationship with a news source qualifies as the same type of privilege. They argue that without a promise of confidentiality, many sources would be reluctant to come forward and the news-gathering process would be severely hindered. In fact, many journalists have been fined and sent to jail for failure to disclose the names of sources or for failing to turn over to the court notes, photos, and videotapes.

Before the 1970s the courts were reluctant to grant any privileges to journalists. Since then, however, journalists are in a better position thanks to several court decisions and the passage of state "shield laws,"

which offer limited protection for journalists. The landmark decision was handed down by the Supreme Court in 1972 in *Branzburg v. Hayes*. Originally regarded as a defeat for the principle of journalistic privilege, the decision actually spelled out guidelines that covered when a reporter might legally refuse to testify. To make a reporter reveal confidential sources and information, the government must pass a three-part test. The three-part test listed below is often used in civil proceedings but seldom used in criminal trials. The government must prove the following:

1. That the journalist has information that bears directly on the case.

2. That the evidence cannot be obtained from any other sources.

3. That the evidence is crucial in the determination of the case.

The government's success in passing this test varies with the legal context. Reporters are most likely to be required to testify before grand juries, particularly if the reporter witnessed criminal activity; they are least likely to be compelled to testify when the defense in a civil trial is trying to obtain information. Civil libel actions where the medium is the defendant create special problems. Some states don't permit the protection of a shield law if it would frustrate a plaintiff's effort to show actual malice.

Thirty-seven states have granted limited protection to journalists by enacting shield laws. These laws, of course, vary from state to state. In some states, protection is given to a journalist who refuses to reveal a source, but protection does not extend to notes, tape, and other media used in the news-gathering process. Moreover, some states have strict definitions of who exactly is a journalist and is covered by the shield law. Several states require the journalist to prove that a source was actually promised confidentiality. Some states require that the information be published before the shield law is triggered. Other state laws list exceptions where the protection is not granted. A federal shield law was introduced in Congress in 2009, but as of mid-2010 the measure was still under consideration.

Cameras in the Courtroom

The controversy over cameras in the courtroom highlights an area where two basic rights come into conflict: the right of a defendant to a fair trial and the right of a free press to report the news.

The controversy began in 1932 during the trial of the man accused of kidnapping and murdering the infant son of national hero Charles Lindbergh. Newspaper, radio, and newsreel reporters helped turn the trial into a media circus, and a special committee of the American Bar Association (ABA) was created after the trial to draw up media guidelines. This group recommended that a canon (labeled **Canon 35**) be added to the code of conduct of the ABA which would prohibit the broadcasting and taking of photographs of a trial. Many states enacted Canon 35 into law.

In 1962 the Supreme Court affirmed the ban on cameras and microphones in the courtroom, but several justices noted that future technological advances in TV and radio might make broadcasting a trial less disruptive and suggested that it would one day be permissible. This prediction came true in 1981 when the Court ruled that televising a trial was not inherently prejudicial and left it up to the states to come up with systems to implement trial coverage.

Since that time, the trend has been toward more access. As of 2010, all 50 states allowed some form of coverage. In most states, the consent of the presiding judge is required and the judge controls the coverage. Cameras are still not allowed in federal district courts; Supreme Court proceedings are not televised either.

REGULATING ADVERTISING

Advertising is a big business: about $50 billion was spent on broadcasting and cable advertising in 2009. Because advertising is such an influential industry, the government has enacted laws and regulations that deal with advertising messages.

Recent decisions by the Supreme Court have established that advertising does deserve some protection under the First Amendment. The Court, however, was unwilling to grant advertising the degree of protection that it gave to other forms of speech. Advertising that is accurate and truthful can be regulated by the state provided the state's regulation passes a three-part test: The regulation must serve a substantial government goal, advance the interests of the state, and be narrowly drawn.

The above paragraph refers to ads that are accurate and truthful. But what about false and deceptive advertising? How is that controlled? The agency most visible in this area is the **Federal Trade Commission (FTC).**

Congress set up the FTC in 1914 to regulate unfair business practices. In 1938 its power was broadened to include jurisdiction over deceptive advertising. Nonetheless, as far as advertising was concerned, the FTC remained an obscure institution until the consumer movement of the 1960s and 1970s when it became highly active in regulating questionable ads. (It even ordered some companies to run "corrective" ads to counteract any misunderstanding caused by their original ads.) After the move toward deregulation in the 1980s, the FTC assumed a much lower profile.

Like the FCC, the FTC is an independent regulatory agency with five commissioners appointed by the president for renewable seven-year terms. The FTC's Bureau of Consumer Protection handles advertising complaints. The FTC is charged with regulating false, misleading, and/or deceptive advertising and may investigate questionable cases on its own or respond to the complaints of competitors or the general public. The FTC may hold formal hearings concerning a complaint and issue a decision. Again, like the FCC, the FTC's decision can be appealed through the federal courts.

The FTC guards mainly against deceptive advertising, and over the years the commission has developed a set of guidelines that define *deception.* Taken as a whole, the ad must have deceived a reasonable person. Any kind of falsehood constitutes deception. For example, a broadcast ad promising buyers a genuine diamond is deceptive if, in fact, what the consumer receives is a zirconium. Even a statement that is literally true might be judged deceptive. Wonder Bread ads claimed that the bread was fortified with vitamins and minerals that are necessary for healthy growth. Although literally true, the ad was ruled deceptive because it did not point out that every fortified bread contained the same vitamins and minerals.

The FTC, however, does recognize that there is room for reasonable exaggeration in advertising. Consequently, the commission permits "puffery" in subjective statements of opinion that the average consumer will probably not take seriously. Thus it would probably be OK for a restaurant to claim that it serves "the world's best coffee" or for a repair shop to advertise the "friendliest service in town." Puffery crosses over into deception when exaggerated claims turn into factual assertions of superiority.

The FTC has several enforcement means at its disposal. At the mildest level, the FTC can simply express its opinion about the questionable content of an ad, as it did in 2010 when it notified cereal makers that they should not promote claims about the health benefits of their products for children without presenting adequate scientific support. Further, it can require that certain statements be carried in the ads to make the ads more accurate. For example, when some Listerine ads claimed the product killed germs that caused sore throats that came with a cold or fever, the FTC ordered the makers of Listerine to include a statement in their ads to the effect that Listerine was not a *cure* for sore throats associated with colds or fever. An appeals court upheld the right of the FTC to order advertisers to engage in such corrective campaigns even though the advertiser objected.

The FTC also can notify an advertiser that its ads are deceptive and ask that the advertiser sign a **consent decree.** By agreeing to a consent decree, the advertiser removes the advertising in question but does not admit that the ad was in fact deceptive. More than 90 percent of all FTC cases are settled by consent decrees. A stronger weapon is a **cease-and-desist order.** In this situation, the FTC issues a formal complaint against an ad and a formal hearing is scheduled. If after the hearing it is ruled that the ad was deceptive, a judge issues a cease-and-desist order and the company must stop airing the offending ad. Failure to do so results in a fine. In rare cases, when an ad might have injurious effects on the public, the FTC can seek an injunction to stop the offending ad quickly.

In practical terms, broadcasters and cable system operators should be encouraged to know that very few of the ads aired in any given year are likely to raise legal questions. In addition, because the advertising industry conducts most of its business in public, it is concerned with the harmful effects that might follow the publication or broadcast of any false or misleading ad. Consequently, the advertising profession has developed an elaborate system of self-regulation (see next chapter) that prevents most deceptive ads from being released. Networks also have departments that screen ads before they are accepted. Nonetheless, an occasional problem ad might crop up, which makes a knowledge of FTC rules and regulations helpful.

Ads for prescription drugs have become common on TV. Thirty-second spots for Prilosec, Lipitor, and other prescription drugs accounted for more than $4.0 billion in advertising revenue in 2009. The **Food and Drug Administration (FDA)** is responsible for regulating these ads. In fact, it was a change in the FDA's advertising policy that opened the door for TV prescription drug advertising. For many years pharmaceutical companies were permitted to advertise only to physicians and not to the general public. The FDA changed that rule in 1997 and allowed direct-to-consumer advertising. Current regulations require that drug ads contain information about the drug's safety and side effects.

SUMMARY

- Broadcasting and cable regulation is based on two rationales: the scarcity theory and the pervasive presence theory. The regulation of the electronic media is influenced by the FCC, Congress, the courts, the White House, industry lobbyists, the public, state and local governments, and the operation of the marketplace.

- The Communications Act of 1934 and the Telecommunications Act of 1996 provide the groundwork for the regulation of the electronic media. The FCC implements these acts by assigning and renewing licenses. Although it does not license cable systems, the FCC does have some regulatory power over the industry. Section 315 of the Communications Act provides equal opportunities for political candidates on television stations.

- Copyright laws are important in broadcasting and cable. Music licensing is the method by which performers and composers are paid for the use of their work by broadcasters and cable operators.

DVR owners can record a program off the air for their personal use without violating copyright laws. The Internet has raised new issues about copyright protection.

- Federal laws pertaining to obscenity apply to broadcasting and cable. In addition, the FCC has drafted special provisions that deal with indecent content on radio and TV.

- Cablecasters and broadcasters are bound by the regulations set down by the Equal Employment Opportunity Commission.

- Several legal areas touch on the practice of broadcast journalism: defamation, invasion of privacy, protecting sources, and using cameras and microphones in the courtroom.

- Advertising qualifies for protection as free speech under the First Amendment. The FTC is the main agency that regulates false and deceptive advertising. Drug advertising is regulated by the FDA.

KEY TERMS

SUGGESTIONS FOR FURTHER READING

Carter, T. B., Franklin, M. A., & Wright, J. B. (2008). *The First Amendment and the fourth estate.* Westbury, NY: Foundation Press.

————. (2007). *The First Amendment and the fifth estate.* Westbury, NY: Foundation Press.

Creech, K. (2007). *Electronic media law and regulation.* Boston: Focal Press.

Krasnow, E., Longley, L., & Terry, H. (1982). *The politics of broadcast regulation.* New York: St. Martin's Press.

Middleton, K., & Lee, W. (2010). *The law of public communication.* Boston: Allyn & Bacon.

Overbeck, W., & Belmas, G. (2010). *Major principles of media law.* New York: HBJ College Division.

Pember, D., & Calvert, C. (2008). *Mass media law.* New York: McGraw-Hill.

Sadler, R. (2005). *Electronic media law.* Thousand Oaks, CA: Sage.

Spitzer, M. (1986). *Seven dirty words and six other stories.* New Haven, CT: Yale University Press.

INTERNET EXERCISES

Visit our Web site at **www.mhhe.com/dominickbib7e** for study-guide exercises to help you learn and apply material in each chapter. You will find ideas for future research as well as useful Web links to provide you with an opportunity to journey through the new electronic media.

11 Self-Regulation and Ethics

Quick Facts

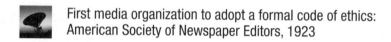 First media organization to adopt a formal code of ethics: American Society of Newspaper Editors, 1923

Date of first National Association of Broadcasters code for broadcasting: 1929

Date code abolished: 1983

Most influential citizens' group in TV history: Action for Children's Television

Percentage of parents who used the V-chip or a set-top cable/satellite box in the past week to control the TV viewing of their children: 12

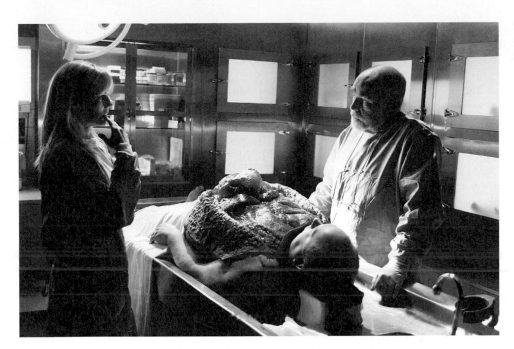

Graphic scenes, such as this one from *CSI*, can cause problems for broadcasters.

The preceding chapter dealt with laws regarding broadcasting and cable. There are many situations, however, that laws or FCC regulations do not cover. In these circumstances, broadcasting and cable professionals must rely on their own ethics, internal standards, and organizational operating policies for guidance.

Consider the following. On broadcast TV during prime time in 2009 and 2010 you could have seen a cartoon character vomiting for 30 seconds (*Family Guy*); a *ménage a trois* involving teenagers (*Gossip Girl*); and ads for models wearing revealing lingerie (courtesy of Victoria's Secret and Lane Bryant).

There's nothing illegal about putting scantily clad models, repulsive scenes, or sexual situations on TV. The decision to air this type of content boils down to a consideration of individual principles, professional standards, and personal ethics. In short, it's a matter of **self-regulation.** A consideration of self-regulation is important because the trend toward fewer formal regulations means that more and more decisions are being left to the discretion of individual broadcasters and program producers. Accordingly, this chapter focuses on (1) the major factors that influence self-regulation in broadcasting and cable and (2) ethics and its relationship to self-regulation.

SELF-REGULATION IN BROADCASTING AND CABLE

This section examines (1) codes of responsibility and good practice, (2) departments devoted to maintaining proper standards, (3) the V-chip, (4) professional groups and organizations, and (5) citizens' groups.

Codes

Codes are written statements of principle that guide the general behavior of those working in a profession. Code statements can be prescriptive—"Thou shalt do this"—or proscriptive—"Thou shalt not do this." At one end of the spectrum they imply the minimum expectations of the profession (journalists should not plagiarize); at the other they embody the ideal way of acting (journalists should tell the truth). Professional codes are common in medicine, law, pharmacy, and journalism.

The NAB Code   Although many group-owned broadcasting stations adopted strict codes, probably the most famous of all in broadcasting was that developed by the National Association of Broadcasters (NAB). The NAB established the first radio code in 1929, just two years after the FRC was founded. In 1952, as TV was growing, the NAB adopted a code for it too. By 1980 the two codes had been amended many times to keep up with the changing social climate. Adherence to the code was voluntary, and figures from 1980 show that about one-half of all radio stations and two-thirds of all TV stations were code subscribers. The NAB had a code authority with a staff of about 33 people who made sure that stations followed the codes. The only punishment the NAB could dish out to the violator, however, was revocation of the right to display the seal of good practice, a penalty that hardly inspired fear among station owners.

A glance at the codes themselves showed that they covered both programming and advertising. Included in the programming area were such diverse topics as news presentation, political broadcasting, religion, community responsibility, and programming aimed at children. The advertising section of the codes contained, among other items, guidelines about what products were acceptable, rules for the presentation of broadcast ads, and time standards suggesting limits on the time per hour that should be devoted to commercials.

The time standard provisions ultimately got the codes into trouble with the Department of Justice, which claimed in an antitrust suit that broadcasters were keeping the prices of ads high by artificially restricting the amount of commercial time available. The NAB, after a negative court decision, suspended the advertising portion of its code. Later, on the advice of lawyers, the NAB revoked the programming sections as well. By 1983 the codes ceased to exist.

Nonetheless, the codes still have some lingering impact. Although the courts said it was anticompetitive for groups of broadcasters to get together to produce common codes, it was still permissible for individual stations and group-owned stations to maintain their own codes. As a result, many stations still informally follow code provisions.

Since its demise there have been various efforts to resurrect the code. In 1997 a bill that would have allowed members of the broadcasting and cable industries to develop a new code without fear of antitrust laws did not pass Congress. The issue surfaced again in 2004 after Janet Jackson's wardrobe malfunction during the Super Bowl's halftime show. As the FCC and various lawmakers considered regulations that would crack down on indecent broadcasts, the National Association of Broadcasters formed a task force to consider options for self-regulation that would address concerns over potentially offensive content. There have been no serious attempts to revive the code since 2005.

Other Codes and Policies   There are other noteworthy industrywide guidelines that deal with broadcast journalism and advertising.

The Radio and Television News Directors Association (RTNDA) has an six-article Code of Broadcast News Ethics that covers items ranging from courtroom coverage to privacy invasions. The Society of Professional Journalists (SPJ) also has a code of ethics that covers all media including broadcasting. This code covers such topics as fair play, accuracy, objectivity, and press responsibility. The language of both codes is general and far-reaching. Examples from the SPJ code include "Seek truth and report it" and "Be accountable."

In the advertising area, the American Advertising Federation and the Association of Better Business Bureaus International have developed a nine-item code that deals with such topics as truth in advertising ("Advertising shall tell the truth . . ."), taste and decency ("Advertising shall be free of statements . . . which are offensive to good taste"), and responsibility ("Advertisers shall be willing to provide substantiation of claims made"). This code has been endorsed by the NAB and many other industry groups.

The absence of a general code of behavior for broadcasting and cable has given station managers and program directors a great deal of discretion in such matters as children's programming, artistic freedom, religious shows, programs devoted to important local issues, and acceptable topics. Management must be sensitive to the political, social, and economic sensibilities of the community; a bad decision can cost a radio, TV, or cable organization credibility, trust, and, in the long run, dollars.

To help guard against bad decisions, many stations have developed their own policy guidelines covering sensitive issues. These station policies generally complement and expand the industrywide codes of conduct. Not surprisingly, the broadcast newsroom is the place where a written policy is most often found.

Written codes, however, are not without controversy. On one hand, proponents of codes argue that they indicate to the general public that the media organization is sensitive to its ethical duties. Moreover, written codes of conduct ensure that every employee understands what the company views as proper or correct behavior; ethical decisions are not left to the whim of each individual. On the other hand, opponents argue that any company policy statement that covers the entire workings of the organization will have to be worded so vaguely that it will be of little use in specific day-to-day decision making. Further, opponents fear that a written code or policy statement might actually be used against a radio or TV station in court. For example, a private citizen who's suing a TV station for libel might argue that the station was negligent because it failed to follow its own written guidelines. Finally, new ethical problems constantly emerge, and new guidelines have to be written. For example, as of 2010 some of the problems facing television journalists included how to handle user-generated content, reporters' blogging activity, and digitally manipulated images.

Many of the company codes that exist today tend to be proscriptive and narrow. Basically they tend to spell out the minimum expectations for an individual employee. For example, many TV station policies forbid journalists from taking gifts from their news sources, or program directors from accepting gifts from program suppliers. Stations also have policies that bar employees from accepting free sports tickets and junkets or from holding outside employment that might conflict with their job at the station.

It's apparent that written guidelines can't do the whole job. This is not surprising because most policy statements and guidelines are directed at the individual, whereas ethical problems are increasingly originating at the corporate level. For example, many stations and cable systems are owned by groups. How much of the profit made by a local operation should be reinvested back into the station and how much should go to shore up unprofitable operations in other communities or to finance new acquisitions? Should a TV station run sensational stories on its TV newscasts during sweep weeks to inflate its ratings? How much local news should be carried on a radio station if it means losing some money in the process? These are questions that codes seldom deal with.

Departments of Standards and Practices

The major broadcast and cable networks maintain staffs to make sure that their commercials and programs do not offend advertisers, affiliated stations and cable systems, audience members, and the FCC.

In prior years these departments, usually called standards and practices (S&P) or something similar, were large and influential. In recent years, however, they have been cut back, and the producers of the various programs now make many of the decisions about what is or is not acceptable.

It's obvious that standards concerning what's acceptable on television have changed dramatically over the years. Back in the 1960s, S&P executives at the TV networks decreed that Barbara Eden of *I Dream of Jeannie* couldn't reveal her navel and that Rob and Laura of the *Dick Van Dyke Show* couldn't be shown in bed together even though they were married. Standards became more liberal in the early 1970s with such shows as *All in the Family* and *Maude*. This trend continued through the 1980s and 1990s. As of 2010, standards had relaxed even more. For example, same-sex kisses are frequently shown. Words that would have been censored 20 years ago are now commonplace. Ads for drugs that treat erectile dysfunction seem to show up everywhere. Series on cable TV push the envelope even further.

What's behind this trend toward greater liberalization? First, society's standards have become more tolerant. Programs about sometimes controversial topics such as homosexuality, abortion, and teenage sex generate few complaints from the viewing audience. Second, the success of such premium cable series as *Sex and the City, Californication,* and *Secret Diary of a Call Girl* encouraged broadcasters and other cable networks to go to greater lengths to compete with the pay channels. Third, the V-chip (discussed in more detail soon) has helped accelerate this trend. The chip allows program creators to alert the audience to possibly objectionable content. Programmers may use labels such as "For Mature Audiences" to include more adult themes in their programs. In short, the V-chip relieves programmers of some of the burden of self-regulation and passes it on to the viewer.

Although they are not as influential as before, networks' standards and practices departments still exercise some authority. CBS, for example, rejected an ad from a gay dating service, and NBC turned down a proposed Super Bowl ad from animal rights group PETA because it was too sexually explicit.

Cable networks, of course, have a little more leeway when it comes to controversial content, but they also follow standards. AMC and the USA Network, for example, edit objectionable content from

Ethics: Deliberate Distortion or Honest Mistake?

On May 22, 2010, President Barack Obama gave the commencement speech at West Point. About one-third of the way through his 32-minute address, Obama said, "[W]e are poised to end our combat mission in Iraq this summer." A video of the speech on the White House Web site shows about 12 seconds of applause after Obama makes that statement. In a two-minute Fox News clip that reported on the event, however, the applause is not heard, and the video footage shows Obama standing silently at the podium for 12 seconds, giving the impression that his pronouncement was met with silence.

Documentary film maker Michael Moore charged that Fox deliberately cut the applause to embarrass the president. The liberal blog *The Progressive Pulse* stated, "Things are getting beyond ridiculous on Fox News. Now they are literally editing out the applause when they air segments of President Obama's speeches." Other liberal blogs were quick to criticize the cable network.

It appears, however, that there may be a more anodyne explanation. The two-minute Fox video clip is actually two sound bites of Obama's speech spliced together. The first was about the war in Iraq while the second was about the war on terror. Networks usually supply sound bites to their affiliates that can be used on their local newscasts. A standard technique in TV news is for the local news to play the clip and then cut back to the local news anchor. The person editing the clip wipes out the audio at the end of a sound bite so there is no overlap between the clip's audio and the voice of the anchor. The abrupt end of the audio is a cue for the anchor to begin talking. In the case of the West Point speech it appears that when the editor joined the two sound bites together, he or she simply left in too much silent "padding" between segments.

Of course, although it might not have been deliberate, the editing did create a misleading impression. Those who edit news clips for on-the-air or online use have a special obligation to maintain accuracy and to preserve the context of what they are editing. In this case, a bit more diligence might have eliminated the controversy.

their movies. MTV has demanded cuts in music videos the network deemed too controversial in their original form. Premium cable channels, such as HBO and Showtime, have the greatest amount of latitude when it comes to presenting mature and sexual content. HBO's *Sex and the City* and *Entourage* both came to broadcast TV only after extensive editing.

At the local level both broadcasting and cable operations pay close attention to questions of taste and appropriateness, but they do not have formalized departments that handle the task. Some group owners of stations have codes that they try to apply to all the stations they own, but most standards-and-practices decisions are made by managers or program executives. Further, not all decisions will be the same. The acceptability of certain TV or radio messages depends on several factors: (1) the size of the market, (2) the time period, (3) the station's audience, and (4) the type of content involved.

To elaborate, what's acceptable in New York City might not be appropriate for Minot, North Dakota. Standards vary widely from city to city and from region to region. The local radio, TV, or cable executive

is usually the best judge of what his or her community will tolerate. For example, in 2009 more than a dozen local Fox affiliates refused to carry *The Osbournes: Reloaded* because the program did not meet their community standards.

The time period also has a lot to do with acceptability. Stations tend to be more careful if there's a good chance that children will be in the audience. Programs and films with adult themes are typically scheduled late in the evening, when few children are presumed to be listening. Cable movie channels generally schedule their racier films after 10:00 p.m.

The audience attracted by a station's programming is another important factor. Radio stations that feature a talk format with controversial topic usually spark few protests because their listeners know what to expect. Listener-sponsored Pacifica radio stations routinely program material that other stations would heartily avoid. Although they do get into occasional trouble (for example, the *Pacifica* case), the audience for Pacifica stations rarely complains.

Finally, the kind of program also makes a difference. Rough language and shocking pictures are sometimes okay for a news or public affairs program.

Cable series, such as MTV's *Jersey Shore*, push the limits of what is acceptable TV content.

The V-Chip

The **V-chip** represents a blend of legal regulation and self-regulation. Section 551 of the Telecommunications Act of 1996 requires TV set manufacturers to install a V-chip content-blocking device in every TV set that is 13 inches or larger.

The V-chip works in concert with the voluntary program rating system developed by the television industry that identifies programs with sexual, violent, or indecent content. After much discussion, the industry came up with a rating system that initially classified TV content according to its acceptability for various age levels:

The ratings can carry two pieces of information: (1) the audience for which the program is appropriate and, if relevant, (2) information about the content of the program. Here are the audience ratings:

TV-Y: Programming suitable for all children.

TV-Y7: Programs directed to children aged 7 or above.

TV-G: General audience.

TV-PG: Parental guidance suggested.

TV-14: Parents strongly cautioned for children under 14.

TV-M: Mature audiences only.

The content labels are these:

FV: Fantasy violence (used with programs in the TV-Y7 category).

D: Suggestive dialogue.

L: Coarse language.

S: Sexual situations.

V: Violence.

Broadcasters and cable networks were initially wary of the V-chip; but after the FCC's crackdown on indecency (see the previous chapter), the industry embraced the device as an alternative to more restrictive legislation. In 2006 broadcasters and cablecasters launched a $300 million publicity campaign to educate parents about the V-chip. In addition, the industry formed TV Watch, a coalition of industry and citizens' groups to promote the use of the chip.

Despite these efforts, parents have generally ignored the V-chip. A 2007 survey noted that nearly 90 percent of parents didn't use the device. Another survey found that 40 percent of respondents didn't know what the V-chip was. A 2007 FCC report to Congress concluded that the V-chip was of limited effectiveness in protecting children from inappropriate content. Yet another campaign to educate viewers about the V-chip ("Parents Say kNOw") was launched by TV Watch in 2010.

Professional Groups

Professional groups are trade and industry organizations that offer their members advice about research, technical, legal, and management issues. The best known of these for broadcasters is the **National Association of Broadcasters (NAB).** The NAB has about 8,300 radio and TV station members, along with more than 1,500 individual members in the broadcasting industry. We have already examined the lobbying component of the NAB; its other services include designing public service campaigns, offering legal advice, conducting technology research, and maintaining an information library. In cable, the **National Cable Television Association (NCTA)** is the most influential group, with a range of services that parallels the NAB's. Other professional groups include the Radio Television News Directors Association, the National Association of Television Program Executives, the National Association of Farm Broadcasters, the National Association of Public

Television Stations, and the National Association of Black-Owned Broadcasters, to name a few.

Professional groups contribute to self-regulation in both formal and informal ways. On the informal level, each group sponsors conventions and meetings where members exchange relevant business and professional information. These meetings offer ways for managers from one part of the country to learn how managers from other regions are handling similar problems. A station in Maine might find that a policy or set of guidelines used by a station in Ohio solves its problem. Organizational meetings let professionals get feedback from their peers. Professional organizations also set examples and demonstrate standards of meritorious behavior that members can emulate. The NAB, for example, reported that in 2009 radio and TV stations nationwide contributed more than $10 billion to community service projects.

The most elaborate system of formal self-regulation by a professional group deals with national advertising. Basically, the process works like this. If a consumer or a competitor thinks an ad is deceptive, a complaint is filed with the **National Advertising Division (NAD)** of the Council of Better Business Bureaus. Most complaints are filed by competitors, but the NAD monitors national radio and TV and can initiate action itself. The NAD can either dismiss the complaint or contact the advertiser for additional information that might refute the complaint. If the NAD is not satisfied with the advertiser's response, it can ask the company to change or stop using the ad. If the advertiser agrees (and most do), that's the end of it. On the other hand, if the advertiser disagrees with the NAD, the case can be taken to the **National Advertising Review Board (NARB).**

The NARB functions much like a court of appeals. A review panel is appointed, the case is examined again, and the complaint is either upheld or dismissed. If the complaint is upheld, the advertiser is asked once again to change or discontinue the ad. If the advertiser still refuses, the case can be referred to the FTC or another government agency for possible legal action.

One problem with this system is that it takes a long time. In many cases, by the time the NAD has weighed the facts of the case, decided that the ad in question was truly deceptive, and notified the company to stop, the advertising campaign has run its course and the ad is already off the air. Nonetheless, although it doesn't have any legal or formal authority, the NAD/NARB system and the implied threat of legal action are taken seriously by most people in the industry.

Last, scholarly and academic organizations, such as the Broadcast Education Association and the Association for Education in Journalism and Mass Communication, contribute to self-regulation through their work with students. These and similar organizations urge colleges and universities to emphasize ethical and professional responsibilities in their curricula. Academic organizations also study and help clarify the norms and standards of the profession so practitioners can have some guidance in making ethical decisions.

Citizens' Groups

In addition to shaping the legal and policy environment of broadcasting, citizens' groups (or pressure groups) exert a force for self-regulation by communicating directly with broadcasters. In recent years citizens' groups have been most vocal about three areas: (1) the portrayal of minorities, (2) the presentation of sex and violence, and (3) children's programming.

Portrayal of Minorities   The concern over the portrayal of minorities began during the civil rights movement of the 1960s. African Americans correctly noted that few blacks appeared in network prime-time programming and that those few who did were usually shown in menial occupations. Their pressure on the networks for more balanced portrayals ultimately led to more important roles for blacks, such as Bill Cosby's in *I Spy* and Diahann Carroll's in *Julia*.

The success of these efforts prompted Latinos to campaign successfully for the removal of a commercial character known as the Frito Bandito, which many found offensive. Ethnic stereotyping in a series called *Chico and the Man* was also a target of Mexican American citizens' groups. Other groups, such as Native Americans, Italian Americans, the Gray Panthers, Arab Americans, and Asian Americans, have also pressured the networks to eliminate stereotyped portrayals.

Presentation of Sex and Violence   The portrayal of sex and violence has been a recurring topic of concern for citizens' groups. The Parents Television Council (PTC) has monitored television programs

According to its Web site, the Parents Television Council (PTC) is a "non-partisan education organization advocating responsible entertainment." Founded in 1995 by conservative L. Brent Bozell III, the organization monitors prime-time television shows, reviews PG and G rated films, and publishes a written description with specific examples of the show's content. The PTC also rates programs according to a traffic light system where green represents a "family-friendly show promoting responsible themes and traditional values" whereas red denotes that the "show may include gratuitous sex, explicit dialogue, violent content, or obscene language, and is unsuitable for children." A yellow light indicates that "the show contains adult-oriented themes and dialogue that may be inappropriate for youngsters." A recent listing of a week of prime-time shows rated, among others, *Cold Case, How I Met Your Mother, America's Next Top Model,* and *Glee* with a red light while shows such as *30 Rock, The Office,* and *The Bachelorette* got yellow lights. Only *Extreme Makeover: Home Edition* received a green light.

In addition to its traffic light ratings, the PTC's Web site also contains reviews, columns, reports, and studies about the current state of electronic entertainment. One report singles out "The Worst Cable TV Show of the Week" (*Neighbors from Hell* on TBS got that distinction one week in 2010). In contrast, the PTC Picks of the Week identify programs that the organization deems acceptable for family viewing. During June 2010, for example, *The Next Food Network Star* and *Family Feud* were Picks of the Week.

Moreover, if parents are concerned about a show's content and wish to complain to the people responsible, the PTC provides contact information for program sponsors and the networks. One of the PTC's main targets has been broadcast indecency. The organization's Web site contains a page that lets parents electronically file an indecency complaint with the FCC. The group has also campaigned for the FCC to have the power to regulate indecency on cable networks as well as on broadcast TV.

Like most citizens' groups, the PTC's actions have drawn both praise and criticism. The organization has about a million members, indicating that many parents find its efforts useful. Its efforts can also remind sponsors that a substantial market exists for family-friendly programming. In 2010, for example, a consortium of companies including Coca-Cola, Procter & Gamble, and Walmart announced the creation of a $10 million fund to support family-friendly shows in prime time. On the other hand, the group has been criticized for trying to legislate morality and for favoring more government restrictions over free speech. Others note that the PTC is a small, self-appointed group whose view of morality should not be imposed on the unwilling majority. In any case, as television programs push the envelope of acceptability further and further, look for the efforts of the PTC and similar groups to increase.

for both violence and sexual content. One PTC report traced the portrayal of violence on TV from 1998 to 2006. A report released in 2009 examined the depiction of violence against women in prime-time broadcasts. The PTC has also examined sexual content in early evening broadcast programs on MTV and on Spanish-language television. The conservative group Morality in Media has campaigned against obscene content on TV and on the Internet.

Children's Programming Programming for children is another recurring concern of many groups, including the national Parent Teacher Association and the National Education Association. Since the passage of the **Children's Television Act of 1990** and the subsequent ruling by the FCC that stations devote three hours a week to children's programs, the major focus of children's television advocates has been the enforcement of these provisions.

Effects Citizens' groups pose special problems for the self-regulatory attempts of the industry. They increase the sensitivity of programmers toward potentially offensive material, but at the same time they severely restrict the creative freedom of writers and producers. Their cumulative effect thus may lead to a kind of self-censorship. In addition, program producers are forced to walk a thin line between alternatives. For example, gay citizens' groups are calling for increased portrayals of homosexuals in TV drama. If the producers accede to the demands, they might risk offending a substantial part of their viewing audience. Similarly, networks and production companies are careful not to allow potentially harmful acts of violence to remain in a show, but even seemingly innocuous acts of aggression may still raise the ire of some citizens' groups. What some consider innocent sexual bantering may be offensive to others. Satisfying everybody is not an easy task.

ETHICS

All of us deal regularly with ethical problems. For example, suppose one of your teachers returns your test with a grade of 95 on it. As you look through the test, you realize your teacher made an addition mistake and your real score is 85. Do you tell your teacher? Or suppose the cashier at the bookstore gives you $25 in change when you were supposed to get only $15. Do you return the extra $10? Personal ethical principles are important in the self-regulation of broadcasting and cable because many decision makers rely on them in situations that are not covered by codes or standards and practices. And because the many crucial ethical decisions of broadcasters and cablecasters are open to public inspection and criticism, ethical behavior is critical to those working in radio and TV. This section takes a brief look at the formal study of ethics and then examines how ethics might apply in the day-to-day world of TV and radio.

The Greek word *ethos* originally meant an abode or an accustomed dwelling place, a place where we would feel comfortable. In like manner, the study of ethics can be thought of as helping us make decisions with which we are comfortable. In formal terms, ethics addresses the question, Which human actions are morally permissible and which are not? Or in more familiar terms, What is the right thing to do?

Ethics and law are related; both limit human activities. Laws, however, are enforced by sanctions and penalties, whereas ethics are enforced by our moral sense of the proper thing. In many cases the law and ethics overlap—the legally correct action is also the morally correct action. In other cases a decision that's perfectly legal may not be the best decision from an ethical standpoint.

Perhaps a brief and basic tour of the philosophical groundwork that underlies ethics might help.

Ethical Theories

Without getting too bogged down in the technical language of the philosophy of ethics, we first need to define two key concepts: teleological theories and deontological theories. A **teleological** (from the Greek *teleos,* an end or a result) **theory** of ethics is one that measures the rightness or wrongness of an action in terms of its consequences. To say that it is unethical for a TV station to show a violent film in prime time when a lot of children are watching because some of them might imitate the film and hurt other people is a

teleological judgment. A policy that forbids reporters from accepting gifts and consideration from the people they cover because it would hurt their journalistic credibility is another teleological judgment.

A **deontological** (from the Greek *deon,* duty) **theory** does not concern itself with consequences; instead it spells out those duties that are morally required of all of us. The source of these moral obligations can come from reason, society, the supernatural, or the human conscience. For example, a policy that forbids investigative TV journalists from assuming a false identity while researching a story because such actions constitute lying, an action forbidden by one of the Ten Commandments, is based on supernatural deontological grounds. Note that it doesn't matter if the consequences of the lying are beneficial to society. A lie is prohibited because it is counter to God's will as expressed in the commandments.

With that as a background, let's examine some specific ethical principles and see how they might relate to broadcasting and cable.

Utilitarianism Probably the most popular and clearest ethical principle is a teleological theory, utilitarianism. **Utilitarianism** holds that a person should act in a way that produces the greatest possible ratio of good over evil. In other words, one should make the decision the consequences of which will yield the greatest good for the greatest number (or the least harm for the fewest number). Under this principle the ethical person is one who adds to the goodness and reduces the evil of human life.

A broadcaster who chose to follow utilitarianism as an ethical standard would first have to calculate the probable consequences that would result from each possible course of action (this is not easy; sometimes it's impossible to predict all the consequences of a given decision). Second, the broadcaster would have to assign a positive or negative value to each probable consequence and then choose the alternative that maximizes benefit and minimizes harm.

To illustrate, suppose the sales manager asks the news director (let's assume that's you) at a given station to kill a story about health code violations at a local restaurant. The restaurant is one of the biggest advertisers on your station and has threatened to cancel if you run the story. From the utilitarian perspective you first define your possible actions: (1) run the story, (2) kill the story, and (3) run an edited version of the story without naming the restaurant involved. The consequences of killing the story are easy to predict. Your station continues to get money and stays in business, thus keeping everyone on your staff employed. It might also help the restaurant stay in business because consumers who are health conscious might have stayed away had the story been aired. On the other hand, failing to run the story or running it minus the name of the offending restaurant might have significant negative effects. First, it might hurt the credibility of your news operation, particularly if other local media identify the restaurant. In the long run this might cause people to stop watching your newscast and hurt your revenues. Second, the morale in your news department might be negatively affected. Third, unwary consumers who eat at the restaurant might have their health jeopardized by the unsanitary conditions. Carrying the full story would help credibil-

ity, improve station morale, and warn unsuspecting members of the general public. In short, our cursory utilitarian analysis suggests that it would be better to carry the story.

Egoism Another teleological theory is known as **egoism.** Its basic premise is simple: Act in the way that is best for you. Any action is judged to be right or wrong in terms of its consequences for one's self. If decision A is more in your self-interest than decision B, then decision A is right.

Egoism was popularized by writer-philosopher Ayn Rand, who argued that a person should not sacrifice self to others. Rather, a person should have the highest regard and owe the greatest obligation to his or her own self. (Rand's book *The Fountainhead* is a forceful interpretation of this view. Incidentally, a movie of the same name, starring Gary Cooper, was based on this book, making it probably the only motion picture ever to be based on a formal ethical theory.)

Egoism sounds like an intellectual rationalization for doing whatever you please. But it goes deeper than that. Egoism doesn't preclude kindness or thoughtfulness toward others. In fact, it requires the individual to make a thoughtful and rational analysis of each choice to determine what exactly is best for the individual. Doing what is best for you frequently also entails doing what is best for others. In any case, egoism is an interesting example of an individualistic ethic that many have criticized as being paradoxical and inconsistent.

In our restaurant example, the news director goes through the same analysis as discussed earlier, but now he or she is not concerned about the consequences for the station, the restaurant, the public, or the news staff. The news director is interested only in what will be best for himself or herself. In this case the news director might well conclude that killing the story would harm his or her reputation as an aggressive, probing journalist and thus would run the story because, in the long run, the action would be beneficial to a news director's career.

Categorical Imperative   Probably the most famous deontological theory was developed by Immanuel Kant. Our proper duty, not the consequences of our actions, must govern our decisions. Kant argued that our proper course of action must be arrived at through reason and an examination of conscience. How do we recognize our proper duty? By subjecting it to the **categorical imperative:** Act only on those principles that you would want to become universal law. This philosophy is close to the famous golden rule in Western cultures. An ethical person should perform only those behaviors that he or she would like all to perform. What is right for one is right for all. In this context, "categorical" means without exception. What's right is right and that's the end of it.

Someone following the categorical imperative might handle the restaurant news story in this manner: Since holding back important information is not something that I would want everybody to do, the story must run. In this instance there is a categorical imperative against squelching the publication of important information. Therefore, it should not be done in this or other situations.

The Golden Mean   Another deontological theory stems from the writings of Aristotle. A natural scientist,

Aristotle grounded his theory of ethics in natural law. He noted that too much or too little of something was harmful. A plant would wither if given too little water but would drown if given too much. The proper course of action is somewhere between these two extremes. Moderation, temperance, equilibrium, and harmony are concepts that are important in his philosophy.

When faced with an ethical dilemma, a person using this theory begins by identifying the extremes and then searches to find some balance point or mean that lies between them—the **golden mean.** This may be easy or hard to do, depending on the situation. In the restaurant example one extreme would be to publish everything; the other, to publish nothing. Perhaps a compromise position between the two would be to air the story completely but also to provide time for the restaurant owner to reply to the charges. Perhaps the story might note that these are the first violations in the restaurant's history or include other tempering remarks.

Cultural Ethics   **Cultural ethics theory,** which is grounded in society as opposed to nature, holds that an individual is shaped by his or her culture. Our moral judgments are shaped by those we experienced when growing up and when entering other socializing environments such as school or work. Cultural ethics suggests that the individual accepts the discipline of society, adjusts to its needs and customs, and finds ethical security within it. There are no universals by which each culture is judged; each is self-legislative, determining its own rules of right and wrong. Moreover, many different subcultures within society may be relevant. An ethical problem encountered on the job might be assessed in the context of the workplace with all of its relevant norms.

In the broadcasting area, the practical application of this theory suggests that a station or cable system owner consult the norms of other media or of other businesses or of the general community before making an ethical decision. In the restaurant example the station involved might see how other stations are treating the story or have treated such stories in the past. Similarly, the way that other media, such as newspapers, handle the situation should be noted. Or the station might consult the managers of other stations throughout the area to get advice about the proper course to follow.

Situational Ethics   The theory of situational ethics also examines ethics in relative terms. Unlike cultural ethics, however, **situational ethics,** or *situationism,* argues that the traditions and norms of society provide inadequate guidance because each individual problem or situation is unique and calls for a creative solution. Decisions regarding how we ought to act must be grounded in the concrete details that make up each circumstance. Universal ethical principles like the categorical imperative might provide some guidance, but they are merely hints as to the correct course; they do not apply in every situation. A general principle that we endorse, such as "TV newscasters should always tell the truth," can be violated if the situation calls for it (such as broadcasting a false story to gain the release of hostages).

Of course, the way we see and analyze situations varies from person to person. No two individuals will define the same situation in exactly the same terms. How we perceive things depends on our moral upbringing and our ethical values. Consequently, different answers are possible depending on how one assesses the situation.

In our restaurant example the entire situation must be examined before making a decision. Was the board of health on a vendetta against this particular restaurant? Has the restaurant recently changed

Immanuel Kant (1724–1804) was a German philosopher who published works that examined ethics, law, religion, and history.

management? How much money will actually be lost if the restaurant cancels its advertising? Could this revenue be replaced from another source? Have all the violations been corrected? These are some aspects of the situation that might be considered before a decision is made. From a situationist point of view there is no single "correct" answer to this problem.

"Doing" Ethics

A knowledge of ethical principles is useful for all those entering the radio and TV profession. First, it is important to have some predefined standard in place when a quick and difficult ethical call is required. Second, a personal code of ethics assures an individual of some measure of consistency from one decision to the next. Third, media professionals are often asked to explain or defend their decisions to the public. A knowledge of ethical principles and the techniques of moral reasoning can give those explanations more credibility and validity. Fourth, and most pragmatically, good ethics and good business generally go hand in hand, at least in the long run.

How can a person develop a set of ethical standards that will be relevant and useful in day-to-day situations? If you have read this far, you already have gotten a head start. The first step is to become familiar with enduring ethical principles, such as those just enumerated, or others that may be germane to your profession. For example, if the classical ethical theories do not seem helpful, you might want to consider the set of ethical principles proposed by Edmund Lambeth in *Committed Journalism*. Although designed for working journalists, his principles have relevance for everyone employed in broadcasting and cable. Lambeth suggests that an individual's decisions should adhere to the following principles:

1. Tell the truth.
2. Behave justly.
3. Respect independence and freedom.
4. Act humanely.
5. Behave responsibly.

Another model for journalists endorsed by many in the profession has seven principles or moral duties:

1. Don't cause harm.
2. Keep all promises.
3. Make up for previous wrongful acts.
4. Act in a just manner.

5. Improve your own virtue.

6. Be good to people who have been good to you.

7. Try to make the world better.

It matters little whether you subscribe to Aristotle's golden mean or principles suggested by Lambeth; the point is that you need to develop some underlying set of ethical principles.

Next you need to develop a model or plan of action that serves as a guide in making ethical choices. When a person is confronted with an ethical dilemma, the model serves as a blueprint for thinking. One possible model might be the following:

> *Stage one.* Determine the situation. Compile all the facts and information that are relevant to the situation. Learn all you can about the circumstances that prompted the problems.
>
> *Stage two.* Examine and clarify all the possible alternatives. Make sure you are aware of all your loyalties and possible courses of action. (If you subscribe to a teleological theory of ethics, you may also have to assess the possible consequences of each action.)
>
> *Stage three.* Determine what ethical theories or principles you will follow in the situation. Try over time to develop some consistency in the choice of theories or principles.
>
> *Stage four.* Decide and act accordingly.

Ethics in the Real World

We have now seen some theories and models promulgated by philosophers who have the luxury of time to reflect on their various ramifications. In the real world of TV and radio, however, rarely do professionals have the time to reflect on their decisions. For example, in New York City a convict with a gun threatened to kill hostages if his demands weren't broadcast immediately by a local TV station. The police on the scene urged the station manager to grant this request. The station involved in this dilemma had about two minutes to decide what to do. That's probably not enough time to do a thorough utilitarian or Kantian analysis of the situation. (In real life the TV station agreed to the request, and bloodshed was averted. Subsequently, however, the station was criticized by local newspapers for giving a forum to a gunman.)

Moreover, many broadcasters and cablecasters enter their profession without a personal code of ethics. Many current media executives were trained in selling, programming, or news but had to pick up informally along the way whatever ethical standards they have. In fact, many executives would probably be hard-pressed to articulate exactly where and how they developed their ethical standards.

Third, although some broadcast and cable organizations have codes of conduct or good practice, they are generally written in broad, general terms and may have little relevance to the individual. Companies rarely conduct education and training sessions in ethics. A new employee who expects the company to provide him or her with a ready-made set of ethics will probably be disappointed.

Finally, recent experience suggests that many ethical problems exist at the corporate level as well as at the individual level. The view that the only responsibility of business is to make a profit has come under attack by those who argue that because corporations have such a significant impact on the environment, their surrounding communities, and the individual consumer, they have an ethical obligation to serve the needs of the larger society. This suggests that employees of broadcasting and cable companies will face ethical decisions throughout their careers. New employees will probably have to make choices about their own personal behaviors, while veterans who have risen to the managerial level will be making decisions regarding proper corporate policy. Personal codes of ethics must also accommodate the corporate situation.

In sum, a theoretical knowledge of ethical principles and analysis is helpful, but it must be tempered by an awareness of the nature of the day-to-day pressures in TV and radio.

Ethics: A Final Word

Many texts on media ethics present case studies that raise ethical problems for discussion. Students spend much time debating alternatives and find that there may be little agreement on the proper choice. Different ethical principles do indeed suggest different courses of action. Many students become frustrated by this and look on ethics as simply a set of mental games that can be used to rationalize almost any decision. This frustration is understandable. It helps, however, to point out that ethical problems are not like algebra problems. There is no one answer that all will come up with. Ethical theories are not like a computer; they do not print out correct answers with mechanical precision. Abstract ethical rules cannot anticipate all possible situations. They necessarily leave room for personal judgment.

Ethical decision making is more an art than a science. The ethical principles and models presented here represent different perspectives from which ethical problems can be viewed. They encourage careful analysis and thoughtful, systematic reflection before making a choice. A system of ethics must be flexible, and it ought to do more than merely rationalize the personal preferences of the person making the choice. As Edmund Lambeth says in *Committed Journalism*, an ethical system "must have bite and give direction." In sum, this brief discussion of ethics is not intended to give everybody the answers. It was designed to present some enduring principles, to encourage a reasoned approach to ethical problems, and to foster a basic concern for ethical issues, recognizing all the while that many ethical decisions have to be made in an uncertain world amid unclear circumstances and with imperfect knowledge.

SUMMARY

- Personal ethics have become an increasingly important issue for broadcasters as the competitive atmosphere, fostered by deregulation, heightens. Station managers now must be accountable for regulating themselves. Codes, departments, professional groups and organizations, and citizens' groups all help promote responsibility.

- The acceptability of a message depends on the size of a market, the time period, the station's audience, and the type of content involved.

- Ethics and law share common threads. Both are restrictive measures. The difference lies in the fact that one is enforced by the state, whereas the other is enforced by personal judgment.

- There are numerous ethical theories that attempt to explain how a person determines right from wrong. Some major theories are utilitarianism, egoism, the categorical imperative, the golden mean, cultural ethics, and situational ethics.

KEY TERMS

self-regulation   265
V-chip   269
National Association of
   Broadcasters (NAB)   269
National Cable Television
   Association
   (NCTA)   269

National Advertising Division
   (NAD)   270
National Advertising Review Board
   (NARB)   270
Children's Television Act
   of 1990   271
teleological theory   272

deontological theory   272
utilitarianism   272
egoism   273
categorical imperative   274
golden mean   274
cultural ethics theory   274
situational ethics   275

SUGGESTIONS FOR FURTHER READING

Christians, C., Rotzoll, K., Fackler, M., & McKee, K., Kreshel, P., & Woods, R. (2008). *Media ethics* (8th ed.). Boston, MA: Allyn & Bacon.

Day, L. 2005. *Ethics in media communications.* Belmont, CA: Wadsworth.

Ess, C. (2009). *Digital media ethics.* Cambridge, UK: Polity Press.

Gordon, D., Kihross, J., Merill, J. G., & Reuss, C. (1998). *Controversies in media ethics.* New York: Addison-Wesley.

Hausman, C. (1992). *Crisis of confidence.* New York: HarperCollins.

Lambeth, E. (1992). *Committed journalism.* Bloomington: Indiana University Press.

Merrill, J., & Odell, S. (1983). *Philosophy and journalism.* New York: Longman.

Meyer, P. (1987). *Ethical journalism.* New York: Longman.

Plaisance, P. (2009). *Media ethics: Key principles for responsible practice.* Thousand Oaks, CA: Sage.

Wilkins, L., & Christians, C. (2009). *The handbook of mass media ethics.* New York: Routledge.

INTERNET EXERCISES

Visit our Web site at **www.mhhe.com/dominickbib7e** for study-guide exercises to help you learn and apply material in each chapter. You will find ideas for future research as well as useful Web links to provide you with an opportunity to journey through the new electronic media.

Part Five   What It Does

Ratings and Audience Feedback   12

Quick Facts

Year of first national radio audience survey: 1927

Number of U.S. households with TV: about 116 million

Number of households in New York City, the largest TV local market: 7.5 million

Number of households in Glendive, Montana, the smallest TV local market: 3,940

Household rating of number one show (*I Love Lucy*) in 1956: 47.5

Household rating of number one show (*American Idol*) in 2010: 16.4

Video on demand, DVRs, Internet video, Internet radio, iPhones, iPods, and iPads have made it difficult to measure how many people are listening to or watching a certain program. Nonetheless, advertisers spend billions every year to purchase time on radio and television for their commercial messages. Not surprisingly, they like to know if their money is well spent. For this to happen, they need information about how many and what kinds of people watch and listen. Enter the ratings.

This chapter discusses how to measure and evaluate what people are listening to or watching. The first part examines how ratings and ratings companies developed in the United States. The next sections will look at how data are collected, analyzed, and reported. The final section explores how additional feedback from the audience is gathered.

HISTORY OF AUDIENCE MEASUREMENT

Audience research first appeared in the 1920s when station owners became curious about the size of their listening audience. Early announcers requested listeners to drop a postcard to the station reporting that they had heard a particular program and indicating whether the signal was clear. The need for more detailed data became important when advertisers, particularly those who bought time on network radio, demanded accurate estimates of audience size. Consequently, the American Association of Advertising Agencies and the Association of National Advertisers formed the **Cooperative Analysis of Broadcasting (CAB)** in 1930.

The CAB collected data on network listening in 35 cities across the United States using the **telephone recall method.** Calls were placed at different times during the day to homes selected at random from phone directories, and respondents were asked to recall the programs they had listened to.

One problem with the credibility of the CAB ratings was in fact this use of the recall method. Although asking a person to remember what he or she had heard in the last few hours is more accurate than asking the person about listening on a previous night, human memory is still open to failure.

The CAB operated until 1946, when it fell victim to another organization with a superior way of measuring the audience. The C. E. Hooper company introduced the **telephone coincidental method,** in which respondents were asked if they were listening to the radio at the time of the call, and, if the answer was

yes, they were asked to name the program or the station to which they were listening. The coincidental method is an improvement over the recall method because it does not rely on the fallible memory of the respondent. The results of the Hooper surveys, called Hooperatings, were sold to advertisers, advertising agencies, and broadcasters.

In 1942 the A. C. Nielsen Company (now the Nielsen Company) started a ratings service that used a different method, one that did not rely on the telephone, to collect data about radio listening. Nielsen connected a mechanical device, called the **audimeter,** to the radios of a randomly selected sample of people. The audimeter consisted of a sharp stylus that made a scratch on a roll of paper tape (later replaced by 16-millimeter film) in synchronization with the radio's tuning dial. After a period of time, listeners sent back the tape or film to Nielsen, where the scratches were analyzed to reveal how long the set was on and to what station it was tuned.

Note that, whereas previous companies measured actual listening, Nielsen measured set use. The audimeter could determine only if the radio was turned on and to what station it was tuned. It could not determine who, if anyone, was listening. Nonetheless, advertisers preferred the Nielsen numbers, and in 1950 Nielsen bought out Hooperatings.

The audimeter moved to TV in the 1950s. A device was attached to every TV set in the home and families were instructed to open up the audimeter at the end of a week's viewing and send the film back to Nielsen for analysis. A Nielsen family received 50 cents per week for their cooperation. Data from the audimeters formed the basis for two Nielsen reports: the **Nielsen Television Index (NTI),** which reported the viewership of network programs, and the **Nielsen Station Index (NSI),** which did the same for local television markets.

Nielsen got a competitor in local TV ratings in 1949 when the American Research Bureau (later called Arbitron) began collecting ratings data. One of the problems with the Nielsen ratings was the lack of demographic data; the audimeter simply measured when the set was on and what channel it was tuned in to—it did not provide information about who, if anybody, was watching or listening. The Arbitron company solved this problem by using yet another data gathering technique—the **diary.** A sample of viewers was asked to record viewing in a specially prepared diary and to mail the finished diary back to Arbitron. In response, Nielsen introduced the diary as a supplement to its audimeters in 1955. Not to be outdone, Arbitron emulated Nielsen and introduced its own version of the audimeter in the 1960s.

Citing increased costs, Nielsen abandoned its radio ratings service in 1963 to concentrate on television. Shortly thereafter, Arbitron announced it would use its diary method to measure local market radio. From the mid-1960s to the 1980s, Nielsen alone provided network TV ratings and competed with Arbitron for local TV market ratings. Arbitron was the dominant company in radio ratings.

The mechanical measurement devices continued to be improved. Nielsen introduced the **storage instantaneous audimeter (SIA)** in several local markets during the 1960s and 1970s. This device sent information directly from the audimeter through phone lines to Nielsen's computers. The SIA made it possible to publish ratings the day after a program was broadcast.

Yet another mechanical device for measuring the audience was introduced in the late 1980s—the **People Meter.** Developed by an English company, AGB Television Research, in an attempt to compete with Nielsen, the People Meter was connected to the TV set and automatically recorded the channel and time. But it also had a new feature—a device that resembled a remote control with a numbered keypad. Each family member was assigned a unique code number. When he or she started watching TV, the family member was supposed to punch in his or her number on the keypad and then punch it again when he or she stopped watching. This information was stored in the People Meter and then transmitted via phone lines to central computers that had detailed demographic information about each family member obtained through a personal interview when the meter was installed. Thus the People Meter could determine exactly who was in the audience. Nielsen quickly introduced its own version of the People Meter for use with its national NTI report. AGB was unable to secure enough clients for its new service and ceased operation in 1988.

People Meters have several advantages over diaries. First, they aren't affected by memory. Many people forget to fill out their diaries. Second, the data are sent electronically to Nielsen, eliminating the problem of people who don't mail back their diaries. Moreover, unlike SIAs, which measure only set usage, the People Meters report data about who is watching.

On the downside, People Meters are relatively expensive to install and maintain. This means that changing homes in the sample is difficult. Second,

children's viewing is hard to measure with the People Meter. When the switch from SIAs to People Meters took place, a 22 percent drop in children's viewing was reported. Children aged 2 to 11 are apparently inconsistent in logging in with the People Meter and get bored with punching the buttons as they watch TV. Finally, like the SIAs, People Meters measure only at-home viewing. TV watching at work, in a bar, or in a college dormitory is not accounted for with the People Meter.

Arbitron, Nielsen's chief rival in providing local market TV ratings, also introduced its own version of the People Meter. The recession of the early 1990s, however, forced many local TV stations, which had previously subscribed to both Nielsen and Arbitron, to cancel one of their contracts in order to save money. The one they canceled was usually Arbitron, and in 1993 the company announced it was abandoning television ratings to concentrate on radio. At the end of the first decade of the new century, Arbitron announced plans to use its PPM system to measure out-of-home TV viewing in the top 50 markets.

The **Portable People Meter (PPM)** was developed in the mid-2000s. PPMs can measure both in-home and out-of-home listening and viewing. The device is about the size of a cell phone and picks up an inaudible tone encoded in the audio signal of radio and TV programs. Individuals clip the PPM to an article of clothing or purse, and the device records the program the person is listening to. At the end of the day, the audience member places the PPM in a special base that recharges the device and sends the collected data back to the ratings company for tabulation.

At the end of the first decade of the new century, competition in the ratings industry was increasing. Nielsen reentered the radio ratings business, using the diary method to measure listening in more than 50 small to midsized U.S. markets. Arbitron announced plans to use its PPM system to measure out-of-home TV viewing in the top 50 markets.

Advertisers were demanding more precise measurement of not only the size of the audience but also the impact of their media investments. Marketers were becoming increasingly dissatisfied with traditional viewing data and were searching for "engagement" measures that show how likely the consumer was to respond to an ad placed within a TV program or online.

Finally, CBS, NBC, and several other media companies set up the Coalition for Innovative Audience Measurement in 2009 to explore methods of gauging traditional TV viewing and online and mobile phone viewing. Moreover, the Nielsen Company announced plans to measure online TV viewing using its national People Meter sample.

In sum, the future of measuring the electronic media will be filled with challenges. It is likely that no single system of data collection will be adequate. There will probably be combinations of high-tech approaches including People Meters, Portable People Meters, Web diaries, SIAs, and even the low-tech paper diary.

THE RATINGS PROCESS

Measuring TV Viewing

Nielsen Media Research draws two different types of samples to measure TV viewing. The national sample used for the NTI is designed to be representative of the entire U.S. population. To draw this sample, Neilsen first selects at random more than 6,000 small geographic areas, usually blocks in urban areas or their equivalent in rural areas, and lists all households in these areas. Next a sample of about 12,000 households (scheduled to increase to 37,000 by 2011) is drawn at random. Each household is then contacted, and, if it agrees to participate in the survey, a Nielsen representative installs a People Meter and trains household members how to use it.

For the local market NSI reports, Nielsen first divides the country into more than 200 markets. Within each market, a sample is drawn from phone books and supplemented by random digit dialing in order to obtain unlisted numbers. Sample sizes vary by market but are usually in the range of 1,000 to 2,000 households.

Nielsen measures local station TV viewing using different techniques depending on market size. In the top 25 markets Nielsen uses the **Local People Meter (LPM),** the same device used with the national ratings but with a local sample. When first introduced, the LPM results were controversial because they were often at odds with data gathered by the older diary method. In response, Nielsen changed its sampling and recruiting procedures. Plans call for the top 50 markets to be measured by LPMs by the end of 2011. In small to midsized markets, SIAs are attached to each TV in the household, and data are gathered about "set tuning behavior." This information is supplemented by diaries that are sent to participating households. In some small mar-

kets, measurement is done by diary only. In the long run, Nielsen plans to eliminate paper diaries. The company will rely on LPMs in the larger markets while the remaining markets are measured by SIAs and/or Internet diaries.

Four times a year (February, May, July, and November) information is collected from all TV markets in the United States. These periods are called "sweeps," and the local stations use the results to set their advertising rates. Sweeps are less important than they once were now that LPMs gather audience data continuously and stations no longer have to wait weeks for results.

In 2005 Nielsen began measuring DVR usage. The company now provides three measures of program viewing. The first is live viewing, the traditional way viewing has been measured. The second is live plus same-day DVR viewing (this number is the one most often reported in rankings of most-watched programs); while the third is live plus seven days of DVR viewing. Two years later Nielsen started to measure viewership of the commercial breaks within the program. The **C3 rating** is the rating of the average commercial minute including live viewing and DVR playback with three days. Advertisers buy time based on the C3 ratings. Finally, Nielsen is stepping up its plans to measure online TV viewing.

Processing the Data

Data from the People Meter and the SIA samples are stored in the home devices until they are automatically retrieved by Nielsen's computers. In addition, program schedules and local system cable information are also checked to make sure the viewing data match up with the correct programs. All of this information is processed overnight and made available for customer access the next day. Diary information takes longer to process. The diaries are first mailed back to Nielsen where they are checked for legibility and consistency. The data are then entered into Nielsen computers and tabulated. It usually takes several weeks before these reports are available.

Reporting the Ratings

In the past, printed copies of the ratings (called "ratings books") were delivered to subscribers. Hard copies of ratings books are no longer published; all

Events: TV Watching and the Three Screens

Americans now have the ability to watch TV on three screens: the traditional TV set, the computer, and the mobile phone. How much viewing do they do on each? The Nielsen Company publishes a quarterly summary titled *Three Screen Report: Television, Internet and Mobile Usage in the U.S.* that contains some revealing data. Here are some findings from its first-quarter 2010 report.

The vast majority of television viewing is still done on the home TV. Overall, Americans watch an average of about 35½ hours of TV per week on traditional TV sets and about another 2 hours per week watching shows recorded on their DVRs. They spend only 20 minutes a week watching video on the Internet and just 4 minutes a week watching video on a mobile phone.

When it comes to traditional TV watching, those aged 65 and above watch most, about 49 hours a week, while teens watch least, about 24 hours per week. In contrast, teens watch the most video on a mobile phone, about 18 minutes a week, whereas those over 65 watch mobile video hardly at all. Teens, however, are not the heaviest viewers of Internet video. Watching Web video is most prevalent among 25- to 34-year-olds, with 35- to 49-year-olds narrowly behind.

Of course much of the difference in viewing times is due to the fact that traditional TV is more available than the newer technologies. As of 2010, more than 98 percent of U.S. households had a TV, and more than half of those had a high-definition set. By comparison, only 63 percent of households had a high-speed broadband hookup, 36 percent had a DVR, and just 22 percent had a smart phone. The time-spent-viewing numbers are likely to change as new technologies become more widespread.

of the information is available online. The NTI contains data on the estimated audience—divided into relevant demographic categories—for each network program broadcast during the measurement period. The report also features a day-by-day comparison of the audience for each of the major networks as well as an estimate of audience watching cable channels, independent broadcast stations, public TV, and premium channels. Nielsen also reports same-day DVR playback.

The NSI is a little more complicated. Each local market ratings report contains a map that divides the market into three areas: (1) the metro area, where most of the population in the market lives; (2) the designated market area (DMA), where the stations in that market get most of their viewers; and (3) the NSI, or total survey area—at portion of the market that surrounds the DMA and accounts for 95 percent of the total viewing audience in that market. NSI areas may overlap, but DMAs do not.

The next section of the NSI contains special information, including the number of homes actually in the sample and demographic characteristics of the market. There are also notes about technical problems the stations may have had during the ratings period, such as being knocked off the air by a thunderstorm or power failure.

Audience estimates appear next. These numbers are broken down by time periods and by programs. Thus a station manager can see how a specific program is doing against its competition and how well it maintains the audience from the program that preceded it.

Nielsen also prepares several specialized reports: The Nielsen Syndication Service reports viewing levels of syndicated programs; and the Nielsen Sports Marketing Service tracks the viewing of particular sports teams. Nielsen also offers a special service that measures the Hispanic television audience.

Terms and Concepts in TV Ratings

There are three important terms in TV ratings. **Households using television (HUT)** represents the number or the percentage of households that have a TV set on during a specific time period.

The second term is **rating.** Specifically, a rating is the percentage or proportion of all households with a TV set watching a particular program at a particular time. A rating of 10 means that 10 percent of all the homes in the market were watching a specific program. Ratings consider all households in the market, not just those with TV sets in use.

The third term is *share of the audience* or **share.** The share is the total number of households watching a particular program at a specific time divided by the total number of households using TV. Thus the share is based only on those households that actually have their TV sets turned on.

Some programs can have the same share but have different ratings. For example, let's pretend there are 1,000 households in our market. At 6 a.m., 100 of those 1,000 households have their TV sets on. Of those 100 households, 20 are watching *The Sunrise Home Shopping Show.* The rating for this program would be 20 divided by 1,000, or 2 percent. The share would be 20 divided by 100, or 20 percent. Later that night, let's say at 9 p.m., 600 households are watch-ing TV, and of those 600, 120 are watching *Glee.* The rating for *Glee* would be 120 divided by 1,000, or 12 percent. The show's share of the audience would be 120 divided by 600, or 20 percent, exactly the same as that of *The Sunrise Home Shopping Show.*

Here are the formulas for calculating ratings and shares:

$$\text{Ratings} = \frac{\text{Number of households watching a program}}{\text{Total number of households in market}}$$

$$\text{Share} = \frac{\text{Number of households watching a program}}{\text{Total number of HUT}}$$

For another calculation example, see the box "Calculating Ratings and Shares."

Measuring Radio Listening

Arbitron is the leading company that provides ratings of local radio stations and network radio listening. Arbitron uses the diary and the Portable People Meter, and many of its procedures are similar to those used by Nielsen Media Research to measure TV viewing.

Arbitron draws its sample by randomly sampling phone numbers from a list compiled by a market research company. Numbers are also randomly generated to account for unlisted phones and cell-phone-only homes. The number of households drawn for the sample varies based on a statistical formula that takes into account the total number of households in the market. Sample sizes may range from 750 to 4,500 for local market surveys, with medium-sized markets having a sample size of about 1,000 diaries.

Those households that are selected by Arbitron for their diary sample are called and asked if they would like to participate in the survey. Arbitron mails a brightly colored package to each household that agrees. Inside the package are envelopes (for each member of the household over 11 years of age) that contain a diary, instructions, a letter of thanks, and a small monetary incentive.

Diaries cover a one-week period beginning on a Wednesday. There is one page per day with a column for indicating when a person started listening to a station and when the person stopped. Another column asks the person to write down the frequency or call letters of the station while another records where the listening took place (in a car, at the office, at home, etc.).

Some simple demographic questions are included at the end of the diary. When the diary is completed, the respondent mails it back to Arbitron, where the next phase begins.

Starting in 2011, Arbitron will measure the top 50 markets using its Portable People Meter system (PPM). As mentioned previously, the PPM collects listening data by detecting an inaudible signal embedded in the transmission of a radio station. Those agreeing to participate in Arbitron's PPM sample provide basic demographic data to Arbitron. Participants are asked to keep the PPM with them throughout the day. The device contains a motion sensor that allows Arbitron to check whether the participants actually carried the meter with them. Participants are instructed to return the PPMs to their base stations at night, where the devices are recharged and their data uploaded to Arbitron's computers.

Processing the Data

Once received by Arbitron, the diaries are subject to several review procedures. The first review removes diaries that Arbitron considers unusable: those that come in late, those that are illegible, those missing demographic information, and so forth. Other reviews look for inconsistent information (e.g., reporting listening to a station that doesn't exist) and other minor errors (e.g., transposing the call letters of a station). The data are then entered into the computer for analysis.

Data from PPMs, of course, are analyzed more quickly, and reports for all stations can be ready in weeks rather than the months it takes to produce a report from diaries.

The Radio Ratings Report

A local market radio ratings report is similar in format to its TV counterpart. The first section contains a map that divides the market into metro, DMA, and total survey areas, much like the NSI. This is followed by general market statistics—number of automobiles, housing values, retail sales data, and the like. Another section reports whether any radio stations conducted unusual promotions designed to artificially increase their audiences during the ratings period. The next section of the book presents demographic data about listeners categorized by dayparts. A station, for example, can easily find its rating among men aged 12 to 24 during the Monday to Friday 6 to 10 a.m. daypart. Other sections of the book summarize total time spent listening to the station, where the listening occurred, and the average audience size per station by quarter-hour estimates.

Arbitron issues its Radio Market Reports for more than 290 local markets. Ratings reports are issued monthly for larger markets. Smaller market reports are issued less frequently.

Arbitron also provides a service called RADAR that measures network radio listening. Network ratings are computed from a nationwide sample of 50,000 radio listening diaries.

Terms and Concepts in Radio Ratings

The basic unit of measurement is different for radio and television ratings. The basic unit for most television ratings is the household. For radio, the basic unit is the person. The formulas for ratings and

Events: Calculating Ratings and Shares

Let's use the following hypothetical data in our calculations. A ratings company samples 24,000 households (all having TVs) in a given market and determines the following for the 7:30 to 7:45 p.m. time period.

Station	Number of Sample Households Watching
WAAA	4,800
WBBB	2,400
WCCC	1,200
Other stations	1,200
	9,600 = HUT

Let's figure out WBBB's rating:

$$\text{WBBB's rating} = \frac{2,400}{24,000} = .10, \text{ or } 10\%$$

To calculate WBBB's share of the audience, we must first determine the total number of households using TV (HUT) during the 7:30 to 7:45 p.m. time period. To do this, we add $4,800 + 2,400 + 1,200 + 1,200 = 9,600$. WBBB's share, then, is

$$\text{Share} = \frac{2,400}{9,600} = .25, \text{ or } 25\%$$

Also note the following relationships:

(1) $\% \text{ HUT} = \dfrac{\text{Rating}}{\text{Share}}$

In our example

$$\% \text{ HUT} = \frac{.10}{.25} = .40, \text{ or } 40\%$$

This means that 40 percent of all the TV homes in the sample were watching TV from 7:30 to 7:45 p.m.

(2) Rating = Share $\times$ % HUT

In our example

Rating = $.25 \times .40 = .10$

This is simply another way to calculate the rating.

(3) Share = $\dfrac{\text{Rating}}{\% \text{ HUT}}$

In our example

$$\text{Share} = \frac{.10}{.40} = .25, \text{ or } 25\%$$

This is another way to calculate the share.

shares for radio listening reflect this difference. Specifically, in radio

$$\text{Ratings} = \frac{\text{Number of persons listening to a station}}{\text{Total number of persons in market}}$$

and

$$\text{Share} = \frac{\text{Number of persons listening to a station}}{\text{Total number of persons using radio}}$$

Two other ratings terms are more commonly associated with radio ratings. The cumulative audience (or **cume**) is an estimate of the total number of different listeners who listen to a given station at least once during the time part under consideration. In other words, cume is a measure of how many different people listen at least once during the week during the given daypart.

Average quarter-hour persons estimates the average number of persons who are listening to a station within a 15-minute period. It is calculated by dividing the estimated number of listeners in a given time period by the number of quarter hours (four per hour) in that time period.

ACCURACY OF THE RATINGS

There are more than 116 million television households in the United States. The Nielsen People Meter sample size is around 10,000, about .00009 of the total. Is it possible for a sample this small to mirror accurately the viewing behaviors of the entire population? The answer to this question is yes, within limits. A sample doesn't have to be large to represent the whole population, as long as it is *representative* of the whole population. To illustrate, when you go to the doctor for a blood test, the doctor does not draw a couple of quarts of blood from your body. A blood test uses only a few milliliters. From this small sample, the doctor can estimate your red cell count, your cholesterol, your hematocrit, and a number of other variables.

Imagine a huge container filled with thousands of coins—pennies, nickels, dimes, and quarters. Let's suppose that 50 percent of the coins are pennies but that this fact is unknown to you. The only way you could be absolutely *sure* what percentage of the coins were pennies would be to count every coin in the huge container, an arduous and time-consuming job. Suppose instead you took a random sample of 100 coins. If sampling were a perfect process, you would find that pennies accounted for 50 percent of your sample. Sometimes this happens, but more often you'll wind up with a little more or a little less than 50 percent pennies. It is also possible, but exceedingly unlikely, that you could draw a sample of 100 percent pennies or another of 0 percent pennies. The bigger the size of your sample, the more likely it is that your results will tend to cluster around the 50 percent mark.

Statisticians have studied the process of sampling and have calculated the accuracy ranges of samples of various sizes. One way of expressing accuracy is to use a concept known as the 95 percent **confidence interval.** Calculated from sample data, this is an interval that has a 95 percent chance of actually including the population value. For example, let's say the Nielsen People Meter sample of 10,000 homes finds that 20 percent of households watched *American Idol.* Similar to our coin example, we probably wouldn't expect that exactly 20 percent of the 110 million TV households in the United States were also watching. By using statistical formulas, however, we can estimate the 95 percent confidence interval, which in this case, ranges roughly from 19 percent to 21 percent. This means that we are 95 percent sure that, in the entire population of 110 million homes, somewhere between 19 percent and 21 percent are watching *Idol.*

To sum up this statistical discussion, Nielsen ratings are not exact estimates. They are subject to sampling error. However, when their margin of error is taken into account, Nielsen ratings (and other ratings based on a random sample) provide rather accurate estimations of audience viewing behavior.

Incidentally, there is an organization that strives to ensure reasonable accuracy in the realm of ratings: the **Media Rating Council (MRC).** (See the box "Media Rating Council.") This council periodically audits Nielsen, Arbitron, and other ratings services to check on their methods and reports. The MRC is an independent body whose fees are paid by the ratings companies.

It should also be noted here that factors other than sampling error also have an impact on accuracy. Note that our discussion was based on the assumption that the ratings were drawn from a random sample of the population. Although both Nielsen and Arbitron go to great lengths to gather data from a truly random sample, that goal is seldom attained: When contacted, many households in the original sample may refuse to cooperate; individuals in the People Meter sample may get tired of pressing

Events: Media Rating Council

The Media Rating Council (MRC) is an organization whose task is to make sure that audience research firms present data that are credible and valid. Formed in 1964, at the urging of the U.S. Congress in the aftermath of hearings on shortcomings in the way that radio and TV stations counted their audiences, the MRC (originally called the Broadcast Ratings Council) relies on the voluntary compliance of its members. All companies that collect audience data are invited to apply for membership.

Members are obligated to provide the MRC with full information about their data collection and analysis procedures and to submit to annual audits of their methods. The MRC hires an independent auditing firm to conduct the evaluation of the member rating services. Auditors check to see if the research company meets the MRC's standards for media research and if the company actually conducts its research in the way that it claims. If the company passes the audit, it is given the MRC's seal of good practice.

In addition to its auditing activities, the MRC also supports research that attempts to improve the quality of audience research. The MRC, for example, played a key role in improving the methods connected with the introduction of the local People Meter.

buttons and stop using it; people in the sample who agree to fill out a diary may get bored after a day or so and not return it; other diaries may be filled out illegibly; and People Meters and SIAs are subject to mechanical errors. All of these factors contribute to a **nonresponse bias.** Nonresponse is a more serious concern for diary samples. In many markets, Arbitron may be able to use fewer than half of all the radio diaries it sends out.

In addition, some people may not tell the truth. During a telephone coincidental survey, one of the authors heard the audio from the TV set in the background that was tuned to a wrestling match. When asked what program he was watching, the respondent replied, "The local newscast." Individuals with SIAs might tune their sets to PBS whenever they leave the house. Diary keepers might fill in many educational programs that they did not watch. These are examples of the **social desirability bias,** or providing answers that the respondent thinks will make him or her look more refined or more educated.

Both of these factors reinforce the fact that ratings are estimates of viewing and listening behavior. They are not exact. Nonetheless, they are the best available means for the industry to determine who is watching or listening to what or which programs.

USES FOR RATINGS

Local stations and networks use ratings to see how they are doing in terms of their total audience. Typically, the bigger the audience, the more money sta-

tions and networks can charge for advertising. This is why *American Idol*, which has a weekly audience of about 20 million households, can charge about $800,000 for a 30-second commercial, while *Cops*, which has a weekly audience of about 4 million homes, charges only $45,000.

In addition, ratings can be used to determine what types of people are watching. Advertisers are interested not only in audience size but also in audience type. A show like MTV's *Jersey Shore*, for example, can charge higher rates, not because its total audience is particularly large, but because the show attracts 18- to 34-year-olds—an audience that many advertisers want to reach.

The sales staff at a station uses ratings to persuade potential advertisers that their stations attract the type of audience most likely to buy the advertiser's product. The salespeople at a radio station with a sports-talk format, for example, can show the owner of a cigar bar that an ad on their station would reach a predominantly male audience, a prime target for a cigar merchant.

The station's news department can use the ratings to see how much viewing occurs in neighboring communities. If the ratings show substantial viewing, the station might want to increase coverage of those areas to encourage continued viewing and better ratings.

These are just a few of the uses for ratings data. Keep in mind, however, that while the ratings are a handy tool, they are only one of several considerations that are used by broadcasters and cablecasters

The personal Portable People Meter comes with its own recharging stand.

to make decisions. They are helpful, but as we have seen, they are not perfect.

MEASURING THE INTERNET AUDIENCE

Having reliable data on the Internet audience is important because without such data advertisers are reluctant to spend money on Net advertising. As in broadcasting and cable, advertisers want to know who is visiting a World Wide Web site, how often they visit, how long they spend at the site, and whether the cost is reasonable. Obtaining such data, however, is difficult. Despite their limits, the Arbitron and Nielsen audience data are generally accepted as industry standards. An industry standard for Internet audience measurement is still evolving.

Early attempts to measure Web page traffic were programs that measured "hits," or the number of times someone logged on to the page. A counter at the bottom of the page kept a running total of the number of visits. These numbers were notoriously unreliable because the programs measured hits in different ways depending on the server. Moreover, there were other programs that called Web sites over and over to inflate the number of hits. Advertisers preferred an independent organization that counts the numbers.

From 1996 to 1998, several companies began to offer Internet measurement services: Media Metrix, NewRatings, RelevantKnowledge, and the Nielsen Company. By 2000, consolidation narrowed the field to two major competitors. Media Metrix merged with RelevantKnowledge and Nielsen joined forces with NetRatings to form Nielsen/NetRatings Inc. Consequently, unlike radio and television, where one ratings company provides the definitive report, two companies provide data on the Internet audience. Nielsen/NetRatings recruits a panel of participants through random-digit dialing and installs software that tracks respondents' online activity. The company provides a report called NetView that is based on a sample of 230,000 Internet users in the United States. In addition, four times a year Nielsen performs a telephone survey to project the total number of U.S. households that have Internet access.

Competing with Nielsen is comScore. ComScore also recruits its members by random phone calls and reports that it uses more than a million consumers worldwide to track Web behavior. Media Metrix, its main U.S. report, is based on a panel of 200,000 consumers who have installed special tracking software. Like Nielsen, comScore also tracks online buying and financial transactions.

Advertisers are perplexed because the two competing services sometimes provide widely conflicting reports of Web traffic. In April 2010, for example, Nielsen/NetRatings reported that Yahoo!'s share of the search engine market was 13.4 percent while comScore reported that Yahoo! had a 17.7 percent share.

Both comScore and NetRatings use a similar methodology. They recruit volunteers who agree to let the companies install software that monitors how the participants surf the Web. Measuring Web site visits, however, is much more difficult than measuring TV viewing or radio listening. A local radio market may only have a couple of dozen stations to monitor; a television market may have a hundred or so stations and networks. Web site researchers have to collect data concerning more than 300,000 sites.

In addition, much Web surfing is done at work. CNN.com and ESPN.com get most of their usage

Events: New Terms Used in Internet Ratings

Ratings and share of audience are common terms used in television and radio ratings, but when it comes to rating the Internet a new vocabulary is needed. Here are the definitions of the terms that are often used by Internet ratings companies:

Active reach: The percentage of all active users over the age of 2 who visited the site. An active user is anyone who used an Internet-enabled computer within the time period (usually a month).

Bounce rate: The percentage of visits where the visitor enters and exits at the same page without visiting any other pages on the site.

Duration of a Web page viewed: Average duration of time that a Web page was viewed per person over the specified reporting period. This is also known as *time per person.*

Hits: The number of times a file (such as a photo, video, or graphic) is requested from an Internet site.

Page view: The number of times a particular Web page is accessed during a measurement period. (Note the difference between hits and page views. A page may contain several files. Thus each page view may contain several hits. For example, if a Web site contained two video files and a photo, a request to view that site would generate four hits: one for the site, two for the video files, and one for the photo.)

Retention rate: The percentage of unique persons visiting a particular Web site two months in a row. For example, if 50 percent of the people who visited eBay in January visited eBay again in February, then the retention rate is 50 percent. This is also known as *loyalty rate.*)

Unique visitors: The number of different people who access a Web site in a measurement period (usually a month). For example, if a user leaves and comes back to the site 50 times during the measurement period, that person is counted as one unique visitor. Unique visitors are often identified by IP address or cookies placed on the visitor's computer. This concept is analogous to the cume measurement in radio ratings.

during the daytime hours. Many businesses and government organizations do not allow ratings companies to install tracking software on office computers because they fear that the software might also be used to access confidential information or sales data. As a result, daytime Web usage might be underestimated. Finally, neither company tracks usage in schools, libraries, or other public places. The next few years will probably see more refinements in the way the Internet audience is measured.

MEASURING WEB AND MOBILE VIDEO

Because a significant amount of current video is viewed on a computer or cell phone, both comScore and Nielsen have developed techniques to capture this information. To measure online viewing, both comScore and Nielsen use similar methods. First, they use the panel technique where thousands of participants install software on their computers that tracks their Web viewing. Second, both firms use "beacons" and "tags," devices placed in the

video host's player that monitor the actions of the viewer. Despite their use of similar methods, there are technical differences in the way each service counts the "playing" of a video. As a result, the two ratings firms often disagree on their estimates of Web viewing.

Nielsen measures video viewing on mobile phones by using a panel of respondents whose phones contain built-in metering software. The device detects and records an inaudible digital signal embedded in the TV program's transmission. In addition, Nielsen uses software that collects information about viewing activity directly from consumers' phone bills. As of 2010, comScore collected cell phone TV data by surveying a panel of mobile phone users.

BEYOND RATINGS: OTHER AUDIENCE RESEARCH

Although audience ratings serve as the primary source of feedback for the electronic media industry, owners and managers often need additional information about who is listening and watching. This section examines two broad categories of audience research that are used to supplement ratings data.

Music Research

Most radio stations play music. All stations want to play the right mix of music so they will attract as large an audience as possible. They want to avoid playing new songs that their listeners dislike and to avoid playing popular songs so many times that listeners get tired of them (a phenomenon called **burnout**). Broadcasters use two methods to test music: call-outs and auditorium testing.

Call-Outs   **Call-out research** refers to a process whereby listeners are surveyed by telephone and asked to rate certain songs. About 20 **hooks**—5 to 10-second cuts of the most memorable parts of the songs—are played, and the listener is asked to rate each song on several rating scales. One scale mea-

sures whether the listener likes the song, while another measures whether the song has reached the burnout stage. Programmers at the station can use the results of the survey to determine those songs that their audience wants to hear as well as those that have peaked in popularity.

The biggest disadvantage of the call-out method is that it can't be used to test new or unfamiliar music. Because it depends on familiar hooks, program directors and music directors must rely on other techniques when evaluating new releases. One possible method is auditorium testing.

Auditorium Testing   **Auditorium testing** consists of gathering a sample of 75 to 100 people in an auditorium or similar facility for about 60 to 90 minutes to evaluate musical selections—both new and familiar. Auditorium testing has two advantages over call-out research: It can test new songs, and it can test a much larger number of hooks. An auditorium test designed to rate familiar songs can test more than 300 hooks at a single session. In addition, entire songs

Focus groups are a popular media research technique. Some groups watch a commercial or a program, and a moderator then leads a discussion about their reactions.

can be played so that the audience can rate music they have never heard before. Radio stations that are considering a format change use auditorium testing to examine reactions to the new format. Instead of a series of hooks, audience members hear longer portions of the proposed format, including music, promotional announcements, and DJ patter.

Market Research

Market research covers a variety of techniques used by broadcasting and cable programmers to gain more knowledge about their audiences and their audiences' reactions to programs and personalities.

Production Research   Before spending huge sums of money to develop a new program or a TV commercial, networks, studios, and ad agencies may want to examine some early responses. **Concept testing** is used by production companies to gauge audience reactions to possible new program ideas. Audience members are given a one- or two-paragraph description of the concept behind a particular show and asked if they would watch it.

Commercials are sometimes tested with a **rough cut,** a simply produced version of the ad using minimal sets, little editing, amateur actors, and no special effects. These rough cuts are used to get a general sense about the direction and the approach of the planned ad. Researchers realize that some low ratings of the rough cut are due to its unfinished nature.

New ads and programs may be tested by using **electronic response indicators (ERIs).** Each seat in a special auditorium is equipped with a dial or a series of buttons that enable a viewer to rate continuously what he or she sees on a screen. One button may be marked "like a lot," while another might be marked "like a little," all the way down to a button marked "don't like at all." The responses are sent directly to a computer that keeps track of the average responses. Thus an advertiser might determine that the first 15 seconds of the commercial were well liked but the rest of the ad rated poorly.

A more realistic method for analyzing viewer reactions to a program is **cable testing.** A research company recruits a sample of 500 to 600 viewers from a typical market. The members of the sample are asked to watch the new program on a cable channel that is not assigned to a broadcast or a cable net-

work. After the show, a survey is conducted among sample members to see what viewers liked or disliked about the program and to ascertain whether they would watch the program if it were regularly scheduled.

Focus groups provide more detailed information about how people think and feel about an ad or a program. A **focus group** is a group of 6 to 12 people and a moderator who have a focused discussion about a topic. The members of the group are screened to ensure that they are appropriate for the research. For example, a radio station conducting a focus group to find out what listeners thought of its music programming would be careful to include only regular listeners in the group. Members are generally paid between $25 and $50 to participate.

The moderator usually has a prepared list of topics for the group to discuss. It is also the moderator's job to elicit responses from everybody in the group and to make sure the group stays on the topic.

Researchers recommend that more than one focus group be conducted for a particular topic. The results from a single group might be unique or idiosyncratic and lead to wrong decisions. The total number of groups used to investigate a topic depends on how much the sponsoring organization can afford to pay, but the typical number of groups used is between four and six per topic.

Focus groups are best thought of as a diagnostic device. Their responses can reveal the reasons behind certain attitudes or behaviors. Because focus groups comprise small, nonrandom samples, it is dangerous to generalize their results to the total population.

Audience Segmentation Research   Radio and television ratings books provide information about the different demographic segments of the audience. Programmers are able to determine whether particular programs do better among males or females and whether a show has a predominantly young or old audience. Demographic breakdowns, however, may not tell the whole story. The listening, viewing, and buying habits of a 20-year-old female living on a farm in Manhattan, Kansas, may be totally different from those of a 20-year-old female living in an apartment in Manhattan, New York City. Accordingly, many market researchers suggest classifying audience members along other dimensions.

Psychographic research segments the audience according to various personality traits. Audience members report their viewing and listening behavior and then rate their personalities on a number of different scales: independent–dependent, active–passive, leader–follower, relaxed–tense, romantic–practical, and so forth. The results can be used by program producers and advertisers. For example, if the audience for CNBC scores high on the practical dimension, commercials that emphasize such themes as "saving money" or "seldom needs repair" might be emphasized.

Lifestyle surveys are similar to psychographic research but put more importance on values that may influence consumer behavior. There are many measurement scales used to segment audiences based on their lifestyles, but the most well-known is VALS—values and lifestyle segmentation—developed at the Stanford Research Institute. The test divides people into eight groups, including "strugglers," "strivers," "achievers," and "actualizers." Advertisers use the VALS results to develop campaigns that are consistent with the values and orientations of their target audiences.

SUMMARY

- Audience estimates, expressed as ratings, are an important tool for broadcasters, cablecasters, Web site operators, and advertisers. Audience reports published by different ratings companies aid decision making in the industry.

- Early ratings companies, such as the Cooperative Analysis of Broadcasting and the C. E. Hooper Company, used telephone surveys to measure radio listening. The A. C. Nielsen Company (now Nielsen Media Research) used a mechanical device attached to a radio or TV set to generate its estimates of the audience.

- Currently the Arbitron Company uses diaries and a Portable People Meter to measure radio listening. Nielsen also uses a People Meter, along with set-top meters and diaries to measure TV viewing. Media Metrix and Nielsen/NetRatings use a panel of computer users to track data on Web site visits.

- Ratings companies calculate ratings, share of the audience, households using TV, people using radio, and cumulative audience figures and publish their results online. The reports contain maps, demographic information, daypart results, and reports concerning specific programs. This information is used by networks, syndication companies, local stations, and advertisers.

- In addition to ratings research, radio stations use call-out research and auditorium testing to fine-tune their playlists.

- Broadcasters and cablecasters also use market research to pretest programs and commercials. Focus groups are conducted to investigate why certain programs and commercials are popular and others aren't.

- Finally, lifestyle research and psychographic research focus on personality traits and values in an effort to understand the audience further.

KEY TERMS

SUGGESTIONS FOR FURTHER READING

Beville, H. M. (1988). *Audience ratings* (2nd ed.). Hillsdale, NJ: Erlbaum.

Chappell, M. N., & Hooper, C. E. (1944). *Radio audience measurement.* New York: Stephen Daye.

Lindlof, T. (1987). *Natural audiences: Qualitative research of media uses and effects.* Norwood, NJ: Ablex.

Webster, J., Phalen, P., & Lichty, L. (2005). *Ratings analysis: The theory and practice of audience research.* Mahwah, NJ: Erlbaum.

Wimmer, R., & Dominick, J. (2010). *Mass media research: An introduction* (8th ed.). Belmont, CA: Wadsworth.

INTERNET EXERCISES

Visit our Web site at **www.mhhe.com/dominickbib7e** for study-guide exercises to help you learn and apply material in each chapter. You will find ideas for future research as well as useful Web links to provide you with an opportunity to journey through the new electronic media.

Quick Facts

Percentage of young people (18–29) naming the Internet as their main source of election news (2004): 21

Percentage of young people (18–29) naming the Internet as their main source of election news (2008): 46

Percentage of female characters in 60 top-selling video games: 14

Average length of sound bite for political candidates on TV news: 9.7 seconds

Most researched television program in history: *Sesame Street*

Do the electronic media have an impact on our lives? Ask yourself the following questions:

1. What rights does a person have when arrested?

2. While on a date, have you ever used a line or clever remark that you heard on TV?

3. When you're preparing for an important occasion, do you worry about dandruff, acne, perspiration, bad breath, or yellow teeth?

4. Did you ever consciously dress like a character you saw on TV?

5. Have you ever voted for a contestant on *American Idol*?

6. Do you vote differently because of televised ads for political candidates?

The answers to these questions will tell you how much of an impact TV and radio have had on your personal life.

Now consider the global scale. What impact have the broadcast media had on society? This question is a little more difficult to answer. Nonetheless, it's an important topic. Radio and TV have been, at various times, the alleged culprits behind a host of social ills. Television, it was claimed, made us more violent and antisocial, hurt our reading skills, decreased our SAT scores, fostered sexual stereotypes, and more. From a pragmatic standpoint society needs to know if, in fact, these allegations are valid, and if so, how to correct them. Consequently, this chapter briefly examines how we go about studying the impact of radio and TV, the changing views concerning media effects over the past 80 years or so, and the most current research about the effects of broadcasting in specific areas.

STUDYING THE EFFECTS OF THE ELECTRONIC MEDIA

There are many ways to examine the social consequences of the electronic media. Some scientists employ qualitative methods, in which they make direct observations and in-depth analyses of mass communication behaviors in natural settings. Other scholars use the critical or cultural studies technique that has been long popular in the humanities to provide a more interpretive look at the process of mass communication. Both the qualitative and critical/ cultural studies approaches suggest new and different

ways of explaining and understanding the nature of the impact of electronic media. This chapter, however, focuses more on the traditional and pragmatic social science approach to mass media effects; it emphasizes research questions that have implications for social policy.

In electronic media research, several techniques are used to gather data about audience effects. These techniques are wide-ranging, partly because historically the effects of mass communication have been studied by psychologists, social scientists, political scientists, and others. Not surprisingly, each discipline has relied on the technique most closely associated with it. Thus psychologists use the experimental method, whereas sociologists use surveys. There are, however, many variations on experimental and survey research. In general, it's possible to say that there are four main social scientific methods:

1. Experimental methods, which can take place either in controlled "laboratory" conditions or in more natural "field" conditions.

2. Survey methods, which can either sample the subjects one time only or continue over time.

3. Content analysis, which is a systematic method for analyzing and classifying communication content.

4. Meta-analysis, which is a method that looks at a number of existing studies about a similar topic and summarizes the main findings by using statistical procedures that highlight which results are consistently found.

Each of these four methods has its own built-in pros and cons. Knowing the advantages and disadvantages of these various techniques is important because they have an impact on the degree of confidence that we have in research results.

Laboratory experiments are done under tightly controlled conditions and allow researchers to focus on the effects of one or more factors that may have an impact on the audience. Usually at least two groups are involved; one group gets treated one way while the other is treated differently. The big advantage of lab experiments over other methods is that they allow researchers to make statements about cause and effect. In an experiment subjects are randomly assigned to experimental conditions, and the researcher has control over most external factors that might bias the results, thus making the claim of cause and effect stronger. Their big disadvantage is that they are done under artificial conditions, so behavior that occurs in the lab might not occur in real life.

Field experiments occur outside the lab. Sometimes a natural event occurs that creates the conditions necessary for an experiment, and sometimes field experiments can be set up by the researcher. To illustrate, suppose one program is fed to one-half the homes on a special cable system while the remainder sees a different program. The effects of this single program could then be examined. The advantage of field experiments is naturalness; people are studied in their typical environments. The big disadvantage is the lack of control. Unlike the lab, field experiments are subject to the contaminating influences of outside events.

Surveys generally consist of a person's answers to a set of predetermined questions. Surveys are done through the mail, over the phone, on the Internet, or in person and usually involve some kind of questionnaire or other instrument. The big advantage of survey research is its realistic approach. People in natural settings are asked questions about their typical behaviors. A big disadvantage with surveys is the fact that they can't establish cause and effect. After a survey a researcher can say only that factor A and factor B are related; that researcher cannot say that A causes B or that B causes A. A survey only establishes a relationship. Another disadvantage is that surveys rely on self-reports. It can only be assumed that respondents give valid and truthful responses.

Surveys can be done one time or they can be **longitudinal** (repeated over time). A **trend study** is one in which the same question or questions are asked of different people at different times. An example of a trend study would be a poll done six months before an election that asks which presidential candidate people intend to vote for and is then repeated with a different group of people a week before the election.

Panel studies are a special type of longitudinal survey in which the same people are studied at different points in time. The advantage in a panel study is that some evidence of cause and effect can be established, usually through sophisticated statistical analysis. The disadvantages include the fact that panel studies take a long time to do and they suffer from attrition—respondents die, move away, or get bored and are no longer part of the study group.

Content analysis studies segments of TV and radio content in order to describe the messages presented by these media. Such studies have been useful in defining media stereotypes and establishing a gauge of the amount of violence in TV programming. The biggest problem with content analysis is that it cannot be used alone as a basis for making statements about the effects of media content. For example, just because a content analysis establishes that cartoons are saturated with violence, it doesn't necessarily follow that children who watch these shows will behave violently. That might be the case, but it would take an audience study to substantiate that claim—a content analysis by itself would be insufficient.

A **meta-analysis** looks at many studies in different settings and across a variety of samples. It provides a macroview of the research in a given area and gives a good synopsis of the major findings. For example, meta-analyses have been conducted on studies that have examined the effects of television violence on aggressive behavior and on the impact of playing video games. Each individual study examined in a meta-analysis provides a different estimate of the strength of the relationship that is being examined. By accumulating the results across a number of studies, we can determine a more accurate picture of the relationship. Meta-analysis, however, is not without disadvantages. Critics have charged that it can oversimplify a complicated pattern of results and that any design flaws in the original studies that are reviewed will produce misleading conclusions. In any case, meta-analysis has become more popular in recent years.

THEORIES OF MEDIA EFFECTS

These methods have been used to study the impact of mass media since the early 1900s. Throughout that time our view about the power of media effects has undergone significant changes as social science learns more about the various factors that affect media impact. As we shall see, there were periods in history when the media (including broadcasting) were thought of as quite powerful and other times when they were thought to have little effect. The current thinking seems to represent a compromise between these two extreme positions. The rest of this section briefly reviews the various theories concerning the effects of mass media that have evolved over the years.

Hypodermic Needle Theory

One of the earliest theories of media effects held that mass-communicated messages would have strong and more or less universal effects on the audience they reached. It was thought that the media would "shoot" beliefs into people's minds much as a doctor inoculates people with a hypodermic needle. Much of this thinking was due to the apparent success of propaganda before and during World War I. For example, in 1914 to 1916, as World War I broke out in Europe, skillful British propaganda stories were considered responsible for bringing the United States into the war on the side of the Allies. After the war, a new medium, radio, further reinforced the hypodermic model. Successful radio rogues, such as Dr. Brinkley (see Chapter 10), and the *War of the Worlds* scare seemed to support the view that mass media can have powerful consequences.

Reexaminations of the development of this model suggest that it was not so thoroughly accepted as once believed. In addition, some social scientists of this early period also argued that other factors should be considered when discussing the impact of the media. In any case, advances in experimental and survey research began to cast serious doubt on the hypodermic needle model. By the mid-1940s it was obvious that the model's assumptions about the way communication affects audiences were too simplistic. The pendulum was about to swing in the other direction.

Limited-Effects Theory

Persuasion, especially the political kind that goes on in election campaigns, was the main focus of this new line of research. Several studies indicated that the media did not have a direct effect on the audience, as was previously believed. The newly developed two-step flow theory suggested that media influence first passed through a group of people known as opinion leaders and then on to the rest of the audience. Further research posited that media influence was filtered through a net of intervening factors, such as a person's prior beliefs and knowledge and the influence of family, friends, and peer groups. The mass media were simply one of a great many determinants of how people think or behave.

This view brought some comfort to those who feared that the public might be brainwashed by skillful

ideologues and clever propaganda techniques because it suggested that they were unlikely to succeed. It also was appealing to mass-media executives, who could use it to counter criticism that the media were the cause of various social ills.

The most complete statement of the limited-effects position (although he doesn't call it that) appears in a book by Joseph Klapper, *The Effects of Mass Communication*, published in 1960. Klapper reviewed the existing research and summed it up in a series of generalizations, the most widely quoted of which held that mass communication alone does not ordinarily cause audience effects but instead functions primarily to reinforce existing conditions.

Klapper's generalizations enjoyed popularity for nearly two decades; in fact, there are some who still subscribe to the limited-effects model even today. Nonetheless, keep in mind that the bulk of the studies reviewed by Klapper were done before TV became the dominant mass medium. In addition, although the most widely quoted of Klapper's conclusions concerned the reinforcement effect of the media, he also noted that there were occasions when the media could exert direct effects or when the mediating factors that generally produce reinforcement are absent or themselves help foster change. As TV became more prevalent and researchers discovered more areas where media effects were direct, the limited-effects model gave way to a new formulation.

Specific-Effects Theory

The most recent theory of media effects represents a middle ground. Researchers realize that media are not all-powerful; they compete with or complement other sources of influence such as friends, family, and teachers. Nonetheless, there are circumstances under which specific types of media content might have a significant effect on certain members of the audience. Although this statement might not be entirely satisfying from a scientific standpoint, in the last few years communication researchers have made great progress in identifying how and when, and sometimes even why, mass media, especially broadcasting, affect individuals and groups. For example, several research studies have identified an agenda-setting effect: The mass media choose to emphasize certain topics, thereby causing the public to perceive these issues as important. Accordingly, the answer to the question, What are the effects of the mass media? has become complex, as social scientists continue to define the circumstances, the topics, and the people for whom specific effects might occur.

The remainder of this chapter examines six of the most investigated topics in recent broadcasting research: (1) the effect of violent TV programming on antisocial behavior, (2) perceptions of social reality, (3) stereotyping, (4) TV and politics, (5) prosocial behavior, and (6) the social impact of the Internet.

VIDEO VIOLENCE

It is appropriate that we first examine the media violence area. This subject is the most controversial, generates the most research, uses all of the four research techniques mentioned earlier, illustrates some of the problems in generalizing from research data, and is the one topic about which communication researchers know the most.

History

Concern about the impact of electronic media violence first surfaced during the 1930s when parents worried that gangster movies would corrupt the morals of young people. When television became popular during the 1950s, video violence became an issue. Congressional hearings examined the topic and concluded that watching TV was an important factor in shaping the attitudes and characters of its younger audience.

The urban violence and general unrest that characterized the mid-1960s sparked a new burst of interest in the topic. A presidential commission, the National Commission on the Causes and Prevention of Violence, reviewed the existing research evidence and concluded that violent behavior as depicted on TV had a negative effect on the audience.

A few years later the U.S. Surgeon General's Office sponsored a research effort involving 50 separate studies that examined this same area. After some debate and further congressional hearings, most researchers who participated in the project agreed that their findings indicated a causal link, albeit a weak one, between watching TV violence and antisocial attitudes and behaviors. In 1982, 10 years after the release of the original Surgeon General's Report, an update reinforced the original conclusion that TV violence was a cause of aggressive behavior.

Many studies appearing since the update have changed their focus to "effect size." This approach gets away from the simple question of whether TV violence has an effect on the audience and considers

The American Psychiatric Association estimates that by the time a child is 18 he or she will have seen nearly 200,000 acts of violence on television and in motion pictures.

instead the more complicated question of how big an effect it has. Several researchers have disagreed over the significance of some of the relatively weak effects that have been discovered.

The issue resurfaced with the passage of the Telecommunications Act of 1996. In response to public and congressional pressure, the act contained a provision mandating that new TV sets be equipped with a V-chip that would allow parents to block out violent content (and other forms of objectionable behavior) from their TV sets. (The V-chip is discussed in more detail in Chapter 11.)

Another reincarnation of this issue occurred after the outbreaks of school violence in Littleton, Colorado; Paducah, Kentucky; and Jonesboro, Arkansas. Congress once again held hearings on media violence; and yet another report, *Youth Violence*, was issued by the U.S. Surgeon General linking exposure to TV violence with some forms of aggressive behavior.

The issue surfaced again in connection with the FCC's increased concern over indecent programming. A group of lawmakers wrote the FCC and asked why the commission worried about the effects of indecent programs but paid little attention to violent programming. Accordingly, in 2004 the FCC held an inquiry about TV violence that covered a wide range of topics from the effects of fantasy violence to the efficacy of the V-chip.

The debate over media violence came up again with regard to violence in video games. Although the research evidence is fuzzy (see the next section), parents, researchers, and politicians were concerned about the impact of this kind of content on young people. In that connection, California (followed by several other states) passed legislation that fined retailers who sold violent video games to minors. A federal judge later overturned this law as a violation of the First Amendment's free speech protection. In 2010, however, the Supreme Court agreed to hear California's appeal of this ruling.

So much for the history of this topic. Next we review specific research evidence, pointing out its strengths and weaknesses, and conclude with an attempt to summarize the research consensus in this area.

Research Evidence

Experiments were one of the first methods used to investigate the impact of media violence. A series of studies done in the early 1960s documented that chil-

dren could easily learn and imitate violent actions that they witnessed on screen.

A second set of experiments from the early 1960s was designed to settle the debate touched off by two competing theories of media effects. On the one hand, the **catharsis theory** posited that watching scenes of media violence would actually reduce the aggressiveness of viewers because their hostile feelings would be purged while watching the media portrayals. Not surprisingly, this viewpoint was popular with many industry executives. On the other hand, the **stimulation theory** predicted that watching scenes of violence actually prompted audience members to behave more aggressively after viewing. The experimental design used to test these competing theories is presented in simplified form in Figure 13–1. The results of these and other experiments showed little support for catharsis. In fact, the bulk of the laboratory research argues for the stimulation effect. This is not to say that the catharsis hypothesis is categorically wrong. There may be some instances where it might occur. Most of the time, however, the likely end product is increased aggression.

These early experiments were criticized for their artificiality. They were done in the lab under controlled conditions and used violent segments that were not typical of what everybody saw on TV. Later experiments used more realistic violent segments and more relevant aggression measures. For example, several experiments used actual programs that contained about the average number of violent acts

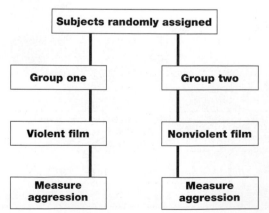

Figure 13–1

Simplified Diagram for Catharsis versus Stimulation Experiment per hour in prime-time TV (about five or six). Additional experiments used more real-life measures of aggression. Several observed the actual interpersonal aggression of children in play groups or in classrooms. These and other more natural measures confirm that watching violence stimulates subsequent real-life aggression.

In sum, the results from laboratory experiments demonstrate that shortly after exposure to media violence, individuals, especially youngsters, are likely to show an increase in their own level of aggression. In fact, since the mid-1970s there has been a marked decrease in the number of lab experiments examining this topic partly because the results have been so consistent. More recent experiments have accepted the fact that exposure to violence facilitates subsequent aggression and have concentrated instead on factors that might increase or decrease the *amount* of aggression performed in response to media portrayals.

Laboratory studies are important because, as mentioned earlier, they help establish a plausible cause-and-effect pattern and control for the effects of extraneous factors. Still, the laboratory is not real life, and to be more sure of our conclusions we need to examine the results of research that is done outside the lab.

Surveys (also called correlational studies) are done in the real world. Although they offer little evidence of cause and effect, they do not have the artificiality of the lab associated with them. Most surveys on this topic incorporate the design of Figure 13–2. If the viewing of media violence is indeed associated with real-world aggression, then people who watch a lot of violent TV should also score high on scales that measure their own aggressive behavior or attitudes toward aggression. The results from a large number of surveys involving literally thousands of respondents across different regions, socioeconomic statuses, and ethnic backgrounds have been remarkably consistent: There is a modest but consistent association between viewing violent TV programs and aggressive tendencies.

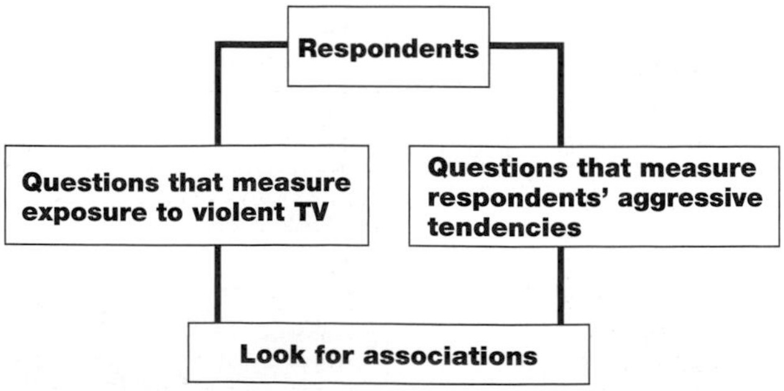

These results, however, are not without problems, such as trying to establish cause and effect. Although viewing TV violence and aggression are related, TV viewing does not necessarily cause aggression. In fact, it's logically possible that aggressive individuals choose to watch more violent TV, which would mean that aggression could cause the viewing of violent TV. Finally, it's also possible that the relationship might be caused by some third factor. Maybe the real cause of aggression is a history of child abuse, and this in turn is associated with watching violent TV. Survey statistics would show a positive relationship between viewing violent TV and aggression, but the real cause might be something else.

Once again, to sum up, correlational studies provide another piece of the puzzle; they show that viewing TV violence and antisocial behavior are linked in the real world, but they don't tell us anything definitive about cause and effect. Remember, however, that lab studies can determine cause and effect and their results are consistent with the notion that TV viewing causes subsequent aggression. So far we have reason to be somewhat comfortable with that conclusion. But there is still other evidence to consider.

In the past 30 years or so, several field experiments were carried out to investigate the potential antisocial effects of TV violence. Recall that field experiments give us some basis for deciding cause and effect but suffer from a lack of control of other, potentially contaminating factors.

The results from field experiments are somewhat inconsistent. At least two done in the early 1970s found no effect from viewing violent TV. One of these two, however, was plagued by procedural problems, and its results should be accepted cautiously. On the other hand, at least five field experiments have yielded data consonant with the lab and survey findings. The main conclusion of these studies seems to be that individuals who watch a diet of violent programs tend to exhibit more antisocial or aggressive behavior. In some studies this effect was stronger than in others, but the direction was consistent.

Figure 13–2

Survey Design Examining Effects of TV Violence

Figure 13–3

Canadian Field Experiment Design

Community	Time one		Time two	
1	No TV	Measure aggression, media exposure, and related variables	One TV channel	Measure aggression, media exposure, and related variables
2	One TV channel		Two TV channels	
3	Four TV channels		Four TV channels	

Figure 13–3 shows the design used in one of these field experiments. In this case the experiment was based on natural circumstances. The researchers were able to identify a Canadian town that was surrounded by mountains and was unable to receive TV signals until 1974. This town was matched with two others, one that could receive only the Canadian Broadcasting Corporation (CBC) and another that could get the CBC plus the three U.S. networks. The towns were studied in 1973 and again two years later. Children in the town that had just gotten TV showed an increase in the rate of aggressive acts that was more than three times higher than those for children living in the other two towns.

On balance, the results from field experiments are not so striking as those using the lab and correlational methods. On the whole, though, they tend to support, although weakly in some cases, the notion that viewing violent TV fosters aggressive behavior.

Panel surveys, as noted earlier, are longitudinal research projects that examine the same individuals at different points in time. They are not plagued by the artificiality of the laboratory, and their design allows us to draw some conclusions about cause and effect. Since the early 1970s the results of several panel studies have become available for analysis.

The panel analysis begins with measurements of both real-life aggression and exposure to TV violence, taken at two different times. Next the researchers determine if TV viewing as measured at time 1 is related to aggression at time 2. At the same time, the relationship between aggression at time 1 and TV viewing at time 2 is also assessed. If early TV viewing is more strongly related to later aggression than early aggression is to later TV violence viewing, then we have evidence that it's the TV viewing causing

the violence and not vice versa. Figure 13–4 diagrams this approach.

Several longitudinal studies done in the United States and Europe, including both panel and trend studies, have found, with some exceptions, similar results. The majority of the studies seem to suggest that the sequence of causation is that viewing TV violence causes viewers to become more aggressive. The degree of the relationship between the two factors is small, influenced by individual and social factors, and sometimes difficult to detect; but it is consistent. In addition, the process seems to be reciprocal. Watching TV violence encourages aggression, which in turn encourages the watching of more violent TV, and so on.

There is one more piece to be added to the puzzle. As already mentioned, a meta-analysis examines the results of many studies and draws general conclusions about the strength of a relationship. One meta-analysis conducted in 2002 looked at more than 280 studies—including lab experiments, field experiments, surveys, and panel studies—concerning TV violence and aggressive behavior. The results of this analysis revealed a positive link between media violence and aggression regardless of the research method. The greatest effect was found in lab experiments, while long-term panel surveys produced the weakest.

Figure 13–4

Longitudinal Design to Study TV Violence

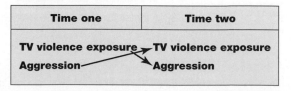

Time one	Time two
TV violence exposure	TV violence exposure
Aggression	Aggression

Having reviewed evidence from four basic research methods, what can we conclude about the effects of violent TV on antisocial behavior? Laboratory experiments demonstrate that under certain conditions, TV can have powerful effects on aggressive behavior. Field experiments provide additional, although less consistent, evidence that TV can exert an impact in the real world. Surveys show a consistent but somewhat weak pattern of association between violence viewing and aggression. Longitudinal studies also show a persistent but weak relationship between the two and suggest a pattern whereby watching TV causes subsequent aggression. Meta-analysis shows consistent results across many samples using different methods. Unfortunately, few findings in areas such as this are unambiguous. Nonetheless, a judgment is in order. Keep in mind that some might disagree, but the consensus among social scientists seems to be the following:

1. Television violence is *a* cause of subsequent aggressive tendencies in viewers; it is not *the* cause since many factors besides TV determine whether people behave aggressively.

2. The precise impact of TV violence will be affected by many other factors, including age, sex, family interaction, and the way violence is presented on the screen.

3. In relative terms, the effect of TV violence on aggression tends to be small.

Does this close the case? Not quite. The third summary statement has been the focus of much current debate. The majority of researchers concede that there is some kind of causal link between viewing video violence and aggression, but several argue that the link is too weak to be meaningful. To be more specific, statisticians characterize the strength of any relationship in terms of the amount of variability in one measure that is accounted for by the other. For example, suppose a person was trying to guess your college grade point average just by looking at you. Chances are the person wouldn't do too well. Now let's show the person your SAT scores and let the person guess again. Chances are that the person will do a little better. Why? Because there is an association (a moderate one, at least) between GPA and SAT scores. In other words, they share some variation. The more shared variability there is between two measures, the better a person can predict. If two factors are strongly related, changes in one might account for 60 to 70 percent (or higher: 100 percent if perfectly related) of the change in the other. A person could make quite accurate predictions in this instance. If two factors are not associated at all, change in one would explain 0 percent of changes in the other. In this case a person's predictions would be no better than chance. Thus the strength of a relationship is measured by the variability explained. As far as TV violence and aggression are concerned, exposure to televised violence typically explains from about 2 to 9 percent of the variability in aggression. Knowing how much TV violence you watch helps a little, but not much, in predicting your aggression level. Put another way, between 91 and 98 percent of the variability in aggression is due to other causes. Given this situation, is the effect of TV on aggression really that meaningful? Does it have any practical or social importance?

This question is more political or philosophical than scientific, but research can offer some guidelines for comparison. The usual effect size found for TV violence's impact on antisocial behavior is only slightly less than that found for the effects of viewing *Sesame Street* and *The Electric Company* on cognitive skills of the audience. It's also only slightly

Issues: Putting Things in Perspective

Which has more violence: TV shows or nursery rhymes? Nursery rhymes by far. A researcher in London analyzed two weeks of television violence and compared it with the violence in 25 popular rhymes such as "Jack and Jill" and "Simple Simon." The results showed that children's rhymes contained 10 times more violence than TV shows broadcast during the early evening hours when most children were watching.

less than the effect that a program of drug therapy has on psychotic patients. Indeed, several drugs in widespread use have therapeutic effects about as great as the effect size of TV violence and aggression. In sum, although the magnitude of the effect may not be great, it is not that much different from effects in other areas that we take to be socially and practically meaningful. Thus even though the effect may be small, this does not mean that it should be dismissed.

Video Game Violence

Early video games were usually played in arcades or on the home TV set. Graphics were relatively and violence was mild (such as PacMan, Missile Command, and Centipede). In the 1990s a new type of video game appeared: the first-person shooter (Doom, Duke Nukem). These games put the player behind the sights of various weapons, and the main object was the killing or wounding of opponents. During the 2000s new game systems with even better graphics were developed (PlayStation, Xbox) that made violent portrayals more realistic. Games such as Grand Theft Auto were linked to violent crimes in several countries. As public concern about the effects of these games increased, researchers intensified their efforts to understand their impact.

One thing is clear: Video games are popular. According to the Entertainment Software Association, nearly 70 percent of all U.S. households have a game console or handheld game device. The average gamer tends to be male (but the female gaming audience is growing) and over 30 years old and spends about 18 hours a week playing games. Young people (ages 8–16) play about 13 hours a week.

Content analysis has shown that many of these games portray violence. One 2004 survey found that more than 70 percent of video games rated "T" (games suitable for teens) contained violence. As of 2010 many popular games were saturated with aggressive and violent behavior. Grand Theft Auto IV features muggings, robberies, and carjacking. Dead Rising 2 lets players kill zombies with lawn mowers, propane tanks, and other assorted items. Halo 3 players can kill aliens with machine guns, bombs, and grenades.

Similar to research about the effects of TV violence, evidence about the effects of video game violence comes from lab experiments, surveys, and meta-analyses. The results of lab experiments are compli-

cated because many variables, including the age of the player, the type of the game, the player's perspective (first person or third person), and the presence or absence of bloody graphics, can have an impact on the outcome. In general, with some exceptions, most lab experiments have found that playing violent video games results in at least a short-term increase in aggressive actions and aggressive thoughts.

Surveys have also been conducted across many age groups and have used a variety of methods to measure aggressive behavior, including self-reports, teacher and peer ratings, and delinquency records. The survey results are a little more consistent. They suggest that video/computer game play is linked to both increases in aggressive behavior and favorable attitudes toward aggression. There was also some evidence of a link between game playing and a decreased self-esteem and an unfavorable self-concept.

One long-term longitudinal study has examined the impact of playing video games on 12- to 18-year-olds in Japan and 9- to 12-year-olds in the United States. Data were gathered at two points in time, separated by three to six months. The results indicated that in both countries those who spent a lot of time playing video games became more physically aggressive.

Unfortunately, meta-analysis has not helped to clarify the situation. Two recent meta-analyses have examined the impact of violent video games, and the authors of each reached different conclusions. (The details can be found in the March 2010 issue of the *Psychological Bulletin*.) One suggested that playing violent video games is a causal risk factor for long-term harmful outcomes, while the other suggested that the existing research has not provided compelling support to indicate a causal relationship between violent game play and actual aggressive behavior. Despite their differing inferences, the authors of the two analyses agreed on one point: The impact of playing violent games was relatively weak. The authors pointed to other factors, such as belonging to a gang or having abusive parents, as much better predictors of violent behavior.

In sum, research into the effects of video games is still at a formative level. Given the large amounts of time that young people spend playing these games and the number of violent themes contained in video/computer games, it is likely that the body of research surrounding this topic will increase in the next few years. It is hoped that future research will help clarify the ultimate impact of this content.

Issues: Violent Video Games and Helping Others

Several research studies have noted that exposure to media violence has a desensitizing effect: People become indifferent to the pain and suffering of others. Is it possible that the same effect might make people less willing to help someone in need? That was the question under investigation in an experiment by Brad Bushman and Craig Anderson published in the March 2009 issue of *Psychological Science*.

Like much social science research, this study looked at the responses of college students. Students were tested individually in a room designed for the experiment. One group of students played a violent video game (such as Mortal Kombat or Duke Nukem) while another group played a nonviolent game (such as Tetras or Pinball). The experimenter told each student to play the game for 20 minutes and then left the room explaining that he had another project to attend to and would return in 40 minutes. He asked the subjects not to leave the room until he returned. Three minutes after the subjects had finished playing the video game, the experimenter played a recording of what sounded like a heated argument between two people taking place just outside the experimental room. The argument appeared to escalate to the point of physical violence, at which point the experimenter threw a chair to floor and kicked the door of the experimental room twice. The recording continued with moans and groans and one of the participants in the scuffle stating that he was on the floor with a twisted ankle. The other person appeared to leave without assisting the injured party.

The researchers then timed how long it took the subject to come out of the experimental room and help the supposedly injured person. Subjects who played the violent video game took significantly longer to help than did those who played the nonviolent game. In addition, when compared with those who played the nonviolent game, the students who played the violent game were less likely to notice that a fight was taking place and also rated the fight as much less serious.

The researchers summed up the results this way: "People exposed to media violence become 'comfortably numb' to the pain and suffering of others and are consequently less helpful."

A MEAN AND SCARY WORLD? PERCEPTIONS OF REALITY

A preceding section traced the impact of TV on the behavior of the audience. This section is more concerned with the impact of TV on how the audience thinks about and perceives reality.

The media, particularly TV, are the source of much of what we know about the world. The media, however, bring us more than simply information. They also, at least to some degree, shape the way we perceive the outside world. Put another way, the media affect the way we construct our social reality. For instance, what is it like to live in southern New Zealand? It seems probable that few of you reading this book have had much of a chance to experience living in southern New Zealand or to talk to people who have. Consequently, a TV show about the life of the people who live there might have tremendous influence on your perceptions in this area. This isn't much of a problem as long as the media presentations accurately represent reality.

There are, however, many areas where the world presented on TV differs greatly from reality. For example, studies of TV entertainment content have shown that far more TV characters work in crime and law enforcement than do people in the real world. Criminals on TV commit violent crime far more often than do their real-life counterparts. Trials on TV are decided by juries more often than they are in reality. More people on soap operas have affairs and illegitimate children than do real people. More unscrupulous and treacherous people are shown on TV than exist in real life. Again, this wouldn't be much of a problem if people were able to separate the two worlds, TV and reality, without any confusion. For some, however, separating the two is not easy.

This is the focus of cultivation theory. **Cultivation theory** was popularized by George Gerbner and his colleagues at the University of Pennsylvania. In simplified form, the theory suggests that the more a person is exposed to TV, the more likely that the person's construction of social reality will be more like that shown on TV and less like reality.

The procedure first used to put the theory to the test requires a content analysis of TV to isolate those portrayals that are at odds with reality. A content analysis is a systematic and objective analysis of the

Figure 13–5

Design for Cultivation Analysis

TV viewing	Number giving TV answer	Number giving non–TV answer
High	A lot	A few
Low	A few	A lot

messages portrayed on TV. The second step requires dividing audience members into heavy-viewing and light-viewing groups and then asking for their perceptions of various social events or situations. If cultivation theory is correct, then a lot of the heavy viewers should give answers more in line with the TV world, whereas a lot of the light viewers should give answers more in keeping with the real world. Figure 13–5 shows the basic model used for analysis.

Gerbner and his colleagues have done several surveys examining the cultivation effect. In one study adolescents were asked how many people were involved in some kind of violence each year, 3 or 10 percent (the TV answer); 83 percent of the heavy viewers gave the TV answer as compared with 62 percent of the light viewers. Another question asked how often a police officer usually draws a gun on an average day. The choices were less than once a day (the real-world answer) and more than five times a day (the answer more in line with the TV world). Three times as many heavy viewers (18 percent) as light viewers (6 percent) said more than five times a day.

Cultivation studies have received a fair amount of publicity in the popular press (*TV Guide* even carried an article by Gerbner and his colleagues), and the theory has a certain commonsense appeal. Recent research, however, suggests that the process of cultivation is much more complex than originally thought.

In the first place, remember that most of the cultivation studies relied on the survey approach. Although the survey method can establish a relationship, it cannot be used to rule out other factors that might be causing the relationship. Consequently, more recent studies suggest that when other factors in the process (like age, sex, race, and education) are simultaneously controlled, the cultivation effect either is weakened or disappears.

In response to these findings, cultivation theory was revised to include two additional concepts—mainstreaming and resonance—that account for the fact that heavy TV viewing may have different out-

comes for various social groups. **Mainstreaming** means that heavy viewers within social subgroups develop common perceptions that differ from those of light viewers in the same subgroup. For example, among light TV viewers, nonwhites are generally more distrusting than whites and are more likely to report that people will take advantage of you if they get the chance. Among heavy viewers, however, the gap between whites and nonwhites on this measure is significantly smaller. Heavy TV viewing has a homogenizing effect in this instance and brings both groups closer to the mainstream.

Resonance refers to a situation in which viewers get a "double dose" from both TV and reality. For example, heavy TV viewers who live in a high-crime area have their belief in a scary world reinforced by both TV and their firsthand experience. They should show an exaggerated cultivation effect when compared with light viewers.

Also remember that surveys cannot establish cause and effect. Cultivation theory assumes that TV viewing is cultivating the subsequent perceptions of reality. It is possible, however, that people who are fearful of going out at night stay home and watch more TV, thus making the perception the cause of the viewing rather than the effect. Of course, the best way to sort out cause and effect would be an experiment, but since cultivation theory talks about the long-term cumulative effect of TV exposure, a definitive experiment would be difficult to design.

Other cultivation studies have tried to specify the conditions that are most likely to foster or inhibit cultivation. Although the results are not entirely consistent, it appears that cultivation depends on the following:

1. *The motivation for viewing:* Ritualistic, low-involvement viewing appears to be more potent than planned and motivated viewing.

2. *Amount of experience with the topic:* Studies have noted that cultivation seems to work best when audience members have only indirect or distant contact with the topic. This seems to contradict the resonance notion.

3. *Perceived realism of the content:* Cultivation appears to be enhanced when the viewer perceives the content of entertainment shows to be realistic.

More recent studies of cultivation theory have demonstrated that the research itself must be done carefully to avoid spurious findings. One study

Issues: Video Games and Cultivation Analysis

Can spending long hours playing video games result in distorted images of social reality? Cultivation theory was originally formulated before playing video games became popular and dealt with exposure to recurrent themes and portrayals on television. In many ways the video game experience is similar to television exposure. The game characters are predictable, the settings are realistic, and the general messages and lessons contained in the game play are consistent. Playing video games, however, also is different from watching TV. The games are available at all times, the experience is more immersive, and the player has more control over the course of the game. All these factors make it likely that some form of cultivation is possible.

A study published in a 2006 issue of the *Journal of Communication* examined this complicated issue. The researcher examined the video game Asheron's Call 2, a game with ample amounts of violence, including featured characters using weapons. One group played the game for a month with an average of about 14 hours per week of game play. Another group did not play the game.

When the two groups were compared, males that played the game believed that people in the real world would be more likely to be robbed by somebody with a weapon than the non–game players. Females who played the game did not exhibit this difference. Perceptions of the frequency of other violent acts not contained in the video game (physical assault, rape, murder) did not differ between game players and those who did not play the game.

In short, the game did produce a specific and limited cultivation effect but only among males. The researcher noted that this finding ran counter to the notion that exposure to TV content should have broad and general cultivation effects. Nonetheless, although the study raised more questions than it answered, it does appear that cultivation can occur in other video channels in addition to TV.

found that the amount of TV viewed that divides the high TV group from the low TV group must be chosen precisely or distortions will appear in the results. Other studies have found that the way the questions are worded and the precise topics to be evaluated will also have an impact.

Finally, the results of a recent meta-analysis of more than two decades of cultivation research encompassing more than 90 studies offer a summary statement about the impact of TV on a person's view of social reality. The analysis concluded that the cultivation literature has demonstrated a weak but persistent relationship between TV viewing and beliefs about the real world. How weak? Recall that viewing TV violence explains about 2 to 9 percent of the variability in aggression level. The impact of cultivation is weaker: TV viewing accounts for about 1 percent of the variation in social perceptions. This is not to say that this is an unimportant consequence. A 1 percent effect that is constant and consistent over the years can turn out to be influential. For example, suppose you're a golfer who uses 100 strokes per 18 holes. If you improved your golf game by about 1 percent per year, at the end of 20 years you would have cut about 20 strokes off your average 18-hole score. The impact of viewing, however, may not necessarily be this predictable. In sum, long-term, cumulative exposure to TV cultivates, to some small but potentially significant degree, the acceptance of ideas and perceptions that are similar to the world portrayed on TV.

It is probably obvious that there is still a lot to learn about cultivation. It represents one of the few topics that has attracted research interest from sociologists, social psychologists, and mass communication researchers. It will likely continue to be an important research area for the foreseeable future.

Racial, Ethnic, and Sex-Role Stereotyping

Somewhat related to cultivation analysis is the research area that examines the impact of stereotyping on viewers' attitudes. The civil rights and the women's movements of the 1960s and 1970s sparked interest in the way that various minority groups and women were portrayed in TV programs.

With regard to sex roles, early content analyses disclosed that men outnumbered women two to one in starring roles and that men appeared in a far greater variety of occupational roles. When they did appear, women were likely to be housewives, secretaries, or nurses. Female characters were also portrayed as passive, deferential, and generally weak, in contrast to male characters, who, on the whole, were active, dominant, and powerful. More recent content analyses have shown that females are now portrayed in a wider range of occupations but that little else has changed.

A number of studies about the effects of exposure to this material began to surface in the early 1970s. Many of these studies used the correlational approach, and, although they were not as rigorous as they could be, their findings generally supported what the cultivation hypothesis would predict: Youngsters who watched a lot of TV should have attitudes and perceptions about sex roles that are in line with the stereotypical portrayals on TV. In one study heavy TV viewers were far more likely than moderate TV watchers to choose a sex-stereotyped profession (for example, boys choosing to be doctors or police officers and girls choosing to be housewives or nurses). Another study noted that children who were heavy viewers scored higher on a standardized test that measured sex stereotyping.

Like cultivation analysis, the major problems with this sort of research are establishing causation and sorting out the impact of TV from other sources of sex-role information (schools, peers, parents, books, and so on). In an attempt to clarify the process, panel studies have examined the correlation between viewing and stereotyping. The results suggested that the causal connection evidently works in both directions: TV viewing led to more stereotypical attitudes and people with more stereotypical attitudes watched more TV, thus reinforcing the effects.

A second popular technique for examining the effects of TV on sex-role attitudes usually takes place in the laboratory and consists of showing subjects (usually youngsters) men and women in counterstereotypical roles (for example, a male nurse, a female mechanic) and then seeing if changes in perceptions occur. Results from these studies have found that exposure to this nontraditional content does seem to decrease sex-role stereotyping. In one typical experiment a group of girls saw commercials in which a woman was shown as a butcher, a welder, and a laborer. Another group saw commercials featuring women as telephone operators, models, and manicurists. After viewing, girls who saw the nontraditional roles expressed a greater preference for traditional male jobs than did the other group. Similar results have been found in at least a half dozen other experiments.

Taken as a whole these studies demonstrate that sex-role beliefs can be affected by the mass media.

Turning to ethnic and racial portrayals, we find that numerous content analyses conducted over the past 40 years have examined the way minorities are portrayed in entertainment programming, commercials, and newscasts. The vast majority of these content analyses have examined the portrayal of African Americans on television; there are few studies that examine the depiction of other ethnic and racial groups. Studies conducted during the 1970s found that African Americans were underrepresented in prime-time TV programs. One analysis found that whites accounted for about 90 percent of characters on TV, while African Americans made up about 7 percent and other nonblack minority groups were almost nonexistent.

More recently, a content analysis of prime-time TV programs from 2000 to 2008 found that whites made up about 80 percent of all characters and African Americans about 14 percent. Both of these figures are in line with the total proportions of whites and African Americans in the U.S. population. This analysis also noted that Asian and Hispanic characters were underrepresented. Keep in mind that these numbers refer to the mainstream broadcast networks. Special cable networks, such as BET or Univision, will regularly feature large numbers of minority characters. A similar trend has been found with TV commercials. African Americans were rarely seen in ads during the 1960s and 1970s, but their numbers have increased in recent years.

Does stereotyping carry over into emerging electronic media? There is limited evidence to suggest that it does. One 2008 study of official video game Web sites disclosed that male characters outnumbered females three to two and Hispanic characters were rarely found. A content analysis of race in online news coverage found that Web news sources were similar to traditional TV newscasts in their portrayals: Whites were overrepresented in positive roles while nonwhites were associated with problematic behaviors. One study of interviews via instant messages found that males were likely to rate male interviewers as more competent than female interviewers.

Studies looking at the impact of these portrayals on racial and ethnic stereotypes are less numerous than the content analyses, and most have focused on the impact of programs depicting African Americans. Researchers have examined the influence of TV programs that feature minorities on both minority and majority audiences. For example, the degree to

Prime-time TV has been criticized many times for its stereotypical portrayal of females. Analyses have shown that women are more likely to be identified by their marital status, while men are identified by their occupation. Further, more male characters were likely to be employed in high-status positions. Females, in contrast, were more likely to be shown in relatively powerless roles, such as homemaker and student.

Are such disparities the result of the gender makeup of the creative personnel who put the show together? Do programs that have a mixed-gender creative team portray females differently from those shows put together by just males? Those were a couple of the questions asked by a 2004 study published in the *Journal of Broadcasting & Electronic Media*.

The authors analyzed on-screen portrayals of one episode of every series on the six broadcast TV networks. For each of the 1,445 characters in their sample, they examined a number of characteristics, including occupational status, success in achieving goals, and leadership activities. To establish the gender of the creative teams, the researchers examined the credits at the end of each program to determine the number of women who worked as creators, writers, or producers. (If a name was ambiguous, they contacted the production company for the correct information.)

The researchers then grouped the shows into six categories: all-male writers versus mixed-gender writers; all-male creators versus mixed-gender creators; and all-male executive producers versus mixed-gender executive producers.

Did having females on the creative team make a difference? On programs with all-male writers, 17 percent of the male characters but only 6 percent of the female characters had leadership roles. On programs with male creators, 16 percent of male characters had leadership roles but only 5 percent of the females. The same pattern was found for shows with all-male executive producers. With one exception, all-male creative teams also portrayed more males than females in positions of power and more males exhibited goal-seeking behaviors.

When it came to mixed-gender creative teams, the results were mixed, but in five of the nine possible comparisons, no meaningful gender differences were found regarding occupational power, leadership roles, or goal-seeking behaviors. As the authors concluded, the results provide evidence that women working behind the scenes were associated with more equitable portrayals of female and male characters.

which white children have personal contact with African Americans affects how white youngsters view TV shows that have black performers: Youngsters who have more personal contact with African Americans judge the TV programs to be less realistic. Moreover, long-term exposure to educational programming, such as *Sesame Street*, has been found to be associated with more positive evaluations of African Americans.

In sum, these studies, like those dealing with sex-role portrayals, suggest that TV programs depicting minority characters can modify racial attitudes and perceptions.

BROADCASTING AND POLITICS

Even the most casual of political observers will concede that the broadcasting media, and TV in particular, have changed American politics. A new term, *telepolitics*, has been coined to describe the way politics is now practiced. This section looks at the obvious and not-so-obvious influences of broadcasting on the political system.

Those who have studied the impact of media on politics generally divide the field into two categories. The first has to do with the influences on the ultimate political act—voting. Studies in this category examine how media help shape our election campaigns, our images of candidates and issues, our knowledge of politics, whether we vote, and for whom we cast a ballot. The second category includes studies of how media, TV especially, are changing the basic political structure and how we perceive it. We shall examine each category, but first let's look at the media, electioneering, and voting.

Media Influences on Voting Behavior

The past 75 years have seen striking changes in the way political scientists and mass communication researchers have viewed the importance of media in political campaigns. Early fears about the political impact of the media were shown to be unjustified by careful studies done in the 1940s and 1950s. Most people reported that factors other than the media, such as their party affiliation and the opinions of respected others, were the most influential factors determining their vote choice. Since 1960, however, TV has assumed dominance as the most potent political medium, and voters have tended to be less influenced by party ties and organizations. Accordingly, the potential for media impact may be on the increase.

One thing is certain: People get a lot of political information from the media during the course of a campaign. Candidates who get extensive coverage also show strong gains in public awareness.

Moreover, the pattern of news coverage during an election campaign can help determine what political issues the public perceives as important, a phenomenon known as **agenda setting.** For example, if the media give extensive coverage to U.S. policy in Central America, audience members may think that this is an important issue and rate it high on their own personal agenda of political issues.

Voters, of course, get more than just issue-related information from the media. Another area of research is concerned with the role of TV and other media in forming voters' images of the candidates. In particular, political ads are designed to project a coherent and attractive image to voters. Studies have suggested that a candidate's image can be the dominant factor in many elections. As party identification weakens, voters tend to rely on a general image to help them make up their minds. This "image effect" seems strongest among uncommitted voters and is most noted during the early stages of a campaign.

When it comes down to the actual choices (1) whether to vote at all and (2) for whom to vote, the research is not so definitive as one might think. Voting behavior is a complex activity, and many factors—interpersonal communication, personal values, social class, age, ethnicity, party affiliation—along with media exposure come into play. To make it even more complicated, some people are unable to distinguish exactly what factors influence their choice. Existing research, however, does offer some conclusions. Not surprisingly, voters who learn a great deal about a particular candidate are likely to vote for that candidate. Certain kinds of media exposure are also related to voter turnout. Print media readership was

found to be related to greater voter participation, whereas people who were heavy TV viewers were less likely to vote. A 2007 meta-analysis of studies examining political advertising concluded that viewing political ads was positively related to learning about issues, increased interest in the campaign, and had an impact on voter choice. Ads did not have an effect on agenda setting or turnout.

Starting with the 1992 and 1996 presidential elections, much research attention has shifted to examining the effects of "new" media such as e-mail, Web sites, and social networks. Early research, done before the growth of social networking sites and blogs, did not find much of an impact. For example, one study of the 2000 presidential election noted that using the Internet for political information was not related to voter turnout. A series of field experiments conducted during the 2002 congressional elections found that an e-mail campaign did not increase registration rates or voter turnout.

Some effects of new media were seen in the 2004 presidential election. Candidate Howard Dean financed his unsuccessful primary campaign through donations raised on his Web site. In addition, political interest groups and political bloggers used their Web sites to raise issues that might not have been covered by the traditional press. At the same time, the traditional media were still important sources of information. A survey by the Pew Research Center found that television was a major source of campaign information for 76 percent of its respondents while the Internet was named as a major source by only 10 percent.

By the 2008 presidential election, however, the Internet had become a more important source of political news. A Pew Center survey noted that one-third of its respondents named the Internet as a major source of campaign news—three times the comparable 2004 figure. Young people were even more likely to rely on the Internet. Half of 18- to 29-year-olds named it as a major source.

In addition, political campaigns had learned how to use the Internet as a campaign tool. All candidates had Web sites, YouTube channels, and Facebook, MySpace, and Twitter accounts. Eventual winner Barack Obama was even called the first Internet president because of his online efforts. During the campaign he was able to amass a database of more than 13 million e-mail addresses, had more than a million friends on Facebook, and sent thousands of messages via Twitter—and his Web site had millions of registered users. His online fund-raising efforts totaled more than a quarter-billion dollars.

Obama's social networking strategy was particularly successful among young people. A Pew Center report found that 50 percent of its survey respondents shared political information with others on a social networking site. Among people under 30, two-thirds had a social networking profile, and half of these used social networking sites to get or share information about the campaign or the candidates. Turnout among young voters was up significantly from 2004, and Obama received a record 66 percent of the under-30 vote.

TV debates between or among presidential candidates have become a fixture of modern campaigns, and their results have been closely studied to determine what, if any, impact they have on voter preference. Numerous studies of the debates of the last six presidential elections generally agree that the debates reinforced preferences that were formed before the debates took place. Almost 6 out of 10 voters have made up their minds by the time the debates occur, and most viewers simply have their choice confirmed.

The two televised debates of the 1996 presidential campaign reinforced these findings. Incumbent President Bill Clinton had a big lead over challenger Bob Dole going into the debates, and public opinion polls detected no change in his lead after the debates were over.

The series of presidential debates between Al Gore and George W. Bush during the 2000 election

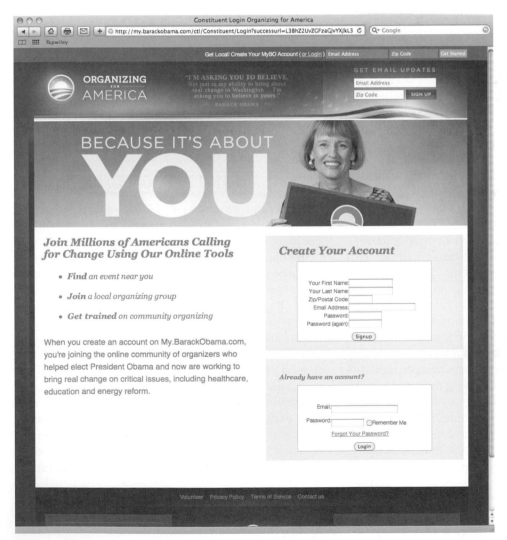

The Internet has forever changed politics. Politicians use Web sites to raise money, campaign for votes, and stay in touch with their constituents.

were notable because they attracted the lowest average number of viewers per debate, thanks to competition from baseball playoffs and entertainment programming on the Fox network. To illustrate, the presidential debates during the 1980s averaged about 68 million viewers per debate; in 2000 that number had dropped to about 40 million.

The effects of viewing the 2000 debates were hard to detect. The race was close all the way and eventually was decided by the Supreme Court. Polls taken after the debates showed small and inconsistent changes in candidate preference. Watching the debates, however, was related to gains in political knowledge and a greater understanding of the issues in the campaign.

Analysis of the impact of the 2004 debates between John Kerry and George W. Bush suggested that presidential debates may matter less than was previously thought. Almost all analysts agreed the Kerry was perceived the victor in the debates, but his performance failed to translate to the polls as Bush won with a comfortable margin.

In 2008 surveys indicated that Barack Obama was perceived as the winner in his series of debates with John McCain. Polls showed that Obama was ahead throughout the campaign, and he went on to win the election with 53 percent of the popular vote.

Media Impact on the Political System

Turning now to the second general area of research, the impact of the media on the political system as a whole, we find that less research is available but the findings are no less important. One line of research suggests that political institutions and the media have become interdependent in a number of ways. Political reporters need information to do their jobs, and the government and politicians need media exposure. Thus public officials hold news conferences early enough to meet media deadlines, presidents have "photo opportunities," and correspondents accompany administration leaders on world trips. Further, many politicians have learned to stage media events that accommodate both sides: The politician gets exposure, and the TV reporter gets a 10-second "sound bite" for the evening news. This interdependence is also demonstrated by the change in political conventions. In prior years, conventions actually selected candidates. These days conventions are more like coronation ceremonies, closely orchestrated to maximize prime-time TV coverage.

The recent trend toward negative political advertising has also been a topic of concern. Definitive results about its impact have yet to be determined. On one hand, many political consultants point to the success of several gubernatorial and senatorial elections in the 1996 campaign that relied on negative advertising and were successful. On the other hand, several surveys and experiments have shown that negative advertising seems to make voters more cynical, less inclined to participate in political campaigns, and even less likely to vote. The level of negative advertising hit a new high in the 1998 midyear elections, and many observers suggested that it had a boomerang effect for several candidates. Negative ads were numerous during the 2008 presidential election with the most negative sponsored by political action groups.

To sum up the rather broad and complicated area of broadcasting and politics, research concerning the political impact of the media demonstrates the specific-effects viewpoint mentioned earlier. In some areas, such as building political knowledge, shaping political images, and setting agendas, the media effects are fairly direct and evident. In other areas, such as voter turnout and voter choice, the media work along with a host of other factors, and their impact is not particularly strong.

TELEVISION AND PROSOCIAL BEHAVIOR

It's tempting, of course, to blame all of society's ills on TV. To be fair, however, we should also point out that TV has had several positive or prosocial effects as well. Prosocial behavior covers a wider range of activity than does antisocial behavior. Usually a prosocial behavior is defined as one that is ultimately good for a person and for society. Some behaviors commonly defined as prosocial are learning cognitive skills associated with school achievement, cooperation, self-control, helping, sharing, resisting temptation, offering sympathy, and making reparation for bad behavior. Many of these prosocial acts are not so obvious or as unmistakable as common antisocial acts; it's a lot easier to see somebody hitting somebody else than it is to see a person resisting temptation. In any case, this section takes a look at the more beneficial results of TV viewing.

First, as noted earlier, specially constructed programs can be effective in preparing young people for school. Without a doubt, the most successful program in this area is *Sesame Street*. On the air for more than 40 years, *Sesame Street* is viewed by nearly 6 million preschoolers every week. Further, *Sesame Street* is the most researched TV series ever, and the available data highlight the success of the series. To summarize some of the major findings:

1. Children who viewed *Sesame Street* regularly, either in school or at home, scored higher on tests measuring school readiness.

2. The more children watched the program, the better their scores were.

3. Disadvantaged children who were frequent viewers showed gains almost as great as their advantaged counterparts.

4. Frequent viewers also seemed to develop more positive attitudes toward school in general.

5. Children who were encouraged to view the program showed more gains than those who were not encouraged.

The success of *Sesame Street* brought it high visibility and criticism. First, it was noted that *Sesame Street* seemed to enlarge the skills gap between advantaged and disadvantaged children. Although disadvantaged children frequently gained as much as advantaged children, fewer disadvantaged children were frequent *Sesame Street* watchers, leading to the net result that a larger proportion of advantaged kids gained by viewing. To cope with this criticism, educators looked for ways to encourage more viewing by the disadvantaged. The second criticism charged that the show's fast-paced style might cause problems when children entered the more slow-paced school environment. It was argued that heavy *Sesame Street* viewers might be bored and/or hyperactive as a consequence. This turned out to be a false alarm, and subsequent research has not linked these problems with frequent viewing.

Other programs that were constructed to get across prosocial messages about mental health or personal social adjustment have proved helpful. For example, viewers of *Mister Rogers' Neighborhood* were found to be more cooperative and more persistent than nonviewers. A two-year study of children who were regular watchers of the Nickelodeon series *Allegra's Window* and *Gullah Gullah Island* disclosed that viewers were better able to solve problems and had more flexible thinking skills than nonviewers. Viewers of another Nickelodeon series, *Blue's Clues,* were better at problem solving than those who didn't watch.

Big Bird and his pals on *Sesame Street* are known the world over. Produced by The Children's Television Workshop, the show has been on the air for more than 40 years.

Surveys that link the viewing of prosocial TV with the performance of prosocial acts in real life are rare. One study done in the 1970s found a weak connection between the two, an association that was even weaker than the correlation between viewing of TV violence and aggression. A 1999 study found a relationship among first graders between watching prosocial situation comedies (*Full House* and *The Cosby Show*) and performing prosocial acts, but the relationship did not show up among third graders, perhaps because of the increased influence of other sources, such as peers. A 2005 meta-analysis of 34 studies found that those children who watched prosocial content in lab experiments were slightly more likely to exhibit prosocial behaviors than those who did not see prosocial material.

In summary, TV seems to have several effects on behaviors that most would define as prosocial:

1. Television teaches certain cognitive skills that are necessary for school success.

2. Television shows can help reduce gender-related stereotypes.

3. Laboratory experiments suggest viewing commercial TV shows with definite prosocial messages can prompt subsequent prosocial behaviors, but this link has not yet been found to carry over in any significant degree to real life.

Before closing this section we should point out that there are many more areas that might have been mentioned. For example, many communications researchers are now devoting increased attention to how individuals process messages in their brain—the study of the cognitive aspects of communication. Moreover, it should be clear by now that the research in many of these areas highlights the thinking embodied in the specific-effects theory discussed earlier in the chapter. Radio and TV usually operate along with a number of other factors to produce an effect, and trying to untangle the unique effects of the media can be quite frustrating. And although the study of media effects is still relatively new, the data are steadily accumulating. It also appears that the electronic media are not necessarily as powerful as many people have charged, although they can exert significant influence in specific instances. Finally, we have a lot more work to do, particularly since new media have transformed the media habits of the audience.

SOCIAL IMPACT OF THE INTERNET

The Internet changes rapidly, and it is difficult to make generalizations about its impact. There are, however, some conclusions that merit reporting.

First, with regard to the audience, nearly 80 percent of all U.S. households were connected to the Internet in 2009. About 230 million people used the Internet in 2010, up from 57 million in 1998. Moreover, the average Internet user was similar to the average American. According to Nielsen/NetRatings data, 52 percent of online users were women, a percentage that almost exactly mirrors that of the general population. In addition, the average household income of the online population was only slightly higher than that of the U.S. population. The Internet

population was still generally younger, with 76 percent of the online users between 18 and 49, compared with 63 percent in the general population. Older Americans, however, were among the fastest-growing age category of Internet users. About 12 percent of the Internet population is Hispanic and 11 percent African American—slightly less than their proportions in the general population.

The Internet is fast becoming a major source of news. A 2008 survey by the Pew Research Center revealed that while television was still the number one source of national and international news, named by 70 percent, the Internet was in second place with 40 percent, with newspapers finishing third. Among young people, the Internet was even more popular with about 60 percent of those under 30 naming the Internet as their main source.

Internet addiction—a psychological dependence on the Internet that may cause people to ignore family, friends, work, and school as they spend most of their time online—is an increasingly popular research topic among social scientists. From 2008 to 2010, more than 100 studies of this topic appeared in scholarly research journals. Internet addiction has been linked to feelings of depression, boredom, attention deficit disorder, anxiety, alcohol use, and substance abuse. The editors of the upcoming fifth edition of *The Diagnostic and Statistical Manual of Mental Disorders* (sometimes called the Bible of psychiatry) were considering adding Internet addiction disorder as an official psychiatric disturbance.

Early studies that examined the Internet's impact on people's social lives found that Internet use appeared to increase feelings of remoteness and isolation. More recent surveys, however, have found the opposite. Internet use was associated with greater community and political involvement and more social contacts. The changing nature of the Internet and its audience is probably responsible for the change. Recent innovations such as instant messages, online communities, photo and video sharing sites, and social networks all encourage more social contacts. In sum, research seems to support the "rich get richer" hypothesis. Internet users with extraverted personalities are the ones who seem to increase their social contacts via the Internet. For these people, the Internet is simply another channel by which they can link up with friends. On the other hand, introverted individuals tend not to use the Internet in this way.

Issues: Internet Addiction

Two recent studies, one in the United States and one in Britain, provide some interesting information about Internet addiction and young people.

The U.S. study was done by the Center for Media and the Public Agenda at the University of Maryland. Researchers asked 200 students to refrain from using all media for just 24 hours—no cell phones, iPods, Facebook, instant messages, texting, TV, radio, or the like. At the end of 24 hours, students were asked to describe their experience. Interestingly, the terms students used to describe their dependence on media were the same as those used by people addicted to drugs or alcohol: "jittery," "in withdrawal," "antsy," "frantically craving." As one student put it, "I clearly am addicted, and the dependence is sickening." The researchers concluded, "[M]ost college students are not just unwilling, but functionally unable to be without their media links to the world."

The British study surveyed more than 1,300 respondents and analyzed their Internet use and depression levels. They concluded that 1.2 percent of their sample could be labeled "Internet addicted." Those who were addicted to the Internet spent more time browsing online gaming sites, online social networks, and sexually oriented Web sites. These same people also reported that they were more depressed than normal users.

Although the 1.2 percent figure may seem small, keep in mind that there are approximately 38 million Internet users in Britain. If 1.2 percent are Internet addicted, that works out to more than 450,000 potentially depressed addicts. The researchers cautioned that their data do not indicate whether Internet addiction causes people to be depressed or if depressed people are simply attracted to the Internet. Nonetheless, they concluded, "[F]or a small subset of people, excessive use of the Internet could be a warning signal for depressive tendencies."

THE FUTURE: SOCIAL CONCERNS

New media technologies, such as 3D TV, iPads, smart phones, game consoles, broadband Internet connections, Blu-ray DVDs, and video on demand, raise new social issues.

First there is the economic issue. All this new technology is expensive and may increase the distance between the media haves and the media have-nots. Low-income households are less likely to own a computer than middle-income or high-income households. A Pew Center study found that 85 percent of households with annual incomes above $75,000 had broadband service compared with 42 percent of households with annual incomes of less than $30,000. Urban residents are more likely to have broadband service than are people living in rural areas. At some point in the future, there will have to be a debate on how to distribute equitably the informational wealth that new technology will bring.

Next are concerns about privacy. Computers and online databases make it easy for people to find out about us. Whenever someone applies for a loan, pays property taxes, files a lawsuit, sells a house, buys a car, or claims unemployment, that information is stored in some digital file that can be easily accessed. Unscrupulous persons can sometimes uncover private information or even steal someone's identity. Personal information can be released by accident or by carelessness. For example, in 2010 an employee of the Social Security Administration lost a computer disk that contained personal information about nearly a thousand people. That same year in Wyoming personal information about 9,000 children enrolled in the state's insurance program was accidentally posted on an unsecured Web page for months before someone noticed the error.

Then there is the problem of information overload. Information overload hardly needs to be defined to college students who are studying 9 or 10 different subjects a year. The term generally refers to the feeling of confusion and helplessness that occurs when a person is confronted with too much stimulation in a limited time period. With 500 or more TV channels, video games, computers, and cell phones, the consumer of the future will have more information available than he or she could ever use.

Last, there is the problem of escapism and isolation. The term *couch potato* came into vogue during the 1980s to describe a type of person who turned away from personal interaction and merely vegetated in front of the TV. How many people will become couch potatoes in the future when 3D TV and realistic video games are routinely available?

The new communication technologies will bring promise and peril. Just like the telegraph, telephone, radio, and TV that preceded them, they will bring fundamental changes to our lives. They will require difficult decisions from policymakers and from consumers alike. They will require us to learn more about them and what they can do. As Loy Singleton pointed out in his book *Telecommunications in the Information Age*, the new technologies will best serve those who know how to use them.

SUMMARY

- The social effects of broadcasting and cable have been studied by using experiments, surveys, panel studies, content analyses, and meta-analyses.

- Over the years various theories have enjoyed popularity as explanations for the effects of the media. The hypodermic needle theory considered the media a powerful persuasive force. This theory held that all people would have more or less the same reaction to a mass-communicated message. The limited-effects theory proposed just the opposite: Because of a variety of intervening variables, the media have little effect. Currently the specific-effects theory is in vogue. This theory argues that there are some circumstances under which the media have a direct effect on some people.

- The most researched topic in broadcasting is the effect of video violence on the audience. After more than 30 years of research, most scientists agree that there is little evidence to support the catharsis theory. Further, most agree that TV violence contributes, although in a small way, to the development of antisocial tendencies. Research about the effects of violent video games has shown a similar pattern of results.

- There is less agreement among scientists about cultivation theory, which states that viewing large amounts of TV will distort a person's perception of reality. Evidence is mixed about this topic, and more research remains to be done. Television also seems to play a part in sex-role and racial stereotyping.

- Broadcasting has had a major effect on politics. It provides political information, sets voters' agendas, establishes candidates' images, and has some limited influence on voters' attitudes.

- Preliminary research into the impact of the Internet suggests that Internet use is generally related to more social contacts and community involvement.

KEY TERMS

laboratory experiments   296
field experiments   297
surveys   297
longitudinal   297
trend study   297

panel studies   297
content analysis   297
meta-analysis   297
catharsis theory   300
stimulation theory   300

cultivation theory   305
mainstreaming   306
resonance   306
agenda setting   310
Internet addiction   314

SUGGESTIONS FOR FURTHER READING

Bryant, J., & Thompson, S. (2002). *Fundamentals of media effects*. New York: McGraw-Hill, 2002.

DeFleur, M., & Ball-Rokeach, S. (1989). *Theories of mass communication*. New York: Longman.

———. (1995). *Milestones in mass communication research*. New York: Longman.

Huesmann, L., & Eron, L. (eds.). (1986). *Television and the aggressive child*. Hillsdale, NJ: Erlbaum.

Liebert, R., & Sprafkin, J. (1988). *The early window*. New York: Pergamon.

Pearl, D., Bouthilet, L., & Lazar, J. (1982). *Television and behavior: Ten years of scientific progress and implications for the eighties* (vol. 2). Washington, DC: U.S. Government Printing Office.

Perse, E., & Lambe, J. (2011). *Media effects and society*. New York: Routledge.

Signorielli, N., & Morgan, M. (1990). *Cultivation analysis*. Newbury Park, CA: Sage.

Sparks, G. (2009). *Media effects research: A basic overview*. Florence, KY: Cengage.

U.S. Department of Health and Human Services. (2001). *Youth violence: A report of the Surgeon General*. Washington, DC: U.S. Government Printing Office.

William, T. (1986). *The impact of television*. New York: Academic Press.

INTERNET EXERCISES

Visit our Web site at **www.mhhe.com/dominickbib7e** for study-guide exercises to help you learn and apply material in each chapter. You will find ideas for future research as well as useful Web links to provide you with an opportunity to journey through the new electronic media.

Glossary

addressable converter   Device that allows pay-per-view cable subscribers to receive their programs.

adjacency   Commercial placement that immediately precedes or follows a specific television, cable, or radio show.

affiliate   Local radio or TV station that has a contractual relationship with a network.

American Society of Composers, Authors, and Publishers (ASCAP)   Group that collects and distributes performance royalty payments to various artists.

amplifier   Device that boosts an electrical signal.

amplitude   Height of a wave above a neutral point.

ARPANET   Early version of the Internet.

audience flow   Movement of audiences from one program to another.

audimeter   Nielsen rating device that indicates if a radio or TV set is in use and to what station the set is tuned. *See also* storage instantaneous audimeter.

audion   Device invented by Lee De Forest that amplified weak radio signals.

auditorium testing   Research technique that tests popularity of records by playing them in front of a large group of people who fill out questionnaires about what they heard.

average quarter-hour persons   In radio, average number of listeners per 15-minute period in a given daypart.

banner ads   Ads that are displayed at the top or sides of a Web page.

barter   Type of payment for syndicated programming in which the syndicator withholds one or more minutes of time in the program and sells these time slots to national advertisers.

Basic penetration   The number of homes subscribing to some level of cable service.

behavioral targeting   Placing web ads tailored to viewers previous websurfing behavior or interests.

blanket rights   Music licensing arrangement in which an organization pays Broadcast Music Incorporated (BMI) or ASCAP a single fee that grants the organization the right to play all of BMI's or ASCAP's music.

block programming   In radio, programming to one target audience for a few hours and then changing the format to appeal to another group. Used by many community radio stations.

blog   A shared online journal where people post entries about their experiences, interests, and attitudes.

BMI   Broadcast Music Incorporated is a music licensing organization that collects license fees on behalf of songwriters, composers and music publisher and distributes them as royalties to those whose works have been performed.

burnout   Tendency of a song to become less popular after repeated playings.

buying power index (BPI)   A weighted measurement describing a specific geographic market's ability to buy goods, based on population, effective income, and retail sales.

C3 rating   The rating of the average commercial minute including live viewing and DVR playback within three days

cable TV   Distributing television signals by wire.

call-out research   Radio research conducted by telephone to evaluate the popularity of recordings.

carrier wave   Basic continuous wave produced by a radio or TV station; modulated to carry information.

catharsis theory   Theory that suggests that watching media violence relieves the aggressive urges of those in the audience. There has been little scientific evidence for this position.

checkerboard   In radio programming, developing a broadcast schedule that is made up of many different types of programs scheduled throughout the broadcast day.

chromakey   Process by which one picture is blended with another in TV production.

churn   The number of people who subscribe to a satellite or cable channel and fail to renew their subscriptions.

clutter   Commercials and other nonprogram material broadcast during program breaks.

compensation   The amount of money networks pay to their affiliates for carrying the network-fed program. Compensation rates are based on market size, ratings, and affiliate strength.

compression   Technique that increases the amount of information that can be carried in a channel.

contextual ads   Web ads that are related to the content of a certain Web page, such as an ad for *Monday Night Football* on ESPN.com.

continuity   Section of the sales department that ensures the daily schedules of broadcast stations have no dead air or interruptions between commercial messages.

convergence   A trend whereby radio, television, and telephone communications are merged with the computer.

cookie   A piece of text saved by a Web browser that can be used to record the actions of a person who visits a Web site.

cooperative advertising   Arrangement in which national advertisers assist local retailers in paying for ads.

cooperative advertising (co-op)   when the cost of advertising is split between the manufacturer and the local merchant.

Copyright Royalty Board (CRB)   Replaced the Copyright Arbitration Royalty Board in 2006. The Board sets royalty rates for streaming music on webcasts.

cost per point   A way of measuring the efficiency of reaching a specific demographic population with a commercial spot.

cost per thousand (CPM)   One measure of efficiency in the media. Defined as the cost to reach 1,000 people.

coventuring   Arrangement by which a TV station's news department shares its newscasts with other local TV stations, cable systems, or radio stations.

cross-media optimization   Using different advertising platforms in a coordinated way to maximize the placement for the target audience.

cultivation theory   Theory suggesting that watching a great deal of stereotyped TV content will cause distorted perceptions of the real world.

dayparts   A way of dividing up the broadcast day to reflect standard time periods for setting advertising rates.

demographics   Science of categorizing people based on easily observed traits. Age and sex, for example, are two common demographic categories.

development process   The process where producers, studio executives, and program creators work out the financial and technical details for a new television or cable program series.

digital audio broadcasting (DAB)   Broadcasting a radio signal by using a binary code (0s and 1s).

digital video disk (DVD)   Device that stores video and audio information by using laser technology.

digital video recorder   Device that records video on a hard disk.

direct broadcast satellite (DBS)   Satellite transmission designed to be received directly by the home.

diversification   Business strategy that involves spreading investments into several different areas.

downconverter   Device that decodes microwave signals.

duopoly   (1) System of broadcasting in which two systems, one public and one private, exist at the same time, as in Canada. (2) Owning more than one AM or FM station in the same market.

effective buying income (EBI)   The amount of disposable income of the average family in a given market.

electronic news gathering (ENG)   Providing information for TV news with the assistance of portable video and audio equipment. Also called electronic journalism (EJ).

electronic response indicator (ERI)   Device that allows viewers to continuously rate a program or a commercial while they are viewing it.

equalizer   Electronic device that adjusts the amplification of certain frequencies; allows for fine-tuning an audio signal.

exclusivity deal   In cable, an arrangement whereby one premium service has the exclusive rights to show the films of a particular motion picture company.

fairness doctrine   Currently defunct policy of the Federal Communications Commission that required broadcast stations to present balanced coverage of topics of public concern.

false light   A type of invasion of privacy in which media coverage creates the wrong impression about a person.

fiber optic   Cable used for transmitting a digital signal via thin strands of flexible glass.

financial interest and syndication rules (fin-syn)   FCC regulations limiting network participation in ownership and subsequent syndication of programs produced for the network.

first-run syndication   Programming developed specifically for the syndication market. Game shows and talk shows are usually first-run syndication.

focus group   Small group of people who discuss predetermined topics, such as a TV newscast.

Food and Drug Administration (FDA)   Federal commission that is responsible for overseeing prescription drug advertising on TV.

format   The type of music or talk that a radio station chooses to program. Formats are usually targeted at a specific segment of the population. *See also* demographics.

frequency   Number of waves that pass a given point in a given time period, usually a second; measured in hertz (Hz).

frequency response   Range of frequencies that a radio set is capable of receiving.

full studio automatic   A fully automated radio station.

future file   Collection of stories to be used in upcoming newscasts.

geosynchronous orbit   A satellite orbit that keeps that satellite over one spot above the earth.

gross impressions   The total number of advertising impressions made during a schedule of commercials. GIs are calculated by multiplying the average persons reached in a specific time period by the number of spots in that period of time.

gross rating points (GRPs)   The total number of rating points gained as a result of scheduling commercials. GRPs are determined by multiplying the specific rating by the number of spots in that time period.

high-definition television (HDTV) Improved resolution TV system that uses approximately 1,100 scanning lines.

homes passed Number of homes that have the ability to receive cable TV; that is, homes passed by the cable.

hot clock A visualization of the format of a radio station's sound hour.

hook Short, easily identifiable segment of a recording.

households using television (HUT) Number of households that are watching TV at a certain time period.

hue Each individual color as seen on color TV.

International Telecommunications Union (ITU) Organization that coordinates the international broadcasting activities of its members

Internet A global network of interconnected computers.

Internet addiction Psychological dependence on the Internet.

Internet service provider (ISP) A company that connects subscribers to the Internet.

interstitial ad Web advertising that is displayed before or after the expected content page is displayed.

inventory The amount of available advertising time a media outlet has to sell; unsold time.

kinescope Early form of recording TV shows in which a film was made of a TV receiver.

local area network (LAN) A group of computers that are linked together.

local market agreement (LMA) Arrangement whereby a company that owns one radio station can manage assets of another station without violating FCC ownership rules.

local origination Program produced by a local TV station or cable system.

low-power television (LPTV) Television stations that operate with reduced coverage and have a coverage area only 12 to 15 miles in diameter.

make good Additional commercial time given to a sponsor when a scheduled ad does not run correctly.

marketing manager In cable operations, the person in charge of promotions.

meta-analysis Research technique that summarizes the findings of many separate studies about a single topic.

Metropolitan statistical area (MSA) The metropolitan area (counties) encompassing the population served by a city's radio stations.

microcasting Transmitting a message to a small group of people.

minidoc Multipart reports that generally air Monday to Friday on local TV stations. Each minidoc segment may only be three or four minutes long.

modulation Encoding a signal by changing the characteristics of the carrier wave.

monopoly The ability to exercise unrestrained power over a market; the existence of no real or effective competition.

MP3 Recording compression technique that makes it possible to share audio files over the Internet.

multichannel, multipoint distribution system (MMDS) System using microwave transmission to provide cable service into urban areas; also called wireless cable.

multiple-system operator (MSO) Company that owns and operates more than one cable system.

multiplexing Sending different signals with the same channel.

National Association of Broadcasters (NAB) Leading professional organization of the broadcasting industry.

National Cable Television Association (NCTA) Leading professional organization of the cable industry.

network compensation Money paid by a network to one of its affiliates in return for the affiliate's carrying network shows and network commercials.

network neutrality Policy that prohibits Internet service providers from favoring one company over another.

Network O & O Television station owned by the network with which is it affiliated. These are the most profitable among all television stations.

network programming Programs that are financed by and shown on TV networks.

news consultants Research companies that advise stations about ways to improve the ratings of their news programs.

noise Unwanted interference in a video or audio signal.

oscillation Vibration of a sound or radio wave.

panel method Research technique in which the same people are studied at different points in time.

Pay households Cable homes who subscribe to one or more pay services such as HBO or Showtime.

pay per view (PPV) System in which cable subscribers pay a one-time fee for special programs such as movies and sporting events. *See also* addressable converter.

People Meter In ratings, handheld device that reports what TV show is being watched. People Meters also gather demographic data about who is watching.

pilot Sample episode of a proposed TV series.

pixel The smallest element in a television picture.

podcasting Distributing audio and video files over the Internet for playback on iPods and similar devices.

pods A cluster of commercials, promotions, or other announcements.

pop up ads Web ads that pop up on the screen when a certain url is entered.

Portable People Meter (PPM)   A device that is carried by an individual to measure radio listening and TV viewing by detecting subaudible tones in the stations' signals.

portal   First page opened by an Internet browser.

preemption   The term used when a television network affiliate refuses to carry the scheduled network program.

prime-time access rule (PTAR)   In general, a regulation that limits the TV networks to three hours of programming during the prime-time period. Exceptions are made for news, public affairs, children's shows, documentaries, and political broadcasts.

psychographic research   Research that uses personality traits to segment the audience.

pulse code modulation (PCM)   Method used in digital recording and reproduction in which a signal is sampled at various points and the resulting value is translated into binary numbers.

rating   In TV, the percentage of households in a market that are viewing a station divided by the total number of households with TV in that market. In radio, the total number of people who are listening to a station divided by the total number of people in the market.

right of first refusal   Network's contractual guarantee to prohibit a production company from producing a specific show for another client.

rough cut   Preliminary rendition of an ad or a TV show produced so that viewers can get a general idea of the content.

satellite news gathering (SNG)   Use of specially equipped mobile units to transmit live and taped remote reports back to a local station.

scatter buying   Purchasing broadcast time over several different time periods of the broadcast day.

share   In radio, the number of people who are listening to a station divided by the total number of people who are listening to radio at a given time. In TV, the total number of households watching a given channel divided by the total number of households using TV.

signal-to-noise ratio   Amount of desired picture or sound information that remains after subtracting unwanted interference.

single-system operator (SSO)   Company that owns and operates one cable system.

standing order   A commercial order that gives a certain time in the broadcast schedule to the same customer until the order is rescinded.

station identification   Station announcement broadcast at the top or bottom of the hour telling call letters and location or having a station logo superimposed on the screen.

step deal   Contractual arrangement by which TV series are produced. Production proceeds in a series of defined steps, with the network having the option to cancel after each step.

stimulation theory   Theory suggesting that watching media violence will stimulate the viewer to perform aggressive acts in real life. Opposite of the catharsis theory.

storage instantaneous audimeter (SIA)   Computer-assisted TV measurement device that makes possible overnight ratings.

storyboard   Drawings illustrating what a finished commercial or segment of a TV show will look like.

streaming   A technique that allows sound and moving pictures to be transmitted on the World Wide Web.

stripping   Scheduling the same show to run in the same time period from Monday through Friday.

supergroup   Radio companies that control large numbers of stations in several different markets.

superstation   Local TV station that is distributed to many cable systems via satellite, giving the station national exposure.

survey   Research method that uses questionnaires or similar instruments to gather data from a sample of respondents.

sweeps   Periods when research companies collect ratings and viewer information in local television markets.

switcher   Device used to switch from one video signal to another. Can also be used to combine more than one video signal.

synchronization pulse   Signal that enables the output of two or more cameras and other video sources to be mixed together and also keeps the scanning process in the camera operating in time to coincide exactly with the retrace process in the TV receiver.

syndication   The sale and distribution of programming directly to the station. First-run syndication involves products that have been specifically produced for airing in the syndication marketplace.

target audience   Specific group a radio or TV program is trying to attract.

telephone coincidental interview   Method of audience research in which a respondent is asked what radio or TV station he or she is listening to at the time of the call.

teletext   Cable service that offers text and graphics displayed on the screen.

tiering   Process of selling cable subscribers increasing levels of service.

time-shifting   Recording something on a VCR to watch at a more convenient time.

traffic   Part of the business operation of a broadcast station, the term applies to programming sales spots and informational messaging into the program schedule.

treatment   Short narrative used to sell an idea for a TV show or series to a production company.

TVRO   Satellite television receive-only earth station.

ultra-high frequency (UHF)   The portion of the electromagnetic spectrum that contains TV channels 14 to 69.

uniform resource locator (URL)   A unique address of an Internet site.

upfront sales   Network television time that is sold in the summer before the actual television season begins. Upfront sales are frequently for dayparts as opposed to actual programs.

V-chip   Device installed in TV sets that blocks out violent programming.

vertical integration   Process by which a firm has interests in the production, distribution, and consumption of a product.

very high frequency (VHF)   The part of the electromagnetic spectrum that contains TV channels 2 to 13.

video news release   A recorded presentation of company news distributed online and to TV stations.

voice-tracking   Radio technique in which a disc jockey records his audio for a program and all other elements are added later by a computer. Makes it possible for one DJ to do programs for several different stations.

Voice over Internet Protocol (VoIP)   Method of sending telephone calls over the Internet.

waveform   Visual representation of a wave as measured by electronic equipment.

wavelength   Distance between two corresponding points on an electromagnetic wave.

WiFi   High-speed networking technology that provides Internet access.

World Wide Web   Part of the Internet that contains sites featuring text and graphics.

Photo Credits

Chapter 1: Page 7 & 10: © Brown Brothers; p. 14 & 15: © Bettmann/Corbis; p. 17 & 21: © Shooting Star; p. 25: © AP Photo/Richard Drew; p. 26: © AP Photo/Kristian Dowling/PictureGroup

Chapter 2: Page 33: © AP/Wide World Photos; p. 36: © Bettmann/Corbis; p. 38: © AP Photo/Sony Corporation; p. 44: Courtesy of the author

Chapter 3: Page 57: © AP/Wide World Photos; p. 62: © AP Images for Best Buy/David Goldman; p. 64: © Blend Images/Inti St Clair/Getty; p. 66: © Alexander Hassenstein/Bongarts/Getty; p. 72: Courtesy of the author; p. 74: © Nick Koudis/Getty RF; p. 80: © AP Photo/PRNewsFoto/Verizon Wireless

Chapter 4: Page 90 (top): © George Frey/Bloomberg via Getty Images; p. 90 (bottom): © AP Photo/Evan Agostini p. 95: © AP Photo/Mark J. Terrill; p. 96: © The McGraw-Hill Companies, Inc./Lars A. Niki, photographer

Chapter 5: Page 113: © AP Images/Michael Becker/PictureGroup/FOX; p. 118: © Everett Collection; p. 120: © AP Photo/Scott Gries/PictureGroup; p. 125: © AP Photo/Paul Sakuma; p. 129: USGS photo by Walter D. Mooney; p. 132: © Digital Vision/SuperStock RF

Chapter 6: Page 140: © The McGraw-Hill Companies, Inc./John Flournoy, photographer; p. 142: © AP Photo/Canadian Press; p. 149: © Keith Eng 2007

Chapter 7: Page 171 (top): © AP Photo for Progressive Insurance/David Adame; p. 171 (bottom): © AP Photo/William Thomas Cain; p. 172: © Jeff Greenberg/Photo Edit; p. 173: © AP photo/Damian Dovarganes

Chapter 8: Page 186: © Scott Gries/Getty; p. 188: © Mark Richards/Photo Edit; p. 192: © AP photo/Paul Sakuma; p. 199: © AP Photo/Kathy Willens; p. 202: © Kevin Horan/Time & Life Pictures/Getty; p. 203: © www.wuog.org, 90.5 FM, University of Georgia

Chapter 9: Page: 208: © Popperfoto/Getty; p. 211: © AP Photo/NASA; p. 214: © Mark Richards/Photo Edit; p. 219: © Neil Jacobs/CBS via Getty; p. 225: © Sonja Flemming/CBS via Getty; p. 228: © David Young-Wolff/Photo Edit; p. 230: © Getty

Chapter 10: Page 244: © FCC; p. 254: © AP Photo/Dan Steinberg

Chapter 11: Page 265: © Michael Yarish/© CBS/Courtesy Everett Collection; p. 269: © AP Photo/Matt Sayles; p. 275: © Pixtal/age Fotostock RF

Chapter 12. Page 289: © Arbitron, Inc.; p. 291: © Ryan McVay/Getty RF

Chapter 13: Page 299: © 20th Century Fox Film Corp. All rights reserved. Courtesy of Everett Collection; p. 313: © Everett Collection

Index